UNIX

Concepts and Applications

FOURTH EDITION

About the Author

Sumitabha Das has a degree in electronics engineering from Calcutta University (1977). He picked up his interest in UNIX when working at the Ministry of Defence. Today, he teaches UNIX and Systems Programming. He is ably supported by his wife and daughter.

For My Mother

A language is not worth knowing unless it teaches you to think differently.

—Larry Wall & Randal Schwartz

Contents

Preface   *xix*
Conventions Used in This Book   *xxiii*

PART I

CHAPTER 1	GETTING STARTED	3

1.1 The Operating System *4*
1.2 The UNIX Operating System *5*
1.3 Knowing Your Machine *6*
1.4 A Brief Session *7*
1.5 How It All Clicked *15*
1.6 Linux and GNU *17*
1.7 Conclusion *18*
      Wrap Up 18
      Test Your Understanding 19
      Flex Your Brain 19

CHAPTER 2	THE UNIX ARCHITECTURE AND COMMAND USAGE	21

2.1   The UNIX Architecture *22*
2.2   Features of UNIX *25*
2.3   POSIX and the Single UNIX Specification *27*
2.4   Locating Commands *28*
2.5   Internal and External Commands *29*
2.6   Command Structure *30*
2.7   Flexibility of Command Usage *32*
2.8   Man Browsing the Manual Pages On-line *33*
2.9   Understanding the man Documentation *34*
2.10 Further Help with man -k, apropos and whatis *37*
2.11 When Things Go Wrong *39*
2.12 Conclusion *41*
       Wrap Up 41
       Test Your Understanding 42
       Flex Your Brain 43

CHAPTER 3	GENERAL-PURPOSE UTILITIES	44

3.1   **cal**: The Calendar   *45*

3.2   **date**: Displaying the System Date   *45*

3.3   **echo**: Displaying a Message   *46*

3.4   **printf**: An Alternative to **echo**   *48*

3.5   **bc**: The Calculator   *49*

3.6   **script**: Recording Your Session   *50*

3.7   Email Basics   *51*

3.8   **mailx**: The Universal Mailer   *52*

3.9   **passwd**: Changing Your Password   *55*

3.10   **who**: Who Are the Users?   *57*

3.11   **uname**: Knowing Your Machine's Characteristics   *58*

3.12   **tty**: Knowing Your Terminal   *59*

3.13   **stty**: Displaying and Setting Terminal Characteristics   *59*

3.14   Conclusion   *61*

     Wrap Up   *61*

     Test Your Understanding   *62*

     Flex Your Brain   *62*

CHAPTER 4	THE FILE SYSTEM	64

4.1   The File   *65*

4.2   What's in a (File)name?   *67*

4.3   The Parent-Child Relationship   *67*

4.4   The HOME Variable: The Home Directory   *68*

4.5   **pwd**: Checking Your Current Directory   *69*

4.6   **cd**: Changing the Current Directory   *69*

4.7   **mkdir**: Making Directories   *71*

4.8   **rmdir**: Removing Directories   *71*

4.9   Absolute Pathnames   *73*

4.10   Relative Pathnames   *74*

4.11   **ls**: Listing Directory Contents   *75*

4.12   The UNIX File System   *79*

4.13   Conclusion   *80*

     Wrap Up   *80*

     Test Your Understanding   *80*

     Flex Your Brain   *81*

CHAPTER 5   HANDLING ORDINARY FILES   **82**

5.1   **cat**: Displaying and Creating Files *83*

5.2   **cp**: Copying a File *84*

5.3   **rm**: Deleting Files *85*

5.4   **mv**: Renaming Files *87*

5.5   **more**: Paging Output *88*

5.6   The lp Subsystem: Printing a File *91*

5.7   **file**: Knowing the File Types *92*

5.8   **wc**: Counting Lines, Words and Characters *93*

5.9   **od**: Displaying Data in Octal *94*

5.10   **cmp**: Comparing Two Files *95*

5.11   **comm**: What is Common? *95*

5.12   **diff**: Converting One File to Other *96*

5.13   **dos2unix** and **unix2dos**: Converting Between DOS and UNIX *97*

5.14   Compressing and Archiving Files *98*

5.15   **gzip** and **gunzip**: Compressing and Decompressing Files *99*

5.16   **tar**: The Archival Program *100*

5.17   **zip** and **unzip**: Compressing and Archiving Together *102*

5.18   Conclusion *103*
       Wrap Up 103
       Test Your Understanding 104
       Flex Your Brain 104

CHAPTER 6   BASIC FILE ATTRIBUTES   **106**

6.1   **ls -l**: Listing File Attributes *106*

6.2   The -d Option: Listing Directory Attributes *108*

6.3   File Ownership *109*

6.4   File Permissions *109*

6.5   **chmod**: Changing File Permissions *110*

6.6   Directory Permissions *115*

6.7   Changing File Ownership *116*

6.8   Conclusion *117*
       Wrap Up 117
       Test Your Understanding 118
       Flex Your Brain 119

CHAPTER 7   THE vi EDITOR   **120**

7.1   **vi** Basics *121*

7.2   Input Mode—Entering and Replacing Text *124*

7.3   Saving Text and Quitting—The ex Mode *128*
7.4   Navigation *131*
7.5   Editing Text *134*
7.6   Undoing Last Editing Instructions (**U** and **U**) *137*
7.7   Repeating the Last Command (**.**) *138*
7.8   Searching for a Pattern (**/** and **?**) *138*
7.9   Substitution—Search and Replace (**:s**) *140*
7.10   Conclusion *141*
       Wrap Up 141
       Test Your Understanding 142
       Flex Your Brain 143

CHAPTER 8   THE SHELL   **145**

8.1   The Shell's Interpretive Cycle *146*
8.2   Shell Offerings *147*
8.3   Pattern Matching—The Wild-cards *147*
8.4   Escaping and Quoting *152*
8.5   Redirection: The Three Standard Files *154*
8.6   /dev/null and /dev/tty: Two Special Files *160*
8.7   Pipes *161*
8.8   **tee**: Creating a Tee *164*
8.9   Command Substitution *165*
8.10   Shell Variables *166*
8.11   Conclusion *169*
       Wrap Up 170
       Test Your Understanding 170
       Flex Your Brain 171

CHAPTER 9   THE PROCESS   **173**

9.1   Process Basics *174*
9.2   **ps**: Process Status *176*
9.3   System Processes (-e or -a) *178*
9.4   Mechanism of Process Creation *179*
9.5   Internal and External Commands *181*
9.6   Process States and Zombies *181*
9.7   Running Jobs in Background *182*
9.8   **nice**: Job Execution with Low Priority *183*
9.9   Killing Processes with Signals *184*
9.10   Job Control *185*

9.11 **at** and **batch**: Execute Later *187*

9.12 **cron**: Running Jobs Periodically *188*

9.13 **time**: Timing Processes *190*

9.14 Conclusion *190*

    Wrap Up 190

    Test Your Understanding 191

    Flex Your Brain 192

CHAPTER 10   CUSTOMIZING THE ENVIRONMENT   **193**

10.1 The Shells *194*

10.2 Environment Variables *194*

10.3 The Common Environment Variables *195*

10.4 Aliases (**bash** and **ksh**) *199*

10.5 Command History (**bash** and **ksh**) *200*

10.6 In-line Command Editing (**bash** and **ksh**) *203*

10.7 Miscellaneous Features (**bash** and **ksh**) *204*

10.8 The Initialization Scripts *205*

10.9 Conclusion *207*

    Wrap Up 208

    Test Your Understanding 208

    Flex Your Brain 209

CHAPTER 11   MORE FILE ATTRIBUTES   **210**

11.1 File Systems and Inodes *211*

11.2 Hard Links *2 12*

11.3 Symbolic Links and **ln** *215*

11.4 The Directory *216*

11.5 **umask**: Default File and Directory Permissions *218*

11.6 Modification and Access Times *218*

11.7 **find**: Locating Files *220*

11.8 Conclusion *224*

    Wrap Up 224

    Test Your Understanding 225

    Flex Your Brain 226

CHAPTER 12   SIMPLE FILTERS   **227**

12.1 The Sample Database *228*

12.2 **pr**: Paginating Files *229*

12.3 **head**: Displaying the Beginning of a File *230*

12.4 **tail**: Displaying the End of a File *231*

12.5 **cut**: Slitting a File Vertically *231*

12.6 **paste**: Pasting Files *233*

12.7 **sort**: Ordering a File *234*

12.8 **uniq**: Locate Repeated and Nonrepeated Lines *238*

12.9 **tr**: Translating Characters *239*

12.10 An Example: Displaying a Word-count List *241*

12.11 Conclusion *242*

Wrap Up *242*

Test Your Understanding *243*

Flex Your Brain *243*

CHAPTER 13 FILTERS USING REGULAR EXPRESSIONS—grep AND sed   245

13.1 **grep**: Searching for a Pattern *246*

13.2 Basic Regular Expressions (BRE)—An Introduction *249*

13.3 Extended Regular Expressions (ERE) and **egrep** *254*

13.4 **sed**: The Stream Editor *255*

13.5 Line Addressing *256*

13.6 Using Multiple Instructions (-E and -F) *257*

13.7 Context Addressing *258*

13.8 Writing Selected Lines to a File (**w**) *258*

13.9 Text Editing *259*

13.10 Substitution (**s**) *260*

13.11 Basic Regular Expressions Revisited *263*

13.12 Conclusion *266*

Wrap Up *266*

Test Your Understanding *267*

Flex Your Brain *268*

CHAPTER 14 ESSENTIAL SHELL PROGRAMMING   270

14.1 Shell Scripts *271*

14.2 **read**: Making Scripts Interactive *272*

14.3 Using Command Line Arguments *273*

14.4 **exit** and Exit Status of Command *275*

14.5 The Logical Operators && and ||—Conditional Execution *276*

14.6 The **if** Conditional *277*

14.7 Using **test** and [] to Evaluate Expressions *278*

14.8 The **case** Conditional *283*

14.9 **expr**: Computation and String Handling *285*

14.10 $0: Calling a Script by Different Names *288*

14.11 **while**: Looping *289*

14.12 **for**: Looping with a List *291*

14.13 **set** and **shift**: Manipulating the Positional Parameters *294*

14.14 The Here Document (<<) *296*

14.15 **trap**: Interrupting a Program *297*

14.16 Debugging Shell Scripts with **set -x** *298*

14.17 Sample Validation and Data Entry Scripts *299*

14.18 Conclusion *302*

Wrap Up 302

Test Your Understanding 303

Flex Your Brain 303

CHAPTER 15 ESSENTIAL SYSTEM ADMINISTRATION 305

15.1 **root**: The System Administrator's Login *306*

15.2 The Administrator's Privileges *307*

15.3 Maintaining Security *308*

15.4 User Management *311*

15.5 Startup and Shutdown *313*

15.6 Managing Disk Space *315*

15.7 Device Files *317*

15.8 Handling Floppy Diskettes *319*

15.9 **cpio**: A Backup Program *321*

15.10 **tar**: The "Tape" Archive Program *325*

15.11 Conclusion *328*

Wrap Up 328

Test Your Understanding 329

Flex Your Brain 330

PART II

CHAPTER 16 THE X WINDOW SYSTEM 333

16.1 X Basics *334*

16.2 The Common Desktop Environment (CDE) *336*

16.3 Starting and Quitting X *338*

16.4 The Terminal Emulator *338*

16.5 Cut-and-Paste Operations *339*

16.6 Running X Clients Remotely *341*

16.7 Command Line Options *343*

16.8   Some Standard X Clients *344*

16.9   The Startup Files *347*

16.10   X Resources *348*

16.11   Conclusion *349*

     Wrap Up 349

     Test Your Understanding 350

     Flex Your Brain 350

CHAPTER 17 NETWORKING TOOLS   351

17.1   TCP/IP Basics *352*

17.2   Resolving IP Addresses *354*

17.3   The Applications *355*

17.4   **ping**: Checking the Network *356*

17.5   **telnet**: Remote Login *356*

17.6   **ftp**: File Transfer Protocol *357*

17.7   Cryptography Basics *360*

17.8   SSH: The Secure Shell *362*

17.9   The SSH Tools *366*

17.10   The Domain Name System (DNS) *368*

17.11   Internet Mail *370*

17.12   MIME: Handling Binary Attachments in Mail *372*

17.13   The World Wide Web *373*

17.14   Multimedia on the Web: MIME Revisited *377*

17.15   Conclusion *378*

     Wrap Up 378

     Test Your Understanding 379

     Flex Your Brain 380

CHAPTER 18 awk—AN ADVANCED FILTER   381

18.1   Simple **awk** Filtering *382*

18.2   Splitting a Line into Fields *383*

18.3   **printf**: Formatting Output *384*

18.4   Variables and Expressions *384*

18.5   The Comparison Operators *385*

18.6   Number Processing *388*

18.7   Variables *388*

18.8   The -f Option: Storing **awk** Programs in a File *388*

18.9   The BEGIN and END Sections *389*

18.10   Built-in Variables *390*

18.11 Arrays *391*

18.12 Functions *393*

18.13 Control Flow—The **if** Statement *394*

18.14 Looping with **for** *396*

18.15 Looping with **while** *398*

18.16 Conclusion *398*

Wrap Up 398

Test Your Understanding 399

Flex Your Brain 400

CHAPTER 19 perl—THE MASTER MANIPULATOR **401**

19.1 **perl** Preliminaries *402*

19.2 The **chop** Function: Removing the Last Character *403*

19.3 Variables and Operators *404*

19.4 The String Handling Functions *405*

19.5 Specifying Filenames in Command Line *406*

19.6 $_: The Default Variable *407*

19.7 Current Line Number ($.) and the Range Operator (..) *408*

19.8 Lists and Arrays *408*

19.9 **foreach**: Looping Through a List *412*

19.10 **split**: Splitting into a List or Array *413*

19.11 **join**: Joining a List *415*

19.12 **dec2bin.pl**: Converting a Decimal Number to Binary *416*

19.13 **grep**: Searching an Array for a Pattern *416*

19.14 Associative Arrays *417*

19.15 Regular Expressions and Substitution *420*

19.16 File Handling *423*

19.17 File Tests *425*

19.18 Subroutines *426*

19.19 Conclusion *427*

Wrap Up 427

Test Your Understanding 428

Flex Your Brain 429

CHAPTER 20 ADVANCED vi **431**

20.1 Operators *431*

20.2 The ex Mode: Handling Multiple Files *435*

20.3 Named Buffers: Storing Multiple Text Sections *437*

20.4 Numbered Buffers: Undoing Multiple Line Deletions *438*

20.5   Entering Control Characters (*[Ctrl-v]*) *439*

20.6   Searching for a Character *439*

20.7   Marking Text *440*

20.8   Customizing **vi** *440*

20.9   Conclusion *444*

Wrap Up 444

Test Your Understanding 444

Flex Your Brain 445

CHAPTER 21 ADVANCED SHELL PROGRAMMING   **446**

21.1   Shells and Sub-shells *447*

21.2   () and {}: Sub-shell or Current Shell? *447*

21.3   **export**: Exporting Shell Variables *448*

21.4   Running a Script in the Current Shell: The **.** Command *449*

21.5   **let**: Computation—a Second Look (Korn and Bash) *450*

21.6   Arrays (Korn and Bash) *450*

21.7   String Handling (Korn and Bash) *452*

21.8   Conditional Parameter Substitution *453*

21.9   Merging Streams *455*

21.10   Shell Functions *456*

21.11   **eval**: Evaluating Twice *459*

21.12   The **exec** Statement *461*

21.13   Conclusion *464*

Wrap Up 464

Test Your Understanding 464

Flex Your Brain 465

CHAPTER 22 PROGRAM DEVELOPMENT TOOLS   **466**

22.1   Handling Multisource C Applications *466*

22.2   A Multisource Application *467*

22.3   **make**: Keeping Programs Up-to-date *471*

22.4   **ar**: Building a Library (Archive) *475*

22.5   Static and Shared Libraries *477*

22.6   Version Control With SCCS and RCS *478*

22.7   An SCCS Session *479*

22.8   Activity and History Information *483*

22.9   Continuing Editing with SCCS *484*

22.10   The Revision Control System (RCS) *486*

22.11   Conclusion *490*

Wrap Up 490
Test Your Understanding 490
Flex Your Brain 491

CHAPTER 23 SYSTEMS PROGRAMMING I—FILES 492

23.1 System Call Basics 493
23.2 Opening and Closing a File 495
23.3 Using the I/O Calls 497
23.4 Buffered and Unbuffered I/O 502
23.5 umask: Modifying File Permissions During Creation 503
23.6 Handling Errors 504
23.7 File Sharing 509
23.8 Directory Navigation 512
23.9 Reading a Directory 513
23.10 Modifying Entries in Directory 514
23.11 Reading the Inode: stat 516
23.12 Checking a File's Access Rights 521
23.13 Modifying File Attributes 526
23.14 Conclusion 529
Wrap Up 530
Test Your Understanding 531
Flex Your Brain 532

CHAPTER 24 SYSTEMS PROGRAMMING II—PROCESS CONTROL 533

24.1 Process Abstractions 534
24.2 process.c: Looking Up Some Process Credentials 536
24.3 Creating a Process 537
24.4 _exit and exit: Process Termination 540
24.5 Waiting to Pick Up Child's Exit Status 542
24.6 Process Groups 545
24.7 Zombies and Orphans 545
24.8 exec: The Final Step in Process Creation 546
24.9 shell.c: A Program with a Shell-like Capability 551
24.10 File Descriptor Manipulation 553
24.11 pipe: Inter-process Communication 557
24.12 Signal Handling 560
24.13 signal: Installing a Signal Handler 563
24.14 killprocess.c: The Final Program Using kill 566
24.15 Conclusion 569

Wrap Up 569
Test Your Understanding 570
Flex Your Brain 571

CHAPTER 25   ADVANCED SYSTEM ADMINISTRATION   572

25.1   Maintaining Security 573
25.2   Partitions and File Systems 574
25.3   The Standard File Systems and Their Types 577
25.4   fdisk: Creating Partitions 578
25.5   mkfs: Creating a File System 580
25.6   Mounting and Unmounting File Systems 580
25.7   fsck: File System Checking 583
25.8   System Startup and init 585
25.9   Shutdown and the sync Operation 589
25.10   Backups 589
25.11   Conclusion 591
        Wrap Up 591
        Test Your Understanding 592
        Flex Your Brain 593

Appendix A   The C Shell—Programming Constructs   594
Appendix B   vi/vim Command Reference   600
Appendix C   The HOWTO   606
Appendix D   Solutions to Test Your Understanding   611
Appendix E   Glossary   632
Appendix F   Bibliography   650
Index   652

Preface

xx Preface

This Fourth Edition

UNIX and the C language have changed the way people used and learned to program with computers. Even though technology changes fast, certain approaches to technology often remain unchanged. UNIX is one of them; it has survived the test of time. Enterprise managers today no longer need to justify the use of UNIX. Thanks partly to Linux, things should remain this way in the foreseeable future too.

Even though this book deals with an operating system in *particular*, it will help you understand operating systems in *general*. This fourth edition was written with this objective in mind. In fact, theoretical courses on operating systems often use the UNIX system to illustrate key features. Although we haven't seen another notable system since the advent of UNIX, it shouldn't surprise us if future operating systems adopt many of the key features of UNIX.

Many people derive comfort from the "user-friendliness" offered by Windows. Why key in a command when one or two mouse clicks can do the job? True, but it doesn't require much effort for a UNIX enthusiast to prove that the mouse can't solve *all* problems. Once you go through Part I of this book, you'll discover several situations where complex jobs are handled—not by mouse clicks—but by combining tools and programming with the shell. Shun the herd and join the select body of people for whom it doesn't matter whether UNIX is user-friendly or not. It's simply a way of life—a life they will never cease to cherish.

Why UNIX Still Remains Important

Even though UNIX was created by the engineering and scientific community, its robustness and absence of a comparable alternative led to its widespread acceptance in the commercial market. UNIX today runs with full vigor on both handhelds and supercomputers. It remains the preferred platform for enterprise databases, ISPs, Web servers and electronic commerce. Further, UNIX is getting better all the time simply because numerous minds spread across the globe are engaged in its improvment and enhancement. Think big and you'll have to think of UNIX.

UNIX offers two of the best text editors (**vi** and **emacs**). Its text processing utilities are unmatched. Complex text manipulation problems are solved in UNIX by using tools in combination. Add the shell's programming features, and you can at once develop noninteractive applications—and even schedule them to run at specific times. It won't take you long to realize that UNIX actually encourages you to innovate using its basic tool set and soon you will love to accept the numerous challenges offered by this operating system.

UNIX fragmentation—once a major irritant—has now been addressed by standards bodies like POSIX and The Open Group. Today, we have a single standard, *The Single UNIX Specification*, that lays down once and for all what an operating system must offer to be called UNIX. This single reference allows you to develop applications that will run without modification on all UNIX systems. We constantly refer to POSIX in this text.

This Fourth Edition

This edition contains fewer chapters but retains the page count. I am of the view that UNIX system administration deserves a separate book by itself, and have, therefore, pruned its coverage in this edition. Also, TCP/IP and networking aren't exactly part of basic UNIX, the reason why there's only a single chapter on networking tools this time. Network administration along with related topics have been moved to the Web site. The remaining key features of this edition are described below:

- Numerous asides, entitled *How It Works*, that explain how a key concept works in UNIX. Even though these asides are for optional reading, they provide a fuller understanding as well as the base for programming in UNIX.

- A separate chapter, *Program Development Tools*, that includes **make** and version control (SCCS and RCS). If you are working on large projects, then you need to use this chapter for program maintenance.

- Coverage on *cryptography* and the tools offered by the Secure Shell suite (SSH). As hackers increasingly threaten the way we live and transact, you need to know why and how data is encrypted.

- A separate command reference for the **vi** editor as Appendix B. This should have been done much earlier, but now it's finally here.

- A specially compiled HOWTO (Appendix C) that helps you locate a command sequence that does a specific job.

This book also discusses Linux—not as an alternative to UNIX—but as an important UNIX implementation. You must treat Linux as a gateway to learning UNIX. Like other UNIX flavors like Solaris, HP-UX and AIX, Linux complies with POSIX and The Single UNIX Specification. In fact, there are more similarities than differences that Linux has with these flavors. This book doesn't encourage the use of Linux-specific features.

A note of caution at this stage would be in order. Unfortunately, many people like UNIX/Linux for its graphical user interface (GUI). You'll have to understand that GUI use is to be reserved for viewing graphics and browsing the Web. *To use UNIX in Windows-style would be self-defeating*. If you appreciate that the UNIX command line is *the* way to interact with the system, then this book is for you. Even though the X Window system still features as a separate chapter in this edition, its coverage would be curtailed in future editions.

The exercises at the end of each chapter have been given a major facelift. There are more and challenging exercises in this edition than in previous ones. The section entitled *Test Your*

Understanding contains mostly simple questions, but you should try to solve them before you switch chapters. The answers to these questions are available in Appendix D. The more involved questions feature in *Flex Your Brains*, whose answers are provided on the book's Web site, *but available only to adopters of the book*.

All examples should run on most UNIX/Linux systems, and you'll find suitable indications when a system-specific feature is encountered. Don't forget to read *Conventions Followed in the Book* before you move into the UNIX mainstream beginning with Chapter 1. Key terms, now shown in a bold and bigger font, would be easier to spot this time.

Acknowledgements

Vibha Mahajan has always been a pleasure to work with, in this as well as in previous editions. Jacob Alexander has never been found wanting in offering valuable suggestions, and has lived up to my expectations very well. Thanks are also due to Mini Narayanan for copyediting and Sohan Gaur for managing the production process. My wife Julie and daughter Sohini continue to remain my main source of inspiration.

And on this note, I wish you an exciting journey to the UNIX world!

SUMITABHA DAS

Conventions Used in This Book

The following conventions have been used in this book:

- Key terms are shown in a large bold font:

  What you see above is an **absolute pathname**, ...

- Commands, program names, user input in examples and system calls are shown in bold constant width font:

  Many commands in **more** including **f** and **b** use a repeat factor.

  The shell features three types of loops—**while**, **until** and **for**.

  Enter your name: **henry**

  The forking mechanism uses the **fork** system call to create a process.

- Apart from command output, filenames, command options, strings, expressions and symbols are shown in constant width font:

  Most commands are located in `/bin` and `/usr/bin`.

  Try doing that with the name `jai sharma`.

  There's adequate scope of using the `-e` and `-f` options.

  The shell looks for the characters `>`, `<` and `<<` in the command line.

- Machine and domain names, email addresses and URLs are displayed in italics:

  This copies a file from the remote machine *saturn*.

  User kumar on this host can be addressed as *kumar@calcs.heavens.com*.

  Google offers comprehensive News services at *http://groups.google.com*.

- Placeholders for filenames, terms, menu options and explanatory comments within examples are displayed in italics:

  When compiled with **cc** *filename*, it produces a file named **a.out**.

  .... to develop a set of standard rules (*protocols*)

  Use *Edit>Preferences* to configure Netscape.

  `$ cd ../..`   *Moves two levels up*

- The following abbreviations, shortcuts and symbols have been used:

  SVR4—System V Release 4

  sh—Bourne shell

  csh—C shell

  ksh—Korn shell

  $HOME/*flname*—The file *flname* in the home directory

  ~/*flname*—The file *flname* in the home directory

  foo and bar—Generic file and directory names as used on USENET

Part I

For the Beginner ...

Getting Started

This chapter begins the tour of the UNIX universe. To understand UNIX, we'll first have to know what an operating system is, why a computer needs one and how UNIX is vastly different from other operating systems that came before—and after. Through a hands-on session, we'll learn to play with the UNIX system and acquire familiarity with some of its commands that are used everyday for interacting with the system. The experience of the introductory session will help us understand the concepts presented in the next chapter.

UNIX has had a rather turbulent background. Knowing this background will help us understand the objectives that guided its development. Even though UNIX owes its origin to AT&T, contributions made by the academic community and industry have also led to the enrichment and fragmentation of UNIX. The emergence of a windowing (GUI) system, however, has often led users to adopt undesirable shortcuts. For the initiated though, Linux offers a superior and cost-effective solution for the mastery of UNIX.

WHAT YOU WILL LEARN

- What an operating system is and how UNIX more than fulfills that role.
- Know the location of the special characters on the keyboard.
- Log in and out of a UNIX system using a username and password.
- Run a few commands like **date**, **who** and **cal**.
- View *processes* with **ps**, and *files* with **ls**.
- Use a special character like the * to match multiple filenames.
- The role of the *shell* in interpreting these special characters (*metacharacters*).
- A brief background of UNIX and Linux.
- How the Internet contributed to the acceptance of UNIX.

TOPICS OF SPECIAL INTEREST

- Examination of the sequence of steps followed by the shell in executing the command **ls > list** to save command output in a file.
- A similar examination of the sequence **ls | wc** to connect two commands to form a *pipeline*.

1.1 THE OPERATING SYSTEM

We use computers freely, but most of us never bother to know what's inside the box. Why should we? After all, we also use TV and never care to find out how this idiot box manages to convert invisible radio waves to real-life colorful pictures. Yes, you can certainly use spreadsheets and word processors without knowing how these programs access the machine's resources. As long as you continue to get all those reports and charts, do you really need to know anything else?

Then the inevitable happens. The great crash occurs, the machine refuses to boot. The expert tells you that the *operating system* has to be reloaded. You are taken in by surprise. You've heard of software, and you have used lots of them. But what is this thing called the operating system? Is it just another piece of software?

Relax, it is. But it's not just any ordinary software that helps you write letters, but a special one—one that gives life to a machine. Every computer needs some basic intelligence to start with. Unlike mortals, a computer is not born with any. This intelligence is used to provide the essential services for programs that run under its auspices—like using the CPU, allocating memory and accessing devices like the hard disk for reading and writing files.

The computer provides yet another type of service, this time for you—the user. You'll always need to copy or delete a file, or create a directory to house files. You'll need to know the people who are working in the network, or send a mail message to a friend. As a system administrator, you'll also have to back up files. No word processor will do all this for you, neither will your Web browser. All this belongs rightly to the domain of what is known as the *operating system*.

So, what is an operating system? An **operating system** is the software that manages the computer's hardware and provides a convenient and safe environment for running programs. It acts as an interface between programs and the hardware resources that these programs access (like memory, hard disk and printer). It is loaded into memory when a computer is booted and remains active as long as the machine is up.

To grasp the key features of an operating system, let's consider the management tasks it has to perform when we run a program. These operations also depend on the operating system we are using, but the following actions are common to most systems:

- The operating system allocates memory for the program and loads the program to the allocated memory.

- It also loads the CPU registers with control information related to the program. The registers maintain the memory locations where each segment of a program is stored.

- The instructions provided in the program are executed by the CPU. The operating system keeps track of the instruction that was last executed. This enables it to resume a program if it had to be taken out of the CPU before it completed execution.

- If the program needs to access the hardware, it makes a call to the operating system rather than attempt to do the job itself. For instance, if the program needs to read a file on disk, the operating system directs the disk controller to open the file and make the data available to the program.

- After the program has completed execution, the operating system cleans up the memory and registers and makes them available for the next program.

Modern operating systems are *multiprogramming*, i.e. they allow multiple programs to be in memory. However, on computers with a single CPU, only one program can run at any instant. Rather than allow a single program to run to completion without interruption, an operating system generally allows a program to run for a small instant of time, save its current state and then load the next program in the queue. The operating system creates a *process* for each program and then control the switching of these processes.

There have been lots of operating systems in the past, one at least from each hardware vendor. They all contributed in their own way to the chaotic situation that made programs written on one machine totally incapable of running on another. Vendors required consumers to purchase expensive proprietary hardware and software if two dissimilar machines needed to talk to each other. We also had DOS and Windows (in all its manifestations) on our desktop computers providing us with a cheaper and user-friendly way of computing.

1.2 THE UNIX OPERATING SYSTEM

Like DOS and Windows, there's another operating system called UNIX. It arrived earlier than the other two, and stayed back late enough to give us the Internet. UNIX is a giant operating system, and is way ahead of them in sheer power. It has practically everything an operating system should have, and several features which other operating systems never had. Its richness and elegance go beyond the commands and tools that constitute it, while simplicity permeates the entire system. It runs on practically every hardware and provided inspiration to the Open Source movement.

However, UNIX also makes many demands of the user. It requires a different type of commitment to understand the subject, even when the user is an experienced computer professional. It introduces certain concepts not known to the computing community before, and uses numerous symbols whose meanings are anything but obvious. It achieves unusual tasks with a few keystrokes, but it takes time to devise a sequence of them for a specific task. Often, it doesn't tell you whether you are right or wrong, and doesn't warn you of the consequences of your actions. That is probably the reason why many people still prefer to stay away from UNIX.

You interact with a UNIX system through a *command interpreter* called the *shell*. Key in a word, and the shell interprets it as a *command* to be executed. A command may already exist on the system as one of several hundred native tools or it could be one written by you. However, the power of UNIX lies in combining these commands in the same way the English language lets you combine words to generate a meaningful idea. As you walk through the chapters of the text, you'll soon discover that this is a major strength of the system.

Kernighan and Pike (*The UNIX Programming Environment*, Prentice-Hall) lamented long ago that "as the UNIX system has spread, the fraction of its users who are skilled in its application has decreased." Many people still use the system as they would use any other operating system, and continue to write comprehensive programs that have already been written before. Beginners with some experience in DOS and Windows think of UNIX in terms of them, quite oblivious of the fact that UNIX has much more to offer. Though references to DOS/Windows have often been made whenever a similar feature was encountered, the similarities end there too. You should not let them get in the way of the UNIX experience.

1.3 KNOWING YOUR MACHINE

Unlike DOS and Windows, UNIX can be used by several users concurrently. In other words, a *single* copy of the operating system installed on disk can serve the needs of hundreds of users. If you have access to such a *multiuser* system, then in all probability you'll be sitting with just a terminal or monitor, and a keyboard. Like you, there will be others working on similar terminals. The rest of the equipment will probably be located in a separate room with restricted access. In this arrangement, you are expected to hook on to your account, do your work, disconnect and leave quietly.

Things are quite different, however, when you are the sole user of the system. This could happen if you work on a desktop machine that has its own *CPU* (the Central Processor Unit), *RAM* (Random Access Memory—the memory), hard disk, floppy and CD-ROM drives, printer and the controllers of these devices. If you own the machine, you are directly responsible for its startup, shutdown and maintenance. If you lose a file, it's your job to get it from a backup. If things don't work properly, you have to try all possible means to set them right before you decide to call the maintenance person.

1.3.1 The Keyboard

Before you start working, you need to know right now the functions of a number of keys on the keyboard. Many of these keys are either not used by DOS/Windows, or have different functions there. The portion of the keyboard at the left having the *QWERTY* layout resembles your typewriter. You need to be familiar with this section of the keyboard initially, in addition to some other keys in its immediate vicinity. If you know typing, you are on familiar terrain, and keyboard phobia should not get in your way.

Apart from the alphanumeric keys, you'll observe a number of symbols as shown below:

`` ` ~ ! @ # $ % ^ & * ( ) - _ = + \ | [ ] { } ; : ' " , . < > / ? ``

Each alphabet, number or symbol is known as a **character**, which represents the smallest piece of information that you can deal with. All of these characters have unique values assigned to them, called the **ASCII value** (ASCII—American Standard Code for Information Interchange). For instance, the letter A has the ASCII value 65, while the bang or exclamation mark (!) has the value 21.

There are some keys that have no counterparts in the typewriter. Note the key *[Enter]* at the right which is used to terminate a line. On some machines this key may be labeled *[Return]*. The significance of this key is taken up in Section 1.4.4.

When you look at a blank screen, you'll see a blinking object called a **cursor**. When you key in a character, it shows up at the location of the cursor, while moving the cursor itself right. Directly above the *[Enter]* key is the key shown with a ◀— or labeled *[Backspace]*. You have to press this key to erase one or more characters that you have just entered, using a feature known as **backspacing**. When this key is pressed, the cursor moves over the character placed on its left and removes it from sight.

Another important key is the one labeled *[Ctrl]* (called Control) which you'll find in duplicate on the lower side of the keyboard. This key is never used singly but always in combination with other keys. We'll be using this key several times in this book. For instance, whenever you are advised to use *[Ctrl-s]* to stop a scrolling display, you should first press the *[Ctrl]* key and then the key labeled s, while *[Ctrl]* is still kept pressed.

At the top-left corner, you can see the *[Esc]* key (called Escape), which you'll require to use when performing file editing with a text editor such as **vi**. This key often takes you to the previous menu in a menu-based program. Then there is the *[Delete]* key, which some systems (like SCO UNIX) use to interrupt a program in the same way *[Ctrl-c]* is used on other UNIX systems (and DOS). On a system running Solaris or Linux, you'll probably be using *[Ctrl-c]*, rather than *[Delete]*, for interrupting a program.

In the same line as the *[Esc]* key are the twelve function keys labeled *[F1]*, *[F2]*, etc., up to *[F12]*. You won't require these keys initially, but much later (for mapping keys in **vi**, for example). The cursor control keys (the ones with four arrows) are required for recalling previous commands in the Bash shell.

1.4 A BRIEF SESSION

Seeing is believing as they say, so without further ado, let's get down to business and see what a UNIX session is really like. If you are migrating from the DOS/Windows environment, you have a bit of mental preparation to do before you start. UNIX isn't very friendly, and the messages that it throws up on the screen can sometimes be confusing. Often, there are no messages at all, and you'll then have to figure out yourself whether the command worked properly. Absorb as much as you can from this session, think for a while, and then move on to the other chapters.

1.4.1 Logging in with Username and Password

UNIX is security-conscious, and can be used only by those persons who maintain an *account* with the computer system. The list of accounts is maintained separately in the computer. You can't simply sit down at any terminal and start banging away if your name doesn't feature in the list. That's both inadvisable and an impossible thing to do.

Because the system can be used by many users, someone has to be given charge of administration of the system. This person is known as the **system administrator**, and he is the person who will grant you the authority to use the system. He opens an account with a name for your use, and gives you a secret code that you have to enter when the system prompts you for it. If you are running UNIX on your desktop, then remember that you are the administrator of the machine.

If you have the name "kumar" for this account, you'll be expected to enter this name when you see a *prompt* similar to this on the terminal:

```
SunOS 5.8                          A Sun machine running Solaris 8

login:
```

The prompt here is preceded by the version of the operating system, SunOS 5.8, which is the operating system of Solaris 8. This is a flavor (brand) of UNIX offered by Sun Microsystems, but your system could show a different string here (if at all). The prompt itself could have a prefix showing the machine name. (Yes, every machine has a name in UNIX.)

The login prompt indicates that the terminal is available for someone to **log in** (i.e., connect to the machine). This message also indicates that the previous user has **logged out** (i.e., finished her work and disconnected). Since you now have an account named 'kumar', enter this string at the prompt. Then press the *[Enter]* key after the string:

```
login: kumar[Enter]
Password:
```

The system now requests you to enter the secret code that was handed to you by your administrator. This code should be known to none except yourself. (The administrator doesn't need to know!) Type the secret code and press *[Enter]*:

```
login: kumar
Password:*********[Enter]                          Entry not displayed
```

You may be surprised to observe that the string you entered at the Password: prompt isn't displayed on the screen. This is another security feature built into the system that doesn't let someone near you see what you have entered (unless, of course, she has been meticulously monitoring your finger movements!).

If you make mistakes while typing, simply press *[Enter]* one or two times until the login prompt reappears on the screen. Be sure to terminate your responses with *[Enter]* to make the system "see" the input that you have entered.

The string that you entered at the first prompt (login:) is known variously as your **login name**, **user-id**, or **username**, and these names will be used interchangeably throughout this book. The secret code that you entered at the next prompt (Password:) is known as the **password**. If you enter either of them incorrectly, the system flashes the following message:

```
Login incorrect
login:
```

Another level of security! You simply don't know what went wrong—your login name or your password. The message Login incorrect is in fact quite deceptive. In most cases, it's the password that's the culprit. Go back to your secret diary where the password should have been noted and restart the session. When you get both these parameters correct, this is what you could see on a Solaris system:

```
Last login: Thu May  9 06:48:39 from saturn.heavens.com
$ _                                    The cursor shown by the _ character
```

The system now shows the $ as the **prompt**, with the cursor constantly blinking beside it. This is a typical UNIX prompt, and many UNIX systems use the $ as the default prompt string. For some users, you might see the % instead of the $, and the system administrator will in all probability be using the #. UNIX allows you to customize the prompt, and it's not unusual to see prompts like these:

```
[/home/kumar]
kumar@saturn:/home/kumar >
```

Both prompts show your "location" in the file system. This should be familiar to DOS users who have used the statement PROMPT [pg] in the AUTOEXEC.BAT file to customize the prompt string. A customized prompt, as you'll see later, helps in a number of ways. For the time being, be content with whatever prompt you have to work with; it won't cause you any harm.

Note: As soon as you log in, a program called the *shell* starts to run at your terminal, and keeps running until you terminate the session. As mentioned before, the shell is your system's *command interpreter*. It displays the prompt and accepts all your input from the keyboard. The UNIX system offers a variety of shells (like Bourne shell, C shell, Korn shell and Bash) for you to choose from. Whether your prompt can display your "location" entirely depends on the shell you use. When the administrator opens a user account, he also sets a specific shell for the user.

Caution: On your first login, the system may force you to change your password. On the other hand, the system may not prompt for the password at all, in which case you'll be taken to the prompt straightaway. This presents a security breach, and you should immediately assign a password to your own account. If others have acquired knowledge of your password, you should change it. Both assignment and change of password can be done with a command named **passwd** (*3.9*). You'll also learn later the terrible consequences that you may have to face if people with mischievous intent somehow come to know what your password is.

1.4.2 The Command

We have now been able to successfully log on to a UNIX system. What do we do now? Let's enter something from the keyboard, press *[Enter]*, and then see what happens:

```
$ unix[Enter]
ksh: unix: command not found        A message from the shell
$ _                                  Shell returns prompt
```

What the system expected was a *command* that it knows, and unix doesn't appear to be a legitimate command. Nevertheless, the prompt returns to accept the next command. UNIX has a large family of commands, some of them quite powerful, and a UNIX expert is expected to know many of them. We'll now acquaint ourselves with a few of these commands.

1.4.3 date: Displaying Both Date and Time

Now that the previous command was rejected by the system, let's use one that it recognizes. UNIX has a **date** command that shows the date and time in the form used on the Internet. Type the four characters in date and press *[Enter]*:

```
$ date[Enter]
Fri Aug 19 13:28:34 IST 2005
$ _
```

date is a valid command, and it displays both the date and time. Notice another security feature of UNIX; the command doesn't prompt you to change either the date or time. This facility is available only to the administrator, and the strange thing is that he uses the same command *(15.2.1)* to do it!

So what is **date**? It's one of several hundred programs available in the UNIX system. Whatever you input through the keyboard is interpreted by the system as a **command**, and when you use one, you are in fact commanding the machine to do something. The **date** command instructs the machine to display the current date and time. Incidentally, most UNIX commands are represented as *files* in the system.

Caution: Tampering with the system date can have adverse effects on a UNIX system. There are many processes that go on in the background without your knowledge, and they are scheduled to start at specific times. If a nonprivileged (ordinary) user (The system administrator is known as the *superuser* simply because he's blessed with enormous powers!) is allowed to change the date and time at will, chaos will ensue.

Note: Henceforth, we'll use the terms *privileged user*, *superuser* and *system administrator* to refer to the root user account that is used by the administrator for logging in, and *nonprivileged user* to mean all other users. It's often important for us to make this distinction because the root user enjoys certain privileges that are denied others.

1.4.4 Two Important Observations

You have had your first interaction with the system by running two commands after logging in. Even though one command worked and the other didn't, you had to terminate each by hitting the *[Enter]* key. The text that you type at the terminal remains hidden from the system until this key is pressed. First-time users often fail to appreciate this point because there's no "*[Enter]* key" in the human information system. Humans register speech or text, as it is being spoken or read, in a continuous manner. In this respect, this key resembles the shutter of a camera; nothing gets into the film until the shutter is pressed.

Also note that the completion of a command, successful or otherwise, is indicated by the return of the prompt (here, a $). The presence of the prompt indicates that all work related to the previous command have been completed, and the system is ready to accept the next command. Henceforth, we'll not indicate the *[Enter]* key or the return of the prompt except in not-so-obvious circumstances.

1.4.5 tput clear: Clearing the Screen

All UNIX systems offer the **tput** command to clear the screen. This is something you'd often like to do to avoid getting distracted by output or error messages of previous commands. However, when you use **tput** as it is, (i.e., without any additional words), this is what UNIX has to say:

```
$ tput
usage:  tput [-T [term]] capname [parm argument...]
OR:     tput -S <<
```

This message makes little sense to a beginner, so we won't attempt to interpret it right now. However, one thing is obvious; **tput** requires additional input to work properly. To make **tput** work, follow **tput** with the word clear:

```
tput clear                                    clear is an argument to tput
```

The screen clears and the prompt and cursor are positioned at the top-left corner. Some systems also offer the **clear** command, but the standard UNIX specifications (like POSIX) don't require UNIX systems to offer this command. You must remember to use **tput clear** to clear the screen because we won't be discussing this command again in this text.

Note: The additional word used with **tput** isn't a command, but is referred to as an *argument*. Here, clear is an argument to **tput**, and the fact that **tput** refused to work alone indicates that it always requires an argument (sometimes more). And, if clear is one argument, there could be others. We'll often refer to the *default* behavior of a command to mean the effect of a using a command without any arguments.

1.4.6 cal: The Calendar

cal is a handy tool that you can invoke any time to see the calendar of any specific month, or a complete year. To see the calendar for the month of July, 2006, provide the month number and year as the two arguments to **cal**:

```
$ cal 7 2006                             Command run with two arguments
        July 2006
Su Mo Tu We Th Fr Sa
                   1
 2  3  4  5  6  7  8
 9 10 11 12 13 14 15
16 17 18 19 20 21 22
23 24 25 26 27 28 29
30 31
```

With **cal**, you can produce the calendar for any month or year between the years 1 and 9999. This should serve our requirements for some time, right? We'll see more of this command later.

1.4.7 who: Who Are the Users?

UNIX is a system that can be concurrently used by multiple users, and you might be interested in knowing the people who are also using the system like you. Use the **who** command:

```
$ who
kumar     console     May  9 09:31    (:0)
vipul     pts/4       May  9 09:31    (:0.0)
raghav    pts/5       May  9 09:32    (saturn.heavens.com)
```

There are currently three users—kumar, vipul and raghav. These are actually the user-ids or usernames they used to log in. The output also includes the username, kumar, which you entered at the login: prompt to gain entry to the system. The second column shows the name of the terminal the user is working on. Just as all users have names, all terminals, disks and printers also have names. You'll see later that these names are represented as *files* in the system. The date and time of login are also shown in the output. Ignore the last column for the time being.

Observe also that the output of **who** doesn't include any headers to indicate what the various columns mean. This is an important feature of the system, and is in some measure responsible for the unfriendly image that UNIX has acquired. After you have completed Chapter 8, you'll discover that it is actually a blessing in disguise.

You logged in with the name kumar, so the system addresses you by this name and associates kumar with whatever work you do. Create a file and the system will make kumar the owner of the file. Execute a program and kumar will be the owner of the *process* (next topic) associated with your program. Send mail to another user and the system will inform the recipient that mail has arrived from kumar.

Note: UNIX isn't just a repository of commands producing informative output. You can extract useful information from command output for using with other commands. For instance, you can extract the day of the week (here, Fri) from the **date** output and then devise a program that does different things depending on the day the program is invoked. You can also "cut" the user-ids from the **who** output and use the list with the **mailx** command to send mail to all users currently logged in. The facility to perform these useful tasks with one or two lines of code makes UNIX truly different from other operating systems.

1.4.8 ps: Viewing Processes

We observed that the shell program is always running at your terminal. Every command that you run gives rise to a *process*, and the shell is a process as well. To view all processes that you are responsible for creating, run the **ps** command:

```
$ ps
   PID TTY      TIME CMD
   364 console  0:00 ksh                              Shell running all the time!
```

Unlike **who**, **ps** generates a header followed by a line containing the details of the **ksh** process. When you run several programs, there will be multiple lines in the **ps** output. **ksh** represents the Korn shell (an advanced shell from AT&T) and is constantly running at this terminal. This process has a unique number 364 (called the *process-id* or PID), and when you log out, this process is killed.

Note: Even though we are using the Korn shell here, you could be using another shell. Instead of **ksh**, you could see **sh** (the primitive Bourne shell), **csh** (C shell—still popular today) or **bash** (Bash shell—a very powerful shell and recommended for use). Throughout this book, we'll be comparing the features of these shells and discover features that are available in one shell but not in another. If a command doesn't produce output as explained in this text, it can often be attributed to the shell.

1.4.9 1s: Listing Files

Your UNIX system has a large number of files that control its functioning, and users also create files on their own. These files are organized in separate folders called *directories*. You can list the names of the files available in this directory with the **ls** command:

```
$ ls
README                          Uppercase first
chap01
chap02
chap03
helpdir
progs
```

ls displays a list of six files, three of which actually contain the chapters of this textbook. Note that the files are arranged alphabetically with uppercase having precedence over lower (which we call the **ASCII collating sequence**).

Since the files containing the first three chapters have similar filenames, UNIX lets you use a special short-hand notation (*) to access them:

```
$ ls chap*
chap01
chap02
chap03
```

Sometimes, just displaying a list of filenames isn't enough; you need to know more about these files. For that to happen, **ls** has to be used with an *option*, -l, between the command and filenames:

```
$ ls -l chap*                                            -l is an option
-rw-r--r--  1 kumar    users     5609 Apr 23 09:30 chap01
-rw-r--r--  1 kumar    users    26129 May 14 18:55 chap02
-rw-r--r--  1 kumar    users    37385 May 15 10:30 chap03
```

The argument beginning with a hyphen is known as an *option*. The characteristic feature of most command options is that they begin with a - (hyphen). An option changes the default behavior (i.e. when used without options) of a command, so if **ls** prints a columnar list of files, the -l option makes it display some of the attributes as well.

1.4.10 Directing Output to a File

UNIX has simple symbols (called *metacharacters*) for creating and storing information in files. Instead of viewing the output of the **ls** command on the terminal, you can save the information in a file, list, by using a special symbol, > (the right chevron character on your keyboard):

```
$ ls > list
$ _                             Prompt returns—no display on terminal
```

You see nothing on the terminal except the return of the prompt. The shell is at work here. It has a mechanism of *redirecting* any output, normally coming to the terminal, to a disk file. To check whether the shell has actually done the job, use the **cat** command with the filename as argument:

```
$ cat list                                            cat displays a file's contents
README
chap01
chap02
chap03
helpdir
progs
```

This single line of code lets us catch a glimpse of the UNIX magic. The shell sees the > *before* ls runs, so it gets to act first. It then opens the file following the > (here, list). ls runs next and it looks up the "table of contents" of the directory to find out the filenames in it. But the shell has already manipulated things in such a way that the ls output doesn't come to the terminal but to the file opened by the shell on its behalf.

Note: You list files in a directory with ls and display file contents with **cat**. You can get more details of a file using the -l option with ls.

1.4.11 wc: Counting Number of Lines in a File

How many lines are there in the file? The **wc** command answers this question:

```
$ wc list
      6       6      42 list
```

Observe once again the brevity that typically characterizes UNIX; it merely echoes three numbers along with the filename. You have to have the manual or this text in front of you to know that the file list contains 6 lines, 6 words and 42 characters.

1.4.12 Feeding Output of One Command to Another

Now you should see something that is often hailed as the finest feature of the system. Previously, you used ls to list files, and then the > symbol to save the output in the file list. You then counted the number of lines, words and characters in this file with **wc**. In this way, you could *indirectly* count the number of files in the directory. The shell can do better; its manipulative capability enables a *direct* count without creating an intermediate file. Using the | symbol, it connects two commands to create a *pipeline*:

```
$ ls | wc
      6       6      42                              No filename this time!
```

See how you can arrive at the same result (except for the filename), this time by simply connecting the output of ls to the input of **wc**. No intermediate file is now needed. On seeing the symbol, | (known as a *pipe*), the shell performs the job of connecting the two commands. If you can connect a number of UNIX commands in this way, you can perform difficult tasks quite easily.

1.4.13 Programming with the Shell

The system also features a programming facility. You can assign a value to a variable at the prompt:

No spaces on either side of =

```
$ x=5
$ _
```

and then evaluate the value of this variable with the **echo** command and a $-prefixed variable name:

A $ required during evaluation

```
$ echo $x
5
```

Apart from playing with variables, UNIX also provides control structures like conditionals and loops, and you'll see a great deal of that in later chapters.

1.4.14 exit: Signing Off

So far, what you have seen is only a small fragment of the UNIX giant, though you have already been exposed to some of its key features. Most of these commands will be considered in some detail in subsequent chapters, and it's a good idea to suspend the session for the time being. You should use the **exit** command to do that:

```
$ exit
login:
```

Alternatively, you may be able to use *[Ctrl-d]* (generated by pressing the *[Ctrl]* key and the character d on the keyboard) to quit the session. The login: message confirms that the session has been terminated, thus making it available for the next user.

Note: Depending on how your environment has been set up, you may not be able to use *[Ctrl-d]* to exit the session. If that happens, try the **logout** command, and if that fails too, use the **exit** command. This command will *always* work.

Caution: Make sure that you log out after your work is complete. If you don't do that, anybody can get hold of your terminal and continue working using your user-id. She may even remove your files! The login prompt signifies a terminated session, so don't leave your place of work until you see this prompt.

1.5 HOW IT ALL CLICKED

Until UNIX came on the scene, operating systems were designed with a particular machine in mind. They were invariably written in a low-level language (like assembler, which uses humanly unreadable code). The systems were fast but were restricted to the hardware they were designed for. Programs designed for one system simply wouldn't run on another. That was the status of the computer industry when Ken Thompson and Dennis Ritchie, of AT&T fame, authored the UNIX system.

In 1969, AT&T withdrew its team from the MULTICS project, which was engaged in the development of a flexible operating system that would run continuously and be used remotely. Thompson and Ritchie then designed and built a small system having an elegant file system, a command interpreter (the shell) and a set of utilities. However, what they wanted was a general operating system running on more than one type of hardware. In 1973, they rewrote the entire system in C—a high-level (more readable than assembler) language that was invented by Ritchie himself. Portability became one of the strong features of UNIX.

1.5.1 Berkeley: The Second School

A U.S. government decree (subsequently revoked) prevented AT&T from selling computer software. The company had no option but to distribute the product to academic and research institutions at a nominal fee, but without any support. The University of California, Berkeley (UCB), created a UNIX of its own. They called it *BSD UNIX* (Berkeley Software Distribution). These versions became quite popular worldwide, especially in universities and engineering circles. Later, UCB gave up all development work on UNIX.

Berkeley filled the gaps left behind by AT&T, and then later decided to rewrite the whole operating system in the way they wanted. They created the standard editor of the UNIX system (**vi**) and a popular shell (C shell). Berkeley also created a better file system, a more versatile mail feature and a better method of linking files (symbolic links). Later, they also offered with their standard distribution a networking protocol software (TCP/IP) that made the Internet possible. Like AT&T, they also offered it practically free to many companies.

1.5.2 The Others

When computer science graduates left academics for the commercial world, they carried their UNIX aspirations with them. It was just a matter of time before business circles developed interest in the product, and they too joined in its development in a spree of unparalleled innovation. UNIX had turned commercial.

Sun used the BSD System as a foundation for developing their own brand of UNIX (then *SunOS*). Today, their version of UNIX is known as *Solaris*. Others had their own brands; IBM had *AIX*, HP offered *HP-UX*, while DEC produced *Digital UNIX*—and now *Tru64 UNIX*. Then the Linux wave arrived, and most of these vendors are offering Linux too. Today, most supercomputers run UNIX, and handheld devices are increasingly using Linux. By making itself available on most hardware, UNIX now gives the customer the "freedom of choice", as opposed to the "freedom from choice" (the way Scott McNealy, the CEO of Sun Microsystems, describes it).

As each vendor modified and enhanced UNIX to create its own version, the original UNIX lost its identity as a separate product. The BSD releases were much different from the AT&T System V releases, and the incompatibilities steadily mounted. While standards were being developed as to what a product had to satisfy to be called UNIX, AT&T took it upon themselves to rework mainly the BSD product, and ultimately unify their own System V 3.2, BSD, SunOS and XENIX flavors into its last release—*System V Release 4* (SVR4). Shortly thereafter, AT&T sold its UNIX business to Novell, who later turned over the UNIX trademark to a standards body called *X/OPEN*, now merged with *The Open Group*.

Note: The UNIX trademark is owned by The Open Group.

1.5.3 The Internet

Even before the advent of SVR4, big things were happening in the U.S. Defense Department. DARPA, a wing of this department, engaged several vendors to develop a reliable communication system using computer technology. Through some brilliant work done by Vinton Cerf and Robert Kahn, DARPA's ARPANET network was made to work using packet-switching technology. In this scenario, data is split into packets, which can take different routes and yet be reassembled in the right order. That was the birth of *TCP/IP*—a set of protocols (rules) used by the Internet for communication.

DARPA commissioned UCB to implement TCP/IP on BSD UNIX. ARPANET converted to TCP/IP in 1983, and in the same year, Berkeley released the first version of UNIX which had TCP/IP built-in. The computer science research community were all using BSD UNIX, and the network expanded like wild fire. The incorporation of TCP/IP into UNIX and its use as the basis of development were two key factors in the rapid growth of the Internet (and UNIX).

1.5.4 The Windows Threat

In the meantime, however, Microsoft was making it big with Windows—a *graphical user interface* (GUI) that uses the mouse rather than arcane and complex command options to execute a job. Options could be selected from drop-down menu boxes and radio buttons, which made handling some of the basic operating system functions easier. Windows first swept the desktop market (with Windows 3.1/95/98) and then made significant inroads into the server market (with Windows NT/2000) which had for long been dominated by UNIX.

When UNIX badly needed a Windows-type interface for its survival, the Massachusetts Institute of Technology (MIT) introduced *X Window*—the first windowing system for UNIX. X Window has many of the important features of Microsoft Windows plus a lot more. Every flavor of UNIX now has X along with a host of other tools that can not only handle files and directories but also update the system's configuration files.

Note: All said and done, the power of UNIX is derived from its commands and their multiple options. No GUI tool can ever replace the **find** command that uses elaborate file attribute-matching schemes to locate files.

1.6 LINUX AND GNU

Although UNIX finally turned commercial, Richard Stallman and Linus Torvalds had different ideas. Torvalds is the father of Linux, the free UNIX that has swept the computer world by storm. Stallman runs the Free Software Foundation (formerly known as GNU—a recursive acronym that stands for "GNU's Not Unix"!). Many of the important Linux tools were written and supplied free by GNU.

Linux is distributed under the GNU General Public License which makes it mandatory for developers and sellers to make the source code public. Linux is particularly strong in networking and Internet features, and is an extremely cost-effective solution in setting up an Internet server or a local internet. Today, development on Linux is carried out at several locations across the globe at the behest of the Free Software Foundation.

The most popular GNU/Linux flavors include Red Hat, Caldera, SuSE, Debian and Mandrake. These distributions, which are shipped on multiple CD-ROMs, include a plethora of software— from C and C++ compilers to Java, interpreters like **perl**, **python** and **tcl**, browsers like Netscape, Internet servers, and multimedia software. Much of the software can also be downloaded free from the Internet. All the major computer vendors (barring Microsoft) have committed to support Linux, and many of them have ported their software to this platform. This book also discusses Linux.

1.7 CONCLUSION

With the goal of building a comfortable relationship with the machine, Thomson and Ritchie designed a system for their own use rather than for others. They could afford to do this because UNIX wasn't initially developed as a commercial product, and the project didn't have any predefined objective. They acknowledge this fact too: "We have not been faced with the need to satisfy someone else's requirements, and for this freedom we are grateful."

UNIX is a command-based system, and you have used a number of them already in the hands-on session. These commands have varied usage and often have a large number of options and arguments. Before we take up each UNIX subsystem along with its associated commands, you need to know more about the general characteristics of commands and the documentation associated with them. The next chapter addresses this issue.

WRAP UP

A computer needs an *operating system* to provide all programs with essential services that involve use of the machine's resources. UNIX is also an operating system but it has more features than is expected out of an operating system.

You enter a UNIX system by entering a username, assigned by the system administrator, and a password. You terminate a session by using the **exit** command or pressing [Ctrl-d].

You can enter any legitimate command at the prompt. The prompt is produced by the *shell*, a program that constantly runs at the terminal as long as the user is logged in.

The **ls** command displays all filenames in a directory. The **ps** command shows the *processes* running in the system.

You can use the * to capture a number of filenames with a simple pattern. The > symbol is used to save the output coming on the screen in a file, while | feeds the output of one command as input to another.

UNIX was developed at AT&T Bell Laboratories by Ken Thompson and Dennis Ritchie. It was finally written in C. Notable work was also done at Berkeley. AT&T introduced System V Release 4 (SVR4) to merge their own version, Berkeley and other variants.

All UNIX flavors today offer a graphical user interface (GUI) in the X Window system. But the strength of UNIX lies in its commands and options.

Linux is a UNIX implementation that is constantly growing with contributions from the Free Software Foundation (formerly, GNU).

Test Your Understanding

1.1   Every character has a value associated with it. What is it called?

1.2   Why is the password string not displayed on the terminal?

1.3   The _____ interacts with the hardware and the _____ interacts with the user.

1.4   Name the commands you used in this chapter to display (i) filenames, (ii) processes, (iii) users.

1.5   Enter this sequence: > user.1st. Note what happens. Repeat the process by removing the space after the >. Does it make any difference?

1.6   Enter this command sequence: **ls | wc -1**. What do you think the output represents?

1.7   Enter the two commands: **echo *** and **ls**. What do you think **echo** did?

1.8   Enter these commands: **echo "$SHELL"** and **echo '$SHELL'**. What difference do you notice?

1.9   A *program* is synonymous with a *process*. True or False?

1.10 Who are the principal architects of the UNIX operating system?

1.11 Why is UNIX more portable than other operating systems?

1.12 What does X/OPEN represent? Who owns the UNIX trademark today?

1.13 Name some of the contributions made by Berkeley in the development of UNIX.

1.14 What is the windowing system of UNIX known as?

1.15 What is the role of the Free Software Foundation in the development of Linux? Who developed the Linux kernel?

Flex Your Brain

1.1   Operating systems like UNIX provide services both for programs and users. Explain.

1.2   What does a program do when it needs to read a file?

1.3   When you log in, a program starts executing at your terminal. What is this program known as? Name four types of this program that are available on a system.

1.4   What exactly happens when you enter this sequence: **ls > list**?

1.5   Attempt the variable assignment x=10 by providing a space on either end of the =. Why doesn't it work?

1.6   Run the following commands and then invoke **ls**. What do you conclude?

```
echo > README[Enter]
echo > readme[Enter]
```

1.7   Enter the following commands and note your observations: (i) **who** and **tty** (ii) **ps** and **echo $$**

1.8   Name the three commands that you would try in sequence to log yourself out of the system. Which one among them will always work?

1.9   What is the significance of your user-id? Where in the system is the name used?

1.10   What is the one thing that is common to directories, devices, terminals and printers?

1.11   Name some of the duties of the system administrator that you have encountered so far.

1.12   What are the two schools of UNIX that initially guided its development?

The UNIX Architecture and Command Usage

UNIX is now more than 25 years old, but fortunately the essentials have remained the same. To appreciate the material presented in the remaining chapters, you must understand the UNIX architecture and its key features. This chapter also introduces the two agencies (the kernel and shell) who between themselves handle all the work of the system.

A major part of the job of learning UNIX is to master the essential command set. UNIX has a vast repertoire of commands that can solve many tasks either by working singly or in combination. We'll examine the generalized UNIX command syntax and understand the significance of its options and arguments. We'll also learn to look up the command documentation from the man pages. UNIX is very well documented, so there's hardly a way that a problem can remain unsolved for long.

WHAT YOU WILL LEARN

- The *multiprogramming*, *multiuser* and *multitasking* nature of UNIX.
- What *system calls* are and how they enrich the UNIX programming environment.
- How UNIX encourages the use of modular tools that can be connected to form complex tasks.
- The other features of UNIX—its vast collection of tools, pattern matching and wide variety of its documentation sources.
- How the shell uses the PATH variable to locate commands.
- The difference between *external* and *internal* commands.
- The breakup of a command into *arguments* and *options*.
- The use of the **man** command to look up the documentation of a command.
- Obtain contextual information on any topic using the **apropos** and **whatis** commands.

TOPICS OF SPECIAL INTEREST

- How two programs—the *kernel* and *shell*—work in a cooperative manner to handle everything.
- The significance of two abstractions—the *file* and *process*—in the UNIX system.

- The importance of the POSIX and Single UNIX Specification standards.
- How to use the man documentation in an effective way and interpret the symbols used.
- The use of keyboard sequences to restore normal operation when commands don't work properly.

2.1 THE UNIX ARCHITECTURE

The entire UNIX system is supported by a handful of essentially simple, though somewhat abstract concepts. The success of UNIX, according to Thompson and Ritchie, "lies not so much in new inventions but rather in the full exploitation of a carefully selected set of fertile ideas, and especially in showing that they can be keys to the implementation of a small and yet powerful operating system." UNIX is no longer a small system, but it certainly is a powerful one. Before we examine the features of UNIX, we need to understand its software architecture—its foundation.

2.1.1 Division of Labor: Kernel and Shell

Foremost among these "fertile ideas" is the division of labor between two agencies—the *kernel* and *shell*. The kernel interacts with the machine's hardware, and the shell with the user. You have seen both of them in action in the hands-on session though the kernel wasn't mentioned by name. Their relationship is depicted in Fig. 2.1.

The **kernel** is the core of the operating system—a collection of routines mostly written in C. It is loaded into memory when the system is booted and communicates directly with the hardware. User programs (the applications) that need to access the hardware (like the hard disk or terminal) use the services of the kernel, which performs the job on the user's behalf. These programs access the kernel through a set of functions called *system calls*, which are taken up shortly.

Apart from providing support to user programs, the kernel has a great deal of housekeeping to do. It manages the system's memory, schedules processes, decides their priorities, and performs other tasks which you wouldn't like to bother about. The kernel has to do a lot of this work even if no user program is running. It is often called *the* operating system—a program's gateway to the computer's resources.

Computers don't have any inherent capability of translating commands into action. That requires a **command interpreter**, a job that is handled by the "outer part" of the operating system—the **shell**. It is actually the interface between the user and kernel. Even though there's only one kernel running on the system, there could be several shells in action—one for each user who is logged in.

When you enter a command through the keyboard, the shell thoroughly examines the keyboard input for special characters. If it finds any, it rebuilds a simplified command line, and finally communicates with the kernel to see that the command is executed. You have already seen the shell in action when you used the > *(1.4.10)* and | *(1.4.12)* symbols. As a simpler example of how the shell examines and tampers with our input, consider this **echo** command which has lots of spaces between the arguments:

```
$ echo Sun                    Solaris
Sun Solaris
```

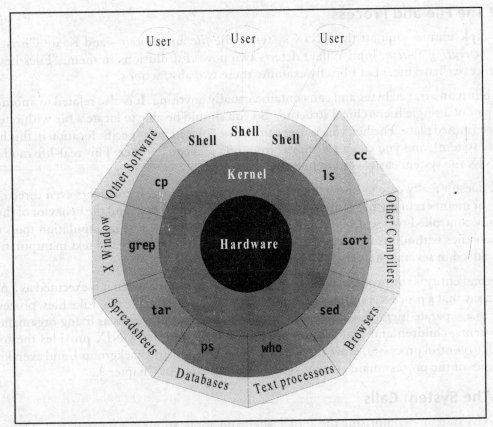

Fig. 2.1 The Kernel-Shell Relationship

In the course of processing, the shell compresses all multiple contiguous spaces in the above command line to a single one. The **echo** command then runs with spaces compressed. But since you may not like this tampering to happen all the time, the shell itself provides features to prevent its own interference. This will be taken up later.

Note: The kernel is represented by the file **/stand/unix**, **/unix** or **/kernel/genunix** (Solaris), depending on the system you are using. The system's bootstrap program loads the kernel into memory at startup. The shell is represented by **sh** (Bourne shell), **csh** (C shell), **ksh** (Korn shell) or **bash** (Bash shell). One of these shells will run to serve you when you log in. To know the one that is running for you, use the command **echo $SHELL**.

LINUX: The kernel is represented by the file **/boot/vmlinuz**. Linux uses the the Bash shell by default, though it offers the C shell and Korn shell as well.

2.1.2 The File and Process

Two simple entities support the UNIX system—the *file* and *process*—and Kaare Christian (*The UNIX Operating System*, John Wiley) detects two powerful illusions in them: "Files have places and processes have life." Let's briefly examine these two abstractions.

A **file** is just an array of bytes and can contain virtually anything. It is also related to another file by being part of a single hierarchical structure. So you should be able to locate a file with reference to a predetermined place. Further, you as user can also be "placed" at a specific location in this hierarchy (the file system), and you can also "move" from one place to another. This real-life model makes the UNIX file system easily comprehensible.

UNIX doesn't really care to know the type of file you are using. It considers even directories and devices as members of the file system. The dominant file type is text, and the behavior of the system is mainly controlled by text files. UNIX provides a vast array of text manipulation tools that can edit these files without using an editor. The file system, its attributes and text manipulation tools are discussed in several chapters.

The second entity is the **process**, which is the name given to a file when it is executed as a program. You can say that a process is simply the "time image" of an executable file. Like files, processes also belong to a separate hierarchical tree structure. We also treat processes as living organisms which have parents, children and grandchildren, and are born and die. UNIX provides the tools that allow us to control processes, move them between foreground and background, and even kill them. The basics of the process management system are discussed in Chapter 9.

2.1.3 The System Calls

The UNIX system—comprising the kernel, shell and applications—is written in C. Though there are over a thousand commands in the system, they all use a handful of functions, called **system calls**, to communicate with the kernel. All UNIX flavors have one thing in common: *They use the same system calls.* These system calls are described in the POSIX specification *(2.3)*. If an operating system uses different system calls, then it won't be UNIX. The reason why Linux can't replace UNIX is that Linux uses the same system calls; Linux is UNIX.

A typical UNIX command writes a file with the **write** system call without going into the innards that actually achieve the write operation. Often the same system call can access both a file and a device; the **open** system call opens both. These system calls are built into the kernel, and interaction through them represents an efficient means of communication with the system. This also means that once software has been developed on one UNIX system, it can easily be ported to another UNIX machine.

C programmers on a Windows system use the *standard library functions* for everything. You can't use the **write** system call on a Windows system; you'll need to use a library function like **fprintf** for the purpose. In contrast, the C programmer in the UNIX environment has complete access to the entire system call library as well as the standard library functions. Chapters 23 and 24 deal with the basic system calls that you need to know to program in the UNIX environment.

2.2 FEATURES OF UNIX

UNIX is an operating system, so it has all the features an operating system is expected to have. However, UNIX also looks at a few things differently and possesses features unique to itself. The following sections present the major features of this operating system.

2.2.1 UNIX: A Multiuser System

From a fundamental point of view, UNIX is a **multiprogramming** system; it permits multiple programs to run and compete for the attention of the CPU. This can happen in two ways:

- Multiple users can run separate jobs.
- A single user can also run multiple jobs.

In fact, you'll see several processes constantly running on a UNIX system. The feature of multiple users working on a single system often baffles Windows users. Windows is essentially a single-user system where the CPU, memory and hard disk are all dedicated to a single user. In UNIX, the resources are actually shared between all users; UNIX is also a **multiuser system**. Multiuser technology is the great socializer that has time for everyone.

For creating the illusory effect, the computer breaks up a unit of time into several segments, and each user is allotted a segment. So at any point in time, the machine will be doing the job of a single user. The moment the allocated time expires, the previous job is kept in abeyance and the next user's job is taken up. This process goes on until the clock has turned full-circle and the first user's job is taken up once again. This the kernel does several times in one second and keeps all ignorant and happy.

2.2.2 UNIX: A Multitasking System Too

A single user can also run multiple tasks concurrently; UNIX is a **multitasking** system. It is usual for a user to edit a file, print another one on the printer, send email to a friend and browse the World Wide Web—all without leaving any of the applications. The kernel is designed to handle a user's multiple needs.

In a multitasking environment, a user sees one job running in the *foreground*; the rest run in the *background*. You can switch jobs between background and foreground, suspend, or even terminate them. Programmers can use this feature in a very productive way. You can edit a C program and then suspend it to run the compiler; you don't have to quit the editor to do that. This feature is provided by most shells (except the original Bourne shell).

Note: Today, we have machines with multiple CPUs that make it possible to actually earmark an entire processor for a single program (in a single-user and single-tasking situation).

2.2.3 The Building-Block Approach

The designers never attempted to pack too many features into a few tools. Instead, they felt "small is beautiful," and developed a few hundred commands each of which performed one simple job only. You have already seen how two commands (**ls** and **wc**) were used with the | (pipe) to count the number of files in your directory *(1.4.12)*. No separate command was designed to perform the job. The commands that can be connected in this way are called *filters* because they filter or manipulate data in different ways.

It's through pipes and filters that UNIX implements the small-is-beautiful philosophy. Today, many UNIX tools are designed with the requirement that the output of one tool be used as input to another. That's why the architects of UNIX had to make sure that commands didn't throw out excessive verbiage and clutter the output—one reason why UNIX programs are not interactive. If the output of the **ls** command contained column headers, or if it prompted the user for specific information, this output couldn't have been used as useful input to the **wc** command.

By interconnecting a number of tools, you can have an large number of combinations of their usage. That's why it's better for a command to handle a specialized function rather than solve multiple problems. *Though UNIX started with this concept, it was somewhat forgotten when tools were added to the system later.*

2.2.4 The UNIX Toolkit

By one definition, UNIX represents the kernel, but the kernel by itself doesn't do much that can benefit the user. To properly exploit the power of UNIX, you need to use the host of applications that are shipped with every UNIX system. These applications are quite diverse in scope. There are general-purpose tools, text manipulation utilities (called filters), compilers and interpreters, networked applications and system administration tools. You'll also have a choice of shells.

This is one area that's constantly changing with every UNIX release. New tools are being added and the older ones are being removed or modified. The shell and utilities form part of the POSIX specification. There are open-source versions for most of these utilities, and after reading Chapter 22, you should be able to download these tools and configure them to run on your machine.

2.2.5 Pattern Matching

UNIX features very sophisticated pattern matching features. You listed the chapters of the text *(1.4.9)* by using the **ls** command with an unusual argument (chap*) instead of explicitly specifying all filenames. The * is a special character used by the system to indicate that it can match a number of filenames. If you choose your filenames carefully, you can use a simple expression to access a whole lot of them.

The * (known as a *metacharacter*) isn't the only special character used by the UNIX system; there are several others. UNIX features elaborate pattern matching schemes that use several characters from this metacharacter set. The matching isn't confined to filenames only. Some of the most advanced and useful tools also use a special expression called a *regular expression* that is framed with characters from this set. This book heavily emphasizes the importance of regular expressions, and shows how you can perform complex pattern matching tasks using them.

2.2.6 Programming Facility

The UNIX shell is also a programming language; it was designed for a programmer, not a casual end user. It has all the necessary ingredients, like control structures, loops and variables, that establish it as a powerful programming language in its own right. These features are used to design *shell scripts*—programs that can also invoke the UNIX commands discussed in this text.

Many of the system's functions can be controlled and automated by using these shell scripts. If you intend taking up system administration as a career, you'll have to know the shell's programming features very well. Proficient UNIX programmers seldom take recourse to any other language (except **perl**) for text manipulation problems. Shell programming is taken up in Chapters 14 and 21.

2.2.7 Documentation

UNIX documentation is no longer the sore point it once was. Even though it's sometimes uneven, at most times the treatment is quite lucid. The principal online help facility available is the **man** command, which remains the most important reference for commands and their configuration files. Thanks to O'Reilly & Associates, one can safely say that there's no feature of UNIX on which a separate textbook is not available. UNIX documentation and the man facility are discussed later in the chapter.

Apart from the online documentation, there's a vast ocean of UNIX resources available on the Internet. There are several *newsgroups* on UNIX where you can fire your queries in case you are stranded with a problem—be it a problem related to shell programming or a network configuration issue. The *FAQ* (Frequently Asked Questions)—a document that addresses common problems— is also widely available on the Net. Then there are numerous articles published in magazines and journals and lecture notes made available by universities on their Web sites. UNIX is easily tamed today.

2.3 POSIX AND THE SINGLE UNIX SPECIFICATION

Dennis Ritchie's decision to rewrite UNIX in C didn't quite make UNIX very portable. UNIX fragmentation and the absence of a single conforming standard adversely affected the development of *portable* applications. First, AT&T created the *System V Interface Definition* (SVID). Later, X/ Open (now The Open Group), a consortium of vendors and users, created the *X/Open Portability Guide* (XPG). Products conforming to this specification were branded UNIX95, UNIX98 or UNIX03 depending on the version of the specification.

Yet another group of standards, the *Portable Operating System Interface for Computer Environments* (POSIX), were developed at the behest of the Institution of Electrical and Electronics Engineers (IEEE). POSIX refers to operating systems in general, but was based on UNIX. Two of the most-cited standards from the POSIX family are known as *POSIX.1* and *POSIX.2*. POSIX.1 specifies the C application program interface—the system calls. POSIX.2 deals with the shell and utilities.

In 2001, a joint initiative of X/Open and IEEE resulted in the unification of the two standards. This is the *Single UNIX Specification, Version 3* (SUSV3). The "write once, adopt everywhere" approach to this development means that once software has been developed on any POSIX-compliant UNIX system, it can be easily ported to another POSIX-compliant UNIX machine with minimum modifications. We make references to POSIX throughout this text, but these references should be interpreted to mean the SUSV3 as well.

Tip: The Single UNIX Specification, Version 3 is available at *http://www.unix.org/version3/pr.html*. You must frequently consult this document when you use a command, an option or a system call to confirm whether the usage is mandated by the specification.

2.4 LOCATING COMMANDS

The UNIX system is command-based, i.e., things happen because of the commands that you key in. UNIX commands are seldom more than four characters long. All UNIX commands are single words like **ls**, **cat**, **who**, etc. These names are all in lowercase, and you must start shedding your old DOS habits of being indifferent to case. For instance, if you enter LS instead of ls, this is how the system will respond:

```
$ LS
bash: LS: command not found
```

This message is from the shell (here, the Bash shell). There's obviously no command named **LS** on the UNIX system. This seems to suggest that there's a "predetermined" list of such commands that the shell first searches before it flashes the message above. These commands are essentially *files* containing programs, mainly written in C. Files are stored in *directories*. For instance, the **ls** command is a file (or program) found in the directory /bin.

The easiest way of knowing the location of an executable program is to use the **type** command:

```
$ type ls
ls is /bin/ls
```                              *Won't work in the C shell*

When you execute the **ls** command, the shell locates this file in the /bin directory and makes arrangements to execute it. **type** looks up only the directories specified in the PATH variable (discussed next).

2.4.1 The PATH

The sequence of directories that the shell searches to look for a command is specified in its own PATH variable. Use **echo** to evaluate this variable and you'll see a directory list separated by colons:

```
$ echo $PATH
/bin:/usr/bin:/usr/local/bin:/usr/ccs/bin:/usr/local/java/bin:.
```

There are six directories in this colon-separated list. To consider the second one, /usr/bin represents a hierarchy of three directory names. The first / indicates the top-most directory called root, so usr is below the root directory and bin is below usr. *Don't confuse the root directory with the root user account.*

When you issue a command, the shell searches this list *in the sequence specified* to locate and execute it. Note that this list also includes the current directory indicated by a singular dot at the end. The following message shows that the **netscape** command is not available in any of these directories:

```
$ netscape
ksh: netscape:  not found
```

The Korn shell is running here and prints the message after failing to locate the file. This doesn't in any way confirm that **netscape** doesn't exist on this system; it could reside in a different directory. In that case we can still run it

- by changing the value of PATH to include that directory.
- by using a pathname (like **/usr/local/bin/netscape** if the command is located in /usr/local/bin).

Windows users also use the same PATH variable to specify the search path, except that Windows uses the ; as the delimiter instead of the colon. We have more to say about pathnames in Chapter 4 and we'll learn to change PATH in Chapter 10.

Note: The essential UNIX commands for general use are located in the directories /bin and /usr/bin. In Solaris, they are all in /usr/bin.

2.5 INTERNAL AND EXTERNAL COMMANDS

Since **ls** is a program or file having an independent existence in the /bin directory (or /usr/bin), it is branded as an **external command**. Most commands are external in nature, but there are some which are not really found anywhere, and some which are normally not executed even if they are in one of the directories specified by PATH. Take for instance the **echo** command:

```
$ type echo
echo is a shell builtin
```

echo isn't an external command in the sense that, when you type echo, the shell won't look in its PATH to locate it (even if it is there in /bin). Rather, it will execute it from its own set of built-in commands that are not stored as separate files. These built-in commands, of which **echo** is a member, are known as **internal commands**.

You must have noted that it's the shell that actually does all this work. This program starts running for you when you log in, and dies when you log out. The shell is an external command with a difference; it possesses its own set of internal commands. So if a command exists both as an internal command of the shell as well as an external one (in /bin or /usr/bin), the shell will accord top priority to its own internal command of the same name.

This is exactly the case with **echo**, which is also found in /bin, but rarely ever executed because the shell makes sure that the internal **echo** command takes precedence over the external. We'll take up the shell in detail later.

2.6 COMMAND STRUCTURE

To exploit the power for which UNIX is well-known, you must know the syntax of the important commands. You have already encountered commands that were used with multiple words (like **tput clear** and **cat list**). The first word (viz., tput and cat) is actually the command; the additional words are called **arguments**. That is to say, clear is an argument to the **tput** command. Because a command often accepts several types of arguments, it can be made to behave in numerous ways.

Commands and arguments have to be separated by spaces or tabs to enable the system to interpret them as *words*. You can use any number of them to separate the words that form a command. A contiguous string of spaces and tabs together form what is known as **whitespace**. Where the system permits the use of one whitespace character to separate words, it generally permits several, as in this command:

```
cat             README
```

The shell possesses a special mechanism of compressing these multiple consecutive spaces or tabs to a single space. You have already seen this happen in Section 2.1.1.

UNIX arguments range from the simple to the complex. They consist of options, expressions, instructions, filenames, etc. The vast majority of commands have simple arguments, but some like **dd** and **find** can make you feel uneasy for a while. You'll have a taste of all of these types as you proceed.

Note: Whitespace refers to a contiguous set of spaces, tabs and newline characters. The tab character is generated by hitting the *[Tab]* key on your keyboard, or using *[Ctrl-i]* in case *[Tab]* doesn't work. The newline character is generated by hitting the *[Enter]* key.

2.6.1 Options

There's a special type of argument that's mostly used with a - sign. For instance, when you use

```
ls -l note
```

-l is an argument to **ls** by definition, but more importantly, it's a special argument known as an **option**. An option is normally preceded by a minus sign (-) to distinguish it from filenames. There must not be any whitespace between - and l. If you inadvertently provide that, many commands could land you in a great deal of trouble!

Options are also arguments, but given a special name because their list is predetermined. When we use **echo hello dolly**, hello and dolly are also arguments, but they are not predetermined. In fact, you can use millions of words legitimately with **echo** and they'll still remain arguments and not options.

LINUX: While most UNIX options use a single - as the option prefix (e.g. -l), Linux also offers options that use two hyphens and a multi-character word. For instance, it offers the synonym **ls --all** in addition to **ls -a**. Though it means more typing load for the user, the words are quite meaningful and easy to remember; it's easier to remember --all than -a.

If you use a command with a wrong option, the shell locates the command all right, but the *command* this time finds the option to be wrong:

```
$ ls -z note
ls: illegal option -- z                              Message from ls, not shell
usage: ls -1RaAdCxmnlogrtucpFbqisfL [files]
```

The above message has been generated by the command, and not by the shell. **ls** does have a large number of options (over 20), but it seems that -z is not one of them. Many commands provide the right syntax and options to use when you use them wrongly.

What you need to keep in mind is something that beginners often forget—the necessity of providing spaces between the command and argument. If you have used **DIR/P** instead of **DIR /P** in DOS, don't expect UNIX to be equally accommodating:

```
$ ls-l
bash: ls-l: command not found
```

Options can normally be combined with only one - sign, i.e., instead of using

```
ls -l -a -t
```

you might as well use

```
ls -lat                                              Same as ls -l -a -t
```

to obtain the same output. This facility reduces your typing load, which becomes significant when you use commands with several options. The command *parses* (breaks up) the option combination into separate options.

Because UNIX was developed by people who had their own ideas as to what options should look like, there will invariably be exceptions to whatever rules we try to formulate. Some commands won't let you combine options in the way you did just now. There are some that use + as an option prefix instead of -. Some even use the =! Let this not deter you; you would have already built up a lot of muscle before you take on these commands.

2.6.2 Filename Arguments

Many UNIX commands use a filename as argument so the command can take input from the file. If a command uses a filename as argument at all, it will generally be its last argument—and after all options. It's also quite common to see many commands working with multiple filenames as arguments:

```
ls -lat chap01 chap02 chap03
cp chap01 chap02 progs                               cp copies files
rm chap01 chap02                                     rm removes files
```

The command with its arguments and options is known as the **command line**. This line can be considered complete only after the user has hit *[Enter]*. The complete line is then fed to the shell as its input for interpretation and execution.

2.6.3 Exceptions

There are, of course, exceptions to the general syntax of commands mentioned above. There are commands (**pwd**) that don't accept any arguments, and some (**who**) that may or may not be specified with arguments. The **ls** command can run without arguments (**ls**), with only options (**ls -l**), with only filenames (**ls chap01 chap02**), or using a combination of both (**ls -la chap01 chap02**). The word *option* turns out to be a misnomer in some instances; some commands compulsorily have to use one (**cut**).

Later on, you'll find that the arguments can take the form of an expression (in **grep**), a set of instructions (in **sed**), or a program (in **awk** and **perl**). You can't really have a catch-all syntax that works for all commands, the syntax pertaining to a specific command is best taken from the UNIX manual. The syntax for some commands have been explicitly specified in this book.

Note: C programmers and shell scripters need to count the number of arguments in their programs. It helps to be aware at this stage that there are some characters in the command line that are not really arguments—the |, > and <, for instance. In Chapter 8, we'll make an amazing discovery that in the command line **who > user.txt**, user.txt is not an argument to **who**!

2.7 FLEXIBILITY OF COMMAND USAGE

The UNIX system provides a certain degree of flexibility in the usage of commands. A command can often be entered in more than one way, and if you use it judiciously, you can restrict the number of keystrokes to a minimum. In this section, we'll see how permissive the shell is to command usage.

2.7.1 Combining Commands

So far, you have been executing commands separately; each command was first processed and executed before the next could be entered. Also, UNIX allows you to specify more than one command in the command line. Each command has to be separated from the other by a ; (semicolon):

```
wc note ; ls -l note
```

When you learn to redirect the output of these commands (8.5.2), you may even like to group them together within parentheses:

```
( wc note ; ls -l note ) > newlist
```

The combined output of the two commands is now sent to the file newlist. Whitespace is provided here only for better readability. You might reduce a few keystrokes like this:

```
(wc note;ls -l note)>newlist
```

When a command line contains a semicolon, the shell understands that the command on each side of it needs to be processed separately. The ; here is known as a *metacharacter*, and you'll come across several metacharacters that have special meaning to the shell.

2.7.2 A Command Line Can Overflow or Be Split into Multiple Lines

A command is often keyed in. Though the terminal width is restricted to 80 characters, that doesn't prevent you from entering a command, or a sequence of them, in one line even though the total width may exceed 80 characters. The command simply overflows to the next line though it is still in a single *logical* line.

Sometimes, you'll find it necessary or desirable to split a long command line into multiple lines. In that case, the shell issues a **secondary prompt**, usually >, to indicate to you that the command line isn't complete. This is easily shown with the **echo** command:

```
$ echo "This is
> a three-line                    A second prompt (>) appears
> text message"
This is
a three-line
text message
```

Tip: Whenever you find the > appear after you have pressed *[Enter]*, it will generally be due to the absence of a matching quote or parenthesis. In case you find that the problem persists even after providing it, just kill the command line with either *[Ctrl-c]* or *[Ctrl-u]*.

2.7.3 Entering a Command Before Previous Command Has Finished

UNIX provides a full-duplex terminal which lets you type a command at any time, and rest assured that the system will interpret it. When you run a long program, the prompt won't appear until program execution is complete. Subsequent commands can be entered at the keyboard (as many commands as you wish) without waiting for the prompt; they may not be even displayed on your screen!

The reason why that happens is this: The command that you key in isn't seen by the shell as its input when it is busy running another program. The input remains stored in a **buffer** (a temporary storage in memory) that's maintained by the kernel for all keyboard input. The command is passed on to the shell for interpretation after the previous program has completed its run. If you type correctly, simply don't bother even if the output from the previous program garbles the display!

2.8 man: BROWSING THE MANUAL PAGES ON-LINE

All said and done, the syntax of some UNIX commands can still be confusing—even to the expert. You may not remember either the command or the required option that will perform a specific job. This is quite understandable considering that there are several hundred commands in /bin and /usr/bin on any UNIX system (around 600 in Solaris).

UNIX offers an online help facility in the **man** command. **man** displays the documentation—often called the **man documentation**— of practically every command on the system. For example, to seek help on the **wc** command, simply run **man** with wc as argument:

`man wc`   *Help on the* `wc` *command*

The entire man page for **wc** is dumped on the screen (Fig. 2.2). **man** presents the first page and pauses. It does this by sending its output to a **pager** program, which displays this output one page (screen) at a time. The pager is actually a UNIX command, and **man** is always preconfigured to be used with a specific pager. UNIX systems currently use these pager programs:

- **more**, Berkeley's pager, that's now available universally as a superior alternative to the original AT&T **pg** command (now obsolete). We'll be considering **more** in this text.
- **less**, the standard pager used on Linux systems, but also available for all UNIX platforms. **less** is modeled on the **vi** editor and is more powerful than **more** because it replicates many of **vi**'s navigational and search functions. The features of **less** are described briefly in Section 5.5.

On a man page that uses **more** as the pager, you'll see a prompt at the bottom-left of the screen which looks something like this:

`--More--(26%)`   `less` *shows a* `:` *as the prompt*

At this prompt you can press a key to perform navigation, or search for a string. The key you press is interpreted as one of **man**'s (rather, the pager's) **internal commands**, and the character often doesn't show up on the screen. Many UNIX utilities like **vi** and **mail** also have their own internal commands. A set of internal commands used by **more** is listed in Table 5.1. We'll discuss only a few of them related to navigation and string search.

To quit the pager, and ultimately **man**, press **q**. You'll be returned the shell's prompt.

2.8.1 Navigation and Search

The navigation commands are numerous and often vary across UNIX implementations. For the time being, you should know these two commands which should work on all systems:

- **f** or spacebar, which advances the display by one screen of text at a time.
- **b**, which moves back one screen.

The man documentation is sometimes quite extensive, and the search facility lets you locate a page containing a keyword quite easily. For example, you can call up the page containing the word `clobber` by using the string with the / (frontslash):

`/clobber[Enter]`

The / and search string show up on the screen this time, and when you press *[Enter]*, you are taken to the page containing `clobber`. If that's not the page you are looking for, you can repeat the search by pressing **n**. Some pager versions even highlight the search term in reverse video.

2.9 UNDERSTANDING THE man DOCUMENTATION

Vendors organize the man documentation differently, but in general you could see eight sections of the UNIX manual (Table 2.1). Later enhancements have added subsections (like 1C, 1M, 3N etc.), but we'll ignore them in this text. Occasional references to other sections can also be reflected in the SEE ALSO section of a man page. You can see from the table that the documentation is not restricted to commands; important system files used by these commands also have separate man pages.

Most of the commands discussed in this text are available in Section 1, and **man** searches the manuals starting from Section 1. If it locates a keyword in one section it won't continue the search even if the keyword occurs in another section. When a keyword is found in multiple sections, you should use the section number additionally as an argument. Depending on the UNIX flavor you are using, you may also need to prefix the -s option to the section number:

```
man 4 passwd                    passwd also occurs in Section 4
man -s4 passwd                  Solaris uses the -s option
```

This displays the documentation for a configuration file named /etc/passwd, from Section 4. There's also an entry for **passwd** in Section 1, but if we had used **man passwd** (without the section number), **man** would have looked up Section 1 only and wouldn't have looked at Section 4 at all.

Note: There are two chapters in this text featuring the important system calls and some standard library functions. Sections 2 and 3 provide detailed documentation on their usage. To look up the **read** system call, you'll have to use **man 2 read** or **man -s2 read**.

2.9.1 Understanding a man Page

A man page is divided into a number of compulsory and optional sections. Every command doesn't have all sections, but the first three (NAME, SYNOPSIS and DESCRIPTION) are generally seen in all man pages. NAME presents a one-line introduction to the command. SYNOPSIS shows the syntax used by the command, and DESCRIPTION (often the largest section) provides a detailed description.

The SYNOPSIS Section is the one that we need to examine closely, and we'll do that with reference to the man page of the **wc** command shown in Fig. 2.2. Here you'll find the syntax—the options and arguments used with the command. The SYNOPSIS follows certain conventions and rules which every user must understand:

- If a command argument is enclosed in rectangular brackets, then it is optional; otherwise, the argument is required. The **wc** man page shows all of its arguments enclosed in three such groups. This means that **wc** can be used without arguments.
- The ellipsis (a set of three dots) implies that there can be more instances of the preceding word. The expression [file ...] signifies that **wc** can be used with more than one filename as argument.
- If you find the | character in any of these areas, it means that only one of the options shown on either side of the pipe can be used. Here, only one of the options, -c, -m and -C, can be used.

All options used by the command are listed in the OPTIONS section. Often, difficult options are supported by suitable examples. There's a separate section named EXIT STATUS which lists possible error conditions and their numeric representation. You need to understand the significance

```
User Commands                                    wc(1)
NAME
     wc - display a count of lines, words and characters in a file
SYNOPSIS
     wc [ -c | -m  | -C ]   [ -lw ]   [ file ... ]
DESCRIPTION
     The wc utility  reads  one  or  more  input  files and,  by
     default,  writes the number of newline characters, words and
     bytes contained in  each input file to the standard output.
     The utility also writes a total count for all named  files,
     if more than one input file is specified.
     wc considers a word to be a non-zero-length string  of  char-
     acters  delimited by white space (for example, SPACE, TAB ).
     See iswspace(3C) or isspace(3C).
OPTIONS
     The following options are supported:
     -c       Count bytes.
     -m       Count characters.
     -C       Same as -m.
     -l       Count lines.
     -w       Count words delimited by white space characters or new
              line  characters.  Delimiting  characters are Extended
              Unix Code (EUC) characters from any code  set  defined
              by iswspace().
     If  no option is specified the default is -lwc (count  lines,
     words, and  bytes.)
OPERANDS
     The following operand is supported:
     file  A path name of an input file. If no file operands  are
           specified, the standard input will be used.
USAGE
     See largefile(5) for the description of the behavior of wc when
     encountering files greater than or equal to 2 Gbyte (2 **31 bytes).
EXIT STATUS
     The following exit values are returned:
     0     Successful completion.
     >0    An error occurred.
SEE ALSO
     cksum(1),        isspace(3C),       iswalpha(3C),       iswspace(3C),
     setlocale(3C), attributes(5), environ(5), largefile(5)
```

Fig. 2.2 man page for **wc** (Solaris)

of these numbers when writing shell scripts in order to determine the actual cause of termination of a command.

2.9.2 Using man to Understand man

Since **man** is also a UNIX command like **ls** or **cat**, you'll probably first like to know how **man** itself is used. Use the same command to view its own documentation:

```
man man
```
Viewing man pages with man

From this man page you'll know that you can choose your pager too. The variable, PAGER, controls the pager **man** uses, and if you set it to **less**, then **man** will use **less** as its pager. This is how you set PAGER at the command prompt before you invoke **man**:

```
PAGER=less ; export PAGER
man wc
```
Set this shell variable and export it and then run man

To evaluate the value of PAGER, use the command **echo $PAGER**. This setting is valid only for the current session. In later chapters, you'll understand the significance of the **export** statement and also learn to make this setting permanent so that its assigned value remains valid for all sessions.

Note: On some systems, **echo $PAGER** may not show you any value at all, in which case **man** is using a default pager. Some systems set this variable in the file /etc/default/man instead.

Table 2.1 Organization of the man Documentation

Section	Subject (SVR4)	Subject (Linux)
1	User programs	User programs
2	Kernel's system calls	Kernel's system calls
3	Library functions	Library functions
4	Administrative file formats	Special files (in /dev)
5	Miscellaneous	Administrative file formats
6	Games	Games
7	Special files (in /dev)	Macro packages and conventions
8	Administration commands	Administration commands

2.10 FURTHER HELP WITH man -k, apropos AND whatis

The POSIX specification requires **man** to support only one option (-k). Most UNIX systems also offer the **apropos** command that emulates **man -k**. When used with this option, **man** searches a summary database and prints a one-line description of the command. To know what **awk** does, use **man** like this:

```
$ man -k awk     Same as apropos awk
awk             awk (1)      - pattern scanning and processing language
nawk            nawk (1)     - pattern scanning and processing language
```

man locates its argument from the NAME line of all man pages. **nawk** is a "newer" version of **awk** (has been new for a long time) that is generally found on all modern UNIX systems. Once you know that **awk** is a processing language, you can use **man awk** to view its detailed documentation. Note that both **awk** and **nawk** are found in Section 1. There's a separate chapter in this textbook that discusses **awk**.

Wanting to know what a command does is one thing, but to find out the commands and files associated with a keyword is quite another. What is FTP? Let's use the **apropos** command this time:

```
$ apropos FTP
ftp           ftp (1)        - file transfer program
ftpd          in.ftpd (1m)   - file transfer protocol server
ftpusers      ftpusers (4)   - file listing users to be disallowed ftp login
privileges
in.ftpd       in.ftpd (1m)   - file transfer protocol server
netrc         netrc (4)      - file for ftp remote login data
```

apropos lists the commands and files associated with FTP—the protocol used to transfer files between two machines connected in a network. There are two commands here, **ftp** and **in.ftpd**, who cooperate with each other for effecting file transfer. There are also two text files, ftpusers and netrc (actually, .netrc), that are looked up by these commands for authenticating users. Don't worry if you don't understand all this now; we still have some way to go before we take on FTP.

The **whatis** command is also available on many UNIX systems. **man** uses the -f option to emulate **whatis** behavior. The command also lists one-liners for a command:

```
$ whatis cp
cp            cp (1)         - copy files
```

This is the command you have to use to copy a file (or directory).

Note: If you don't have the **apropos** command on your system, you can use **man -k**. You can also use **man -f** in place of **whatis**. The commands search a database that is built separately from man pages. It may or may not be installed on your system. **apropos** and **whatis** are not included in the POSIX specification, but **man -k** is (but not -f).

LINUX: The --help Option

Some commands have just too many options, and sometimes a quick lookup facility is what you need. Most Linux commands offer the --help option that displays a compact listing of all options. You can spot the **find** option you are looking for by using this:

```
$ find --help
Usage: find [path...] [expression]
default path is the current directory; default expression is -print
expression may consist of:
operators (decreasing precedence; -and is implicit where no others are given):
      ( EXPR ) ! EXPR -not EXPR EXPR1 -a EXPR2 EXPR1 -and EXPR2
      EXPR1 -o EXPR2 EXPR1 -or EXPR2 EXPR1 , EXPR2
options (always true): -daystart -depth -follow --help
```

```
        -maxdepth LEVELS -mindepth LEVELS -mount -noleaf --version -xdev
tests (N can be +N or -N or N): -amin N -anewer FILE -atime N -cmin N
      -cnewer FILE -ctime N -empty -false -fstype TYPE -gid N -group NAME
      -ilname PATTERN -iname PATTERN -inum N -ipath PATTERN -iregex PATTERN
      -links N -lname PATTERN -mmin N -mtime N -name PATTERN -newer FILE
      -nouser -nogroup -path PATTERN -perm [+-]MODE -regex PATTERN
      -size N[bckw] -true -type [bcdpfls] -uid N -used N -user NAME
      -xtype [bcdpfls]
actions: -exec COMMAND ; -fprint FILE -fprint0 FILE -fprintf FILE FORMAT
      -ok COMMAND ; -print -print0 -printf FORMAT -prune -ls
```

A Linux command invariably offers far more options than its UNIX counterpart. You'll find this lookup facility quite useful when you know the usage of the options but can't recollect the one you require.

2.11 WHEN THINGS GO WRONG

Terminals and keyboards have no uniform behavioral pattern. Terminal settings directly impact keyboard operation, and you may sometimes need to check the value of the TERM variable. We'll discuss TERM later, but as of now, you should at least be able to wriggle out of some common traps. You must know which keys to press when things don't quite work as expected.

Backspacing Doesn't Work   Consider that you misspelled passwd (a legitimate command) as password, and when you pressed the backspace key to erase the last three characters, you saw this:

$ **password**^H^H^H

Backspacing is not working here; that's why you see the symbol ^H every time you press the key. This often happens when you log on to a remote machine whose terminal settings are different from your local one. In this case you should try these two key sequences; one of them should see you through:

  [Ctrl-h] or [Delete]   *The erase character*

Killing a Line   If the command line contains many mistakes, you could prefer to kill the line altogether without executing it. In that case, use

  [Ctrl-u]   *The line-kill character*

The line-kill character erases everything in the line and returns the cursor to the beginning of the line.

Interrupting a Command   Sometimes, a program goes on running for an hour and doesn't seem to complete. You can interrupt the program and bring back the prompt by using either of the two sequences:

  [Ctrl-c] or [Delete]   *The interrupt character*

This is an important key sequence, and in this book, you'll often be advised to use the *interrupt key*. Note, however, that if *[Delete]* works as the erase character on your machine, it can't also be the interrupt character at the same time.

Terminating a Command's Input   You know that the **cat** command is used with an argument representing the filename *(1.4.10)*. What happens if you omit the filename and simply press *[Enter]*?

$ **cat***[Enter]*

Nothing happens; the command simply waits for you to enter something. Even if you do some text entry, you must know how to terminate your input. For commands that expect user input, enter a *[Ctrl-d]* to bring back the prompt:

```
$ cat
[Ctrl-d]                                          The end-of-file or eof character
$ _
```

This is another important key sequence; we'll often refer to *[Ctrl-d]* as the *eof* or end-of-file character. Sometimes pressing the interrupt key also works in this situation.

The Keyboard is Locked   When this happens, you won't be able to key in anything. It could probably be due to accidental pressing of the key sequence *[Ctrl-s]*. Try using *[Ctrl-q]* to release the lock and restore normal keyboard operation. These two sequences are actually used by the system to control the flow of command output.

At times, you may consciously like to use *[Ctrl-s]* and *[Ctrl-q]*. If the display from a command is scrolling too fast for you to see on the terminal, you can halt the output temporarily by pressing *[Ctrl-s]*. To resume scrolling, press *[Ctrl-q]*. With modern hardware where the output scrolls off very fast, this facility is now practically ineffective, but it pays to know what they do because inadvertent pressing of *[Ctrl-s]* can lock your terminal.

The [Enter] Key Doesn't Work   This key is used to complete the command line. If it doesn't work, you can use either *[Ctrl-j]* or *[Ctrl-m]*. These key sequences generate the linefeed and carriage return characters, respectively.

The Terminal Behaves in an Erratic Manner   Your terminal settings could be disturbed; it may display everything in uppercase or simply garbage when you press the printable keys. Try using the command **stty sane** to restore sanity. Since the *[Enter]* key may not work either in these situations, use *[Ctrl-j]* or *[Ctrl-m]* to simulate *[Enter]*.

These key functions are summarized in Table 2.2. We have provided names to some of these key sequences (like eof and interrupt), but don't be surprised if you find some of them behaving differently on your system. Much of UNIX is configurable by the user, and you'll learn later to use the **stty** command to change these settings. If you have problems, seek assistance of the system administrator.

Tip: At this early stage, it may not be possible for you to remember all of these key sequences. But do keep these two keys in mind: *[Ctrl-c]*, the interrupt character, used to interrupt a running program and *[Ctrl-d]*, the eof character, used to terminate a program that's expecting input from the terminal. On machines running Solaris or Linux, *[Ctrl-c]* can interrupt a command even when it is expecting input.

Also keep in mind that some UNIX programs (like `mailx`) are interactive and have their own set of internal commands (those understood only by the program). These commands have specific key sequences for termination. You may not remember them, so try using **q**, **quit**, **exit** or *[Ctrl-d]*; one of them might just work.

Table 2.2 Keyboard Commands to Try When Things Go Wrong

Keystroke or Command	*Function*
[Ctrl-h]	Erases text (The *erase* character)
[Ctrl-c] or *[Delete]*	Interrupts a command (The *interrupt* character)
[Ctrl-d]	Terminates login session or a program that expects its input from the keyboard (The *eof* character)
[Ctrl-s]	Stops scrolling of screen output and locks keyboard
[Ctrl-q]	Resumes scrolling of screen output and unlocks keyboard
[Ctrl-u]	Kills command line without executing it (The *line-kill* character)
[Ctrl-\]	Kills running command but creates a core file containing the memory image of the program (The *quit* character)
[Ctrl-z]	Suspends process and returns shell prompt; use **fg** to resume job (The *suspend* character)
[Ctrl-j]	Alternative to *[Enter]*
[Ctrl-m]	As above
`stty sane`	Restores terminal to normal status (a UNIX command)

2.12 CONCLUSION

This chapter should prepare you well for the forthcoming tour of UNIX. You can now expect to encounter UNIX commands used with a wide variety of options and arguments. The man documentation will be your most valuable help tool and you must develop the habit of looking it up whenever you are stranded with a problem related to command usage. Also, things will go wrong and keyboard sequences won't sometimes work as expected. So don't forget to look up Section 2.11 for remedial action when that happens.

WRAP UP

The *kernel* addresses the hardware directly. The *shell* interacts with the user. It processes a command, scans it for special characters and rebuilds it in a form that the kernel can understand.

The shell and applications communicate with the kernel using *system calls*, which are special routines built into the kernel.

The *file* and *process* are two basic entities that support the UNIX system. UNIX considers everything as a file. A process represents a program (a file) in execution.

Several users can use the system together (*multiuser*), and a single user can also run multiplejobs concurrently(*multitask*).

Some UNIX commands are designed to perform simple jobs. UNIX lets you develop complex command routines by connecting these tools.

UNIX is a command-based system. The commands used by all users are located in /bin and /usr/bin. The shell variable, PATH, specifies the search list of directories for locating commands.

External commands exist on disk as separate files. An *internal command* is built into the shell, and is normally executed even if there's an external command of the same name.

A command is used with *options* and *arguments*. Commands and arguments must be separated by any number of spaces or tabs (*whitespace*).

A command line can contain more than one command, and a command sequence can be split into multiple lines. You don't have to wait for the previous command to complete before you enter another one.

The **man** command contains the documentation of commands in Section 1. System calls and library functions are found in Sections 2 and 3. Use the section number when a keyword is not found in Section 1.

There are various key sequences that you can use when things go wrong. They are listed in Table 2.2.

Test Your Understanding

2.1   _____ have places and _____ have life.

2.2   There can be multiple kernels and shells running on your system. True or False?

2.3   Why is the shell called a *command interpreter*?

2.4   Two UNIX systems may or may not use the same system calls. True or False?

2.5   To obtain help on any feature of the system, what are the possible help sources available to you?

2.6   Enter a : and press *[Enter]*. Next run **type** **:**. What do you conclude?

2.7   UNIX commands must be in lowercase and must not have extensions. True or False?

2.8   Why are the directories /bin and /usr/bin usually found first in the output of **echo $PATH**?

2.9   If two commands with the same filename exist in two directories in PATH, how can they be executed?

2.10   How is the current directory indicated in the value of PATH?

2.11   Use the **type** command with the following arguments—**cd, date, pwd** and **ls**. Which are the internal commands in the list?

2.12   What is the difference between an *argument* and an *option*?

2.13   If the command **ls --all** works on your system, which flavor of UNIX could you be using?

2.14   What does the secondary prompt look like and when does it appear?

2.15   You located the string **crontab** in a man page by searching with **/crontab***[Enter]*. How do you find out the other occurrences of this string in the page?

2.16   What is a pager? Name the two standard pagers used by **man**.

2.17 If a command doesn't seem to complete, which key will you press to interrupt it?

2.18 Do you need to wait for a command to finish before entering the next one?

Flex Your Brain

2.1 Describe briefly the UNIX architecture explaining the role played by the kernel and shell in sharing the workload.

2.2 Explain briefly the significance of a UNIX file and the relation it has to a process. Why do UNIX systems predominantly use text files?

2.3 What do *multiprogramming*, *multiuser* and *multitasking* mean?

2.4 What are *system calls* and what role do they play in the system? How is C programming so different and powerful in the UNIX environment compared to Windows?

2.5 Why are many UNIX commands designed to perform simple rather than complex tasks?

2.6 The **wc** command was designed to count characters, lines and words *only* in files. Explain whether the statement is true or not with a suitable example.

2.7 Name three major differences between UNIX commands and Windows programs.

2.8 A program file named foo exists in the current directory, but when we try to execute it by entering foo, we see the message foo: command not found. Explain how that can happen.

2.9 What is *whitespace*? Explain the treatment the shell metes out to a command that contains a lot of whitespace.

2.10 If a command, filename and system call have the same name and are available in Sections 1, 5 and 2 respectively, how will you display the man pages of each one of them?

2.11 What do the | and the three dots in the SYNOPSIS section of these man pages indicate as shown below?

```
/usr/xpg4/bin/tail [ -f | -r ]
/usr/bin/ls [ -aAbcCdfFgilLmnopqrRstux1 ] [ file ... ]
```

2.12 Explain the significance of the interrupt and eof characters. With which keys are they associated on your system?

2.13 How do you direct **man** to use a specific pager, say, **less**?

General-Purpose Utilities

The best way to start acquiring knowledge of the UNIX command set is to try your hand at some of the general-purpose utilities of the system. These commands have diverse functions, but can be broadly divided into two categories. Some of them act as handy accessories that can perform calculations or handle your mail, for instance. Others tell you the state the system is in, and even manipulate it.

Every command featured in this chapter is useful, and has not been included here for cosmetic effect. Many of them have been reused in later chapters, especially in shell programming. A few are true dark horses. You'll need these commands in all situations in your daily life at the machine. The commands are simple to use, have very few options (except for **stty**), and don't require you to know much about the files they may access.

WHAT YOU WILL LEARN

- Display the calendar of a month or year with **cal**.
- Display the current system date and time in a variety of formats using **date**.
- Use **echo** with escape sequences to display a message on the terminal.
- Use **bc** as a calculator with a decimal, octal or hexadecimal number as base.
- The basics of electronic mail and its addressing scheme.
- Handle your mail with the character-based **mailx** program.
- Change your password with **passwd**.
- Display the list of users currently working on the system with **who**.
- Display the characteristics of your operating system with **uname**.
- Display the filename of your terminal with **tty**.
- Use **stty** to display and change your terminal's settings.

TOPICS OF SPECIAL INTEREST

- Features of the POSIX-recommended **printf** command as a portable replacement of **echo**.
- Record your login session including all keystrokes with **script**.

- The advantage character-based mailers have over graphic programs.
- The significance of the *mailbox* and *mbox* in the mailing system.

3.1 cal: THE CALENDAR

You can invoke the **cal** command to see the calendar of any specific month or a complete year. The facility is totally accurate and takes into account the leap year adjustments that took place in the year 1752. Let's have a look at its syntax drawn from the Solaris man page:

```
cal [ [ month ] year ]
```

Everything within rectangular brackets is optional, so we are told *(2.9.1)*. So, **cal** can be used without arguments, in which case it displays the calendar of the current month:

```
$ cal
      August 2005
Su Mo Tu We Th Fr Sa
    1  2  3  4  5  6
 7  8  9 10 11 12 13
14 15 16 17 18 19 20
21 22 23 24 25 26 27
28 29 30 31
```

The syntax also tells us that when **cal** is used with arguments, the month is optional but the year is not. To see the calendar for the month of March 2006, you need two arguments:

```
$ cal 03 2006
     March 2006
Su Mo Tu We Th Fr Sa
          1  2  3  4
 5  6  7  8  9 10 11
12 13 14 15 16 17 18
19 20 21 22 23 24 25
26 27 28 29 30 31
```

You can't hold the calendar of a year in a single screen page; it scrolls off too rapidly before you can use *[Ctrl-s]* to make it pause. To make **cal** pause in the same way **man** pauses, use **cal** with a pager (**more** or **less**) using the | symbol to connect them. A single argument to **cal** is interpreted as the year:

```
cal 2003 | more
```
                                              Or use less *instead of more*

The | symbol connects two commands (in a pipeline) where **more** takes input from the **cal** command. We have used the same symbol in Chapter 1 to connect the **ls** and **wc** commands *(1.4.12)*. You can now scroll forward by pressing the spacebar, or move back using **b**.

3.2 date: DISPLAYING THE SYSTEM DATE

The UNIX system maintains an internal clock meant to run perpetually. When the system is shut down, a battery backup keeps the clock ticking. This clock actually stores the number of seconds elapsed since the **Epoch**; this is January 1, 1970. A 32-bit counter stores these seconds (except on 64-bit machines), and the counter will overflow sometime in 2038.

You can display the current date with the **date** command, which shows the date and time to the nearest second:

```
$ date
Wed Aug 31 16:22:40 IST 2005                    Time zone here is IST
```

The command can also be used with suitable format specifiers as arguments. Each format is preceded by the + symbol, followed by the % operator, and a single character describing the format. For instance, you can print only the month using the format +%m:

```
$ date +%m
08
```

or the month name:

```
$ date +%h
Aug
```

or you can combine them in one command:

```
$ date +"%h %m"
Aug 08
```

There are many other format specifiers, and the useful ones are listed below:

d—The day of the month (1 to 31).

y—The last two digits of the year.

H, M and S—The hour, minute and second, respectively.

D—The date in the format *mm/dd/yy*.

T—The time in the format *hh:mm:ss*.

When you use multiple format specifiers (as shown in the previous example), you must enclose them within quotes (single or double), and use a single + symbol before it.

Note: You can't change the date as an ordinary user, but the system administrator uses the same command with a different syntax to set the system date! This is discussed in Chapter 15.

3.3 echo: DISPLAYING A MESSAGE

We have used the **echo** command a number of times already in this text. This command is often used in shell scripts to display diagnostic messages on the terminal, or to issue prompts for taking user input. So far, we have used it in two ways:

- To display a message (like **echo Sun Solaris**).
- To evaluate shell variables (like **echo $SHELL**).

Originally, **echo** was an external command *(2.5)*, but today all shells have **echo** built-in. There are some differences in **echo**'s behavior across the shells, and most of these differences relate to the way **echo** interprets certain strings known as escape sequences.

An **escape sequence** is generally a two character-string beginning with a \ (backslash). For instance, \c is an escape sequence. When this escape sequence is placed at the end of a string used as an argument to **echo**, the command interprets the sequence as a directive to place the cursor and prompt in the same line that displays the output:

```
$ echo "Enter filename: \c"
Enter filename: $ _                     Prompt and cursor in same line
```

This is how **echo** is used in a shell script to accept input from the terminal. Like \c, there are other escape sequences (Table 3.1). Here are two commonly used ones:

\t—A tab which pushes text to the right by eight character positions.

\n—A newline which creates the effect of pressing *[Enter]*.

All escape sequences are not two-character strings. ASCII characters can also be represented by their octal values (numbers using the base 8 contrasted with the standard decimal system which uses the base 10). **echo** interprets a number as octal when it is preceded by \0. For instance, *[Ctrl-g]*, which results in the sounding of a beep, has the octal value 7 (i.e., \07). You can use this value as an argument to **echo**, but only after preceding it with \0:

```
$ echo '\07'                            Double quotes will also do
..... beep heard .....
```

This is the first time we see ASCII octal values used by a UNIX command. Later, you'll see the **tr**, **awk** and **perl** commands also using octal values.

Caution: **echo** escape sequences are a feature of System V. BSD doesn't recognize them but it supports the -n option as an alternative to the \c sequence:

```
echo "Enter filename: \c"               System V
echo -n "Enter filename: "              BSD
```

Even though we don't use the disk version nowadays, the bad news is that the shells too respond in different ways to these escape sequences. Rather than go into these details, a word of caution from POSIX would be appropriate: Use **printf**.

LINUX: Bash, the standard shell used in Linux, interprets the escape sequences only when **echo** is used with the -e option:

```
echo -e "Enter your name:\c"
```

We'll be using these escape sequences extensively in this text, so if you are a Bash user (which most Linux users are), you must either commit this option to memory or make a special setting in the shell that makes **echo** behave in the normal way *(14.1—Tip)*.

Table 3.1 Escape Sequences Used by **echo** and **printf**

Escape Sequence	Significance
\a	Bell
\b	Backspace
\c	No newline (cursor in same line)
\f	Formfeed
\n	Newline
\r	Carriage return
\t	Tab
\v	Vertical tab
\\	Backslash
\0n	ASCII character represented by the octal value n, where n can't exceed 0377 (decimal value 255)

3.4 printf: AN ALTERNATIVE TO echo

The **printf** command is available on most modern UNIX systems, and is the one you should use instead of **echo** (unless you have to maintain a lot of legacy code that use **echo**). Like **echo**, it exists as an external command; it's only the Bash shell that has **printf** built-in. The command in its simplest form can be used in the same way as **echo**:

```
$ printf "No filename entered\n"                              \n is explicitly specified
No filename entered
$ _
```

printf also accepts all escape sequences used by **echo**, but unlike **echo**, it doesn't automatically insert a newline unless the \n is used explicitly. Though we don't need to use quotes in this example, it's good discipline to use them. **printf** also uses formatted strings in the same way the C language function of the same name uses them:

```
$ printf "My current shell is %s\n" $SHELL                    No comma before $
My current shell is /usr/bin/bash
```

The %s format string acts as a placeholder for the value of $SHELL (the argument), and **printf** replaces %s with the value of $SHELL. %s is the standard format used for printing strings. **printf** uses many of the formats used by C's **printf** function. Here are some of the commonly used ones:

%s — String

%30s — As above but printed in a space 30 characters wide

%d — Decimal integer

%6d — As above but printed in a space 6 characters wide

%o — Octal integer

%x — Hexadecimal integer

%f — Floating point number

Note that the formats also optionally use a number to specify the width that should be used when printing a string or number. You can also use multiple formats in a single **printf** command. But then you'll have to specify as many arguments as there are format strings—and in the right order.

While **printf** can do everything that **echo** does, some of its format strings can convert data from one form to another. Here's how the number 255 is interpreted in octal (base 8) and hexadecimal (base 16):

```
$ printf "The value of 255 is %o in octal and %x in hexadecimal\n" 255 255
The value of 255 is 377 in octal and ff in hexadecimal
```

The %o and %x format strings are also used by **awk** and **perl** (and by C) to convert a decimal integer to octal and hex, respectively; it's good to know them. Note that we specified 255 twice to represent the two arguments because it's the same number that we want to convert to octal and hex.

Note: C language users should note some syntactical differences in **printf** usage. **printf** is a function in C and hence uses the parentheses to enclose its arguments. Moreover, arguments are separated from one another as well as from the format string by commas. Here's how the previous command line is implemented as a C statement:

```
printf("The value of 255 is %o in octal and %x in hexadecimal\n", 255, 255);
```

The discussion on **printf** should prepare you well for eventually using the **printf** function in C, but remember that this C function uses many format specifiers not used by the UNIX **printf** command.

3.5 bc: THE CALCULATOR

UNIX provides two types of calculators—a graphical object (the **xcalc** command) that looks like one, and the text-based **bc** command. The former is available in the X Window system and is quite easy to use. The other one is less friendly, extremely powerful and remains one of the system's neglected tools.

When you invoke **bc** without arguments, the cursor keeps on blinking and nothing seems to happen. **bc** belongs to a family of commands (called *filters*) that expect input from the keyboard when used without an argument. Key in the following arithmetic expression and then use *[Ctrl-d]* to quit **bc**:

```
$ bc
12 + 5
17                                  Value displayed after computation
[Ctrl-d]                            The eof character
$ _
```

bc shows the output of the computation in the next line. Start **bc** again and then make multiple calculations in the same line, using the **;** as delimiter. The output of each computation is, however, shown in a separate line:

```
12*12 ; 2^32                        ^ indicates "to the power of"
144
4294967296                          Maximum memory possible on a 32-bit machine
```

bc performs only integer computation and truncates the decimal portion that it sees. This shows up clearly when you divide two numbers:

```
9/5
1                                     Decimal portion truncated
```

To enable floating-point computation, you have to set **scale** to the number of digits of precision before you key in the expression:

```
scale=2                               Truncates to 2 decimal places
17/7
2.42                                  Not rounded off, result is actually 2.42857.....
```

bc is quite useful in converting numbers from one base to another. For instance, when setting IP addresses *(17.1.3)* in a network, you may need to convert binary numbers to decimal. Set **ibase** (input base) to 2 before you provide the number:

```
ibase=2
11001010
202                                   Output in decimal—base 10
```

The reverse is also possible, this time with **obase**:

```
obase=2
14
1110                                  Binary of 14
```

In this way, you can convert from one base to the other (not exceeding 16). **bc** also comes with a library for performing scientific calculations. It can handle very, very large numbers. If a computation results in a 900-digit number, **bc** will show each and every digit!

3.6 script: RECORDING YOUR SESSION

This command, virtually unknown to many UNIX users, lets you "record" your login session in a file. This command is not included in POSIX, but you'll find it useful to store in a file all keystrokes as well as output and error messages. You can later view the file. If you are doing some important work and wish to keep a log of all your activities, you should invoke this command immediately after you log in:

```
$ script
Script started, file is typescript
$ _                                   Another shell—child of login shell
```

The prompt returns and all your keystrokes (including the one used to backspace) that you now enter here get recorded in the file typescript. After your recording is over, you can terminate the session by entering **exit**:

```
$ exit
Script done, file is typescript       Or use [Ctrl-d]
$ _                                   Back to login shell
```

You can now view this file with the **cat** command. **script** overwrites any previous typescript that may exist. If you want to append to it, or want to use a different log file, you can consider using these arguments:

```
script -a            Appends to existing file typescript
script logfile       Logs activities to file logfile
```

There are some activities that won't be recorded properly, for instance, the commands used in the full-screen mode (like **vi** and **emacs**).

3.7 EMAIL BASICS

A UNIX system is used by multiple users, so communication through the system seems natural and necessary. It's no wonder that electronic mail (email) is one of the first applications that UNIX users are familiar with. Email is fast and cheap, and can be used today to exchange graphics, sound and video files. Because a message is usually received in a few seconds, post office mail is often referred to as "snail mail".

An email message never appears on your terminal the moment it is received. It is deposited in your *mailbox* even when you are not logged in. The shell regularly checks this mailbox, and when it detects the arrival of new mail, it issues a message similar to this:

```
You have new mail in /var/mail/romeo            romeo is the user
```

You can see this message either when you log in or after a program run by you completes execution. It's good practice to see incoming mail immediately upon arrival rather than defer it for future viewing. After viewing it, you can do these things with it:

- Reply to the sender and all recipients.
- Forward it to others.
- Save it in a mailbox folder or separate file.
- Delete it.
- Print it.
- Add the address of the sender and all recipients to the address book.
- Call up a helper application to view it if it is not in plain text format.

The characteristic feature of most character-based mail programs (like **mailx**, **mail**, **pine**, etc.) is that mail doesn't remain in the mailbox after it is viewed. The message moves from the mailbox to the *mbox* (a secondary file), where it remains until it is explicitly deleted.

3.7.1 Mail Addressing Scheme

A recipient is identified by her email address. The addressing scheme in the early days simply used the recipient's username as the email address. However, in a single network, the email address also uses the machine name as a component. Here are the two forms:

```
mailx henry                                    henry on same host
mailx henry@saturn                             henry on networked host saturn
```

The second example uses a combination of the username and machine name (called *hostname*); this email address is unique in a network. A similar form is also used in Internet addressing except that the Internet uses *domain names* (called FQDNs) instead of simple hostnames:

```
mailx henry@heavens.com                        Email address unique on the Internet
```

Because of the way domains (like *heavens*) are allotted, no two individuals or organizations can have the same email address on the Internet. We'll now discuss **mailx**, a standard mail handling tool.

3.8 mailx: THE UNIVERSAL MAILER

One of the strengths of UNIX lies in its command line tools. Even though we may use a sophisticated mailer (like Netscape or Mozilla) for handling our mail, we also need a simple mail program that can run noninteractively from shell scripts. We should be able to execute this program with its various command line options, using redirection and piping, to generate the mail headers and message body on the fly. In this chapter, we discuss **mailx**, a character-based mail agent that can do that.

mailx finds place in the POSIX specification, which no longer requires UNIX systems to support the earliest mail agent of all—the **mail** command. Linux doesn't support **mailx**, so you must use **mail** or BSD-based **Mail**, which have a lot in common with **mailx**.

There are two ways of invoking **mailx**—in the sending and receiving modes. In the sending mode, **mailx** is used with the email address of the recipient as argument. In the receiving mode, you *generally* use it without arguments to handle your received mail. In this mode, you can perform all mail functions listed at the beginning of Section 3.7. In the following paragraphs, we'll discuss both modes while communicating with another user on the same host.

3.8.1 Sending Mail

In the sending mode, **mailx** turns interactive, prompting for the subject first. You have to key it in before entering the message body. The same conventions apply: Use the standard input to key in your input and then use *[Ctrl-d]* (or a solitary .). This is how user henry sends mail to charlie:

```
$ mailx charlie                                charlie is on same host
Subject: New System
The new system will start functioning from next month.
Convert your files by next week - henry
[Ctrl-d]                                       Some systems use a dot here
EOT                                            System indicates end of text
```

Sending a message is as simple as this. The sent message doesn't directly appear on charlie's terminal but lands in his mailbox, which is usually /var/mail/charlie. How charlie handles this mail is considered shortly.

Sending Mail Noninteractively   Since we often need to send mail from a shell script, we can use a shell feature called *redirection (8.5)* to take the message body from a file and the -s option to specify the subject:

```
mailx -s "New System" charlie < message.txt
```

Though POSIX doesn't require **mailx** to support options that copy messages to other people, on most systems, **mailx** can be used to send copies using the -c option. Multiple recipients should be enclosed in quotes:

```
mailx -s "New System" -c "jpm,sumit" charlie < message.txt
```

This command sends a message to charlie with copies to jpm and sumit. Now, pay attention to this: If this command line is placed in a shell script, mail will be sent *without user intervention (no mouse clicks)*. You can now well understand why UNIX is considered to be a versatile system.

Note: What makes this method of invocation remarkable is that the subject and recipients need not be known in advance, but can be obtained from shell variables. The message body could come from the output of another program. You can use this feature to design automated mailing lists.

Tip: You can send mail to yourself also using your own user-id as argument. Mail sent to oneself in this way serves as a reminder service provided the user is disciplined enough to read all incoming mail immediately on logging in.

3.8.2 Receiving Mail

All incoming mail is appended to the **mailbox**. This is a text file named after the user-id of the recipient. UNIX systems maintain the mailbox in a directory which is usually /var/mail (/var/spool/mail in Linux). charlie's mail is appended to /var/mail/charlie. By default, **mailx** reads this file for viewing received mail.

Referring to the message sent by henry, the shell on charlie's machine regularly checks his mailbox to determine the receipt of new mail. If charlie is currently running a program, the shell waits for program execution to finish before flashing the following message:

```
You have new mail in /var/mail/charlie
```

When charlie logs in, he may also see this message. He now has to invoke the **mailx** command in the receiving mode (without using an argument) to see the mail henry has sent him. The system first displays the headers and some credentials of all incoming mail *that's still held in the mailbox*:

```
$ mailx
mailx version 5.0 Wed Jan  5 16:00:40 PST 2000  Type ? for help.
"/var/mail/charlie": 5 messages 2 new 5 unread
U  1 henry@jack.hill.com   Fri Apr  3 16:38  19/567   "sweet dreams"
U  2 MAILER-DAEMON@jack.h  Sat Apr  4 16:33  69/2350  "Warning: could not se"
```

```
U  3 MAILER-DAEMON@jack.h  Thu Apr  9 08:31  63/2066  "Returned mail: Cannot"
N  4 henry@jack.hill.com   Thu Apr 30 10:02  17/515   "Away from work"
>N 5 henry@jack.hill.com   Thu Apr 30 10:39  69/1872  "New System"
?  _
```
The ? prompt

The pointer (>) is positioned on the fifth message. This is the *current message*. To view the message body, charlie has to input either the message number shown in the second column, or press *[Enter]*. The following message is typically seen on charlie's screen:

```
Message 5:
>From henry@saturn.heavens.com  Tue Jan 13 10:06:14 2003
Date: Tue, 13 Jan 2003 10:06:13 +0530
From: "henry blofeld" <henry@saturn.heavens.com>
To: charlie@saturn.heavens.com
Subject: New System

The new system will start functioning from next month.
Convert your files by next week - henry
? q
Saved 1 message in /users1/home/staff/charlie/mbox
$ _
```
Quitting mailx *with* q

As we mentioned before, after a message has been seen by the recipient, it moves from the mailbox to the **mbox**, the secondary storage. The name of this file is generally mbox, to be found in the user's home directory (where a user is placed on logging in).

Note: All mail handling commands are presumed to work in a network. That's why the sender's address shows @saturn.heavens.com appended. This is the sender's domain name whose significance is taken up in Chapter 17.

3.8.3 `mailx` Internal Commands

Like the pager used by `man`, the `mailx` command supports a number of internal commands (Table 3.2) that you can enter at the ? prompt. Enter **help** or a **?** at this prompt to see the list of these commands.

You can see the next message by using a **+** (or *[Enter]*), and a **-** to display the previous message. Since messages are numbered, a message can also be accessed by simply entering the number itself:

```
3
```
Shows message number 3

Replying to mail The **r** (reply) command enables the recipient to reply when the sent message is on display at her terminal. `mailx` has a way of deducing the sender's details, and consequently, the **r** command is usually not used with an address:

```
? r
To: henry@saturn.heavens.com
Subject: Re: File Conversion
```
Sender's address automatically inserted

I am already through.
[Ctrl-d]
EOT

When charlie invokes the **r** command, **mailx** switches to the sending mode. The rules for replying to a message are the same as for sending.

Saving Messages   Generally, all mail commands act on the current message by default. With the **w** command, you can save one or more messages in separate files rather than the default mbox (the file mbox) used by the system:

w note3	*Appends current message to* note3
w 1 2 3 note3	*Appends first three messages to* note3

In either case, the message is saved without header information. To save messages with headers, use the **s** command.

Deleting Mail   To delete a message from the mailbox, use the **d** (delete) command. It simply *marks* mail for deletion; the mail actually gets deleted only when quitting **mailx**.

There's still a lot to know about email. We need to examine mail headers, and domain names that are used in email addresses. We must also understand how multimedia files are sent as part of a mail message. We visit email again in Chapter 17.

Table 3.2 Internal Commands used by **mailx**

Command	Action
+	Prints next message
-	Prints previous message
N	Prints message numbered *N*
h	Prints headers of all messages
d *N*	Deletes message *N* (The current message if *N* is not specified)
u *N*	Undeletes message *N* (The current message if *N* is not specified)
s *flname*	Saves current message with headers in *flname* ($HOME/mbox if *flname* is not specified)
w *flname*	Saves current message without headers in *flname* ($HOME/mbox if *flname* is not specified)
m *user*	Forwards mail to *user*
r *N*	Replies to sender of message *N* (The current message if *N* is not specified)
q	Quits **mailx** program
! *cmd*	Runs UNIX command *cmd*

3.9 passwd: CHANGING YOUR PASSWORD

The remaining commands in this chapter relate to our UNIX system, and we'll first take up the command that changes the user's password. In Chapter 1, you have seen how keying in a wrong password prevents you from accessing the system. If your account doesn't have a password or has one that is already known to others, you should change it immediately. This is done with the **passwd** command:

```
$ passwd
passwd:  Changing password for kumar
Enter login password: *******
New password: ********
Re-enter new password: ********
passwd (SYSTEM): passwd successfully changed for kumar
```

Asks for old password

passwd (note the spelling) expects you to respond three times. First, it prompts for the old password. Next, it checks whether you have entered a valid password, and if you have, it then prompts for the new password. Enter the new password using the password naming rules applicable to your system. Finally, **passwd** asks you to reenter the new password. If everything goes smoothly, the new password is registered by the system.

When you enter a password, the string is *encrypted* by the system. Encryption generates a string of seemingly random characters that UNIX subsequently uses to determine the authenticity of a password. This encryption is stored in a file named shadow in the /etc directory. Even if a user is able to see the encryption in the file, she can't work backwards and derive the original password string from the encryption.

***

Note: This is the first time you have changed the *state* of the system; you have indirectly modified a file (shadow) *that is otherwise not available to you for direct editing.* There's a special feature of UNIX that allows you to do that, and we'll be examining it at the end of Part I of this text.

3.9.1 Password Framing Rules and Discipline

Depending on the way they are configured, many systems conduct certain checks on the string that you enter as password. There is often a minimum length of the string. Many systems insist on using a mix of letters with numerals. They may either disallow you from framing easy-to-remember passwords or advise you against choosing a bad password. The following messages are quite common:

```
passwd(SYSTEM): Password too short - must be at least 6 characters.
passwd(SYSTEM): Passwords must differ by at least 3 positions.
passwd(SYSTEM): The first 6 characters of the password must contain at least
two alphabetic characters and at least one numeric or special character.
BAD PASSWORD: it is based on a dictionary word.
BAD PASSWORD: is too similar to the old one.
passwd(SYSTEM): Too many failures - try later.
```

These messages suggest that you are not able to choose any password you like. These are some of the rules that you are expected to follow when handling your own password:

- Don't choose a password similar to the old one.
- Don't use commonly used names like names of friends, relatives, pets and so forth. A system may check with its own dictionary and throw out those passwords that are easily guessed.

- Use a mix of alphabetic or numeric characters. Enterprise UNIX systems won't allow passwords that are wholly alphabetic or numeric.
- Don't write down the password in an easily accessible document.
- Change the password regularly.

You must remember your password, but if you still forget it, rush to your system administrator. You'll learn later of the terrible consequences that you may have to face if people with mischievous intent somehow come to know what your password is. The command also behaves differently when used by the system administrator; it doesn't ask for the old password. The **passwd** command is revisited in Chapter 15.

3.10 who: WHO ARE THE USERS?

UNIX maintains an account of all users who are logged on to the system. It's often a good idea to know their user-ids so you can mail them messages. The **who** command displays an informative listing of these users:

```
$ who
root        console      Aug  1 07:51      (:0)
kumar       pts/10       Aug  1 07:56      (pc123.heavens.com)
sharma      pts/6        Aug  1 02:10      (pc125.heavens.com)
project     pts/8        Aug  1 02:16      (pc125.heavens.com)
sachin      pts/14       Aug  1 08:36      (mercury.heavens.com)
```

The first column shows the usernames (or user-ids) of five users currently working on the system. The second column shows the device names of their respective terminals. These are actually the filenames associated with the terminals. kumar's terminal has the name pts/10 (a file named 10 in the pts directory). The third, fourth and fifth columns show the date and time of logging in. The last column shows the machine name from where the user logged in. Users can log in remotely to a UNIX system, and all users here except root have logged in remotely from four different machines.

While it's a general feature of most UNIX commands to avoid cluttering the display with header information, this command does have a header option (-H). This option prints the column headers, and when combined with the -u option, provides a more detailed list:

```
$ who -Hu
NAME        LINE         TIME          IDLE   PID    COMMENTS
root        console      Aug  1 07:51  0:48   11040  (:0)
kumar       pts/10       Aug  1 07:56  0:33   11200  (pc123.heavens.com)
sachin      pts/14       Aug  1 08:36  .      13678  (mercury.heavens.com)
```

Two users have logged out, so it seems. The first five columns are the same as before, but it's the sixth one (IDLE) that is interesting. A . against sachin shows that activity has occurred in the last one minute before the command was invoked. kumar seems to be idling for the last 33 minutes. The PID is the process-id, a number that uniquely identifies a process. You have seen it when you used the **ps** command in Section 1.4.8 to list the processes running at your terminal.

One of the users shown in the first column is obviously the user who invoked the **who** command. To know that specifically, use the arguments am and i with **who**:

```
$ who am i
kumar      pts/10      Aug  1 07:56    (pc123.heavens.com)
```

Note: UNIX provides a number of tools (called *filters*) to extract data from command output for further processing. For instance, you can use the **cut** command to extract the first column from the **who** output, and then use this list with **mailx** to send a message to these users. The ability to combine commands to perform tasks that are not possible to achieve using a single command is what makes UNIX so different from other operating systems. We'll be combining commands several times in this text.

3.11 uname: KNOWING YOUR MACHINE'S CHARACTERISTICS

The **uname** command displays certain features of the operating system running on your machine. By default, it simply displays the name of the operating system:

```
$ uname
SunOS
```
Linux shows Linux

This is the operating system used by Sun Solaris. Linux systems simply show the name Linux. Using suitable options, you can display certain key features of the operating system, and also the name of the machine. The output will depend on the system you are using.

The Current Release (-r)   Since UNIX comes in many flavors, vendors have customized a number of commands to behave in the way they want, and not as AT&T decreed. A UNIX command often varies across versions so much so that you'll need to use the -r option to find out the version of your operating system:

```
$ uname -r
5.8
```
This is SunOS 5.8

This is a machine running SunOS 5.8, the name given to the operating system used by the Solaris 8 environment. If a command doesn't work properly, it could either belong to a different "implementation" (could be BSD) or a different "release" (may be 4.0, i.e., System V Release 4 of AT&T).

The Machine Name (-n)   If your machine is connected to a network, it must have a name (called *hostname*). If your network is connected to the Internet, then this hostname is a component of your machine's *domain name* (a series of words separated by dots, like *mercury.heavens.com*). The -n option tells you the hostname:

```
$ uname -n
mercury
```
The first word of the domain name

The same output would be obtained with the **hostname** command. Many UNIX networking utilities use the hostname as argument. To copy files from a remote machine named *mercury* running the FTP service, you have to run **ftp mercury**.

LINUX: `uname -n` may show either the host name (like `mercury`) or the complete domain name (like `mercury.heavens.com`), depending on the flavor of Linux you are using. `uname` and `uname -r` display the operating system name and version number of the kernel, respectively:

```
$ uname
Linux
$ uname -r
2.4.18-14
```
Kernel version is 2.4

The first two numbers of the kernel version (here, 2.4) are something every Linux user must remember. Before installing software, the documentation may require you to use a kernel that is "at least" 2.2. The same software should run on this machine whose kernel version is 2.4.

3.12 tty: KNOWING YOUR TERMINAL

Since UNIX treats even terminals as files, it's reasonable to expect a command that tells you the filename of the terminal you are using. It's the **tty** (teletype) command, an obvious reference to the device that has now become obsolete. The command is simple and needs no arguments:

```
$ tty
/dev/pts/10
```

The terminal filename is 10 (a file named 10) resident in the pts directory. This directory in turn is under the /dev directory. These terminal names were seen on a Solaris machine; your terminal names could be different (say, /dev/tty01).

You can use **tty** in a shell script to control the behavior of the script depending on the terminal it is invoked from. If a program must run from only one specified terminal, the script logic must use **tty** to make this decision.

3.13 stty: DISPLAYING AND SETTING TERMINAL CHARACTERISTICS

Different terminals have different characteristics, and your terminal may not behave in the way you expect it to. For instance, command interruption may not be possible with *[Ctrl-c]* on your system. Sometimes you may like to change the settings to match the ones used at your previous place of work. The **stty** command helps straighten these things out; it both displays and changes settings.

stty uses a very large number of *keywords* (options that look different), but we'll consider only a handful of them. The -a (all) option displays the current settings. A trimmed output is presented below:

```
$ stty -a
speed 38400 baud; rows = 25; columns = 80; ypixels = 0; xpixels = 0;
intr = ^c; quit = ^\; erase = ^?; kill = ^u;
eof = ^d; eol = <undef>; eol2 = <undef>; swtch = <undef>;
start = ^q; stop = ^s; susp = ^z; dsusp = ^y;
isig icanon -xcase echo echoe echok -echonl -noflsh
-tostop echoctl -echoprt echoke -defecho -flusho -pendin iexten
```

The output shows, among other things, the baud rate (the speed) of the terminal—in this case 38,400. It also shows many of the parameters that were discussed in a previous chapter *(2.11)*. The other keywords take two forms:

- *keyword = value*
- *keyword* or *-keyword*. The - prefix implies that the option is turned off.

The setting intr = ^c signifies that *[Ctrl-c]* interrupts a program. The erase character is *[Ctrl-h]* and the kill character is *[Ctrl-u]*. The eof (end-of-file) character is set to *[Ctrl-d]*, the same key sequence that was used with the **bc** *(3.5)* and **mailx** *(3.8)* commands. For commands that accept input from the keyboard, this key signifies the end of input.

Let's understand the significance of some of the other keywords and then use **stty** to change the settings.

3.13.1 Changing the Settings

*Whether Backspacing Should Erase Character (*echoe*)*   If you have worked on a number of terminals, you would have noticed that backspacing over a character sometimes removes it from sight and sometimes doesn't. This is decided by the keyword echoe. Since it is set here (no - prefix to it), backspacing removes the character from display.

You can use the same keyword to reverse this setting. Here you need to prefix a - to the echoe keyword:

```
stty -echoe
```

Backspacing now doesn't remove a character from sight. This setting is inoperative on some systems.

*Entering a Password through a Shell Script (*echo*)*   The echo setting has to be manipulated to let shell programs accept a password-like string that must not be displayed on the screen. By default, the option is turned on, but you can turn it off in this way:

```
stty -echo                                    Turns off keyboard input
```

With this setting, keyboard entry is not echoed. You should turn it off after the entry is complete by using **stty echo**, which again is not displayed, but makes sure that all subsequent input is.

*Changing the Interrupt Key (*intr*)*   **stty** also sets the functions for some of the keys. For instance, if you like to use *[Ctrl-c]* as the interrupt key instead of *[Delete]*, you'll have to use

```
stty intr \^c                                      ^ and c
```

Here, the keyword intr is followed by a space, the \ (backslash) character, a ^ (caret), and finally the character c. This is the way **stty** indicates to the system that the interrupt character is *[Ctrl-c]*.

When you insert control characters into a file, you'll see a ^ symbol apparently prefixed to the character. For example, *[Ctrl-l]* is seen as ^l (or ^L). However, it's actually a single character, occupying two slots on the terminal; no caret is actually present. However, for using a control character in an **stty** setting, you'll have to use a literal caret preceded by a backslash.

Changing the End-of-File Key (eof)   When using **mailx**, you used *[Ctrl-d]* to terminate input. This eof character is also selectable. Instead of *[Ctrl-d]*, you can use *[Ctrl-a]* as the eof character:

```
stty eof \^a
```

[Ctrl-a] will now terminate input for those commands that expect input from the keyboard when invoked in a particular way. The **cat**, **bc** and **mailx** commands can be made to work in this way.

When Everything Else Fails (sane)   **stty** also provides another argument to set the terminal characteristics to values that will work on most terminals. Use the word sane as a single argument to the command:

```
stty sane                                    Restores sanity to the terminal
```

There are other options, but you are advised against tampering with too many settings.

3.14 CONCLUSION

The commands featured in this chapter were all used in standalone mode. But UNIX provides a number of commands (called *filters*) that can be combined with one another to process command output. In fact, UNIX is most effective when used in these ways. In later chapters, we'll often be combining commands to perform useful tasks. The next four chapters examine one of the two illusions *(2.1.2)* that support the UNIX system—files.

WRAP UP

cal produces the calendar of a month or year.

date can display any component of the system date and time in a number of formats.

echo displays a message on the screen. It can work with escape sequences like \c and \t as well as octal numbers like \007. The command has portability problems, the reason why **printf** should be used. **printf** works like **echo** but can also use format specifiers like %d and %s.

bc is the calculator. You can use any numbering system or degree of precision you want. You can also store intermediate results in variables.

script is the UNIX system's recorder which logs all activities of a user in a separate file.

Electronic mail can be used to send messages to a user on the same host, any host in a network or on the Internet. A mail message is appended to a *mailbox* from where it moves to *mbox*.

mailx is invoked with the email address of the recipient in the sending mode, and without arguments in the receiving mode. The command can also be used noninteractively from shell scripts.

passwd is used to change a user's password but is not displayed on the screen. The command prompts for the old password before the new one.

who shows the users working on the system and the time of logging in.

uname reveals details of your machine's operating system (-r). It also displays the hostname (-n) that is used by networking commands.

> **tty** displays the device name of your terminal.
>
> **stty** displays and sets various terminal attributes. You can define the key that interrupts a program (intr) and marks end-of-file (eof). Use **stty sane** to set the terminal to some standard values.

Test Your Understanding

3.1   Observe the calendar for the year 1752. Do you notice anything unusual?

3.2   How will you browse the above output, moving forward and back as necessary?

3.3   Display the current date in the form *dd/mm/yyyy*.

3.4   Can you change the system date with the **date** command?

3.5   [Ctrl-g] sounds a beep. How do you use escape sequences in **echo** to do the same?

3.6   How will you ensure that **bc** displays the results of all divisions using 3 decimal places?

3.7   How will you record your login session in the file session.1st?

3.8   What is the default location of a user's mailbox on UNIX and Linux systems?

3.9   When do you use **mailx** with and without an argument?

3.10 If you find a message in $HOME/mbox, what does that indicate?

3.11 Can you have the same login name more than once in the **who** output?

3.12 Interpret the following output of **who am i**:

```
romeo       pts/10      Aug  1 07:56    (pc123.heavens.com)
```

3.13 Where is the password stored and in what form?

3.14 If you find that your keystrokes are not being echoed, what remedies will you try?

Flex Your Brain

3.1   How do you display both date and time in the format *dd-mm-yy/hh:mm:ss*?

3.2   What is an *escape sequence*? Name three escape sequences used by the **echo** command, and explain the significance of each.

3.3   The command **echo "Filename: \c"** didn't place the cursor at the end of the line. How will you modify the command to behave correctly if your shell is (i) Bash, (ii) any other shell?

3.4   Why doesn't this command run in the way it is meant to? **printf "Filename: %s\n", fname**

3.5   Convert the decimal number 192 to octal and hexadecimal using (i) **bc** and (ii) **printf**. Which one will you use to display the number in binary?

3.6   Run **ps**, the **script** command and run **ps** again. What do you notice?

3.7   In what way is the **mailx** command superior to a GUI program like Netscape or Mozilla?

3.8   Explain the significance of the terms *mailbox* and *mbox*.

3.9   You need to accept a secret code through a shell script. What command will you run in the script to make sure that your keyboard input is not displayed? How do you then revert to the normal setting?

3.10 Both your local and remote machines use identical versions of UNIX. How do you confirm whether you are logged on to a remote machine or not?

3.11 How do you determine the erase, kill and eof characters on your system?

3.12 What will you do to ensure that *[Ctrl-c]* interrupts any program? Will it work the next time you log in?

The File System

4

In this chapter, we begin our study of one of the two pillars that support UNIX—the file system. UNIX looks at everything as a file and any UNIX system has thousands of files. If you write a program, you add one more file to the system. When you compile it, you add some more. Files grow rapidly, and if they are not organized properly, you'll find it difficult to locate them. Just as an office has separate file cabinets to group files of a similar nature, UNIX also organizes its own files in *directories* and expects you to do that as well.

The file system in UNIX is one of its simple and conceptually clean features. It lets users access other files not belonging to them, but it also offers an adequate security mechanism so outsiders are not able to tamper with a file's contents. In this chapter, you'll learn to create directories, move around within the system, and list filenames in these directories. We'll deal with file attributes, including the ones related to security, in a later chapter.

WHAT YOU WILL LEARN

- The initial categorization of files into three types—*ordinary*, *directory* and *device*.
- The features of a UNIX filename.
- The hierarchical structure containing files and directories, and the parent—child relationship that exists between them.
- The significance of the *home directory* and HOME variable.
- Navigate the file system with the **cd** and **pwd** commands.
- Create and remove directories with **mkdir** and **rmdir**.
- The significance of *absolute* and *relative* pathnames.
- Use **ls** to list filenames in a directory in different formats.

TOPICS OF SPECIAL INTEREST

- The significance of the important directories of the UNIX file system from a functional point of view.
- How It Works: A graphic that shows how **mkdir** and **rmdir** affect a directory.

4.1 THE FILE

The **file** is a container for storing information. As a first approximation, we can treat it simply as a sequence of characters. If you name a file foo and write three characters a, b and c into it, then foo will contain only the string abc and nothing else. Unlike the old DOS files, a UNIX file doesn't contain the eof (end-of-file) mark. A file's size is not stored in the file, nor even its name. All file attributes are kept in a separate area of the hard disk, not directly accessible to humans, but only to the kernel.

UNIX treats directories and devices as files as well. A directory is simply a folder where you store filenames and other directories. All physical devices like the hard disk, memory, CD-ROM, printer and modem are treated as files. The shell is also a file, and so is the kernel. And if you are wondering how UNIX treats the main memory in your system, it's a file too!

So we have already divided files into three categories:

- *Ordinary file*—Also known as *regular file*. It contains only data as a stream of characters.
- *Directory file*—It's commonly said that a directory contains files and other directories, but strictly speaking, it contains their *names* and a number associated with each name.
- *Device file*—All devices and peripherals are represented by files. To read or write a device, you have to perform these operations on its associated file.

There are other types of files, but we'll stick to these three for the time being. The reason why we make this distinction between file types is that the significance of a file's attributes often depends on its type. Read permission for an ordinary file means something quite different from that for a directory. Moreover, you can't directly put something into a directory file, and a device file isn't really a stream of characters. While many commands work with all types of files, some don't. For a proper understanding of the file system you must understand the significance of these files.

4.1.1 Ordinary (Regular) File

An **ordinary file** or **regular file** is the most common file type. All programs you write belong to this type. An ordinary file itself can be divided into two types:

- Text file
- Binary file

A **text file** contains only printable characters, and you can often view the contents and make sense out of them. All C and Java program sources, shell and **perl** scripts are text files. A text file contains lines of characters where every line is terminated with the *newline* character, also known as *linefeed* (LF). When you press *[Enter]* while inserting text, the LF character is appended to every line. You won't see this character normally, but there is a command (**od**) which can make it visible.

A **binary file**, on the other hand, contains both printable and unprintable characters that cover the entire ASCII range (0 to 255). Most UNIX commands are binary files, and the object code and executables that you produce by compiling C programs are also binary files. Picture, sound and video files are binary files as well. Displaying such files with a simple **cat** command produces unreadable output and may even disturb your terminal's settings.

4.1.2 Directory File

A **directory** contains no data, but keeps some details of the files and subdirectories that it contains. The UNIX file system is organized with a number of directories and subdirectories, and you can also create them as and when you need. You often need to do that to group a set of files pertaining to a specific application. This allows two or more files in separate directories to have the same filename.

A directory file contains an entry for every file and subdirectory that it houses. If you have 20 files in a directory, there will be 20 entries in the directory. Each entry has two components:

- The filename.
- A unique identification number for the file or directory (called the *inode number*).

If a directory bar contains an entry for a file foo, we commonly (and loosely) say that the directory bar contains the file foo. Though we'll often be using the phrase "contains the file" rather than "contains the filename", you must not interpret the statement literally. *A directory contains the filename and not the file's contents.*

You can't write a directory file, but you can perform some action that makes the kernel write a directory. For instance, when you create or remove a file, the kernel automatically updates its corresponding directory by adding or removing the entry (inode number and filename) associated with the file.

Note: The name of a file can only be found in its directory; the file itself doesn't contain its own name or any of its attributes, like its size or access rights.

4.1.3 Device File

You'll also be printing files, installing software from CD-ROMs or backing up files to tape. All of these activities are performed by reading or writing the file representing the device. For instance, when you restore files from tape, you read the file associated with the tape drive. It is advantageous to treat devices as files as some of the commands used to access an ordinary file also work with device files.

Device filenames are generally found inside a single directory structure, /dev. A device file is indeed special; it's not really a stream of characters. *In fact, it doesn't contain anything at all.* You'll soon learn that every file has some attributes that are not stored in the file but elsewhere on disk. The operation of a device is entirely governed by the attributes of its associated file. The kernel identifies a device from its attributes and then uses them to operate the device.

Now that you understand the three types of files, you shouldn't feel baffled by subsequent use of the word in the book. The term "file" will often be used in this book to refer to any of these types, though it will mostly be used to mean an ordinary file. The real meaning of the term should be evident from its context.

4.2 WHAT'S IN A (FILE)NAME?

On most UNIX systems today, a filename can consist of up to 255 characters, though this figure is normally not reached. Files may or may not have extensions, and can consist of practically any ASCII character except the / and the NULL character (ASCII value 0). You are permitted to use control characters or other unprintable characters in a filename. The following are valid filenames in UNIX:

```
.last_time      list.      ^V^B^D-++bcd      -{}[]      @#$%*abcd      a.b.c.d.e
```

The third filename contains three control characters (*[Ctrl-v]* being the first). These characters should definitely be avoided in framing filenames. Moreover, since the UNIX system has a special treatment for characters like $, ~, ?, *, & among others, it is recommended that only the following characters be used in filenames:

- Alphabetic characters and numerals.
- The period (.), hyphen (-) and underscore (_).

UNIX imposes no rules for framing filename extensions. A shell script doesn't need to have the .sh extension, even though it helps in identification. In all cases, it's the application that imposes the restriction. Thus the C compiler expects C program filenames to end with .c, Oracle requires SQL scripts to have the .sql extension, and so forth. DOS/Windows users must also keep these two points in mind:

- A file can have as many dots embedded in its name; a.b.c.d.e is a perfectly valid filename. A filename can also begin with a dot or end with one.
- UNIX is sensitive to case; chap01, Chap01 and CHAP01 are three different filenames, and it's possible for them to coexist in the same directory.

Caution: Never use a - at the beginning of a filename. You'll have a tough time getting rid of it! A command that uses a filename as argument often treats it as an option and reports errors. For instance, if you have a file named -z, **cat -z** won't display the file but interpret it as an invalid option.

4.3 THE PARENT-CHILD RELATIONSHIP

All files in UNIX are "related" to one another. The file system in UNIX is a collection of all of these related files (ordinary, directory and device files) organized in a hierarchical (an inverted tree) structure. This system has also been adopted by DOS and Windows, and is visually represented in Fig. 4.1.

The implicit feature of every UNIX file system is that there is a top, which serves as the reference point for all files. This top is called *root* and is represented by a / (frontslash). *root is actually a directory*. It is conceptually different from the user-id root used by the system administrator to log in. In this text, we'll be using both the name "root" and the symbol / to represent the root directory.

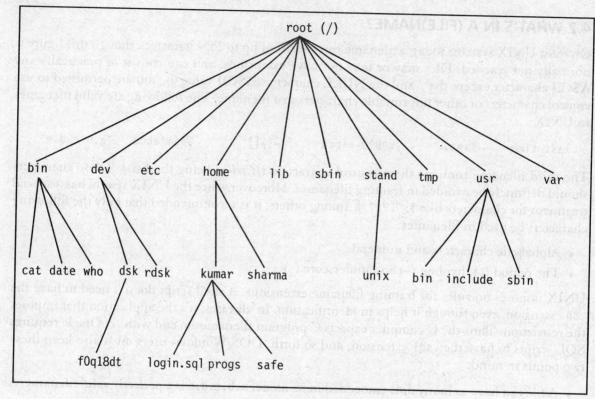

Fig. 4.1 The UNIX File System Tree

The root directory (/) has a number of subdirectories under it. These subdirectories in turn have more subdirectories and other files under them. For instance, bin and usr are two directories directly under /, while a second bin and kumar are subdirectories under usr.

Every file, apart from root, must have a parent, and it should be possible to trace the ultimate parentage of a file to root. Thus, the home directory is the parent of kumar, while / is the parent of home, and the grandparent of kumar. If you create a file login.sql under the kumar directory, then kumar will be the parent of this file.

It's also obvious that, in these parent—child relationships, the parent is always a directory. home and kumar are both directories as they are both parents of at least one file or directory. login.sql is simply an ordinary file; it can't have any directory under it.

4.4 THE HOME VARIABLE: THE HOME DIRECTORY

When you log on to the system, UNIX automatically places you in a directory called the **home directory**. It is created by the system when a user account is opened. If you log in using the login name kumar, you'll land up in a directory that could have the pathname /home/kumar (or something else). You can change your home directory when you like, but you can also effect a quick return to it, as you'll see soon.

The shell variable HOME knows your home directory:

```
$ echo $HOME
/home/kumar                              First / represents the root directory
```

What you see above is an **absolute pathname**, which is simply a sequence of directory names separated by slashes. An absolute pathname shows a file's location with reference to the top, i.e., root. These slashes act as delimiters to file and directory names, except that *the first slash is a synonym for root*. The directory kumar is placed two levels below root.

It's often convenient to refer to a file foo located in your home directory as $HOME/foo. Further, most shells (except Bourne) also use the ~ symbol for this purpose. So, $HOME/foo is the same as ~/foo in these shells. The ~ symbol is a little tricky to use because it can refer to any user's home directory and not just your own. If user sharma has the file foo in his home directory, then kumar can access it as ~sharma/foo. The principle is this:

A tilde followed by / (like ~/foo) refers to one's own home directory, but when followed by a string (~sharma) refers to the home directory of that user represented by the string.

Note: The home directory is determined by the system administrator at the time of opening a user account. Its pathname is stored in the file /etc/passwd. On many UNIX systems, home directories are maintained under /home, but your home directory could be different (say, in /export/home). Even if you have moved away from your "home", you can use the cd command to effect a quick return to it, as you'll see soon.

4.5 pwd: CHECKING YOUR CURRENT DIRECTORY

UNIX encourages you to believe that, like a file, a user is *placed* in a specific directory of the file system on logging in. You can move around from one directory to another, but at any point of time, you are located in only one directory. This directory is known as your **current directory**.

At any time, you should be able to know what your current directory is. The **pwd** (print working directory) command tells you that:

```
$ pwd
/home/kumar
```

Like HOME, **pwd** displays the absolute pathname. As you navigate the file system with the **cd** command, you'll be using **pwd** to know your current directory.

Note: It's customary to refer to a file foo located in the home directory as $HOME/foo. Depending on the shell you use, it may be possible to even access foo as ~/foo. One form is shell-dependent but the other isn't, but both naming conventions are followed in this text.

4.6 cd: CHANGING THE CURRENT DIRECTORY

You can move around in the file system by using the **cd** (change directory) command. When used with an argument, it changes the current directory to the directory specified as argument, for instance, progs:

```
$ pwd
/home/kumar
$ cd progs                                          progs must be in current directory
$ pwd
/home/kumar/progs
```

Though **pwd** displays the absolute pathname, **cd** doesn't need to use one. The command **cd progs** here means this: "Change your subdirectory to progs under the current directory." Using a pathname causes no harm either; use **cd /home/kumar/progs** for the same effect.

When you need to switch to the /bin directory where most of the commonly used UNIX commands are kept, you should use the absolute pathname:

```
$ pwd
/home/kumar/progs
$ cd /bin                                           Absolute pathname required here because
$ pwd                                               bin isn't in current directory
/bin
```

We can also navigate to /bin (or any directory) using a different type of pathname; we are coming to that shortly.

cd can also be used without any arguments:

```
$ pwd
/home/kumar/progs
$ cd
$ pwd                                               cd used without arguments
/home/kumar                                         reverts to the home directory
```

Attention, DOS users! This command invoked without an argument doesn't indicate the current directory. It simply switches to the home directory, i.e., the directory where the user originally logged into. Therefore, if you wander around in the file system, you can force an immediate return to your home directory by simply using **cd**:

```
$ cd /home/sharma
$ pwd
/home/sharma
$ cd                                                Returns to home directory
$ pwd
/home/kumar
```

The **cd** command can sometimes fail if you don't have proper permissions to access the directory. This doesn't normally happen unless you deliberately tamper with the permissions of the directory. The technique of doing that is described in Section 6.5.

Note: Unlike in DOS, when **cd** is invoked without arguments, it simply reverts to its home directory. It doesn't show you the current directory!

4.7 mkdir: MAKING DIRECTORIES

Directories are created with the **mkdir** (make directory) command. The command is followed by names of the directories to be created. A directory patch is created under the current directory like this:

```
mkdir patch
```

You can create a number of subdirectories with one **mkdir** command:

```
mkdir patch dbs doc
```
Three directories created

So far, simple enough, but the UNIX system goes further and lets you create directory trees with just one invocation of the command. For instance, the following command creates a directory tree:

```
mkdir pis pis/progs pis/data
```
Creates the directory tree

This creates three subdirectories—pis and two subdirectories under pis. The order of specifying the arguments is important; you obviously can't create a subdirectory before creation of its parent directory. For instance, you can't enter

```
$ mkdir pis/data pis/progs pis
mkdir: Failed to make directory "pis/data"; No such file or directory
mkdir: Failed to make directory "pis/progs"; No such file or directory
```

Note that even though the system failed to create the two subdirectories, progs and data, it has still created the pis directory.

Sometimes, the system refuses to create a directory:

```
$ mkdir test
mkdir: Failed to make directory "test"; Permission denied
```

This can happen due to these reasons:

- The directory test may already exist.
- There may be an ordinary file by that name in the current directory.
- The permissions set for the current directory don't permit the creation of files and directories by the user. You'll most certainly get this message if you try to create a directory in /bin, /etc or any other directory that houses the UNIX system's files.

We'll take up file and directory permissions in Chapter 6 featuring file attributes.

4.8 rmdir: REMOVING DIRECTORIES

The **rmdir** (remove directory) command removes directories. You simply have to do this to remove the directory pis:

```
rmdir pis
```
Directory must be empty

Like **mkdir**, **rmdir** can also delete more than one directory in one shot. For instance, the three directories and subdirectories that were just created with **mkdir** can be removed by using **rmdir** with a reversed set of arguments:

```
rmdir pis/data pis/progs pis
```

Note that when you delete a directory and its subdirectories, a reverse logic has to be applied. The following directory sequence used by **mkdir** is invalid in **rmdir**:

```
$ rmdir pis pis/progs pis/data
rmdir: directory "pis": Directory not empty
```

Have you observed one thing from the error message? **rmdir** has silently deleted the lowest level subdirectories progs and data. This error message leads to two important rules that you should remember when deleting directories:

- You can't delete a directory *with* **rmdir** unless it is empty. In this case, the pis directory couldn't be removed because of the existence of the subdirectories, progs and data, under it.
- You can't remove a subdirectory unless you are placed in a directory which is hierarchically *above* the one you have chosen to remove.

The first rule follows logically from the example above, but the highlight on **rmdir** has significance that will be explained later. (A directory can also be removed without using **rmdir**.) To illustrate the second cardinal rule, try removing the progs directory by executing the command from the same directory itself:

```
$ cd progs
$ pwd
/home/kumar/pis/progs
$ rmdir /home/kumar/pis/progs          Trying to remove the current directory
rmdir: directory "/home/kumar/pis/progs": Directory does not exist
```

To remove this directory, you must position yourself in the directory above progs, i.e., pis, and then remove it from there:

```
$ cd /home/kumar/pis
$ pwd
/home/kumar/pis
$ rmdir progs
```

The **mkdir** and **rmdir** commands work only in directories *owned* by the user. Generally, a user is the owner of her home directory, and she can create and remove subdirectories (as well as regular files) in this directory or in any subdirectories created by her. However, she normally won't be able to create or remove files and directories in other users' directories. The concept of ownership will be discussed in Section 6.3.

Note: A subdirectory can't be removed with **rmdir** unless it's empty, and one is positioned in its parent directory or above it. But we can remove a directory without using **rmdir** also (discussed later).

HOW IT WORKS: How Files and Directories are Created and Removed

As mentioned in Section 4.1.2, a file (ordinary or directory) is associated with a name and a number, called the *inode number*. When a directory is created, an entry comprising these two parameters is made in the file's parent directory. The entry is removed when the directory is removed. The same holds good for ordinary files also. Figure 4.2 highlights the effect of **mkdir** and **rmdir** when creating and removing the subdirectory progs in /home/kumar.

Filename	Inode Number
.	386444
..	417585
foo	499770

mkdir progs →

Filename	Inode Number
.	386444
..	417585
foo	499770
progs	162112

rmdir progs →

Filename	Inode Number
.	386444
..	417585
foo	499770

Fig. 4.2 Directory Entry after **mkdir** and **rmdir**

Later in this chapter, we'll discuss the significance of the entries, . and .., that you'll find in every directory. In this chapter and Chapters 5 and 11, we'll be progressively monitoring this directory for changes that are caused by some of the file-handling commands.

4.9 ABSOLUTE PATHNAMES

Many UNIX commands use file and directory names as arguments, which are presumed to exist in the current directory. For instance, the command

    cat login.sql

will work only if the file login.sql exists in your current directory. However, if you are placed in /usr and want to access login.sql in /home/kumar, you can't obviously use the above command, but rather the pathname of the file:

    cat /home/kumar/login.sql

As stated before, if the first character of a pathname is /, the file's location must be determined with respect to root (the first /). Such a pathname, as the one above, is called an **absolute pathname**. When you have more than one / in a pathname, for each such /, you have to descend one level in the file system. Thus, kumar is one level below home, and two levels below root.

When you specify a file by using frontslashes to demarcate the various levels, you have a mechanism of identifying a file uniquely. No two files in a UNIX system can have identical absolute pathnames. You can have two files with the same name, but in different directories; their pathnames will also be different. Thus, the file /home/kumar/progs/c2f.pl can coexist with the file /home/kumar/safe/c2f.pl.

4.9.1 Using the Absolute Pathname for a Command

More often than not, a UNIX command runs by executing its disk file. When you specify the **date** command, the system has to locate the file date from a list of directories specified in the PATH variable, and then execute it. However, if you know the location of a particular command, you can precede its name with the complete path. Since **date** resides in /bin (or /usr/bin), you can also use the absolute pathname:

```
$ /bin/date
Thu Sep  1 09:30:49 IST 2005
```

Nobody runs the **date** command like that. For any command that resides in the directories specified in the PATH variable, you don't need to use the absolute pathname. This PATH, you'll recall *(2.4.1)*, invariably has the directories /bin and /usr/bin in its list.

If you execute programs residing in some other directory that isn't in PATH, the absolute pathname then needs to be specified. For example, to execute the program **less** residing in /usr/local/bin, you need to enter the absolute pathname:

```
/usr/local/bin/less
```

If you are frequently accessing programs in a certain directory, it's better to include the directory itself in PATH. The technique of doing that is shown in Section 10.3.

4.10 RELATIVE PATHNAMES

You would have noted that in a previous example *(4.8)*, we didn't use an absolute pathname to move to the directory progs. Nor did we use one as an argument to **cat** *(4.9)*:

```
cd progs
cat login.sql
```

Here, both progs and login.sql are presumed to exist in the current directory. Now, if progs also contains a directory scripts under it, you still won't need an absolute pathname to change to that directory:

```
cd progs/scripts                              progs is in current directory
```

Here we have a pathname that has a /, but it is not an absolute pathname because it doesn't begin with a /. In these three examples, we used a rudimentary form of relative pathnames though they are generally not labeled as such. Relative pathnames, in the sense they are known, are discussed next.

4.10.1 Using . and .. in Relative Pathnames

In a preceding example *(4.8)*, you changed your directory from /home/kumar/pis/progs to its parent directory (/home/kumar/pis) by using **cd** with an absolute pathname:

```
cd /home/kumar/pis
```

Navigation often becomes easier by using a common ancestor (here, /home) as reference. UNIX offers a shortcut—the **relative pathname**—that uses either the current or parent directory as reference, and specifies the path relative to it. A relative pathname uses one of these cryptic symbols:

- . (a single dot)—This represents the current directory.
- .. (two dots)—This represents the parent directory.

We'll now use the .. to frame relative pathnames. Assuming that you are placed in /home/kumar/progs/data/text, you can use .. as an argument to **cd** to move to the parent directory, /home/kumar/progs/data:

```
$ pwd
/home/kumar/progs/data/text
$ cd ..                              Moves one level up
$ pwd
/home/kumar/progs/data
```

This method is compact and more useful when ascending the hierarchy. The command **cd ..** translates to this: "Change your directory to the parent of the current directory." You can combine any number of such sets of .. separated by /s. However, when a / is used with .. it acquires a different meaning; instead of moving down a level, it moves one level *up*. For instance, to move to /home, you can always use **cd /home**. Alternatively, you can also use a relative pathname:

```
$ pwd
/home/kumar/pis
$ cd ../..                           Moves two levels up
$ pwd
/home
```

Now let's turn to the solitary dot that refers to the current directory. Any command which uses the current directory as argument can also work with a single dot. This means that the **cp** command *(5.2)* which also uses a directory as the last argument can be used with a dot:

```
cp ../sharma/.profile .              A filename can begin with a dot
```

This copies the file .profile to the current directory (.). Note that you didn't have to specify the filename of the copy; it's the same as the original one. This dot is also implicitly included whenever we use a filename as argument, rather than a pathname. For instance, **cd progs** is the same as **cd ./progs**.

Note: Absolute pathnames can get very long if you are located a number of "generations" away from root. However, whether you should use one depends solely on the number of keystrokes required when compared to a relative pathname. In every case here, the relative pathname required fewer key depressions. Depending on where you are currently placed, an absolute pathname can be faster to type.

4.11 ls: LISTING DIRECTORY CONTENTS

You have already used the **ls** command *(1.4.9)* to obtain a list of all filenames in the current directory. Let's execute it again:

```
$ ls
08_packets.html                              Numerals first
TOC.sh                                       Uppercase next
calendar                                     Then lowercase
cptodos.sh
dept.lst
emp.lst
helpdir
progs
usdsk06x
usdsk07x
usdsk08x
```

What you see here is a complete list of filenames in the current directory arranged in **ASCII collating sequence** (numbers first, uppercase and then lowercase), with one filename in each line. It includes directories also, and if you are using Linux, you would probably see the directories and ordinary files in different colors.

LINUX: If your Linux system doesn't show these colors, make sure that you create this *alias* after logging in:

```
alias ls='ls --color=tty'
```

Aliases are discussed in Section 10.4, but note that they are not supported by the Bourne shell.

Directories often contain many files, and you may simply be interested in only knowing whether a particular file is available. In that case, just use **ls** with the filename:

```
$ ls calendar
calendar
```

and if **perl** isn't available, the system clearly says so:

```
$ ls perl
perl: No such file or directory
```

ls can also be used with multiple filenames, and has options that list most of the file attributes. In the following sections, you'll see some of these options.

4.11.1 ls Options

ls has a large number of options (Table 4.1), but in this chapter, we'll present a handful of them. The other options will be taken up in later chapters. The section numbers are appropriately indicated in the table.

Output in Multiple Columns (-x)   When you have several files, it's better to display the filenames in multiple columns. Modern versions of **ls** do that by default (i.e., when used without options), but if that doesn't happen on your system, use the -x option to produce a multicolumnar output:

```
$ ls -x
```

```
08_packets.html   TOC.sh        calendar      cptodos.sh
dept.lst          emp.lst       helpdir       progs
usdsk06x          usdsk07x      usdsk08x      ux2nd06
```

If your system needs to use the -x option to display multicolumnar output, you can later customize the command to display in this format by default *(10.4)*.

Identifying Directories and Executables (-F)   The output of **ls** that you have seen so far merely showed the filenames. You didn't know how many of them, if any, were directory files. To identify directories and executable files, the -F option should be used. Combining this option with -x produces a multicolumnar output as well:

```
$ ls -Fx
08_packets.html   TOC.sh*       calendar*     cptodos.sh*
dept.lst          emp.lst       helpdir/      progs/
usdsk06x          usdsk07x      usdsk08x      ux2nd06
```

Note the use of two symbols, * and /, as type indicators. The * indicates that the file contains executable code and the / refers to a directory. You can now identify the two subdirectories in the current directory—helpdir and progs.

Showing Hidden Files Also (-a)   **ls** doesn't normally show all files in a directory. There are certain hidden files (filenames beginning with a dot), often found in the home directory, that normally don't show up in the listing. The -a option (all) lists all hidden files as well:

```
$ ls -axF
./                ../           .exrc         .kshrc
.profile          .rhosts       .sh_history   .xdtsupCheck
.xinitrc          08_packets.html*  TOC.sh*   calendar*
.....
```

The file .profile contains a set of instructions that are performed when a user logs in. It is conceptually similar to AUTOEXEC.BAT of DOS, and you'll know more about it later. The other file, .exrc, contains a sequence of startup instructions for the **vi** editor. To display these hidden filenames, you can either use the -a option or specify the filenames in the command line.

The first two files (. and ..) are special directories. Recall that we used the same symbols in relative pathnames to represent the current and parent directories *(4.10.1)*. These symbols have the same meaning here. Whenever you create a subdirectory, these "invisible" directories are created automatically by the kernel. You can't remove them, nor can you write into them. They help in holding the file system together.

Note: All filenames beginning with a dot are displayed only when **ls** is used with the -a option. The directory . represents the current directory and .. signifies the parent directory.

Listing Directory Contents   In the last example, you specified some ordinary filenames to **ls** to have a selective listing. However, the situation will be quite different if you specify the two directory names, helpdir and progs, instead:

```
$ ls -x helpdir progs
helpdir:
forms.obd      graphics.obd    reports.obd

progs:
array.pl       cent2fah.pl     n2words.pl      name.pl
```

This time the *contents* of the directories are listed, consisting of the Oracle documentation in the helpdir directory and a number of **perl** program files in progs. Note that **ls**, when used with directory names as arguments, doesn't simply show their names as it does with ordinary files.

Recursive Listing (-R) The -R (recursive) option lists all files and subdirectories in a directory tree. Similar to the **DIR /S** command of DOS, this traversal of the directory tree is done recursively until there are no subdirectories left:

```
$ ls -xR
08_packets.html    TOC.sh          calendar        cptodos.sh
dept.lst           emp.lst         helpdir         progs
usdsk06x           usdsk07x        usdsk08x        ux2nd06

./helpdir:
forms.hlp          graphics.hlp    reports.hlp

./progs:
array.pl           cent2fah.pl     n2words.pl      name.pl
```

The list shows the filenames in three sections—the ones under the home directory and those under the subdirectories helpdir and progs. Note the subdirectory naming conventions followed; ./helpdir indicates that helpdir is a subdirectory under . (the current directory). Since /home/kumar happens to be the current directory, the absolute pathname of this file expands to /home/kumar/helpdir.

Table 4.1 Options to **ls**

Option	Description
-x	Multicolumnar output
-F	Marks executables with *, directories with / and symbolic links with @
-a	Shows all filenames beginning with a dot including . and ..
-R	Recursive list
-r	Sorts filenames in reverse order (ASCII collating sequence by default)
-l	Long listing in ASCII collating sequence showing seven attributes of a file *(6.1)*
-d *dirname*	Lists only *dirname* if *dirname* is a directory *(6.2)*
-t	Sorts filenames by last modification time *(11.6)*
-lt	Sorts listing by last modification time *(11.6)*
-u	Sorts filenames by last access time *(11.6)*
-lu	Sorts by ASCII collating sequence but listing shows last access time *(11.6)*
-lut	As above but sorted by last access time *(11.6)*
-i	Displays inode number *(11.1)*

4.12 THE UNIX FILE SYSTEM

We have learned to use the basic command set for handling files and directories. Let's conclude this chapter by taking a cursory look at the structure of the UNIX file system. This structure has been changing constantly over the years until AT&T proposed one in its SVR4 release. Though vendor implementations vary in detail, broadly the SVR4 structure has been adopted by most vendors.

Refer to Fig. 4.1 which shows a heavily trimmed structure of a standard UNIX file system. In real life, the root directory has many more subdirectories under it than shown, but for our initial comprehension, we'll stick to the ones presented below. It helps, from the administrative point of view at least, to view the entire file system as comprising two groups of files. The first group contains the files that are made available during system installation:

- /bin and /usr/bin—These are the directories where all the commonly used UNIX commands (binaries, hence the name bin) are found. Note that the PATH variable always shows these directories in its list.

- /sbin and /usr/sbin—If there's a command that you can't execute but the system administrator can, then it would probably be in one of these directories. You won't be able to execute most (some, you can) commands in these directories. Only the system administrator's PATH shows these directories.

- /etc—This directory contains the configuration files of the system. You can change a very important aspect of system functioning by editing a text file in this directory. Your login name and password are stored in files /etc/passwd and /etc/shadow.

- /dev—This directory contains all device files. These files don't occupy space on disk. There could be more subdirectories like pts, dsk and rdsk in this directory.

- /lib and /usr/lib—Contain all library files in binary form. You'll need to link your C programs with files in these directories.

- /usr/include—Contains the standard header files used by C programs. The statement #include <stdio.h> used in most C programs refers to the file stdio.h in this directory.

- /usr/share/man—This is where the man pages are stored. There are separate subdirectories here (like man1, man2, etc.) that contain the pages for each section. For instance, the man page of ls can be found in /usr/share/man/man1, where the 1 in man1 represents Section 1 of the UNIX manual. These subdirectories may have different names on your system (like sman1, sman2, etc. in Solaris).

Over time, the contents of these directories would change as more software and utilities are added to the system. Users also work with their own files; they write programs, send and receive mail and also create temporary files. These files are available in the second group shown below:

- /tmp—The directories where users are allowed to create temporary files. These files are wiped away regularly by the system.

- /var—The variable part of the file system. Contains all your print jobs and your outgoing and incoming mail.

- /home—On many systems users are housed here. kumar would have his home directory in /home/kumar. However, your system may use a different location for home directories.

On a busy system, it's in directories belonging to the second group that you could experience rapid depletion of available disk space. You'll learn later to house some of these directory structures on separate *file systems* so that depletion of space in one file system doesn't affect other file systems. File system internals and administration are taken up toward the end of this text.

4.13 CONCLUSION

Though UNIX is known to make little distinction between the various types of files, that wasn't really established in this chapter. You used exclusive commands to handle directories (like **pwd**, **cd**, **mkdir** and **rmdir**). These commands have no relevance when applied to ordinary or device files. It appears that UNIX does care to some extent about the type of file it handles. In the next chapter, we look at ordinary files using yet another set of commands meant for them.

WRAP UP

Files have been assumed to be of three types. An *ordinary* file contains what you put into it. A *directory* maintains the filename and its associated *inode number*. A *device* file contains no data but the kernel uses the attributes of the file to operate the device.

Executable files don't need any specific extensions. A file doesn't contain its attributes nor does it contain the end-of-file mark.

The file system is a hierarchical structure, and the top-most directory is called *root*. Files and directories have a parent—child relationship.

pwd tells you the current directory, and **cd** is used to change it. When used by itself, it switches to the *home* directory. The home directory is available in the shell variable HOME. A file foo in the home directory is often referred to as $HOME/foo or ~/foo.

mkdir and **rmdir** are used to create or remove directories. To remove a directory bar with **rmdir**, **bar** must be empty and you must be positioned above bar.

A pathname is a sequence of directory and filenames separated by slashes. An *absolute* pathname begins with a / and denotes the file's location with respect to root. A *relative* pathname uses the symbols . and .. to represent the file's location relative to the current and parent directory, respectively.

By default, **ls** displays a list of filenames in *ASCII collating sequence*, which accords priority in this sequence—numbers, uppercase, lowercase. It can also display hidden filenames beginning with a dot (-a) and a recursive list (-R). However, when used with a directory name as argument, **ls** displays the *filenames* in the directory.

Test Your Understanding

4.1   How long can a UNIX filename be? Which characters can't be used in a filename?

4.2   State two reasons for not having a filename beginning with a hyphen.

4.3   Can the files note and Note coexist in the same directory?

4.4   In how many ways can you find out what your home directory is?

4.5   Switch to the root directory with **cd** and then run **cd ..** followed by **pwd**. What do you notice?

4.6   What is the easiest way of changing from /var/spool/lp/admins to /var/spool/mail?

4.7   Explain the significance of these two commands: **ls ..** ; **ls -d ..**

4.8   Look up the man page of **mkdir** to find out the easiest way of creating this directory structure: share/man/cat1

4.9   If **rmdir c_progs** fails, what could be the possible reasons?

4.10   If the file /bin/echo exists on your system, are the commands **echo** and **/bin/echo** equivalent?

4.11   How do you run **ls** to (i) mark directories and executables separately, (ii) display also hidden files?

4.12   How will you obtain a complete listing of all files and directories in the whole system?

Flex Your Brain

4.1   Name the two types of ordinary files and explain the difference between them. Provide three examples of each type of file.

4.2   How does the device file help in accessing the device?

4.3   Which of these commands will work? Explain with reasons: (i) **mkdir a/b/c** (ii) **mkdir a a/b** (iii) **rmdir a/b/c** (iv) **rmdir a a/b** (v) **mkdir /bin/foo**

4.4   If **mkdir test** fails, what could be the possible reasons?

4.5   Which of these files or directories can you create? Explain with reasons: ., .., ... and ....

4.6   The command **rmdir bar** fails with the message that the directory is not empty. On running **ls bar**, no files are displayed. Why did the **rmdir** command fail?

4.7   Suppose you have to develop a script that refers to a file in charlie's home directory. How will you specify the location of this file in your script to make sure that it works even when charlie's home directory changes?

4.8   Explain the difference between the commands **cd ~charlie** and **cd ~/charlie**. Is it possible for both commands to work?

4.9   Why do we sometimes run a command like this — **./update.sh** instead of **update.sh**?

4.10   What is the sort order prescribed by the ASCII collating sequence?

4.11   Assuming that you are positioned in the directory /home/kumar, what are these commands presumed to do and explain whether they will work at all: (i) **cd ../..** (ii) **mkdir ../bin** (iii) **rmdir ..** (iv) **ls ..**

5

Handling Ordinary Files

The last chapter examined the tools that handle directories. But users actually do most of their work with ordinary (or regular) files, and it's natural that the UNIX system should feature a host of commands to handle them. Although all of these commands use filenames as arguments, they were not designed *only* to read files. In fact, many of them don't need to read a file at all. However, to understand their basic functionality, we'll use them with filenames in this chapter.

We'll first consider the common file-handling commands that the DOS environment also offers, except that the UNIX variety has more features. We'll also discuss those commands that show differences between two files and convert files between DOS and UNIX formats. Finally, we'll examine the important compression utilities with which we handle documents and software found on the Internet. As we progressively discover the shell's features in later chapters, we'll learn to use the same commands in other ways.

WHAT YOU WILL LEARN

- View text files with **cat** and **more** (or **less**)
- Use **cat** to create a file.
- The essential file functions—copy with **cp**, remove with **rm** and rename with **mv**.
- Print a file with **lp** (**lpr** in Linux).
- Classify files with **file**.
- Count the number of lines, words and characters with **wc**.
- Display the ASCII octal value of text with **od**.
- Compare two files with **cmp**, **comm** and **diff**.
- Compress and decompress files with **gzip** and **gunzip**.
- Create an *archive* comprising multiple files with **tar**.
- Perform both functions (compressing and archiving) with **zip** and **unzip**.

TOPICS OF SPECIAL INTEREST

- A discussion on the issues related to file compression and archival.
- Convert between UNIX and DOS files with **unix2dos** and **dos2unix**.
- How It Works: A graphic showing how a directory is affected by **cp**, **mv** and **rm**.

5.1 cat: DISPLAYING AND CREATING FILES

cat is one of the most well-known commands of the UNIX system. It is mainly used to display the contents of a small file on the terminal:

```
$ cat dept.lst
01|accounts|6213
02|progs|5423
03|marketing|6521
04|personnel|2365
05|production|9876
06|sales|1006
```

cat, like several other UNIX commands, also accepts more than one filename as arguments:

```
cat chap01 chap02
```

The contents of the second file are shown immediately after the first file without any header information. In other words, **cat** concatenates the two files—hence its name.

5.1.1 cat Options (-v and -n)

There are two **cat** options that you may find useful, though POSIX doesn't require **cat** to support either one.

Displaying Nonprinting Characters (-v)   **cat** is normally used for displaying text files only. Executables, when seen with **cat**, simply display junk. If you have nonprinting ASCII characters in your input, you can use **cat** with the -v option to display these characters.

Numbering Lines (-n)   The -n option numbers lines. C compilers indicate the line number where errors are detected, and this numbering facility often helps a programmer in debugging programs. But then your **vi** editor can show line numbers too, and if your version of **cat** doesn't support -n, you can use the **pr** *(12.2)* command to do the same job.

5.1.2 Using cat to Create a File

cat is also useful for creating a file. Though the significance of the following sequence can be appreciated only after reading Section 8.5.2, you should now know how to create small files. Enter the command **cat**, followed by the > (the right chevron) character and the filename (for example, foo):

```
$ cat > foo
A > symbol following the command means that the
output goes to the filename following it. cat used
in this way represents a rudimentary editor.
[Ctrl-d]
$ _                                          Prompt returns
```

When the command line is terminated with *[Enter]*, the prompt vanishes. **cat** now waits to take input from the user. Enter the three lines, each followed by *[Enter]*. Finally press *[Ctrl-d]* to signify the end of input to the system. This is the eof character used by UNIX systems and is shown in the

stty output *(3.13)*. When this character is entered, the system understands that no further text input will be made. The file is written and the prompt returned. To verify this, simply "cat" this file:

```
$ cat foo
A > symbol following the command means that the
output goes to the filename following it. cat used
in this way represents a rudimentary editor.
```

Note: The *[Ctrl-d]* character is used to terminate input not only with **cat**, but with all commands that accept input from the keyboard.

---

cat is a versatile command. It can be used to create, display, concatenate and append to files. More importantly, it doesn't restrict itself to handling files only; it also acts on a *stream*. You can supply the input to **cat** not only by specifying a filename, but also from the output of another command. You'll learn about all this in Chapter 8.

5.2 cp: COPYING A FILE

The **cp** (copy) command copies a file or a group of files. It creates an exact image of the file on disk with a different name. The syntax requires at least two filenames to be specified in the command line. When both are ordinary files, the first is copied to the second:

```
cp chap01 unit1
```

If the destination file (unit1) doesn't exist, it will first be created before copying takes place. If not, it will simply be overwritten without any warning from the system. So be careful when you choose your destination filename. Just check with the **ls** command whether or not the file exists.

If there is only one file to be copied, the destination can be either an ordinary or directory. You then have the option of choosing your destination filename. The following example shows two ways of copying a file to the progs directory:

```
cp chap01 progs/unit1            chap01 copied to unit1 under progs
cp chap01 progs                  chap01 retains its name under progs
```

cp is often used with the shorthand notation, . (dot), to signify the current directory as the destination. For instance, to copy the file .profile from /home/sharma to your current directory, you can use either of the two commands:

```
cp /home/sharma/.profile .profile        Destination is a file
cp /home/sharma/.profile .                Destination is the current directory
```

Obviously, the second one is preferable because it requires fewer keystrokes.

cp can also be used to copy more than one file with a single invocation of the command. In that case, the last filename *must* be a directory. For instance, to copy the files chap01, chap02 and chap03 to the progs directory, you have to use **cp** like this:

```
cp chap01 chap02 chap03 progs
```

The files retain their original names in progs. If these files are already resident in progs, they will be overwritten. For the above command to work, the progs directory must exist because **cp** won't create it.

You have already seen *(5.3)* how the UNIX system uses the * to frame a pattern for matching more than one filename. If there were only three filenames in the current directory having the common string chap, you can compress the above sequence using the * as a suffix to chap:

    cp chap* progs   *Copies all files beginning with* chap

We'll continue to use the * as a shorthand for multiple filenames. There are other metacharacters too, and they are discussed in complete detail in Section 8.3.

Note: In the previous example, **cp** doesn't look for a file named chap*. Before it runs, the shell expands chap* to regenerate the command line arguments for **cp** to use.

Caution: cp overwrites without warning the destination file if it exists! Run **1s** before you use **cp** unless you are sure that the destination file doesn't exist or deserves to be overwritten.

5.2.1 cp Options

Interactive Copying (-i)   The -i (interactive) option warns the user before overwriting the destination file. If unit1 exists, **cp** prompts for a response:

```
$ cp -i chap01 unit1
cp: overwrite unit1 (yes/no)? y
```

A y at this prompt overwrites the file, any other response leaves it uncopied.

Copying Directory Structures (-R)   Many UNIX commands are capable of **recursive** behavior. This means that the command can descend a directory and examine all files in its subdirectories. The **cp -R** command behaves recurvely to copy an entire directory structure, say, progs to newprogs:

    cp -R progs newprogs   newprogs *must not exist*

Attention! How **cp** behaves here depends on whether newprogs also exists as a directory. If newprogs doesn't exist, **cp** creates it along with the associated subdirectories. But if newprogs exists, progs becomes a subdirectory under newprogs. This means that the command run twice in succession will produce different results!

Caution: Sometimes, it's not possible to copy a file. This can happen if it's read-protected or the destination file or directory is write-protected. File permissions are discussed in Section 6.4.

5.3 rm: DELETING FILES

The **rm** (remove) command deletes one or more files. It normally operates silently and should be used with caution. The following command deletes three files:

```
rm chap01 chap02 chap03
```
                                                    rm chap* *could be dangerous to use!*

A file once deleted can't be recovered. **rm** won't *normally* remove a directory, but it can remove files from one. You can remove two chapters from the progs directory without having to "cd" to it:

```
rm progs/chap01 progs/chap02
```
                                        Or rm progs/chap0[12]

You may sometimes need to delete all files in a directory as part of a cleanup operation. The *, when used by itself, represents all files, and you can then use **rm** like this:

```
$ rm *
$ _
```
                                              All files gone!

DOS users, beware! When you delete files in this fashion, the system won't prompt you with the message All files in directory will be deleted! before removing the files! The $ prompt will return silently; the work has been done. The * used here is equivalent to *.* used in DOS.

Note: Whether or not you are able to remove a file depends, not on the file's permissions, but on the permissions you have for the *directory*. Directory permissions are taken up in Section 6.6.

5.3.1 rm Options

Interactive Deletion (-i)   Like in **cp**, the -i (interactive) option makes the command ask the user for confirmation before removing each file:

```
$ rm -i chap01 chap02 chap03
rm: remove chap01 (yes/no)? ?y
rm: remove chap02 (yes/no)? ?n
rm: remove chap03 (yes/no)? [Enter]
```
                                        No response—file not deleted

A y removes the file, any other response leaves the file undeleted.

Recursive Deletion (-r or -R)   With the -r (or -R) option, **rm** performs a tree walk—a thorough recursive search for all subdirectories and files within these subdirectories. At each stage, it deletes everything it finds. **rm** *won't normally remove directories, but when used with this option, it will.* Therefore, when you issue the command

```
rm -r *
```
                                          Behaves partially like rmdir

you'll delete all files in the current directory and all its subdirectories. If you don't have a backup, then these files will be lost forever.

Forcing Removal (-f)   **rm** prompts for removal if a file is write-protected. The -f option overrides this minor protection and forces removal. When you combine it with the -r option, it could be the most risky thing to do:

```
rm -rf *
```
                              Deletes everything in the current directory and below

Caution: Make sure you are doing the right thing before you use `rm *`. Be doubly sure before you use `rm -rf *`. The first command removes only ordinary files in the current directory. The second one removes everything—files and directories alike. If the root user (the super user) invokes `rm -rf *` in the / directory, the entire UNIX system will be wiped out from the hard disk!

5.4 `mv`: RENAMING FILES

The `mv` command renames (moves) files. It has two distinct functions:

- It renames a file (or directory).
- It moves a group of files to a different directory.

`mv` doesn't create a copy of the file; it merely renames it. No additional space is consumed on disk during renaming. To rename the file chap01 to man01, you should use

```
mv chap01 man01
```

If the destination file doesn't exist, it will be created. For the above example, `mv` simply replaces the filename in the existing directory entry with the new name. By default, `mv` doesn't prompt for overwriting the destination file if it exists. So be careful again.

Like `cp`, a group of files can be moved to a directory. The following command moves three files to the progs directory:

```
mv chap01 chap02 chap03 progs
```

`mv` can also be used to rename a directory, for instance, pis to perdir:

```
mv pis perdir
```

Like in `cp -R`, there's a difference in behavior depending on whether perdir exists or not. You can check that out for yourself.

There's a `-i` option available with `mv` also, and behaves exactly like in `cp`. The messages are the same and require a similar response.

HOW IT WORKS: How a Directory is Affected by cp, mv and rm

cp, mv and rm work by modifying the directory entries of the files they access. As shown in Fig. 5.1, cp adds an entry to the directory with the name of the destination file and inode number that is allotted by the kernel. mv replaces the name of an existing directory entry without disturbing its inode number. rm removes from an entry from the directory.

This is a rather simplistic view, and is true only when source and destination are in the same directory. When you "mv" a file to a directory that resides on a separate hard disk, the file is *actually* moved. You'll appreciate this better after you have understood how multiple file systems create the illusion of a single file system on your UNIX machine.

Fig. 5.1 Directory Status after **cp**, **mv** and **rm**

The action of **rm** also needs to be studied further. A file is not actually removed by deleting its directory entry. There could be "similar" entries (ones having the same inode number) for this file in this or another directory. We'll examine this directory table again along with its permissions when we take up file attributes in Chapter 11.

5.5 more: PAGING OUTPUT

The **man** command displays its output a page at a time. This is possible because it sends its output to a pager program. UNIX offers the **more** pager (originally from Berkeley) which has today replaced **pg**, the original pager of UNIX. Linux also offers **more** but **less** is its standard pager. We'll discuss more in this section and note the exclusive features of **less** separately in the aside on Linux.

To view the file **chap01**, enter the command with the filename:

```
more chap01
```
Press q *to exit*

You'll see the contents of chap01 on the screen, one page at a time. At the bottom of the screen, you'll also see the filename and percentage of the file that has been viewed:

```
--More--(17%)
```

more has a couple of internal commands that don't show up on the screen when you invoke them. **q**, the command used to exit **more**, is an internal command.

The AT&T and BSD versions of **more** differ widely in their capabilities and command usage. The POSIX specification on **more** is based on the BSD version. You have to try out the commands shown in Table 5.1, as well as look up the man pages, to know whether they apply to your system. **more** has a fairly useful help screen too; hitting an **h** invokes this screen.

5.5.1 Navigation

Irrespective of version, **more** uses the spacebar to scroll forward a page at a time. You can also scroll by small and large increments of lines or screens. To move forward one page, use

   f or the spacebar

and to move back one page, use

   b

5.5.2 The Repeat Features

The Repeat Factor   Many navigation commands in **more**, including **f** and **b**, use a *repeat factor*. This is the term used in **vi** *(7.1.1)* to prefix a number to a **vi** internal command. Use of the repeat factor as a command prefix simply repeats the command that many times. This means you can use **10f** for scrolling forward by 10 pages and **30b** for scrolling back 30 pages. Just remember that the commands themselves are not displayed on the screen—even for a moment.

Repeating The Last Command (.)   **more** has a repeat command, the dot (same command used by **vi**), that repeats the last command you used. If you scroll forward with **10f**, you can scroll another 10 pages by simply pressing a dot. This is a great convenience available in **more**!

5.5.3 Searching for a Pattern

You can perform a search for a pattern with the **/** command followed by the string. For instance, to look for the first **while** loop in your program, you'll have to enter this:

   /while   *Press [Enter] also*

You can repeat this search for viewing the next **while** loop section by pressing **n**, and you can do that repeatedly until you have scanned the entire file. Move back with **b** (using a repeat factor, if necessary) to arrive at the first page.

Note: The search capability in **more** is not restricted to simple strings. Like many UNIX commands (**grep**, **sed** and **vi**), **more** lets you use a *regular expression* to match multiple similar strings. Regular expressions are discussed in several chapters of this text beginning with Chapter 13.

5.5.4 Using more in a Pipeline

The **man** syntax doesn't indicate this (except mention that **more** is a filter), but we often use **more** to page the output of another command. The **ls** output won't fit on the screen if there are too many files, so the command has to be used like this:

```
ls | more
```
No filename with more!

We have a *pipeline* here of two commands where the output of one is used as the input of the other. Pipes are a feature of the shell and the topic is taken up in Chapter 8.

Tip: You can start up the **vi** editor from inside **more** by pressing **v**. When you finish editing, exit from **vi** returns you to **more** once again.

LINUX: less—The Standard Pager

Even though every Linux system also offers **more**, **less** is its standard pager. It's ironic that it bears such a name because it's more powerful than **more**. **less** is modeled on the **vi** editor, so learning **less** should be a breeze for **vi** users.

Navigation is **vi**-compatible. You have to work with these keys:

f, *[Ctrl-f]* or spacebar	Scroll forward one screen
b or *[Ctrl-b]*	Scroll backward one screen
j	One line up
k	One line down

Pattern searching techniques are similar. Unlike **more**, **less** can search for a pattern in the reverse direction also using the sequence ?*pattern*. But **less** does have one serious limitation. Unlike **more** (which uses the **.**), it can't repeat the last command.

Table 5.1 Internal Commands of **more** and **less**

more	less	*Action*
Spacebar or f	Spacebar or f or z	One page forward
20f	–	20 pages forward
b	b	One page back
15b	–	15 pages back
[Enter]	j or [Enter]	One line forward
–	k	One line back
–	p or 1G	Beginning of file
–	G	End of file
/pat	/pat	Searches forward for expression *pat*
n	n	Repeats search forward
–	?pat	Searches back for expression *pat*
. (a dot)	–	Repeats last command
v	v	Starts up vi editor
!cmd	!cmd	Executes UNIX command *cmd*
q	q	Quit
h	h	View Help

5.6 THE lp SUBSYSTEM: PRINTING A FILE

No user is allowed direct access to the printer. Instead, one has to *spool* (line up) a job along with others in a print queue. Spooling ensures the orderly printing of jobs and relieves the user from the necessity of administering the print resources. The spooling facility in System V is provided by the **lp** (line printing) command. Systems derived from BSD (like Linux) use the **lpr** command instead.

The following **lp** command prints a single copy of the file rfc822.ps (a document containing an Internet specification in the form of a Request For Comment):

```
$ lp rfc822.ps                          A Postscript file
request id is pr1-320 (1 file)
$ _
```

Note that the prompt is returned immediately after the job is submitted. The file isn't actually printed at the time the command is invoked, but later, depending on the number of jobs already lined up in the queue. Several users can print their files in this way without conflict.

lp notifies the request-id—a combination of the printer name (pr1) and the job number (320)—which can later be accessed with other commands. The hard copy of the file is often preceded by a title page mentioning the username, request-id and date.

5.6.1 lp Options

lp accepts the above request because a default printer has been defined by the administrator. If it is not, or if there is more than one printer in the system, you have to use the -d option with the printer name (say, laser):

```
lp -dlaser chap01.ps                    Can also provide space after -d
```

The -t (title) option, followed by the title string, prints the title on the first page:

```
lp -t"First chapter" chap01.ps
```

After the file has been printed, you can notify the user with the -m (mail) option. You can also print multiple copies (-n):

```
lp -n3 -m chap01.ps                     Prints three copies and mails user a message
```

Even though we used **lp** with filenames, this will not always be the case. You are aware that the shell's | symbol allows us to use **ls | more**. The same symbol also lets us use **ls | lp**.

5.6.2 Other Commands in the lp Subsystem

The print queue is viewed with the **lpstat** command. By viewing this list, you can use the **cancel** command to cancel any jobs submitted by you. **cancel** uses the request-id or printer name as argument:

```
cancel laser                            Cancels current job on printer laser
cancel pr1-320                          Cancels job with request-id pr1-320
```

You can cancel only those jobs that you own (i.e., you have submitted yourself), but the system administrator can cancel any job. **cancel** is effective only when a job remains in the print queue. If it is already being printed, **cancel** can't do a thing.

Note: Most UNIX printers are of the *Postscript* variety, i.e., they can properly print files formatted in Postscript, like the files `rfc822.ps` and `chap01.ps` used in the examples. (Postscript files are easily identified by the extension `.ps`.) When you select *Print* from the *File* menu of any GUI program, the program converts the data to Postscript which serve as input to the printer. No such conversion takes place when you use **lp** to print a text file like `/etc/passwd`. If you have a text file to print, use a Postscript conversion utility before you use **lp**. On Solaris, you can use the program **/usr/lib/lp/postscript/postprint** before running **lp**.

LINUX: Printing with **lpr**, **lpq** and **lprm**

Linux uses Berkeley's printing system which supports the **lpr** command for printing. You must have your printer configured properly before you can use **lpr**. The command normally doesn't throw out the job number:

```
lpr /etc/group
```

Linux has a rich set of tools that convert text files to Postscript. Check whether you have the programs **a2ps** or **enscript** on your system. Both eventually call up **lpr**; you don't have to do that on your own.

Like in System V, you can print a specific number of copies, choose the title and direct output to a specific printer. You can also mail completion of the job:

```
lpr -P hp4500 foo.ps              Prints on printer hp4500
lpr -T "The List of RFCs" foo.ps  Uses this title
lpr -#3 foo.ps                    Prints 3 copies
lpr -m foo.ps                     Mails message after completion
```

lpq displays the print queue showing job numbers. Using one or more job numbers as arguments to **lprm**, you can remove from the print queue only those jobs owned by you:

```
lprm 31         Removes job number 31
lprm -          Removes all jobs owned by user
```

The **lpc** command is used by the administrator to configure the printer. We'll not discuss printer administration in this text.

5.7 `file`: KNOWING THE FILE TYPES

Even though we know (so far) that files are of three types, you may often need to know more about these files. For instance, a regular file may contain plain text, a C program or executable code. UNIX provides the **file** command to determine the type of file, especially of an ordinary file. You can use it with one or more filenames as arguments:

```
$ file archive.zip
archive.zip:    ZIP archive
```

file correctly identifies the basic file types (regular, directory or device). For a regular file, it attempts to classify it further. Using the * to signify all files, this is how **file** behaves on this system having regular files of varying types:

```
$ file *
CW6.Eval.exe:     DOS executable (EXE)
User_Guide.ps:    PostScript document
archive.tar.gz:   gzip compressed data - deflate method , original file name
create_user.sh:   commands text
fatal.o:          ELF 32-bit MSB relocatable SPARC Version 1
fork1.c:          c program text
os_Lec03.pdf:     Adobe Portable Document Format (PDF) v1.2
```

This command identifies the file type by examining the **magic number** that is embedded in the first few bytes of the file. Every file type has a unique magic number. **file** recognizes text files, and can distinguish between shell programs, C source and object code. It also identifies DOS executables, compressed files, PDF documents and even empty files. While this method of identifying files is not wholly accurate, it's a reliable indicator.

5.8 wc: COUNTING LINES, WORDS AND CHARACTERS

UNIX features a universal word-counting program that also counts lines and characters. It takes one or more filenames as arguments and displays a four-columnar output. Before you use **wc** on the file infile, just use **cat** to view its contents:

```
$ cat infile
I am the wc command
I count characters, words and lines
With options I can also make a selective count
```

You can now use **wc** without options to make a "word count" of the data in the file:

```
$ wc infile
   3      20      103 infile
```

wc counts 3 lines, 20 words and 103 characters. The filename has also been shown in the fourth column. The meanings of these terms should be clear to you as they are used throughout the book:

- A **line** is any group of characters not containing a newline.
- A **word** is a group of characters not containing a space, tab or newline.
- A **character** is the smallest unit of information, and includes a space, tab and newline.

wc offers three options to make a specific count. The –l option counts only the number of lines, while the –w and –c options count words and characters, respectively:

```
$ wc -l infile
   3 infile                    Number of lines
$ wc -w infile
  20 infile                    Number of words
$ wc -c infile
 103 infile                    Number of characters
```

When used with multiple filenames, `wc` produces a line for each file, as well as a total count:

```
$ wc chap01 chap02 chap03
    305   4058  23179 chap01
    550   4732  28132 chap02
    377   4500  25221 chap03
   1232  13290  76532 total
```
A total as a bonus

`wc`, like `cat`, doesn't work with only files; it also acts on a data stream. You'll learn all about these streams in Chapter 8.

5.9 od: DISPLAYING DATA IN OCTAL

Many files (especially executables) contain nonprinting characters, and most UNIX commands don't display them properly. The file `odfile` contains some of these characters that don't show up normally:

```
$ more odfile
White space includes a
The ^G character rings a bell
The ^L character skips a page
```

The apparently incomplete first line actually contains a tab (entered by hitting *[Tab]*). The **od** command makes these commands visible by displaying the ASCII octal value of its input (here, a file). The -b option displays this value for each character separately. Here's a trimmed output:

```
$ od -b odfile
0000000 127 150 151 164 145 040 163 160 141 143 145 040 151 156 143 154
0000020 165 144 145 163 040 141 040 011 012 124 150 145 040 007 040 143
.....Output trimmed....
```

Each line displays 16 bytes of data in octal, preceded by the offset (position) in the file of the first byte in the line. In the absence of proper mapping it's difficult to make sense of this output, but when the -b and -c (character) options are combined, the output is friendlier:

```
$ od -bc odfile
0000000 127 150 151 164 145 040 163 160 141 143 145 040 151 156 143 154
          W   h   i   t   e       s   p   a   c   e       i   n   c   l
0000020 165 144 145 163 040 141 040 011 012 124 150 145 040 007 040 143
          u   d   e   s       a      \t  \n   T   h   e      007      c
0000040 150 141 162 141 143 164 145 162 040 162 151 156 147 163 040 141
          h   a   r   a   c   t   e   r       r   i   n   g   s       a
0000060 040 142 145 154 154 012 124 150 145 040 014 040 143 150 141 162
              b   e   l   l  \n   T   h   e      \f       c   h   a   r
  .....
```

Each line is now replaced with two. The octal representations are shown in the first line. The printable characters and escape sequences are shown in the second line. The first character in the first line is the letter W having the octal value 127. You'll recall having used some of the escape sequences with **echo** *(3.3)*. Let's have a look at their various representations:

- The tab character, *[Ctrl-i]*, is shown as \t and the octal value 011.
- The bell character, *[Ctrl-g]*, is shown as 007. Some systems show it as \a.
- The formfeed character, *[Ctrl-l]*, is shown as \f and 014.
- The LF (linefeed or newline) character, *[Ctrl-j]*, is shown as \n and 012. Note that **od** makes the newline character visible too.

Like **wc**, **od** also takes a command's output as its own input, and in Section 5.13, we'll use it to display nonprintable characters in filenames.

5.10 cmp: COMPARING TWO FILES

You may often need to know whether two files are identical so one of them can be deleted. There are three commands in the UNIX system that can tell you that. In this section, we'll have a look at the **cmp** (compare) command. Obviously, it needs two filenames as arguments:

```
$ cmp chap01 chap02
chap01 chap02 differ: char 9, line 1
```

The two files are compared byte by byte, and the location of the first mismatch (in the ninth character of the first line) is echoed to the screen. By default, **cmp** doesn't bother about possible subsequent mismatches but displays a detailed list when used with the -1 (list) option.

If two files are identical, **cmp** displays no message, but simply returns the prompt. You can try it out with two copies of the same file:

```
$ cmp chap01 chap01
$ _
```

This follows the UNIX tradition of quiet behavior. This behavior is also very important because the comparison has returned a *true* value, which can be subsequently used in a shell script to control the flow of a program.

5.11 comm: WHAT IS COMMON?

Suppose you have two lists of people and you are asked to find out the names available in one and not in the other, or even those common to both. **comm** is the command you need for this work. It requires two *sorted* files, and lists the differing entries in different columns. Let's try it on these two files:

```
$ cat file1
c.k. shukla
chanchal singhvi
s.n. dasgupta
sumit chakrobarty
```

```
$ cat file2
anil aggarwal
barun sengupta
c.k. shukla
lalit chowdury
s.n. dasgupta
```

Both files are sorted and have some differences. When you run **comm**, it displays a three-columnar output:

```
$ comm file[12]                           Comparing file1 and file2
        anil aggarwal
        barun sengupta
                c.k. shukla
chanchal singhvi
        lalit chowdury
                s.n. dasgupta
sumit chakrobarty
```

The first column contains two lines unique to the first file, and the second column shows three lines unique to the second file. The third column displays two lines common (hence its name) to both files.

This output provides a good summary to look at, but is not of much use to other commands that take **comm**'s output as their input. These commands require single-column output from **comm**, and **comm** can produce it using the options -1, -2 or -3. To drop a particular column, simply use its column number as an option prefix. You can also combine options and display only those lines that are common:

```
comm -3 foo1 foo2                         Selects lines not common to both files
comm -13 foo1 foo2                        Selects lines present only in second file
```

The last example and one more with the other matching option (-23) has more practical value than you may think, but we'll not discuss their application in this text.

5.12 diff: CONVERTING ONE FILE TO OTHER

diff is the third command that can be used to display file differences. Unlike its fellow members, **cmp** and **comm**, it also tells you which lines in one file have to be *changed* to make the two files identical. When used with the same files, it produces a detailed output:

```
$ diff file1 file2                        Or diff file[12]
0a1,2                                     Append after line 0 of first file
> anil aggarwal                           this line
> barun sengupta                          and this line
2c4                                       Change line 2 of first file
< chanchal singhvi                        Replacing this line
--                                        with
> lalit chowdury                          this line
4d5                                       Delete line 4 of first file
< sumit chakrobarty                       containing this line
```

diff uses certain special symbols and **instructions** to indicate the changes that are required to make two files identical. You should understand these instructions as they are used by the **sed** command, one of the most powerful commands on the system.

Each instruction uses an **address** combined with an **action** that is applied to the first file. The instruction **0a1,2** means appending two lines after line 0, which become lines 1 and 2 in the second file. **2c4** changes line 2 which is line 4 in the second file. **4d5** deletes line 4.

Tip: If you are simply interested in knowing whether two files are identical or not, use **cmp** without any options.

Maintaining Several Versions of a File (-e)   **diff -e** produces a set of instructions only (similar to the above), but these instructions can be used with the **ed** editor (not discussed in this text) to convert one file to the other. This facility saves disk space by letting us store the oldest file in its entirety, and only the changes between consecutive versions. We have a better option of doing that in the *Source Code Control System* (SCCS), but **diff** remains quite useful if the differences are few. SCCS is discussed in Chapter 22.

5.13 dos2unix AND unix2dos: CONVERTING BETWEEN DOS AND UNIX

Life being the way it is, you'll encounter DOS/Windows files in the course of your work. Sometimes, you'll need to move files between Windows and UNIX systems. Windows files use the same format as DOS, where the end of line is signified by two characters—CR (\r) and LF (\n). UNIX files, on the other hand, use only LF. Here are two lines from a DOS file, foo, viewed on a UNIX system with the **vi** editor:

```
Line 1^M                                    The [Ctrl-m] character at end
Line 2^M
```

There's a ^M (*[Ctrl-m]*) representing the CR sequence at the end of each line. An octal dump confirms this:

```
$ od -bc foo
0000000 114 151 156 145 040 061 015 012 114 151 156 145 040 062 015 012
        L   i   n   e       1  \r  \n   L   i   n   e       2  \r  \n
```

The CR-LF combination is represented by the octal values 015-012 and the escape sequence \r\n. Conversion of this file to UNIX is just a simple matter of removing the \r. This is often done automatically when downloading a UNIX file from a Windows machine using **ftp**, but sometimes you have to do that job yourself.

For this purpose, some UNIX systems feature two utilities—**dos2unix** and **unix2dos**—for converting files between DOS and UNIX. Sometimes, systems differ in their implementation. This is how we use **dos2unix** to convert this file foo to UNIX format on a Solaris system:

```
dos2unix foo foo.dos
```

The output is written to foo.dos. When you use **od** again, you'll find that the CR character is gone:

```
$ od -bc foo.dos
0000000 114 151 156 145 040 061 012 114 151 156 145 040 062 012
        L   i   n   e       1  \n   L   i   n   e       2  \n
```

One some systems (like Solaris), the first and second filenames could be the same. Others (like Linux) require only one filename, in which case the command rewrites the input file. Some may even require redirection. Browse through the man page to identify the form that works on your machine:

```
dos2unix foo foo                          foo rewritten in UNIX format
dos2unix foo                              Same
dos2unix foo > foo.dos                    Taking shell's help
```

unix2dos inserts CR before every LF, and thus increases the file size by the number of lines in the file. The syntactical form that works for **dos2unix** also works for **unix2dos**.

Tip: You can use **dos2unix** to delete the ^M character that occurs at the end of every line in the file typescript. This is the file used by **script** to record a login session *(3.6)*.

Note: If you view the UNIX file foo on Windows using Notepad but without performing the conversion, then you'll see a single line: Line 1line2. In fact, whenever you see a single line on a Windows machine that should have been multiple lines, satisfy yourself that you are viewing an unconverted UNIX file.

Caution: Never perform this conversion on a binary file. If you have downloaded a Windows program (say, a .EXE file) on a UNIX machine, the file must be transferred to the Windows machine without conversion. Otherwise, the program simply won't execute.

5.14 COMPRESSING AND ARCHIVING FILES

To conserve disk space you'll need to compress large and infrequently used files. Moreover, before sending a large file as an email attachment, it's good etiquette to compress the file first. Every UNIX system comes with some or all of the following compression and decompression utilities:

- **gzip** and **gunzip** (.gz)
- **bzip2** and **bunzip2** (.bz2)
- **zip** and **unzip** (.zip)

You'll find all of these programs on Solaris and Linux. The extension acquired by the compressed filename is shown in parentheses. The degree of compression that can be achieved depends on the type of file, its size and the compression program used. Large text files compress more, but GIF and JPEG image files (the types used on the World Wide Web) compress very little because they hold data in compressed form.

Apart from compressing, you'll also need to group a set of files into a single file, called an **archive**. The **tar** and **zip** commands can pack an entire directory structure into an archive. You can send this archive as a single file, either using **ftp** or as an email attachment, to be used on a remote machine. An additional layer of compression helps bring down the file size, the reason why **tar** is often used with **gzip** and **bzip2** for creating a compressed archive. **zip** handles both functions itself. In the next few sections, we'll be discussing these compression and archival utilities.

Note: Modern versions of WINZIP that run on Windows can read all of these formats though it can write only in the ZIP format. So you can choose any of these formats for compressing and archiving files even if you have to restore them on a Windows system. However, do check the WinZip documentation on the other system before you select the format to write an archive.

5.15 gzip AND gunzip: COMPRESSING AND DECOMPRESSING FILES

We'll monitor the size of one HTML and one PostScript file as they go through a number of compression and archival agents. We'll start with **gzip**, a very popular program, that works with one or more filenames. It provides the extension .gz to the compressed filename and removes the original file.

How well do HTML files compress? In the following example, we run **gzip** on the file libc.html (documentation for the GNU C library). We also note the file size, both before and after compression, using **wc -c** which counts characters:

```
$ wc -c libc.html
   3875302 libc.html
$ gzip libc.html
$ wc -c libc.html.gz
    788096 libc.html.gz
```

We seem to have achieved very high compression here, but before we go in for the statistics, let's repeat the previous exercise on a Postscript file:

```
$ wc -c User_Guide.ps ; gzip User_Guide.ps ; wc -c User_Guide.ps.gz

    372267 User_Guide.ps          Before compression
    128341 User_Guide.ps.gz       After compression
```

How much compression did we actually achieve for both files? Use the -l option with the compressed or original filenames as arguments:

```
$ gzip -l libc.html.gz User_Guide.ps.gz         .gz not necessary
compressed   uncompr. ratio uncompressed_name
   788096    3875302  79.6% libc.html
   128341     372267  65.5% User_Guide.ps
   916437    4247569  78.4% (totals)
```

HTML compressed better than Postscript (79.6% vs. 65.5%). This may not always be the case.

5.15.1 gzip Options

Uncompressing a "gzipped" File (-d)   To restore the original and uncompressed file, you have two options: Use either **gzip -d** or **gunzip** with one or more filenames as arguments; the .gz extension is optional yet again:

```
gunzip libc.html.gz                      Retrieves lib.html
gzip -d libc.html                        Same—.gz assumed
gunzip libc.html.gz User_Guide.ps.gz     Works with multiple files
```

You can now browse the files with their respective viewers—a browser like Netscape or Mozilla for HTML files, and **gv** for Postscript documents.

Recursive Compression (-r)   Like **cp**, you can also descend a directory structure and compress all files found in subdirectories. You need the -r option, and the arguments to **gzip** must comprise at least one directory:

```
gzip -r progs                            Compresses all files in progs
```

This option can be used for decompression also. To decompress all files in this directory you need to use **gunzip -r progs** or **gzip -dr progs**.

Tip: To view compressed text files, you really don't need to "gunzip" (decompress) them. Use the **gzcat** and **gzmore** (or **zcat** and **zmore**) commands if they are available on your system. In most cases, the commands run **gunzip -c**.

Note: For some years, **gzip** reigned as the most favored compression agent. Today, we have a better agent in **bzip2** (and **bunzip2**). **bzip2** is slower than **gzip** and creates .bz2 files. We are beginning to see .bz2 files on the Internet. **bzip2** options are modeled on **gzip**, so if you know **gzip** you also know **bzip2**.

5.16 tar: THE ARCHIVAL PROGRAM

For creating a disk archive that contains a group of files or an entire directory structure, we need to use **tar**. The command is taken up in some detail in Chapter 15 to back up files to tape (or floppy), but in this section we need to know how the command is used to create a disk archive. For this minimal use of **tar** we need to know these *key* options:

-c	Create an archive
-x	Extract files from archive
-t	Display files in archive
-f *arch*	Specify the archive *arch*

Only one these key options can be used at a time. We'll also learn to use **gzip** and **gunzip** to compress and decompress the archive created with **tar**.

5.16.1 Creating an Archive (-c)

To create an archive, we need to specify the name of the archive (with -f), the copy or write operation (-c) and the filenames as arguments. Additionally, we'll use the -v (verbose) option to display the progress while **tar** works. This is how we create a file archive, archive.tar, from the two uncompressed files used previously:

```
$ tar -cvf archive.tar libc.html User_Guide.ps
a libc.html 3785K
a User_Guide.ps 364K
```
                                              -v *(verbose) displays list*
                                              a *indicates append*

By convention, we use the .tar extension, so you'll remember to use the same **tar** command for extraction. We created an archive containing two ordinary files, but **tar** also behaves recursively to back up one or more directories. In the following example, **tar** fills the archive progs.tar with three directory structures:

```
tar -cvf progs.tar c_progs java_progs shell_scripts
```

We'll soon use the same **tar** command to extract files from this archive. But before we do that, let's **see** how we can compress this archive.

Using gzip *with* tar   If the created archive is very big, you may like to compress it with **gzip**:

```
gzip archive.tar
```
                                                        Archived and compressed

This creates a "tar-gzipped" file, archive.tar.gz. This file can now be sent out by FTP or as an email attachment to someone. A great deal of open-source UNIX and Linux software are available as .tar.gz files on the Internet. To use the files in this archive, the recipient needs to have both **tar** and **gzip** at her end.

5.16.2 Extracting Files from Archive (-x)

tar uses the -x option to extract files from an archive. You can use it right away on a .tar file, the one we just used to archive three directories:

```
tar -xvf progs.tar
```
                                                        Extracts the three directories

But to extract files from a .tar.gz file (like archive.tar.gz), you must first use **gunzip** to decompress the archive and then run **tar**:

```
$ gunzip archive.tar.gz                              Retrieves archive.tar
$ tar -xvf archive.tar                               Extracts files
x libc.html, 3875302 bytes, 7569 tape blocks         x indicates extract
x User_Guide.ps, 372267 bytes, 728 tape blocks
```

You'll now find the two files in the current directory. Selective extraction is also possible. Just follow the above command line with one or more filenames that have to be extracted:

```
tar -xvf archive.tar User_guide.ps
```
                                                        Extracts only User_guide.ps

This extracts a single file from the archive. If you use a pathname, it must be exactly in the same form that was used during the copying operation. This has been discussed later *(15.9.2—Tip).*

5.16.3 Viewing the Archive (-t)

To view the contents of the archive, use the -t (table of contents) option. It doesn't extract files, but simply shows their attributes in a form that you'll see more often later:

```
$ tar -tvf archive.tar
-rw-r--r-- 102/10  3875302 Aug 24 19:49 2002 libc.html
-rw-r--r-- 102/10   372267 Aug 24 19:48 2002 User_Guide.ps
```

You'll understand the significance of these columns after you have learned to interpret the **ls -l** output *(6.1).* But you can at least see the individual file size (third column) and their names (last column) in this output.

Both **tar** and **gzip** can be made to behave like *filters* (a group of programs whose input and output are quite flexible). After you have understood how filters work, you'll be able to perform both activities without creating an intermediate file.

LINUX: **tar** and **gzip** are so often used together that GNU **tar** has a -z option that compresses and archives together (and decompresses and extracts together). This dual activity is reflected in the following commands:

```
tar -cvzf archive.tar.gz libc.html User_Guide.ps
tar -xvzf archive.tar.gz
tar -xvzf archive.tar.gz User_Guide.ps
tar -tvzf archive.tar.gz
```

Compresses also
Decompresses also
Extracts one file only
Displays list

Note that whether you should use the -z option with -x or -t depends on whether the archive was compressed in the first place with -c. The archive's extension (.tar.gz) should provide this hint, but that's no guarantee. A wrong extension could have been provided by the user at the time of archival.

GNU **tar** also has a --bzip option that uses **bzip2** for handling compression. If you decide to use it, provide the extension .tar.bz2 to the compressed archive so the person at the other end knows how to handle it.

5.17 zip AND unzip: COMPRESSING AND ARCHIVING TOGETHER

Phil Katz's popular PKZIP and PKUNZIP programs are now available as **zip** and **unzip** on UNIX and Linux systems. **zip** generally doesn't compress as much as **bzip2** but it combines the compressing function of **gzip** with the archival function of **tar**. So instead of using two commands to compress a directory structure, you can use only one—**zip**. All the letters of the alphabet are available as its options but we'll consider just a few of them.

zip requires the first argument to be the compressed filename; the remaining arguments are interpreted as files and directories to be compressed. The compression in the previous example could have been achieved with **zip** in the following way:

```
$ zip archive.zip libc.html User_Guide.ps
  adding: libc.html (deflated 80%)
  adding: User_Guide.ps (deflated 66%)
```

The unusual feature of this command is that it doesn't overwrite an existing compressed file. If archive.zip exists, files will either be updated or appended to the archive depending on whether they already exist in the archive.

Recursive Compression (-r)   For recursive behavior, **zip** uses the -r option. It descends the tree structure in the same way **tar** does except that it also compresses files. You can easily compress your home directory in this way:

```
cd ; zip -r sumit_home.zip .
```

cd *is same as* cd $HOME

Using unzip   Files are restored with the **unzip** command, which in its simplest form, uses the compressed filename as argument. **unzip** does a noninteractive restoration if it doesn't overwrite any existing files:

```
$ unzip archive.zip
Archive:  archive.zip
  inflating: libc.html
  inflating: User_Guide.ps
```

But if the uncompressed file exists on disk, **unzip** makes sure that it's doing the right thing by seeking user confirmation:

```
replace libc.html? [y]es, [n]o, [A]ll, [N]one, [r]ename: y
```

You can respond with y or n. You can also rename the file (r) to prevent overwriting or direct **unzip** to perform the decompression on the remaining files noninteractively (A).

Viewing the Archive (-v)   You can view the compressed archive with the -v option. The list shows both the compressed and uncompressed size of each file in the archive along with the percentage of compression achieved:

```
$ unzip -v archive.zip
Archive:  archive.zip
 Length  Method    Size  Ratio   Date    Time   CRC-32     Name
 ------  ------    ----  ----    ----    ----   ------     ----
3875302  Defl:N  788068   80%  08-24-02  19:49  fae93ded   libc.html
 372267  Defl:N  128309   66%  08-24-02  19:48  7839e6b3   User_Guide.ps
 ------          ------   --                                -------
4247569          916377   78%                              2 files
```

Tip: If you have to move files between UNIX and Windows machines, you can take advantage of the end-of-line conversion options offered by **zip**. Use -l to convert from LF to CR-LF, and -ll to do the opposite. However, use them only when there are no binary files in your archive.

5.18 CONCLUSION

The commands discussed in this chapter don't always take input from files. Some commands (like **more** and **lp**) use, as alternate sources of input, the keyboard or the output of another command. Most of the other commands (like **wc**, **cat**, **cmp**, **od**, **gzip** and **tar**) can also send output to a file or serve as input to another command. Some examples in this chapter (and previous ones) have shown this to be possible with the > and | symbols. The discussion on these techniques is taken up in Chapter 8.

You would have also noted that we can use **gzip -d** instead of **gunzip** to decompress files. You'll have to understand why two commands have been offered to do the same job when one of them would have sufficed. Are **gzip** and **gunzip** one and the same file? This question is related to file attributes, and we begin our discussion on file attributes in the next chapter.

WRAP UP

cat is not only used to display one or more files but also to create a file.

You can copy files with **cp**, remove them with **rm**, and rename them with **mv**. All of them can be used interactively (-i), and the first two can be used to work on a complete directory tree (-r or -R) i.e., recursively. **rm -r** can remove a directory tree even if is not empty.

more is a pager that supports a *repeat factor*. You can search for a pattern (/) and repeat the search (n). Linux offers **less** as a superior pager.

lp prints a file and can *directly* print Postscript documents. You can cancel any submitted job with **cancel**. Linux uses the **lpr** command instead of **lp**.

file identifies the file type beyond the normal three categories. **wc** counts the number of lines, words and characters. **od** displays the octal value of each character and is used to display invisible characters.

We discussed three file comparison utilities. **cmp** tells you where the first difference was encountered. **comm** shows the lines that are common and optionally shows you lines unique to either or both *sorted* files. **diff** lists file differences as a sequence of **sed**-like instructions.

The **dos2unix** and **unix2dos** commands convert files between DOS and UNIX. DOS files use CR-LF as the line terminator, while UNIX uses only LF.

We also discussed several compression and archival tools. **gzip** and **gunzip** compresses and decompresses individual files (extension—.gz). **tar** always works recursively to archive a group of files into an *archive*. **tar** and **gzip** are often used together to create compressed archives (extension—.tar.gz).

zip and **unzip** can perform all functions that are found in **gzip**, **gunzip** and **tar**. **zip** alone can create a compressed archive from directory structures (-r).

Test Your Understanding

5.1   What will **cat foo foo foo** display?

5.2   How will you copy a directory structure bar1 to bar2? Does it make any difference if bar2 exists?

5.3   Run the command **tty** and note the device name of your terminal. Now use this device name (say, /dev/pts/6) in the command, **cp /etc/passwd /dev/pts/6**. What do you observe?

5.4   How will you remove a directory tree even when it's not empty and without using **rmdir**?

5.5   How does the command **mv bar1 bar2** behave, where both bar1 and bar2 are directories, when (i) bar2 exists, (ii) bar2 doesn't exist?

5.6   Use the **file** command on all files in the /dev directory. Can you group these files into two categories?

5.7   How do you print three copies of /etc/passwd on the printer named arjun?

5.8   Run the **script** command and then issue a few commands before you run **exit**. What do you see when you run **cat -v typescript**?

5.9   How will you find out the ASCII octal values of the numerals and alphabets?

5.10 How will you display *only* the lines common to two files?

5.11 The command **cmp foo1 foo2** displays nothing. What does it indicate?

Flex Your Brain

5.1   Describe the contents of a directory, explaining the mechanism by which its entries are updated. Why is the size of a directory usually small?

5.2   What is the difference between **cat foo** and **cat > foo**? Why do you have to use *[Ctrl-d]* in one and not in the other?

5.3   Will the command **cp foo bar** work if (i) foo is an ordinary file and bar is a directory, (ii) both foo and bar are directories?

5.4   Assuming that bar is a directory, explain what the command **rm -rf bar** does. How is the command different from **rmdir bar**?

5.5   What is the significance of these commands? (i) **mv $HOME/include .** (ii) **cp -r bar1 bar2** (iii) **mv * ../bin**

5.6   The command **cp hosts backup/hosts.bak** didn't work even though all files exist. Name three possible reasons.

5.7   You have a directory structure $HOME/a/a/b/c where the first a is empty. How do you remove it and move the lower directories up?

5.8   Explain the significance of the repeat factor used in **more**. How do you search for the pattern include in a file and repeat the search? What is the difference between this repeat command and the dot command?

5.9   A file with the .ps extension should be a Postscript file, but how can you be sure? What is the importance of this file type in the printing subsystem?

5.10 A file foo contains a list of filenames, with one filename in each line. One of the filenames appears to have an embedded space. How will you (i) count the number of filenames, (ii) check whether there's actually an embedded space in a filename?

5.11 How do DOS and UNIX text files differ? Name the utilities that convert files between these two formats?

5.12 You have two lists, foo1 and foo2, containing names of users. How do you create a third list of those users in foo2 who are absent in foo1? When will the command not work properly?

5.13 How do you use **tar** to add two files, foo.html and bar.html, to an archive and then compress the archive? How will you reverse the entire process and extract the files in their original uncompressed form?

5.14 Name three advantages **zip** has over **gzip**. How do you use **zip** to send a complete directory structure to someone by email? How does the recipient recreate the directory structure at her end?

5.15 What is meant by *recursive* behavior of a command? Name four commands, along with a suitable example of each, that can operate recursively.

6

Basic File Attributes

In the previous two chapters, you created files and directories, navigated the file system, and copied, moved and removed files without any problem. In real life, however, matters may not be so rosy. You may have problems when handling a file or directory. Your file may be modified or even deleted by others. A restoration from a backup may be unable to write to your directory. You must know why these problems happen and how to rectify and prevent them.

The UNIX file system lets users access other files not belonging to them and without infringing on security. A file also has a number of *attributes* (properties) that are stored in the inode. In this chapter, we'll use the **ls -l** command with additional options to display these attributes. We'll mainly consider the two basic attributes—permissions and ownership—both of which are changeable by well-defined rules. The remaining attributes are taken up in Chapter 11.

WHAT YOU WILL LEARN
- Interpret the significance of the seven fields of the **ls -l** output (*listing*).
- How to obtain the listing of a specific directory.
- The importance of *ownership* and *group ownership* of a file and how they affect security.
- The significance of the nine permissions of a file as applied to different *categories* of users.
- Use **chmod** to change all file permissions in a relative and absolute manner.
- Use **chown** and **chgrp** to change the owner and group owner of files on BSD and AT&T systems.

TOPICS OF SPECIAL INTEREST
- The importance of directory permissions (discussion on individual permissions deferred to Chapter 11).
- An introductory treatment of the relationship that exists between file ownership, file permissions and directory permissions.

6.1 ls -l: LISTING FILE ATTRIBUTES

We have already used the **ls** command with a number of options. It's the -l (long) option that reveals most. This option displays most attributes of a file—like its permissions, size and ownership details. The output in UNIX lingo is often referred to as the **listing**. Sometimes we combine this option with other options for displaying other attributes, or ordering the list in a different sequence.

`ls` looks up the file's inode to fetch its attributes. Let's use `ls -l` to list seven attributes of all files in the current directory:

```
$ ls -l
total 72
-rw-r--r--   1 kumar    metal        19514 May 10 13:45 chap01
-rw-r--r--   1 kumar    metal         4174 May 10 15:01 chap02
-rw-rw-rw-   1 kumar    metal           84 Feb 12 12:30 dept.lst
-rw-r--r--   1 kumar    metal         9156 Mar 12  1999 genie.sh
drwxr-xr-x   2 kumar    metal          512 May  9 10:31 helpdir
drwxr-xr-x   2 kumar    metal          512 May  9 09:57 progs
```

The list is preceded by the words `total 72`, which indicates that a total of 72 blocks are occupied by these files on disk, each block consisting of 512 bytes (1024 in Linux). We'll now briefly describe the significance of each field in the output.

File Type and Permissions   The first column shows the type and *permissions* associated with each file. The first character in this column is mostly a -, which indicates that the file is an ordinary one. This is, however, not so for the directories `helpdir` and `progs`, where you see a d at the same position.

You then see a series of characters that can take the values r, w, x and -. In the UNIX system, a file can have three types of permissions—read, write and execute. You'll see how to interpret these permissions and also how to change them in Sections 6.4 and 6.5.

Links   The second column indicates the number of *links* associated with the file. This is actually the number of filenames maintained by the system of that file. UNIX lets a file have as many names as you want it to have, even though there is a single file on disk. This attribute will be discussed in Chapter 11.

Note: A link count greater than one indicates that the file has more than one name. That doesn't mean that there are two copies of the file.

Ownership   When you create a file, you automatically become its *owner*. The third column shows kumar as the owner of all of these files. The owner has full authority to tamper with a file's contents and permissions—a privilege not available with others except the root user. Similarly, you can create, modify or remove files in a directory if you are the owner of the directory.

Group Ownership   When opening a user account, the system administrator also assigns the user to some group. The fourth column represents the *group owner* of the file. The concept of a group of users also owning a file has acquired importance today as group members often need to work on the same file. It's generally desirable that the group have a set of privileges distinct from others as well as the owner. Ownership and group ownership are elaborated in Section 6.7.

File Size   The fifth column shows the size of the file in bytes, i.e., the amount of data it contains. The important thing to remember is that it is only a character count of the file and not a measure of disk space that it occupies. The space occupied by a file on disk is usually larger than this figure since files are written to disk in blocks of 1024 bytes or more. In other words, even though the file dept.1st contains 84 bytes, it would occupy 1024 bytes on disk on systems that use a block size of 1024 bytes. We'll discuss the significance of block size much later in the text.

The two directories show smaller file sizes (512 bytes each). This is to be expected as a directory maintains a list of filenames along with an identification number (the inode number) for each file. The size of the directory file depends on the size of this list—whatever be the size of the files themselves.

Last Modification Time   The sixth, seventh and eighth columns indicate the last modification time of the file, which is stored to the nearest second. A file is said to be modified only if its contents have changed in any way. If you change only the permissions or ownership of the file, the modification time remains unchanged. If the file is less than a year old since its last modification date, the year won't be displayed. Note that the file genie.sh has been modified more than a year ago.

You'll often need to run automated tools that make decisions based on a file's modification time. This column shows two other time stamps when **ls** is used with other options. The time stamps are discussed in Chapter 11.

Filename   The last column displays the filenames arranged in ASCII collating sequence. You already know *(4.2)* that UNIX filenames can be very long (up to 255 characters). If you would like to see an important file at the top of the listing, then choose its name in uppercase— at least, its first letter.

The order of the list can be changed by combining the -1 option with other options. In the rest of the chapter, we'll discuss permissions and ownership, and also learn how to change them.

6.2 THE -d OPTION: LISTING DIRECTORY ATTRIBUTES

You'll recall *(4.11.1)* that **ls**, when used with directory names, lists files in the directory rather than the directory itself. To force **ls** to list the attributes of a directory, rather than its contents, you need to use the -d (directory) option:

```
$ ls -ld helpdir progs
drwxr-xr-x   2 kumar    metal        512 May  9 10:31 helpdir
drwxr-xr-x   2 kumar    metal        512 May  9 09:57 progs
```

Directories are easily identified in the listing by the first character of the first column, which here shows a d. For ordinary files, this slot always shows a - (hyphen), and for device files, either a b or c. The significance of the attributes of a directory differ a good deal from an ordinary file. Directories will be considered in some detail in Chapter 11.

Tip: To see the attributes of a directory rather than the files contained in it, use **ls -ld** with the directory name. Note that simply using **ls -d** will *not* list all subdirectories in the current directory. Strange though it may seem, **ls** has no option to list only directories!

6.3 FILE OWNERSHIP

Before we take up file permissions, you need to understand the significance of file ownership. When you create a file, your username shows up in the third column of the file's listing; you are the **owner** of the file. Your group name is seen in the fourth column; your group is the **group owner** of the file. If you copy someone else's file, you are the owner of the copy. If you can't create files in other users' home directories, it's because those directories are not owned by you (and the owner has not allowed you write access).

Several users may belong to a single group. People working on a project are generally assigned a common group, and all files created by group members (who have separate user-ids) will have the same group owner. However, make no mistake: The privileges of the group are set by the owner of the file and not by the group members.

When the system administrator creates a user account, he has to assign these parameters to the user:

- The user-id (UID)—both its name and numeric representation.
- The group-id (GID)—both its name and numeric representation.

The file /etc/passwd maintains the UID (both the number and name) and GID (but only the number). /etc/group contains the GID (both number and name). We'll discuss these two files when learning to add a user account in Chapter 15.

Tip: To know your own UID and GID without viewing /etc/passwd and /etc/group, use the **id** command:

```
$ id
uid=655537(kumar) gid=655535(metal)
```

The uid is kumar, and if this name matches the one shown in the ownership field of the listing (**ls -l** output), then you are the owner of those files. It also means that you have the authority to change the file's attributes.

6.4 FILE PERMISSIONS

UNIX has a simple and well-defined system of assigning permissions to files. Let's issue the **ls -l** command once again to view the permissions of a few files:

```
$ ls -l chap02 dept.1st dateval.sh
-rwxr-xr--  1 kumar   metal    20500 May 10 19:21 chap02
-rwxr-xr-x  1 kumar   metal      890 Jan 29 23:17 dateval.sh
-rw-rw-rw-  1 kumar   metal       84 Feb 12 12:30 dept.1st
```

Observe the first column that represents file permissions. These permissions are also different for the three files. UNIX follows a three-tiered file protection system that determines a file's access rights. To understand how this system works, let's break up the permissions string of the file chap02 into three groups. The initial - (in the first column) represents an ordinary file and is left out of the permissions string:

```
r w x    r - x    r - -
```

Each group here represents a **category** and contains three slots, representing the read, write and execute permissions of the file—in that order. r indicates read permission, which means **cat** can display the file. w indicates write permission; you can edit such a file with an editor. x indicates execute permission; the file can be executed as a program. The - shows the absence of the corresponding permission.

The first group (rwx) has all three permissions. The file is readable, writable and executable by the *owner* of the file, kumar. But do we know who the owner is? Yes we do. The third column shows kumar as the owner and the first permissions group applies to kumar. You have to log in with the username kumar for these privileges to apply to you.

The second group (r-x) has a hyphen in the middle slot, which indicates the absence of write permission by the *group owner* of the file. This group owner is metal, and all users belonging to the metal group have read and execute permissions only.

The third group (r--) has the write and execute bits absent. This set of permissions is applicable to *others*, i.e., those who are neither the owner kumar nor belong to the metal group. This category (others) is often referred to as the *world*. This file is not world-writable.

You can set different permissions for the three categories of users—owner, group and others. It's important that you understand them because a little learning here can be a dangerous thing. A faulty file permission is a sure recipe for disaster.

Note: The group permissions here don't apply to kumar (the owner) even if kumar belongs to the metal group. The owner has its own set of permissions that override the group owner's permissions. However, when kumar renounces the ownership of the file, the group permissions then apply to him.

6.5 chmod: CHANGING FILE PERMISSIONS

Before we take up **chmod**, let's decide to change a habit. Henceforth, we'll refer to the owner as *user* because that's how the **chmod** command (which changes file permissions) refers to the owner. In this section, whenever we use the term *user*, we'll actually mean *owner*.

A file or directory is created with a default set of permissions, and this default is determined by a simple setting (called *umask*), which we'll discuss later. Generally, the default setting write-protects a file from all except the user (new name for owner), though all users *may* have read access. However, this may not be so on your system. To know your system's default, create a file xstart:

```
$ cat /usr/bin/startx > xstart          Actually copies the file startx
$ ls -l xstart
-rw-r--r--   1 kumar    metal       1906 Sep  5 23:38 xstart
```

It seems that, by default, a file doesn't also have execute permission. So how does one execute such a file? To do that, the permissions of the file need to be changed. This is done with **chmod**.

The **chmod** (change mode) command is used to set the permissions of one or more files for all three categories of users (user, group and others). It can be run only by the user (the owner) and the superuser. The command can be used in two ways:

- In a relative manner by specifying the changes to the current permissions.
- In an absolute manner by specifying the final permissions.

We'll consider both ways of using **chmod** in the following sections.

6.5.1 Relative Permissions

When changing permissions in a relative manner, **chmod** only changes the permissions specified in the command line *and leaves the other permissions unchanged*. In this mode it uses the following syntax:

chmod *category operation permission filename(s)*

chmod takes as its argument an expression comprising some letters and symbols that completely describe the user category and the type of permission being assigned or removed. The expression contains three components:

- User *category* (user, group, others)
- The *operation* to be performed (assign or remove a permission)
- The type of *permission* (read, write, execute)

By using suitable abbreviations for each of these components, you can frame a compact expression and then use it as an argument to **chmod**. The abbreviations used for these three components are shown in Table 6.1.

Now let's consider an example. To assign execute permission to the user (We won't remind again that user here is the owner.) of the file xstart, we need to frame a suitable expression by using appropriate characters from each of the three columns of Table 6.1. Since the file needs to be executable only by the user, the expression required is u+x:

```
$ chmod u+x xstart
$ ls -l xstart
-rwxr--r--   1 kumar    metal       1906 May 10 20:30 xstart
```

The command assigns (+) execute (x) permission to the user (u), but other permissions remain unchanged. You can now execute the file if you are the owner of the file but the other categories (i.e., group and others) still can't. To enable all of them to execute this file, you have to use multiple characters to represent the user category (ugo):

```
$ chmod ugo+x xstart ; ls -l xstart
-rwxr-xr-x   1 kumar    metal        1906 May 10 20:30 xstart
```

The string ugo combines all the three categories—user, group and others. UNIX also offers a shorthand symbol a (all) to act as a synonym for the string. And, as if that wasn't enough, there's an even shorter form that combines these three categories. When it is not specified, the permission applies to all categories. So the previous sequence can be replaced by either of the following:

```
chmod a+x xstart                          a implies ugo
chmod +x xstart                           By default, a is implied
```

chmod accepts multiple filenames in the command line. When you need to assign the same set of permissions to a group of files, this is what you should do:

```
chmod u+x note note1 note3
```

Permissions are removed with the - operator. To remove the read permission from both group and others, use the expression go-r:

```
$ ls -l xstart
-rwxr-xr-x   1 kumar    metal        1906 May 10 20:30 xstart
$ chmod go-r xstart ; ls -l xstart
-rwx--x--x   1 kumar    metal        1906 May 10 20:30 xstart
```

chmod also accepts multiple expressions delimited by commas. For instance, to restore the original permissions to the file xstart, you have to remove the execute permission from all (a-x) and assign read permission to group and others (go+r):

```
$ chmod a-x,go+r xstart ; ls -l xstart
-rw-r--r--   1 kumar    metal        1906 May 10 20:30 xstart
```

More than one permission can also be set; **u+rwx** is a valid **chmod** expression. So setting write and execute permissions for others is no problem:

```
$ chmod o+wx xstart ; ls -l xstart
-rw-r--rwx   1 kumar    metal        1906 May 10 20:30 xstart
```

We described relative permissions here, but **chmod** also uses an absolute assignment system, which is taken up in the next topic.

Table 6.1 Abbreviations Used by **chmod**

Category	*Operation*	*Permission*
u—User	+—Assigns permission	r—Read permission
g—Group	-—Removes permission	w—Write permission
o—Others	=—Assigns absolute permission	x—Execute permission
a—All (ugo)		

6.5.2 Absolute Permissions

Sometimes you don't need to know what a file's current permissions are, but want to set all nine permission bits explicitly. The expression used by **chmod** here is a string of three octal numbers (base 8). You may or may not be familiar with this numbering system, so a discussion would be in order.

Octal numbers use the base 8, and octal digits have the values 0 to 7. This means that a set of three bits can represent one octal digit. If we represent the permissions of each category by one octal digit, this is how the permissions can be represented:

- Read permission—4 (Octal 100)
- Write permission—2 (Octal 010)
- Execute permission—1 (Octal 001)

For each category we add up the numbers. For instance, 6 represents read and write permissions, and 7 represents all permissions as can easily be understood from Table 6.2.

Table 6.2

Binary	Octal	Permissions	Significance
000	0	---	No permissions
001	1	--x	Executable only
010	2	-w-	Writable only
011	3	-wx	Writable and executable
100	4	r--	Readable only
101	5	r-x	Readable and executable
110	6	rw-	Readable and writable
111	7	rwx	Readable, writable and executable

We have three categories and three permissions for each category, so three octal digits can describe a file's permissions completely. The most significant digit represents user and the least one represents others. **chmod** can use this three-digit string as the expression.

You can use this method to assign read and write permission to all three categories. Without octal numbers, you should normally be using **chmod a+rw xstart** to achieve the task (assuming there was no execute permission initially). Now you can use a different method:

```
$ chmod 666 xstart ; ls -l xstart
-rw-rw-rw-  1 kumar    metal          1906 May 10 20:30 xstart
```

The 6 indicates read and write permissions (4 + 2). To restore the original permissions to the file, you need to remove the write permission (2) from group and others:

```
$ chmod 644 xstart ; ls -l xstart
-rw-r--r--  1 kumar    metal          1906 May 10 20:30 xstart
```

To assign all permissions to the owner, read and write permissions to the group, and only execute permission to the others, use this:

```
chmod 761 xstart
```

Now it should be quite easy for you to understand that the expression 777 signifies all permissions for all categories, while 000 indicates absence of all permissions for all categories. But can we delete a file with permissions 000? Yes, we can. Can we prevent a file with permissions 777 from being deleted? We can do that too. We'll soon learn that it's the directory that determines whether a file can be deleted, not the file itself.

Note: Remember that a file's permissions can only be changed by the owner (understood by **chmod** as user) of the file. One user can't change the protection modes of files belonging to another user. However, the system administrator can tamper with all file attributes including permissions, irrespective of their ownership.

6.5.3 The Security Implications

To understand the security implications behind these permissions and the role played by **chmod**, consider the default permissions of the file xstart that was shown at the beginning of Section 6.5:

```
-rw-r--r--   1 kumar    metal        1906 May 10 20:30 xstart
```

These permissions are fairly safe; only the user can edit the file. What are the implications if we remove all permissions in either of these ways?

```
chmod u-rw,go-r xstart
chmod 000 xstart
```

The listing in either case will look like this:

```
----------   1 kumar    metal        1906 May 10 20:30 xstart
```

This setting renders the file virtually useless; you simply can't do anything useful with it. *But the user can still delete this file!* To understand why that can happen, you need to understand directory permissions and how they are related to file permissions.

On the other hand, you must not be too generous (and careless, too) to have all permissions enabled for all categories of users, using either of these commands:

```
chmod a+rwx xstart
chmod 777 xstart
```

The resulting permissions setting is simply dangerous:

```
-rwxrwxrwx   1 kumar    metal        1906 May 10 20:30 xstart
```

It's the universal write permission here that concerns us most. This file can be written by all. You shouldn't be able to read, write or execute every file. If that were possible, you can never have a secure system. The UNIX system, by default, never allows that, and no sensible user will compromise security so easily.

Note: We ignored the directory permissions in our discussions, but they also have a major role to play in setting a file's access rights. No matter how careful you are with your file permissions, a faulty directory permission will affect the security of all files housed in that directory. It doesn't matter who owns the file or whether the file itself has write permission for that user. Directory permissions are taken up later.

6.5.4 Using chmod Recursively (-R)

It's possible to make **chmod** descend a directory hierarchy and apply the expression to every file and subdirectory it finds. This is done with the -R (recursive) option:

```
chmod -R a+x shell_scripts
```

This makes all files and subdirectories found in the tree-walk (that commences from the shell_scripts directory) executable by all users. You can provide multiple directory and filenames, and if you want to use **chmod** on your home directory tree, then "cd" to it and use it in one of these ways:

```
chmod -R 755 .          Works on hidden files also
chmod -R a+x *          Leaves out hidden files
```

When you know the shell metacharacters well, you'll appreciate that the * doesn't match filenames beginning with a dot. The dot is generally a safer bet but note that both commands change the permissions of directories also. What do permissions mean when they are applied to a directory? The directory is taken up first in Section 6.6 and then again in Chapter 11.

6.6 DIRECTORY PERMISSIONS

Directories also have their own permissions and the significance of these permissions differ a great deal from those of ordinary files. You may not have expected this, but be aware that read and write access to an ordinary file are also influenced by the permissions of the directory housing them. It's possible that a file can't be accessed even though it has read permission, and can be removed even when it's write-protected. In fact, it's very easy to make it behave that way.

If the default directory permissions are not altered, the **chmod** theory still applies. However, if they are changed, unusual things can happen. Though directory permissions are taken up later *(11.4)*, it's worthwhile to know what the default permissions are on your system:

```
$ mkdir c_progs; ls -ld c_progs
drwxr-xr-x   2 kumar    metal          512 May  9 09:57 c_progs
```

The default permissions of a directory on this system are rwxr-xr-x (or 755); that's what it should be. *A directory must never be writable by group and others.* If you find that your files are being tampered with even though they appear to be protected, check up the directory permissions. If the permissions differ from what you see here, look up Chapter 11 for remedial action.

Caution: If a directory has write permission for group and others also, be assured that every user can remove every file in the directory! As a rule, you must not make directories universally writable unless you have definite reasons to do so.

Note: The default file and directory permissions on your machine could be different from what has been assumed here. The defaults are determined by the *umask* setting of your shell. This topic is discussed in Section 11.5.

6.7 CHANGING FILE OWNERSHIP

File ownership is a feature often ignored by many users. By now you know well enough that when a user kumar of the metal group creates a file foo, he becomes the owner of foo, and metal becomes the group owner. It's only kumar who can change the major file attributes like its permissions and group ownership. No member of the metal group (except kumar) can change these attributes. However, when sharma copies foo, the ownership of the copy is transferred to sharma, and he can then manipulate the attributes of the copy at will.

There are two commands meant to change the ownership of a file or directory—**chown** and **chgrp**. UNIX systems differ in the way they restrict the usage of these two commands. On BSD-based systems, only the system administrator can change a file's owner with **chown**. On the same systems, the restrictions are less severe when it comes to changing groups with **chgrp**. On other systems, only the owner can change both.

6.7.1 chown: Changing File Owner

We'll first consider the behavior of BSD-based **chown** (change owner) that has been adopted by many systems including Solaris and Linux. The command is used in this way:

```
chown options owner [:group] file(s)
```

chown transfers ownership of a file to a user, and it seems that it can optionally change the group as well. The command requires the user-id (UID) of the recipient, followed by one or more filenames. Changing ownership requires superuser permission, so let's first change our status to that of superuser with the **su** command:

```
$ su
Password: ********                       This is the root password!
# _                                      This is another shell
```

After the password is successfully entered, **su** returns a # prompt, the same prompt used by root. **su** lets us acquire superuser status if we know the root password. To now renounce the ownership of the file note to sharma, use **chown** in the following way:

```
# ls -l note
-rwxr----x    1 kumar    metal         347 May 10 20:30 note
# chown sharma note ; ls -l note
-rwxr----x    1 sharma   metal         347 May 10 20:30 note
```

```
# exit                                    Switches from superuser's shell
$ _                                       to user's login shell
```

Once ownership of the file has been given away to sharma, the user file permissions that previously applied to kumar now apply to sharma. Thus, kumar can no longer edit note since there's no write privilege for group and others. He can't get back the ownership either. But he can copy the file to his own directory, in which case he becomes the owner of the copy.

6.7.2 chgrp: Changing Group Owner

By default, the group owner of a file is the group to which the owner belongs. The **chgrp** (change group) command changes a file's group owner. On systems that implement the BSD version of **chgrp** (like Solaris and Linux), a user can change the group owner of a file, but only to a group to which she also belongs. Yes, a user can belong to more than one group, and the one shown in /etc/passwd is the user's main group. We'll discuss *supplementary groups* in Chapter 15 featuring system administration.

chgrp shares a similar syntax with **chown**. In the following example, kumar changes the group ownership of dept.1st to dba (no superuser permission required):

```
$ ls -l dept.1st
-rw-r--r--   1 kumar    metal          139 Jun  8 16:43 dept.1st
$ chgrp dba dept.1st ; ls -l dept.1st
-rw-r--r--   1 kumar    dba            139 Jun  8 16:43 dept.1st
```

This command will work on a BSD-based system if kumar is also a member of the dba group. If he is not, then only the superuser can make the command work. Note that kumar can reverse this action and restore the previous group ownership (to metal) because he is still owner of the file and consequently retains all rights related to it.

Using chown *to Do Both*   As an added benefit, UNIX allows the administrator to use only **chown** to change both owner and group. The syntax requires the two arguments to be separated by a :

```
chown sharma:dba dept.1st              Ownership to sharma, group to dba
```

Like **chmod**, both **chown** and **chgrp** use the -R option to perform their operations in a recursive manner.

6.8 CONCLUSION

In this chapter we considered two important file attributes—permissions and ownership. After we complete the first round of discussions related to files, we'll take up the other file attributes—the links and time stamps (Chapter 15). We also need to examine the inode that stores all of these attributes. In the next chapter, we'll discuss file editing with the **vi** editor.

WRAP UP

The **ls -l** command lists seven file attributes, and the output is often called the *listing*. **ls -ld** used with a directory name lists directory attributes.

A file can have more than one *link*, i.e., more than one name without having multiple copies on disk.

A file has an *owner*, usually the name of the user (UID) who creates the file. A file is also owned by a group (GID), by default, the group to which the user belongs. Both UID and GID are maintained in /etc/passwd. Apart from the superuser, it's only the owner who can change all file attributes.

The file size displayed by the listing is not the actual space the file occupies on disk, but the number of bytes it contains.

A file can have read (r), write (w) or execute (x) permission, and there are three sets of such permissions for the *user* (u), *group* (g) and *others* (o).

A file's owner uses **chmod** to alter file permissions. The permissions can be *relative* when used with the + or - symbols, or *absolute* when used with octal numbers. The octal digit 7 includes read (4), write (2) and execute permission (1) bits.

For security reasons, a regular file shouldn't normally have write permission for group and others. A file's access rights are also influenced by the permissions of its directory which usually has read and execute permission for all.

chown and **chgrp** are used to transfer ownership and group ownership, respectively. They can be used by the owner of the file on AT&T systems. On BSD systems, **chown** can be used only by the superuser, and a user can use **chgrp** to change her group to another to which she also belongs.

Test Your Understanding

6.1   A file contains 1026 bytes. How many bytes of disk space will it occupy on a system where the size of a disk block is 1024 bytes?

6.2   Where are the UID and GID of a file stored?

6.3   Show the octal representation of these permissions: (i) rwxr-xrw- (ii) rw-r----- (iii) --x-w-r--

6.4   What will the permissions string look like for these octal values? (i) 567 (ii) 623 (iii) 421

6.5   If a file's permissions are 000, can the superuser still read and write the file?

6.6   Which important file attribute changes when you copy a file from another user's home directory?

6.7   Copy a file with permissions 444. Copy it again and explain your observations.

6.8   Try creating a directory in the system directories /bin and /tmp. What do you notice and why does that happen?

6.9   If the owner doesn't have write permission on a file but her group has, can she edit it?

6.10   How is **chown** different from **chgrp** on a BSD-based system when it comes to renouncing ownership?

6.11   Explain with reference to the dot and * what the following commands do: (i) **chown -R project .** (ii) **chgrp -R project ***

Flex Your Brain

6.1 How will you obtain a complete listing of all files and directories in the whole system and save the output in a file?

6.2 Explain briefly the significance of the first four fields of the **ls -l** output. Who can change these attributes? Is there any attribute that can be changed *only* by the superuser?

6.3 Explain the significance of the following commands: (i) **ls -ld .** (ii) **ls -l ..**

6.4 The commands **ls bar** and **ls -d bar** display the same output—the string bar. This can happen in two ways. Explain.

6.5 Does the owner always belong to the same group as the group owner of a file?

6.6 Create a file foo. How do you assign all permissions to the owner and remove all permissions from others using (i) relative assignment, (ii) absolute assignment? Do you need to make any assumptions about foo's default permissions?

6.7 You tried to copy a file foo from another user's directory, but you got the error message cannot create file foo. You have write permission in your own directory. What could be the reason and how do you copy the file?

6.8 Explain the consequences, from the security viewpoint, of a file having the permissions (i) 000 (ii) 777. Assume that the directory has write permission.

6.9 Examine the output of the two commands on a BSD-based system. Explain whether kumar can (i) edit, (ii) delete, (iii) change permissions, (iv) change ownership of foo:

```
$ who am i ; ls -l foo
kumar
-r--rw----    1 sumit     kumar         78 Jan 27 16:57 foo
```

6.10 Assuming that a file's current permissions are rw-r-xr--, specify the **chmod** expression required to change them to (i) rwxrwxrwx (ii) r--r----- (iii) --r--r-- (iv) --------, using both relative and absolute methods of assigning permissions.

6.11 Use **chmod -w .** and then try to create and remove a file in the current directory. Can you do that? Is the command the same as **chmod a-w foo**?

6.12 How will you determine whether your system uses the BSD or AT&T version of **chown** and **chgrp**?

7

The vi Editor

No matter what work you do with the UNIX system, you'll eventually write some C programs or shell (or **perl**) scripts. You may have to edit some of the system files at times. For all this you must learn to use an editor, and UNIX provides a very versatile one—**vi**. Bill Joy created this editor for the BSD system. The program is now standard on all UNIX systems. Bram Moolenaar improved it and called it **vim** (vi improved). In this text we discuss the **vi** editor and also note the features of **vim** available in Linux.

Like any editor, **vi** uses a number of internal commands to navigate to any point in a text file and edit the text there. It also allows you to copy and move text within a file and also from one file to another. **vi** offers cryptic, and sometimes mnemonic, internal commands for editing work. It makes complete use of the keyboard where practically every key has a function. You don't need to master **vi** right now; a working knowledge is all that is required initially. The advanced features of **vi** are taken up in Part II of this book.

WHAT YOU WILL LEARN

- The three modes in which **vi** operates for sharing the workload.
- Use a *repeat factor* to repeat a command multiple times.
- Use the *Input Mode* to insert and replace text.
- Use the *ex Mode* to save your work.
- Use the *Command Mode* to perform navigation.
- Use the *word* as a navigation unit for movement along a line.
- Delete, yank (copy) and move text using *operators*.
- Undo the last editing action and repeat the last command.
- Search for a pattern and repeat the search.
- Use the ex Mode to perform string substitution.

TOPICS OF SPECIAL INTEREST

- Master the technique of using a three-function sequence to (i) search for a pattern (ii) take some action and (iii) repeat the search and action.

- Learn to use the two powerful features available in **vim**—word completion and multiple undoing.

7.1 vi BASICS

For a quick tour of **vi**, let's add some text to a file. Invoke **vi** with the filename **sometext**:

```
vi sometext
```

In all probability, the file doesn't exist, and **vi** presents you a full screen with the filename shown at the bottom with the qualifier, [New File]. The cursor is positioned at the top and all remaining lines of the screen (except the last) show a ~. You can't take your cursor there yet; they are nonexistent lines. The last line is reserved for commands that you can enter to act on text. This line is also used by the system to display messages.

You are now in the *Command Mode*, one of the three modes used by **vi**. This is the mode where you can pass commands to act on text, using most of the keys of the keyboard. Pressing a key doesn't show it on screen but may perform a function like moving the cursor to the next line, or deleting a line. You can't use the Command Mode to enter or replace text.

For text editing, **vi** uses 24 of the 25 lines that are normally available in a terminal. To enter text, you must switch to the *Input Mode*. First press the key marked i, and you are in this mode ready to input text. Subsequent key depressions will then show up on the screen as text input. Start inserting a few lines of text, each line followed by *[Enter]*, as shown in Fig. 7.1.

After text entry is complete, the cursor is positioned on the last character of the last line. This is known as the **current line** and the character where the cursor is stationed is the **current cursor position**. If you see something that shouldn't be there, use the backspace key to wipe it out. If a word has been misspelled, use *[Ctrl-w]* to erase the entire word.

Now press the *[Esc]* key to revert to Command Mode. Press it again and you'll hear a beep; a beep in **vi** indicates that a key has been pressed unnecessarily.

```
This is the vi editor[Enter]
It is slow in getting started but is quite powerful[Enter]
It operates in three modes[Enter]
All the features of ex are also available[Enter]
You can even escape to the UNIX shell[Enter]
It maintains 26 buffers for storing chunks of text
~
~
~
```

Fig. 7.1 Inserting Some Text

The file sometext doesn't exist yet. Actually, the text that you entered hasn't been saved on disk but exists in some temporary storage called a *buffer*. To save the entered text, you must switch to the *ex Mode* (also known as *Last Line Mode*). Invoke the ex Mode from the Command Mode by entering a : (colon), which shows up in the last line. Enter an x and press *[Enter]*:

```
:x[Enter]
"sometext" 6 lines, 232 characters
$ _                                        Quits editor—back to shell prompt
```

The file is saved on disk and **vi** returns the shell prompt. To modify this file, you'll have to invoke **vi sometext** again. But before moving ahead, let's summarize the modes used by **vi**:

- **Command Mode**—The default mode of the editor where every key pressed is interpreted as a command to run on text. You'll have to be in this mode to copy and delete text. Unnecessary pressing of *[Esc]* in this mode sounds a beep but also confirms that you are in this mode.

- **Input Mode**—Every key pressed after switching to this mode actually shows up as text. This mode is invoked by pressing one of the keys shown in Table 7.1.

- **ex Mode** (or Last Line Mode)—The mode used to handle files (like saving) and perform substitution. Pressing a : in the Command Mode invokes this mode. You then enter an ex Mode command followed by *[Enter]*. After the command is run, you are back to the default Command Mode.

Much of the chapter deals with Command Mode commands where most of the action is. Some of these commands also have ex Mode equivalents which are sometimes easier to use. But all three modes also have their own exclusive features and an editing session in **vi** involves constant switching between modes as depicted in Fig. 7.2.

7.1.1 The Repeat Factor

When discussing **more** (5.5), we introduced the *repeat factor* as a command prefix to repeat the command as many times as the prefix. **vi** also provides the repeat factor with many of its Command Mode and Input Mode commands. So if the Command Mode command **k** moves the cursor up one line, then **10k** moves it up 10 lines. The repeat factor thus speeds up operations. You'll be using it several times in this chapter.

7.1.2 The File .exrc

The default behavior of **vi** is adequate for novices, but as you get comfortable with it, you'll feel the need to customize it to behave in a way that makes writing programs and documents easier. **vi** reads the file $HOME/.exrc (same as ~/.exrc in some shells) on startup. If **ls -a** doesn't show this file in your home directory, you can create or copy one. Linux users must note that **vim** generally doesn't use .exrc but .vimrc (with exceptions).

Many ex Mode commands can be placed in this file so they are available in every session. You can create abbreviations, redefine your keys to behave differently and also make variable settings. Your .exrc will progressively develop into an exclusive "library" containing all shortcuts and settings that you use regularly. It could be your most prized possession, so always keep a backup of this file.

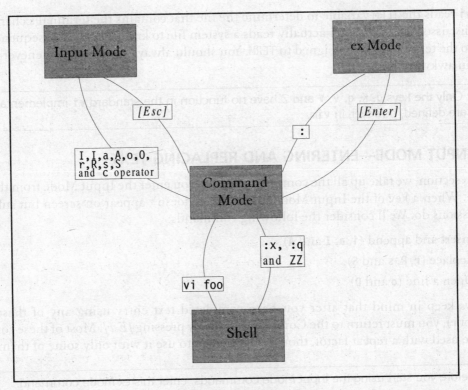

Fig. 7.2 The Three Modes

7.1.3 A Few Tips First

We are about to take off, but before we do that, a few tips at this stage will stand you in good stead. You must keep them in mind at all times when you are doing work with **vi**:

- *Undo whenever you make a mistake.* If you have made a mistake in editing, either by wrongly deleting text or inserting it at a wrong location, then as a first measure, just press *[Esc]* and then **u** to undo the last action. If that makes matters worse, use **u** again. Linux users should instead use *[Ctrl-r]*.

- *Clearing the screen* If the screen gets garbled for some reason, use *[Ctrl-l]* (el) in the Command Mode to redraw the screen. If you hit *[Ctrl-l]* in the Input Mode, you'll see the symbol ^L on the screen. Use the backspace key to wipe it out, press *[Esc]* and then hit *[Ctrl-l]*.

- *Don't use [CapsLock]* **vi** commands are case-sensitive; **a** and **A** are different commands. Even if you activate this key to enter a large block of text in uppercase, make sure you deactivate it after text entry is complete.

- *Avoid using the PC navigation keys* As far as possible, avoid using all the standard navigation keys like Up, Down, Left and Right, *[PageUp]* and *[PageDown]*. Many of them could fail when you use **vi** over a network connection. **vi** provides an elaborate set of keys for navigation purposes.

- **vi** reads the TERM variable to determine the file that contains the terminal's characteristics. As discussed later *(10.3)*, vi actually reads a system file to know the control sequences that apply to the terminal name assigned to TERM. You should always check TERM whenever **vi** behaves in an awkward manner.

Note: Only the keys g, K, q, v, V and Z have no function in the standard **vi** implementation. Some of them are defined, however, in **vim**.

7.2 INPUT MODE—ENTERING AND REPLACING TEXT

In this section, we take up all the commands that let you enter the Input Mode from the Command Mode. When a key of the Input Mode is pressed, it doesn't appear on screen but subsequent key depressions do. We'll consider the following commands:

- Insert and append (**i**, **a**, **I** and **A**)
- Replace (**r**, **R**, **s** and **S**)
- Open a line (**o** and **0**)

Always keep in mind that after you have completed text entry using any of these commands (except **r**), you must return to the Command Mode by pressing *[Esc]*. Most of these commands can also be used with a repeat factor, though you'll need to use it with only some of them.

Tip: Before you start using the Input Mode commands, enter this ex Mode command:

`:set showmode[Enter]`

Enter a : (the ex Mode prompt) and you'll see it appear in the last line. Follow it with the two words and press *[Enter]*. showmode sets one of the parameters of the **vi** environment. Messages like INSERT MODE, REPLACE MODE or CHANGE MODE, etc. will now appear in the last line when you run an Input Mode command. We'll learn later to make the setting permanent by placing it in $HOME/.exrc.

7.2.1 Insertion of Text (i and a)

The simplest type of input is insertion of text. Just press

i
                                                    Existing text will be shifted right

Pressing this key changes the mode from Command to Input. Since the showmode setting was made at the beginning (with :set showmode), you'll see the words INSERT MODE at the bottom-right corner of the screen. Further key depressions will result in text being entered and displayed on the screen.

If the **i** command is invoked with the cursor positioned on existing text, text on its right will be shifted further without being overwritten. The insertion of text with **i** is shown in Fig. 7.3, along with the position of the cursor.

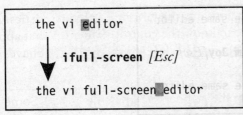

Fig. 7.3 Text Insertion with **i**

Fig. 7.4 Text Appending with **a**

There are other methods of inputting text. To append text to the right of the cursor position, use

a   *Existing text will also be shifted right*

followed by the text you wish to key in (Fig. 7.4). After you have finished editing, press *[Esc]*. With **i** and **a**, you can append several lines of text in this way.

7.2.2 Insertion of Text at Line Extremes (I and A)

I and **A** behave somewhat like **i** and **a** except that they work at line extremes by performing the necessary navigation to move there:

I   Inserts text at beginning of line.
A   Appends text at end of line.

These two commands are suitable for converting code to comment lines in a C program (Fig. 7.5). A comment line in C is of the form /* *comment* */. Use **I** on an existing line that you now wish to convert to a comment, and then enter the symbols /*. After pressing *[Esc]*, use **A** to append */ at the end of the line and press *[Esc]* again. A document author often needs to use **A** to continue text entry from the point work was suspended—adding a sentence to a paragraph, for instance.

Fig. 7.5 Using **I** and **A** to Create a Comment Line in a C Program

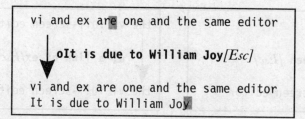

Fig. 7.6 Opening a New Line with **o**

Tip: C language programmers sometimes precede a block of comment lines with a pattern like this:

```
/*******************************************************************
```

It seems that there are 70 asterisks here, and to draw them you should use a repeat factor. After you have entered / in the Input Mode, press *[Esc]*, and then enter **70a***[Esc]*. You'll see 70 asterisks appended to the /.

7.2.3 Opening a New Line (o and 0)

Many a time it has been observed that people migrating from a word-processing environment use a convoluted sequence to open a new line below the current line. They move the cursor past the end of the current line and press *[Enter]*. In **vi**, you use **o** and **0** instead. To open a line below from anywhere in a line, simply press

o   *Opens new line below current line*

This inserts an empty line below the current line (Fig. 7.6). **0** also opens a line but above the current line. You are free to enter as much text as you choose, spanning multiple lines if required. Press the *[Esc]* key after completing text input.

7.2.4 Replacing Text (r, s, R and S)

To change existing text, **vi** provides mainly four commands (actually, more) as shown in the heading. To replace a single character with another, you should use

r   *No [Esc] required*

```
this is the vi full-screen editor

   rT

This is the vi full-screen editor
```

Fig. 7.7 Replacing a Single Character with **r**

Fig. 7.8 Replacing Text with **s**

Fig. 7.9 Replacing Text with **R**

followed by the character that replaces the one under the cursor (Fig. 7.7). You can replace a single character only in this way. **vi** momentarily switches from Command Mode to Input Mode when **r** is pressed. It returns to Command Mode as soon as the new character is entered. There's no need to press *[Esc]* when using **r** and the replacement character, since **vi** expects a single character anyway.

When you want to replace the letter d with 10f in a **printf** statement in C, you need to replace one character with three. In that case, press

s   *Replaces one character with many*

vi deletes the character under the cursor and switches to Input Mode. It may also show a $ at that location to indicate that replacement will not affect text on its right. Now enter **10f** and press *[Esc]*. To replace multiple characters, use a repeat factor. **3s** replaces three characters with new text. Use of **s** is shown in Fig. 7.8.

R and **S** act in a similar manner compared to their lowercase ones except that they act on a larger group of characters:

R   Replaces all text on the right of the cursor position.

S   Replaces the entire line irrespective of cursor position. (Existing line disappears)

Try using the repeat factor with **R** and **S** and see whether you can take advantage of this feature. Use of **R** is shown in Fig. 7.9.

You have now been able to enter the Input Mode in ten ways. The functions of these ten keys are summarized in Table 7.1.

Caution: You must press *[Esc]* to switch to Command Mode after you have keyed in text. Repeated pressing of *[Esc]* won't make any difference to **vi** except that it has a built-in capability to indicate with a beep if a key has been pressed unnecessarily. Try this by pressing *[Esc]* several times. You are now in the Command Mode.

LINUX: A superb text completion feature is available in **vim**. If the string printf is available in the file, you don't need to enter the entire string eve. Just key in as much as is necessary to make the string unique (say, up to pr), and then press

[Ctrl-p]   **vim** *attempts to complete string*

vim expands pr to printf if this is the *only* word beginning with pr. In case there are other words, repeated pressing of the key shows all matching words in turn. In case you have to view the list backwards, use *[Ctrl-n]*.

Table 7.1 Input Mode Commands

Command	Function
i	Inserts text to left of cursor (Existing text shifted right)
a	Appends text to right of cursor (Existing text shifted right)
I	Inserts text at beginning of line (Existing text shifted right)
A	Appends text at end of line
o	Opens line below
O	Opens line above
rch	Replaces single character under cursor with *ch* (No *[Esc]* required)
R	Replaces text from cursor to right (Existing text overwritten)
s	Replaces single character under cursor with any number of characters
S	Replaces entire line

7.3 SAVING TEXT AND QUITTING—THE ex MODE

When you edit a file using **vi**—or for that matter, any editor—the original file isn't disturbed as such, but only a copy of it that is placed in a **buffer** (a temporary form of storage). From time to time, you should save your work by writing the buffer contents to disk to keep the disk file current (or, as we say, in *sync*). When we talk of saving a file, we actually mean saving this buffer. You may also need to quit **vi** after or without saving the buffer. These features are adequately handled by the ex Mode. The basic file handling features are shown in Table 7.2.

7.3.1 Saving Your Work (:w)

We have already used the ex Mode command, **:x**, to save the buffer and exit the editor *(7.1)*. For extended sessions with **vi**, you must able to save the buffer and *remain* in the editor. From time to time, you must use the **:w** command to write the buffer to disk. Enter a :, which appears on the last line of the screen, then w and finally *[Enter]*:

```
:w[Enter]
"sometext", 8 lines, 275 characters
```

You can now continue your editing work normally, but make sure that you execute this command regularly. With the **:w** command you can optionally specify a filename as well. In that case, the contents are separately written to another file.

Tip: It's common practice to ignore the readonly label on opening a file that doesn't have the write permission bit set. When you attempt to save the file with :w, vi retorts with the message File is read only. You should have been careful in the first place, but there's hope: Just save the file with a different name (say, :w foo) after making sure that foo doesn't exist. Look up Table 7.2 for the command to use when foo exists.

7.3.2 Saving and Quitting (:x and :wq)

The previous command returns you to the Command Mode so you can continue editing. However, to save and quit the editor (i.e., return to the shell), use the **:x** (exit) command instead:

```
:x[Enter]
"sometext", 8 lines, 303 characters
$ _
```

You can also use **:wq** to save and quit the editor. But that requires an additional keystroke and is not recommended for use.

Tip: The best way to save and quit the editor is to use **ZZ**, a Command Mode command, instead of **:x** or **:wq**.

7.3.3 Aborting Editing (:q)

It's also possible to abort the editing process and quit the editing mode without saving the buffer. The **:q** (quit) command does that job:

```
:q[Enter]                          Won't work if buffer is unsaved
$ _
```

vi also has a safety mechanism that prevents you from aborting accidentally if you have modified the file (buffer) in any way. The following message is typical when you try to do so:

```
No write since last change (:quit! overrides)
```

If the buffer has been changed and you still want to abandon the changes, then use

```
:q!                                Ignores all changes made and quits
```

to return you to the prompt irrespective of the status of the buffer—no questions asked. **vi** suggests appending a ! to an ex Mode command every time it feels that you could be doing something that is potentially unsafe.

Note: In general, any ex Mode command used with a ! signifies an abort of some type. It can be used to switch to another file without saving the current one, or reload the last saved version of a file. You can even use it to overwrite a separate file.

7.3.4 Writing Selected Lines

The **:w** command is an abbreviated way of executing the ex Mode instruction **:1,$w**. w can be prefixed by one or two *addresses* separated by a comma. The command

```
:10,50w n2words.pl                 Writes 41 lines to another file
```

saves lines 10 through 50 to the file n2words.pl. You can save a single line as well:

```
:5w n2words.pl                     Writes 5th line to another file
```

There are two symbols used with **w** that have special significance—the dot and $. The dot represents the current line while $ represents the last line of the file. You can use them singly or in combination:

`:.w tempfile`	*Saves current line (where cursor is positioned)*
`:$w tempfile`	*Saves last line*
`:.,$w tempfile`	*Saves current line through end*

If `tempfile` exists and is writable by you, **vi** issues yet another warning:

`"tempfile" File exists - use "w! tempfile" to overwrite`

The message is clear: **vi** is telling you to suffix the **!** to the **:w** command to overwrite `tempfile`. As mentioned before, the **!** is the universal overriding operator in the ex Mode and you'll be using it often.

Note: In the ex Mode, the current line number is represented by **.** (dot) and the last line is denoted by **$**. **:w** is the same as **:1,$w**. Both commands address the entire file.

7.3.5 Escape to the UNIX Shell (:sh and [Ctrl-z])

How do do you edit and compile your C program repeatedly? You need to make a temporary escape to the shell to run the **cc** command. There are two ways; the first method is to use the ex Mode command, **:sh**:

```
:sh
$ _
```
You haven't quit vi yet

This returns a shell prompt. Execute **cc** or any UNIX command here and then return to the editor using *[Ctrl-d]* or **exit**. Don't make the mistake of running **vi** once again, as you'll then have two instances of **vi**—an undesirable situation.

If your shell supports job control (which most shells do), you can also *suspend* the current **vi** session. Just press *[Ctrl-z]* and you'll be returned a shell prompt. Run your commands and then use the **fg** command to return to the editor. Job control is discussed in Section 9.10.

7.3.6 Recovering from a Crash (:recover and -r)

Accidents can and will happen. The power can go off, leaving work unsaved. However, don't panic, **vi** stores most of its buffer information in a hidden swap file. Even though **vi** removes this file on successful exit, a power glitch or an improper shutdown procedure lets this swap file remain on disk. **vi** will then complain the next time you invoke it with the same file.

The complaint usually also contains some advice regarding the salvage operation. You'll be advised to use either the ex Mode command **:recover**, or **vi -r foo** to recover as much of **foo** as possible. After you have done that, have a look at the buffer contents and satisfy yourself of the success of the damage control exercise. If everything seems fine, save the buffer and remove the swap file if **vi** doesn't do that on its own.

Note: You can't be assured of complete recovery every time. Sometimes, **vi** may show you absolute junk when using the -r option (or :recover). In that case, don't save the file and simply quit (with :q!). Start **vi** again normally; recovery is not possible here. Linux users should note that in these situations, they need to delete the file having a .swp extension manually; otherwise the file will not be editable.

Table 7.2 Save and Exit Commands of the ex Mode

Command	Action
:w	Saves file and remains in editing mode
:x	Saves file and quits editing mode
:wq	As above
:w n2w.pl	Like *Save As* ..... in Microsoft Windows
:w! n2w.pl	As above, but overwrites existing file
:q	Quits editing mode when no changes are made to file
:q!	Quits editing mode but after abandoning changes
:*n1*,*n2*w build.sql	Writes lines *n1* to *n2* to file build.sql
:.w build.sql	Writes current line to file build.sql
:$w build.sql	Writes last line to file build.sql
:!*cmd*	Runs *cmd* command and returns to Command Mode
:sh	Escapes to UNIX shell
:recover	Recovers file from a crash

7.4 NAVIGATION

We'll now consider the functions of the Command Mode. This is the mode you come to when you have finished entering or changing your text. A Command Mode command doesn't show up on screen but simply performs a function. We begin with navigation. Don't forget to avoid the cursor control keys for navigation as advised in Section 7.1.3.

7.4.1 Movement in the Four Directions (h, j, k and 1)

vi provides the keys **h, j, k** and **1** to move the cursor in the four directions. These keys are placed adjacent to one another in the middle row of the keyboard. Without a repeat factor, they move the cursor by one position. Use these keys for moving the cursor vertically:

k	Moves cursor up
j	Moves cursor down

To move the cursor along a line, use these commands:

h	Moves cursor left
1	Moves cursor right

Fig. 7.10 Relative Navigation with **h**, **j**, **k** and **l**

The repeat factor can be used as a command prefix with all these four commands. Thus, **4k** moves the cursor 4 lines up and **20h** takes it 20 characters to the left. Navigation with the four keys is shown in Fig. 7.10. Note that this motion is relative; you can't move to a specific line number with these keys.

Tip: To remember the keys that move the cursor left or right, observe these four keys on your keyboard. The left-most key, **h**, moves the cursor to the left, and the right-most key, **l** (el), moves it right.

7.4.2 Word Navigation (b, e and w)

Moving by one character is not always enough; you'll often need to move faster along a line. **vi** understands a *word* as a navigation unit which can be defined in two ways, depending on the key pressed. If your cursor is a number of words away from your desired position, you can use the word-navigation commands to go there directly. There are three basic commands:

b	Moves back to beginning of word
e	Moves forward to end of word
w	Moves forward to beginning of word

A repeat factor speeds up cursor movement along a line. For example, **5b** takes the cursor five words back, while **3w** takes the cursor three words forward. A word here is simply a string of alphanumeric characters and the _ (underscore). Bash is one word; so is sh_profile. tcp-ip is three words; the hyphen by definition becomes a word too.

The keys **B**, **E** and **W** perform functions similar to those of their lowercase counterparts except that punctuation is skipped. The word definition also gets changed here, but we'll ignore these minor details.

7.4.3 Moving to Line Extremes (0, | and $)

Moving to the beginning or end of a line is a common requirement. This is handled by the keys **0**, **|** and **$**. To move to the first character of a line, use

    0 *(zero) or* | 30| *moves cursor to column 30*

The **|** takes a repeat factor and using that, you can position the cursor on a certain column. To position the cursor on column 30, use **30|**.

We used **$** as the line address in the ex Mode to represent the last line of the file. The same symbol in the Command Mode represents the end of line. To move to the end of the current line, use

    $ *Moves to end of line*

The use of these two commands along with those that use units of words (**b**, **e** and **w**) is shown in Fig. 7.11.

Note: When you use the keys **b**, **e** and **w**, remember that a word is simply a string of alphanumeric characters and the _ (underscore).

7.4.4 Scrolling ([Ctrl-f], [Ctrl-b], [Ctrl-d] and [Ctrl-u])

Faster movement can be achieved by scrolling text in the window using the control keys. The two commands for scrolling a page at a time are

    [Ctrl-f]   Scrolls forward
    [Ctrl-b]   Scrolls backward

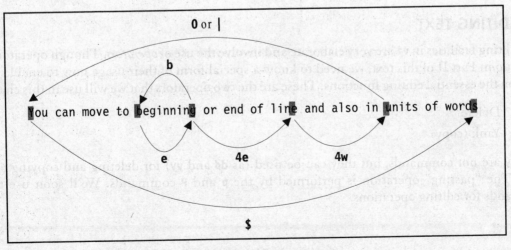

Fig. 7.11 Navigation Along a Line

You can use the repeat factor, like in **10**[*Ctrl-f*], to scroll 10 pages and navigate faster in the process. You can scroll by half a page as well:

[*Ctrl-d*]	Scrolls half page forward
[*Ctrl-u*]	Scrolls half page backward

The repeat factor can also be used here.

7.4.5 Absolute Movement (G)

Upon startup, **vi** displays the total number of lines in the last line. At any time, you can press [*Ctrl-g*] to know the current line number:

```
"/etc/passwd" [Read only] line 89 of 179 --49%--
```

The cursor is on line 89 (49% of 179), and this read-protected file has 179 lines in all. Compilers also indicate line numbers in their error messages. You need to use the **G** command with the line number as repeat factor to locate the offending lines. To move to the 40th line, use

40G	*Goes to line number 40*

and to move to the beginning of the file, use

1G	*Goes to line number 1*

The end of the file is reached by simply using

G	*Goes to end of file*

Note: The ex Mode offers equivalent commands for moving between lines. The previous three commands can be replaced with **:40**, **:1** and **:$**, respectively (along with [*Enter*]).

7.5 EDITING TEXT

The editing facilities in **vi** are very elaborate and involve the use of *operators*. Though operators are taken up in Part II of this text, we need to know a special form of their usage now to enable us to perform the essential editing functions. These are the two operators that we will use in this chapter:

d	Delete
y	Yank (copy)

d and **y** are not commands, but they can be used (as **dd** and **yy**) for deleting and copying entire lines. The "pasting" operation is performed by the **p** and **P** commands. We'll soon use these commands for editing operations.

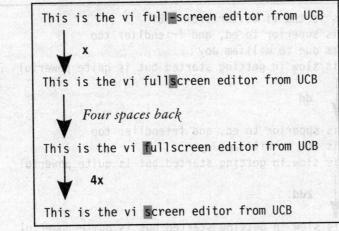

```
This is the vi full screen editor from UCB

        ↓ x

This is the vi full screen editor from UCB

        ↓   Four spaces back

This is the vi fullscreen editor from UCB

        ↓ 4x

This is the vi  screen editor from UCB
```

Fig. 7.12 Deleting Text with **x**

7.5.1 Deleting Text (x and dd)

The simplest text deletion is achieved with the **x** command. This command deletes the character under the cursor. Move the cursor to the character that needs to be deleted and then press

x   *Deletes a single character*

The character under the cursor gets deleted, and the text on the right shifts left to fill up the space. A repeat factor also applies here, so **4x** deletes the current character as well as three characters from the *right* (Fig. 7.12).

A Windows Notepad user would be surprised to note that when the cursor is at the end of a line, **x** doesn't pull up the following line but works instead on text on the *left* of the cursor. Deletion of text from the left is otherwise handled by the **X** command. Keep it pressed, and you'll see that you have erased all text to the beginning of the line.

Entire lines are removed with the **dd** "command" (rather a doubled operator). Move the cursor to any line and then press

dd   *Cursor can be anywhere in line*

6dd deletes the current line and five lines below. Fig. 7.13 illustrates the use of **dd** both with and without a repeat factor. There are other forms of deletion available in **vi** and you'll know them all after you have understood the **d** operator well (*20.1.1*).

7.5.2 Moving Text (p)

Text movement requires you to perform an additional task: Put the text at the new location with **p** or **P**. **vi** uses these two commands for all "put" operations that follow delete or copy operations. The significance of **p** and **P** depends on whether they are used on parts of lines or complete lines. We need some examples to illustrate their behavior.

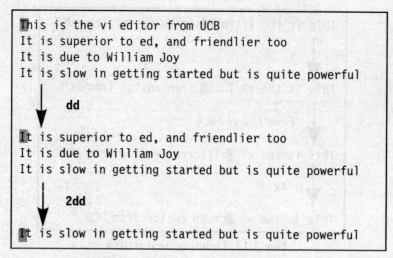

Fig. 7.13 Deleting Lines with **dd**

For instance, to correct sdtio.h to stdio.h, you'll have to transpose the characters d and t, i.e. delete the d and put it after the t. Move your cursor to the d in sdtio.h and use these two commands:

x	sdtio.h *becomes* stio.h—*cursor on t*
p	d *put on right*—stio.h *becomes* stdio.h

Since we worked on parts of lines, associate the word "right" with **p** and "left" with **P**. **P** places text on the left of the cursor.

To put entire (deleted) lines at a different location, you'll need to use the same commands, except that we have to think in terms of "below" and "above" the current line. **p** places text below the current line and **P** places text above.

Note: p and **P** place text on right and left only when you delete parts of lines. But the same keys get associated with "below" and "above" when you delete complete lines.

7.5.3 Copying Text (y and p)

vi uses the term **yanking** for copying text, the reason why the operator is named **y**. The principles are exactly the same as compared to deletion with **d**. For instance, to copy (or yank) one or more lines, use the **yy** "command":

yy	*Yanks current line*
10yy	*Yanks current line and 9 lines below*

This yanked text has to be placed at the new location. The put commands are the same—**p** and **P**. Since we copied entire lines, we can only place the copied text below or above the current line, and not on the left or right. But suppose you need to place an entire line at the end of another line. You have to place it below the line first and then join the two lines. Just read on.

7.5.4 Joining Lines (J)

In word processors, you join the current and next line by moving the cursor to the end of line and pressing *[Delete]*. This technique won't work in **vi**. To join the current line and the line following it, use

J   4J *joins following 3 lines with current one*

J removes the newline character between the two lines to pull up the line below it. Joining, however, is restricted to the maximum line size that your **vi** editor can support. It could be below 2000 (as in Solaris) or unlimited (in Linux).

To solve the problem posed at the end of the previous section, if you place a line below the current line with **p**, you can use **J** to join the two lines.

7.6 UNDOING LAST EDITING INSTRUCTIONS (u and U)

If you have inadvertently made an editing change that you shouldn't have, **vi** provides the **u** command to undo the last change made. Before you do anything else, reverse the last change you made to the buffer by pressing

u   *Must use in Command Mode; press [Esc] if necessary*

This will undo the most recent single editing change by restoring the position before the change. Another **u** at this stage will undo this too, i.e., restore the original status (doesn't apply to Linux). This facility is very useful, especially for beginners, who may accidentally delete a group of lines. Any deletion can be undone with **u** provided it is pressed *immediately* after deletion, and before fresh editing action has been performed.

When a number of editing changes have been made to a single line, **vi** allows you to discard all changes *before you move away from the line*. The command

U   *Don't move away from current line*

reverses all changes made to the current line, i.e., all modifications that have been made since the cursor was moved to this line.

Caution: Make sure the cursor has not been moved to another line before invoking **U**, in which case it won't work.

LINUX: *Multiple Undoing and Redoing*   **vim** lets you undo and redo multiple editing instructions. **u** behaves differently here; repeated use of this key progressively undoes your previous actions. You could even have the original file in front of you! Further, **10u** reverses your last 10 editing actions. The function of **U** remains the same.

You may overshoot the desired mark when you keep **u** pressed, in which case use *[Ctrl-r]* to redo your undone actions. Further, undoing with **10u** can be completely reversed with **10[Ctrl-r]**. The undoing limit is set by the ex Mode command **:set undolevels=**n, where n is set to 1000 by default.

7.7 REPEATING THE LAST COMMAND (.)

Most editors don't have the facility to repeat the last *editing* instruction, but **vi** has. The **.** (dot) command is used for repeating both Input and Command Mode commands that perform editing tasks. The principle is this: Use the actual command only once, and then repeat it at other places with the dot command.

To take a simple example, if you have deleted two lines of text with **2dd**, then to repeat this operation elsewhere, all you have to do is to position the cursor at the desired location and press

Use u to undo this repeat

This will repeat the last editing instruction performed, i.e., it will also delete two lines of text.

The **.** command is indeed a very handy tool. As another example, consider that you have to indent a group of lines by inserting a tab at the beginning of each line. You need to use **i**[*Tab*][*Esc*] only once, say on the first line. You can then move to each line in turn by hitting [*Enter*], and simply press the dot. A group of lines can be indented in no time. The dot is specially suited for substitution work also, as you'll see in Section 7.8.1.

The **.** command can be used to repeat only the most recent *editing* operation— be it insertion, deletion or any other action that modifies the buffer. This, obviously, doesn't include the search commands (that don't modify the buffer contents in any way) which have their own set of characters for repeating a search. It doesn't also include the navigation or paging commands because they don't alter the buffer either.

Note: The dot command can be applied to repeat the last editing instruction only, i.e., an instruction that changes the contents of a file. The dot retains its meaning even after undoing, so you can use it again at another location.

7.8 SEARCHING FOR A PATTERN (/ and ?)

vi is extremely strong in search and replacement activities. Searching can be made in both forward and reverse directions, and can be repeated. It is initiated from the Command Mode by pressing a /, which shows up in the last line. For example, if you are looking for the string printf, enter this string after the /:

/printf[*Enter*]   *Searches forward*

The search begins forward to position the cursor on the first instance of the word. **vi** searches the entire file, so if the pattern can't be located until the end of file is reached, the search **wraps around** to resume from the beginning of the file. If the search still fails, **vi** responds with the message Pattern not found.

Likewise, the sequence

?*pattern*[*Enter*]

searches backward for the most previous instance of the pattern. The wraparound feature also applies here but in the reverse manner.

7.8.1 Repeating the Last Pattern Search (n and N)

The **n** and **N** commands repeat a search where **n** and **N** don't exactly play the roles you'd expect them to. For repeating a search in the direction the previous search was made with **/** or **?**, use

   n   *Repeats search in same direction of original search*

The cursor will be positioned at the beginning of the pattern. In this way, you can press **n** repeatedly to scan all instances of the string. **N** reverses the direction pursued by **n**, which means that you can use it to retrace your search path. The search and repeat actions are illustrated in Fig. 7.14 and the commands are summarized in Table 7.3.

Note: n doesn't necessarily repeat a search in the forward direction; the direction depends on the search command used. If you used **?printf** to search in the reverse direction in the first place, then **n** also follows the same direction. In that case, **N** will repeat the search in the forward direction, and not **n**.

Tip: The three commands, **/** (search), **n** (repeat search) and **.** (repeat last editing command), form a wonderful trio of search—search-repeat—edit-repeat commands. You'll often be tempted to use this trio in many situations where you want the same change to be carried out at a number of places.

For instance, if you want to replace some occurrences of int with double, then first search for int with **/int**, change int to double with **3s**, repeat the search with **n**, and press the **.** wherever you want the replacement to take place. Yes, you wouldn't like printf to also show up (int is embedded there), which means you need to use a *regular expression* to throw printf out. Like more, **vi** also recognizes regular expressions as search patterns; these expressions are first discussed in Section 13.2.

```
/echo [Enter]    if [ -z "$pname" ]
                 then
                     echo "You have not entered the string"
                     exit 1
            n    else
                     echo "Enter the file to be used: \c"
            n        read flname
                     if [ ! -n "$flname" ] ; then
            N            echo "You have not entered the filename" ; exit 2
                     else
```

Fig. 7.14 Search and Repeat with **/** and **n**

Note: You can start up **vi** by specifying a pattern. Use the +/ symbols before the pattern:

```
vi +/scheduling chap01
```
Cursor at scheduling

The cursor will be located at the first instance of the pattern. You can then use **n** and **N** in the usual way for locating the next instance of the string. If the pattern contains multiple words, enclose them within quotes.

Table 7.3 Search and Repeat Commands

Command	Function
/pat	Searches forward for pattern *pat*
?pat	Searches backward for pattern *pat*
n	Repeats search in same direction along which previous search was made
N	Repeats search in direction opposite to that along which previous search was made

7.9 SUBSTITUTION—SEARCH AND REPLACE (:s)

vi offers yet another powerful feature, that of substitution, which is achieved with the ex Mode **s** (substitute) command. It lets you replace a pattern in the file with something else. The syntax is shown below:

:address/source_pattern/target_pattern/flags

The *source_pattern* here is replaced with *target_pattern* in all lines specified by *address*. The *address* can be one or a pair of numbers, separated by a comma. For instance, 1,$ addresses all lines in a file. The most commonly used flag is g, which carries out the substitution for all occurrences of the pattern in a line. The following example shows a typical substitution command:

```
:1,$s/director/member/g
```
Can also use % instead of 1,$

Here, director is replaced with member globally throughout the file. If the pattern can't be found, **vi** responds with the message Substitute pattern match failed. If you leave out the g, the substitution will be carried out for the *first* occurrence in each addressed line.

The target pattern is optional. If you leave it out, then you'll delete all instances of the source pattern in all lines matched by the address:

```
:1,50s/unsigned//g
```
Deletes unsigned *everywhere in lines 1 to 50*

As shown above, you can choose the range of lines that are to be affected by the substitution. The following examples should make addressing clear:

```
:3,10s/director/member/g
:.s/director/member/g
:$s/director/member/g
```
Substitute lines 3 through 10
Only the current line
Only the last line

Interactive Substitution   Sometimes you may like to selectively replace a string. In that case, add the c (confirmatory) parameter as the flag at the end:

```
:1,$s/director/member/gc
```

Each line is selected in turn, followed by a sequence of carets in the next line, just below the pattern that requires substitution. The cursor is positioned at the end of this caret sequence, waiting for your response:

```
9876|jai sharma      |director |production|03/12/50|7000
                      ~~~~~~~~y
2365|barun sengupta   |director |personnel |05/11/47|7800
                      ~~~~~~~n
1006|chanchal singhvi |director |sales     |09/03/38|6700
                      ~~~~~~~y
6521|lalit chowdury   |director |marketing |09/26/45|8200
                      ~~~~~~~n
```

A y performs the substitution, any other response doesn't. This sequence is repeated for each of the matched lines in turn. In the present case, the substitution is performed for only two of the four lines.

LINUX: The interactive substitution feature in **vim** is both friendlier and more powerful than its UNIX counterpart. The string to be replaced is shown in reverse video, and a prompt appears in the last line of the screen:

```
replace with msg (y/n/a/q/^E/^Y)?
```

Apart from responding with y or n, you have the option of aborting (q) the substitution process or making it noninteractive (a).

7.10 CONCLUSION

The features of **vi** that have been highlighted so far are good enough for a beginner who shouldn't proceed any further before mastering most of them. There are many more functions that make **vi** a very powerful editor. Can you copy three words or even the entire file using simple keystrokes? Can you copy or move multiple sections of text from one file to another in a single file switch? How do you compile your C and Java programs without leaving the editor? **vi** can do all that, and if you already know this editor quite well, then skip to Chapter 20.

With the completion of the first round of discussions on files, we need to examine the other areas of UNIX. The shell is taken up in the next chapter.

> **WRAP UP**
>
> **vi** operates in three modes. The *Command Mode* is used to enter commands that operate on text or control cursor motion. The *Input Mode* is used to enter text. The *ex Mode* (or *Last Line Mode*) is used for file handling and substitution.

Most of the Input and Command Mode commands also work with a *repeat factor* which performs the command multiple times.

The Input Mode is used to insert (**i** and **I**), append (**a** and **A**), replace (**r** and **R**), change (**s** or **S**) text and open a line (**o** and **0**). The mode is terminated by pressing *[Esc]*.

Using the ex Mode you can save your work (**:w**), exit the editor after saving (**:x**) and quit without saving (**:q** and **:q!**). The current line in this mode is represented by a dot and the last line by a $.

Navigation is performed in the Command Mode. You can move in the four directions (**h**, **j**, **k** and **1**) or move along a line, using a *word* as a navigation unit. You can move back (**b**) and forward (**w**) to the beginning of a word.

Editing functions are also performed in the Command Mode. You can delete characters (**x** and **X**) and lines (**dd**), and yank or copy lines (**yy**). Deleted and yanked text can be put at another location (**p** and **P**).

vi can repeat (**.**) and undo (**u**) the last editing instruction. **vim** in Linux can perform multiple levels of undo and redo with **u** and *[Ctrl-r]*, respectively.

You can search for a pattern (**/** and **?**) and also repeat (**n** and **N**) the search in both directions. The **/**, **n** and **.** commands form a very useful trio for interactive replacement work.

The ex Mode is also used for substitution (**:s**). Both search and replace operations also use *regular expressions* for matching multiple patterns.

Test Your Understanding

7.1   You pressed **50k** to move the cursor 50 lines up but you see **50k** input as text. What mistake did you make and how do you remove the three characters?

7.2   How will you replace has with have in the current line?

7.3   How will you insert a line (i) above the current line, (ii) below the current line?

7.4   How do you abort an editing session?

7.5   Name three ways exiting a **vi** session after saving your work.

7.6   How will you quickly move to the fifth word of a line and replace its four characters with the string counter?

7.7   Find out the number of words in this string as interpreted by (i) **vi**, (ii) wc—29.02.2000 is_last_day_of_February.

7.8   In the current line, how do you take your cursor to (i) the 40th character, (ii) the beginning, (iii) the end?

7.9   Explain which of the following commands can be repeated or undone: (i) **40k** (ii) *[Ctrl-f]* (iii) **5x** iv) **J**

7.10 You have wrongly entered the word Comptuer. How will you correct it to Computer?

7.11 From a conceptual point of view, how are **d** and **y** different from Command Mode commands like **j** and **$**?

7.12 How do you combine five lines into a single line?

7.13 How will you search for a pattern printf and then repeat the search in the opposite direction the original search was made?

7.14 Every time you press a . (dot), you see a blank line inserted below your current line. Why does that happen?

Flex Your Brain

7.1 Name the three modes of **vi** and explain how you can switch from one mode to another.

7.2 How will you add /* at the beginning of a line and */ at the end?

7.3 How do you remove the characters that you just inserted above without using the undo feature?

7.4 How do you move to line number 100 and then write the remaining lines (including that line) to a separate file?

7.5 **vi** refuses to quit with :q. What does that indicate and how do you exit anyway?

7.6 Explain what the following commands do: (i) :.,10w foo (ii) :$w! foo. In which mode are the commands executed and what difference does it make if foo exists?

7.7 Assuming that the cursor is at the beginning of the line, name the commands required to replace (i) echo 'Filename: \c' with echo -n "Filename: " (ii) printf("File not found\n"); with fprintf(stderr, "File not found\n");

7.8 In the midst of your work, how can you see the list of users logged in? If you have a number of UNIX commands to execute, which course of action will you take?

7.9 Name the sequence of commands to execute to move to the line containing the string #include, deleting four lines there, and then placing the deleted lines at the beginning of the file.

7.10 Mention the sequence of commands to execute that will replace printf(with fprintf(stderr,? How will you repeat the action globally?

7.11 How do **u** and **U** differ? When will **U** fail to work?

7.12 Name the commands required to noninteractively replace all occurrences of cnt with count in (i) the first 10 lines, (ii) the current line, (iii) all lines. How do you repeat the exercise in an interactive manner?

7.13 If the power to the machine is cut off while a **vi** session is active, how does it affect your work? What salvage operation will you try?

7.14 You made some changes to a read-only file and then find that you can't save the buffer. What course of action will you take without quitting the editor?

7.15 Copy /etc/passwd to passwd. Name the **vi** commands required to save the first 10 lines in passwd1, the next 10 in passwd2 and the rest in passwd3.

7.16 List the editing and navigation commands required to convert the following text:

```
# include<errno.h>
void quit (char *message)
{
        printf("Error encountered\n");
        printf("error number %d, ", errno);
```

```
            printf("quitting program\n");
            exit(1);
    }
```

to this:

```
    #include <stdio.h>
    #include <errno.h>
    void quit (char *message, int exit_status) {
            /* printf("Error encountered\n"); */
            fprintf(stderr, "Error number %d, quitting program\n", errno);
            exit(exit_status);
    }
```

8

The Shell

This chapter introduces the agency that sits between the user and the UNIX system. It is called the *shell*. All the wonderful things that you can do with UNIX are possible because the shell does a lot of work on our behalf that could be tedious for us to do on our own. The shell looks for some special symbols in the command line, performs the tasks associated with them and finally executes the command. For example, it opens a file to save command output whenever it sees the > symbol.

The shell is a unique and multi-faceted program. It is a command interpreter and a programming language rolled into one. From another viewpoint, it is also a process that creates an environment for you to work in. All of these features deserve separate chapters for discussion, and you'll find the shell discussed at a number of places in this book. In this chapter, we focus on the shell's basic interpretive activities. We have seen some of these activities in previous chapters (like `rm *` or `ls | wc`), but it is here that we need to examine them closely.

WHAT YOU WILL LEARN

- An overview of the shell's interpretive cycle.
- The significance of *metacharacters* and their use in *wild-cards* for matching multiple filenames.
- The use of *escaping* and *quoting* to remove the meaning of a metacharacter.
- The significance of the three *standard files (streams)* that are available to every command.
- How the shell manipulates the default source and destination of these streams to implement *redirection* and *pipelines*.
- Understand what *filters* are and why they are so important in UNIX.
- The significance of the files /dev/null and /dev/tty.
- The use of *command substitution* to obtain the arguments of a command from the standard output of another.
- Shell variables and why they are so useful.

TOPICS OF SPECIAL INTEREST

- The difference between use of double and single quotes.
- The importance of making the command ignorant of the source of its input and destination of its output.

8.1 THE SHELL'S INTERPRETIVE CYCLE

When you log on to a UNIX machine, you first see a prompt. This prompt remains there until you key in something. Even though it may appear that the system is idling, a UNIX command is in fact running at the terminal. But this command is special; it's with you all the time and never terminates unless you log out. This command is the **shell**.

Even though the shell appears not to be doing anything meaningful when there's no activity at the terminal, it swings into action the moment you key in something. If you provide this input in the form of a **ps** command (that shows processes owned by you), you'll see the shell running:

```
$ ps
   PID TTY      TIME CMD
   328 pts/2    0:00 bash                            Bash shell running
```

The Bash shell is running at the terminal /dev/pts/2. When you key in a command, it goes as input to the shell. The shell first scans the command line for **metacharacters**. These are special characters that mean nothing to the command, but mean something special to the shell. The previous example (**ps**) had none of these characters, but we did encounter these characters before (section numbers shown in parentheses):

```
cat > foo           (5.1.2)
rm -r *             (5.3.1)
ls | more           (5.5.4)
comm file[12]       (5.11)
```

So what does the shell do when it sees metacharacters like the >, |, *, etc. in the command line? It performs all actions represented by the symbols *before* the command can be executed. For instance, the * makes no sense to **rm**, so the shell replaces it with all filenames in the current directory. **rm** ultimately runs with these filenames as arguments. The > means nothing to **cat**, so the shell creates the file foo and connects **cat**'s output to it.

When all pre-processing is complete, the shell passes on the command line to the kernel for ultimate execution. The command line now has none of the metacharacters that were originally seen by the shell. While the command is running, the shell has to wait for notice of its termination from the kernel. After the command has completed execution, the shell once again issues the prompt to take up your next command.

To summarize, the following activities are typically performed by the shell in its interpretive cycle:

- The shell issues the prompt and waits for you to enter a command.
- After a command is entered, the shell scans the command line for metacharacters and expands abbreviations (like the * in **rm ***) to recreate a simplified command line.
- It then passes on the command line to the kernel for execution.
- The shell waits for the command to complete and normally can't do any work while the command is running.
- After command execution is complete, the prompt reappears and the shell returns to its waiting role to start the next cycle. You are now free to enter another command.

You can change this behavior and instruct the shell not to wait so you can fire one job after another without waiting for the previous one to complete. We'll be discussing the role of the & metacharacter in running jobs in the background in Chapter 9.

8.2 SHELL OFFERINGS

Your UNIX system offers a variety of shells for you to choose from. Over time, shells have become more powerful by the progressive addition of new features. The shells we consider in this text can be grouped into two categories:

- The Bourne family comprising the Bourne shell (**/bin/sh**) and its derivatives—the Korn shell (**/bin/ksh**) and Bash (**/bin/bash**).
- The C Shell (**/bin/csh**) and its derivative, Tcsh (**/bin/tcsh**).

The absolute pathname of the shell's command file is shown in parentheses. This chapter discusses the common features of the Bourne family of shells. Everything that applies to Bourne also applies to its supersets, Korn and Bash. However, just a few of the shell's features discussed in this chapter don't apply to the C shell. We note the shell-specific features in separate asides in this text.

When you run **echo $SHELL**, the output displays the absolute pathname of the shell's command file. If $SHELL evaluates to /bin/bash, your login shell is Bash. Bash is near POSIX-compliant and is probably the best shell to use. Korn should be the next choice. Decide on the shell you would like to use for interpretive work and make that your login shell.

Note: Some systems (like Linux) offer the **chsh** command that can change your login shell. In case you don't find it on your system, you'll have to ask the administrator to make the change for you. He'll either use the **usermod** command or directly edit the last field in the relevant line of /etc/passwd. You may not like to know all this right now, but it does pay at this stage to know the shell that you are using or one that you should henceforth use.

8.3 PATTERN MATCHING—THE WILD-CARDS

We begin with the special set of characters that the shell uses to match filenames. In previous chapters, you used commands with more than one filename as arguments (e.g., **cat chap01 chap02**). Often, you may need to enter multiple filenames in a command line. To illustrate this point, try listing all filenames beginning with chap. The most obvious solution is to specify all the filenames separately:

```
ls chap chap01 chap02 chap03 chap04 chapx chapy chapz
```

If filenames are similar (as above), we can use the facility offered by the shell of representing them by a single pattern or model. For instance, the pattern chap* represents all filenames beginning with chap. This pattern is framed with ordinary characters (like chap) and a metacharacter (like *) using well-defined rules. The pattern can then be used as an argument to the command, and the shell will expand it suitably *before the command is executed*.

The metacharacters that are used to construct the generalized pattern for matching filenames belong to a category called **wild-cards** (something like the joker that can match any card). In the following sections, we'll discuss the significance of the various metacharacters in the wild-card set that are listed in Table 8.1.

Table 8.1 The Shell's Wild-Cards

Wild-Card	Matches
*	Any number of characters including none
?	A single character
[ijk]	A single character—either an i, j or k
[x-z]	A single character that is within the ASCII range of the characters x and z
[!ijk]	A single character that is not an i, j or k (Not in C shell)
[!x-z]	A single character that is not within the ASCII range of the characters x and z (Not in C shell)
{pat1,pat2...}	pat1, pat2, etc. (Not in Bourne Shell)

8.3.1 The * and ?

In the first chapter, you used the command **ls chap*** *(1.4.9)* to list some filenames beginning with **chap**. The metacharacter, *, is one of the characters of the shell's wild-card set. It matches any number of characters (including none). It thus matches all filenames specified in the previous command line which can now be shortened in this way:

```
$ ls chap*
chap      chap01  chap02  chap03  chap04  chap15  chap16  chap17  chapx  chapy
chapz
```

Observe that chap* also matches the string chap. When the shell encounters this command line, it identifies the * immediately as a wild-card. It then looks in the current directory and recreates the command line as below from the filenames that match the pattern chap*:

```
ls chap chap01 chap02 chap03 chap04 chap15 chap16 chap17 chapx chapy chapz
```

The shell now hands over this command line to the kernel which uses its process creation facilities to run the command.

What happens when you use **echo** with only the * as argument?

```
$ echo *
array.pl back.sh calendar cent2fah.pl chap chap01 chap02 chap03 chap04 chap15 ch
ap16 chap17 chapx chapy chapz count.pl date_array.pl dept.lst desig.lst n2words.
pl name.pl name2.pl odfile operator.pl profile.sam rdbnew.lst rep1.pl
```

You simply see a list of files! All filenames in the current directory match a solitary *, so you see all of them in the output. If you use **rm *** in this directory, all these files will be deleted.

Note: DOS/Windows users may be surprised to know that the * may occur anywhere in a filename and not merely at the end. Thus, *chap* matches all the following filenames—chap newchap chap03 chap03.txt.

Caution: Be careful when you use the * with **rm** to remove files. You could land yourself in a real mess if, instead of typing **rm *.o** which removes all the C object files, you inadvertently introduce a space between * and .o:

```
$ rm * .o                                       Very dangerous!
rm: .o: No such file or directory
```

The error message here masks a disaster that has just occurred; **rm** has removed all files in this directory! In such situations, you should pause and check the command line before you finally press *[Enter]*.

The next wild-card is the ?, which matches a single character. When used with same string chap (chap?), the shell matches all five-character filenames beginning with chap. Appending another ? creates the pattern chap??, which matches six-character filenames. Use both expressions separately, and the meaning becomes obvious:

```
$ ls chap?
chapx   chapy   chapz
$ ls chap??
chap01   chap02   chap03   chap04   chap15   chap16   chap17
```

Both the * and ? operate with some restrictions that are taken up in the next topic.

8.3.2 Matching the Dot

The behavior of the * and ? in relation to the dot isn't as straightforward as it may seem. The * doesn't match all files *beginning* with a . (dot) or the / of a pathname. If you want to list all hidden filenames in your directory having at least three characters after the dot, the dot must be matched explicitly:

```
$ ls .???*
.bash_profile   .exrc   .netscape   .profile
```

However, if the filename contains a dot anywhere but at the beginning, it need not be matched explicitly. For example, the expression emp*1st matches a dot embedded in the filename:

```
$ ls emp*1st
emp.1st     emp1.1st     emp221st     emp2.1st     empn.1st
```

Note: There are two things that the * and ? can't match. First, they don't match a filename beginning with a dot, but they can match any number of embedded dots. For instance, apache*gz matches apache_1.3.20.tar.gz. Second, these characters don't match the / in a pathname. You can't use **cd /usr?local** to switch to /usr/local.

8.3.3 The Character Class

The patterns framed in the preceding examples are not very restrictive. With the knowledge we have, it's not easy to list only chapy and chapz. Nor is it easy to match only the first four chapters from the numbered list. You can frame more restrictive patterns with the **character class**.

The character class comprises a set of characters enclosed by the rectangular brackets, [and], but it matches a *single* character in the class. The pattern [abcd] is a character class, and it matches a single character—an a, b, c, or d. This can be combined with any string or another wild-card expression, so selecting chap01, chap02 and chap04 now becomes a simple matter:

```
$ ls chap0[124]
chap01   chap02   chap04
```

Range specification is also possible inside the class with a - (hyphen); the two characters on either side of it form the range of characters to be matched. Here are two examples:

```
ls chap0[1-4]          Lists chap01, chap02, chap03 and chap04
ls chap[x-z]           Lists chapx, chapy and chapz
```

A valid range specification requires that the character on the left have a lower ASCII value than the one on the right.

Note: The expression [a-zA-Z]* matches all filenames beginning with an alphabet, irrespective of case.

Negating the Character Class (!)   How about framing a pattern that reverses the above matching criteria? The solution that we prescribe here unfortunately doesn't work with the C shell, but with the other shells, you can use the ! as the first character in the class to negate the class. The two examples below should make this point amply clear:

```
*.[!co]       Matches all filenames with a single-character extension but not the .c or .o files.
[!a-zA-Z]*    Matches all filenames that don't begin with an alphabetic character.
```

Even though the character class is meant to be used with a group of characters, it's the only way you can negate a match for a single character. Thus, to match all files except those ending with .o (i.e., C object files), you have to use a character class as a "dummy class":

```
*.[!o]                 Not the .o files
```

C Shell: The ! can't be used to negate a character class at all. In fact, the C shell has no mechanism for doing so.

8.3.4 Matching Totally Dissimilar Patterns

This feature, not available in the Bourne shell, enables us to match totally dissimilar patterns. How does one copy all the C and Java source programs from another directory? Delimit the patterns with a comma, and then put curly braces around them (no spaces please!):

```
cp $HOME/prog_sources/*.{c,java} .
```
                                    Won't work in Bourne shell

This works in the Korn, Bash and C shells. The Bourne shell would need two separate invocations of **cp** to do this job. Using the curly brace form, you can also access multiple directories:

```
cp /home/kumar/{project,html,scripts}/*
```
                                    Won't work in Bourne shell

This copies all files from three directories (project, html and scripts) to the current directory. Isn't this convenient?

Note: Wild-cards mean nothing to a command but only to the shell. The shell interprets the wild-cards and produces a clean list of filenames, which is easily understood by the command.

8.3.5 Rounding Up

Some of the wild-card characters have different meanings depending on where they are placed in the pattern. The * and ? lose their meaning when used inside the class, and are matched literally. Similarly, - and ! also lose their significance when placed outside the class. There are other restrictions but we can ignore them for now.

Whether or not you are able to devise a suitable pattern that matches a group of filenames depends, apart from your ingenuity, on the way the filenames were chosen in the first instance. When organizing information in groups of files, you should choose these names with care so you don't need to use too many patterns to match them. If you don't do that, be prepared to specify them separately every time you use a command that accesses all of them!

To summarize what has been discussed so far, a sample set of command lines is presented below:

`ls *.c`	Lists all files with extension .c.
`mv * ../bin`	Moves all files to bin subdirectory of parent directory.
`cp foo foo*`	Copies foo to foo* (* loses meaning here).
`cp ?????? progs`	Copies to progs directory all files with six-character names.
`lp note[0-1][0-9]`	Prints files note00, note01 ..... through note19.
`rm *.[!l][!o][!g]`	Removes all files with three-character extensions except the ones with the .log extension.
`cp -r /home/kumar/{include,lib,bin} .`	Copies recursively the three directories, include, lib and bin from /home/kumar to the current directory. (Not in Bourne shell)

It's the shell that interprets these expressions. Sometimes we don't want this interpretation to take place. This could be on account of a mistake that has occurred (like creating a file named foo*) but there could be other reasons as well. In the next topic, we discuss two techniques of removing the special meaning of metacharacters.

8.4 ESCAPING AND QUOTING

At this stage, you might well think that if the shell uses some special characters to match filenames, then the filenames themselves must not contain any of these characters. That's right thinking but the real world is far from perfect. One of the sample lines featured in the previous section shows how easy it is to actually create a file named foo*. Because the pattern foo* also matches the filename foo*, the shell will include it in its list if it actually finds a file with this name. The output below shows a file named chap*:

```
$ ls chap*
chap    chap*  chap01  chap02  chap03  chap04  chap15  chap16  chap17  chapx
chapy   chapz
```

This file can be a great nuisance and should be removed immediately. But that won't be easy. Trying **rm chap*** would be dangerous; it would remove the other filenames beginning with chap also. We must be able to protect all special characters (including wild-cards) so the shell is not able to interpret them. The shell provides two solutions to prevent its own interference:

- **Escaping**—Providing a \ (backslash) before the wild-card to remove (escape) its special meaning.

- **Quoting**—Enclosing the wild-card, or even the entire pattern, within quotes (like 'chap*'). Anything within these quotes (barring few exceptions) are left alone by the shell and not interpreted.

In most cases you can use either mechanism, but some situations warrant the use of quotes. Sometimes you also need to make a distinction between single and double quotes, but more of that later.

8.4.1 Escaping

Let's take up escaping first. Placing a \ immediately before a metacharacter turns off its special meaning. For instance, in the pattern *, the \ tells the shell that the asterisk has to be matched literally instead of being interpreted as a metacharacter. This means that we can remove the file chap* without affecting the other filenames that also begin with chap by using

```
rm chap\*
```
                                                        Doesn't remove chap1, chap2

The \ suppresses the wild-card nature of the *, thus preventing the shell from performing filename expansion on it. This feature is known as **escaping**. You'll see this concept of using the \ in other areas also.

To consider another example, if you have files chap01, chap02 and chap03 in your current directory, and still dare to create a file chap0[1-3] by using

```
echo > chap0[1-3]
```
                                                        Creates a file chap0[1-3]

then you should escape the two rectangular brackets when accessing the file:

```
$ ls chap0\[1-3\]
chap0[1-3]
```
                                                        Must escape the [*and*]

```
$ rm chap0\[1-3\]
$ ls chap0\[1-3\]
chap0[1-3] not found                    File removed
```

Escaping the Space   Apart from metacharacters, there are other characters that are special—like the space character. The shell uses it to delimit command line arguments. So to remove the file My Document.doc which has a space embedded, a similar reasoning should be followed:

```
rm My\ Document.doc                     Without the \ rm would see two files
```

Escaping the \ Itself   Sometimes you may need to interpret the \ itself literally. You need another \ before it, that's all:

```
$ echo \\
\
$ echo The newline character is \\n
The newline character is \n
```

Escaping the Newline Character   The newline character is also special; it marks the end of the command line. Some command lines that use several arguments can be long enough to overflow to the next line. To ensure better readability, you need to split the wrapped line into two lines, but make sure that you input a \ before you press *[Enter]*:

```
$ find /usr/local/bin /usr/bin -name "*.pl" -mtime +7 -size +1024 \[Enter]
> -size -2048 -atime +25 -print                          Note the >
```

This is the **find** command at work, a command often used with several arguments. The \ here escapes the meaning of the newline character generated by *[Enter]*. It also produces the second prompt (which could be a > or a ?), which indicates that the command line is incomplete. Command lines involving multiple commands (as in pipelines) can also be very long. For better readability, you should split them into multiple lines wherever possible.

Note: The space, \ and LF (the newline character generated by *[Enter]*) are also special and need to be escaped if the shell is to be prevented from interpreting them in the way it normally does.

8.4.2 Quoting

There's another way to turn off the meaning of a metacharacter. When a command argument is enclosed in quotes, the meanings of all enclosed special characters are turned off. Here's how we can run some of the previous commands, using a mix of single- and double-quoting this time:

```
echo '\'                                Displays a \
rm 'chap*'                              Removes file chap*
rm "My Document.doc"                    Removes file My Document.doc
```

Escaping also turns out to be a tedious affair when there are just too many characters to protect. Quoting is often a better solution. The following example shows the protection of four special characters using single quotes:

```
$ echo 'The characters |, <, > and $ are also special'
The characters |, <, > and $ are also special
```

We could have used escaping here, but then we would need to use four \s in front of each of these four metacharacters. We used single quotes because they protect all special characters (except the single quote). Double quotes are more permissive; they don't protect (apart from the double quote itself) the $ and the ` (backquote):

```
$ echo "Command substitution uses `` while TERM is evaluated using $TERM"
Command substitution uses  while TERM is evaluated using vt100
```

Observe that the pair of backquote characters (``) and the variable $TERM have been interpreted by the shell inside double quotes. $TERM is vt100 for this terminal, and `` evaluated to a null command. Now try out the same example using single quotes:

```
$ echo 'Command substitution uses `` while TERM is evaluated using $TERM'
Command substitution uses `` while TERM is evaluated using $TERM
```

> **Note:** It's often crucial to select the right type of quote, so bear in mind that single quotes protect all special characters. Double quotes, however, let a pair of backquotes (``) be interpreted as *command substitution* characters, and the $ as a variable prefix. There is also a reciprocal relationship between the two types of quotes; double quotes protect single quotes, and single quotes protect double quotes.

8.4.3 Escaping in echo

We used **echo** in Section 3.3 with escape sequences like \n and \t. The \ has a reverse meaning there; it treats the characters n and t as special rather than remove their special meanings. This is obviously the case because n and t don't have special meanings. These escape sequences are always used within quotes to keep the shell out. But what is **echo**?

```
$ type echo
echo is a shell builtin
```

It's a funny situation that we have here. We quoted **echo**'s arguments to keep the shell out of the picture only to learn that **echo** is built into the shell! For this purpose, the shell treats **echo** as an external command (which it once was).

8.5 REDIRECTION: THE THREE STANDARD FILES

Before we commence our discussions on redirection, let's first understand what the term "terminal" means since we'll be using it often. In the context of redirection, the terminal is a generic name that represents the screen, display or keyboard (or even an X window that emulates a terminal). Just as we refer to a directory as a file, we'll also sometimes refer to the keyboard as a terminal.

We see command output and error messages on the terminal (display), and we sometimes provide command input through the terminal (keyboard). The shell associates three files with the terminal—two for the display and one for the keyboard. Even though our terminal is also represented by a specific device name (/dev/tty), commands don't usually read from or write to this file. They perform all terminal-related activity with the three files that the shell makes available to every command.

These special files are actually **streams** of characters which many commands see as input and output. A stream is simply a sequence of bytes. When a user logs in, the shell makes available three files representing three streams. Each stream is associated with a default device, and—generically speaking—this device is the terminal:

- *Standard Input*—The file (or stream) representing input, which is connected to the keyboard.
- *Standard Output*—The file (or stream) representing output, which is connected to the display.
- *Standard Error*—The file (or stream) representing error messages that emanate from the command or shell. This is also connected to the display.

Every command that uses streams will always find these files open and available. The files are closed when the command completes execution. Even though the shell associates each of these files with a default physical device, this association is not permanent. The shell can easily unhook a stream from its default device and connect it to a disk file (or to any command) the moment it sees some special characters in the command line. You, as user, have to instruct the shell to do that by using symbols like > and < in the command line.

8.5.1 Standard Input

We have used the **cat** and **wc** commands to read disk files. These commands have an additional method of taking input. When they are used without arguments, they read the file representing the **standard input**. This file is indeed special; it can represent three input sources:

- The keyboard, the default source.
- A file using *redirection* with the < symbol (a metacharacter).
- Another program using a *pipeline*.

When you use **wc** without an argument and have no special symbols like the < and | in the command line, **wc** obtains its input from the default source. You have to provide this input from the keyboard and mark the end of input with *[Ctrl-d]*:

```
$ wc
Standard input can be redirected
It can come from a file
or a pipeline
[Ctrl-d]
      3        14       71
```

This situation is similar to the one encountered when creating a file with **cat** (*5.1.2*). Enter the three lines of text and signify the end of input with *[Ctrl-d]*. **wc**, which takes the stream from standard input, immediately counts 3 lines, 14 words and 71 characters. We have used **wc** before (*5.8*), but then it showed the filename in the fourth column. This time no filename was specified, so no filename was output. And yet it remains true that **wc** read a file—the standard input file.

The shell's manipulative nature finds place here. It can reassign the standard input file to a disk file. This means it can **redirect** the standard input to originate from a file on disk. This reassignment or redirection requires the < symbol:

```
$ wc < sample.txt
        3      14      71
```
File containing the above 3 lines

The filename is missing once again, which means that **wc** didn't open `sample.txt`. It read the standard input file as a stream but only after the shell reassigned this stream to a disk file.

You may have already framed your next question. Why bother to redirect the standard input from a file if the command can read the file itself? After all, **wc** can also use a filename as argument! The answer is that there are times when you need to keep the command *ignorant* of the source of its input. This aspect, representing one of the most deep-seated features of the system, will gradually expose itself as you progress through these chapters.

HOW IT WORKS: How Input Redirection Works

Command: `wc < sample.txt`

1. On seeing the <, the shell opens the disk file, `sample.txt`, for reading.
2. It unplugs the standard input file from its default source and assigns it to `sample.txt`.
3. **wc** reads from standard input which has earlier been reassigned by the shell to `sample.txt`.

The important thing here is that **wc** has no idea where the stream came from; it is not even aware that the shell had to open the file `sample.txt` on its behalf!

Note: When the standard input is redirected to come from a file (with <), it's the shell that opens the file. The command here is totally ignorant of what the shell is doing to provide it with input. However, when you invoke a command with a filename as argument, it's the command that opens the file and not the shell.

Taking Input Both from File and Standard Input   When a command takes input from multiple sources—say a file and standard input, the - symbol must be used to indicate the sequence of taking input. The meaning of the following sequences should be quite obvious:

```
cat - foo
cat foo - bar
```
First from standard input and then from foo
First from foo, *then standard input, and then* bar

The third source of standard input is the pipe, which is discussed later (8.7). There's a fourth form of standard input which we have not mentioned here. It's the *here document* that has application in shell programming and hence discussed in Chapter 14.

8.5.2 Standard Output

All commands displaying output on the terminal actually write to the **standard output** file as a stream of characters, and not *directly* to the terminal as such. There are three possible destinations of this stream:

- The terminal, the default destination.
- A file using the redirection symbols > and >>.
- As input to another program using a pipeline (to be taken up later).

The shell can effect redirection of this stream when it sees the > or >> symbols in the command line. You can replace the default destination (the terminal) with any file by using the > (right chevron) operator, followed by the filename:

```
$ wc sample.txt > newfile
$ cat newfile
      3      14      71  sample.txt
```

The first command sends the word count of sample.txt to newfile; nothing appears on the terminal screen. If the output file doesn't exist, the shell creates it before executing the command. If it exists, the shell overwrites it, so use this operator with caution. The shell also provides the >> symbol (the right chevron used twice) to append to a file:

```
wc sample.txt >>newfile
```
                                                    Doesn't disturb existing contents

HOW IT WORKS: How Output Redirection Works

Command: wc sample.txt > newfile

1. On seeing the >, the shell opens the disk file, newfile, for writing.
2. It unplugs the standard output file from its default destination and assigns it to newfile.
3. wc (and not the shell) opens the file sample.txt for reading.
4. wc writes to standard output which has earlier been reassigned by the shell to newfile.

And all this happens without wc knowing that it is in fact writing to newfile! Any command that uses standard output is ignorant about the destination of its output also.

Redirection also becomes a useful feature when concatenating the standard output of a number of files. The following example that uses a wild-card saves all C programs in a single file:

```
cat *.c > c_progs_all.txt
```

This concatenated output stream provides no visual indication of the name of the files, so we can do somewhat better by preceding this output with a list of filenames. A single > does the job, but this requires the use of the (and) symbols for grouping commands:

```
( ls -x *.c ; echo ; cat *.c ) > c_progs_all.txt
```

The **echo** command in the middle serves to insert a blank line between the multicolumn file list and the code listings. The program names now feature in the front page, so you have a table of contents preceding your code listings. But better still would be to precede each program listing with its filename. You can do this using a loop construct after you have learned shell programming.

The standard output of one command can also be used by another command as its standard input. This is the third destination of standard output and is taken up in the discussion on pipes *(8.7)*.

Note: When the output of a command is redirected to a file, the output file is created by the shell before the command is executed. Any idea what **cat foo > foo** does?

8.5.3 Standard Error

Before we proceed any further, you should know that each of the three standard files is represented by a number, called a **file descriptor**. A file is opened by referring to its pathname, but subsequent read and write operations identify the file by this file descriptor. The kernel maintains a table of file descriptors for every process running in the system. The first three slots are generally allocated to the three standard streams in this manner:

0—Standard input
1—Standard output
2—Standard error

These descriptors are *implicitly* prefixed to the redirection symbols. For instance, > and 1> mean the same thing to the shell, while < and 0< also are identical. If your program opens a file, in all probability, the file will be allocated the descriptor 3.

We need to explicitly use one of these descriptors when handling the standard error stream. When you enter an incorrect command or try to open a nonexistent file, certain diagnostic messages show up on the screen. This is the **standard error** stream whose default destination is the terminal. Trying to "cat" a nonexistent file produces the error stream:

```
$ cat foo
cat: cannot open foo
```

cat fails to open the file and writes to standard error. If you are not using the C shell, you can redirect this stream to a file. Using the symbol for standard output obviously won't do:

```
$ cat foo > errorfile
cat: cannot open foo
```
Error stream can't be captured with >

The diagnostic output has not been sent to errorfile. It's obvious that standard error can't be redirected in the same way standard output can (with > or >>). Even though standard output and standard error use the terminal as the default destination, the shell possesses a mechanism for capturing them individually. Redirecting standard error requires the use of the 2> symbols:

```
$ cat foo 2>errorfile
$ cat errorfile
cat: cannot open foo
```

This works. You can also append diagnostic output in a manner similar to the one in which you append standard output:

```
cat foo 2>> errorfile
```

If you have a program that runs for a long time and is not error-free, you can direct the standard error to a separate file and then stay away from the terminal. On return, you can examine this file for errors.

Now that you have separate symbols for the output and error streams, you can redirect them separately:

```
foo.sh > bar1 2>bar2
```

What about saving both streams in the same file? You need to use the stream merging mechanism (which uses the symbols 1>&2 and 2>&1), but these are required in shell scripts and are appropriately taken up in Chapter 14.

HOW IT WORKS: How Redirection Makes Use of File Descriptors

The concepts related to redirection are pretty simple. A command like **ls** writes to file descriptor 1, and this remains true even when you use **ls > foo**. To save the **ls** output in **foo**, the shell has to manipulate this file descriptor before running **ls**. It closes standard output and then opens **foo**. Since the kernel allocates the lowest unallocated integer in the file descriptor table, **foo** is assigned the value 1. The **ls** output is thus captured in **foo**.

Even though the concept appears simple, its implementation requires two processes. After all, if the shell closes its own standard output file, how does it display the prompt after the command has completed execution? In reality, the shell creates a copy of its own process, performs the descriptor manipulation in the copied process and even runs the **ls** command in that process. The shell's own file descriptors are then left undisturbed. Chapter 24 discusses how the **dup**, **dup2** and **fcntl** system calls are used to implement redirection.

C Shell: The standard error is handled differently by the C shell, so the examples of this section won't work with it. In fact, the C shell merges the standard error with the standard output; it has no separate symbol for handling standard error only. The command **cat foo >& bar** saves both standard output and standard error in **bar**.

8.5.4 Filters: Using Both Standard Input and Standard Output

We return to the subject of input and output streams to ask ourselves this question: Do all commands use the features of standard input and standard output? No, certainly not. From this viewpoint, the UNIX commands can be grouped into four categories:

- Directory-oriented commands like **mkdir**, **rmdir** and **cd**, and basic file handling commands like **cp, mv** and **rm** use neither standard input nor standard output.
- Commands like **ls, pwd, who**, etc. don't read standard input but they write to standard output.
- Commands like **lp** that read standard input but don't write to standard output.
- Commands like **cat, wc, od, cmp, gzip**, etc. that use both standard input and standard output.

Commands in the fourth category are called, in UNIX parlance, **filters**, and the dual stream-handling feature makes filters powerful text manipulators. Note that most filters can also read *directly* from files whose names are provided as arguments. Four separate chapters are earmarked for filters in this text.

Some of the commands discussed in previous chapters are actually filters. To see how their capabilities get enhanced when used as filters, let's use the **bc** command as a filter this time. Consider this file containing some arithmetic expressions:

```
$ cat calc.txt
2^32                                      Maximum memory on a 32-bit computer
25*50
30*25 + 15^2
```

You can redirect **bc**'s standard input to come from this file and save the output in yet another:

```
$ bc < calc.txt > result.txt              Using both standard input and output
$ cat result.txt
4294967296                                This is 2 ^ 32
1250                                       This is 25*50
975                                        This is 30*25 + 15 ^ 2
```

bc obtained the expressions from redirected standard input, processed them and sent out the results to a redirected output stream. Though we used the < first and then the >, there's no restriction in the sequence we use or in the use of whitespace around the symbols:

```
bc > result.txt < calc.txt
bc>result.txt<calc.txt                     No whitespace!
> result.txt < calc.txt bc                 As above, but command at end
```

The last example illustrates a departure from the statement made previously (2.6) that the first word in the command line is the command. In the last example, **bc** is the last word in the command line. Rather than use these combinations, you'll find it more convenient to stick to the first form.

The indifference of a command to the source of its input and destination of its output is one of the most profound features of the UNIX system. It raises the possibility of commands "talking" to one another so the output of one command can be used as input to another. Very soon we'll discuss pipes when you'll see how two or more commands communicate with one another.

8.6 /dev/null AND /dev/tty: TWO SPECIAL FILES

/dev/null   Quite often, and especially in shell programming, you'll like to check whether a program runs successfully without seeing its output on the screen. You may not want to save this output in a file either. You have a special file that simply accepts any stream without growing in size—the file /dev/null:

```
$ cmp foo1 foo2 >/dev/null
$ cat /dev/null
$ _                                        Size is always zero
```

Check the file size; it's always zero. /dev/null simply incinerates all output written to it. Whether you direct or append output to this file, its size always remains zero. This facility is useful in redirecting error messages away from the terminal so they don't appear on the screen. /dev/null is actually a pseudo-device because, unlike all other device files, it's not associated with any physical device.

Why did we run **cmp** to compare two files if we are not interested in its output? Later, you'll learn how to examine a special shell variable (\$?) to know whether two files are identical or not. It's this value that we are often interested in and not the actual output that lists the differences.

/dev/tty The second special file in the UNIX system is the one indicating one's terminal—/dev/tty. But make no mistake: *This is not the file that represents standard output or standard error.* Commands generally don't write to this file, but you'll need to redirect some statements in shell scripts to this file.

Consider, for instance, that romeo is working on terminal /dev/pts/1 and juliet on /dev/pts/2. However, both romeo and juliet can refer to their own terminals with the same filename—/dev/tty. Thus, if romeo issues the command

```
who >/dev/tty
```

the list of current users is sent to the terminal he is currently using—/dev/pts/1. Similarly, juliet can use an identical command to see the output on her terminal, /dev/pts/2. Like /dev/null, /dev/tty can be accessed independently by several users without conflict.

You may ask why one should need to specifically redirect output to one's own terminal since the default output goes to the terminal anyway. The answer is that sometimes you need to specify that explicitly as the following real-world example suggests.

Consider redirecting a shell script to a file, say, by using **foo.sh > redirect.txt**. Redirecting a script implies redirecting the standard output of all statements in the script. That's not always desirable. Your script may contain some **echo** commands that provide helpful messages for the user, and you would obviously like to see them on the terminal. If these statements are explicitly redirected to /dev/tty inside the script, redirecting the script won't affect these statements. We'll use this feature later in our shell scripts.

Apart from its use in redirection, /dev/tty can also be used as an argument to some UNIX commands. Section 8.8 makes use of this feature, while some situations are presented in Chapter 14 (featuring shell programming).

Note: The size of /dev/null is always zero and all terminals can be represented by /dev/tty.

8.7 PIPES

Standard input and standard output constitute two separate streams that can be individually manipulated by the shell. If that be so, can't the shell connect these streams so that one command takes input from the other? That is not only possible but forms the cornerstone of the building-block approach that UNIX advocates to solve all text manipulation problems.

You know the **who** command produces a list of users, one user per line. Let's use redirection to save this output in a file:

```
$ who > user.txt
$ cat user.txt
root        console      Aug  1 07:51    (:0)
romeo       pts/10       Aug  1 07:56    (pc123.heavens.com)
juliet      pts/6        Aug  1 02:10    (pc125.heavens.com)
project     pts/8        Aug  1 02:16    (pc125.heavens.com)
andrew      pts/14       Aug  1 08:36    (mercury.heavens.com)
```

Let's now use **wc** to make a complete count of this file's contents. We'll use the -1 option to count the number of lines only, and redirect **wc**'s input so that the filename doesn't appear in the output:

```
$ wc -1 < user.txt
        5                                   Counts the number of users
```

Using an intermediate file (user.txt), we effectively counted the number of users. This method of running two commands separately has two obvious disadvantages:

• For long-running commands, this process can be slow. The second command can't act unless the first has completed its job.

• You need an intermediate file that has to be removed after completion of the job. When handling large files, temporary files can build up easily and eat up disk space in no time.

Here, **who**'s standard output was redirected, and so was **wc**'s standard input, and both used the same disk file. The shell can connect these streams using a special operator, the | (pipe), and avoid creation of the disk file. You can make **who** and **wc** work in tandem so that one takes input from the other:

```
$ who | wc -1                              No intermediate files created
        5
```

Here, the output of **who** has been passed directly to the input of **wc**, and **who** is said to be **piped** to **wc**. When multiple commands are connected this way, a **pipeline** is said to be formed. It's the shell that sets up this connection and the commands have no knowledge of it.

The pipe is the third source and destination of standard input and standard output, respectively. You can now use one to count the number of files in the current directory:

```
$ ls | wc -1
        15
```

Note that no separate command was designed to tell you that, though the designers could easily have provided another option to **ls** to perform this operation. And because **wc** uses standard output, you can redirect this output to a file:

```
ls | wc -1 > fkount
```

There's no restriction on the number of commands you can use in a pipeline. But you must know the behavioral properties of these commands to place them there. Consider this command sequence which prints the man page of **grep** on the printer:

```
man grep | col -b | lp
```

The online man pages of a command often show the keywords in boldface. These pages contain a number of control characters which are removed here by the **col** **-b** command. Like **col**, **lp** also reads standard input, this time from **col**'s output and prints the file. For a pipeline to be feasible, the leftmost command (here, **man**) must be able to write to standard output while the rightmost command (here, **lp**) must be able to read standard input. Intermediate commands (here, **col**) must be able to do both.

In a pipeline, all programs run simultaneously. A pipe also has a built-in mechanism to control the flow of the stream. Since a pipe is both being read and written, the reader and writer have to act in unison. If one operates faster than the other, then the appropriate driver has to readjust the flow. This happens when you use the following command sequence:

```
ls | more
```

Since the standard output from **more** freezes as long as you don't scroll forward, the kernel makes sure that **ls** writes to the pipe only as much as **more** can absorb at a time.

8.7.1 When a Command Needs to Be Ignorant of Its Source

We mentioned several times about a command being ignorant of its source and destination. When and why is this ignorance essential for us? To appreciate this point, let's use the **wc** command to display the *total* size of all C programs:

```
$ wc -c *.c
   2078 backtalk.c
    231 beyond_array.c
   .......
   1944 dog.c
    884 hexdump.c
    214 swap.c
 940101 total
```

Output trimmed here

The display shows the total usage at 940,101 bytes, but it also shows the usage for each file. We are not interested in individual statistics this time, what we need is a single figure representing the total size. To be able to do that, you must make **wc** ignorant of its input source. You can do that by feeding the concatenated output stream of all of these files to **wc** **-c** as its input:

```
$ cat *.c | wc -c
940101
```

Since **wc** acts on a stream this time, it displays a single figure. When do we need a single figure? We can use this command sequence as a control command in a shell script to determine whether the files will fit in a floppy diskette:

```
if [ `cat *.c | wc -c` -lt 1474560 ] ; then
    echo 'These files will fit in a single 3.5" diskette'
fi
```

Note how the single quotes protect the double quote in the **echo** statement. We'll learn to use the **if** construct in Chapter 14 that features shell programming. The two backquotes (``` `` ```) denote command substitution which is discussed shortly.

Note: In a pipeline, the command on the left of the | must use standard output and the one on the right must use standard input.

The feature of pipelining represents one of the most important aspects of the UNIX system. It implements the UNIX philosophy that difficult jobs can be done by combining some tools that do simple jobs in isolation. The UNIX manual doesn't tell you the combinations of commands required for each task, and this makes pipelines difficult to conceive initially. A lot is left to knowledge of filters, perseverance and imagination.

8.8 tee: CREATING A TEE

tee is an external command and not a feature of the shell. It handles a character stream by duplicating its input. It saves one copy in a file and writes the other to standard output. Being also a filter (which uses standard input and standard output), **tee** can be placed anywhere in a pipeline. **tee** doesn't perform any filtering action on its input; it gives out exactly what it takes.

The following command sequence uses **tee** to display the output of **who** and saves this output in a file as well:

```
$ who | tee user.txt
romeo      pts/2        Sep  7 08:41    (pc123.heavens.com)
juliet     pts/3        Sep  7 17:58    (pc122.heavens.com)
sumit      pts/5        Sep  7 18:01    (mercury.heavens.com)
```

`user.txt` also contains this output, but how can we be sure without using **cat** to view `user.txt`? Since **cmp** compares two files and one of them can be represented by the standard input file, we can arrange to provide this input from the output of **who**:

```
$ who | cmp user.txt -                        Second file is standard input
$ _
```

The comparison *succeeded*, so **who**'s output and the contents saved earlier by **tee** are identical. We'll later understand what "success" here means.

How do you use **tee** to display both the list of users and its count on the terminal? Since the terminal is also a file, you can use the device name /dev/tty as an argument to **tee**:

```
$ who | tee /dev/tty | wc -l                   /dev/tty used as command argument
romeo      pts/2        Sep  7 08:41    (pc123.heavens.com)
juliet     pts/3        Sep  7 17:58    (pc122.heavens.com)
sumit      pts/5        Sep  7 18:01    (mercury.heavens.com)
        3                                        It's like running who | wc -l
```

tee "saved" the **who** output in /dev/tty, thus effectively showing it on screen. **wc -l** counted the other stream. The advantage of treating the terminal as a file is apparent from the above example. You couldn't have done this if **tee** (or for that matter, any UNIX command) had placed restrictions on the type of file it could handle.

8.9 COMMAND SUBSTITUTION

The shell enables the connecting of two commands in yet another way. While a pipe enables a command to obtain its standard input from the standard output of another command, the shell enables one or more command *arguments* to be obtained from the standard output of another command. This feature is called **command substitution**.

To consider a simple example, suppose you need to display today's date with a statement like this:

```
The date today is Sat Sep  7 19:01:16 IST 2002
```

The last part of the statement (beginning from Sat) represents the output of the **date** command. How does one incorporate **date**'s output into the **echo** statement? With command substitution it's a simple matter. Use the expression `date` as an argument to **echo**:

```
$ echo The date today is `date`
The date today is Sat Sep  7 19:01:56 IST 2002
```

When scanning the command line, the ` (backquote or backtick) is another metacharacter that the shell looks for. There's a special key on your keyboard (generally at the top-left) that generates this character, and it should not be confused with the single quote ('). The shell then executes the enclosed command and replaces the enclosed command line with the output of the command. For command substitution to work, the command so "backquoted" must use standard output. **date** does; that's why command substitution worked.

You can use this feature to generate useful messages. For example, you can use two commands in a pipeline and then use the output as the argument to a third:

```
$ echo "There are `ls | wc -l` files in the current directory"
There are 58 files in the current directory
```

The command worked properly even though the arguments were double-quoted. It's a different story altogether when single quotes are used:

```
$ echo 'There are `ls | wc -l` files in the current directory'
There are `ls | wc -l` files in the current directory
```

This was to be expected because we had already tried out a similar exercise earlier *(8.4.2)*. The ` is one of the few characters interpreted by the shell when placed within double quotes. If you want to echo a literal `, you have to use single quotes.

Command substitution has interesting application possibilities in shell scripts. It speeds up work by letting you combine a number of instructions in one. You'll see more of this feature in subsequent chapters.

Note: Command substitution is enabled when backquotes are used within double quotes. If you use single quotes, it's not.

Korn Shell, Bash Shell: POSIX recommends the use of the form $ (*command*) rather than the archaic `command` for command substitution. The Korn and Bash shells offer both forms. The POSIX form requires you to place the command inside parentheses and have a $ before them:

```
$ echo The date today is $(date)
The date today is Sat Sep  7 19:15:33 IST 2002
```

Whether or not you should use the POSIX notation is something you have to decide for yourself. Make sure that you don't have to run your shell scripts with the Bourne shell before you decide to adopt this form.

8.10 SHELL VARIABLES

The shell supports variables that are useful both in the command line and shell scripts. You have already encountered some of them like TERM and SHELL. Variable usage in the Bourne family differs from that in the C shell. In this section and elsewhere, we discuss Bourne-type variables. The features of C shell variables are noted in the aside at the end of this section.

A variable assignment is of the form *variable=value* (no spaces around =), but its evaluation requires the $ as prefix to the variable name:

```
$ count=5                        No $ required for assignment
$ echo $count                    but needed for evaluation
5
```

A variable can also be assigned the value of another variable:

```
$ total=$count                   Assigning a value to another variable
$ echo $total
5
```

When the shell reads the command line, it interprets any word preceded by a $ as a variable, and replaces the word by the value of the variable. Programmers must note that there must not be any whitespace on either side of the = symbol. The command line x =5 is interpreted by the shell as the x command running with the =5 argument!

Variable names begin with a letter but can contain numerals and the _ as the other characters. Names are case-sensitive; x and X are two different variables. Unlike in programming languages, shell variables are not typed; you don't need to use a char, int or long prefix when you define them. In fact, you don't even have to declare them before you use them. All shell variables are of the string type, which means even a number like 123 is stored as a string rather than in binary. (This may not remain true in future.)

All shell variables are initialized to null strings by default. While explicit assignment of null strings with x="" or x='' is possible, you can also use this as a shorthand:

```
x=                               A null string
```

A variable can be removed with **unset** and protected from reassignment by **readonly**. Both are shell internal commands:

```
unset x                          x is now undefined
readonly x                       x can't be reassigned
```

Tip: By convention, variable names used by the UNIX system and software packages are in uppercase. You are advised to use lowercase variable names in your shell scripts simply to distinguish them from system variables.

C Shell: The C shell uses the **set** statement to set variables. There either has to be whitespace on both sides of the = or none at all:

```
set count = 1                    Both statements are valid
set count=1                      but set count= 1 won't work
```

The evaluation is done in the normal manner (**echo $count**). The C shell uses another statement, **setenv**, to set an *environment variable*. These variables are discussed in Chapter 10.

8.10.1 Effects of Quoting and Escaping

To assign a multiword string to a variable, you can escape each space character, but quoting (single or double) is the preferred solution:

```
message=You\ didn\'t\ enter\ the\ filename     ' also needs to be escaped
message="You didn't enter the filename"
```

Now that you have another special character ($) that is gobbled up by the shell, you may still need to interpret it literally without it being evaluated. This time we have escaping and single-quoting as our options:

```
$ echo The average pay is \$1000
The average pay is $1000
$ echo 'The average pay is $1000'
The average pay is $1000
```

Like the backquote, the $ is also evaluated by the shell when it is double-quoted. Here are two examples:

```
$ echo "The PATH is $PATH and the current directory is `pwd`"
The PATH is /bin:/usr/bin:. and the current directory is /home/kumar/workc
$ echo "The average pay is $1000"
The average pay is 000
```

The first example shows both command substitution and variable evaluation at work, but have a look at the second example. Here, the shell evaluated a "variable" $1. It is not defined, so a null string was output. $1 belongs to a set of parameters that are called *positional parameters, (14.3)* signifying the arguments that you pass to a script.

Note: Whether you should use double quotes or single quotes depends on whether you want command substitution and variable evaluation to be enabled or not. Double quotes permit their evaluation but single quotes don't.

8.10.2 Where to Use Shell Variables

Setting Pathnames   If a pathname is used several times in a script, you should assign it to a variable. You can then use it as an argument to any command. Let's use it with **cd** in this manner:

```
$ progs='/home/kumar/c_progs'
$ cd $progs ; pwd
/home/kumar/c_progs
```

A shell script would generally contain this definition at the beginning, and then it could be used everywhere—both in the script and in other scripts run from that script. It means lesser typing, but there's another advantage. In a later reorganization, if the location of c_progs changes to, say, /export/home/kumar/c_progs, then you simply need to change the variable definition, and everything will work in the same way as before.

Using Command Substitution   You can also use the feature of command substitution to set variables:

```
$ mydir=`pwd` ; echo $mydir
/home/kumar/c_progs
```

You can store the size of a file in a variable too:

```
size=`wc -c < foo.txt`
```

We used the < symbol to leave out the filename in the value assigned to size. If we had used foo.txt as an argument instead, size would have contained a two-word string.

Concatenating Variables and Strings   In your shell scripts, you'll often need to concatenate a variable with another variable or string. In a later chapter, we'll use this feature to change a file's extension. To concatenate two variables you can either place them side by side:

```
base=foo ; ext=.c               Two assignments in one line
file=$base$ext                  This is foo.c
```

or use curly braces to delimit them:

```
file=${base}$ext
```

In either case, you can finally run a compilation command in this way:

```
cc -o $base $file               Creates executable foo from foo.c
```

A similar technique can be used to concatenate a variable and a string. Note that some situations require you to use quotes:

```
file=$base'.c'                  This is foo.c; quotes not required
file=${base}.c                  Same but more readable
file=$base'01'                  This is foo01; quotes required
```

Note: This concatenation feature finds application in adding a directory name to the shell's PATH variable. You can append a directory to the existing PATH in this way:

```
PATH=$PATH:/usr/local/bin
```

You can make this assignment at the prompt in which case the setting will be valid only for the current session. Later, you'll learn to make this setting permanent.

The UNIX system also uses a number of variables to control its behavior. There are variables that tell you the type of terminal you are using, the prompt string you use or the directory where incoming mail is kept. These variables are often called *environment variables* because they are available in all processes. A detailed discussion of the significance of these special shell (environment) variables will be taken up in Chapter 10.

8.11 CONCLUSION

Now that you have seen the major interpretive features of the shell, it's time we made a summary of these activities. After the command line is terminated by hitting the *[Enter]* key, the shell goes ahead with processing the command line in one or more passes. The sequence varies with the shell you use, but broadly assumes the following order:

- *Parsing* The shell first breaks up the command line into words using spaces and tabs as delimiters, unless quoted. All consecutive occurrences of a space or tab are replaced here with a single space.

- *Variable evaluation* All $-prefixed strings are evaluated as variables, unless quoted or escaped.

- *Command substitution* Any command surrounded by backquotes is executed by the shell, which then replaces the standard output of the command into the command line.

- *Redirection* The shell then looks for the characters >, < and >> to open the files they point to.

- *Wild-card interpretation* The shell finally scans the command line for wild-cards (the characters *, ?, [and]). Any word containing a wild-card is replaced by a sorted list of filenames that match the pattern. The list of these filenames then forms the arguments to the command.

- PATH *evaluation* It finally looks for the PATH variable to determine the sequence of directories it has to search in order to hunt for the command.

The preceding sequence can be considered as a simplistic treatment of the shell's behavioral pattern. There are many more characters that the shell looks for that have been ignored here. And the shell itself can be viewed from different perspectives. The next chapter examines the process; the shell is also a process. Later chapters discuss the shell's environment (Chapter 10) and its programming features (Chapters 14 and 21).

WRAP UP

The shell is a process that runs when a user logs in and terminates when she logs out. It scans the command line for *metacharacters* and rebuilds it before turning it over to the kernel for execution.

The shell matches filenames with *wild-cards* that have to be expanded before the command is executed. It can match any character (*) or a single one (?). It can also match a range ([ ]) and negate a match ([!]). The * and ? don't match a filename beginning with a dot.

A wild-card is escaped with a \ to be treated literally, and if there are a number of them, then they should be *quoted*. These techniques also work on the space, the newline and the \, which the shell interprets specially.

The shell makes available three files representing *standard input, standard output* and *standard error* to every command that it runs. It can manipulate the default source and destination of input and output streams by assigning them to disk files. These files are accessed with small integers called *file descriptors*.

The file /dev/null never grows in size and every user can access her own terminal as /dev/tty.

Pipes connect the standard output of one command to the standard input of another. Commands using standard output and standard input are called *filters*, which serve as powerful text manipulators.

Command substitution enables a command's output to serve as arguments to another command. The shell supports *variables* which are evaluated by prefixing a $ to the variable name.

Single quotes protect all special characters, while double quotes enable command substitution and variable evaluation.

You should use either Korn or Bash as your login shell.

Test Your Understanding

8.1   Why does the shell need to expand wild-cards? How does it treat the * when used as an argument to a command (like **echo** *)?

8.2   What is the significance of the command **ls** *.*?

8.3   How do you remove only the hidden files of your directory? Does **rm** * remove these files as well?

8.4   Match the filenames chapa, chapb, chapc, chapx, chapy and chapz with a wild-card expression.

8.5   Is the wild-card expression [3-h]* valid?

8.6   Frame wild-card patterns (i) where the last character is not numeric, (ii) that have at least four characters.

8.7   When will **cd** * work?

8.8   Name the three sources of standard input and standard output.

8.9   How do you save your entire home directory structure including the hidden files in a file?

8.10   How will you add the tags <html> and </html> to the beginning and end respectively of foo.html?

8.11 The commands, **cat** and **bc**, when used without arguments don't seem to do anything. What does that indicate and how do you return to the shell prompt?

8.12 A directory bar contains a number of files including one named -foo. How do you remove the file?

8.13 How will you create a filename containing just one space character? How will you later confirm from the **ls** output that it indeed contains a space?

8.14 Is this a legitimate command and what does it appear to do? **>foo <bar bc**

8.15 How do you split a long command sequence into multiple lines?

8.16 Command substitution requires the command to use (i) standard input (ii) standard output (iii) both (iv) none of these.

8.17 How do you send mail to all users whose names are stored in a file foo and the message is stored in message.txt?

8.18 Enter the commands **echo "$SHELL"** and **echo '$SHELL'**. What difference do you notice?

8.19 Attempt the variable assignment x = 10 (space on both sides of the =). Does it work if you are not using the C shell?

8.20 Interpret these statements and the message displayed (if any) (i) $x=5 (ii) directory='pwd'=`pwd`

8.21 To append .c to a variable x, you have to use the expression (i) $x.c (ii) $x".c" (iii) ${x}.c (iv) any of these (v) only the first two.

Flex Your Brain

8.1 When the shell finds metacharacters in the command line what does it do? When is the command finally executed?

8.2 Devise wild-card patterns to match the following filenames: (i) foo1, foo2 and Foo5 (ii) quit.c, quit.o and quit.h (iii) watch.htm, watch.HTML and Watch.html (iv) all filenames that begin with a dot and end with .swp

8.3 Devise wild-card patterns to match all filenames comprising at least three characters (i) where the first character is numeric and the last character is not alphabetic, (ii) not beginning with a dot, (iii) containing 2004 as an embedded string except at the beginning or end.

8.4 Explain what these wild-card patterns match: (i) [A-z]????* (ii) *[0-9]* (iii) *[!0-9] (iv) *.[!s][!h]

8.5 Devise a command that copies all files named chap01, chap02, chap03 and so forth, and up to chap26 to the parent directory. Can a single wild-card pattern match them all?

8.6 Explain what the commands **ls .*** and **ls *.** display.

8.7 You have a file named * and a directory named My Documents in the current directory. How do you remove them?

8.8 Explain the significance of single- and double-quoting including when one is preferred to the other.

8.9 How do the commands **wc foo** and **wc < foo** differ? Who opens the file in each case?

8.10 You want to concatenate two files, foo1 and foo2, but also insert some text after foo1 and before foo2 from the terminal. How will you do this?

8.11 What happens when you use (i) **cat > foo** if foo contains data, (ii) **who >> foo** if foo doesn't exist, (iii) **cat foo > foo** (iv) **echo 1> foo**?

8.12 Execute the command **ls > newlist**. What interesting observation can you make from the contents of **newlist**?

8.13 What are *file descriptors* and why is 2> used as the redirection symbol for standard error?

8.14 Explain why the error message is seen on the terminal in spite of having used the 2> symbol:

```
$ cat < foo 2>bar
ksh: cannot open foo: No such file or directory
```

8.15 What are the conditions that need to be satisfied to make this sequence work?
prog1 | prog2 | prog3

8.16 How do you find out the number of users logged in?

8.17 Use command substitution to print the (i) calendar of the current month, (ii) listing of a group of filenames stored in a file.

8.18 How will you store in a variable count (i) the total size of all C source files (.c), (ii) the total number of lines in a file?

8.19 A file foo contains a list of filenames. Devise a single statement, with suitable explanation, that stores in a variable count the total character count of the *contents* of these files. (HINT: Both command substitution and **cat** have to be used twice.)

9

The Process

Everything, they say, in UNIX is a file. In this chapter, we look at everything as a process. A process is a UNIX abstraction that enables us to look at files and programs in another way. A file is treated as a simple file when it lies in a dormant state on disk. It can also be understood as a process when it is executed. Like living organisms, processes are born, they give birth to other processes and also die. Processes make things "happen" in UNIX.

UNIX being a multitasking system, hundreds or even thousands of processes can run on a large system. Processes belong to the domain of the kernel, which is responsible for their management. We'll examine the process attributes and understand the process creation mechanism. We must also be able to control these processes by moving them between foreground and background and killing them when they get out of control. We'll also examine the process scheduling facilities offered by UNIX.

WHAT YOU WILL LEARN

- An overview of the kernel's role in process management.
- The similarities between files and processes.
- Examine process attributes and the inheritance mechanism.
- View process attributes with **ps**.
- Run a job in the background with & and **nohup**.
- Reduce the priority of a job with **nice**.
- Use **kill** to terminate processes.
- Use *job control* commands to switch control from one job to another.
- Schedule jobs for one-time execution with **at** and **batch**.
- Use the **cron** scheduler to schedule jobs to run periodically.
- Time a process with **time**.

TOPICS OF SPECIAL INTEREST

- How a process is created using three primitives—**fork**, *exec* and **wait**.

- Understand how the shell is created using these primitives.
- A brief introduction to *signals* whose coverage is to be expanded in Chapter 24.

9.1 PROCESS BASICS

A **process** is simply an instance of a running program. A process is said to be **born** when the program starts execution and remains alive as long as the program is active. After execution is complete, the process is said to **die**. A process also has a name, usually the name of the program being executed. For example, when you execute the **grep** command, a process named **grep** is created. However, a process can't be considered synonymous with a *program*. When two users run the same program, there's one program on disk but two processes in memory.

The kernel is responsible for the management of processes. It determines the time and priorities that are allocated to processes so that multiple processes are able to share CPU resources. It provides a mechanism by which a process is able to execute for a finite period of time and then relinquish control to another process. The kernel has to sometimes store *pages* (sections) of these processes in the swap area of the disk before calling them again for running. All this happens more than once a second, making the user oblivious to the switching process.

Files have attributes and so do processes. Some attributes of every process are maintained by the kernel in memory in a separate structure called the **process table**. You could say that the process table is the inode for processes. Two important attributes of a process are:

- *The Process-id (PID)* Each process is uniquely identified by a unique integer called the **Process-id (PID)** that is allotted by the kernel when the process is born. We need this PID to control a process, for instance, to kill it.
- *The Parent PID (PPID)* The PID of the parent is also available as a process attribute. When several processes have the same PPID, it often makes sense to kill the parent rather than all its children separately.

The other attributes are inherited by the child from its parent and are discussed in Section 9.4.

Things do go wrong at times. A process may go berserk and multiply rapidly, bringing the system to a complete standstill. A process may not complete in the expected time, and you may decide to suspend it, move it to the background, or even kill it. UNIX provides us with the tools to understand the process hierarchy and also control these processes.

9.1.1 The Shell Process

When you log on to a UNIX system, a process is immediately set up by the kernel. This process represents a UNIX command which may be **sh** (Bourne shell), **ksh** (Korn shell), **csh** (C shell) or **bash** (Bash). Any command that you key in is actually the standard input to the shell process. This process remains alive until you log out, when it is killed by the kernel. We'll mostly assume and use the Bash shell for the examples of this chapter.

The shell maintains a set of environment variables, and you have already encountered some of them like PATH and SHELL. The shell's pathname is stored in SHELL, but its PID is stored in a special "variable", $$. To know the PID of your current shell, type

```
$ echo $$
291
```

The PID of your login shell can't obviously change as long as you are logged in. A low PID indicates that the process was initiated quite early. When you log out and log in again, your login shell will be assigned a different PID. Knowledge of the PID is often necessary to control the activities at your terminal, especially when things go wrong.

9.1.2 Parents and Children

Just as a file has a parent, every process also has one. This **parent** itself is another process, and a process born from it is said to be its **child**. When you run the command

```
cat emp.1st
```

from the keyboard, a process representing the **cat** command, is started by the shell process. This **cat** process remains active as long as the command is active. The shell (which could be **sh, ksh, bash** or **csh**) is said to be the parent of **cat**, while **cat** is said to be the child of the shell.

Since every process has a parent, you can't have an "orphaned" process (though a process can remain in this state for a small moment). The ancestry of every process is ultimately traced to the first process (PID 0) that is set up when the system is booted. It's like the root directory of the file system.

The analogy with files and directories doesn't stop here. Like a file, a process can have only one parent. Moreover, just as a directory can have more than one file under it, the multitasking nature of UNIX permits a process to generate (or *spawn*) one or more children. The command

```
cat emp.1st | grep 'director'
```

sets up two processes for the two commands. These processes have the names **cat** and **grep**, and both are spawned by the shell.

9.1.3 Wait or Not Wait?

While the analogy between processes and mortals is striking, you could be amused by two different attitudes that can be taken by the parent toward its child:

- It may wait for the child to die so that it can spawn the next process. The death is informed by the kernel to the parent. When you execute a command from the shell, the shell process waits for the command to die before it returns the prompt to take up the next command.

- It may not wait for the child to die at all and may continue to spawn other processes. This is what the **init** process does, the reason why **init** is the parent of several processes. Your shell can also create a process without waiting for it to die.

In this chapter, we'll experience both behavioral patterns displayed by the shell.

Note: All commands don't set up processes. Built-in commands of the shell like **pwd**, **cd** etc. don't create processes.

9.2 ps: PROCESS STATUS

Let's now use the **ps** command to display some process attributes. **ps** can be seen as the process counterpart of the file system's **ls** command. The command reads through the kernel's data structures and process tables to fetch the characteristics of processes.

By default, **ps** displays the processes owned by the user running the command. If you execute the command immediately after logging in, what you see could look like this:

```
$ ps
    PID TTY        TIME CMD
    291 console   0:00 bash
```
                                                The login shell of this user

Ignoring the header, each line (here, only one) shows the PID, the terminal (TTY) with which the process is associated (the *controlling terminal*), the cumulative processor time (TIME) that has been consumed since the process has been started, and the process name (CMD).

You can see that your login shell (**bash**) has the PID 291, the same number echoed by the special variable, $$. On some systems, you might see the **ps** command itself in the output. Since the login shell isn't doing much work, its CPU usage is negligible. Here, the user is running the Bash shell; your shell could be different.

9.2.1 ps Options

ps is a highly variant command; its actual output varies across different UNIX flavors. BSD and System V are at war here; there are hardly any options common to both systems. For instance, **ps -e** on System V *approximates* to **ps aux** (no hyphens) on BSD. Solaris uses the System V version while Linux accepts both type of options. Table 9.1 shows the options used by both systems, showing their equivalence wherever possible.

Full Listing (-f)   To get a detailed listing which also shows the parent of every process, use the -f (full) option:

```
$ ps -f
     UID    PID  PPID  C    STIME TTY       TIME CMD
   sumit    367   291  0 12:35:16 console  0:00 vi create_user.sh
   sumit    291     1  0 10:24:58 console  0:00 -bash
   sumit    368   367  0 12:35:18 console  0:00 /usr/bin/bash -i
```

Now you can see the parent (PPID) and owner (UID) of every process. The login shell (PID 291) has the PPID 1, the second process of the system. (The first process has the PID 0). This is **init**, the creator of all login shells and parent of all services offered by the system. We'll be discussing **init** soon.

Apart from the **vi** editor, there are two shells running here, and the -f option easily identifies a login shell by the hyphen preceding the command name. We'll ignore the C header for the time being. STIME shows the time the process started. CMD displays the entire command line with its arguments.

Table 9.1 Options to **ps**

POSIX Option	BSD Option	Significance
-f	f	Full listing showing the PPID of each process
-e or -A	aux	All processes including user and system processes
-u *usr*	U *usr*	Processes of user *usr* only
-a		Processes of all users excluding processes not associated with terminal
-l	l	Long listing showing memory-related information
-t *term*	t *term*	Processes running on terminal *term* (say, /dev/console)

Caution: The display of the entire command line by the -f option lets one user know what the other is doing. This can arguably be considered as a demerit of the system. When a user is working on a file, it's difficult for her to keep the filename a closely guarded secret.

Displaying Processes of a User (-u)   The system administrator needs to use the -u (user) option to know the activities of any user. The following output shows a user working on the X Window system rather than a character terminal and X running a number of processes on the user's behalf:

```
$ ps -u sumit
   PID TTY     TIME CMD
   378 ?       0:05 Xsun
   403 ?       0:00 Xsession
   339 pts/3   0:00 bash
   346 pts/3   0:00 vi
   347 pts/3   0:00 bash
   478 ?       0:00 dtfile
   460 pts/5   0:00 dtsessio
   467 ?       0:01 dtwm       The window manager of CDE
   479 ??      0:00 dtterm     A terminal window in CDE
```

It's the Common Desktop Environment (CDE) that's running as X Window on this Solaris machine. All commands beginning with the string dt are components of CDE. You'll learn about some of these commands in Chapter 16 that features X Window and CDE. The terminal name pts/3 refers to a pseudo-terminal, like an **xterm** window that runs under X.

Displaying All User Processes (-a)   The -a (all) option lists processes of all users but doesn't display the system processes:

```
$ ps -a
   PID    TTY        TIME CMD
   662    pts/01     00:00:00 ksh
   705    pts/04     00:00:00 sh
  1005    pts/01     00:00:00 ksh
  1017    pts/01     00:00:04 vi
   680    pts/03     00:00:00 ksh
  1056    pts/02     00:00:00 sort
  1058    pts/05     00:00:00 bash
  1069    pts/02     00:00:00 ps
```

Several users are at work here, as evident from the terminal names displayed. Most of them seem to be users of the Korn shell. Not much work seems to be going on here except for sorting and a file editing operation with **vi**. The list is usually much larger than this but has been condensed here for obvious reasons.

9.3 SYSTEM PROCESSES (-e or -A)

Apart from the processes a user generates, a number of system processes keep running all the time. Most of them are not associated with any terminal (having no *controlling terminal*—term explained soon). They are spawned during system startup and some of them start when the system goes to the multiuser state. To list all processes running on your machine, use the -e or -A option to **ps**. On a busy system, this list could be very long; we produce below a trimmed and annotated list showing some important system processes:

```
$ ps -e
  PID TTY        TIME CMD
    0 ?         0:01 sched          Takes care of swapping
    1 ?         0:00 init           Parent of all shells
    2 ?         0:00 pageout        Part of the kernel—not exec'd
    3 ?         4:36 fsflush        Part of the kernel—not exec'd
  194 ?         0:00 syslogd        Logs all system messages
  170 ?         0:00 inetd          Server side of FTP and TELNET
  231 ?         0:00 lpsched        The printer daemon
  200 ?         0:00 cron           Schedules your jobs
  247 ?         0:00 sendmail       Handles all your mail
 2931 ?         0:00 in.telne       Serves your TELNET requests
  292 ?         0:00 dtlogin
 1436 ?         0:00 in.rlogi       Serves your RLOGIN requests
 3054 pts/2     0:00 bash
 3006 ?         0:01 dtwm           Handles windows on X Window
 2908 pts/4     0:00 vi
 2993 pts/6     0:00 bash
```

System processes are easily identified by the ? in the TTY column; they generally don't have a **controlling terminal** (term used twice before). This means that the standard input and standard output of these processes are not connected to the terminal. You can't press *[Ctrl-c]* to interrupt these processes either. These processes are known as **daemons** because they are called without a specific request from a user. Many of these daemons are actually sleeping and wake up only when they receive input.

Daemons do important work for the system. The **lpsched** daemon controls all printing activity. **sendmail** handles both your incoming and outgoing mail. Your TCP/IP network won't run FTP and TELNET without the **inetd** daemon. **cron** looks at its control file once a minute to decide what it should do. You'll learn about some of these daemons and other system processes in subsequent chapters. We'll consider the **cron** daemon in this chapter.

Note: Many system daemons act as *server* components of a TCP/IP network. They listen at certain *ports* for user requests and then wake up when they receive input. For each of these daemons, there's a corresponding *client* component (another program) that a user may run on another machine. For instance, the **ftp** command on your machine communicates with the **inetd** daemon (server). Your mail handling program like **mailx** or Mozilla connects to **sendmail** to send out mail.

9.4 MECHANISM OF PROCESS CREATION

There are three distinct phases in the creation of a process and uses three important system calls or functions—**fork**, *exec* and **wait**. Knowledge of the process creation cycle will enable you to write programs that create processes (Chapter 24) and also help you debug shell scripts. The three phases are discussed below:

- **Fork**   A process in UNIX is created with the **fork** system call, which creates a copy of the process that invokes it. The process image is practically identical to that of the calling process, except for a few parameters like the PID. When a process is *forked* in this way, the child gets a new PID. The forking mechanism is responsible for the multiplication of processes in the system.

- **Exec**   Forking creates a process but it is not enough to run a new program. To do that, the forked child needs to overwrite its own image with the code and data of the new program. This mechanism is called exec, and the child process is said to *exec* a new program. No new process is created here, the PID and PPID of the exec'd process remain unchanged.

- **Wait**   The parent then executes the **wait** system call to *wait* for the child process to complete. It picks up the *exit status* of the child (explained shortly) and then continues with its other functions. As observed before *(9.1.3)*, a parent may not decide to wait for the death of its child.

All this means that when you run a command (say, **cat**) from the shell, the shell first forks another shell process. The newly forked shell then overlays itself with the executable image of **cat**, which then starts to run. The parent (the shell) waits for **cat** to terminate and then picks up the exit status of the child. This is a number returned by the child to the kernel, and has great significance in both shell programming and systems programming. You'll meet the exit status in Chapters 14 and 24; the latter chapter discusses the entire process creation scheme in detail.

When a process is forked, the child has a different PID and PPID from its parent. However, it inherits most of the environment of its parent. The important attributes that are inherited are:

- The **real UID** and **real GID** of the process. These are attributes that we relate to a file, but here they represent the UID and GID of the user running the program (and not of the file that is executed). These parameters are stored in the entry for the user in /etc/passwd.

- The **effective UID** and **effective GID** of the process. These are generally the same as their "real" cousins but some processes behave differently. (See Inset)

- The current directory from where the process was run. This is something you must remember to understand why you can't create a process to change your current directory.

- The descriptors of all files opened by the parent process. Recall that these are small integers that are used to identify a file (8.5.3). The file descriptor table reserves the first three slots (0, 1 and 2) for the shell's standard streams.

- Environment variables (like HOME and PATH). Every process knows the user's home directory and the path used by the shell to look for commands.

Some conclusions are inescapable. First, by virtue of ownership, one user can't kill or otherwise control another user's process. However, this doesn't apply to the root user, who can manipulate every user process. Moreover, inheritance here implies that the child has its own *copy* of these parameters and can thus alter the operating environment it has inherited. However, in that case, the modified environment is not available to the parent process and disappears as soon as the child dies.

Note: A process remembers the directory from where it was run. This attribute acquires importance when a process also changes a directory.

HOW IT WORKS: When Real UID Differs from Effective UID

Why does every process have two UIDs and two GIDs (real and effective) as shown in the list of inherited process attributes? Most programs we run have the real UID and GID the same as the effective UID and GID. Now consider the listing of these two programs:

```
$ ls -l /bin/cat /usr/bin/passwd
-rwxr-xr-x   1 root     root        14264 2002-09-10 18:43 /bin/cat
-rwsr-xr-x   1 root     shadow      68680 2002-09-11 00:43 /usr/bin/passwd
```

When kumar runs **cat**, the real and effective UID of the **cat** process are the same—kumar. Being a nonprivileged user, kumar can't use **cat** to open a file that is readable only by root.

Now notice the bit marked s in the permissions field of **passwd**. This bit, called the *set-user-id* (SUID), changes the normal ownership scheme. When kumar runs **passwd**, the real UID is still kumar, *but the effective UID is root, the owner of the program*. Because it's the effective UID, not the real UID, that determines the access rights of the process, the **passwd** process run by kumar can open any file that is readable by root. We have more to say about SUID in Chapters 15, 23 and 24.

9.4.1 How the Shell is Created

With this knowledge of the elements of process creation, let's now see how the shell itself is created. When the system moves to multiuser mode, **init** forks and execs a **getty** for every active communication port (or line). Each one of these **getty**s prints the login prompt on the respective terminal and then goes off to sleep.

When a user attempts to log in, **getty** wakes up and fork-execs the **login** program to verify the login name and password entered. On successful login, **login** forks-execs the process representing the login shell. Repeated overlaying ultimately results in **init** becoming the immediate ancestor of the shell as can be seen from this sequence:

```
init  ══════▷  getty  ══════▷  login  ══════▷  shell
         fork           fork-exec         fork-exec
```

init goes off to sleep, waiting for the death of its children. The other processes **getty** and **login** have extinguished themselves by overlaying. When the user logs out, her shell is killed and the death is intimated to **init**. **init** then wakes up and spawns another **getty** for that line to monitor the next login. We'll see in Chapter 25 how all this is implemented in /etc/inittab, the configuration file used by **init**.

9.5 INTERNAL AND EXTERNAL COMMANDS

From the process viewpoint, the shell recognizes three types of commands:

- *External Commands*—The most commonly used ones are the UNIX utilities and programs, like **cat**, **ls,** etc. The shell creates a process for each of these commands that it executes while remaining their parent.

- *Shell Scripts*—The shell executes these scripts by spawning another shell, which then executes the commands listed in the script. The child shell becomes the parent of the commands that feature in the script.

- *Internal Commands*—The shell has a number of built-in commands as well. Some of them like **cd** and **echo** don't generate a process, and are executed directly by the shell. Similarly, variable assignment with the statement x=5, for instance, doesn't generate a process either.

9.5.1 Why Directory Change Can't Be Made in Separate Process

It's just as well that certain commands are built into the shell because it would be either difficult or impossible to implement them as separate external commands. You know that a child process inherits the current working directory from its parent as one of its environmental parameters. This inheritance has important consequences for the **cd** command.

It's necessary for the **cd** command not to spawn a child to achieve a change of directory. If it did so through a separate child process, then after **cd** had completed its run, control would revert to the parent and the original directory would be restored. It would then be impossible to change directories.

9.6 PROCESS STATES AND ZOMBIES

At any instant of time, a process is in a particular **state**. A process after creation is in the *runnable* state before it actually runs (state *running*). While the process is running, it may be invoke a disk I/O operation when it has nothing to do except wait for the I/O to complete. The process then moves to the *sleeping* state to be woken up when the I/O operation is over. A process can also be *suspended* by pressing a key (usually, *[Ctrl-z]*). Processes whose parents don't wait for their death move to the *zombie* state.

When a process dies, it immediately moves to the **zombie** state. It remains in this state until the parent picks up the child's exit status (the reason for waiting) from the process table. When that is done, the kernel frees the process table entry. A zombie is a harmless dead child but you can't kill it.

It's also possible for the parent itself to die before the child dies. The child then becomes an **orphan** and the kernel makes **init** the parent of all orphans. When this adopted child dies, **init** waits for its death.

9.7 RUNNING JOBS IN BACKGROUND

A multitasking system lets a user do more than one job at a time. Since there can be only one job in the *foreground*, the rest of the jobs have to run in the *background*. There are two ways of doing this—with the shell's & operator and the **nohup** command. The latter permits you to log out while your jobs are running, but the former doesn't allow that (except in the C shell and Bash).

9.7.1 &: No Logging Out

The & is the shell's operator used to run a process in the background. The parent in this case doesn't wait for the child's death. Just terminate the command line with an &; the command will run in the background:

```
$ sort -o emp.lst emp.lst &
550                                                          The job's PID
```

The shell immediately returns a number—the PID of the invoked command (550). The prompt is returned and the shell is ready to accept another command even though the previous command has not been terminated yet. The shell, however, remains the parent of the background process. Using an & you can run as many jobs in the background as the system load permits.

Depending on the shell you are using, the standard output and standard error of a job running in the background may or may not come to the terminal. If they do, then make sure both streams are redirected suitably, using /dev/null, if necessary. This precaution has to be taken when you are using the C shell. This shell, along with Bash, allows you to log out without aborting the job.

Background execution of a job is a useful feature that you should utilize to relegate time-consuming or low-priority jobs to the background, and run the important ones in the foreground. Here, discipline is very important as significant deterioration of CPU performance can occur. It can also be a disservice to other users who might find the machine practically at a standstill owing to the multiplicity of these processes. UNIX can't prevent users from running multiple jobs.

9.7.2 nohup: Log Out Safely

Background jobs cease to run, however, when a user logs out (the C shell and Bash excepted). That happens because her shell is killed. And when the parent is killed, its children are also normally killed (subject to certain conditions). The UNIX system permits a variation in this default behavior. The **nohup** (no hangup) command, when prefixed to a command, permits execution of the process even after the user has logged out. You must use the & with it as well:

```
$ nohup sort emp.lst &
586
Sending output to nohup.out
```

The shell returns the PID this time too, and some shells display this message as well. When the **nohup** command is run in these shells, **nohup** sends the standard output of the command to the file nohup.out. If you don't get this message, then make sure that you have taken care of the output, using redirection if necessary. You can now safely log out of the system without aborting the command.

When you use the **ps** command after using **nohup** from another terminal (and if it has not been completed already), you'll notice something quite significant:

```
$ ps -f -u kumar
    UID    PID  PPID  C   STIME TTY  TIME COMMAND
  kumar    586     1  45 14:52:09  01  0:13 sort emp.1st
```

Look what's happened this time. The shell died (rather, was killed) on logging out but its child (**sort**) didn't; it turned into an orphan. The kernel handles such situations by reassigning the PPID of the orphan (**sort**) to the system's **init** process (PID 1)—the parent of all shells. When the user logs out, **init** takes over the parentage of any process run with **nohup**. *In this way, you can kill a parent (the shell) without killing its child (sort).*

If you run more than one command in a pipeline, you should use the **nohup** command at the beginning of each command in the pipeline:

```
nohup grep 'director' emp.1st & | nohup sort &
```

C shell, Bash Shell: Jobs run in the background continue to send their standard output and standard error to the terminal, and have to be redirected to avoid screen clutter. The jobs are not aborted even after the user has logged out. This is not the case with the Bourne and Korn shells. Moreover, the **nohup** command in the C shell doesn't send the standard output of the command to nohup.out. It has to be separately redirected to a file.

9.8 nice: JOB EXECUTION WITH LOW PRIORITY

Processes in the UNIX system are usually executed with equal priority. This is not always desirable since high-priority jobs must be completed at the earliest. UNIX offers the **nice** command, which is used with the & operator to *reduce* the priority of jobs. More important jobs can then have greater access to the system resources (being "nice" to your neighbors).

To run a job with a low priority, the command name should be prefixed with **nice**:

```
nice wc -l uxmanual
```

or better still with

```
nice wc -l uxmanual &
```

nice is a built-in command in the C shell. nice values are system-dependent and typically range from 1 to 19. Commands execute with a nice value that is generally in the middle of the range—usually 10. A higher nice value implies a lower priority. **nice** reduces the priority of any process, thereby raising its nice value. You can also specify the nice value explicitly with the -n option:

```
nice -n 5 wc -l uxmanual &          Nice value increased by 5 units
```

A nonprivileged user can't increase the priority of a process; that power is reserved for the superuser. The nice value is displayed with the **ps -o nice** command.

9.9 KILLING PROCESSES WITH SIGNALS

The UNIX system often requires to communicate the occurrence of an event to a process. This is done by sending a **signal** to the process. Each signal is identified by a number and is designed to perform a specific function. Because the same signal number may represent two different signals on two different machines, signals are better represented by their symbolic names having the SIG prefix. They can be generated from the keyboard or by the **kill** command, which we'll be discussing soon.

If a program is running longer than you anticipated and you want to terminate it, you normally press the interrupt key. This sends the process the SIGINT signal (numbered 2). The default action of this signal is to kill the process. A process may also ignore a signal or execute some user-defined code written to handle that signal. Chapter 24 discusses all of these options in detail; in this chapter we are concerned with a signal's default action only.

Irrespective of what you do, there are two signals that a process can't ignore or run user-defined code to handle it. They are the SIGKILL and SIGSTOP signals which always perform the default action associated with them. We'll now learn to use the **kill** command to send specific signals to processes.

9.9.1 kill: Premature Termination of a Process

The **kill** command sends a signal, *usually* with the intention of killing one or more processes. **kill** is an internal command in most shells; the external **/bin/kill** is executed only when the shell lacks the kill capability. The command uses one or more PIDs as its arguments, and by default uses the SIGTERM (15) signal. Thus,

```
kill 105                            It's like using kill -s TERM 105
```

terminates the job having PID 105. To facilitate premature termination, the & operator displays the PID of the process that's run in the background. If you don't remember the PID, use **ps** to know that and then use **kill**.

If you run more than one job—either in the background or in different windows in the X Window system—you can kill them all with a single **kill** statement. Just specify all their PIDs with **kill**:

```
kill 121 122 125 132 138 144
```

If all these processes have the same parent, you may simply kill the parent in order to kill all its children. However, when you use **nohup** with a set of commands and log out, you can't kill the parent as **init** acquires their parentage. You then have to kill the processes individually because you can't kill **init**.

Note: Like files, you also own processes spawned by commands that you execute. It's natural that you can kill only those processes that you own, and you can't kill processes of other users. Moreover, certain system processes having the PIDs 0, 1, 2, 3 and 4 simply can't be killed in this manner.

Killing the Last Background Job   For most shells, the system variable $! stores the PID of the last background job—the same number seen when the & is affixed to a command. So you can kill the last background process without using the **ps** command to find out its PID:

```
$ sort -o emp.lst emp.lst &
345
$ kill $!                          Kills the sort command
```

If your shell supports job control (as most shells do), you can use **kill** with a slightly different syntax to terminate a job. We'll be discussing job control shortly.

Using kill *with Other Signals*   By default, **kill** uses the SIGTERM signal (15) to terminate the process. You would have noticed that some programs simply ignore it and continue execution normally. In that case, the process can be killed with the SIGKILL signal (9). This signal can't be generated at the press of a key, so you must use **kill** with the signal name (without the SIG) preceded by the -s option:

```
kill -s KILL 121                   Recommended way of using kill
kill -9 121                        Same as above but not recommended
```

A simple **kill** command (with TERM) won't kill the login shell. You can kill your login shell by using any of these commands:

```
kill -9 $$                         $$ stores PID of current shell
kill -s KILL 0                     Kills all processes including the login shell
```

Tip: To view the list of all signal names and numbers that are available on your machine, use the command **kill -1** (list) or view the file /usr/include/sys/signal.h.

Note: In early days, **kill** was used only to terminate a process. Today, with so many signals available, the name "kill" today has turned a misnomer; all signals don't kill a process. In Chapter 24, we'll examine the **kill** system call to learn that **kill** can also suspend a job or even direct a suspended job to continue!

9.10 JOB CONTROL

A **job** is the name given to a group of processes. The easiest way of creating a job is to run a pipeline of two or more commands. Now consider that you expect a job to complete in 10 minutes and it goes on for half an hour. If you kill the job now, you'll lose a lot of work. If you are using the C shell, Korn shell or Bash, you can use their **job control** facilities to manipulate jobs. Job control in these shells means that you can

- Relegate a job to the background (**bg**).
- Bring it back to the foreground (**fg**).
- List the active jobs (**jobs**).
- Suspend a foreground job (*[Ctrl-z]*).
- Kill a job (**kill**).

The commands needed to perform these activities are shown in parentheses. To begin our discussion, if you have invoked a command and the prompt hasn't yet returned, you can suspend the job by pressing *[Ctrl-z]*. You'll then see the following message:

```
[1] + Stopped                       spell uxtip02 > uxtip02.spell
```

Observe that the job has not been terminated yet; it's only suspended ("stopped"). You can now use the **bg** command to push the current foreground job to the background:

```
$ bg
[1]     spell uxtip02 > uxtip02.spell&             A single-process job
```

The & at the end of the line indicates that the job is now running in the background. So a foreground job goes to the background, first with *[Ctrl-z]*, and then with the **bg** command. You can start more jobs in the background any time:

```
$ sort permuted.index > sorted.index &
[2]    530     [2] indicates second job
$ wc -l uxtip?? > word_count &
[3]    540
```

Each of these jobs comprises a single process. Now that you have three jobs running, you can have a listing of their status with the **jobs** command:

```
$ jobs
[3] + Running                  wc -l uxtip?? > word_count &
[1] - Running                  spell uxtip02 > uxtip02.spell &
[2]   Running                  sort permuted.index > sorted.index &
```

You can now bring any of the background jobs to the foreground with the **fg** command. To bring the current (most recent) job to the foreground, use

```
fg
```

This will bring the **wc** command in the foreground. The **fg** and **bg** commands can also be used with the job number, job name or a string as arguments, prefixed by the % symbol:

fg %1	Brings first job to foreground
fg %sort	Brings sort job to foreground
bg %2	Sends second job to background
bg %?perm	Sends to background job containing string **perm**

At any time, however, you can terminate a job with the **kill** command using the same identifiers as above. Thus, **kill %1** kills the first background job with SIGTERM, while **kill -s KILL %spell** terminates the spell-checking program with SIGKILL.

At this point, it must be mentioned that the reason why we used *[Ctrl-z]* for suspending a job is that, by default, this is the character set by the **stty** command *(3.13)* for this purpose. When you use this command in those shells that support job control, you'll probably see a line of output similar to this:

```
start = ^q; stop = ^s; susp = ^z; dsusp = ^y;
```

The third assignment shows the suspend character as ^z, which is **stty**'s way of representing *[Ctrl-z]*. You can change it if you want but that normally won't be necessary.

9.11 at AND batch: EXECUTE LATER

UNIX provides sophisticated facilities to schedule a job to run at a specified time of day. If the system load varies greatly throughout the day, it makes sense to schedule less urgent jobs at a time when the system overheads are low. The **at** and **batch** commands make such scheduling possible.

9.11.1 at: ONE-TIME EXECUTION

at takes as its argument the time the job is to be executed and displays the at> prompt. Input has to be supplied from the standard input:

```
$ at 14:08
at> empawk2.sh
[Ctrl-d]
commands will be executed using /usr/bin/bash
job 1041188880.a at Sun Dec 29 14:08:00 2002
```

The job goes to the queue, and at 2:08 p.m. today, the script file **empawk2.sh** will be executed. **at** shows the job number, the date and time of scheduled execution. This job number is derived from the number of seconds that have elapsed since the Epoch *(3.2)*. It's the most meaningful method of making such numbers unique across several years.

at doesn't indicate the name of the script to be executed; that is something the user has to remember. The standard output and standard error of the program are mailed to the user, who can use any mail reading program to view it. Alternatively, a user may prefer to redirect the output of the command itself:

```
at 15:08
empawk2.sh > rep.lst
```

You can also use the -f option to take commands from a file. However, any error messages that may be generated when executing a program will, in the absence of redirection, continue to be mailed to the user. To mail job completion to the user, use the -m option.

at also offers the key words now, noon, midnight, today and tomorrow. Moreover, it accepts the + symbol to act as an operator. The words that can be used with this operator include hours, days, weeks, months and years. The following forms show the use of some of the key words and operators:

at 15	*24-hour format assumed*
at 5pm	
at 3:08pm	
at noon	*At 12:00 hours today*
at now + 1 year	*At current time after one year*
at 3:08pm + 1 day	*At 3:08 p.m. tomorrow*
at 15:08 December 18, 2001	
at 9am tomorrow	

The month name and day of the week, when used at all, must be either fully spelled out or abbreviated to three letters.

Jobs can be listed with the **at -l** command and removed with **at -r**. Unfortunately, there's no way you can find out the name of the program scheduled to be executed. This can create problems, especially when you are unable to recall whether a specific job has actually been scheduled for later execution.

9.11.2 batch: Execute in Batch Queue

The **batch** command also schedules jobs for later execution, but unlike **at**, jobs are executed as soon as the system load permits. The command doesn't take any arguments but uses an internal algorithm to determine the execution time. This prevents too many CPU-hungry jobs from running at the same time. The response of **batch** is similar to **at** otherwise:

```
$ batch < empawk2.sh
commands will be executed using /usr/bin/bash
job 1041185673.b at Sun Dec 29 13:14:33 2002
```

Any job scheduled with **batch** goes to a special **at** queue from where it can be removed with **at -r**.

Note: The system administrator controls the use of **at** and **batch** on your system. For details, look up Section 15.2.4.

9.12 cron: RUNNING JOBS PERIODICALLY

The **ps -e** command always shows the **cron** daemon running. This is the UNIX system's chronograph, ticking away every minute. Unlike **at** and **batch** that are meant for one-time execution, **cron** executes programs at regular intervals. It is mostly dormant, but every minute it wakes up and looks in a control file (the **crontab** file) in /var/spool/cron/crontabs for instructions to be performed at that instant. After executing them, it goes back to sleep, only to wake up the next minute.

A user may also be permitted to place a crontab file named after her login name in the crontabs directory. kumar has to place his crontab commands in the file /var/spool/cron/crontabs/kumar. This location is, however, system-dependent. A specimen entry in the file /var/spool/cron/crontabs/kumar can look like this:

```
00-10 17 * 3,6,9,12 5  find / -newer .last_time -print > backuplist
```

Each line contains a set of six fields separated by whitespace. The complete command line is shown in the last field. All of these fields together determine when and how often the command will be executed. **cron** uses an unusual number matching system for matching fields. A set of numbers is delimited by a comma. A * used in any of the first five fields implies that the command is to be executed every period depending on the field where it is placed.

The first field (legal values 00 to 59) specifies the number of minutes after the hour when the command is to be executed. The range 00-10 schedules execution every minute in the first 10 minutes of the hour. The second field (17, i.e., 5 p.m.) indicates the hour in 24-hour format for scheduling (legal values 1 to 24).

The third field (legal values 1 to 31) controls the day of the month. This field (here, an asterisk), read with the other two, implies that the command is to be executed every minute, for the first 10 minutes, starting at 5 p.m. every day. The fourth field (3,6,9,12) specifies the month (legal values 1 to 12). The fifth field (5—Friday) indicates the days of the week (legal values 0 to 6), Sunday having the value 0.

So what is the frequency of execution of this command? Even though the third field uses a * to indicate execution every day, the fifth field overrides the entry and limits execution to every Friday. The **find** command will thus be executed every minute in the first 10 minutes after 5 p.m., every Friday of the months March, June, September and December (of every year).

Note: Linux additionally looks up the file /etc/crontab, which has the instructions in a different format.

9.12.1 crontab: Creating a crontab File

You can also create your own crontab files with **vi** in the format shown previously. You'll then need to use the **crontab** command to place the file in the directory containing crontab files for **cron** to read the file again:

```
crontab cron.txt
```
           cron.txt contains cron commands

If kumar runs this command, a file named **kumar** will be created in /var/spool/cron/crontabs containing the contents of cron.txt. In this way, different users can have crontab files named after their user-ids.

It's also possible to enter **cron** commands by using **crontab** with the -e option. **crontab** calls up the editor defined in the EDITOR variable (often, **vi**). After you have edited your commands and quit **vi**, the commands are automatically scheduled for execution.

You can see the contents of your crontab file with **crontab -l** and remove them with **crontab -r**.

cron is mainly used by the system administrator to perform housekeeping chores, like removing outdated files or collecting data on system performance. It's also extremely useful to periodically dial up to an Internet mail server to send and retrieve mail.

Note: Like **at** and **batch**, the use of **cron** is controlled by some system files, which can be edited only by the system administrator (15.2.4).

9.13 time: TIMING PROCESSES

When you have multiple versions of a program, you'll want to find out how efficiently they use the system resources. The **time** command accepts the entire command line to be timed as its argument and does this work. It executes the program and also displays the time usage on the terminal. This enables programmers to tune their programs to keep CPU usage at an optimum level.

You can find out the time taken to perform a sorting operation by preceding the **sort** command with **time**:

```
$ time sort -o newlist invoice.lst
real       0m29.811s
user       0m1.370s
sys        0m9.990s
```

The *real* time shown is the clock elapsed time from the invocation of the command until its termination. The *user* time shows the time spent by the program in executing itself. In Chapter 23, you'll see how control shifts to the kernel when a program executes a system call, and *sys* indicates the time used by the kernel in doing work on behalf of the user process. The sum of the user time and the sys time actually represents the CPU time. This could be significantly less than the *real* time on a heavily loaded system (as is the case above).

9.14 CONCLUSION

This chapter examined the process—the other key subsystem of the UNIX operating system. In Chapter 24, we'll have a second look at processes and use the **fork**, *exec* and **wait** system calls to actually create them. We'll also have a close look at the signaling facility to change the default signal-handling behavior of these processes. Knowledge of processes is also key to customizing the shell's operating environment, and that is what we are going to take up in the next chapter.

> ### WRAP UP
>
> A *process* is an instance of a running program. The multitasking nature of UNIX allows a process to spawn one or more processes.
>
> Process attributes like the *process-id* (PID) and *parent PID* (PPID) are maintained in the *process table*. The kernel decides which process to run and for how long before another process is given a chance.
>
> The login shell is a process that keeps running as long as the user is logged in. Its PID is stored in the shell parameter $$.
>
> You can list your own processes with **ps**, view the process ancestry (-f), all users' processes (-a) and all system processes (-e). BSD uses a different set of options.
>
> System processes, often called *daemons*, are generally not attached to a terminal and not invoked specifically by a user. They often act as *servers* in a client-server framework.

A process is created with the **fork** system call, which creates a copy of itself. The child then execs to overwrite itself with the image of the program to be run.

The parent normally waits for the death of the child so that it can pick up the child's *exit status* by issuing the **wait** system call. Until that is done (if at all), the dead child remains in *zombie* state.

The child's environment inherits some parameters from the parent, like the real and effective UID and GID, the file descriptors, the current directory and environment variables. However, changes in the child are *not* made available in the parent.

Built-in shell commands like **pwd** and **cd** don't fork a separate process. Shell scripts use a subshell to run the commands in a script.

A job can run in the background using the &. **nohup** ensures that a background job remains alive even after the user has logged out. Premature death of the parent makes the child an *orphan*, and **init** takes over the parentage of all orphans.

The UNIX kernel communicates with a process by sending it a *signal* from the keyboard or by invoking the **kill** command. Use **kill -s KILL** if a simple **kill** doesn't do the job.

A *job* is a collection of processes. The C shell, Korn and Bash shells enable job control. You can move jobs between foreground and background (**fg** and **bg**) and suspend (*[Ctrl-z]*) them.

You can schedule a job for one-time execution with **at**, or run it when the system load permits with **batch**. **cron** lets you schedule jobs so that they run repeatedly.

Jobs are timed with **time**, a useful tool for the programmer for making comparisons between different versions of a program.

Test Your Understanding

9.1 What is the significance of the PID and PPID?

9.2 Which process do you think may have the maximum number of children?

9.3 How do you display all processes running on your system?

9.4 Which programs are executed by spawning a shell? What does the second shell do?

9.5 Name some commands that don't require a separate process.

9.6 How do you find out the complete command line of a process run by user timothy?

9.7 How will you use **kill** to (i) ensure that a process is killed, (ii) display the signal list on your system?

9.8 How will you kill the last background job without knowing its PID?

9.9 Using **mailx**, how do you send the **ps** output showing all system processes to user charlie?

9.10 Should you run a command like this? **nohup compute.sh**

9.11 You are editing a file with **vi**, and you want to make a temporary exit to the shell. How will you do it and then come back to **vi** again?

9.12 Interpret the following crontab entry without examining the **find** command line:
30 21 * * * find /tmp /usr/tmp -atime +30 -exec rm -f {} \;

9.13 How do you compare the efficiency of the programs foo1 and foo2?

Flex Your Brain

9.1   Mention the significance of the two shell parameters, $$ and $!.

9.2   Mention the similarities that you find between processes and files.

9.3   What are the two options available to a parent after it has spawned a child? How can the shell be made to behave in both ways?

9.4   Explain what *daemon* processes are and their behavioral pattern. Name three examples of daemons and the tasks they perform. How do you identify these processes?

9.5   How is a process created? Mention briefly the role of the fork-exec mechanism in process creation.

9.6   Name five important process attributes that are inherited by the child from its parent.

9.7   Unlike the built-in commands, **pwd** and **echo**, which also exist as separate disk files, why is there no file named **cd** on any UNIX system?

9.8   Explain the sequence of steps followed by **init** that allows us to log in and work at the shell prompt. What does **init** do when a user logs out?

9.9   What is a *zombie*, and how is it killed?

9.10   What is the difference between a process run with & and one run with **nohup**?

9.11   What are *signals*? Name a way of generating a signal from the keyboard. Why should we use **kill** with signal names rather than their numbers?

9.12   Explain whether the following are true or false: (i) A script can be made to ignore all signals. (ii) The parent process always picks up the exit status of its children. (iii) One program can give rise to multiple processes.

9.13   The **jobs** command issued the message jobs: not found. When does that normally happen?

9.14   What is the difference between a *job* and a *process*? How do you (i) suspend the foreground job, (ii) move a suspended job to the background, (iii) bring back a suspended job to the foreground?

9.15   Interpret these crontab entries and explain if they will work: (i) * * * * * dial.sh (ii) 00-60 22-24 30 2 * find.sh

9.16   Frame a crontab entry to execute the connect.sh script every 30 minutes on every Monday, Wednesday and Friday between the times 8 a.m. and 6 p.m.

Customizing the Environment

Interaction with the operating system takes away a significant chunk of the user's time. She has to constantly change directories, list files, edit and compile programs and repeat previous commands. Incorrect or inconvenient environmental settings can also make life miserable for the UNIX programmer. As a user, you must strive to set a pleasant environment for yourself. The task is not difficult at all as UNIX is second to none in environment control.

UNIX can be highly customized by manipulating the settings of the shell alone. Commands can be made to change their default behavior. In fact, the degree of customization possible depends mainly on the shell you use. The Bourne shell has the minimum number of features, but its derivatives—the Korn shell and Bash—are feature-rich and highly customizable. You'll have a headstart over others if you select one of the two as your login shell. After reading this chapter, you may want to make this decision.

WHAT YOU WILL LEARN

- The evolution of the four shells—Bourne shell, C shell, Korn shell and Bash.
- The difference between *local* and *environment* variables.
- The significance of environment variables like HOME, SHELL, MAIL, and so forth.
- How to customize the prompt string in Bash and Korn.
- Use *aliases* to invoke commands with short names.
- Use the *history* mechanism to recall, edit and run previously executed commands.
- Prevent accidental overwriting of files and logging out with *[Ctrl-d]* using **set -o**.
- Use the *tilde substitution* feature to shorten pathnames that refer to the home directory.
- How the initialization scripts function in the various shells while noting the distinction between the *profiles* and *rc* scripts.

TOPICS OF SPECIAL INTEREST

- Use the history mechanism to repeatedly edit and compile a program using the minimum number of keystrokes.
- Use the $_ shortcut with any command to represent the last argument to the previous command.
- Edit any previous command line using the **vi**-like *in-line editing* feature.

10.1 THE SHELLS

The UNIX shell is both an interpreter and a scripting language. It's one way of saying that a shell can be interactive or noninteractive. When you log in, an *interactive shell* presents a prompt and waits for your requests. This type of shell supports job control, aliases and history. An interactive shell runs a *noninteractive shell* when executing a shell script.

Every feature used in a shell script can also be used in an interactive shell, but the reverse is not true. Job control and history have no meaning in a shell script. In this chapter we are mostly concerned with interactive shells.

Steve Bourne developed the first shell for UNIX. The Bourne shell was weak as an interpreter but had reasonably strong programming features. The C shell was created by Bill Joy at Berkeley to improve the interpretive features of Bourne. But Joy's shell wasn't suitable for programming. For some time, it was normal to use the C shell for interpretive work and the Bourne shell for programming. Had this trend continued till this day, this chapter would have focused almost entirely on the C shell.

Things changed when David Korn developed the Korn shell. It combined the best of both worlds—the interactive features of the C shell and the programming features of Bourne. Korn offered important features likes aliases and command history (which the Bourne shell lacked) and also offered additional programming constructs not available in Bourne. While Korn was a complete superset of Bourne, it lacked some features of the C shell like directory stack manipulation. Korn's alias handling is also somewhat weak.

Bash was developed by GNU as a Bourne-again shell. It was a grand superset in that in combined the features of the Korn and C shells. Bash was developed to ultimately conform to the POSIX shell specification. It is arguably the best shell to use.

10.2 ENVIRONMENT VARIABLES

Shell variables are of two types—local and environment. PATH, HOME and SHELL are **environment variables**. They are so called because they are available in the user's total environment—the sub-shells that run shell scripts, and mail commands and editors. Local variables are more restricted in scope as shown by this example:

```
$ DOWNLOAD_DIR=/home/kumar/download
$ echo $DOWNLOAD_DIR
/home/kumar/download
```

DOWNLOAD_DIR is a local variable; its value is not available to child processes. Run a Bourne sub-shell with **sh** and check whether you can see the variable there:

```
$ sh                              Create a child shell
$ echo $DOWNLOAD_DIR              Is DOWNLOAD_DIR visible in child
                                  It is not!
$ echo $PATH                      But is PATH visible?
PATH=/bin:/usr/bin::.:/usr/ccs/bin   It is!
$ exit                            Terminate child
$ _                               and come back to login shell
```

The **set** statement displays all variables available in the current shell, but the **env** command displays only environment variables. We show below a concise list:

```
$ env
HOME=/home/henry
IFS='
'
LOGNAME=kumar
MAIL=/var/mail/kumar
MAILCHECK=60
PATH=/bin:/usr/bin:.:/usr/ccs/bin
PS1='$ '
PS2='> '
SHELL=/usr/bin/bash
TERM=xterm
```

IFS includes newline
So closing quote is on next line

By convention, environment variable names are defined in uppercase though nothing prevents you from using a different scheme. **env** is an external command and runs in a child process. It thus lists only those variables that it has inherited from its parent, the shell. But **set** is a shell built-in and shows all variables visible in the current shell. **set** will display the value of DOWNLOAD_DIR but not **env**.

Applications often obtain information on the process environment through these environment variables. **vi** reads TERM and **mailx** looks up MAIL. Applications are not designed to run from a specific shell, so environment variables always present information in the *name=value* format. They may, however, be assigned differently in the different shells (like the C shell).

A local variable can be converted to an environment variable using the shell's **export** statement. This statement has been discussed in Chapter 21.

10.3 THE COMMON ENVIRONMENT VARIABLES

Environment variables (Table 10.1) control the behavior of the system. They determine the environment in which you work. If they are not set properly, you may not be able to use some commands without a pathname, use **vi** on a remote connection or obtain notification on receipt of mail. You can set or reset these variables to your liking.

We begin our study by examining the environment variables that are common to the Bourne family of shells (**sh**, **bash** and **ksh**). Later, we'll examine some variables specific to Bash and Korn.

The Command Search Path (PATH) The PATH variable instructs the shell about the route it should follow to locate any executable command. This has already been discussed *(2.4.1)*. Its current value as displayed by **env** shows a list of four directories. To include the directory /usr/xpg4/bin in your search list you'll have to reassign this variable:

```
PATH=$PATH:/usr/xpg4/bin
```
                                    Appending new value to old value—OK

Note: If there are two commands having the same name in two different directories, that command will be executed whose directory name appears first in the PATH list.

Your Home Directory (HOME)   When you log in, UNIX normally places you in a directory named after your login name. This directory is called the home or login directory *(4.4)* and is available in the variable HOME:

```
$ echo $HOME
/home/henry
```

The home directory ($HOME) for a user is set by the system administrator in /etc/passwd. The line for this user could look like this:

```
henry:x:208:50::/home/henry:/bin/ksh
```

Note that the home directory is set in the last but one field. This file can be edited by the system administrator, either manually, or by invoking the **useradd** or **usermod** commands. You only have to tell the administrator if you desire a change of HOME.

You can manually reassign this variable, but it will *not* change the home directory as such, but only the directory that **cd** switches to when used without arguments. This happens because a simple **cd** implies **cd $HOME**.

Mailbox Location and Checking (MAIL *and* MAILCHECK)   The UNIX mail handling system doesn't inform the user that mail has arrived; that job is done by the shell. It knows the location of a user's mailbox from MAIL. This mailbox is generally /var/mail or /var/spool/mail (Linux). henry's mail is saved in /var/mail/henry on an SVR4 system.

MAILCHECK determines how often the shell checks the file for the arrival of new mail (The **env** output shows 60). If the shell finds the file modified since the last check, it informs the user with this familiar message:

```
You have mail in /var/mail/henry
```

The Prompt Strings (PS1 *and* PS2)   The shell has two prompts. The primary prompt string PS1 is the one you normally see. You have also seen when discussing the **echo** command *(2.7.2)*, how a multiline command makes the shell respond with a >. The > is the secondary prompt string stored in PS2. Normally, PS1 and PS2 in the Bourne shell are set to the characters $ and >, respectively.

You can change the primary prompt string to C> if you find the Windows environment more reassuring:

```
$ PS1="C> "
C> _
```

While the $ is the primary prompt string for nonprivileged users, the system administrator uses the # as the prompt. We have something more to discuss about PS1 when we take up the Bash and Korn shells.

Shell Used by Commands with Shell Escapes (SHELL)   SHELL tells you the shell you are using. There are some programs like **more** and **vi** that provide you with a *shell escape* to let you run a UNIX command. SHELL determines the shell these programs use.

The system administrator usually sets up your login shell in /etc/passwd when creating a user account, though he can change it whenever you make a request. Just have a look at the sample line in the discussion on the HOME variable; the last field sets the value of SHELL.

The Terminal Type (TERM)   TERM indicates the terminal type that is used. Every terminal has certain characteristics that are defined in a separate control file in the terminfo directory (in /usr/lib or /usr/share/lib). This directory contains a number of subdirectories named after the letters of the alphabet. A terminal's control file is available in a directory having a one-letter name that is the same as the first letter of the terminal name. For instance, vt100 terminals use the file /usr/share/lib/terminfo/v/vt100.

Some utilities like the **vi** editor are terminal-dependent, and they need to know the type of terminal you are using. If TERM isn't set correctly, **vi** won't work and the display will be faulty. TERM is also important when you log on to a remote machine.

Your Username (LOGNAME)   This variable shows your username. When you wander around in the file system, you may sometimes forget your login name. (It's strange, but it happens when you have multiple accounts!) From time to time, just make sure you know which account you logged in to:

```
$ echo $LOGNAME                              Or try who am i
henry
```

Where else can you use this variable? You can use it in a shell script which does different things depending on the user invoking the script.

Field Separator for Command and Arguments (IFS)   IFS contains a string of characters that are used as word separators in the command line. The string normally consists of the space, tab and newline characters. All of these characters are invisible but the blank line following it suggests that the newline character is part of this string. You can confirm the contents of this variable by taking its octal dump:

```
$ echo "$IFS" | od -bc
0000000  040 011 012 012
             \t \n \n
0000004
```

You can see the three whitespace characters that comprise IFS. Shell programmers sometimes need to make a temporary change to IFS. We'll also do that in Chapter 21.

10.3.1 Variables Used in Bash and Korn

Current Directory in Prompt (PWD *and* PS1)   Bash and Korn dispense with the need to use the pwd command which displays the current directory. They offer a separate variable PWD whose value can be assigned to PS1:

```
$ PS1='[$PWD] '                              Value to be enclosed within quotes
[/home/henry] _
```

See how the prompt changes from $ to [/home/henry]. If you change your directory now to tulec2, the prompt changes to reflect the new directory:

Table 10.1 Common Environment Variables

Variable	Significance
HOME	Home directory—the directory a user is placed on logging in
PATH	List of directories searched by shell to locate a command
LOGNAME	Login name of user
USER	Login name of user
MAIL	Absolute pathname of user's mailbox file
MAILCHECK	Mail checking interval for incoming mail
TERM	Type of terminal
PWD	Absolute pathname of current directory (Korn and Bash only)
CDPATH	List of directories searched by cd when used with a nonabsolute pathname
PS1	Primary prompt string
PS2	Secondary prompt string
SHELL	User's login shell and one invoked by programs having shell escapes

```
[/home/henry] cd tulec2
[/home/henry/tulec2] _
```

PWD is a rather unusual variable; it is reevaluated every time the working directory changes. The prompt accordingly changes to reflect the new value of PWD.

Using Event Number in PS1 *(!)*   Bash and Korn also support a *history* facility that treats a previous command as an *event* and associates it with a number. You can recall and execute previous commands by their event numbers. Using the !, you can set the PS1 prompt to show the current event number:

```
$ PS1='[!] '                                    Bash requires \ before !
[42] _
```

or better still, include the PWD variable to also reflect the current directory:

```
$ PS1='[! $PWD] '                               Variable evaluation within single quotes!
[43 /home/henry/tulec2]
```

Every time you execute a command, the event number is incremented (here, from 42 to 43). Knowledge of the event number is quite useful because you can reexecute a previous command by referring to this number.

Customizing PS1 *in Bash*   Bash uses a number of escape sequences to make your prompt string as informative as possible. For instance, the \h string shows the hostname of your computer:

```
$ PS1="\h> "
saturn> _                                       saturn is the machine's name
```

When you use **telnet** or **ssh** to get into other machines in the network, you often get confused as to where you actually are. This prompt keeps you informed at all times. If you set PS1 to include your hostname and see some other name in the prompt string, then you must be logged on to a remote machine. Look up the Bash documentation for the other escape sequences.

The other variables used by Bash and Korn will be discussed in later sections that feature the history facility, in-line editing and the startup files.

10.4 ALIASES (bash and ksh)

Bash and Korn support the use of **aliases** that let you assign shorthand names to frequently used commands. For instance, many people customize the **ls** command to always execute **ls -xF**. Aliasing is done with the **alias** statement and an alias is defined in the same way as a variable.

A UNIX user often uses the **ls -l** command, so if you don't have the **ll** command or alias on your system, you can create an alias:

```
alias ll='ls -l'                        Quoting necessary for multiple words
```

As with shell variables, there must not be any whitespace on either side of the = symbol. Once the alias is defined, you can execute the **ls -l** command simply by using

```
ll                                      This executes ls -l
```

To consider another example, we often use the **cd** command with long pathnames. If there's a sequence that you use often, it would be sensible to convert it into an alias like this:

```
alias cdsys="cd /usr/include/sys"
```

Now you can simply invoke **cdsys** to change to this directory.

You can also use aliasing to redefine an existing command so it is always invoked with certain options. Here are two useful aliases:

```
alias cp="cp -i"
alias rm="rm -i"
```

The **cp -i** command behaves interactively when the destination file exists. **rm -i** always behaves interactively. With aliases now defined for them, every time you invoke these commands, their aliased versions are executed. How can you now use the original external commands? Just precede the command with a \. This means that you have to use **\cp foo1 foo2** to override the alias.

You can display an alias definition by using **alias** with the name:

```
$ alias cp
cp='cp -i'                              Bash output differs a little
```

Let's briefly examine the other features of aliases. An alias is recursive, which means that if **a** is aliased to **b** and **b** is aliased to **c**, **a** should run **c**. You can list all aliases by using **alias** without arguments and unset an alias with the **unalias** statement. To unset the alias **cp**, use **unalias cp**.

Exercise some restraint in using aliases; too much aliasing can be confusing and difficult to remember. Moreover, aliases have been entirely superseded by *shell functions (21.10)*, which offer a superior form of aliasing. Aliases are good to begin with but eventually you'll be using shell functions.

Note: Just because the alias **cp** works with two filenames as arguments, don't interpret that to mean that the alias accepts arguments. It's simply that the shell expands the alias before running the command line. Bash and Korn aliases don't use arguments, but C shell aliases do.

10.5 COMMAND HISTORY (bash and ksh)

A serious drawback of the Bourne shell is that a command has to be retyped to be reexecuted. Bash and Korn support a versatile **history** feature that treats a previous command as an **event** and associates it with an event number. Using this number, you can recall previous commands (even those executed in previous sessions), edit them if required and reexecute them. The shell may (depending on the shell used) also save all commands in a history file.

The **history** command displays the history list showing the event number of every previously executed command. A command is recalled by using this event number with a symbol like **!** or **r**. The maximum size and name of this file are determined by two shell-specific variables.

While Bash displays the complete history list with **history**, Korn lists the 16 commands most recently used, but we can easily find out the last five commands by using a numeric argument:

```
history 5           Bash
history -5          Korn
```

The output shows the event number and command associated with that number, and it could look like this:

```
35 set -o ignoreeof
36 exit
37 alias l='ls -l'
38 tar cvf /dev/fd0 *.doc
39 fc -l
40 history            Also includes command invoked to obtain list
```

By default, Bash stores all previous commands in $HOME/.bash_history ($HOME/.sh_history in Korn). When a command is entered and executed, it is appended to the list.

Knowing the event number may not be enough; you may need to repeat a previous command. Sometimes you may also have to edit it a bit before reexecuting it. Both Bash and Korn allow you to do that, and these features are taken up in the following sections.

10.5.1 Accessing Previous Commands by Event Numbers (! and r)

The **!** symbol (**r** in Korn) is used to repeat previous commands. For repeating the last command, you have to use this:

```
!!                  Repeats previous command—Bash
r                   Same—Korn
```

Just one or two characters, nothing could be simpler than that! You can repeat other commands using **!** or **r**, but with the event number as argument:

```
$ !38                                          Use r 38 in Korn
38 tar cvf /dev/fd0 *.c
```

The command line is displayed and executed. Working like this, you might execute a wrong command (like **rm**), so using the p (print) modifier you can display the command without executing it. However, this works only in Bash:

```
$ !38:p                                        Use fc -l 38 38 in Korn
38 tar cvf /dev/fd0 *.doc                       Copies files from disk to diskette
```

This **tar** command copies files between disk and diskette. You should make sure of what you are doing by using the :p modifier first. If the command you recalled had xvf instead of cvf as arguments, data would flow in the reverse direction—from diskette to disk *(15.10)*. But if the above command line is the one you want to run again, simply use **!!**.

Relative Addressing   If you don't know the event number but want to execute the command prior to the previous one, you can use a negative argument with **!** or **r**:

```
!-2                                            Bash—no space between ! and -
r -2                                           Korn
```

Tip: Programmers will find this form of relative addressing very useful for repeatedly editing and compiling programs. For instance, if you use the command **vi app1.c** and **cc app1.c** alternately, you need to explicitly invoke the commands only once. Subsequently, you can continue using **!-2 (r -2** in Korn) until the compilation generates no errors.

10.5.2 Executing Previous Commands by Context

You probably won't remember the event numbers of the commands except for the immediately preceding two or three, but you could at least remember that the command started with a specific letter or a string. If you know that the last command name *beginning* with v was the **vi** command, you can use **!** or **r** with either v or vi to repeat the last **vi** command:

```
!v                                             Repeats last command beginning with v—Bash
r v                                            Same—Korn
```

Like in the previous example discussed in the Tip, you can also use **!c** for compiling a C program and **!v** for editing (**r c** and **r v** in Korn); this is even simpler!

10.5.3 Substitution in Previous Commands

Often you need to execute a previous command but only after replacing a string in the command line with another. The same history symbols (**!** in Bash and **r** in Korn) allow you to do that by following the normal repeat command with a substitution instruction. This instruction takes on different forms in Bash and Korn.

Bash uses the **vi**-style **:s** command and the **/** as delimiter of the old and new patterns. Korn uses the form *old=new*. So if you want to repeat the previous **tar** command, but this time using the .bak instead of the .doc files, you have to replace doc with bak in this way:

```
!tar:s/doc/bak                          Bash—vi also uses :s for substitution
r tar doc=bak                           Korn
```

You can well guess that to perform a substitution on the immediately previous command, you only have to use **!!** or **r** with the substitution instruction. However, Bash offers an additional shortcut; it's the **^** (caret). Restore the original command line by replacing bak with doc in this way:

```
!!:s/bak/doc                            Bash—Substitution in previous command
^bak^doc                                Bash—Same; a shortcut
r bak=doc                               Korn
```

Note that this substitution is made only for the *first* occurrence in a line; two or more substitutions are not permitted in Korn. However, Bash permits global substitution also.

10.5.4 Using Last Argument to Previous Command ($_)

We often run several commands on the same file, and instead of specifying the filename every time, we can now use $_ as the abbreviated filename. This expression signifies the *last* argument to the previous command. For instance, we create a directory with **mkdir progs** and then change to it with **cd progs**. We can use $_ as a shorthand feature to represent the directory used by the previous command:

```
mkdir progs
cd $_                                   Changes directory to progs
```

To consider another example, if you have edited a shell script cronfind.sh with **vi**, you can execute this file by simply entering this:

```
$_                                      Executes cronfind.sh
```

What better way can you imagine of executing a shell or **perl** script that you just edited with **vi**! Bash has several other parameters that can access every argument to any previous command, but discussion on that is beyond the scope of this text. For details, look up this author's *Your UNIX: The Ultimate Guide* (Tata McGraw-Hill).

10.5.5 The History Variables

There are a few environment variables that influence the behavior of the history mechanism in Bash and Korn. First, the HISTFILE variable determines the filename that saves the history list. If it is not set, Bash and Korn use the following as the default history files in the home directory:

```
.bash_history                           Bash
.sh_history                             Korn
```

The history list is maintained in memory also. Bash uses two separate variables, HISTSIZE and HISTFILESIZE, for setting the size of the history list in memory and on disk. Korn uses only HISTSIZE for both purposes. Here are two examples:

```
HISTSIZE=500                            Bash and Korn
HISTFILESIZE=1000                       Bash only—determines size of disk file
```

With memory and disk space going cheap today, you should set these variables to large values so you can store commands of multiple login sessions.

10.6 IN-LINE COMMAND EDITING (bash and ksh)

Bash and Korn provide a "vi-like" capability of editing the command line, both of the current command and its predecessors in the history list. Before you are able to do that, you have to make the following setting:

```
set -o vi                          Use set +o vi to reverse this setting
```

You can switch off either mode by using the +o option instead. The editing features of the **vi** editor are built into the Bash and Korn shells, and this setting enables their use for **in-line editing**. Since you are familiar with the editing commands used in **vi**, you would be delighted to be able to use them without specifically invoking **vi**.

10.6.1 Editing a Command Line

In **vi** jargon, when you enter a command at the shell prompt, you are always in the Input Mode, i.e., the mode where every key pressed is entered as text. With in-line editing enabled, if you notice a mistake in the current command line, you need no longer erase all previous text to take the cursor to that point. All you have to do is to press *[Esc]*. This key, you'll recall, takes you to the Command Mode. After you have done that, you can use all **vi** navigation commands to move across a line, using a repeat factor too if necessary and relevant.

For instance, you can invoke the commands used to enter the Input Mode, like **i**, **a**, **A**, etc. You can also delete a character with **x** and three characters with **3x**. You can even put this word elsewhere with **p** or **P**! Once all changes are made, the command can be executed by hitting *[Enter]*.

To edit previous commands, recall that the **k** command in **vi** takes the cursor one line up. However, when the same command is used for in-line editing, the previous command is presented. And since the repeat factor applies here too, you can also use **5k** to present the fifth-most recent command (barring the present). If that's not the command you are looking for, use **j** to show the next line. Once you have located the line, you can navigate along it and make the necessary changes.

Tip: To recall a previous command, first press *[Esc]* and then **k** as many times as required until you locate the command. If you overshoot, use **j** until you get the line you are looking for.

10.6.2 Searching History List for Previous Commands

You can use **vi**'s search techniques to recall previous commands from the history list. Even though the search is in the reverse direction, you'll have to use the */pattern* sequence:

```
/cvf[Enter]                        Locates last occurrence of string cvf
```

You can repeat the search by pressing **n** repeatedly. If you overshoot, come back with **N**. Edit the line and run it again. Now, isn't this something!

Tip: A proficient **vi** user will easily exploit these editing facilities to run a command with selected arguments of previous commands. If you remember having executed the command **vi foo1 foo2 foo3 foo4**, you can easily run the **gzip** command with some or all of these arguments. Press *[Esc]*, search for the command with **/vi**, change vi to gzip with **2s**, and hit *[Enter]*. If you need to delete the last argument, move to the fourth argument with **4w** and press **d$**. It's as simple as that!

10.7 MISCELLANEOUS FEATURES (bash and ksh)

Before moving on to the shell's initialization scripts, let's consider a few features available in Bash and Korn which you'll find quite useful. Two of them use the shell's **set** statement. We'll also consider the significance of the ~ (tilde) in these shells.

10.7.1 Using set -o

The **set** statement by default displays the variables in the current shell *(10.2)*, but in Bash and Korn, it can make several environment settings with the -o option. This option, followed by a keyword, takes care of some of the common hazards faced by users, like overwriting files and accidental logging out.

File Overwriting (noclobber) The shell's > symbol overwrites (clobbers) an existing file, and to prevent such accidental overwriting, you have to use the noclobber argument in this way:

```
set -o noclobber                                    No more overwriting files with >
```

This means that if you redirect output to an existing file foo, the shell will retort with a message:

```
bash: foo: cannot overwrite existing file          Bash
ksh: foo: file already exists                       Korn
```

To override this protection feature, use the | after the >:

```
head -n 5 emp.lst >| foo
```

Accidental Logging Out (ignoreeof) Users often inadvertently press *[Ctrl-d]* with intent to terminate standard input, but end up logging out of the system. The ignoreeof keyword offers protection from accidental logging out:

```
set -o ignoreeof                                    [Ctrl-d] won't log you out
```

Now, when you use *[Ctrl-d]* to terminate your session, the shell typically responds like this:

```
Use 'exit' to terminate this shell
```

You now have to use the **exit** command to take you out of the session; *[Ctrl-d]* won't do any more (unless executed repeatedly!).

A **set** option is turned off with **set +o** *keyword*. To reverse the noclobber feature, use **set +o noclobber**. The complete list of **set**'s special options is obtained by using **set -o** or **set +o** without any additional arguments.

10.7.2 Tilde Substitution

The ~ acts as a shorthand representation of the home directory. When the ~ is followed by a login name, the shell understands the entire argument as the absolute pathname of the login directory. Thus, when the shell encounters the following command line

```
cd ~sharma                              Effectively becomes $HOME/sharma
```

it switches to sharma's home directory. If the value of $HOME is /home/sharma/tulec1, this is the directory where **cd ~sharma** switches to.

Interestingly, the ~ when used by itself or when immediately followed by a /, refers to the home directory of the user using it. If you have logged in as juliet, you can access the html directory under your home directory by using **cd ~/html**. That's why we often find a configuration file like .profile referred to both as $HOME/.profile and ~/.profile. The former works in the Bourne shell also but not the latter.

You can also toggle between the directory you switched to most recently and your current directory. This is done with the ~- symbols (or simply -, a hyphen). For instance, either of the commands

```
cd ~-                                   Change to your previous directory
cd -                                    Same
```

changes your current working directory to the one you used most recently. Here's how you use the **cd** command:

```
[/home/image] cd /bin                   Changes to /bin from /home/image
[/bin] cd -                             Reverts to /home/image
/home/image                             Shell displays this
[/home/image] _                         Current directory shown by PS1
```

This toggling effect is like the button many TV remote units have to let you alternate between the current and last visited channels.

10.8 THE INITIALIZATION SCRIPTS

We have assigned values to many of the environment variables, defined aliases and used **set** options. These settings are applicable only for the session; they revert to their default values when the user logs out. To make these settings permanent, you'll have to place them in certain startup scripts.

Every shell uses at least one startup script in the user's home directory—much like the AUTOEXEC.BAT file of DOS. This script is executed when the user logs in. Some shells also make use of a separate file that is run before logging out. Look in your home directory with **ls -a** and you'll find one or more of these files:

- .profile (Bourne shell)
- .profile and .kshrc (Korn Shell)
- .bash_profile (or .profile or .bash_login) and .bashrc (Bash)

Bash has an elaborate startup system, but the system is not as complex as it may appear. We have two types of files here—the "profiles" and "rc" files. The profiles are executed only once, upon login. The rc files are designed to be executed every time a separate shell is created. Let's now examine these files and consider the entries that we can place in them.

10.8.1 The Profile (.profile and .bash_profile)

The Bourne family uses .profile as the login script. As an added feature, the profile used by Bash can have one of three names—.bash_profile, .profile and .bash_login. Bash looks for one of these files in the sequence specified and identifies the one it spots first as its profile.

Issue the **ls -a** command and see whether you can locate one of these files in your home directory. This login script should be added to your home directory at the time of user creation, but you can create one even if it's not there. It is really a shell script that is executed by the shell when one logs on to the system. These "profiles" can be quite large depending on users' requirements, but an abridged one should do for initial comprehension:

```
$ cat .profile
# User $HOME/.profile - commands executed at login time

MAIL=/var/mail/$LOGNAME                           # mailbox location
PATH=$PATH:$HOME/bin:/usr/ucb:.
PS1='$ '
PS2=>
TERM=vt100
MOZILLA_HOME=/opt/netscape ; export MOZILLA_HOME
stty stop ^S intr ^C erase ^?
echo "Today's date is `date`"
```

The profile contains commands that are meant to be executed only *once* in a session. Some of the system variables have been assigned in this script. The later statements show that the file has been edited to taste. The PATH has been modified to contain three more directories. Some **stty** settings have also been made here. All of these commands and variables are understood by the Bourne shell, so this script will work in all shells of the Bourne family.

The .profile lets you customize your operating environment to suit your requirements. This environment remains in effect throughout the login session. Every time you make changes to this file, you should either log out and log in again or use a special command (called dot) to execute the file:

. .profile   *Used by the Bourne family*

Additionally, Bash offers the use of the C shell-styled **source** command, so you can also use **source .profile**. Both **source** and . execute a script in a special way—without creating a separate process (like **cd**). That's why there are certain things you can do with this file that are difficult or impossible to do otherwise.

Note: The `.profile` must be located in your home directory and it is executed after `/etc/profile`, the universal profile for all users. Universal environment settings are kept by the administrator in `/etc/profile` so they are available to all users.

10.8.2 The rc File (bash and ksh)

There's no rc file in Bourne, but Bash and Korn use one. This file is defined by an environment variable (BASH_ENV in Bash and ENV in Korn), which should be specified in the profile (`.profile` or `.bash_profile`). You should have one of these settings in your profile depending on the shell you use:

```
export BASH_ENV=$HOME/.bashrc          Bash; can also use BASH_ENV=~/.bashrc
export ENV=$HOME/.kshrc                Korn; can also use ENV=~/.kshrc
```

This file is executed every time a second shell is called up (when running a shell script, for instance). However, there's a little difference in the way Bash and Korn use their rc file. Korn automatically executes `.kshrc` during login if ENV is defined in the way shown above. However, the above Bash definition merely ensures that a sub-shell executes this file. If the login shell also has to execute this file, then a separate statement must be added in the profile:

```
. ~/.bashrc                            Bash; can also use source ~/.bashrc
```

The environment file should be used to hold only Bash- or Korn-specific features. History list settings (like HISTSIZE and HISTFILE), command editing settings (like **set -o vi**) and alias definitions should all be made in the environment file. This is a cleaner arrangement because should you decide to change your shell any time later, you won't be saddled with a `.profile` ridden with irrelevant entries. Here are some sample entries:

```
alias cp="cp -i"
alias rm="rm -i"
set -o noclobber
set -o vi
set -o ignoreeof
```

This rc file will be executed after the profile. However, if the BASH_ENV or ENV variable isn't set, the shell executes only the profile.

10.9 CONCLUSION

In this chapter, we had a look at the environment-related features of the shells, and found weaknesses in the Bourne shell. Knowledge of Bash and Korn only supplements your knowledge of Bourne and doesn't take anything away. It's always advisable to use Bash or Korn as your default login shell. If you are convinced, ask your system administrator to set it that way. You are assured of a fruitful and rewarding experience. This experience will include the shell programming language and there are two chapters that examine this language. We are not done with the shell yet.

> ### WRAP UP
>
> The UNIX shell sets the user's environment and can be tailored to behave in the way you want. Bash and Korn are feature-rich and recommended for use.
>
> *Environment variables* are available in the login shell and all its child processes. You can set the command search path (PATH), the home directory (HOME), terminal (TERM) and prompts (PS1 and PS2). You can also set the location of your mailbox (MAIL) and frequency of checking it (MAILCHECK).
>
> Bash and Korn offer *aliases* that let you abbreviate any command sequence to a string. Aliases are also useful in redefining existing commands to always run with specific options.
>
> These shells also offer a *history* feature that lets you recall, edit and reexecute previous commands without retyping them. Previous commands can be accessed by their *event number* or context, and substitution can be performed on them.
>
> These shells also offer an *in-line editing* facility that lets us edit a previous command line with **vi**-like commands.
>
> Using **set -o** in Bash and Korn, you can protect your files from accidental overwriting (noclobber) and accidental logout (ignoreeof).
>
> *Tilde substitution* lets you access a file foo in the home directory with ~/foo, and use a shortcut like **cd ~henry** to switch to henry's home directory.
>
> The shell executes a "profile" on login (~/.profile or ~/.bash_profile). It also executes an "rc" file when a sub-shell is created. These files are executed without creating a process using the **.** or **source** commands. Commands to be executed only once are placed in the profile. Aliases, history settings and **set -o** commands should be kept in the rc file.

Test Your Understanding

10.1 How is the home directory set—by the HOME variable or /etc/passwd?

10.2 If TERM has the value vt220, where will you expect to find its control file?

10.3 How will you add the parent directory to your existing PATH?

10.4 Write a Korn or Bash alias to show *only* the hidden files of the current directory.

10.5 How will you repeat the last command in (i) Korn, (ii) Bash?

10.6 You have just used the command **tar -cvf /dev/fd0 *.sh**. How will you repeat the command to use the .pl files this time in (i) Korn, (ii) Bash?

10.7 To enable **vi**-like editing of the command line, what setting will you make first?

10.8 Suppose you have just viewed a file with **cat calc_km.java**. How will you now display it with **more** if you are using the Korn or Bash shells?

10.9 You issued the command **$_** and got the message foo: Permission denied. What does the message indicate?

10.10 You don't know the absolute pathname of the home directory of henry. How will you "cd" to it in the Bash and Korn shells?

10.11 You repeatedly have to toggle between /usr/include and /usr/lib. How do you use a shortcut to do that repeatedly?

10.12 There is a file profile (no dot) in /etc. When is this file executed?

10.13 If you have the files .bash_profile and .profile in your home directory, will Bash read them both on login?

10.14 A shell script also runs the login file. True or False?

Flex Your Brain

10.1 What is the difference between an *interactive* and *noninteractive* shell? Which features of the shell have significance only in an interactive shell?

10.2 Why are all environment variables represented in a fixed format regardless of the shell you use?

10.3 Which two environment variables are set by reading /etc/passwd?

10.4 Explain the significance of the MAIL and MAILCHECK variables. How do you come to know that mail has arrived?

10.5 Mention the steps needed to (i) change the prompt to look like this: [jupiter-henry ~/project8] (user—henry, machine name—*jupiter* and current directory—project8) (ii) revert to your original prompt.

10.6 Create an alias named **rm** that always deletes files recursively. How can you execute the original **rm** command without unaliasing it?

10.7 How can you prevent your files from being overwritten using the redirection symbols in Korn and Bash? How will you overwrite these files?

10.8 What is the significance of these commands in Bash? (i) **!50** (ii) **!-2:p** (iii) **!!** (iv) **^doc^bak**. What are their equivalents in Korn?

10.9 In the Korn shell, the command **r ca** runs from the history list (i) the last command having ca embedded. (ii) the first command beginning with ca (iii) the last command beginning with ca. (iv) all commands beginning with ca.

10.10 Can you condense these sequences? (i) **cp *.c c_progs ; cd c_progs** (ii) **cmp foo foo.bak ; cmp foo foo.doc**

10.11 Using the history facility, how can you repeatedly execute this sequence in (i) Korn, (ii) Bash? **vi signal.c; cc signal.c**

10.12 You want to recall all the **tar** commands that you executed for viewing. How can you see them in turn by pressing a single key repeatedly in Korn and Bash?

10.13 Explain the significance of these commands: (i) **cd ~henry** (ii) **cd ~/henry** (iii) **cd ~-** (iv) **cd -**

10.14 Why do all shells use a profile as well as an rc file? What type of entries do you place in each?

10.15 How can you make all aliases placed in ~/.alias available in all sub-shells? Will the aliases be available in a shell script in (i) Korn, (ii) Bash?

10.16 Name two ways of making the changes made to .profile available in the environment.

More File Attributes

Apart from permissions and ownership, a UNIX file has several other attributes, and in this chapter, we look at most of the remaining ones. A file also has properties related to its time stamps and links. It's important to know how these attributes are interpreted when applied to a directory or a device. We need to revisit the **ls** command and see some of its other options that reveal these attributes. We'll also discuss **find**—one of the most versatile attribute-handling tools of the UNIX system.

This chapter also introduces the concept of a *file system*. It also looks at the *inode*, the lookup table that contains almost all file attributes. Though a detailed treatment of file systems is taken up later, knowledge of its basics is essential to our understanding of the significance of some of the file attributes. Moreover, some administration tools act and report on individual file systems separately.

WHAT YOU WILL LEARN

- The concept of the *file system* and how multiple file systems are seen as one.
- The use of the *inode* to store file attributes and **ls** to display the inode number.
- Use **ln** to create a *hard link* by providing a file with a different name.
- The limitations of hard links and how they are overcome by *symbolic links*.
- The concept of the *user mask* and how **umask** changes the default file and directory permissions.
- How to display the listing in order of a file's time stamps.
- Use **touch** to change a file's modification and access times.

TOPICS OF SPECIAL INTEREST

- Three possible situations where hard links can be very useful.
- The significance of directory permissions and how they ultimately impact a file's access rights.
- The elaborate syntax used by **find** to match one or more file attributes, and take action on selected files.
- How It Works: A graphic that shows how **ln** and **rm** affect the inode and directory.

11.1 FILE SYSTEMS AND INODES

We now need to have some idea of the way files are organized in a UNIX system. So far, we have been referring to the UNIX file hierachy as a "file system" as if all files and directories are held together in one big superstructure. That is seldom the case, and never so in large systems. The hard disk is split into distinct **partitions** (or *slices*), with a separate file system in each partition (or slice).

Every **file system** has a directory structure headed by root. If you have three file systems on one hard disk, then they will have three separate root directories. When the system is up, we see only a *single* file system with a single root directory.

Of these multiple file systems, one of them is considered to be the main one, and contains most of the essential files of the UNIX system. This is the **root file system**, which is more equal than others in at least one respect; its root directory is also the root directory of the combined UNIX system. At the time of booting, all secondary file systems *mount* (attach) themselves to the main file system, creating the illusion of a single file system to the user.

Every file is associated with a table that contains all that you could possibly need to know about a file—except its name and contents. This table is called the **inode** (shortened from index node) and is accessed by the **inode number**. The inode contains the following attributes of a file:

- File type (regular, directory, device, etc.).
- File permissions (the nine permissions and three more).
- Number of links (the number of aliases the file has).
- The UID of the owner.
- The GID of the group owner.
- File size in bytes.
- Date and time of last modification.
- Date and time of last access.
- Date and time of last change of the inode.
- An array of pointers that keep track of all disk blocks used by the file.

Observe that *neither the name of the file nor the inode number is stored in the inode*. It's the directory that stores the inode number along with the filename. When you use a command with a filename as argument, the kernel first locates the inode number of the file from the directory and then reads the inode to fetch data relevant to the file.

Every file system has a separate portion set aside for storing inodes, where they are laid out in a contiguous manner. This area is accessible only to the kernel. The inode number is actually the *position* of the inode in this area. The kernel can locate the inode number of any file using simple arithmetic. Since a UNIX machine usually comprises multiple file systems, you can conclude that the inode number for a file is unique in a *single* file system.

The **ls** command reads the inode to fetch a file's attributes, and it can list most of them using suitable options. One of them is the **-i** (inode) option that tells you the **inode** number of a file:

```
$ ls -il tulec05
9059 -rw-r--r--    1 kumar    metal           51813 Jan 31 11:15 tulec05
```

The file tulec05 has the inode number 9059. No other file *in the same file system* can have this number unless the file is removed. When that happens, the kernel will allocate this inode number to a new file.

Note: The inode contains all attributes of a file except the filename. The filename is stored in the directory housing the file. The inode number is also not stored in the inode, but the kernel can locate any inode by its position since its size is fixed.

HOW IT WORKS: How cat and ls Work

When you run **cat foo**, the kernel first locates the inode number of foo from the current directory. It then reads the inode for foo to fetch the file size and addresses of the disk blocks that contain the file's data. It then goes to each block and reads the data until the the number of characters displayed is equal to the file size.

When you execute **ls -l progs** where progs is a directory, the kernel looks up the directory progs and reads all entries. For every entry, the kernel looks up the inode to fetch the file's attributes.

11.2 HARD LINKS

Why is the filename not stored in the node? So that a file can have multiple filenames. When that happens, we say the file has more than one **link**. We can then access the file by any of its links. All names provided to a single file have one thing in common; they all have the same inode number.

The link count is displayed in the second column of the listing. This count is normally 1 (as shown in the previous listing), but the following files have two links:

```
-rwxr-xr--    2 kumar    metal           163 Jul 13 21:36 backup.sh
-rwxr-xr--    2 kumar    metal           163 Jul 13 21:36 restore.sh
```

All attributes seem to be identical, but the "files" could still be copies (which have different inode numbers). It's the link count that seems to suggest that the "files" are linked to each other. But this can only be confirmed by using the -i option to **ls**:

```
$ ls -li backup.sh restore.sh
 478274 -rwxr-xr--    2 kumar    metal           163 Jul 13 21:36 backup.sh
 478274 -rwxr-xr--    2 kumar    metal           163 Jul 13 21:36 restore.sh
```

Both "files" indeed have the same inode number, so there's actually only one file with a single copy on disk. We can't really refer to them as two "files", but only as two "filenames". This file simply has two aliases; changes made in one alias (link) are automatically available in the others. There are two entries for this file in the directory, both having the same inode number.

11.2.1 1n: Creating Hard Links

A file is linked with the **1n** (link) command, which takes two filenames as arguments. The command can create both a *hard* and a *soft* link (discussed later) and has a syntax similar to the one used by **cp**. The following command (hard) links emp.1st with employee:

```
ln emp.1st employee                          employee must not exist
```

The -i option to **1s** shows that they have the same inode number, meaning that they are actually one and the same file:

```
$ ls -li emp.1st employee
29518 -rwxr-xr-x   2 kumar     metal         915 May  4 09:58 emp.1st
29518 -rwxr-xr-x   2 kumar     metal         915 May  4 09:58 employee
```

The link count, which is normally one for unlinked files, is shown to be two. You can link a third filename, emp.dat, and increase the number of links to three:

```
$ ln employee emp.dat ; ls -l emp*
29518 -rwxr-xr-x   3 kumar     metal         915 May  4 09:58 emp.dat
29518 -rwxr-xr-x   3 kumar     metal         915 May  4 09:58 emp.1st
29518 -rwxr-xr-x   3 kumar     metal         915 May  4 09:58 employee
```

You can link multiple files (i.e., create a link for each), but then the destination filename must be a directory. Here's how you create links for all the chapters of this text in the directory project8_dir:

```
ln chap?? project8_dir                       project8_dir is a directory
```

If chap?? matches 25 files, there will be 25 linked filenames in project8_dir, i.e., there will be 25 entries in that directory. The **rm** command removes a file by deleting its directory entry, so we expect the same command to remove a link also:

```
$ rm emp.dat ; ls -l emp.1st employee
-rwxr-xr-x   2 kumar     metal         915 May  4 09:58 emp.1st
-rwxr-xr-x   2 kumar     metal         915 May  4 09:58 employee
```

The link count has come down to two. Another **rm** will further bring it down to one. A file is considered to be completely removed from the system when its link count drops to zero.

Tip: **1n** returns an error when the destination file exists. Use the -f option to force the removal of the existing link before creation of the new one.

11.2.2 Where to Use Hard Links

Links are an interesting feature of the file system, but where does one use them? We can think of three situations straightaway:

1. Let's consider that you have written a number of programs that read a file foo.txt in $HOME/input_files. Later, you reorganized your directory structure and moved foo.txt to $HOME/data instead. What happens to all the programs that look for foo.txt at its original location? Simple, just link foo.txt to the directory input_files:

HOW IT WORKS: ln and rm Affect the Directory and Inode

The role of **rm** and **ln** are complementary which is evident from the names of their corresponding system calls—**link** and **unlink**. The **ln** command adds an entry in the directory and also increases the link count in the inode by one. The **rm** command simply reverses the action of **ln**. The effect they have on the inode and directory is depicted in Fig. 11.1.

Directory	
Filename	*Inode Number*
.	386444
..	417585
date.sh	254414
Inode for date.sh	
Link Count = 1	

Directory	
Filename	*Inode Number*
.	386444
..	417585
date.sh	254414
who.sh	254414
Inode for date.sh	
Link Count = 2	

Directory	
Filename	*Inode Number*
.	386444
..	417585
date.sh	254414
Inode for date.sh	
Link Count = 1	

```
ln date.sh who.sh                    rm who.sh
```

Fig. 11.1 Effect of **ln** and **rm** on Directory and Inode

```
ln data/foo.txt input_files                 Creates link in directory input_files
```

With this link available, your existing programs will continue to find foo.txt in the input_files directory. It's more convenient to do this that modify all programs to point to the new path.

2. Links provide some protection against accidental deletion, especially when they exist in different directories. Referring to the previous application, even though there's only a single file foo.txt on disk, you have effectively made a backup of this file. If you inadvertently delete input_files/foo.txt, one link will still be available in data/foo.txt; your file is not gone yet.

3. Because of links, we don't need to maintain two programs as two separate disk files if there is very little difference between them. A file's name is available to a C program (as argv[0]) and to a shell script (as $0). A single file with two links can have its program logic make it behave in two different ways depending on the name by which it is called. There's a shell script using this feature in Section 14.10.

Many UNIX commands are linked. Refer to Section 5.18, where we posed the question whether **gzip** and **gunzip** were two separate files. This question can now easily be answered by looking at their inode numbers:

```
13975 -r-xr-xr-x  3 root   bin    60916 Jan  5 2000 gunzip
13975 -r-xr-xr-x  3 root   bin    60916 Jan  5 2000 gzip
```

They are, in fact, one and the same file. The listing shows the existence of a third link as well, but how does one locate it? Doing an **ls -li** and then looking for entries with the same inode number isn't a practical approach. It may not also work since links could be spread across multiple directories. For this task, we need the **find** command which is discussed at the end of this chapter.

11.3 SYMBOLIC LINKS AND ln

We have seen how links let us have multiple names for a file. These links are often called **hard links**, and have two limitations:

- You can't have two linked filenames in two file systems. In other words, you can't link a filename in the /usr file system to another in the /home file system.
- You can't link a directory even within the same file system.

This serious limitation was overcome when **symbolic links** made their entry. Until now, we have divided files into three categories (ordinary, directory and device). The symbolic link is the fourth file type considered in this text. Unlike the hard link, a symbolic link doesn't have the file's contents, but simply provides the pathname of the file that actually has the contents. Being more flexible, a symbolic link is also known as a **soft link**. Windows shortcuts are more like symbolic links.

The **ln** command creates symbolic links also, except that you have to use the -s option. This time the listing tells you a different story:

```
$ ln -s note note.sym
$ ls -li note note.sym
9948 -rw-r--r--   1 kumar    group          80 Feb 16 14:52 note
9952 lrwxrwxrwx   1 kumar    group           4 Feb 16 15:07 note.sym -> note
```

You can identify symbolic links by the character l (el) seen in the permissions field. The pointer notation -> note suggests that note.sym contains the pathname for the filename note. It's note, and not note.sym, that actually contains the data. When you use **cat note.sym**, you don't actually open the symbolic link, note.sym, but the file the link points to. Observe that the size of the symbolic link is 4; this is the length of the pathname it contains (note).

It's important you realize that this time we indeed have two "files", and they are not identical. Removing note.sym won't affect us much because we can easily recreate the link. But if we remove note, we would lose the file containing the data. In that case, note.sym would point to a nonexistent file and become a *dangling* symbolic link.

Symbolic links can also be used with relative pathnames. Unlike hard links, they can also span multiple file systems and also link directories. If you have to link *all* filenames in a directory to another directory, it makes sense to simply link the directories. Like other files, a symbolic link has a separate directory entry with its own inode number. This means that **rm** can remove a symbolic link even if its points to a directory (or even a device).

LINUX: A symbolic link has an inode number separate from the file that it points to. In most cases, the pathname is stored in the symbolic link and occupies space on disk. However, Linux uses a *fast symbolic link* which stores the pathname in the inode itself provided it doesn't exceed 60 characters.

11.4 THE DIRECTORY

A directory has its own permissions, owners and links. However, the significance of the file attributes change a great deal when applied to a directory. For example, the size of a directory is in no way related to the size of files that exist in the directory, but rather to the *number* of files housed by it. The higher the number, the larger is the directory.

Permissions too acquire a different meaning when the term is applied to a directory. Before we take up directory permissions, let's see what its default permissions are on this system:

```
$ ls -l -d progs
drwxr-xr-x   2 kumar      metal        320 May  9 09:57 progs
```

The default permissions are different from those of ordinary files. The user has all permissions, and group and others have read and execute permissions only. The permissions of a directory also impact the security of its files. To understand how that can happen, we must know what permissions for a directory really mean.

11.4.1 Read Permission

Read permission for a directory means that the *list* of filenames stored in that directory is accessible. Since **ls** reads the directory to display filenames, if a directory's read permission is removed, **ls** won't work. Consider removing the read permission first from the directory progs:

```
$ ls -ld progs
drwxr-xr-x   2 kumar      metal        128 Jun 18 22:41 progs
$ chmod -r progs ; ls progs
progs: Permission denied
total 2
```

Being unreadable, the progs directory couldn't be accessed by **ls**, and hence the error message. *However, this doesn't prevent you from reading the files separately if you know their names.*

11.4.2 Write Permission

Be aware that you can't write to a directory file; only the kernel can do that. If that were possible, any user could destroy the integrity of the file system. Write permission for a directory implies that you are permitted to create or remove files in it (that would make the kernel modify the directory entries). To try that out, restore the read permission and remove the write permission from the directory before you try to copy a file to it:

```
$ chmod 555 progs ; ls -ld progs
dr-xr-xr-x   2 kumar      metal        128 Jun 18 22:41 progs
$ cp emp.1st progs
cp: cannot create progs/emp.1st: Permission denied
```

The directory doesn't have write permission; you can't create, copy or delete a file in it. But can you modify its existing files? This question often confuses beginners, and if you are confused too, then follow this line of reasoning:

- The write permission for a directory determines whether you can create or remove files in it because these actions modify the directory.
- Whether you can modify a file depends solely on whether the file itself has write permission. Changing a file doesn't in any way modify its directory entry.

Note: The term "write-protected" has a limited meaning in the UNIX file system. A write-protected file can't be written, but it can be removed if the directory has write permission.

11.4.3 Execute Permission

Executing a directory just doesn't make any sense, so what does its execute privilege mean? It only means that a user can "pass through" the directory in searching for subdirectories. When you use a pathname with any command

```
cat /home/kumar/progs/emp.sh
```

you need to have execute permission for each of the directories involved in the complete pathname. The directory home contains the entry for kumar, and the directory kumar contains the entry for progs, and so forth. If a single directory in this pathname doesn't have execute permission, then it can't be searched for the name of the next directory. That's why the execute privilege of a directory is often referred to as the *search* permission.

A directory has to be searched for the next directory, so the **cd** command won't work if the search permission for the directory is turned off:

```
$ chmod 666 progs ; ls -ld progs
drw-rw-rw-   2 kumar   metal        128 Jun 18 22:41 progs
$ cd progs
bash: cd: progs: Permission denied
```

Like for regular files, directory permissions are extremely important because system security is heavily dependent upon them. If you tamper with the permissions of your directories, make sure you set them correctly. If you don't, then be assured that an intelligent user could make life miserable for you!

Let's now add a qualifier to the two bulleted observations made regarding write permission for a directory. To be able to create or remove files, write permission for the directory is not enough; the directory must have search (execute) permission as well.

Caution: Danger arises when you mistakenly assign the permissions 775 or 777 to a directory. In the present scenario, 775 allows any user of the metal group to create or remove files in the directory. 777 extends this facility to the world. As a rule, you should never make directories group- or world-writable unless you have definite reasons to do so.

11.5 umask: DEFAULT FILE AND DIRECTORY PERMISSIONS

When you create files and directories, the permissions assigned to them depend on the system's default setting. The UNIX system has the following default permissions for all files and directories:

- rw-rw-rw- (octal 666) for regular files.
- rwxrwxrwx (octal 777) for directories.

However, you don't see these permissions when you create a file or directory. Actually, this default is transformed by subtracting the **user mask** from it to remove one or more permissions. To understand what this means, let's evaluate the current value of the mask by using **umask** without arguments:

```
$ umask
022
```

This is an octal number which has to be subtracted from the system default to obtain the *actual* default. This becomes 644 (666 - 022) for ordinary files and 755 (777 - 022) for directories. When you create a file on this system, it will have the permissions rw-r--r--.

umask is a shell built-in command though it also exists as an external command. A user can also use this command to set a new default. Here's an extreme setting:

```
umask 000                                          All read-write permissions on
```

A umask value of 000 means that you haven't subtracted anything, and this could be dangerous. The system's default then applies (666 for files and 777 for directories). All files and directories are then writable by all; nothing could be worse than that! However, a mask value of 666 or 777 doesn't make much sense either; you'll then be creating files and directories with no permissions.

The important thing to remember is that, no one—not even the administrator—can use **umask** to turn on permissions not specified in the systemwide default settings. However, you can always use **chmod** as and when required. The systemwide umask setting is placed in one of the machine's startup scripts, and is automatically made available to all users.

11.6 MODIFICATION AND ACCESS TIMES

A UNIX file has three time stamps associated with it. In this section, we'll be discussing just two of them (the first two):

• Time of last file modification	*Shown by* ls -l
• Time of last access	*Shown by* ls -lu
• Time of last inode modification	*Shown by* ls -lc

Whenever you write to a file, the time of last modification is updated in the file's inode. A directory can be modified by changing its entries—by creating, removing and renaming files in the directory. Note that changing a file's contents only changes its last modification time but not that of its directory. **ls -l** displays the last modification time.

A file also has an access time, i.e., the last time someone read, wrote or executed the file. This time is distinctly different from the modification time that gets set only when the contents of the file are changed. For a directory, the access time is changed by a read operation only; creating or removing a file or doing a "cd" to a directory doesn't change its access time. The access time is displayed when **ls -l** is combined with the **-u** option.

Even though **ls -l** and **ls -lu** show the time of last modification and access, respectively, the sort order remains standard, i.e. ASCII. However, when you add the **-t** option to **-l** or **-lu**, the files are actually displayed in *order* of the respective time stamps:

ls -lt	Displays listing in order of their modification time
ls -lut	Displays listing in order of their access time

Knowledge of a file's modification and access times is extremely important for the system administrator. Many of the tools used by him look at these time stamps to decide whether a particular file will participate in a backup or not. A file is often incorrectly stamped when extracting it (using an option) from a backup with a file restoration utility (like **tar** or **cpio**). If that has happened to you, you can use **touch** to reset the times to certain convenient values without actually modifying or accessing the file. **touch** is discussed next.

11.6.1 touch: Changing the Time Stamps

As has just been discussed, you may sometimes need to set the modification and access times to predefined values. The **touch** command changes these times, and is used in the following manner:

    touch options expression filename(s)

When **touch** is used without *options* or *expression*, both times are set to the current time. The file is created if it doesn't exist:

    touch emp.lst   Creates file if it doesn't exist

When **touch** is used without options but with *expression*, it changes both times. The *expression* consists of an eight-digit number using the format *MMDDhhmm* (month, day, hour and minute). Optionally, you can suffix a two- or four-digit year string:

```
$ touch 03161430 emp.lst ; ls -l emp.lst
-rw-r--r--   1 kumar    metal          870 Mar 16 14:30 emp.lst
$ ls -lu emp.lst
-rw-r--r--   1 kumar    metal          870 Mar 16 14:30 emp.lst
```

It's also possible to change the two times individually. The -m and -a options change the modification and access times, respectively:

```
$ touch -m 02281030 emp.lst ; ls -l emp.lst
-rw-r--r--   1 kumar    metal          870 Feb 28 10:30 emp.lst
$ touch -a 01261650 emp.lst ; ls -lu emp.lst
-rw-r--r--   1 kumar    metal          870 Jan 26 16:50 emp.lst
```

The system administrator often uses **touch** to "touch up" these times so a file may be included in or excluded from an *incremental backup* (that backs up only changed files). The **find** command can then be used to locate files that have changed or have been accessed after the time set by **touch**. **find** is the last command we discuss in this chapter and is taken up next.

11.7 find: LOCATING FILES

find is one of the power tools of the UNIX system. It *recursively* examines a directory tree to look for files matching some criteria, and then takes some action on the selected files. It has a difficult command line, and if you have ever wondered why UNIX is hated by many, then you should look up the cryptic **find** documentation. However, **find** is easily tamed if you break up its arguments into three components:

find *path_list selection_criteria action*

This is how **find** operates:

- First, it recursively examines all files in the directories specified in *path_list*.
- It then matches each file for one or more *selection_criteria*.
- Finally, it takes some *action* on those selected files.

The *path_list* comprises one or more subdirectories separated by whitespace. There can also be a host of *selection_criteria* that you can use to match a file, and multiple *actions* to dispose of the file. This makes the command difficult to use initially, but it is a program that every user must master since it lets her make file selection under practically any condition.

As our first example, let's use **find** to locate all files named a.out (the executable file generated by the C compiler):

```
$ find / -name a.out -print
/home/kumar/scripts/a.out
/home/tiwary/scripts/reports/a.out
/home/sharma/a.out
```

The path list (/) indicates that the search should start from the root directory. Each file in the list is then matched against the selection criteria (-name a.out), which always consists of an expression in the form -*operator argument*. If the expression matches the file (i.e., the file has the name a.out), the file is selected. The third section specifies the action (-print) to be taken on the files; in this case, a simple display on the terminal. All **find** operators start with a -, and the *path_list* can never contain one.

LINUX: **find** in UNIX displays the file list only if the -print operator is used. However, Linux doesn't need this option; it prints by default. Linux also doesn't need the path list; it uses the current directory by default. Linux even prints the entire file list when used without any options whatsoever! This behavior is not required by POSIX.

You can also use relative names (like the .) in the path list, and **find** will then output a list of relative pathnames. When **find** is used to match a group of filenames with a wild-card pattern, the pattern should be quoted to prevent the shell from looking at it:

```
find . -name "*.c" -print                    All files with extension .c
find . -name '[A-Z]*' -print                 Single quotes will also do
```

The first command looks for all C program source files in the current directory tree. The second one searches for all files whose names begin with an uppercase letter. You must not forget to use the -print option because without it, **find** on UNIX systems will look for files all right but won't print the list.

-name is not the only operator used in framing the selection criteria; there are many others (Table 11.1). The actual list is much longer, and takes into account practically every file attribute. Let's now take a look at some of the important ones. We'll consider the selection criteria first, and then the possible actions we can take on the selected files.

11.7.1 Selection Criteria

Locating a File by Inode Number (-inum)   Refer to Section 11.2.2, where we found that **gzip** has three links and **gunzip** was one of them. **find** allows us to locate files by their inode number. Use the -inum option to find all filenames that have the same inode number:

```
$ find / -inum 13975 -print                  Inode number obtained from Section 11.2.2
find: cannot read dir /usr/lost+found: Permission denied
/usr/bin/gzip
/usr/bin/gunzip
/usr/bin/gzcat                               "Cats" a compressed file
```

Now we know what the three links are. Note that **find** throws an error message when it can't change to a directory. Sometimes, there will be so many of them on your screen that you would find it difficult to spot the files that actually show up as **find**'s output. To avoid these messages, simply redirect the standard error to /dev/null.

File Type and Permissions (-type and -perm)   The -type option followed by the letter f, d or l selects files of the ordinary, directory and symbolic link type. Here's how you locate all directories of your home directory tree:

```
$ cd; find . -type d -print 2>/dev/null
.                                            Shows the . also
./.netscape                                  Displays hidden directories also
./java_progs
./c_progs
./c_progs/include
./c_progs/lib
./shell_scripts
./.ssh
```

Note the relative pathname **find** displays, but that's because the pathname itself was relative (.). **find** also doesn't necessarily display an ASCII sorted list. The sequence in which files are displayed depends on the internal organization of the file system.

The -perm option specifies the permissions to match. For instance, -perm 666 selects files having read and write permission for all categories of users. Such files are security hazards. You'll often want to use two options in combination to restrict the search to only directories:

```
find $HOME -perm 777 -type d -print
```

find uses an AND condition (an implied -a operator between -perm and -type) to select directories that provide all access rights to everyone. It selects files only if both selection criteria (-perm and -type) are fulfilled.

Finding Unused Files (-mtime and -atime)   Files tend to build up incessantly on disk. Some of them remain unaccessed or unmodified for months—even years. **find**'s options can easily match a file's modification (-mtime) and access (-atime) times to select them. -mtime helps in backup operations by providing a list of those files that have been modified, say, in less than 2 days:

```
find . -mtime -2 -print
```

-2 here means *less* than 2 days. To select from the /home directory all files that have not been accessed for more than a year, a positive value has to be used with -atime:

```
find /home -atime +365 -print | mailx root
```

Because **find** uses standard output, the list can be stored in a file or used to mail a message.

Note: +365 means greater than 365 days, -365 means less than 365 days. For specifying exactly 365, use 365.

11.7.2 The find Operators (!, -o and -a)

There are three operators that are commonly used with **find**. The ! operator is used before an option to negate its meaning. So,

```
find . ! -name "*.c" -print
```

selects all but the C program files. To look for both shell and **perl** scripts, use the -o operator which represents an OR condition. We need to use an escaped pair of parentheses here:

```
find /home \( -name "*.sh" -o -name "*.pl" \) -print
```

The (and) are special characters that are interpreted by the shell to group commands (2.7.1). The same characters are used by **find** to group expressions using the -o and -a operators, the reason why they need to be escaped.

The -a operator represents the AND condition, and is implied by default whenever two selection criteria are placed together.

Table 11.1 Major Expressions Used by **find** (Meaning gets reversed when - is replaced by +, and vice versa)

Selection Criteria	Selects File
-inum *n*	Having inode number *n*
-type *x*	If of type *x*; *x* can be f (ordinary file), d (directory) or l (symbolic link)
-type f	If an ordinary file
-perm *nnn*	If octal permissions match *nnn* completely
-links *n*	If having *n* links
-user *usname*	If owned by *usname*
-group *gname*	If owned by group *gname*
-size +*x*[c]	If size greater than *x* blocks (characters if *c* is also specified) (Chapter 15)
-mtime -*x*	If modified in less than *x* days
-newer *flname*	If modified after *flname* (Chapter 25)
-mmin -*x*	If modified in less than *x* minutes (Linux only)
-atime +*x*	If accessed in more than *x* days
-amin +*x*	If accessed in more than *x* minutes (Linux only)
-name *flname*	*flname*
-iname *flname*	As above, but match is case-insensitive (Linux only)
-follow	After following a symbolic link
-prune	But don't descend directory if matched
-mount	But don't look in other file systems (Chapter 25)

Action	Significance
-print	Prints selected file on standard output
-ls	Executes **ls -lids** command on selected files
-exec *cmd*	Executes UNIX command *cmd* followed by {} \;

11.7.3 Options Available in the Action Component

Displaying the Listing (-ls)   The -print option belongs to the *action* component of the **find** syntax. In real life, you'll often want to take some action on the selected files and not just display the filenames. For instance, you may like to view the listing with the -ls option:

```
$ find . -type f -mtime +2 -mtime -5 -ls        -a option implied
475336    1 -rw-r--r--   1 romeo    users      716 Aug 17 10:31 ./c_progs/fileinout.c
```

find here runs the **ls -lids** command to display a special listing of those regular files that are modified in more than two days and less than five days. In this example, we see two options in the selection criteria (both -mtime) simulating an AND condition. It's the same as using \(-mtime +2 -a -mtime -5 \).

Taking Action on Selected Files (-exec and -ok)   The -exec option is the dark horse of the **find** tool. It lets you take any action by running a UNIX command on the selected files. -exec takes the command to execute as its own argument, followed by {} and finally the rather cryptic symbols \; (backslash and semicolon). This is how you can reuse a previous **find** command quite meaningfully:

```
find $HOME -type f -atime +365 -exec rm {} \;                    Note the usage
```

This will use **rm** to remove all ordinary files unaccessed for more than a year. This can be a risky thing to do, so you can consider using **rm**'s -i option. But all commands don't have interactive options, in which case you should use **find**'s -ok option:

```
$ find $HOME -type f -atime +365 -ok mv {} $HOME/safe \;
< mv ... ./archive.tar.gz > ? y
< mv ... ./yourunix02.txt > ? n
< mv ... ./yourunix04.txt > ? y
   .......
```

mv turns interactive with -i but only if the destination file exists. Here, -ok seeks confirmation for every selected file to be moved to the $HOME/safe directory irrespective of whether the files exist at the destination or not. A y deletes the file.

find is the system administrator's tool. You'll see it used for a number of tasks in Chapter 15. It is specially suitable for backing up files and for use in tandem with the **xargs** command (25.10.3).

Note: The pair of {} is a placeholder for a filename. So, **-exec cp {} {}.bak** provides a .bak extension to all selected files. Don't forget to use the **\;** symbols at the end of every -exec or -ok keyword.

11.8 CONCLUSION

This chapter is a sequel to Chapter 6, and examined practically all the common file attributes. The inode is at the heart of it all, but it contains 12 permissions for a file, and not 9, as you might be tempted to think. We'll be examining the three remaining permission bits—the SUID, SGID and the sticky bit—in Chapter 15. At this point we have covered most of the concepts, so it's time we applied them. The next chapter is the first of four chapters devoted to those powerful text manipulators that we call *filters*.

WRAP UP

The UNIX directory tree is actually a collection of multiple *file systems* that are *mounted* at boot time to appear as a single file system. Every file is identified by the *inode number* and has its attributes stored in the *inode*. The inode number is unique in a single file system.

A file can have more than one name or *link*, and is linked with **ln**. Two linked filenames have the same inode number. Links provide protection against accidental deletion. A C or shell programmer takes advantage of the linking feature to write code that does different things depending on the name by which the file is invoked.

A *symbolic link* is a file which contains the pathname of another file or directory even if it is in another file system. It is created with **ln -s**. Accidental deletion of the file pointed to is dangerous and creates a *dangling* symbolic link.

Permissions have different significance for directories. Read permission means that the filenames stored in the directory are readable. Write permission implies that you are permitted to create or remove files in the directory. Execute (or *search*) permission means that you can change to that directory with the **cd** command.

The UNIX system creates files and directories with 666 and 777 as the default permissions. But this default is generally changed by **umask** in the system's startup scripts. A umask value of 022 changes the system default to 644 and 755 for a file and directory, respectively.

The inode stores the time of last modification and access of a file. You can use **touch** to change both these times to either the current time, by default, or to specific values.

find looks for files by matching one or more file attributes. A file can be specified by type (-type), name (-name), permissions (-perm) or by its time stamps (-mtime and -atime). -print is the action commonly used, but any UNIX command can be run on the selected files (-ls, -exec and -ok) with or without user confirmation.

Test Your Understanding

11.1 Which important file attribute is not maintained in the inode? Where is it stored then?

11.2 What do you mean by saying that a file has three links?

11.3 How do you link all C source files in the current directory and place the links in another directory, bar?

11.4 State whether the following are true or false: (i) The **rm** command removes only a hard link but not a symbolic link. (ii) A symbolic link has the same inode number as the file it is linked to.

11.5 How do you link foo1 to foo2 using (i) a hard link, (ii) a symbolic link? If you delete foo2, does it make any difference?

11.6 How can you make out whether two files are copies or links?

11.7 What do you do to make sure that no one is able see the names of the files you have?

11.8 A file was not writable by group and others and yet could be deleted by users of those categories. How?

11.9 How do you ensure that all files created by you will have the default permissions rw-rw----?

11.10 When you invoke **ls -l foo** the access time of foo changes. True or false?

11.11 How can you find out whether a program has been executed today?

11.12 What does the command **touch foo** do? Why is the command important for the system administrator?

11.13 Copy the file /etc/passwd to your current directory and then observe the listing of the copy. Which attributes have changed?

11.14 How do you change the modification time of a file to Sep 30, 10:30 a.m.?

11.15 Use **find** to locate in /bin and /usr/bin all filenames that (i) begin with z, (ii) have the extension .html or .java.

11.16 How will you count the number of ordinary files in the directory tree, /home/henry?

11.17 Observe the access time of a file with **ls -lu foo**. Next, append the **date** command output to it and observe the access time of foo again. What do you see?

Flex Your Brain

11.1 Explain whether the following statement is true: The UNIX file system has many root directories even though it actually shows one.

11.2 What are the three time stamps maintained in the inode and how do you display two of them for the file foo?

11.3 What change takes place in the inode and directory when a file is linked and later removed?

11.4 What happens when you invoke the command **ln foo bar** if (i) bar doesn't exist, (ii) bar exists as an ordinary file, (iii) bar exists as a directory?

11.5 Explain two application areas of hard links. What are the two main disadvantages of the hard link?

11.6 Explain the significance of *fast symbolic links* and *dangling symbolic links*.

11.7 You have a number of programs in $HOME/progs which are called by other programs. You have now decided to move these programs to $HOME/internet/progs. How can you ensure that users don't notice this change?

11.8 The command **cd bar** failed. When can that happen even if bar exists?

11.9 If a file has the permissions 000, you may or may not be able to delete the file. Explain how both situations can happen. Does the execute permission have any role to play here?

11.10 If **umask** shows the value (i) 000 (ii) 002, what implications do they have from the security viewpoint?

11.11 Explain the difference between (i) **ls -l** and **ls -lt** (ii) **ls -lu** and **ls -lut**.

11.12 Use **find** to locate from your home directory tree all (i) files with the extension .html or .HTML, (ii) files having the inode number 9076, (iii) directories having permissions 666, (iv) files modified yesterday. Will any of these commands fail?

11.13 Use **find** to (i) move all files modified within the last 24 hours to the posix directory under your parent directory, (ii) locate all files named a.out or core in your home directory tree and remove them interactively, (iii) locate the file login.sql in the /oracle directory tree, and then copy it to your own directory, (iv) change all directory permissions to 755 and all file permissions to 644 in your home directory tree.

Simple Filters

This chapter features the simple filters of the system—commands which accept data from standard input, manipulate it and write the results to standard output. Filters are the central tools of the UNIX tool kit, and each filter featured in this chapter performs a simple function. This chapter shows their use both in standalone mode and in combination with other tools using redirection and piping.

Many UNIX files have lines containing *fields*—strings of characters representing a meaningful entity. Some commands expect these fields to be separated by a suitable delimiter that's not used by the data. Typically this delimiter is a : (as in /etc/passwd and $PATH), but we have used the | (pipe) as delimiter for some of the sample files in this and other chapters. Many filters work well with delimited fields, and some simply won't work without them.

WHAT YOU WILL LEARN

- Use **pr** to format text to provide margins and headers, doublespacing and multiple column output.
- Pick up lines from the beginning with **head**, and from the end with **tail**.
- Extract characters or fields with **cut**.
- Join two files laterally, and multiple lines to a single line with **paste**.
- Sort, merge and remove repeated lines with **sort**.
- Find out the unique and nonunique lines with **uniq**.
- Change, delete or squeeze individual characters with **tr**.

TOPICS OF SPECIAL INTEREST

- A special feature of **paste** to form a singe line from multiple lines.
- The counting facility available in **uniq**.
- Use all of these commands in an example to perform content manipulating tasks.

Filters Reviewed

Filters were introduced in Section 8.5.4 as a category of commands that take advantage of the shell's redirection features. A filter has the capability of reading standard input and writing to standard output. By default, a filter writes to standard output. It reads from standard input when used without a filename as argument, and from the file otherwise.

The piping mechanism of the shell lets the standard output of one filter serve as standard input of another. This feature lets us design pipelines containing a series of filters. Section 12.10 shows their use in combination for performing content manipulations tasks—tasks which these tools can't do when acting alone.

12.1 THE SAMPLE DATABASE

Henceforth, you'll be learning the features of several UNIX commands, including the advanced ones, text editing and shell programming with reference to a file emp.1st. It's a good idea to have a close look at the file now and understand the organization:

```
$ cat emp.1st
2233|a.k. shukla       |g.m.     |sales     |12/12/52|6000
9876|jai sharma         |director |production|12/03/50|7000
5678|sumit chakrobarty  |d.g.m.   |marketing |19/04/43|6000
2365|barun sengupta     |director |personnel |11/05/47|7800
5423|n.k. gupta         |chairman |admin     |30/08/56|5400
1006|chanchal singhvi   |director |sales     |03/09/38|6700
6213|karuna ganguly     |g.m.     |accounts  |05/06/62|6300
1265|s.n. dasgupta      |manager  |sales     |12/09/63|5600
4290|jayant Choudhury   |executive|production|07/09/50|6000
2476|anil aggarwal      |manager  |sales     |01/05/59|5000
6521|lalit chowdury     |director |marketing |26/09/45|8200
3212|shyam saksena      |d.g.m.   |accounts  |12/12/55|6000
3564|sudhir Agarwal     |executive|personnel |06/07/47|7500
2345|j.b. saxena        |g.m.     |marketing |12/03/45|8000
0110|v.k. agrawal       |g.m.     |marketing |31/12/40|9000
```

This is a text file designed in fixed format and containing a personnel database. There are 15 lines in the file, where each line has six fields separated from one another by the delimiter |. The details of an employee are stored in one line. A person is identified by the emp-id, name, designation, department, date of birth and salary, as indicated by the fields (in the same order). You'll be using this files, or ones derived from them, in various ways to see the extent of manipulation that is possible with the UNIX tool kit.

12.2 pr: PAGINATING FILES

The **pr** command prepares a file for printing by adding suitable headers, footers and formatted text. A simple invocation of the command is to use it with a filename as argument:

```
$ pr dept.lst

May 06 10:38 1997   dept.lst Page 1

01:accounts:6213
02:admin:5423
03:marketing:6521
04:personnel:2365
05:production:9876
06:sales:1006
```
These six lines are the original contents of dept.lst *shown in Section 5.1*

  ...blank lines...

pr adds five lines of margin at the top and five at the bottom. The lower portion of the page has not been shown in the examples for reasons of economy. The header shows the date and time of last modification of the file along with the filename and page number.

12.2.1 pr Options

pr's -k option (where k is an integer) prints in k columns. If a program outputs a series of 20 numbers, one in each line, then this option can make good use of the screen's empty spaces. And because **pr** is a filter, it can obtain its input from the standard output of another program. Let's use the -t option also to suppress the headers and footers:

```
$ a.out | pr -t -5
0           4           8           12          16
1           5           9           13          17
2           6           10          14          18
3           7           11          15          19
```

If you are not using the -t option, then you can have a header of your choice with the -h option. This option is followed by the header string. There are some more options that programmers will find useful:

- -d Doublespaces input, reduces clutter.
- -n Numbers lines, helps in debugging code.
- -o n Offsets lines by n spaces, increases left margin of page.

Combine these various options to produce just the format you need:

```
$ pr -t -n -d -o 10 dept.lst
       1   01:accounts:6213

       2   02:admin:5423
```

```
3    03:marketing:6521

4    04:personnel:2365

5    05:production:9876

6    06:sales:1006
```

There's one option that uses a number prefixed by a + to print from a specific page number. Another option (-1) sets the page length:

```
pr +10 chap01                                    Starts printing from page 10
pr -l 54 chap01                                  Page length set to 54 lines
```

Because **pr** formats its input by adding margins and a header, it's often used as a "pre-processor" before printing with the **lp** command:

```
pr -h "Department list" dept.lst | lp           Use lpr in Linux
```

Since **pr** output often lands up in the hard copy, **pr** and **lp** form a common pipeline sequence.

Note: For numbering lines, you can also use the **nl** command (not covered in this edition). It's easier to use **nl foo** than **pr -t -n foo**.

12.3 head: DISPLAYING THE BEGINNING OF A FILE

The **head** command, as the name implies, displays the top of the file. When used without an option, it displays the first ten lines of the file:

```
head emp.lst                                     Shows first ten lines
```

You can use the -n option (POSIX mandated) to specify a line count and display, say, the first three lines of the file:

```
$ head -n 3 emp.lst                              Or head -3 emp.lst on some systems
2233|a.k. shukla       |g.m.     |sales      |12/12/52|6000
9876|jai sharma         |director |production |12/03/50|7000
5678|sumit chakrobarty|d.g.m.    |marketing  |19/04/43|6000
```

head can be used in imaginative ways. Consider that you are resuming an editing session the next day and find that you are unable to recall the name of the file you last edited. Since **ls -t** displays filenames in order of their modification time, the job is easily done by picking up the first filename from the list and using it as an argument to **vi**. This requires command substitution:

```
vi `ls -t | head -n 1`                           Opens last modified file for editing
```

You can define this as an *alias (10.4)* so the aliased command is always available for you to use.

12.4 tail: DISPLAYING THE END OF A FILE

Complementing its **head** counterpart, the **tail** command displays the end of the file. It provides an additional method of addressing lines, and like **head**, it displays the last ten lines by default. The last three lines are displayed in this way:

```
$ tail -n 3 emp.1st                              Or use tail -3 emp.1st
3564|sudhir Agarwal    |executive|personnel |06/07/47|7500
2345|j.b. saxena       |g.m.      |marketing |12/03/45|8000
0110|v.k. agrawal      |g.m.      |marketing |31/12/40|9000
```

You can also address lines from the beginning of the file instead of the end. The +*count* option allows you to do that, where *count* represents the line number from where the selection should begin. Since the file contains 15 lines, selecting the last five implies using

```
tail +11 emp.1st                      11th line onwards, possible with + symbol
```

12.4.1 tail Options

tail has more options than **head**, and can also extract in units of bytes rather than lines.

Monitoring File Growth (-f)   Many UNIX programs constantly write to the system's log files as long as they are running. System administrators need to monitor the growth of these files to view the latest messages. **tail** offers the -f (follow) option for this purpose. This is how you can monitor the installation of Oracle by watching the growth of the log file install.log from another terminal:

```
tail -f /oracle/app/oracle/product/8.1/orainst/install.log
```

The prompt doesn't return even after the work is over. With this option, you have to use the interrupt key to abort the process and exit to the shell.

Extracting Bytes Rather than Lines (-c)   POSIX requires **tail** to support the -c option followed by a positive or negative integer depending on whether the extraction is performed relative to the beginning or end of a file. Solaris supports this option only in its XPG4 version, but this is no problem in Linux:

```
tail -c -512 foo                 Copies last 512 bytes from foo
tail -c +512 foo                 Copies everything after skipping 511 bytes
```

Tip: Use **tail -f** when you are running a program that continuously writes to a file, and you want to see how the file is growing. You have to terminate this command with the interrupt key.

12.5 cut: SLITTING A FILE VERTICALLY

The features of the **cut** and **paste** commands will be illustrated with specific reference to the file shortlist, which stores the first five lines of emp.1st:

```
$ head -n 5 emp.lst | tee shortlist
2233|a.k. shukla       |g.m.     |sales     |12/12/52|6000
9876|jai sharma        |director |production|03/12/50|7000
5678|sumit chakrobarty|d.g.m.   |marketing |04/19/43|6000
2365|barun sengupta    |director |personnel |05/11/47|7800
5423|n.k. gupta        |chairman |admin     |08/30/56|5400
```

Note the use of the **tee** facility that saves the output in shortlist and also displays it on the terminal. We can extract both columns and fields from this file with the **cut** command. Columns are specified with the -c option and fields with -f. We'll take up columns first.

12.5.1 Cutting Columns (-c)

To extract specific columns, you need to follow the -c option with a list of column numbers, delimited by a comma. Ranges can also be used using the hyphen. Here's how we extract the name and designation from shortlist:

```
$ cut -c 6-22,24-32 shortlist
a.k. shukla       g.m.
jai sharma        director
sumit chakrobartyd.g.m.
barun sengupta    director
n.k. gupta        chairman
```

Note that there should be no whitespace in the column list. Moreover, **cut** uses a special form for selecting a column from the beginning and up to the end of a line:

```
cut -c -3,6-22,28-34,55- shortlist          Must be an ascending list
```

The expression 55- indicates column number 55 to end of line. Similarly, -3 is the same as 1-3.

12.5.2 Cutting Fields (-f)

The -c option is useful for fixed-length lines. Most UNIX files (like /etc/passwd and /etc/group) don't contain fixed-length lines. To extract useful data from these files you need to cut fields rather than columns. **cut** uses the tab as the default field delimiter, but can also work with a different delimiter. Two options need to be used here: -d for the field delimiter and -f for the field list. This is how you cut the second and third fields of our sample file:

```
$ cut -d \| -f 2,3 shortlist | tee cutlist1
a.k. shukla       |g.m.
jai sharma        |director
sumit chakrobarty|d.g.m.
barun sengupta    |director
n.k. gupta        |chairman
```

The | was escaped to prevent the shell from interpreting it as the pipeline character; alternatively, it can also be quoted (-d"|"). To cut out fields numbered 1, 4, 5 and 6 and save the output in cutlist2, follow a similar procedure:

```
cut -d "|" -f 1,4- shortlist > cutlist2          Here | is quoted
```

Extracting User List from who *Output*   **cut** can be used to extract the first word of a line by specifying the space as the delimiter. The example used in Section 3.10 now run in tandem with **cut** displays the list of users only:

```
$ who | cut -d " " -f1                    Space is the delimiter
root
kumar
sharma
project
sachin
```

cut is a powerful text manipulator often used in combination with other commands or filters. You'll be using the command a number of times in this text.

Note: You must indicate to **cut** whether you are extracting fields or columns. One of the options -f and -c must be specified. These options are really not optional; one of them is compulsory.

12.6 paste: PASTING FILES

What you cut with **cut** can be pasted back with the **paste** command—but vertically rather than horizontally. You can view two files side by side by pasting them. In the previous topic, **cut** was used to create the two files cutlist1 and cutlist2 containing two cut-out portions of the same file. Using **paste**, you can fix them laterally:

```
$ paste cutlist1 cutlist2
a.k. shukla      |g.m.              2233|sales      |12/12/52|6000
jai sharma       |director          9876|production|12/03/50|7000
sumit chakrobarty|d.g.m.            5678|marketing  |19/04/43|6000
barun sengupta   |director          2365|personnel  |11/05/47|7800
n.k. gupta       |chairman          5423|admin      |30/08/56|5400
```

The original contents have been restored to some extent, except that the fields have different relative locations, and pasting has taken place on whitespace. Like **cut**, **paste** also uses the tab as the default delimiter, but you can specify *one or more delimiters* with -d:

```
$ paste -d"|" cutlist1 cutlist2
a.k. shukla      |g.m.     |2233|sales      |12/12/52|6000
jai sharma       |director |9876|production|12/03/50|7000
sumit chakrobarty|d.g.m.   |5678|marketing  |19/04/43|6000
barun sengupta   |director |2365|personnel  |11/05/47|7800
n.k. gupta       |chairman |5423|admin      |30/08/56|5400
```

Even though **paste** uses at least two files for concatenating lines, the data for one file can be supplied through the standard input. If, for instance, cutlist2 doesn't exist, you can provide the character stream by cutting out the necessary fields from shortlist and piping the output to **paste**:

```
$ cut -d \| -f 1,4- shortlist | paste -d "|" cutlist1 -
a.k. shukla      |g.m.     |2233|sales      |12/12/52|6000
jai sharma       |director |9876|production|12/03/50|7000
```

```
sumit chakrobarty|d.g.m.    |5678|marketing |19/04/43|6000
barun sengupta   |director  |2365|personnel |11/05/47|7800
n.k. gupta       |chairman  |5423|admin     |30/08/56|5400
```

You can also reverse the order of pasting by altering the location of the - sign:

```
cut -d "|" -f 1,4- shortlist | paste -d "|" - cutlist1
```

Joining Lines (-s)   **paste** is more useful than you might think. Consider this address book that contains details of three persons, with three lines for each:

```
$ cat addressbook
anup kumar                           Name
anup_k@yahoo.com                     Email address
24569083                             Telephone number
vinod sharma
vinod_sharma@hotmail.com
34586532
madhuri bahl
madhuri@heavens.com
39034943
```

The -s option joins lines in the same way **vi**'s **J** command does *(7.5.4)*. Using this option on this file (with **paste -s addressbook**) would join all of these nine lines to form a single line. This won't be of much use, so we'll learn to use the -d option with multiple delimiters to join three lines at a time.

If we specify the delimiter string as ||\n with -d, the delimiters are used in a circular manner. The first and second lines would be joined with the | as delimiter, and the same would be true for the second and third line. The third and fourth line would be separated by a newline. After the list is exhausted it is reused. This is exactly what we want:

```
$ paste -s -d"||\n" addressbook
anup kumar|anup_k@yahoo.com|24569083
vinod sharma|vinod_sharma@hotmail.com|34586532
madhuri bahl|madhuri@heavens.com|39034943
```

Just see how **paste** works (with a single file this time) to concatenate lines in a specified manner. Table data is often split with each column on a separate line, and it's in situations like these that **paste** can be so useful.

12.7 sort: ORDERING A FILE

Sorting is the ordering of data in ascending or descending sequence. The **sort** command orders a file. Like **cut**, it identifies fields and it can sort on specified fields. We'll consider the important **sort** options by sorting the file **shortlist** (created in Section 12.5) in different ways. By default, the entire line is sorted:

```
$ sort shortlist
2233|a.k. shukla    |g.m.     |sales     |12/12/52|6000
2365|barun sengupta |director |personnel |11/05/47|7800
```

```
5423|n.k. gupta         |chairman |admin     |30/08/56|5400
5678|sumit chakrobarty|d.g.m.     |marketing |19/04/43|6000
9876|jai sharma         |director |production|12/03/50|7000
```

By default, **sort** reorders lines in ASCII collating sequence—whitespace first, then numerals, uppercase letters and finally lowercase letters. This default sorting sequence can be altered by using certain options. You can also sort on one or more keys (fields) or use a different ordering rule.

12.7.1 sort Options

The important **sort** options are summarized in Table 12.1. We'll be using the -k (key) POSIX option to identify *keys* (the fields) instead of the +*n* and -*n* forms (where *n* is the field number) that were used earlier. Unlike **cut** and **paste**, **sort** uses one or more contiguous spaces as the default field separator (tab in **cut** and **paste**). We'll use the -t option to specify the delimiter.

Sorting on Primary Key (-k)   Let's now use the -k option to sort on the second field (name). The option should be -k 2:

```
$ sort -t"|" -k 2 shortlist
2233|a.k. shukla      |g.m.     |sales     |12/12/52|6000
2365|barun sengupta   |director |personnel |11/05/47|7800
9876|jai sharma       |director |production|12/03/50|7000
5423|n.k. gupta       |chairman |admin     |30/08/56|5400
5678|sumit chakrobarty|d.g.m.   |marketing |19/04/43|6000
```

The sort order can be reversed with the -r (reverse) option. The following sequence reverses a previous sorting order:

```
$ sort -t"|" -r -k 2 shortlist
5678|sumit chakrobarty|d.g.m.   |marketing |19/04/43|6000
5423|n.k. gupta       |chairman |admin     |30/08/56|5400
9876|jai sharma       |director |production|12/03/50|7000
2365|barun sengupta   |director |personnel |11/05/47|7800
2233|a.k. shukla      |g.m.     |sales     |12/12/52|6000
```

sort combines options in a rather unusual way. The previous command sequence could also have been written as:

```
sort -t"|" -k 2r shortlist
```

Sorting on Secondary Key   You can sort on more than one key, i.e., you can provide a secondary key to **sort**. If the primary key is the third field, and the secondary key is the second field, then you need to specify for every -k option, where the sort ends. This is done in this way:

```
$ sort -t"|" -k 3,3 -k 2,2 shortlist
5423|n.k. gupta       |chairman |admin     |30/08/56|5400
5678|sumit chakrobarty|d.g.m.   |marketing |19/04/43|6000
2365|barun sengupta   |director |personnel |11/05/47|7800
9876|jai sharma       |director |production|12/03/50|7000
2233|a.k. shukla      |g.m.     |sales     |12/12/52|6000
```

This sorts the file by designation and name. -k 3,3 indicates that sorting starts on the third field and ends on the same field.

Sorting on Columns   You can also specify a character position within a field to be the beginning of sort. If you are to sort the file according to the year of birth, then you need to sort on the seventh and eighth column positions within the fifth field:

```
$ sort -t"|" -k 5.7,5.8 shortlist
5678|sumit chakrobarty|d.g.m.    |marketing |19/04/43|6000
2365|barun sengupta    |director |personnel |11/05/47|7800
9876|jai sharma         |director |production|12/03/50|7000
2233|a.k. shukla        |g.m.     |sales     |12/12/52|6000
5423|n.k. gupta         |chairman |admin     |30/08/56|5400
```

The -k option also uses the form -k *m*.*n* where *n* is the character position in the *m*th field. So, 5.7,5.8 means that sorting starts on column 7 of the fifth field and ends on column 8.

Numeric Sort (-n)   When **sort** acts on numerals, strange things can happen. When you sort a file containing only numbers, you get a curious result:

```
$ sort numfile
10
2
27
4
```

This is probably not what you expected, but the ASCII collating sequence places 1 above 2, and 2 above 4. That's why 10 preceded 2 and 27 preceded 4. This can be overridden by the -n (numeric) option:

```
$ sort -n numfile
2
4
10
27
```

Removing Repeated Lines (-u)   The -u (unique) option lets you remove repeated lines from a file. If you "cut" out the designation field from emp.lst, you can pipe it to **sort** to find out the unique designations that occur in the file:

```
$ cut -d"|" -f3 emp.lst | sort -u | tee desigx.lst
chairman
d.g.m.
director
executive
g.m.
manager
```

We used three commands to solve a text manipulation problem. Here, **cut** select the third field from shortlist for **sort** to work on.

Other sort *Options*   Even though **sort**'s output can be redirected to a file, we can use its -o option to specify the output filename. Curiously enough, the input and output filenames can even be the same:

```
sort -o sortedlist -k 3 shortlist        Output stored in sortedlist
sort -o shortlist shortlist              Output stored in same file
```

To check whether the file has actually been sorted in the default order, use the -c (check) option:

```
$ sort -c shortlist
$ _                                      File is sorted
```

You can also add the -k option to the above to check whether a specific field is sorted:

```
$ sort -t"|" -c -k 2 shortlist
sort: shortlist:2: disorder: 2365|barun sengupta    |director |personnel |11/05/4
7|7800
```

When **sort** is used with multiple filenames as arguments, it concatenates them and sorts them collectively. When large files are sorted in this way, performance often suffers. The -m (merge) option can merge two or more files that are sorted individually:

```
sort -m foo1 foo2 foo3
```

This command will run faster than the one used without the -m option only if the three files are sorted.

Tip: Commit to memory the default delimiter used by **cut**, **paste** and **sort**. **cut** and **paste** use the tab, but **sort** uses a contiguous string of spaces as a single delimiter.

Table 12.1 sort Options

Option	Description
-t*char*	Uses delimiter *char* to identify fields
-k *n*	Sorts on *n*th field
-k *m* ,*n*	Starts sort on *m*th field and ends sort on *n*th field
-k *m* .*n*	Starts sort on *n*th column of *m*th field
-u	Removes repeated lines
-n	Sorts numerically
-r	Reverses sort order
-f	Folds lowercase to equivalent uppercase (case-insensitive sort)
-m *list*	Merges sorted files in *list*
-c	Checks if file is sorted
-o *flname*	Places output in file *flname*

12.8 uniq: LOCATE REPEATED AND NONREPEATED LINES

When you concatenate or merge files, you'll face the problem of duplicate entries creeping in. You saw how **sort** removes them with the -u option. UNIX offers a special tool to handle these lines—the **uniq** command. Consider a sorted file dept.1st that includes repeated lines:

```
$ cat dept.lst
01|accounts|6213
01|accounts|6213
02|admin|5423
03|marketing|6521
03|marketing|6521
03|marketing|6521
04|personnel|2365
05|production|9876
06|sales|1006
```

uniq simply fetches one copy of each line and writes it to the standard output:

```
$ uniq dept.lst
01|accounts|6213
02|admin|5423
03|marketing|6521
04|personnel|2365
05|production|9876
06|sales|1006
```

Since **uniq** requires a sorted file as input, the general procedure is to sort a file and pipe its output to **uniq**. The following pipeline also produces the same output, except that the output is saved in a file:

```
sort dept.lst | uniq -  uniqlist
```

uniq is indeed unique; if provided with two filenames as arguments, **uniq** will read the first file and write its output to the second. Here, it reads from the standard input and writes to uniqlist.

12.8.1 uniq Options

To select unique lines, it's preferable to use **sort -u** that does the job with a single command. But **uniq** has a couple of useful options; they can be used to make simple database queries.

Selecting the Nonrepeated Lines (-u)   To determine the designation that occurs uniquely in emp.1st, cut out the third field, sort it, and then pipe it to **uniq**. The -u (unique) option selects only lines that are not repeated:

```
$ cut -d"|" -f3 emp.lst | sort | uniq -u
chairman
```

Selecting the Duplicate Lines (-d)   The -d (duplicate) option selects only one copy of the repeated lines:

```
$ cut -d"|" -f3 emp.lst | sort | uniq -d
d.g.m.
director
executive
g.m.
manager
```

Counting Frequency of Occurrence (-c)   The -c (count) option displays the frequency of occurrence of all lines, along with the lines:

```
$ cut -d"|" -f3 emp.lst | sort | uniq -c
   1 chairman
   2 d.g.m.
   4 director
   2 executive
   4 g.m.
   2 manager
```

> *In SQL, you would be using this:*
> *SELECT COUNT(*), JOB FROM EMP*
> *GROUP BY JOB ;*

This is an extremely useful option, and we'll make best use of it in an example that is taken up at the end of this chapter. It raises the possibility of printing a word-count list that displays the frequency of occurrence of each word.

Caution: Like **sort**, **uniq** also accepts the output filename as an argument, but without using an option (unlike -o in **sort**). If you use **uniq foo1 foo2**, **uniq** simply processes foo1 and overwrites foo2 with its output. Never use **uniq** with two filenames unless you know what you are doing.

12.9 tr: TRANSLATING CHARACTERS

So far, the commands have been handling either entire lines, or columns. The **tr** (translate) filter manipulates *individual characters* in a line. More specifically, it translates characters using one or two compact expressions:

   tr *options expression1 expression2 standard input*

Note that **tr** *takes input only from standard input; it doesn't take a filename as argument.* By default, it translates each character in *expression1* to its mapped counterpart in *expression2*. The first character in the first expression is replaced with the first character in the second expression, and similarly for the other characters.

Let's use **tr** to replace the | with a ~ (tilde) and the / with a -. Simply specify two expressions containing these characters in the proper sequence:

```
$ tr '|/' '~-' < emp.lst | head -n 3
2233~a.k. shukla       ~g.m.     ~sales     ~12-12-52-6000
9876~jai sharma        ~director ~production~12-03-50-7000
5678~sumit chakrobarty~d.g.m.    ~marketing ~19-04-43-6000
```

Note that the lengths of the two expressions should be equal. If they are not, the longer expression will have unmapped characters (not in Linux). Single quotes are used here because no variable evaluation or command substitution is involved. It's just as easy to define the two expressions as two separate variables, and then evaluate them in double quotes:

```
exp1='|/' ; exp2='~-'
tr "$exp1" "$exp2" < emp.lst
```

Like wild-cards, **tr** also accepts ranges in the expressions. The same rules apply; the character on the right of the - must have an ASCII value higher than that of the character on the left. The escaping rules should also be obvious; the character [needs to be escaped if the special meaning is to be removed from it.

Changing Case of Text   Since **tr** doesn't accept a filename as argument, the input has to be redirected from a file or a pipe. The following sequence changes the case of the first three lines from lower to upper:

```
$ head -n 3 emp.lst | tr '[a-z]' '[A-Z]'
2233|A.K. SHUKLA      |G.M.    |SALES     |12/12/52|6000
9876|JAI SHARMA       |DIRECTOR |PRODUCTION|12/03/50|7000
5678|SUMIT CHAKROBARTY|D.G.M.   |MARKETING |19/04/43|6000
```

Reversing the two expressions will convert case from upper to lower. **tr** is often used to change the case of a file's contents.

12.9.1 tr Options

Deleting Characters (-d)   The file emp.lst has fields separated by delimiters and the date formatted in readable form with a /. In nondatabase setups, delimiters are not used, and the date is generally represented as a six-character field in the format *ddmmyy*. To convert this file to the traditional format, use the -d (delete) option to delete the characters | and / from the file. The following command does it for the first three lines:

```
$ tr -d '|/' < emp.lst | head -n 3
2233a.k. shukla      g.m.     sales     1212526000
9876jai sharma       director production1203507000
5678sumit chakrobartyd.g.m.   marketing 1904436000
```

Compressing Multiple Consecutive Characters (-s)   UNIX tools work best with fields rather than columns (like above), so it's preferable to use files with delimited fields. In that case, lines need not be of fixed length; you can eliminate all redundant spaces with the -s (squeeze) option, which squeezes multiple consecutive occurrences of its argument to a single character. We can then have compressed output with lines in free format:

```
$ tr -s ' ' <emp.lst | head -n 3
2233|a.k. shukla |g.m. |sales |12/12/52|6000
9876|jai sharma |director |production|12/03/50|7000
5678|sumit chakrobarty|d.g.m. |marketing |19/04/43|6000
```

Tip: You can use the -s option to compress all contiguous spaces in the output of several UNIX commands and then use **cut** to extract individual fields from this compressed output. For instance, you can "cut" out any field from the listing.

Complementing Values of Expression (-c)   Finally, the -c (complement) option complements the set of characters in the expression. Thus, to delete all characters except the | and /, you can combine the -d and -c options:

```
$ tr -cd '|/' <emp.1st
|||||//|||||//|||||//|||||//|||||//|||||//|||||//|||||//|||||//|||||//||||
|//|||||//|||||//|||||//|$ _
```

Unusual output indeed! **tr** has deleted all characters except the | and / from the file. The appearance of the prompt at the immediate end of output shows that the newline character has also not been spared. We'll use the -c and -d options to place each word in a separate line in our example section *(12.10)*.

Using ASCII Octal Values and Escape Sequences   Like **echo**, **tr** also uses octal values and escape sequences to represent characters. This facility is specially suited for using nonprintable characters in the expression. So to have each field on a separate line, replace the | with the LF character (octal value 012):

```
$ tr '|' '\012' < emp.1st | head -n 6          Can also use \n
2233                                            instead of \012
a.k. shukla
g.m.
sales
12/12/52
6000
```

If you reverse the two expressions, you'll make the newline character visible. Study these **tr** options closely, and you'll discover many areas where you can apply them. We'll be using some of the **tr** options in the example that's considered next.

12.10 AN EXAMPLE: DISPLAYING A WORD-COUNT LIST

Armed with the knowledge of the basic UNIX filters, let's devise a command sequence that uses a number of filters in a pipeline. Document authors sometimes like to view a list that displays the frequency of usage of each word in the document. For this to be possible, each word has to be placed in a separate line. **tr** can do that by converting all spaces and tabs (octal 011) to newlines:

```
tr " \011" "\012\012" < foo1          Space is \040
```

There's a space before \011; we won't be displaying the symbol subsequently. If we define a word as a contiguous group of alphabetic characters, we have to use **tr** again to delete all nonalphabetic characters (apart from the newline) from the output of the first **tr** command. This requires the use of the complementary (-c) and delete (-d) options:

```
tr " \011" "\012\012" < foo1 | tr -cd "[a-zA-Z\012]"
```

You now have a list of words, with each word on a separate line. Now sort this output and pipe it to **uniq -c**:

```
$ tr " \011" "\012\012" < foo1 | tr -cd "[a-zA-Z\012]" | sort | uniq -c
      32 Apache                                      Apache used 32 times
      18 DNS
      10 Directory
      16 FQDN
      25 addresses
      56 directory
```

You had to use four commands to display the word count. You'll need two more to sort the list in reverse numeric sequence and print it in three columns:

```
$ tr " \011" "\012\012" < foo1 | tr -cd "[a-zA-Z\012]" | sort | uniq -c \
> | sort -nr | pr -t -3
      56 directory          25 addresses          16 FQDN
      32 Apache             18 DNS                 10 Directory
```

For the sake of readability, we split the command line into two lines by using \ to escape the *[Enter]* key.

12.11 CONCLUSION

This chapter presented some of the commonly used filters available in the UNIX system. These filters mostly work on entire lines or fields; it's only **tr** that manipulates individual characters. These filters have limited use when they are used in standalone mode. But you also used a number of them in pipelines to perform tasks that apparently seem so difficult to achieve by conventional means. We still have four other filters to discuss—**grep**, **sed**, **awk** and **perl**, but three of them actually deviate from the do-one-thing-well approach to UNIX tool building.

> ### WRAP UP
>
> The **pr** command formats input to print headings and page numbers but can also drop them (-t). The output can be numbered (-n), doublespaced (-d) and offset from the left (-o).
>
> **head** displays the beginning of a file, while **tail** displays the end. Unlike **head**, **tail** can also be used with a line number (with the + option) from where extraction should begin. It is most useful in monitoring the growth of a file (-f).
>
> **cut** selects columns (-c) from its input, as well as fields (-f). You can join two files laterally with **paste**. By using the delimiter in a circular manner, **paste** can join multiple lines into one.
>
> Using **sort**, you can sort on one or more fields or keys (-k), and columns within these fields. You can sort numerically (-n), reverse the sort order (-r), make a case-insensitive sort (-f), and remove repeated lines (-u).
>
> **uniq** removes repeated or nonrepeated lines. The command is often combined with **sort** to order the input first.
>
> **tr** translates characters using two expressions, but accepts only standard input. It can be used to change the case of letters. You can compress multiple consecutive occurrences (-s) or delete a specific character (-d). You can also use it with ASCII octal values and escape sequences to transform nonprintable characters.

Test Your Understanding

12.1   How will you (i) doublespace a file, (ii) produce a list of all files in the current directory without headers but in three columns?

12.2   What happens when you use **head** with multiple filenames?

12.3   How do you display the **ps** output without the header line?

12.4   You need to run a program, a.out, that continuously writes to a file foo. How will you run the program and then monitor the growth of this file from the *same* terminal?

12.5   Will this command work? **cut -d: -c1 -f2 foo**

12.6   Write a **sort** sequence to order emp.lst on the month of birth.

12.7   Produce from emp.lst, a list of the birth years along with the number of people born in that year.

12.8   Generate a numbered code list for the departments in shortlist in the form *code_number code_description* (like 1 admin).

12.9   Devise a sequence to reset the PATH variable so that the first directory is removed from its list.

12.10 How do you remove repeated lines from an unsorted file where the repeated lines are (i) contiguous, (ii) not contiguous?

12.11 How do you convert the contents of the file emp.lst to uppercase?

Flex Your Brain

12.1   How will you use **pr**, **sort** and **cut** to read a file in reverse?

12.2   Write a Korn or Bash shell alias that always brings up the last modified file for editing with **vi**.

12.3   How do you select from a file (i) lines 5 to 10, (ii) last but one line?

12.4   How do you display the **date** output with each field on a separate line? How do you now join the fields to get back the original output?

12.5   How do you display a list of all processes without the **ps** header line where processes with the same name are grouped together?

12.6   How will you find out the number of times the character ? occurs in a file?

12.7   Extract the names of the users from /etc/passwd after ignoring the first 10 entries.

12.8   How do you display a listing of all directories in the PATH list?

12.9   Devise a **sort** command to order the file /etc/passwd on GID (primary) and UID (secondary) so that users with the same GID are placed together. Users with a lower UID should be placed higher in the list.

12.10 Devise a pipeline which lists the five largest files in the current directory.

12.11 Use a pipeline and command substitution to set the length of a line in emp.lst to a variable.

12.12 You have two files, foo1 and foo2, copied from two /etc/passwd files on two machines. How do you print a list of users who are (i) present in foo1 but not in foo2, (ii) present in foo2 and not in foo1, (iii) present in both files?

12.13 Assuming that a user may be logged in more than once, how do you (i) list only those users, (ii) mail root a sorted list of all users currently logged in, where a user is mailed only once?

12.14 How are these two commands similar and different? **sort -u foo ; uniq foo**

12.15 A feature provided in a user's startup file appends the output of the **date** command to a file foo whenever a user logs in. How can the user print a report showing the day along with the number of times she logged in on that day?

Filters Using Regular Expressions—grep and sed

You often need to search a file for a pattern, either to see the lines containing (or not containing) it or to have it replaced with something else. This chapter discusses two important filters that are specially suited for these tasks—**grep** and **sed**. **grep** takes care of all search requirements you may have. **sed** goes further and can even manipulate the individual characters in a line. In fact **sed** can do several things, some of them quite well.

This chapter also takes up one of the fascinating features of UNIX—*regular expressions*. When discussing **more** and **vi**, we observed that the search patterns in those programs can also take on special expressions. In this chapter, you'll see regular expressions in all their manifestations. This chapter should prepare you well for **awk** and **perl** because they too use these expressions.

WHAT YOU WILL LEARN

- Use **grep** to search a file for a pattern and display both matching and nonmatching lines.

- The various **grep** options to display a count, line numbers or filenames.

- The concept of a *regular expression* as a mechanism for matching multiple similar patterns.

- The significance of the characters of the *Basic Regular Expression* (BRE) set.

- The significance of the characters of the *Extended Regular Expression* (ERE) set.

- Use **sed** to edit an input stream and understand its addressing mechanism.

- The *substitution* feature and how it is enhanced when used with regular expressions.

- The significance of the *repeated* and *remembered* patterns.

TOPICS OF SPECIAL INTEREST

- Use the *interval regular expression* (IRE) to locate or replace patterns at specific locations.

- Use the *tagged regular expression* (TRE) to use *part* of the source pattern in the target pattern.

13.1 grep: SEARCHING FOR A PATTERN

UNIX has a special family of commands for handling search requirements, and the principal member of this family is the **grep** command. **grep** scans its input for a pattern and displays lines containing the pattern, the line numbers or filenames where the pattern occurs. The command uses the following syntax:

```
grep options pattern filename(s)
```

grep searches for *pattern* in one or more *filename(s)*, or the standard input if no filename is specified. The first argument (barring the options) is the pattern and the remaining arguments are filenames. Let's use **grep** to display lines containing the string sales from the file emp.1st; the contents of this file are shown in Section 12.1:

```
$ grep "sales" emp.1st
2233|a.k. shukla      |g.m.     |sales      |12/12/52|6000
1006|chanchal singhvi |director |sales      |03/09/38|6700
1265|s.n. dasgupta    |manager  |sales      |12/09/63|5600
2476|anil aggarwal    |manager  |sales      |01/05/59|5000
```

Because **grep** is also a filter, it can search its standard input for the pattern, and also save the standard output in a file:

```
who | grep kumar > foo
```

Though we have used the pattern both with ("sales") and without quotes (kumar), it's generally safe to quote the pattern. In fact, quoting is essential if the search string consists of more than one word or uses any of the shell's characters like *, $, etc.

grep also silently returns the prompt in case the pattern can't be located:

```
$ grep president emp.1st          No quoting necessary here
$ _                               No president found
```

The command *failed* because the string president couldn't be located. Though the feature of scanning a file for a pattern is available in both **sed** and **awk**, these commands are *not* considered to fail if they can't locate the patterns in their input. The success or failure of a command is yet another important feature of the UNIX system, and you'll see in Chapter 14 (shell programming) how this feature is used in the command line of the shell's programming constructs.

When **grep** is used with multiple filenames, it displays the filenames along with the output. In the next example, **grep** searches two files. Don't bother about what they contain; just observe how each line is preceded by the filename:

```
$ grep "director" emp1.1st emp2.1st
emp1.1st:1006|chanchal singhvi |director |sales      |03/09/38|6700
emp1.1st:6521|lalit chowdury   |director |marketing  |26/09/45|8200
emp2.1st:9876|jai sharma       |director |production |12/03/50|7000
emp2.1st:2365|barun sengupta   |director |personnel  |11/05/47|7800
```

Though we need not have quoted the patterns in these examples, quoting is essential when the pattern contains multiple words:

```
$ grep 'jai sharma' emp.lst
9876|jai sharma        |director |production|12/03/50|7000
```

Though quotes are redundant in single-word fixed strings, it's better to enforce their use. It sets up a good habit with no adverse consequences. You can then use regular expressions inside them.

Note: Quote the pattern used with **grep** if it contains multiple words or special characters that can be interpreted otherwise by the shell. You can generally use either single or double quotes, but if the special characters in the pattern require command substitution or variable evaluation to be performed, you must use double quotes.

13.1.1 grep Options

grep is one of the most important UNIX commands, and you must know the options that POSIX requires **grep** to support. Table 13.1 shows only the POSIX options. Linux supports all of these options, but Solaris has two versions of **grep** (in /usr/bin and /usr/xpg4/bin), and between them they support all POSIX options.

Ignoring Case (-i)   When you look for a name but are not sure of the case, use the -i (ignore) option. This option ignores case for pattern matching:

```
$ grep -i 'agarwal' emp.lst
3564|sudhir Agarwal   |executive|personnel |06/07/47|7500
```

This locates the name Agarwal using the pattern agarwal.

Deleting Lines (-v)   **grep** can play an inverse role too; the -v (inverse) option selects all lines *except* those containing the pattern. Thus, you can create a file otherlist containing all but directors:

```
$ grep -v 'director' emp.lst > otherlist
$ wc -l otherlist
  11 otherlist                       There were 4 directors initially
```

More often than not, when we use **grep -v**, we also redirect its output to a file as a means of getting rid of unwanted lines. Obviously, the lines are not deleted from the original file as such.

Note: The -v option removes lines from **grep**'s output, but doesn't actually change the argument file. This option is frequently used with redirection.

Displaying Line Numbers (-n)   The -n (number) option displays the line numbers containing the pattern, along with the lines:

```
$ grep -n 'marketing' emp.lst
3:5678|sumit chakrobarty|d.g.m.   |marketing |19/04/43|6000
11:6521|lalit chowdury  |director |marketing |26/09/45|8200
14:2345|j.b. saxena     |g.m.     |marketing |12/03/45|8000
15:0110|v.k. agrawal    |g.m.     |marketing |31/12/40|9000
```

The line numbers are shown at the beginning of each line, separated from the actual line by a :. Now that you know how to use **cut**, it's a simple matter to extract only the line numbers from this output.

Counting Lines Containing Pattern (-c)   How many directors are there in the file? The -c (count) option counts the number of lines containing the pattern (which is not the same as number of occurrences). The following example reveals that there are four of them:

```
$ grep -c 'director' emp.lst
4
```

If you use this command with multiple files, the filename is prefixed to the line count:

```
$ grep -c director emp*.lst
emp.lst:4
emp1.lst:2
emp2.lst:2
empold.lst:4
```

Sometimes, you need to get a single count from all of these files so that you can use it in script logic. You have already handled a similar situation before *(8.7.1)*, so you should be able to use **grep** in a manner that drops the filenames from the output.

Displaying Filenames (-l)   The -l (list) option displays only the names of files containing the pattern:

```
$ grep -l 'manager' *.lst
desig.lst
emp.lst
emp1.lst
empn.lst
```

So if you have forgotten the filename where you last saw something, just use this option to find out.

Matching Multiple Patterns (-e)   With the -e option (Solaris has it only in the XPG4 version.), you can match the three *agarwals* by using **grep** like this:

```
$ grep -e "Agarwal" -e "aggarwal" -e "agrawal" emp.lst
2476|anil aggarwal    |manager  |sales     |05/01/59|5000
3564|sudhir Agarwal   |executive|personnel |07/06/47|7500
0110|v.k. agrawal     |g.m.     |marketing |12/31/40|9000
```

You could question the wisdom of entering such a long command line when the patterns don't differ much from one another. Yes, **grep** supports sophisticated pattern matching techniques that can display the same lines but with a *single* expression. This is the ideal forum for regular expressions to make their entry.

Taking Patterns from a File (-f)   You can place all the three patterns in a separate file, one pattern per line. **grep** uses the -f option to take patterns from a file:

```
grep -f pattern.lst emp.lst
```

In Solaris, the -f option is available only in its XPG4 version. There's no problem with this option in Linux.

Table 13.1 Options Used by **grep**

Option	Significance
-i	Ignores case for matching
-v	Doesn't display lines matching expression
-n	Displays line numbers along with lines
-c	Displays count of number of occurrences
-l	Displays list of filenames only
-e *exp*	Specifies expression with this option. Can use multiple times. Also used for matching expression beginning with a hyphen.
-x	Matches pattern with entire line (doesn't match embedded patterns)
-f *file*	Takes patterns from *file*, one per line
-E	Treats pattern as an extended regular expression (ERE)
-F	Matches multiple fixed strings (in **fgrep**-style)

13.2 BASIC REGULAR EXPRESSIONS (BRE)—AN INTRODUCTION

View the file emp.lst (12.1) once again and locate all the agarwals. On close examination, you'll see three lines containing similar, but not identical patterns—Agarwal, aggarwal and agrawal. It's tedious to specify each pattern separately with the -e option. This is where searches in UNIX become truly remarkable; you can locate an agarwal without knowing exactly how his name is spelled.

Like the shell's wild-cards (8.3) which match similar filenames with a single expression, **grep** uses an expression of a different type to match a group of similar patterns. Unlike wild-cards, however, this expression is a feature of the *command* that uses it and has nothing to do with the shell. It uses an elaborate metacharacter set (Table 13.2), overshadowing the shell's wild-cards, and can perform amazing matches. If an expression uses any of these characters, it is termed a **regular expression**. Some of the characters used by regular expressions are also meaningful to the shell—enough reason why these expressions should be quoted.

Regular expressions take care of some common query and substitution requirements. You may want the system to present a list of similar names so you can select exactly the one you need. Or you may want to replace multiple spaces with a single space, or display lines that begin with a #. You may even be looking for a string at a specific column position in a line. All of this is possible (and much more) with regular expressions as you'll discover in the three rounds of discussions that feature the subject in this chapter.

POSIX identifies regular expressions as belonging to two categories—*basic* and *extended*. **grep** supports basic regular expressions (BRE) by default and extended regular expressions (ERE) with the -E option. **sed** supports only the BRE set. We'll first start with a minimal treatment of the BRE set and then take up the ERE set in the next section. We'll later expand the coverage of the BRE when we discuss **sed**.

Note: Regular expressions are interpreted by the command and not by the shell. Quoting ensures that the shell isn't able to interfere and interpret the metacharacters in its own way.

Table 13.2 The Basic Regular Expression (BRE) Character Subset

Symbols or Expression	Matches
*	Zero or more occurrences of the previous character
g*	Nothing or g, gg, ggg, etc.
.	A single character
.*	Nothing or any number of characters
[pqr]	A single character p, q or r
[c1-c2]	A single character within the ASCII range represented by c1 and c2
[1-3]	A digit between 1 and 3
[^pqr]	A single character which is not a p, q or r
[^a-zA-Z]	A nonalphabetic character
^pat	Pattern pat at beginning of line
pat$	Pattern pat at end of line
bash$	bash at end of line
^bash$	bash as the only word in line
^$	Lines containing nothing

13.2.1 The Character Class

A regular expression lets you specify a group of characters enclosed within a pair of rectangular brackets, [ ], in which case the match is performed for a *single* character in the group. This form resembles the one used by the shell's wild-cards. Thus, the expression

    [ra]

matches either an r or an a. The metacharacters [and] can now be used to match Agarwal and agrawal. The following regular expression

    [aA]g[ar][ar]wal

matches the two names. The character class [aA] matches the letter a in both lowercase and uppercase. The model [ar][ar] matches any of the four patterns:

    aa   ar   ra   rr

of which the second and third are relevant to the present problem. As a first step, let's use this regular expression with **grep**:

```
$ grep "[aA]g[ar][ar]wal" emp.lst
3564|sudhir Agarwal    |executive|personnel |07/06/47|7500
0110|v.k. agrawal      |g.m.     |marketing |12/31/40|9000
```

A single pattern has matched two similar strings; that's what regular expressions are all about. You can also use ranges, both for alphabets and numerals. The pattern [a-zA-Z0-9] matches a single alphanumeric character. When you use a range, make sure that the character on the left of the hyphen has a lower ASCII value than the one on the right. Also bear in mind that uppercase precedes lowercase in the ASCII sequence.

Negating a Class (^)   Regular expressions use the ^ (caret) to negate the character class, while the shell uses the ! (bang). When the character class *begins* with this character, all characters other than the ones grouped in the class, are matched. So, [^a-zA-Z] matches a single nonalphabetic character string.

Note: The character class feature is similar to the wild-cards except that negation of the class is done by a ^ (caret), while in the shell it's done by the ! (bang). Like in wild-cards, the character class is the only way you can negate a single character. For instance, [^p] represents any character other than p.

13.2.2 The *

The * (asterisk) refers to the *immediately preceding* character. However, its interpretation is the trickiest of the lot as it bears absolutely no resemblance whatsoever with the * used by wild-cards or DOS (or the * used by Amazon or Ebay in search strings). Here, it indicates that the *previous* character can occur many times, or not at all. The pattern

    g*

matches the single character g, or any number of gs. Because the previous character may not occur at all, it also matches a null string. Thus, apart from this null string, it also matches the following strings:

    g   gg   ggg   gggg   .....

Mark the key words "zero or more occurrences of the previous character" that are used to describe the significance of the *. Don't make the mistake of using g* to match a string beginning with g; use gg* instead. The * used here has a different significance from the * used by wild-cards, where it doesn't relate to the previous character at all.

How do you match all three patterns? The third pattern aggarwal contains an extra g, while the other patterns don't. To include this string also, you can use the * to enhance the previous expression. Observe carefully that the regular expression

    [aA]gg*[ar][ar]wal

matches all three patterns. Now use this expression with **grep**, and you'll find that it solves the problem:

```
$ grep "[aA]gg*[ar][ar]wal" emp.lst
2476|anil aggarwal     |manager   |sales     |05/01/59|5000
3564|sudhir Agarwal     |executive|personnel |07/06/47|7500
0110|v.k. agrawal      |g.m.      |marketing |12/31/40|9000
```

A simple regular expression matches all three names! You don't have to use the -e option three times to get this result. But note that these are not the only strings it can match; the expression is general enough to include other patterns. It would have also matched Agggaawal had there been such a pattern in the file.

Note: C programmers should note that the expression s*printf matches sprintf, ssprintf, sssprintf and so forth, but it also matches printf, because the previous character, s, which the * refers to, may not occur at all.

13.2.3 The Dot

A . matches a single character. The shell uses the ? character to indicate that. The pattern

    2...

matches a four-character pattern beginning with a 2. The shell's equivalent pattern is 2????.

The Regular Expression .*   The dot along with the * (.*) constitutes a very useful regular expression. It signifies any number of characters, or none. Consider that you want to look up the name j. saxena but are not sure whether it actually exists in the file as j.b. saxena or as joginder saxena. No problem, just embed the .* in the search string:

```
$ grep "j.*saxena" emp.lst
2345|j.b. saxena      |g.m.      |marketing |03/12/45|8000
```

Note that if you look for the name j.b. saxena, the expression should be j\.b\.saxena. The dots need to be escaped here with the \, the same character you used in the shell *(8.4.1)* for despecializing the next character.

Note: A regular expression match is made for the longest possible string. Thus, when you use the expression 03.*05, it will match 03 and 05 as close to the left and right of the line, respectively.

13.2.4 Specifying Pattern Locations (^ and $)

Most of the regular expression characters are used for matching patterns, but there are two that can match a pattern at the beginning or end of a line. Anchoring a pattern is often necessary when it can occur in more than one place in a line, and you are interested in its occurrence only at a particular location. These are the two characters that are used:

^ (caret) — For matching at the beginning of a line.

$ — For matching at the end of a line.

Consider a simple example. Try to extract those lines where the emp-id begins with a 2. What happens if you simply use

    2...

as the expression? This won't do because the character 2, followed by three characters, can occur anywhere in the line. You must indicate to **grep** that the pattern occurs at the beginning of the line, and the ^ does it easily:

```
$ grep "^2" emp.lst
2233|a.k. shukla       |g.m.      |sales     |12/12/52|6000
2365|barun sengupta    |director  |personnel |05/11/47|7800
2476|anil aggarwal     |manager   |sales     |05/01/59|5000
2345|j.b. saxena       |g.m.      |marketing |03/12/45|8000
```

Similarly, to select those lines where the salary lies between 7000 and 7999, you have to use the $ at the end of the pattern:

```
$ grep "7...$" emp.lst
9876|jai sharma        |director  |production|03/12/50|7000
2365|barun sengupta    |director  |personnel |05/11/47|7800
3564|sudhir Agarwal    |executive |personnel |07/06/47|7500
```

How can you reverse the search and select only those lines where the emp-ids *don't* begin with a 2? You need the expression ^[^2]:

```
grep "^[^2]" emp.lst
```

UNIX has no command that lists only directories. However, we can use a pipeline to "grep" those lines from the listing that begin with a d:

```
ls -l | grep "^d"                          Shows only directories
```

You should convert this into an *alias (10.4)* or a *shell function (21.10)* so that it is always available for you to use.

Note: The caret has a triple role to play in regular expressions. When placed at the beginning of a character class (e.g. [^a-z]), it negates every character of the class. When placed outside it, and at the beginning of the expression (e.g. ^2...), the pattern is matched at the beginning of the line. At any other location (e.g. a^b), it matches itself literally.

13.2.5 When Metacharacters Lose Their Meaning

It is possible that some of these special characters actually exist as part of the text. If a literal match has to be made for any of them, the "magic" of the characters should be turned off. Sometimes, that is automatically done if the characters violate the regular expression rules. Like the caret, the meaning of these characters can change depending on the place they occupy in the expression.

The - loses its meaning inside the character class if it's not enclosed on either side by a suitable character, or when placed outside the class. The . and * lose their meanings when placed inside the character class. The * is also matched literally if it's the first character of the expression. For instance, when you use **grep "*"**, you are in fact looking for an asterisk.

Sometimes, you may need to escape these characters, say, when looking for a pattern g*. In that case, **grep "g*"** won't do, and you have to use the \ for escaping. Similarly, to look for a [, you should use \[, and to look for the literal pattern .*, you should use \.*.

Regular expressions are found everywhere in the UNIX system. Apart from **grep**, some of the most powerful UNIX commands like **vi, sed, awk, perl** and **expr** also use regular expressions, a reason why these commands have become indispensable to the UNIX tool kit. You must understand them because they hold the key to the mastery of the UNIX system.

13.3 EXTENDED REGULAR EXPRESSIONS (ERE) AND egrep

Extended regular expressions (ERE) make it possible to match dissimilar patterns with a single expression. This set uses some additional characters (Table 13.3) and POSIX-compliant versions of **grep** use them with the -E option. Linux **grep** has this option, but Solaris users must use **/usr/xpg4/bin/grep** to use EREs. If your version of **grep** doesn't support this option, then use **egrep** but without the -E option.

13.3.1 The + and ?

The ERE set includes two special characters, + and ?. They are often used in place of the * to *restrict* the matching scope. They signify the following:

+ — Matches one or more occurrences of the previous character.

? — Matches zero or one occurrence of the previous character.

In both cases, the emphasis is on the *previous* character. This means that b+ matches b, bb, bbb, etc., but unlike b*, it doesn't match nothing. The expression b? matches either a single instance of b or nothing. These characters restrict the scope of match as compared to the *.

Using this extended set, you can now have a different regular expression for matching Agarwal and aggarwal. Note that the character g occurs only once or twice. So, gg? now restricts the expansion to one or two gs only. This time we need to use **grep**'s -E option to use an ERE:

```
$ grep -E "[aA]gg?arwal" emp.lst
2476|anil aggarwal    |manager  |sales     |01/05/59|5000
3564|sudhir Agarwal    |executive|personnel |06/07/47|7500
```

The + is a pretty useful character too. When you are looking for a multiword string like #include <stdio.h>, but don't know how many spaces separate the #include and <stdio.h>, you can use the expression #include +<stdio.h> to match them all. This expression matches the following patterns:

```
#include <stdio.h>      #include  <stdio.h>      #include      <stdio.h>
```

And if you are not sure whether there's a space between # and include, include the ? in the expression:

```
# ?include +<stdio.h>
```

But there could be tabs here instead of spaces as well, so how does one handle them?

13.3.2 Matching Multiple Patterns (|, (and))

The | is the delimiter of multiple patterns. Using it, we can locate both sengupta and dasgupta from the file and without using the -e option twice:

```
$ grep -E 'sengupta|dasgupta' emp.lst
2365|barun sengupta    |director |personnel |11/05/47|7800
1265|s.n. dasgupta     |manager  |sales     |12/09/63|5600
```

The ERE thus handles the problem easily, but offers an even better alternative. The characters, (and), let you group patterns, and when you use the | inside the parentheses, you can frame an even more compact pattern:

```
$ grep -E '(sen|das)gupta' emp.lst
2365|barun sengupta    |director |personnel |11/05/47|7800
1265|s.n. dasgupta     |manager  |sales     |12/09/63|5600
```

EREs when combined with BREs form very powerful regular expressions. For instance, the expression agg?[ar]+wal contains characters from both sets. All EREs can also be placed in a file in exactly the same way they are used in the command line. You then have to use **grep** both with the -E and -f options to take the patterns from the file.

Note: If **grep** doesn't support the -E option on your machine, use **egrep** without the -E option for all examples considered in this section.

Table 13.3 The Extended Regular Expression (ERE) Set Used by **grep**, **egrep** and **awk**

Expression	Significance
ch+	Matches one or more occurrences of character *ch*
ch?	Matches zero or one occurrence of character *ch*
exp1|*exp1*	Matches *exp1* or *exp2*
GIF|JPEG	Matches GIF or JPEG
(*x1*|*x2*)*x3*	Matches *x1x3* or *x2x3*
(lock|ver)wood	Matches lockwood or verwood

13.4 sed:THE STREAM EDITOR

sed is a multipurpose tool which combines the work of several filters. It is derived from **ed**, the original UNIX editor (not discussed in this text). **sed** performs noninteractive operations on a data stream—hence its name. It uses very few options but has a host of features that allow you to select lines and run instructions on them. Learning **sed** will prepare you well for **perl** which uses many of these features.

Like the **diff** command *(5.12)*, **sed** uses **instructions** to act on text. An instruction combines an **address** for selecting lines, with an **action** to be taken on them, as shown by the syntax:

    sed options 'address action' file(s)

The address and action are enclosed within single quotes. Addressing in **sed** is done in two ways:

- By one or two line numbers (like 3,7).
- By specifying a /-enclosed pattern which occurs in a line (like /From:/).

In the first form, *address* specifies either one line number to select a single line or a set of two (3,7) to select a group of contiguous lines. Likewise, the second form uses one or two patterns. The *action* component is drawn from **sed**'s family of internal commands (Table 13.4). It can either be a simple display (print) or an editing function like insertion, deletion or substitution of text. We'll refer to these actions as *commands*.

sed processes several instructions in a sequential manner. Each instruction operates on the output of the previous instruction. In this context, two options are relevant, and probably they are the only ones you'll use with **sed**—the -e option that lets you use multiple instructions, and the -f option to take instructions from a file. Both options are used by **grep** in identical manner.

13.5 LINE ADDRESSING

To consider **line addressing** first, the instruction **3q** can be broken down to the address 3 and the action **q** (quit). When this instruction is enclosed within quotes and followed by one or more filenames, you can simulate **head -n 3** in this way:

```
$ sed '3q' emp.lst                          Quits after line number 3
2233|a.k. shukla        |g.m.     |sales      |12/12/52|6000
9876|jai sharma         |director |production|03/12/50|7000
5678|sumit chakrobarty|d.g.m.   |marketing |04/19/43|6000
```

Generally, we'll be using the **p** (print) command to display lines. However, this command behaves in a seemingly strange manner; it outputs both the selected lines as well as *all* lines. So the selected lines appear twice. We must suppress this behavior with the -n option and remember to use this option whenever we use the **p** command. Thus,

```
$ sed -n '1,2p' emp.lst
2233|a.k. shukla        |g.m.     |sales      |12/12/52|6000
9876|jai sharma         |director |production|03/12/50|7000
```

prints the first two lines. To select the last line of the file, use the $:

```
$ sed -n '$p' emp.lst
0110|v.k. agrawal       |g.m.     |marketing |31/12/40|9000
```

Selecting Lines from Anywhere   The two command invocations above emulate the **head** and **tail** commands, but **sed** can also select a contiguous group of lines from anywhere in the file. To select lines 9 through 11, you have to use the following command:

```
sed -n '9,11p' emp.lst
```

Selecting Multiple Groups of Lines   **sed** is not restricted to selecting a single group of lines. You can select as many sections from just about anywhere:

```
sed -n '1,2p                     3 addresses in one command, using only a single
7,9p                             pair of quotes
$p' emp.lst                      Selects the last line
```

In the next section, we'll be considering alternative methods of running the above **sed** command.

Negating the Action (!)   **sed** also has a negation operator (!), which can be used with any action. For instance, selecting the first two lines is the same as *not* selecting lines 3 through the end. A previous command sequence (**1,2p**) can be written in this way too:

```
sed -n '3,$!p' emp.lst
```
                                            Don't print lines 3 to end

The address and action are normally enclosed within a pair of single quotes. As you have already learned by now, you should use double quotes only when variable evaluation or command substitution is embedded in the quoted string.

Tip: Use the -n option whenever you use the **p** command, unless you deliberately want to select lines twice. Usually, that requirement doesn't arise.

13.6 USING MULTIPLE INSTRUCTIONS (-e and -f)

In the previous section, we encountered multiple instructions in a single **sed** command, the one that selected three segments from a file. There's adequate scope of using the -e and -f options whenever **sed** is used with multiple instructions. The -e option allows you to enter as many instructions as you wish, each preceded by the option. We can repeat the command prior to the previous one with this:

```
sed -n -e '1,2p' -e '7,9p' -e '$p' emp.lst
```

When you have too many instructions to use or when you have a set of common instructions that you execute often, they are better stored in a file. For instance, the above three instructions can be stored in a file, with each instruction on a separate line:

```
$ cat instr.fil
1,2p
7,9p
$p
```

You can now use the -f option to direct **sed** to take its instructions from the file using the command
sed -n -f instr.fil emp.lst.

sed is quite liberal in that it allows a great deal of freedom in using and repeating options. You can use the -f option with multiple files. You can also combine the -e and -f options as many times as you want:

```
sed -n -f instr.fil1 -f instr.fil2 emp.lst
sed -n -e '/saxena/p' -f instr.fil1 -f instr.fil2 emp?.lst
```

These are some of the features of **sed** that make it so versatile, and at the same time easy to work with. The second example uses context addressing (/saxena/) in an instruction. This is the other form of addressing used by **sed**, and is considered next.

13.7 CONTEXT ADDRESSING

The second form of addressing, called **context addressing**, lets you specify one or two patterns to locate lines. The pattern must be bounded by a / on either side. When you specify a single pattern, all lines containing the pattern are selected. You can "grep" the directors in this way:

```
$ sed -n '/director/p' emp.1st
9876|jai sharma        |director |production|03/12/50|7000
2365|barun sengupta    |director |personnel |05/11/47|7800
1006|chanchal singhvi  |director |sales     |09/03/38|6700
6521|lalit chowdury    |director |marketing |09/26/45|8200
```

You can also specify a comma-separated pair of context addresses to select a group of lines. Line and context addresses can also be mixed:

```
sed -n '/dasgupta/,/saksena/p' emp.1st
sed -n '1,/dasgupta/p' emp.1st
```

Using Regular Expressions   Context addresses also uses regular expressions, which you first saw used in **grep**. The following command lines should refresh your memory:

```
sed -n '/[aA]gg*[ar][ar]wal/p' emp.1st        All the agarwals
sed -n '/sa[kx]s*ena/p                          Either the saxenas or
        /gupta/p' emp.1st                       gupta
```

You can use the anchoring characters, ^ and $, as part of the regular expression syntax. This is how you locate all people born in the year 1950:

```
$ sed -n '/50.....$/p' emp.1st
9876|jai sharma        |director |production|03/12/50|7000
4290|jayant Choudhury  |executive|production|09/07/50|6000
```

Regular expressions in **grep** and **sed** are actually more powerful than the ones we have used so far. They use some more special characters, and we'll meet them in the third round of discussions at the end of the chapter.

Tip: C programmers should use the command **sed -n '/{/,/}/p' foo.c** to select the *first* block of code delimited by { and }. **sed** won't select the subsequent blocks.

Note: We used single quotes here, but if the pattern itself contains a single quote, you must use double quotes. In that case, make sure that a $ (if present) in the pattern is not interpreted as a variable unless you want it treated that way.

13.8 WRITING SELECTED LINES TO A FILE (w)

Irrespective of the way you select lines (by line or context addressing), you can use the **w** (write) command to write the selected lines to a separate file. Save the lines of directors in dlist in this way:

```
sed -n '/director/w dlist' emp.1st              No display when using -n option
```

Since **sed** accepts more than one address, you can perform a full context splitting of the file emp.1st. You can store the lines pertaining to the directors, managers and executives in three separate files:

```
sed -n '/director/w dlist
        /manager/w mlist
        /executive/w elist' emp.1st
```

The same applies to line addressing also. For a file foo.main containing 1000 lines, you can save the two halves separately:

```
sed -n '1,500w foo1                    Saves first 500 lines in foo1
501,$w foo2' foo.main                  and the rest in foo2
```

Note: The -n option is required with the **w** command only to suppress printing of all lines on the terminal. However, even without it, the selected lines will be written to the respective files.

13.9 TEXT EDITING

This section discusses some of the editing commands available in **sed**'s action component. **sed** can insert text and change existing text in a file. A **vi** user would be relieved to learn that the commands are also the same—**i** (insert), **a** (append), **c** (change) and **d** (delete). But there are important differences too.

13.9.1 Inserting and Changing Lines (i, a, c)

The **i** command inserts text. A C programmer can add two common "include" lines at the beginning of a program, foo.c in this way:

```
$ sed '1i\                        Need to use \ before [Enter] here ...
> #include <stdio.h>\             and here only
> #include <unistd.h>            No \ in last line of input
> ' foo.c > $$                    Redirect output to a temporary file
```

First enter the instruction **1i**, which inserts text at line number 1. Then enter a \ before pressing *[Enter]*. You can now key in as many lines as you wish. Each line *except the last* has to be terminated by the \ before hitting *[Enter]*. **sed** identifies the line without the \ as the last line of input. This technique has to be followed when using the **a** and **c** commands also.

The above command writes the concatenated output of the two lines of inserted text and existing lines to standard output, which we redirected to a temporary file, $$. We must move this file to foo.c to be able to use it. The first two lines show that the **i** command worked fine:

```
$ mv $$ foo.c ; head -n 2 foo.c
#include <stdio.h>
#include <unistd.h>
```

Doublespacing Text   What is the consequence of not using an address with these commands? The inserted or changed text is then placed after or before *every* line of the file. The following command

```
sed 'a\
                                              Inserts after every line
' emp.lst                                     this blank line
```

inserts a blank line *after* each line of the file is printed. This is another way of doublespacing text *(12.2.1)*. Using **i** here would have inserted a blank line *before* each selected line.

13.9.2 Deleting Lines (d)

sed uses the **d** (delete) command to emulate **grep**'s **-v** option of selecting lines not containing the pattern. Either of the following commands

```
sed '/director/d' emp.lst > olist
sed -n '/director/!p' emp.lst > olist                    -n option not to be used with d
```

selects all lines except those containing director, and saves them in olist.

Deleting Blank Lines   A blank line consists of any number of spaces, tabs or nothing. How do you delete these lines from a file? Frame a pattern which matches zero or more occurrences of a space or tab:

```
sed '/^[□→]*$/d' foo                          A space and a tab inside [ ]
```

You need to press the *[Tab]* key or *[Ctrl-i]* inside the character class—immediately after the space. Providing a ^ at the beginning and a $ at the end matches lines that contain only whitespace. Note that this expression also matches lines containing nothing.

13.10 SUBSTITUTION (s)

Substitution is easily the most important feature of **sed**, and this is one job that **sed** does exceedingly well. It lets you replace a pattern in its input with something else. The use of regular expressions enhances our pattern matching capabilities, and in this chapter we feature some more regular expression characters that make the use of **sed** so compelling. You have encountered the substitution syntax in **vi** before *(7.9)*:

*[address]*s/*expression1*/*expression2*/*flags*

Here, *expression1* (which can also be a regular expression) is replaced with *expression2* in all lines specified by *[address]*. Unlike in **vi**, however, if the address is not specified, the substitution is performed for all matching lines. This means that there's no need to use 1,$ as the address. To bring *flags* into the picture, let's first avoid its use and replace the | with a colon:

```
$ sed 's/|/:/' emp.lst | head -n 2
2233:a.k. shukla     |g.m.      |sales      |12/12/52|6000
9876:jai sharma      |director  |production|12/03/50|7000
```

Just look at what **sed** has done; only the first (left-most) instance of the | in a line has been replaced. You need to use the g (global) flag to replace all the pipes:

```
$ sed 's/|/:/g' emp.lst | head -n 2
2233:a.k. shukla     :g.m.      :sales      :12/12/52:6000
9876:jai sharma      :director  :production:12/03/50:7000
```

We used global substitution to replace all pipes with colons. **s** here is the same as **1,$s**. Though we see two lines here, the substitution has been carried out for the entire file. You can limit the vertical boundaries too by specifying an address:

```
sed '1,3s/|/:/g' emp.lst                          First three lines only
```

Substitution is not restricted to a single character; it can be any string. Let's replace the word director with member in the first five lines of emp.lst:

```
$ sed '1,5s/director/member  /' emp.lst
2233|a.k. shukla       |g.m.      |sales     |12/12/52|6000
9876|jai sharma        |member    |production|03/12/50|7000
5678|sumit chakrobarty |d.g.m.    |marketing |04/19/43|6000
2365|barun sengupta    |member    |personnel |05/11/47|7800
5423|n.k. gupta        |chairman  |admin     |08/30/56|5400
1006|chanchal singhvi  |director  |sales     |09/03/38|6700
....more lines....
```

sed also uses regular expressions for patterns to be substituted. To replace all occurrences of agarwal, aggarwal and agrawal with simply Agarwal, use the regular expression you had used earlier with **grep** (13.2.2):

```
sed 's/[Aa]gg*[ar][ar]wal/Agarwal/g' emp.lst
```

You can also use the anchoring characters, ^ and $, with the same meaning. Further, when either is used as a sole character in the source pattern, it implies that the target pattern has to be placed at that location. This is how you can add the 2 prefix to all emp-ids:

```
$ sed 's/^/2/' emp.lst | head -n 1
22233|a.k. shukla       |g.m.      |sales     |12/12/52|6000
```

There are five digits now in the first field. Likewise, you can add the suffix .00 to the salary:

```
$ sed 's/$/.00/' emp.lst | head -n 1
2233|a.k. shukla       |g.m.      |sales     |12/12/52|6000.00
```

Note: When a g is used at the end of a substitution instruction, the change is performed globally along the line. Without it, only the left-most occurrence is replaced.

Performing Multiple Substitutions   You can perform multiple substitutions with one invocation of **sed**. Simply press *[Enter]* at the end of each instruction and finally close the quote at the end. This is how you replace three HTML tags:

```
$ sed 's/<I>/<EM>/g
> s/<B>/<STRONG>/g
> s/<U>/<EM>/g' form.html
```

sed is a stream editor; it works on a data stream. This means that an instruction processes the output of the previous one. This is something users often forget; they don't get the sequence right. Note that the following sequence finally converts all <I> tags to <STRONG>:

```
$ sed 's/<I>/<EM>/g
> s/<EM>/<STRONG>/g' form.html
```

Tip: When there are a group of instructions to execute, you should place these instructions in a file instead and use **sed** with the -f option.

Compressing Multiple Spaces   How do you delete trailing spaces from the second, third and fourth fields? The regular expression required in the source string needs to signify one or more occurrences of a space, followed by a |:

```
$ sed 's/ *|/|/g' emp.1st | tee empn.1st | head -n 3
2233|a.k. shukla|g.m.|sales|12/12/52|6000
9876|jai sharma|director|production|12/03/50|7000
5678|sumit chakrobarty|d.g.m.|marketing|19/04/43|6000
```

Most UNIX system files (like /etc/passwd) follow this variable-length format because the commonly used filters can easily identify a field by seeing the delimiter. Using **tee**, we created the file empn.1st. This is the file you'll be using with the **awk** command later.

13.10.1 The Remembered Pattern (//)

So far, we have looked for a pattern and then replaced it with something else. Truly speaking, the three commands below do the same job:

```
sed 's/director/member/' emp.1st
sed '/director/s//member/' emp.1st
sed '/director/s/director/member/' emp.1st
```

The second form suggests that **sed** "remembers" the scanned pattern, and stores it in // (2 frontslashes). The // representing an empty (or null) regular expression is interpreted to mean that the search and substituted patterns are the same. We'll call it the **remembered pattern**.

However, when you use // in the target string, it means you are removing the pattern totally:

```
sed 's/|//g' emp.1st                          Removes every | from file
```

The address /director/ in the third form appears to be redundant. However, you must understand this form also because it widens the scope of substitution. It's possible that you may like to replace a string in all lines containing a different string:

```
$ sed -n '/marketing/s/director/member   /p' emp.1st
6521|lalit chowdury   |member   |marketing |09/26/45|8200
```

Note: The significance of // depends on its position in the instruction. If it is in the source string, it implies that the scanned pattern is stored there. If the target string is //, it means that the source pattern is to be removed.

13.11 BASIC REGULAR EXPRESSIONS REVISITED

To master **sed**, you must appreciate the numerous possibilities that regular expressions throw up with this command—more so than in **grep**. This third round of discussions feature some more characters from the BRE set. Both **grep** and **sed** use these characters, but **sed** simply exploits them to the hilt. This time be prepared to see and use a \ before every metacharacter discussed in this section, except the &. We'll learn to use three types of expressions:

- The *repeated pattern*—This uses a single symbol, &, to make the entire source pattern appear at the destination also.
- The *interval regular expression* (IRE)—This expression uses the characters { and } with a single or a pair of numbers between them.
- The *tagged regular expression* (TRE)—This expression groups patterns with (and) and represents them at the destination with numbered tags.

In the last two types of expressions, the metacharacters need escaping so the *command* understands them as special. The expressions themselves are quoted so the shell can't interpret them.

13.11.1 The Repeated Pattern (&)

We sometimes encounter situations when the source pattern also occurs at the destination. We can then use the special character & to represent it. All of these commands do the same thing:

```
sed 's/director/executive director/' emp.lst
sed 's/director/executive &/' emp.lst
sed '/director/s//executive &/' emp.lst
```

All of these commands replace director with executive director. The &, known as the **repeated pattern**, here expands to the entire source string. Apart from the numbered tag (discussed soon), the & is the only other special character you can use in the target expression.

13.11.2 Interval Regular Expression (IRE)

We have matched a pattern at the beginning and end of a line. But what about matching it at any specified location—or within a zone? **sed** and **grep** also use the **interval regular expression** (IRE) that uses an integer (or two) to specify the number of characters preceding a pattern. The IRE uses an escaped pair of curly braces and takes three forms:

- *ch*\{*m*\}—The metacharacter *ch* can occur *m* times.
- *ch*\{*m*,*n*\}—Here, *ch* can occur between *m* and *n* times.
- *ch*\{*m*,\}—Here, *ch* can occur at least *m* times.

All of these forms have the single character regular expression *ch* as the first element. This can either be a literal character, a . (dot), or a character class. It is followed by a pair of escaped curly braces containing either a single number *m*, or a range of numbers lying between *m* and *n* to determine the number of times the character preceding it can occur. The values of *m* and *n* can't exceed 255.

To illustrate the first form, let's consider this small telephone directory where a person has either a wired phone (8 digits) or a mobile phone (10 digits):

```
$ cat teledir.txt
jai    sharma 25853670
chanchal singhvi 9831545629
anil   aggarwal 9830263298
shyam  saksena 23217847
lalit  chowdury 26688726
```

Let's use **grep** to select only those users who have a mobile phone. We must use an IRE to indicate that a numeral can occur 10 times:

```
$ grep '[0-9]\{10\}' teledir.txt
chanchal singhvi 9831545629
anil   aggarwal 9830263298
```

Let's now consider the second form of the IRE, using **sed** this time. Since this matches a pattern within a "zone," we can display the listing for those files that have the write bit set either for group or others:

```
$ ls -l | sed -n '/^.\{5,8\}w/p'
-r-xr-xrwx  3 sumit    dialout      426 Feb 26 19:58 comj
-r-xr-xrwx  3 sumit    dialout      426 Feb 26 19:58 runj
-r-xrw-r-x  1 sumit    dialout      527 Apr 23 07:42 valcode.sh
-r-xrw-r-x  2 sumit    dialout      289 Apr 23 07:42 vvi.sh
```

Extracting Lines Based on Length With the IRE, you can use the following commands to select lines longer than 100 characters. The second one additionally imposes a limit of 150 on the maximum length:

```
sed -n '/.\{101,\}/p' foo          Line length at least 101
grep '^.\{101,150\}$' foo          Line length between 101 and 150
```

The ^ and $ are required in the second example; otherwise lines longer than 150 characters would also be selected. Remember that a regular expression always tries to match the longest pattern possible (13.2.3—Note).

13.11.3 The Tagged Regular Expression (TRE)

This is the most complex of all regular expressions, and possibly the finest. It relates to breaking up a line into groups and then extracting one or more of these groups. The tagged regular expression (TRE) requires two regular expression to be specified—one each for the source and target patterns.

This is how the TRE works. You have to identify the segments of a line that you wish to extract and enclose each segment with a matched pair of escaped parentheses. For instance, if you need to extract a number, you'll have to represent that number as \([0-9]*\). A series of nonalphabetic characters can be represented as \([^a-zA-Z]*\). Every grouped pattern automatically acquires the numeric label n, where n signifies the nth group from the left. To reproduce a group at the destination, you have to use the tag \n. This means that the first group is represented as \1, the second one as \2 and so forth.

Let's illustrate this with a simple example. Consider the telephone directory that was considered in the previous section. Apart from telephone numbers, this file also contains names in the sequence *first_name last_name*. Some lines may have more than one space between the two name components, and our job is to use the TRE to take care of these imperfections.

We'll create a new list from this file that shows the surname first, followed by a , and then the first name and the rest of the line. For instance, the first name in the file should appear as sharma, jai 5853670. We'll have to frame two groups of alphabetic characters and then reverse them in the target pattern, while inserting a comma between them. This is how we obtain a sorted list:

```
$ sed 's/\([a-z]*\) *\([a-z]*\)/\2, \1/' teledir.txt | sort
aggarwal, anil 9830263298
chowdury, lalit 6688726
saksena, shyam 3217847
sharma, jai 5853670
singhvi, chanchal 9831545629
```

The first group, \([a-z]*\), represents zero or more occurrences of alphabetic characters; this effectively captures the first name. An identical pattern takes care of the surname. These two groups are separated by zero or more occurrences of space (▢*). In the target pattern, we recreate these groups but in a reverse sequence with the tags \2 and \1. The comma between them is treated by **sed** literally.

Taking the cue from here, you can now add the century prefix to the year in the fifth field representing the date of birth in our sample database. We'll also convert the date format to *yyyymmdd*. To do that, consider the date field as comprising three pattern groups, representing the day, month and year. This group can be represented by \(..\). Now use the TRE to generate the *19yymmdd* format from the existing one:

```
$ sed 's^\(..\)/\(..\)/\(..\)^19\3\2\1^' emp.lst | head -n 3
2233|a.k. shukla     |g.m.     |sales      |19521212|6000
9876|jai sharma      |director |production |19500312|7000
5678|sumit chakrobarty|d.g.m.  |marketing  |19430419|6000
```

Each group is separated from the next one by /. In the target pattern, we added the string 19, dropped the /, and totally inverted the pattern groups (shown as \3\2\1).

You may be wondering what the ^ is doing here, when a / was expected. The fact is that **sed** doesn't compulsorily use a / to delimit patterns for substitution; *you can use any character provided it doesn't occur in the entire command line*. Choosing a different delimiter has allowed us to get away without escaping the / which actually occurs in the pattern.

You'll find numerous uses for the TRE when using **sed**. Though it's quite cryptic and difficult to comprehend initially, you must understand it if you want **sed** to serve as a gateway to learning **perl**. **perl** also uses these numbered tags but in a more readable form.

Table 13.4 Internal Commands Used by **sed**

Command	Description
i, a, c	Inserts, appends and changes text
d	Deletes line(s)
10q	Quits after reading the first 10 lines
p	Prints line(s) on standard output
3,$p	Prints lines 3 to end (-n option required)
$!p	Prints all lines except last line (-n option required)
/begin/,/end/p	Prints lines enclosed between begin and end (-n option required)
q	Quits after reading up to addressed line
r *flname*	Places contents of file *flname* after line
w *flname*	Writes addressed lines to file *flname*
=	Prints line number addressed
s/*s1*/*s2*/	Replaces first occurrence of expression *s1* in all lines with expression *s2*
10,20s/-/:/	Replaces first occurrence of - in lines 10 to 20 with a :
s/*s1*/*s2*/g	Replaces all occurrences of expression *s1* in all lines with expression *s2*
s/-/:/g	Replaces all occurrences of - in all lines with a :

13.12 CONCLUSION

While **grep** is pretty to easy to comprehend, **sed** is best mastered by sheer practice, by repeated attempts to figure out the exact command sequence that will perform a specific job. You don't always get it right the first time, but don't worry; hardly anybody does—not with this command at least.

This completes our discussion on filters for Part I of this book. We'll visit filters and regular expressions again in Part II when we examine the two heavyweights—**awk** and **perl**. In the next chapter, you'll see how filters are used in shell scripts.

> ### WRAP UP
>
> The **grep** filter searches a file or standard input for a pattern. You can ignore case when performing a match (-i) and select lines not containing the pattern (-v). You can also display a count (-c), the filenames (-1) and line numbers (-n).
>
> **grep** can also be used with a *regular expression* using two sets of metacharacters—the *basic regular expression set* (BRE) and *extended regular expression set* (ERE). **sed** doesn't use the ERE set. All regular expressions must be quoted to prevent the shell from interfering.
>
> In the BRE set, the . matches a single character, while * matches zero or more occurrences of the *previous* character. The character class is similar to the one used by wild-cards except that the ^ negates the class. The pattern .* matches anything and is often embedded in a regular expression. The ^ and $ serve as anchoring characters.

grep uses the ERE with the -E option, but **egrep** does the same without requiring this option. The ERE uses the | to delimit multiple patterns and the (and) to group patterns. The + and ? are similar to the * used in the BRE except that they are more restrictive.

A **sed** *instruction* comprises an *address* and an *action* (command). Lines can be addressed by line numbers or context. The -n option makes sure that lines are not printed twice when using the **p** command. Lines can be inserted (**i**), appended (**a**), changed (**c**) and deleted (**d**).

sed is mostly used for substitution (**s**). The g flag at the end makes the substitution global. The search and substitution patterns can be regular expressions, but only of the BRE type.

A set of two slashes (//) as the source pattern represents the expression used for scanning a pattern (the *remembered pattern*). The & reproduces the entire source pattern at the target (the *repeated pattern*).

The *interval regular expression* (IRE) uses a single or a pair of numbers surrounded by escaped curly braces—like ch\{m,n\}. The expression signifies that *ch* can occur between *m* and *n* times.

The *tagged regular expression* (TRE) uses \(and \) to enclose a pattern. The grouped pattern gets a tag \1, \2, etc. The feature is useful in reproducing a portion of the source pattern at the target.

Test Your Understanding

13.1   What do these commands do? (i) **grep a b c** (ii) **grep <HTML> foo**

13.2   What does **grep "^*"** look for? Is the \ really necessary?

13.3   What do these regular expressions match? (i) a.*b (ii) ..* (iii) ^}$

13.4   How do you use **grep** to locate lines containing these patterns? (i) SIGSTOP or SIGTSTP (ii) SIGTTIN or SIGTTOU (iii) harris or harrison

13.5   How is the expression g* different from gg*?

13.6   Devise a command sequence to locate the line containing the last occurrence of a pattern.

13.7   How can you extract from the output of **find . -name "*.c" -print** only filenames in the current directory and not in its subdirectories?

13.8   What does this command do and what are the two $s doing here?

        grep "$SHELL$" /etc/passwd | cut -d: -f1

13.9   How do you store in the variable numb the number of .c files that contain the string printf?

13.10 Use extended regular expressions to extract all section headers from this book. (Each section is numbered.)

13.11 Devise a sequence to display the listing, ordered by last access time, of the .c files in the current directory that contain the string wait.

13.12 Write a Korn or Bash alias which displays, from the current directory, the listing of only directories.

13.13 How will you display, from all files in the current directory, lines containing the string printf or fprintf without prefixing the filename to each line?

13.14 How will you select from a file (i) lines 3 to 10, (ii) all but the last line?

13.15 How do you (i) print every line of a file twice, (ii) insert a blank line after each line that is read?

13.16 What shortcut does **sed** offer to replace the string Linux with Red Hat Linux?

13.17 How do you add two spaces to the beginning of every line?

13.18 Invert the name of the individual in emp.1st so that the surname occurs first.

Flex Your Brain

13.1 What is the difference between a wild-card and a regular expression?

13.2 Explain the significance of the * in this command: **grep 'botswana.*birds' *.htm***.

13.3 How will you list the *ordinary* files in your current directory that are not user-writable?

13.4 How many lines does **grep '.*' foo** display? What happens if you remove the quotes?

13.5 What is the significance of this command? **grep -l "`echo '\t'`" foo**

13.6 Use command substitution with **grep** to list the names of the persons from emp.1st who were born today.

13.7 How do these expressions differ? (i) [0-9]* and [0-9][0-9]* (ii) ^[^^] and ^^^

13.8 Are the following commands equivalent? **grep "^[^a-z]" foo** and **grep -v "^[a-z]" foo**

13.9 Frame regular expressions to match these patterns: (i) jefferies jeffery jeffreys (ii) hitchen hitchin hitching (iii) Heard herd Hird (iv) dix dick dicks dickson dixon (v) Mcgee mcghee magee

13.10 How will you remove blank lines from a file using (i) **grep**, (ii) **sed**? (A blank line may contain either nothing or only whitespace characters.)

13.11 How do you locate lines containing only printf but not fprintf using (i) **grep** (ii) **sed**? (Note that printf can also occur at the beginning of a line.)

13.12 How do you locate all nonblank lines that don't begin with #, /* or //?

13.13 Locate lines longer than 100 and smaller than 150 characters using (i) **grep**, (ii) **sed**.

13.14 Find out the occurrences of **three** consecutive and identical word characters (like aaa or bbb) using (i) **grep**, (ii) **sed**.

13.15 Devise a sequence to locate those users who have logged in yesterday or earlier but have not logged out, and mail the list to root. Users logged in more than once should feature only once in the list.

13.16 **grep -c ENCRYPTION foo** outputs the number of lines containing ENCRYPTION, but if the pattern sometimes occurs more than once in a line, how do you then obtain a count of all these *occurrences*? (HINT: Use **sed** also.)

13.17 Frame a command sequence that looks at romeo's mailbox to tell him that either he has received a message from henry or the Subject: line contains the word urgent or immediate in lower- or uppercase.

13.18 Using **sed**, how do you add the tags <HTML> at the beginning and </HTML> at the end of a file?

13.19 How do you delete all leading and trailing spaces in all lines of a file?

13.20 How do you locate lines beginning and ending with a dot using (i) **grep**, (ii) **sed**

13.21 Explain what these commands do and if there's anything wrong with them:

  (i) **`sed -e 's/print/printf/g' -e 's/printf/print/g' foo`**
 (ii) **`sed -e 's/compute/calculate/g' -e 's/computer/host/g' foo`**

13.22 Every <B> tag in an HTML file has a closing </B> tag as well. Convert them to <STRONG> and </STRONG>, respectively, using **sed** with a single **s** command.

13.23 Specify the command sequence needed to remove the directory /usr/local/bin from the PATH defined in $HOME/.profile.

Essential Shell Programming

The activities of the shell are not restricted to command interpretation alone. The shell has a whole set of internal commands that can be strung together as a language. We need two chapters to discuss this language. In this chapter, we focus on the Bourne shell—the lowest common denominator of all shells. We have reserved the discussion of the advanced features of the Korn and Bash shells for Part II of the book. However, everything discussed here applies to both these shells too. The C shell uses totally different programming constructs and has been separately treated in Appendix A.

A shell program runs in *interpretive* mode. It is not compiled into a separate executable file as a C program is. Each statement is loaded into memory when it is to be executed. Shell scripts consequently run slower than those written in high-level languages. However, what makes shell programs powerful is that external UNIX commands blend easily with the shell's internal constructs. Speed is not a factor in many jobs we do, and in many cases, using the shell is an advantage—especially in system administrative tasks. *The UNIX system administrator must be an accomplished shell programmer.*

WHAT YOU WILL LEARN

- How shell scripts are executed, and the role of the *interpreter line*.
- Make shell scripts interactive using **read**.
- Use *positional parameters* to read command line arguments.
- The role of the **exit** statement in terminating a script.
- Elementary decision making with the || and && operators.
- Comprehensive decision making with the **if** conditional.
- Use **if** in tandem with **test** to perform numeric and string comparison, and test a file's attributes.
- Use the wild-card pattern matching features of **case** for decision making.
- Integer computing and string handling using **expr**.
- Use a **while** loop to repeatedly execute a set of commands.
- Use a **for** loop with a list.
- Manipulate the positional parameters with the **set** and **shift** statements.
- Use **trap** to control the behavior of a shell script when it receives signals.

TOPICS OF SPECIAL INTEREST

- Redirect some statements to /dev/tty so the other statements can be manipulated collectively.
- Exploit the hard linking feature with $0 to make a script behave in different ways depending on the name by which it is invoked.
- Use a *here document* as the fourth source of standard input to run any interactive shell script noninteractively.

14.1 SHELL SCRIPTS

When a group of commands have to be executed regularly, they should be stored in a file, and the file itself executed as a **shell script** or **shell program**. Though it's not mandatory, we normally use the .sh extension for shell scripts. This makes it easy to match them with wild-cards.

Shell scripts are executed in a separate child shell process, and this sub-shell need not be of the same type as your login shell. In other words, even if your login shell is Bourne, you can use a Korn sub-shell to run your script. By default, the child and parent shells belong to the same type, but you can provide a special *interpreter line* in the first line of the script to specify a different shell for your script.

Tip: Generally, Bourne shell scripts run without problem in the Korn and Bash shells. There are two issues in Bash, however. First, Bash evaluates $0 differently. This has to be handled by appropriate code in the script. Second, it doesn't recognize escape sequences used by **echo** (like \c and \n) unless the -e option is used. To make **echo** behave in the normal manner, place the statement **shopt -s xpg_echo** in your rc file (probably, ~/.bashrc).

Use your **vi** editor to create the shell script, **script.sh** (Fig. 14.1). The script runs three **echo** commands and shows the use of variable evaluation and command substitution. It also prints the calendar of the current month.

```
#!/bin/sh
# script.sh: Sample shell script
echo "Today's date: `date`"
echo "This month's calendar:"
cal `date "+%m 20%y"`               # This month's calendar
echo "My shell: $SHELL"
```

Fig. 14.1 script.sh

Note the comment character (#) that can be placed anywhere in a line; the shell ignores all characters placed on its right. However, this doesn't apply to the first line which also begins with a #. This is the **interpreter line** that was mentioned previously. It always begins with #! and is followed by the pathname of the shell to be used for running the script. Here, this line specifies the Bourne shell.

To run the script, make it executable first and then invoke the script name:

```
$ chmod +x script.sh
$ script.sh
Today's date: Mon Jan  6 10:02:42 IST 2003
This month's calendar:
     January 2003
Su Mo Tu We Th Fr Sa
          1  2  3  4
 5  6  7  8  9 10 11
12 13 14 15 16 17 18
19 20 21 22 23 24 25
26 27 28 29 30 31

My shell: /bin/sh
```

PATH must include the .
or else use ./script.sh

The script is too simple to need any explanation—no inputs, no command line arguments and no control structures. We'll be progressively adding these features to our future scripts.

We mentioned that shell scripts are executed by a child shell. Actually, the child shell reads and executes each statement in sequence (in interpretive mode). You can also *explicitly* spawn a child of your choice with the script name as argument:

```
sh script.sh
```

Will spawn a Bourne shell

When used in this way, the Bourne sub-shell opens the file but ignores the interpreter line. The script doesn't need to have execute permission either. We'll make it a practice to use the interpreter line in all our scripts.

Tip: The pathname of the shell specified in the interpreter line may not match the actual pathname on your system. This sometimes happens with downloaded scripts. To prevent these scripts from breaking, make a symbolic link between the two locations. Note that root access is required to make a symbolic link between **/bin/ksh** and **/usr/bin/ksh**.

14.2 read: MAKING SCRIPTS INTERACTIVE

The **read** statement is the shell's internal tool for taking input from the user, i.e., making scripts interactive. It is used with one or more variables. Input supplied through the standard input is read into these variables. When you use a statement like

```
read name
```

the script pauses at that point to take input from the keyboard. Whatever you enter is stored in the variable name. Since this is a form of assignment, no $ is used before name. The script, **emp1.sh** (Fig. 14.2), uses **read** to take a search string and filename from the terminal.

Shell scripts accept comments prefixed by # anywhere in a line. You know what the sequence \c does *(3.3)*. Run the script and specify the input when the script pauses twice:

```
#!/bin/sh
# emp1.sh: Interactive version - uses read to take two inputs
#
echo "Enter the pattern to be searched: \c"        # No newline
read pname
echo "Enter the file to be used: \c"               # Use echo -e or
read flname                                        # shopt -s xpg_echo in Bash
echo "Searching for $pname from file $flname"
grep "$pname" $flname
echo "Selected records shown above"
```

Fig. 14.2 <code>emp1.sh</code>

```
$ emp1.sh
Enter the pattern to be searched: director
Enter the file to be used: emp.1st
Searching for director from file emp.1st
9876|jai sharma       |director |production|12/03/50|7000
2365|barun sengupta   |director |personnel |11/05/47|7800
Selected records shown above
```

The script first asks for a pattern to be entered. Input the string director, which is assigned to the variable pname. Next, the script asks for the filename; enter the string emp.1st, which is assigned to the variable flname. **grep** then runs with these two variables as arguments.

A single **read** statement can be used with one or more variables to let you enter multiple arguments:

```
read pname flname
```

If the number of arguments supplied is less than the number of variables accepting them, any leftover variables will simply remain unassigned. However, when the number of arguments exceeds the number of variables, the remaining words are assigned to the *last* variable.

14.3 USING COMMAND LINE ARGUMENTS

Like UNIX commands (which are written in C), shell scripts also accept arguments from the command line. They can, therefore, run noninteractively and be used with redirection and pipelines. When arguments are specified with a shell script, they are assigned to certain special "variables"—rather **positional parameters**.

The first argument is read by the shell into the parameter $1, the second argument into $2, and so on. You can't technically call them shell variables because all variable names start with a letter. In addition to these positional parameters, there are a few other special parameters used by the shell. Their significance is noted below:

$* — It stores the complete set of positional parameters as a single string.

$# — It is set to the number of arguments specified. This lets you design scripts that check whether the right number of arguments have been entered.

```
#!/bin/sh
# emp2.sh: Non-interactive version  - uses command line arguments
#
echo "Program: $0                  # $0 contains the program name
The number of arguments specified is $#
The arguments are $*"               # All arguments stored in $*
grep "$1" $2
echo "\nJob Over"
```

Fig. 14.3 emp2.sh

$0— Holds the command name itself. You can link a shell script to be invoked by more than one name. The script logic can check $0 to behave differently depending on the name by which it is invoked.

The next script, **emp2.sh** (Fig. 14.3), runs **grep** with two positional parameters that are set by the script arguments, director and emp.1st:

```
$ emp2.sh director emp.1st
Program: emp2.sh
The number of arguments specified is 2
The arguments are director emp.1st
1006|chanchal singhvi |director |sales     |03/09/38|6700
6521|lalit chowdury   |director |marketing |26/09/45|8200

Job Over
```

When arguments are specified in this way, the first word (the command itself) is assigned to $0, the second word (the first argument) to $1, and the third word (the second argument) to $2. You can use more positional parameters in this way up to $9 (and using the **shift** statement, you can go beyond).

When you use a multiword string to represent a single command line argument, you must quote it. To look for chanchal singhvi, use **emp2.sh "chanchal singhvi" emp.1st**. You have noted this quoting requirement when using **grep** also *(13.1)*.

All assignments to positional and special parameters are made by the shell. You can't really tamper with their values, except in an indirect fashion, but you can use them to great advantage in several ways. They will be used over and over again in shell scripts, and are listed in Table 14.1.

Bash Shell: $0 in Bash prepends the ./ prefix to the script name. In the example above, it would have shown ./emp2.sh instead of emp2.sh. You need to keep this in mind when you make use of $0 to develop portable scripts.

Table 14.1 Special Parameters Used by the Shell

Shell Parameter	*Significance*
$1, $2...	Positional parameters representing command line arguments
$#	Number of arguments specified in command line
$0	Name of executed command
$*	Complete set of positional parameters as a single string
"$@"	Each quoted string treated as a separate argument (recommended over $*)
$?	Exit status of last command
$$	PID of the current shell *(9.1.1)*
$!	PID of the last background job *(9.9.1)*

14.4 exit AND EXIT STATUS OF COMMAND

C programs and shell scripts have a lot in common, and one of them is that they both use the same command (or function in C) to terminate a program. It has the name **exit** in the shell and **exit()** in C. We'll take up the **exit** function in Part II of this book, but in this section, we'll examine the shell's **exit** command. The command is generally run with a numeric argument:

```
exit 0                          Used when everything went fine
exit 1                          Used when something went wrong
```

These are two very common **exit** values. You don't need to place this statement at the end of every shell script because the shell understands when script execution is complete. Rather, it's quite often used with a command when it fails.

Once **grep** couldn't locate a pattern *(13.1)*; we said then that the command *failed*. What we meant was that the **exit** function in the **grep** code was invoked with a nonzero argument (**exit(1)**). This value (1) is communicated to the calling program, usually the shell.

It's through the **exit** command or function that every command returns an **exit status** to the caller. Further, a command is said to return a *true* exit status if it executes successfully, and *false* if it fails. The **cat** command as used below:

```
$ cat foo
cat: can't open foo
```

returns a nonzero exit status because it couldn't open the file. The shell offers a variable ($?) and a command (**test**) that evaluates a command's exit status.

The Parameter $?   The parameter $? stores the exit status of the last command. It has the value 0 if the command succeeds and a nonzero value if it fails. This parameter is set by **exit**'s argument. If no exit status is specified, then $? is set to zero (true). Try using **grep** in these ways and you'll see it returning three different exit values:

```
$ grep director emp.lst >/dev/null; echo $?
0                                                    Success
$ grep manager emp.lst >/dev/null; echo $?
1                                                    Failure—in finding pattern
```

```
$ grep manager emp3.1st >/dev/null; echo $?
grep: can't open emp3.1st                                          Failure—in opening file
2
```

The exit status is extremely important for programmers. They use it to devise program logic that branches into different paths depending on the success or failure of a command. For example, there's no point in continuing with script execution if an important file doesn't exist or can't be read.

Tip: To find out whether a command executed successfully or not, simply use **echo $?** after the command. 0 indicates success, other values point to failure.

Note: Success or failure isn't as intuitive as it may seem. The designer of **grep** interpreted **grep**'s inability to locate a pattern as failure. The designer of **sed** thought otherwise. The command **sed -n '/manager/p' emp.1st** returns a true value even if manager is not found!

14.5 THE LOGICAL OPERATORS && AND ||—CONDITIONAL EXECUTION

The script **emp1.sh** has no logic to prevent display of the message, Selected lines shown above, when the pattern search fails. That is because we didn't use **grep**'s exit status to control the flow of the program. The shell provides two operators that allow conditional execution—the && and ||, which typically have this syntax:

cmd1 && *cmd2*
cmd1 || *cmd2*

The && delimits two commands; the command *cmd2* is executed only when *cmd1* succeeds. You can use it with **grep** in this way:

```
$ grep 'director' emp.1st && echo "pattern found in file"
1006|chanchal singhvi |director |sales     |03/09/38|6700
6521|lalit chowdury   |director |marketing |26/09/45|8200
pattern found in file
```

The || operator plays an inverse role; the second command is executed only when the first fails. If you "grep" a pattern from a file without success, you can notify the failure:

```
$ grep 'manager' emp.1st || echo "Pattern not found"
Pattern not found
```

The || goes pretty well with the **exit** command. You often need to terminate a script when a command fails. The script **emp2.sh** can be modified to include this feature. The following two lines ensure that the program is aborted when the **grep** command fails and a message is printed if it succeeds:

```
grep "$1" $2 || exit 2                              No point continuing if search fails
echo "Pattern found - Job Over"                     Executed only if grep succeeds
```

This segment makes rudimentary decisions which the previous scripts couldn't. In fact, the && and || operators are recommended for making simple decisions. When complex decision making is involved, they have to make way for the **if** statement.

14.6 THE if CONDITIONAL

The **if** statement makes two-way decisions depending on the fulfillment of a certain condition. In the shell, the statement uses the following forms, much like the one used in other languages:

if *command is successful*
then
    execute commands
else
    execute commands
fi
	if *command is successful*
	then
	    execute commands
	fi
		if *command is successful*
		then
		    execute commands
		elif *command is successful*
		then...
		else...
		fi

Form 1	**Form 2**	**Form 3**

As in BASIC, **if** also requires a **then**. It evaluates the success or failure of the *command* that is specified in its "command line." If *command* succeeds, the sequence of commands following it is executed. If *command* fails, then the **else** statement (if present) is executed. This statement is not always required, as shown in Form 2. Every **if** is closed with a corresponding **fi**, and you'll encounter an error if one is not present.

What makes shell programming so powerful is that a command's exit status solely determines the course of action pursued by many of the shell's important constructs like **if** and **while**. All commands return an exit status as we saw with **cat** and **grep**, so you can imagine where shell programming can lead us.

In the next script, **emp3.sh** (Fig. 14.4), **grep** is first executed and a simple **if-else** construct tests the exit status of **grep**. This time we'll search /etc/passwd for the existence of two users; one exists in the file and the other doesn't:

```
$ emp3.sh ftp
ftp:*:325:15:FTP User:/users1/home/ftp:/bin/true
Pattern found - Job Over
$ emp3.sh mail
Pattern not found
```

```
#!/bin/sh
# emp3.sh: Using if and else
#
if grep "^$1" /etc/passwd 2>/dev/null    # Search username at beginning of line
then
        echo "Pattern found - Job Over"
else
        echo "Pattern not found"
fi
```

Fig. 14.4 emp3.sh

We'll discuss the third form of the **if** statement when we discuss **test**. The condition placed in the command line of the **if** statement will henceforth be referred to as the **control command**. You can use **if** in this way with any executable program. Amazing power indeed!

14.7 USING test AND [] TO EVALUATE EXPRESSIONS

When you use **if** to evaluate expressions, you need the **test** statement because the true or false values returned by expressions can't be *directly* handled by **if**. **test** uses certain operators to evaluate the condition on its right and returns either a true or false exit status, which is then used by **if** for making decisions. **test** works in three ways:

- Compares two numbers.
- Compares two strings or a single one for a null value.
- Checks a file's attributes.

These tests can be made by **test** in association with the shell's other statements also, but for the present we'll stick with **if**. **test** doesn't display any output but simply sets the parameter $?. In the following sections, we'll check this value.

14.7.1 Numeric Comparison

The numerical comparison operators (Table 14.2) used by **test** have a form different from what you would have seen anywhere. They always begin with a - (hyphen), followed by a two-letter string, and enclosed on either side by whitespace. Here's a typical operator:

```
-ne     Not equal
```

The operators are quite mnemonic; -eq implies equal to, -gt implies greater than, and so on. Numeric comparison in the shell is confined to integer values only; decimal values are simply truncated. To illustrate how numeric tests are performed, we'll assign some values to three variables and numerically compare them:

```
$ x=5; y=7; z=7.2
$ test $x -eq $y ; echo $?
1                                          Not equal
$ test $x -lt $y ; echo $?
0                                          True
$ test $z -gt $y ; echo $?
1                                          7.2 is not greater than 7!
$ test $z -eq $y ; echo $?
0                                          7.2 is equal to 7!
```

The last two tests prove conclusively that numeric comparison is restricted to integers only. Having used **test** as a standalone feature, you can now use it as **if**'s control command. The next script, **emp3a.sh** (Fig. 14.5) uses **test** in an **if-elif-else-fi** construct (Form 3) to evaluate the shell parameter, $#. It displays the usage when no arguments are input, runs **grep** if two arguments are entered and displays an error message otherwise.

```
#!/bin/sh
# emp3a.sh: Using test, $0 and $# in an if-elif-if construct
#
if test $# -eq 0 ; then
    echo "Usage: $0 pattern file" >/dev/tty
elif test $# -eq 2 ; then
    grep "$1" $2 || echo "$1 not found in $2" >/dev/tty
else
    echo "You didn't enter two arguments" >/dev/tty
fi
```

Fig. 14.5 `emp3a.sh`

Why did we redirect the **echo** output to /dev/tty? Simple, we want the script to work both with and without redirection. In either case, the output of the **echo** statements must appear *only* on the terminal. These statements are used here as "error" messages even though they are not directed to the standard error. Now run the script four times and redirect the output every time:

```
$ emp3a.sh > foo
Usage: emp3a.sh pattern file
$ emp3a.sh ftp > foo
You didn't enter two arguments
$ emp3a.sh henry /etc/passwd > foo
henry not found in /etc/passwd
$ emp3a.sh ftp /etc/passwd > foo
$ cat foo
ftp:*:325:15:FTP User:/users1/home/ftp:/bin/true
```

The importance of /dev/tty as a mechanism of explicitly redirecting an output stream shows up in this example. You must appreciate this and use this feature in shell scripts when you like to have the redirection option open. The above script works just as well even if you don't redirect it.

Tip: An application may need to be designed in a flexible manner to allow redirection of an entire script or its participation in a pipeline. In that case, you need to ensure that messages meant to draw the attention of the user (mainly from **echo**) are redirected to >/dev/tty.

Table 14.2 Numerical Comparison Operators Used by **test**

Operator	Meaning
-eq	Equal to
-ne	Not equal to
-gt	Greater than
-ge	Greater than or equal to
-lt	Less than
-le	Less than or equal to

Shorthand for test   **test** is so widely used that fortunately there exists a shorthand method of executing it. A pair of rectangular brackets enclosing the expression can replace it. Thus, the following two forms are equivalent:

```
test $x -eq $y
[ $x -eq $y ]
```

Note that you must provide whitespace around the operators (like -eq), their operands (like $x) and inside the [and]. The second form is easier to handle and will be used henceforth. But don't forget to be liberal in the use of whitespace here!

Note: It is a feature of most programming languages that you can use a condition like **if (x)**, where x is a variable or expression. If x is greater than 0, the statement is said to be true. We can also apply the same logic here and use **if [$x]** as a shorthand form of **if [$x -gt 0]**.

14.7.2 String Comparison

test can be used to compare strings with yet another set of operators (Table 14.3). Equality is performed with = and inequality with the C-type operator !=. Other **test** checks can be negated by the ! too. Thus, [! -z $string] negates [-z $string].

Our next script, **emp4.sh** (Fig. 14.6) behaves both interactively and noninteractively. When run without arguments, it turns interactive and takes two inputs from you. It then runs **emp3a.sh**, the script developed previously, with the supplied inputs as arguments. However, when **emp4.sh** itself is run with at least one argument, it runs **emp3a.sh** with the same arguments. In either case, **emp3a.sh** is run, which finally checks for the actual number of arguments entered before making a search with **grep**.

When the script runs in the interactive mode, the check for a null string is made with [-z "$pname"] as well as with [! -n "$flname"], since they are really two different ways of saying the same thing. Note the use of $* in the noninteractive mode; this is the way you can use the same set of arguments to run another script. Very soon, we'll find a good reason to change $* to "$@". Let's first run the script interactively:

```
$ emp4.sh
Enter the string to be searched: [Enter]
You have not entered the string
$ emp4.sh
Enter the string to be searched: root
Enter the filename to be used: /etc/passwd
root:x:0:1:Super-User:/:/usr/bin/bash                    From emp3a.sh
```

See how two scripts cooperated in displaying root's entry from /etc/passwd. When we run the script with arguments, **emp4.sh** bypasses all of the above activities and calls **emp3a.sh** to perform all validation checks:

```
$ emp4.sh jai
You didn't enter two arguments
```

```
#!/bin/sh
# emp4.sh: Checks user input for null values - Finally runs emp3a.sh
#                                    developed previously
if [ $# -eq 0 ] ; then
    echo "Enter the string to be searched: \c"
    read pname
    if [ -z "$pname" ] ; then            # -z checks for a null string
        echo "You have not entered the string" ; exit 1
    fi
    echo "Enter the filename to be used: \c"
    read flname
    if [ ! -n "$flname" ] ; then         # ! -n is the same as -z
        echo "You have not entered the filename" ; exit 2
    fi
    emp3a.sh "$pname" "$flname"          # Runs the script that will do the job
else
    emp3a.sh $*                          # We'll change $* to "$@" soon
fi
```

Fig. 14.6 emp4.sh

```
$ emp4.sh jai emp.lst
9876|jai sharma          |director |production|12/03/50|7000
$ emp4.sh "jai sharma" emp.lst
You didn't enter two arguments
```

The last message could take you by surprise as jai sharma should have been treated as a single argument by the script. Indeed it has been, but $* doesn't understand it as such; jai and sharma are embedded in $* as separate arguments. $# thus makes a wrong argument count. The solution to this is simple: Replace $* in the script with "$@" (with quotes) and then run the script again:

```
$ emp4.sh "jai sharma" emp.lst
9876|jai sharma          |director |production|12/03/50|7000
```

Tip: It's safer to use "$@" instead of $*. When you employ multiword strings as arguments to a shell script, it's only "$@" that interprets each quoted argument as a separate argument. As the output above suggests, if you use $*, the shell makes a wrong count of the arguments.

---

test also permits the checking of more than one condition in the same line, using the -a (AND) and -o (OR) operators. You can now simplify the earlier script to illustrate this feature. Accept both inputs in succession and then make the check with a compound **if** statement:

```
if [ -n "$pname" -a -n "$flname" ] ; then
    emp3a.sh "$pname" "$flname"
else
    echo "At least one input was a null string" ; exit 1
fi
```

The **test** output is true only if both variables are nonnull strings, i.e., the user enters some nonwhitespace characters when the script pauses twice.

Tip: Observe that we have been quoting our variables wherever possible. Quoting is essential when you assign multiple words to a variable. To try that out, drop the quotes to use the statement **if [-z $pname]**. When you input two words, or even a null string to be assigned to pname, you'll often encounter an error. Quoting is safe with no adverse consequences.

Table 14.3 String Tests Used by **test**

Test	True if
s1 = *s2*	String *s1* = *s2*
s1 != *s2*	String *s1* is not equal to *s2*
-n *stg*	String *stg* is not a null string
-z *stg*	String *stg* is a null string
stg	String *stg* is assigned and not null
s1 == *s2*	String *s1* = *s2* (Korn and Bash only)

14.7.3 File Tests

test can be used to test the various file attributes like its type (file, directory or symbolic link) or its permissions (read, write, execute, SUID, etc.). Both **perl** and the UNIX system call library also offer these facilities (Table 14.4). Let's test some attributes of the file emp.1st at the prompt:

```
$ ls -l emp.1st
-rw-rw-rw-   1 kumar      group            870 Jun  8 15:52 emp.1st
$ [ -f emp.1st ] ; echo $?                             An ordinary file?
0                                                      Yes
$ [ -x emp.1st ] ; echo $?                             An executable file?
1                                                      No
$ [ ! -w emp.1st ] || echo "False that file is not writable"
False that file is not writable
```

The ! negates a test, so [! -w foo] negates [-w foo]. Using these features, you can design a script, **filetest.sh** (Fig. 14.7), that accepts a filename as argument and then performs a number of tests on it. Test the script with two filenames—one that doesn't exist and one that does:

```
$ filetest.sh emp3.1st
File does not exist
$ filetest.sh emp.1st
File is both readable and writable
```

This completes the discussion on the three domains of **test**—numeric comparison, testing of strings and file attributes. Even though we used **test** with the **if** statement in all of our examples, **test** returns an **exit** status only, and can thus be used with any shell construct that uses an exit status. **test** also finds wide application in the **while** statement.

```
#!/bin/sh
# filetest.sh: Tests file attributes
#
if [ ! -e $1 ] ; then
     echo "File does not exist"
elif [ ! -r $1 ] ; then
     echo "File is not readable"
elif [ ! -w $1 ] ; then
     echo "File is not writable"
else
     echo "File is both readable and writable"
fi
```

Fig. 14.7 `filetest.sh`

Table 14.4 File-related Tests with **test**

Test	True if File
-f *file*	*file* exists and is a regular file
-r *file*	*file* exists and is readable
-w *file*	*file* exists and is writable
-x *file*	*file* exists and is executable
-d *file*	*file* exists and is a directory
-s *file*	*file* exists and has a size greater than zero
-e *file*	*file* exists (Korn and Bash only)
-u *file*	*file* exists and has SUID bit set
-k *file*	*file* exists and has sticky bit set
-L *file*	*file* exists and is a symbolic link (Korn and Bash only)
f1 -nt *f2*	*f1* is newer than *f2* (Korn and Bash only)
f1 -ot *f2*	*f1* is older than *f2* (Korn and Bash only)
f1 -ef *f2*	*f1* is linked to *f2* (Korn and Bash only)

14.8 THE case CONDITIONAL

The **case** statement is the second conditional offered by the shell. It doesn't have a parallel either in C (**switch** is similar) or **perl**. The statement matches an expression for more than one alternative, and uses a compact construct to permit multiway branching. **case** also handles string tests, but in a more efficient manner than **if**. The general syntax of the **case** statement is as follows:

```
case expression in
     pattern1) commands1 ;;
     pattern2) commands2 ;;
     pattern3) commands3 ;;
     .....
esac
```

```
#!/bin/sh
# menu.sh: Uses case to offer 5-item menu
#
echo "          MENU\n
1. List of files\n2. Processes of user\n3. Today's Date
4. Users of system\n5. Quit to UNIX\nEnter your option: \c"
read choice
case "$choice" in
    1) ls -l ;;
    2) ps -f ;;
    3) date ;;
    4) who  ;;
    5) exit ;;
    *) echo "Invalid option"        # ;; not really required for the last option
esac
```

Fig. 14.8 menu.sh

case first matches *expression* with *pattern1*. If the match succeeds, then it executes *commands1*, which may be one or more commands. If the match fails, then *pattern2* is matched, and so forth. Each command list is terminated with a pair of semicolons, and the entire construct is closed with **esac** (reverse of **case**).

Consider a simple script, **menu.sh** (Fig. 14.8) that uses **case**. The script accepts values from 1 to 5, and performs some action depending on the number keyed in. The five menu choices are displayed with a multi-line **echo** statement.

case matches the value of $choice with the strings 1, 2, 3, 4 and 5. If the user enters a 1, the **ls -l** command is executed. Option 5 quits the program. The last option (*) matches any option not matched by by the previous options. We'll make good use of the * later.

You can see today's date by choosing the third option:

```
$ menu.sh
          MENU

1. List of files
2. Processes of user
3. Today's Date
4. Users of system
5. Quit to UNIX
Enter your option: 3
Tue Jan  7 18:03:06 IST 2003
```

case can't handle relational and file tests, but it matches strings with compact code. It is also very effective when the string is fetched by command substitution. If you cut out the first field from the **date** output, you can use this **case** construct to do different things, depending on the day of the week:

```
case `date | cut -d" " -f1` in
```
                                    Outputs three-character day string

```
    Mon) tar -cvf /dev/fd0 $HOME ;;
    Wed) scp -r $HOME mercury:/home/henry ;;
    Fri) find $HOME -newer .last_full_backup_time -print > tarilist ;;
      *) ;;
esac
```

case can also handle numbers, but only by treating them as strings. Some of our previous programs used **if** and **test** to check the value of $#. You can use **case** to match $# *directly* (without using **test**) with specific values (0, 1, 2, etc.), but you can't use it to make numeric checks (of the type $# -gt 2).

14.8.1 Matching Multiple Patterns

case can also specify the same action for more than one pattern. Programmers frequently encounter a logic that has to test a user response for both y and Y (or n and N). Like **grep** **-E** and **egrep**, **case** uses the | to delimit multiple patterns. For instance, the expression y|Y can be used to match y in both upper and lowercase:

```
echo "Do you wish to continue? (y/n): \c"
read answer
case"$answer" in
    y|Y) ;;                    Null statement, no action to be performed
    n|N) exit ;;
esac
```

The same logic would require a larger number of lines if implemented with **if**. **case** becomes an automatic choice when the number of matching options is high.

14.8.2 Wild-Cards: case Uses Them

case has a superb string matching feature that uses wild-cards. It uses the filename matching metacharacters *, ? and the character class *(8.3.3)—but only to match strings and not files in the current directory*. The revised **case** construct of a previous example lets the user answer the question in several ways:

```
case "$answer" in
    [yY][eE]*) ;;              Matches YES, yes, Yes, YEs, yES, etc.
    [nN][oO]) exit ;;          Matches NO, no, nO and No
          *) echo "Invalid response"When everything else fails
esac
```

Wild-card usage in the first two options appears simple enough. Note that the * appears in two options. In the first option, it behaves like a normal wild-card. In the last option, it provides a refuge for all other nonmatched options. Note that the last **case** option doesn't need ;; but you can provide them if you want.

14.9 expr: COMPUTATION AND STRING HANDLING

The Bourne shell can check whether an integer is greater than another, but it doesn't have any computing features at all. It has to rely on the external **expr** command for that purpose. This command combines two functions in one:

- Performs arithmetic operations on integers.
- Manipulates strings.

We'll use **expr** to perform both these functions, but with not-very-readable code when it comes to string handling. If you are using the Korn shell or Bash, you have better ways of handling these things (*21.7*), but you must also understand the helplessness of Bourne. It's quite possible that you have to debug someone else's script which contains **expr**.

14.9.1 Computation

expr can perform the four basic arithmetic operations as well as the modulus (remainder) function:

```
$ x=3 y=5                                     Multiple assignments without a ;
$ expr 3 + 5
8
$ expr $x - $y
-2
$ expr 3 \* 5                                 Asterisk has to be escaped
15
$ expr $y / $x
1
$ expr 13 % 5                                 Decimal portion truncated
3
```

The operand, be it +, -, * etc., must be enclosed on either side by whitespace. Observe that the multiplication operand (*) has to be escaped to prevent the shell from interpreting it as the filename metacharacter. Since **expr** can handle only integers, division yields only the integral part.

expr is often used with command substitution to assign a variable. For example, you can set a variable z to the sum of two numbers:

```
$ x=6 y=2 ; z=`expr $x + $y`
$ echo $z
8
```

Perhaps the most common use of **expr** is in incrementing the value of a variable. All programming languages have a shorthand method of doing that, and it is natural that UNIX should also have its own:

```
$ x=5
$ x=`expr $x + 1`                             This is the same as C's x++
$ echo $x
6
```

If you are using the Korn shell or Bash, then you can turn to Section 21.5 for a discussion on the **let** statement that both shells use to handle computation.

14.9.2 String Handling

Though **expr**'s string handling facilities aren't exactly elegant, Bourne shell users hardly have any choice. For manipulating strings, **expr** uses two expressions separated by a colon. The string to be worked upon is placed on the left of the :, and a regular expression is placed on its right. Depending on the composition of the expression, **expr** can perform three important string functions:

- Determine the length of the string.
- Extract a substring.
- Locate the position of a character in a string.

The Length of a String   The length of a string is a relatively simple matter; the regular expression .* signifies to **expr** that it has to print the number of characters matching the pattern, i.e., the length of the entire string:

```
$ expr "abcdefghijkl" : '.*'                Space on either side of : required
12
```

Here, **expr** has counted the number of occurrences of any character (.*). This feature is useful in validating data entry. Consider that you want to validate the name of a person accepted through the keyboard so that it doesn't exceed, say, 20 characters in length. The following **expr** sequence can be quite useful for this task:

```
while echo "Enter your name: \c" ; do              echo always returns true
    read name
    if [ `expr "$name" : '.*'` -gt 20 ] ; then
        echo "Name too long"
    else
        break                                      break terminates a loop
    fi
done
```

Extracting a Substring   **expr** can extract a string enclosed by the escaped characters \(and \). If you wish to extract the 2-digit year from a 4-digit string, you must create a pattern group and extract it this way:

```
$ stg=2003
$ expr "$stg" : '..\(..\)'                   Extracts last two characters
03
```

Note the pattern group \(..\). This is the tagged regular expression (TRE) used by **sed** *(13.11.3)*, but it is used here with a somewhat different meaning. It signifies that the first two characters in the value of $stg have to be ignored and two characters have to be extracted from the third character position. (There's no \1 and \2 here.)

Locating Position of a Character   **expr** can also return the location of the first occurrence of a character inside a string. To locate the position of the character d in the string value of $stg, you have to count the number of characters which are not d ([^d]*), followed by a d:

```
$ stg=abcdefgh ; expr "$stg" : '[^d]*d'
4
```

expr duplicates some of the features of the **test** statement, and also uses the relational operators in the same way. They are not pursued here because **test** is a built-in feature of the shell, and is consequently faster. The Korn shell and Bash have built-in string handling facilities; they don't need **expr**. These features are taken up in Chapter 21.

14.10 $0: CALLING A SCRIPT BY DIFFERENT NAMES

In our discussion on links *(11.2.2)*, we raised the possibility of invoking a file by different names and doing different things depending on the name by which it is called. In fact, there are a number of UNIX commands that do exactly that. Now that we know how to extract a string with **expr**, it's time we designed a single script, **comc.sh** (Fig. 14.9), that compiles, edits or runs the last modified C program. The script file will have three more names, but before developing it, let's understand the compiling mechanism used by the **cc** or **gcc** compiler.

A C program has the .c extension. When compiled with cc *filename*, it produces a file named a.out. However, we can provide a different name to the executable using the -o option, For instance, **cc -o foo foo.c** creates an executable named foo. We must be able to extract the "base" filename after dropping the extension, and with **expr** it should be a simple matter.

First, we store the name of the C program that was last modified, in the variable lastfile. Next, we extract the base filename by dropping the .c extension using the TRE feature of **expr**. The **case** conditional now checks the name (saved in the variable command) by which the program is invoked. Observe that the first option (runc) simply executes the value evaluated by the variable executable. The only thing left to do now is to create three links:

```
ln comc.sh comc
ln comc.sh runc
ln comc.sh vic
```

Now you can run **vic** to edit the program, **comc** to compile it and **runc** to execute the object code. We'll only compile it here:

```
$ comc
hello.c compiled successfully
```

Note that this script works only with a C program that is stored, along with any functions, in one file. If functions are stored in separate files, this script won't work. In that case, **make** is the solution and is discussed in Chapter 22.

```
#!/bin/sh
# comc.sh: Script that is called by different names
#
lastfile=`ls -t *.c | head -n 1`
command=$0                      # Assigning a special parameter to a variable - OK
executable=`expr $lastfile : '\(.*\).c'`     # Removes .c; foo.c becomes foo
case $command in
        *runc) $executable ;;                # Runs the executable
         *vic) vi $lastfile ;;
        *comc) cc -o $executable $lastfile &&
               echo "$lastfile compiled successfully" ;;
esac
```

Fig. 14.9 comc.sh

14.11 while: LOOPING

None of the pattern scanning scripts developed so far offers the user another chance to rectify a faulty response. Loops let you perform a set of instructions repeatedly. The shell features three types of loops—**while**, **until** and **for**. All of them repeat the instruction set enclosed by certain keywords as often as their control command permits.

The **while** statement should be quite familiar to most programmers. It repeatedly performs a set of instructions until the control command returns a true exit status. The general syntax of this command is as follows:

```
while condition is true
do                                Note the do keyword
      commands
done                              Note the done keyword
```

The *commands* enclosed by **do** and **done** are executed repeatedly as long as *condition* remains true. You can use any UNIX command or **test** as the *condition*, as before.

We'll start with an orthodox **while** loop application. The script, **emp5.sh** Fig. 14.10), accepts a code and description in the same line, and then writes the line to newlist. It then prompts you for more entries. The loop iteration is controlled by the value of $answer.

We have redirected the output of two **echo** statements to /dev/tty for reasons that will be apparent later. We'll make a small but significant modification later, but let's run it first:

```
$ emp5.sh
Enter the code and description: 03 analgesics
Enter any more (y/n)? y
```

```
#!/bin/sh
# emp5.sh: Shows use of the while loop
#
answer=y          # Must set it to y first to enter the loop
while [ "$answer" = "y" ]      # The control command
do
      echo "Enter the code and description: \c" >/dev/tty
      read code description      # Read both together
      echo "$code|$description" >> newlist    # Append a line to newlist
      echo "Enter any more (y/n)? \c" >/dev/tty
      read anymore
      case $anymore in
          y*|Y*) answer=y ;;    # Also accepts yes, YES etc.
          n*|N*) answer=n ;;    # Also accepts no, NO etc.
             *) answer=y ;;    # Any other reply means y
      esac
done
```

Fig. 14.10 **emp5.sh**

```
Enter the code and description: 04 antibiotics
Enter any more (y/n)? [Enter]                                    No response, assumed to be y
Enter the code and description: 05 OTC drugs
Enter any more (y/n)? n
```

When you see the file newlist, you'll know what you have achieved:

```
$ cat newlist
03|analgesics
04|antibiotics
05|OTC drugs
```

Did redirection with /dev/tty achieve anything here? No, nothing yet, but after we make a small change in the script, it will. Note that you added a record to newlist with the >> symbol. This causes newlist to be opened every time **echo** is called up. The shell avoids such multiple file openings and closures by providing a redirection facility at the **done** keyword itself:

```
done > newlist
```

Make this change in the script and remove the redirection provided with the >> symbols. This form of redirection speeds up execution time as newlist is opened and closed only once. Because this action redirects the standard output of all commands inside the loop, we redirected some statements to /dev/tty because we want their output to come to the terminal.

Note: Redirection is also available at the **fi** and **esac** keywords, and includes input redirection and piping:

done < param.lst	*Statements in loop take input from* param.lst
done | while true	*Pipes output to a* while *loop*
fi > foo	*Affects statements between* if *and* fi
esac > foo	*Affects statements between* case *and* esac

14.11.1 Using while to Wait for a File

Let's now consider an interesting **while** loop application. There are situations when a program needs to read a file that is created by another program, but it also has to wait until the file is created. The script, **monitfile.sh** (Fig. 14.11), periodically monitors the disk for the existence of the file, and then executes the program once the file has been located. It makes use of the external **sleep** command that makes the script pause for the duration (in seconds) as specified in its argument.

The loop executes repeatedly as long as the file invoice.lst can't be read (! -r means not readable). If the file becomes readable, the loop is terminated and the program alloc.pl is executed. This script is an ideal candidate to be run in the background like this:

```
monitfile.sh &
```

We used the **sleep** command to check every 60 seconds for the existence of the file. **sleep** is also quite useful in introducing some delay in shell scripts.

```
#!/bin/sh
# monitfile.sh: Waits for a file to be created
#
while [ ! -r invoice.lst ]      # While the file invoice.lst can't be read
do
    sleep 60                    # sleep for 60 seconds
done
alloc.pl                        # Execute this program after exiting loop
```

Fig. 14.11 `monitfile.sh`

14.11.2 Setting Up an Infinite Loop

Suppose you, as system administrator, want to see the free space available on your disks every five minutes. You need an infinite loop, and it's best implemented by using **true** as a dummy control command with **while**. **true** does nothing except return a true exit status. Another command named **false** returns a false value. You can set up this loop in the background as well:

```
while true ; do                 This form is also permitted
    df -t                       df reports free space on disk
    sleep 300
done &                          & after done runs loop in background
```

With the job now running in the background, you can continue your other work, except that every five minutes you could find your screen filled with **df** output *(15.6.1)*. You can't now use the interrupt key to kill this loop; you'll have to use **kill $!**, which kills the last background job *(9.9.1)*.

Note: The shell also offers an **until** statement which operates with a reverse logic used in **while**. With **until**, the loop body is executed as long as the condition remains *false*. Some people would have preferred to have written a previous **while** control command as **until [-r invoice.lst]**. This form is easily intelligible.

14.12 for: LOOPING WITH A LIST

The shell's **for** loop differs in structure from the ones used in other programming languages. There is no three-part structure as used in C, **awk** and **perl**. Unlike **while** and **until**, **for** doesn't test a condition, but uses a list instead:

```
for variable in list
do
    commands                                    Loop body
done
```

The loop body also uses the keywords **do** and **done**, but the additional parameters here are *variable* and *list*. Each whitespace-separated word in *list* is assigned to *variable* in turn, and *commands* are executed until *list* is exhausted. A simple example can help you understand things better:

```
$ for file in chap20 chap21 chap22 chap23 ; do
>     cp $file ${file}.bak
>     echo $file copied to $file.bak
> done
chap20 copied to chap20.bak
chap21 copied to chap21.bak
chap22 copied to chap22.bak
chap23 copied to chap23.bak
```

The *list* here comprises a series of character strings (chap20 and onwards, representing filenames) separated by whitespace. Each item in the list is assigned to the variable file. file first gets the value chap20, then chap21, and so on. Each file is copied with a .bak extension and the completion message displayed after every file is copied.

14.12.1 Possible Sources of the List

The list can consist of practically any of the expressions that the shell understands and processes. **for** is probably the most often used loop in the UNIX system, and it's important that you understand it thoroughly.

List from Variables   You can use a series of variables in the command line. They are evaluated by the shell before executing the loop:

```
$ for var in $PATH $HOME $MAIL ; do echo "$var" ; done
/bin:/usr/bin:/home/local/bin:/usr/bin/X11:.:/oracle/bin
/home/henry
/var/mail/henry
```

You have to provide the semicolons at the right places if you want to enter the entire loop in a single line. The three output lines represent the values of the three environment variables.

List from Command Substitution   You can also use command substitution to create the list. The following **for** command line picks up its list from the file clist:

```
for file in `cat clist`
```

This method is most suitable when the list is large and you don't consider it practicable to specify its contents individually. It's also a clean arrangement because you can change the list without having to change the script.

List from Wild-cards   When the list consists of wild-cards, the shell interprets them as *filenames*. **for** is thus indispensable for making substitutions in a set of files with **sed**. Take, for instance, this loop which works on every HTML file in the current directory:

```
for file in *.htm *.html ; do
    sed 's/strong/STRONG/g
    s/img src/IMG SRC/g' $file > $$
    mv $$ $file
    gzip $file
done
```

```
#!/bin/sh
# emp6.sh -- Using a for loop with positional parameters
#
for pattern in "$@" ; do                    # Decided not to use $* - Section 14.7.2
    grep "$pattern" emp.lst || echo "Pattern $pattern not found"
done
```

Fig. 14.12 `emp6.sh`

In this loop, each HTML filename is assigned to the variable `file` in turn. **sed** performs some substitution on each file and writes the output to a temporary file. This filename is numeric—expanded from the variable $$ (the PID of the current shell). The temporary file is written back to the original file with **mv**, and the file is finally compressed with **gzip**.

List from Positional Parameters **for** is also used to process positional parameters that are assigned from command line arguments. The next script, **emp6.sh** (Fig. 14.12), scans a file repeatedly for each argument. It uses the shell parameter "$@" (and not $*) to represent all command line arguments.

Execute the script by passing four arguments, one of which is a multiword string:

```
$ emp6.sh 2345 1265 "jai sharma" 4379
2345|j.b. saxena      |g.m.      |marketing  |12/03/45|8000
1265|s.n. dasgupta    |manager   |sales      |12/09/63|5600
9876|jai sharma        |director  |production |12/03/50|7000
Pattern 4379 not found
```

Since **for** is mostly used with "$@" to access command line arguments, a blank list defaults to this parameter. Thus, these two statements mean the same thing:

```
for pattern in "$@"
for pattern                                    "$@" is implied
```

Note that the script won't work properly if we replaced "$@" with $*. Make this change and then see for yourself how the script behaves.

14.12.2 basename: Changing Filename Extensions

We'll discuss yet another external command, **basename**, only because it's most effective when used inside a **for** loop. Working in tandem, they are quite useful in changing the extensions of a group of filenames. **basename** extracts the "base" filename from an absolute pathname:

```
$ basename /home/henry/project3/dec2bin.pl
dec2bin.pl
```

When **basename** is used with two arguments, it strips off the second argument from the first argument:

```
$ basename ux2nd.txt txt
ux2nd.                                         txt stripped off
```

You can now use this feature to rename filename extensions from txt to doc:

```
for file in *.txt ; do
  leftname=`basename $file txt`          Stores left part of filename
  mv $file ${leftname}doc
done
```

If **for** picks up seconds.txt as the first file, leftname stores seconds. (with a dot). **mv** simply adds a doc to the extracted string (seconds.). You don't need **expr** for this job at all!

14.13 set AND shift: MANIPULATING THE POSITIONAL PARAMETERS

Some UNIX commands like **date** produce single-line output. We also pass command output through filters like **grep** and **head** to produce a single line. Recall that we had to use an external command (**cut**) to extract a field from the **date** output *(14.8)*:

```
case `date | cut -d" " -f1` in
```

This is overkill; the shell has an internal command to do this job—the **set** statement. **set** assigns its arguments to the positional parameters $1, $2, and so on. This feature is especially useful for picking up individual fields from the output of a program. But before we do that, let's use **set** to convert its arguments to positional parameters:

```
$ set 9876 2345 6213
$ _
```

This assigns the value 9876 to the positional parameter $1, 2345 to $2 and 6213 to $3. It also sets the other parameters $# and $*. You can verify this by echoing each parameter in turn:

```
$ echo "\$1 is $1, \$2 is $2, \$3 is $3"
$1 is 9876, $2 is 2345, $3 is 6213
$ echo "The $# arguments are $*"
The 3 arguments are 9876 2345 6213
```

We'll now use command substitution to extract individual fields from the **date** output and without using **cut**:

```
$ set `date`
$ echo $*
Wed Jan 8 09:40:35 IST 2003
$ echo "The date today is $2 $3, $6"
The date today is Jan 8, 2003
```

The day of the week is available in $1. Using the **set** feature, the **case** construct simplifies to case $1 in.

Tip: **set** parses its arguments on the delimiters specified in the environment variable IFS, which, by default, is whitespace. You can change the value of this variable to make **set** work on a different delimiter. This means that you can easily extract any field in a line from /etc/passwd without using **cut**! One of our sample validation scripts *(14.17.1)* makes use of this feature.

14.13.1 `shift`: Shifting Arguments Left

Many scripts use the first argument to indicate a separate entity—say a filename. The other arguments could then represent a series of strings—probably different patterns to be selected from a file. For this to be possible, **for** should start its iteration from the second parameter onwards. This is possible with the **shift** statement.

shift transfers the contents of a positional parameter to its immediate lower numbered one. This is done as many times as the statement is called. When called once, $2 becomes $1, $3 becomes $2, and so on. Try this on the positional parameters that were previously filled up with **date**:

```
$ echo "$@"                          Here, "$@" and $* are interchangeable
Wed Jan 8 09:48:44 IST 2003
$ echo $1 $2 $3
Wed Jan 8
$ shift
$ echo $1 $2 $3
Jan 8 09:48:44
$ shift 2                            Shifts 2 places
$ echo $1 $2 $3
09:48:44 IST 2003
```

Note that the contents of the leftmost parameter, $1, are lost every time **shift** is invoked. In this way, you can access $10 by first shifting it and converting it to $9. So if a script uses twelve arguments, you can shift thrice and then use the ninth parameter. We need the **set-shift** duo for the next script, **emp7.sh** (Fig. 14.13), which is run with a filename and a set of patterns as arguments.

Since the script requires at least two arguments, you should verify their presence before you act on the patterns. We stored $1 in the variable flname because the next **shift** operation would wipe it away. Now you can use the script with a variable number of arguments (not less than 2):

```
$ emp7.sh emp.lst
Insufficient number of arguments
$ emp7.sh emp.lst saxena 1006 9876
2345|j.b. saxena      |g.m.       |marketing |12/03/45|8000
```

```
#!/bin/sh
# emp7.sh: Script using shift -- Saves first argument; for works with rest
#
case $# in
    0|1) echo "Usage: $0 file pattern(s)" ; exit 2 ;;
    *) flname=$1    # Store $1 as a variable before it gets lost
       shift
       for pattern in "$@" ; do       # Starts iteration with $2
           grep "$pattern" $flname || echo "Pattern $pattern not found"
       done ;;
esac
```

Fig. 14.13 `emp7.sh`

```
1006|chanchal singhvi |director |sales     |03/09/38|6700
Pattern 9876 not found
```

Here flname stores emp.lst, and the **for** loop iterates with the three strings, saxena, 1006, 9876.

Tip: Every time you use **shift**, the leftmost variable gets lost; so it should be saved in a variable before using **shift**. If you have to start iteration from the fourth parameter, save the first three parameters and then use **shift 3**.

14.13.2 set --: Helps Command Substitution

You'll often need to use **set** with command substitution. There's a small problem though, especially when the output of the command begins with a -:

```
$ set `ls -l unit01`
-rw-r--r--: bad option(s)
```

Since the permissions string begins with a - (for regular files), **set** interprets it as an option and finds it to be a "bad" one. **set** creates another problem when its arguments evaluate to a null string. Consider this command:

```
set `grep PPP /etc/passwd`
```

If the string PPP can't be located in the file, **set** will operate with no arguments and puzzle the user by displaying all variables on the terminal (its default output)! The solution to both these problems lies in the use of -- (two hyphens) immediately after **set**:

```
set -- `ls -l unit01`          First - now taken care of
set -- `grep PPP /etc/passwd`  Null output is no problem
```

set now understands that the arguments following -- are not to be treated as options. The two hyphens also direct **set** to suppress its default behavior if its arguments evaluate to a null string.

14.14 THE *HERE DOCUMENT* (<<)

There are occasions when the data your program reads is fixed and fairly limited. The shell uses the << symbols to read data from the same file containing the script. This is referred to as a **here document**, signifying that the data is here rather than in a separate file. Any command using standard input can also take input from a here document.

This feature is useful when used with commands that don't accept a filename as argument (like the **mailx** command, for instance). If the message is short (which any mail message is normally expected to be), you can have both the command and message in the same script:

```
mailx sharma << MARK
Your program for printing the invoices has been executed
on `date`. Check the print queue          Command substitution permitted
The updated file is known as $flname      Variable evaluation too
MARK                                       No spaces permitted here
```

The here document symbol (<<) is followed by three lines of data and a delimiter (the string MARK). The shell treats every line following the command and delimited by MARK as input to the command. sharma at the other end will see the three lines of message text with the date inserted by command substitution and the evaluated filename. The word MARK itself doesn't show up. When this sequence is placed inside a script, execution is faster because **mailx** doesn't have to read an external file; it's here.

Note: The contents of a here document are interpreted and processed by the shell before they are fed as input to a command. This means you can use command substitution and variables in its input. You can't do that with normal standard input.

14.14.1 Using the Here Document with Interactive Programs

Many commands require input from the user. Often, it's the same input that is keyed in, in response to a series of questions posed by the command. For instance, you may have to enter a y two or three times when the command pauses, but the questions may not come in quick succession. Rather than wait for the prompt, we can instruct the script to take input from a here document.

We'll now attempt something that has far-reaching consequences. Recall that we used an interactive script **emp1.sh** *(14.2)* by keying in two parameters. We can make that script work noninteractively by supplying the inputs through a here document:

```
$ emp1.sh << END
> director
> emp.lst
> END
Enter the pattern to be searched: Enter the file to be used: Searching for
director from file emp.lst
9876|jai sharma        |director |production|12/03/50|7000
2365|barun sengupta    |director |personnel |11/05/47|7800
Selected records shown above
```

Even though the prompts are displayed in a single line, the important thing is that the script worked. We have been able to run an interactive script noninteractively!

Tip: If you write a script that uses the **read** statement, and which often assumes a predefined set of replies, you can make the script behave noninteractively by supplying its input from a here document.

14.15 trap: INTERRUPTING A PROGRAM

By default, shell scripts terminate whenever the interrupt key is pressed. It's not always a good idea to terminate shell scripts in this way because that can leave a lot of temporary files on disk. The **trap** statement lets you do the things you want in case the script receives a signal. The statement is normally placed at the beginning of a shell script and uses two lists:

```
trap 'command_list' signal_list
```

When a script is sent any of the signals in *signal_list*, **trap** executes the commands in *command_list*. The signal list can contain the integer values or names (without the SIG prefix) of one or more signals—the ones you use with the **kill** command. So instead of using 2 15 to represent the signal list, you can also use INT TERM (the recommended approach).

If you habitually create temporary files named after the PID number of the shell, you should use the services of **trap** to remove them whenever an interrupt occurs:

```
trap 'rm $$* ; echo "Program interrupted" ; exit' HUP INT TERM
```

trap is a signal handler. Here, it first removes all files expanded from $$*, echoes a message and finally terminates the script when the signals SIGHUP (1), SIGINT (2) or SIGTERM (15) are sent to the shell process running the script. When the interrupt key is pressed, it sends the signal number 2. It's a good idea to include this number in your scripts.

You may also like to ignore the signal and continue processing. In that case, you should make the script ignore such signals by using a null command list. A script containing the following **trap** statement will not be affected by three signals; this time we'll use the signal numbers:

```
trap '' 1 2 15
```
                                              Script can't be killed by normal means

The Korn and Bourne shells don't execute a file on logging out, but using **trap**, you can make them do that. You'll have to use the signal name EXIT (or 0) as a component of the signal list. These shells also use the statement **trap -** to reset signals to their default values. You can also use multiple **trap** commands in a script; each one overrides the previous one.

Note: It's not mandatory to have a **trap** statement in your shell scripts. However, if you have one, don't forget to include the **exit** statement at the end of the command list unless you want the script to ignore the specific signals.

14.16 DEBUGGING SHELL SCRIPTS WITH set -x

Apart from assigning values to positional parameters, **set** serves as a useful debugging tool with its -x option. When used inside a script (or even at the $ prompt), it echoes each statement on the terminal, preceded by a + as it is executed. Modify any previous script to turn on the **set** option by placing the following statement at the beginning of the script:

```
set -x
```

set +x turns off **set -x**, and you can place the latter statement at the end of the script. This is what you'll see when you invoke the script, **emp7.sh**, in the following manner:

```
$ emp7.sh emp.1st 2233 1265 0110
+ flname=emp.1st
+ shift
+ grep 2233 emp.1st
2233|a.k. shukla      |g.m.     |sales    |12/12/52|6000
+ grep 1265 emp.1st
1265|s.n. dasgupta    |manager  |sales    |12/09/63|5600
```

```
+ grep 0110 emp.lst
0110|v.k. agrawal      |g.m.      |marketing |31/12/40|9000
```

This is an ideal tool to use if you have trouble finding out why scripts don't work in the manner expected. Note how the shell prints each statement as it is being executed, affixing a + to each. It even shows you what the **grep** command line looks like at every iteration!

14.17 SAMPLE VALIDATION AND DATA ENTRY SCRIPTS

It's time to consolidate our knowledge by devising two interactive shell scripts that accept input from the user. One script looks up a code list while the other adds an entry to a text database.

14.17.1 `valcode.sh`: Script to Look Up a Code List

This script, **valcode.sh** (Fig. 14.14), uses the **set** and **shift** features to accept and validate a department code. It looks up a code list maintained as a here document in the script file itself, and flashes the department name on the terminal.

Since **echo** always produces a true exit status, the statement issuing the prompt is itself used as the control command of the **while** loop. The pattern selected by **grep** is split by **set** on the | into three positional parameters. This is done by changing the IFS setting that normally consists of whitespace. **shift 3** flushes the positional parameters before starting the next iteration. When you execute the script, this is how it behaves:

```
#!/bin/sh
# valcode.sh: Uses a here document to look up a code list
#
IFS="|"              # Reset field separator to pipe
while echo "Enter department code  : \c" ; do
    read dcode
    set -- `grep "^$dcode" << limit
01|accounts|6213
02|admin|5423
03|marketing|6521
04|personnel|2365
05|production|9876
06|sales|1006
limit`                       # Closing ` marks end of standard input

    case $# in
        3) echo "Department name        : $2\nEmp-id of head of dept : $3\n"
           shift 3 ;;        # Flush out the positional parameters
        *) echo "Invalid code"   ; continue
    esac
done
```

Fig. 14.14 `valcode.sh`

```
$ valcode.sh
Enter department code  : 99
Invalid code
Enter department code  : 02
Department name        : admin
Emp-id of head of dept : 5423

Enter department code  : 04
Department name        : personnel
Emp-id of head of dept : 2365

Enter department code  : [Ctrl-c]
```

The script doesn't terminate normally, but you can use the interrupt key at any time to abort the program.

14.17.2 dentry1.sh: A Data Entry Script

Our final script, **dentry1.sh** (Fig. 14.15), accepts a designation code and its description from the terminal, performs some rudimentary validation checks, and then adds an entry to a file (desig.1st). It validates the code entered with the ones that already exist in the file. The script repeatedly prompts the user until the right response is obtained.

Before you examine the script, you must know two keywords, **break** and **continue**, which are used by the shell's loops. They have their counterparts in the C language with the same names. **continue** suspends execution of all statements following it, and switches control to the top of the loop for the next iteration. **break**, on the other hand, causes control to break out of the loop.

The script prompts for two fields, the designation code and description, and uses two **while** loops, one enclosed by the other. The code has to be reentered if it exists in the file or if it doesn't have a two-digit structure. Similarly, the description has to be reentered if it contains a nonalphabetic character other than a space (*[!\ a-zA-Z]*). The **continue** statements let you reenter the data or start a fresh cycle. The **break** statement in the inner loop quits the loop after adding the line.

The logic becomes convincing after you undertake a dialog with the script, but before that let's see the entries in desig.1st:

```
$ cat desig.1st
01|accounts
02|admin
03|marketing
04|personnel
05|production
06|sales
$ dentry1.sh
Designation code: 01
Code exists
Designation code: 07
Description     : security officer

Wish to continue? (y/n): Y
```

```
#!/bin/sh
# dentry1.sh: Data entry script - Runs in a loop
#
trap 'echo Not to be interrupted' INT        # [Ctrl-c] won't work
trap 'echo Signal received ; exit' HUP TERM   # but these two signals will
file=desig.lst                                # The file that is looked up and appended to
while echo "Designation code: \c" >/dev/tty ; do
    read desig
    case "$desig" in              # First check if the code exists
    [0-9][0-9]) if grep "^$desig" $file >/dev/null ; then
                    echo "Code exists"
                    continue          # Go to loop beginning
                fi ;;
            *) echo "Invalid code"
               continue ;;
    esac

    while echo "Description       : \c"  >/dev/tty ; do
        read desc
        case "$desc" in
    *[!\ a-zA-Z]*) echo "Can contain only alphabets and spaces" >/dev/tty
                   continue ;;        # Go to inner loop beginning
               "") echo "Description not entered" >/dev/tty
                   continue ;;
                *) echo "$desig|$desc"
                   break              # Terminate this inner loop
        esac
    done >> $file                     # Appends to same file that is looked up

    echo "\nWish to continue? (y/n): \c"
    read answer
    case "$answer" in
        [yY]*) continue ;;             # Go to outer loop beginning
           *) break ;;                 # Terminate outer loop
    esac
done

echo "Normal exit"
```

Fig. 14.15 dentry1.sh

```
Designation code: 8
Invalid code
Designation code: 08
Description     : vice president 1
Can contain only alphabets and spaces
Description     : vice president

Wish to continue? (y/n): n
Normal exit
```

When you see the last two lines of desig.lst, you'll see the two appended entries:

```
$ tail -n 2 desig.1st
07|security officer
08|vice president
```

The **while** structure is ideal for developing data entry shell scripts with extensive validation features. You have had a taste of this in this section. If you have found this script difficult, you should flip back and reassimilate the material. It isn't difficult at all, be assured.

14.18 CONCLUSION

This chapter presented the essential programming constructs offered by the shell. If you have written C programs, you can realize that the domain of shell programming is quite different from that of any high-level language. Shell scripts are ideal for integrating your existing applications. You should now be able to write scripts up to moderate complexity. If you are the system administrator, you'll need the services of shell scripting to automate the routine functions, using **cron** scheduling when needed. In Part II, we revisit the shell to consider its advanced features.

The shell is also a programming language that executes shell scripts in the *interpretive mode*—one line at a time. The *interpreter line* signifies the sub-shell that runs the script.

The **read** statement is used with one or more variables to provide input to a script from the keyboard. Command line arguments passed to a script are read into *positional parameters* (like $1, $2, etc.). $# stores the number of arguments. Both $* and "$@" contain all arguments, but use of "$@" is preferred. $0 contains the name of the script itself.

WRAP UP

The **exit** statement terminates a script. The numeric argument used with it is available in the shell's special variable, $?, and signifies *success* or *failure* of the command or script.

The && and || operators are used as simple conditionals. The **if** statement has three forms, and is normally used with the **test** statement or its synonym [ ]. **test** can be used with operators to compare numbers and strings, as well as check the various file attributes.

case is a compact string matching construct. It accepts the shell's wild-cards for matching patterns, and can also match multiple patterns of the type used in extended regular expressions (ERE).

expr can perform basic integer computing (like incrementing a variable). It can also be used for extracting a substring and evaluating the length of a string.

All loops use the keywords **do** and **done**. A **while** loop is used for repeatedly executing a group of commands. The **for** loop iterates through a list. You can use **basename** inside a **for** loop to change the extensions of filenames. Both **while** and **for** use **continue** and **break** to alter the loop iteration.

set places values into positional parameters. Every time **shift** is invoked, the left-most parameter is lost, so it should be saved in a variable before using **shift**. **set --** is recommended for use when using command substitution. To debug shell scripts, use **set -x** at the beginning so every command line is echoed to the screen.

The *here document* (<<) is used in the same script as the command to provide nominal standard input. It can be used with both command substitution and variables.

Use **trap** as a signal handler if you want your script to respond to a signal in a specific way. You can also make a script ignore signals by using a null command list.

Test Your Understanding

14.1   If x has the value 10, what is the value of (i) xx (ii) xx?

14.2   Mention two ways you can run a script developed for the Korn shell (**/usr/bin/ksh**) even if your login shell is different.

14.3   A shell script stopped running when its name was changed. Why?

14.4   What is the *exit status* of a command and where is it stored?

14.5   Develop script logic that allows only romeo and henry to execute a program, and only from the terminals tty05 and tty06.

14.6   A script named **test** containing the **df** and **du** commands displays nothing when executed. Why does that happen? State two ways of making the script behave properly.

14.7   Search for a pattern with **grep** and **sed**, and look for a file with **find**. Test the return value of each command when it displays no output. What conclusions would you draw?

14.8   Write shell code to accept a string from the terminal, and echo a suitable message if it doesn't have at least 10 characters using (i) **case**, (ii) **expr**

14.9   Use **expr** to extract the parent directory from the absolute pathname of a file stored in a variable x.

14.10 Write a script that accepts a filename as argument and displays the last modification time if the file exists and a suitable message if it doesn't.

14.11 Devise a script that accepts two directory names, bar1 and bar2, and deletes those files in bar2 which are identical to their namesakes in bar1.

14.12 Write a script that accepts a compressed filename as argument (which could be .gz, .bz2 or .zip). It looks at the extension and decompresses the file using the correct decompression program, but only if the decompressed file (or one with the same name) doesn't exist.

14.13 Write a shell script that searches for a pattern (supplied as argument) in all files in the current directory and then calls up the **vi** editor with those files containing the pattern. How will you repeat the search in the current file and other files?

14.14 Explain whether these **while** loops will run: (i) **while [5]** (ii) **while [x"$1" != x]**

14.15 Write a script that accepts filenames as arguments. For every filename, it should first check whether it exists in the current directory and then convert its name to uppercase, but only if a file with the new name doesn't exist.

14.16 Devise a script that looks at every component of PATH and checks whether the directory exists and is also accessible.

Flex Your Brain

14.1   Devise a script that takes a filename as argument (which must exist in the current directory) and locates from your home directory tree all pathnames of its links. The list should be mailed to self.

14.2 Use a script to take two numbers as arguments and output their sum using (i) **bc**, (ii) **expr**. Include error-checking to test whether two arguments were entered. Should you use **bc** or **expr** for computation?

14.3 Write a script that lists files by modification time when called with **lm** and by access time when called with **la**. By default, the script should show the listing of all files in the current directory.

14.4 Expand the scope of the script in 14.13 (Test Your Understanding) to perform the search recursively.

14.5 Write a script that behaves both in interactive and noninteractive mode. When no arguments are supplied, it picks up each C program from the current directory and lists the first 10 lines. It then prompts for deletion of the file. If the user supplies arguments with the script, then it works on those files only.

14.6 Display the processes in the system every 30 seconds five times using a (i) **while** loop, (ii) **for** loop. What is the unusual feature of the **for** loop?

14.7 You are moving files to a handheld which accepts only 8+3 type filenames. Produce a list of those files in your current directory that fail in this test.

14.8 Write a script that displays a special formatted listing showing the (i) permissions, (ii) size, (iii) filename, (iv) last modification time, (v) last access time of filenames supplied as arguments. Provide suitable headers using the **printf** command.

14.9 Find out the pathname of the Korn shell on your machine and then change the interpreter line in all shell scripts in the current directory that show a different pathname for **ksh**.

14.10 Observe this command; does it make any sense? **set `set`**

14.11 Write a script which looks up every .c file in the current directory for the strings printf or fprintf. If found, the script adds the statement #include <stdio.h> at the beginning of the file but only if it doesn't already have it included.

14.12 Write a script that compares two directories bar1 and bar2 (supplied as arguments) and copies or overwrites to bar1 from bar2 every file that is either not present in bar1 or is newer than its namesake in bar1. (HINT: Use the **find** command.)

14.13 You have a number of C programs that contain comment lines at the beginning of each program. The lines begin with /* followed by the first line of comment, but the terminator line has */ as the *only* characters in the line. Remove these comments from all files.

14.14 Write a script that monitors the creation of .pdf or .PDF files in the current directory. Every minute it should display a list of those filenames created after the previous display.

14.15 Write a shell script that uses **find** to look for a file and echo a suitable message if the file is not found. You must not store the **find** output in a file.

14.16 Write a script that checks each minute and reports on who logs in and who logs out.

14.17 Assume that you have a number of files, downloaded from the Internet, in the /home/kumar/download directory. The table of contents (TOC) is available in the file TOC_download.txt in the form *filename:description*. The script should check each file in the download directory that doesn't have a description in the TOC file and prompt the user for the description. The TOC should be updated to maintain the list in sorted condition. The script must be immune to signals.

Essential System Administration

In the concluding act for Part I of this book, it's time to make a visit to the world of system administration. This task is usually entrusted to a single person—the **system administrator**, also known as the **superuser** or **root user**. The administrator has vast powers, having access to practically everything. The success and stability of any UNIX installation depends, in great measure, on the effectiveness of the system administrator. Today, every user must know some of the important administrative functions that she may be called upon to perform at any time.

The job of system administration involves the management of the entire system—ranging from maintaining user accounts, security and managing disk space to performing backups. The burden is not overwhelming though because UNIX is more easily maintained and well documented than most other systems. However, UNIX gets greatly fragmented in this area, and POSIX makes no attempt to address administrative issues. We consider the routine duties in this chapter and the more involved ones in Chapter 25.

WHAT YOU WILL LEARN

- Log in to root and become a *superuser* with **su**.
- The administrator's powers in changing the attributes of any file and in killing any process.
- Control access to the scheduling services, **at** and **cron**.
- Create, modify and delete user accounts with **useradd**, **usermod** and **userdel**.
- The concept of *run levels* and their role in startup and shutdown operations.
- Use **df** and **du** to report on both free and used disk space.
- The significance of the attributes of device files.
- Format and copy diskettes with **format**, **fdformat** and **dd**.
- Handle DOS files on diskettes with a set of "dos" commands.
- Use **cpio** to back up and restore files.
- Use **tar** to back up a directory tree and append files to an archive.

┌──┐
│ ┌── TOPICS OF SPECIAL INTEREST
│ • The significance of the three special file permissions bits—*SUID*, *SGID* and *sticky bit*, and
│   how the administrator uses them in enforcing security.
│ • Understanding how disk read/write operations take place.
└──┘

15.1 root: THE SYSTEM ADMINISTRATOR'S LOGIN

The UNIX system provides a special login name for the exclusive use of the administrator; it is called **root**. This account doesn't need to be separately created but comes with every system. Its password is generally set at the time of installation of the system and has to be used on logging in:

```
login: root
password: *******[Enter]
# _
```

The prompt of root is #, unlike the $ or % used by nonprivileged users. Once you log in as root, you are placed in root's home directory. Depending on the system, this directory could be / or /root.

On modern systems, most administrative commands are resident in /sbin and /usr/sbin, but if you are using an older system, you could find them in /etc. root's PATH list is also different from the one used by other users:

```
/sbin:/bin:/usr/sbin:/usr/bin:/usr/dt/bin
```

Since the superuser has to constantly navigate the file system, it's possible that he might inadvertently execute programs and scripts written by other users. That's why the PATH for a superuser doesn't include the current directory.

Many of the standard scripts supplied with UNIX systems for system administration work (especially the scripts related to booting) rely on the Bourne shell for execution. As administrator, you have to carefully weigh the consequences of using the Korn shell since scripts developed under this shell may not run on another host, which may not have this shell. But you must not under **any** circumstances use C shell scripts. Linux uses Bash for normal and system administrative activities; there's no problem there.

15.1.1 su: Acquiring Superuser Status

Any user can acquire superuser status with the **su** command if she knows the root password. For example, the user juliet (with the home directory /home/juliet) becomes a superuser in this way:

```
$ su
Password: ********                          root's password
# pwd
/home/juliet                                Prompt changes, but directory doesn't
```

Though the current directory doesn't change, the # prompt indicates that juliet now has powers of a superuser. To be in root's home directory on superuser login, use **su -l**.

Creating a User's Environment   Users often rush to the administrator with the complaint that a program has stopped running. The administrator first tries running it in a simulated environment.

su, when used with a **-**, recreates the user's environment without taking the login-password route:

```
su - henry                              No password required
```

This sequence executes henry's .profile (or the relevant startup scripts), and temporarily creates henry's environment. **su** runs a separate sub-shell, so this mode is terminated by hitting *[Ctrl-d]* or using **exit**.

15.2 THE ADMINISTRATOR'S PRIVILEGES

The superuser has enormous powers, and any command invoked by him has a greater chance of success than when issued by others. The command may also behave differently or be reserved for his exclusive use. The superuser's authority is mainly derived from the power to

- Change the contents or attributes of any file like its permissions and ownership. He can delete any file even if the directory is write-protected!
- Initiate or kill any process. The administrator can directly kill all processes except the ones essential for running the system.
- Change any user's password without knowing the existing one.
- Set the system clock with **date**.
- Address all users concurrently with **wall**.
- Limit the maximum size of files that users are permitted to create with **ulimit**.
- Control users' access to the scheduling services like **at** and **cron**.
- Control users' access to many networking services like FTP, SSH, etc.

The administrator has to use these powers with utmost caution. An apparently innocent and unplugged loophole can cause disaster if that knowledge is acquired by a mischievous person. Let's now see how the administrator exercises some of the powers listed above.

15.2.1 date: Setting the System Date

We have used **date** as a "passive" command before *(3.2)*—to display the system date. The administrator uses the same command with a numeric argument to *set* the system date. This argument is usually an eight-character string of the form *MMDDhhmm*, optionally followed by a two- or four-digit year string:

```
# date 01092124
Thu Jan  9 21:24:00 IST 2003
```

UNIX systems will continue to understand the century for some time (until the year 2038, at least). Ensure that the date is reasonably accurate as the **cron** scheduler *(9.12)* uses the clock time to run jobs.

15.2.2 wall: Communicating with Users

The **wall** command addresses all users simultaneously. Most UNIX systems don't permit users to run this command (Linux excepted), and reserve it for the sole use of the administrator:

```
# wall
The machine will be shut down today
at 14:30 hrs. The backup will be at 13:30 hrs
[Ctrl-d]
```

All users currently logged in will receive this message on their terminal. This command is routinely executed by the administrator—especially before shutdown of the system.

15.2.3 ulimit: Setting Limits on File Size

Faulty programs or negligence can eat up disk space in no time. The **ulimit** command (now a builtin in all shells) imposes a restriction on the maximum size of a file that a user is permitted to create. Though an ordinary user can only reduce this default value, the superuser can increase it:

    ulimit 20971510   *Measured in 512-byte blocks*

You'll often place this statement in /etc/profile so that every user has to work within these restrictions. When used by itself, **ulimit** displays the current setting. Solaris and Linux show unlimited as the default output, but it could be different on your system.

15.2.4 Controlling Use of at and cron

The access to the use of **at** and **batch** is restricted and controlled by the files at.allow and at.deny in /etc/cron.d (/etc in Linux). If at.allow is present, only users listed in the file are permitted to use **at** and **batch**. If it is not present, the system checks at.deny for users who are barred from using these commands. If neither file is present, only the system administrator is permitted to invoke **at** and **batch**.

The **cron** scheduler *(9.12)* is used by the administrator to make commands like **find** and **du** compile useful information about the system, or for automating the backup operations. Like **at** and **batch**, the authorization to use it is controlled in identical manner by two files, cron.allow and cron.deny, in /etc/cron.d (/etc in Linux).

15.3 MAINTAINING SECURITY

Because security in a computer system eventually involves files, a faulty file permission can easily be exploited by a malicious user in a destructive manner. As administrator, you have to ensure that the system directories (/bin, /usr/bin, /etc, /sbin etc.) and the files in them are not writable by others. We'll now discuss some important security-related features found on a UNIX system.

15.3.1 passwd: Changing Any Password

passwd prompts for the existing password when the command is used by a nonprivileged user *(3.9)*. However, when the superuser uses the command, the system behaves in a more lenient manner:

```
# passwd
Changing password for root
Enter the new password (minimum of 5, maximum of 8 characters)
Please use a combination of upper and lower case letters and numbers.
```

```
New password: *********
Re-enter password: *********          To be entered twice
Password changed.
```

Note that the system doesn't prompt for the old password this time. The administrator must closely guard the superuser password. Otherwise, the entire UNIX system may have to be reloaded! UNIX also allows the administrator the privilege of changing anybody's password without knowing it:

```
passwd henry
```

Once again, the old password is not prompted for; the new one has only to be entered twice. As users often give out their passwords to others, passwords tend to be known to others over time. What makes matters worse is that users themselves are quite averse to changing their own passwords. The **passwd** command offers features that force users to change their passwords after a specific time. For details look up Chapter 25.

Note: passwd doesn't prompt for the old password when the command is used by the superuser for changing the root password.

15.3.2 Set-User-Id (SUID): Power for a Moment

Recall the discussions on process attributes (9.4) where we mentioned that sometimes the *effective UID* may not be the same as the *real UID*. The time has now come to discuss a security feature which exploits this fact. Many UNIX programs have a special permissions mode that lets users update sensitive system files—like /etc/shadow—something they can't do directly with an editor. This is true of the **passwd** program:

```
-rwsr-xr-x  1 root      shadow      34808 Nov 30 17:55 /usr/bin/passwd
```

The letter **s** in the user category of the permissions field represents a special mode known as the **set-user-id** (SUID). This mode lets a process have the privileges of the *owner* of the file during the instance of the program. Thus, when a nonprivileged user executes **passwd**, the *effective* UID of the process is not the user's, but of root's—the owner of the program. This SUID privilege is then used by **passwd** to edit /etc/shadow.

The SUID for any file can be set by the superuser using the **chmod** command. The syntax uses the character **s** as the permission:

```
# chmod u+s a.out ; ls -l a.out
-rwsr-xr-x  1 root      staff       2113 Mar 24 11:18 a.out
```

To assign SUID in an absolute manner, simply prefix 4 to whatever octal string you would otherwise use (like 4755 instead of 755). The **set-group-id** (SGID) is similar to SUID except that a program with SGID set allows the user to have the same power as the group which owns the program. The SGID bit is 2, and some typical examples could be **chmod g+s a.out** or **chmod 2755 a.out**.

The SUID mechanism, invented by Dennis Ritchie, is a potential security hazard. It lets a user acquire hidden powers by running such a file owned by root. As administrator, you must keep track of all SUID programs owned by root that a user may try to create or copy. The **find** command easily locates them:

```
find /home -perm -4000 -print | mailx root
```

The extra octal bit (4) signifies the SUID mode, *but* **find** *treats the – before* 4000 *as representing any other permissions.* You can use **cron** to run this program at regular intervals and mail the file list to root.

Note: The fourth permission bit is used only when a special mode of a file needs to be set. It has the value 4 for SUID, 2 for SGID and 1 for the sticky bit. The other 3 bits have their usual significance.

15.3.3 The Sticky Bit

The **sticky bit** (also called the *saved text bit*) is the last permission bit remaining to be discussed. It applies to both regular files and directories. When applied to a regular file, it ensures that the text image of a program with the bit set is permanently kept in the swap area so it can be reloaded quickly when the program's turn to use the CPU arrives. Previously, it made sense to have this bit set for programs like **vi** and **emacs**. Today, machines with ultra-fast disk drives and lots of cheap memory don't need this bit for ordinary files.

However, the sticky bit becomes a useful security feature when used with a directory. The UNIX system allows users to create files in /tmp and /var/tmp, but no one can delete files not owned by her. Strange, isn't it? That's possible because both directories have their sticky bits set:

```
# ls -ld /tmp /var/tmp
drwxrwxrwt   5 root      sys        377 Jan  9 13:28 /tmp
drwxrwxrwt   2 root      sys       7168 Jan  9 13:34 /var/tmp
```

The directories are *apparently* writable by all, but that extra t (sticky) bit ensures that kumar can't remove sharma's files in these directories. Using **chmod**, you can set the bit on a directory by using 1 as the additional bit:

```
# chmod 1775 bar                                          Or chmod +t bar
# ls -l bar
drwxrwxr-t   2 sumit     dialout    1024 Apr 13 08:25 bar
```

The sticky bit is extremely useful for implementing group projects. To let a group of users work on a set of files without infringing on security, you'll have to do this:

1. Create a common group for these users in /etc/group.

2. Create separate user accounts for them but specify the same home directory.

3. Make sure the home directory and all subdirectories are not owned by any of the users. Use **chown** to surrender ownership to root.

4. Make the directories group-writable and set their sticky bits with **chmod 1775**.

In this scenario, every user of the group has write permission on the directory and can create files and subdirectories, but can only delete those she owns. A very useful feature indeed!

15.4 USER MANAGEMENT

The term *user* in UNIX is not meant to be only a person; it can represent a project or an application as well. A group of users performing similar functions may use the same username to use the system. It's thus quite common to have usernames like marketing, accounts, and so forth. For the creation and maintenance of user accounts, UNIX provides three commands—**useradd**, **usermod** and **userdel**.

When opening a user account, you have to associate the user with a group. A group usually has more than one member with a different set of privileges. People working on a common project should be able to read one another's files, which is possible only if they belong to the same group.

- Creating a user involves defining the following parameters:
- A user identification number (UID) and username.
- A group identification number (GID) and group name.
- The home directory.
- The login shell.
- The mailbox in /var/mail.
- The password.

Most of these parameters are found in a single line identifying the user in /etc/passwd. We'll now create a group for a user and then add that user to the system.

15.4.1 groupadd: Adding a Group

If the user is to be placed in a new group, an entry for the group has to be created first in /etc/group. A user always has one primary group and may also have one or more **supplementary groups**. This file contains all of the named groups of the system, and a few lines of this file reveal the structure:

```
root:x:0:root
bin:x:1:root,bin,daemon
lp:x:7:
uucp:x:14:uucp,fax,root,fnet,sumit
users:x:100:henry,oracle,image,enquiry
```

Each line contains four colon-delimited fields. Let's focus our attention on the group named users shown in the first field. This is the same name you see in the group ownership column of the listing. The second field once represented the group password but is hardly used today; it is either blank or an x. The third field shows the user's GID (here, 100). The last field contains a list of comma-delimited usernames (henry,oracle,image,enquiry) for whom this is the supplementary group. A blank at this position doesn't mean that no one is a member of this group; it's just that it's not the supplementary group for any user. Note that primary group for a user is shown in /etc/passwd.

To create a new group, dba, with a GID of 241, you have to use the **groupadd** command:

```
groupadd -g 241 dba
```
241 is the GID for dba

The command places this entry in /etc/group which you can also insert manually:

```
dba:x:241:
```

Once an entry for the group has been made, you are now ready to add a user of this group to the system.

15.4.2 useradd: Adding a User

The **useradd** command adds new users to the system. All parameters related to the user have to be provided in the command line itself:

```
# useradd -u 210 -g dba -c "THE RDBMS" -d /home/oracle -s /bin/ksh -m oracle
# _
```

This quietly creates the user oracle with a UID of 210 and group name dba. The home directory is /home/oracle, and the user will use the Korn shell. The -m option ensures that the home directory is created if it doesn't already exist and copies a sample .profile and .kshrc to the user's home directory. The line **useradd** creates in /etc/passwd is shown below:

```
oracle:x:210:241:THE RDBMS:/home/oracle:/bin/ksh
```

useradd also sets up the user's mailbox and sets the MAIL variable to point to that location (in /var/mail or /var/spool/mail). You now have to set the new user's password with the command **passwd oracle**. Once all this is done, the oracle user account is ready for use.

15.4.3 /etc/passwd and /etc/shadow: User Profiles

All user information except the password encryption is now stored in /etc/passwd. This file contained the password once, the reason why it continues to be known by that name. The encryption itself is stored in /etc/shadow. This is now the control file used by **passwd** to ascertain the legitimacy of a user's password.

Let's take the line pertaining to oracle in /etc/passwd. There are seven fields here, and their significance is noted below (in the order they appear in /etc/passwd):

- Username—The name you use to log on to a UNIX system (oracle).
- Password—No longer stores the password encryption but contains an x.
- UID—The user's numerical identification (210). No two users *should* have the same UID. **ls** prints the owner's name by matching the UID obtained from the inode with this field.
- GID—The user's numerical group identification (241). This number is also the third field in /etc/group.
- Comment or GCOS—User details, e.g., her name, address and so forth (The RDBMS). This name is used at the front of the email address for this user. Any mail sent from this user account will show the sender as *"The RDBMS"* <*oracle@heavens.com*>—assuming that the user belongs to the domain shown.

- Home directory—The directory where the user ends up on logging in (/home/oracle). The **login** program reads this field to set the variable HOME.
- Login shell—The first program executed after logging in. This is usually the shell (**/bin/ksh**). **login** sets the variable SHELL by reading this entry, and also fork-execs the shell process *(9.4.1)*.

For every line in /etc/passwd, there's a corresponding entry in /etc/shadow. The relevant line in this file could look something like this:

```
oracle:PR1hjiDhRM2Lg:12032::::::
```

The password encryption is shown in the second field. It's impossible to generate the password from this encryption. However, an intelligent hacker can use an encryption algorithm to generate a sequence of encrypted patterns. It's quite possible that she might just find a match, so this file must be made unreadable to all but the superuser.

Note: The last field in /etc/passwd is actually the command to be executed when a user logs in. This is usually the shell, but the administrator may choose a different program to restrict the user's actions.

15.4.4 usermod and userdel: Modifying and Removing Users

usermod is used for modifying some of the parameters set with **useradd**. Users sometimes need to change their login shell, and the following command line sets Bash as the login shell for the user oracle:

```
usermod -s /bin/bash oracle
```

Users are removed from the system with **userdel**. The following command removes the user oracle from the system:

```
userdel oracle                              Doesn't delete user's files
```

This removes all entries pertaining to oracle from /etc/passwd, /etc/group and /etc/shadow. The user's home directory doesn't get deleted in the process and has to be removed separately if required.

15.5 STARTUP AND SHUTDOWN

Startup　　　　　After a machine is powered on, the system looks for all peripherals and then goes through a series of steps that may take up to a few minutes to complete the boot cycle. The exact sequence is system-dependent, but the first major event is the loading of the kernel (**/kernel/genunix** in Solaris and **/boot/vmlinuz** in Linux) into memory. The kernel then spawns **init** (PID 1) which, in turn, spawns further processes. Some of these processes monitor all of the terminal lines, activate the network and printer. Eventually, **init** becomes the parent of all shells.

A UNIX system boots to a specific **state** (or mode), and this state is represented by a number or letter, called the **run level**. The default run level as well as the action to take for each run level are controlled by **init**. We'll consider **init**'s role in detail later *(25.8)*, but as of now you should know these two states:

- **Single-user** mode—This mode is important for the administrator, who uses it to perform his administrative tasks, like checking or backing up individual file systems. Other users are prevented from operating the system in single-user mode.

- **Multiuser** mode—In this mode, individual file systems are mounted *(25.6)*, and system daemons *(9.3)* are also started. Printing is possible only in multiuser mode and when the **lpsched** daemon is running.

The **who -r** command displays the run level for your system:

```
$ who -r
.         run-level 3  Jan  9 09:39        3       0  S
```

This machine is at run level 3, a state which supports multiuser and network operations. We'll have more to discuss about run levels and the role of **init** in Part II of the text.

Shutdown   The administrator also has the duty of shutting down the machine at the end of the day (if it is ever shut down). The **shutdown** command controls this sequence. **shutdown** usually performs the following activities:

- Notifies users with **wall** about the system going down with a directive to log out. Users are then expected to close their files and log out. **shutdown** itself sleeps for a minute after mailing the first message and may issue a reminder or two.

- Sends signals to all running processes so they can terminate normally.

- Logs users off and kills remaining processes.

- Unmounts *(25.6)* all secondary file systems.

- Writes information about file system status to disk *(25.9)* to preserve the integrity of the file system.

- Notifies users to reboot or switch off, or moves the system to single-user mode.

shutdown finally displays a message that could look something like these:

```
Reboot the system now or turn power off
System halted
```

The machine can now be considered to have completed the shutdown sequence successfully. You can now turn the power off unless your machine supports a power management feature that does this job automatically.

The -g option to **shutdown** overrides the default waiting time of one minute. The command can be used in these ways:

```
shutdown -g2           Powers down machine after 2 minutes
shutdown -y -g0        Immediate shutdown
shutdown -y -g0 -i6    Shut down and reboot
```

Some systems like Solaris have the **reboot** and **halt** commands that also shut the system down without warning the users. Unless you know what you are doing, you should stick to **shutdown** if you are administering a multiuser system.

LINUX: Linux uses the -t option to override the default waiting time of one minute. **shutdown** can also be used in these ways:

```
shutdown 17:30             Shut down at 17:30 hours
shutdown -r now            Shut down immediately and reboot
shutdown -h now            Shut down immediately and halt
```

Linux also permits the use of the Windows-styled *[Ctrl][Alt][Del]* sequence to shut down the system.

15.6 MANAGING DISK SPACE

No matter how many disks are added to the system, there will always be a scramble for space. Users often forget to remove the files they no longer require. Files tend to accumulate during the day, thus slowing down the system. If this buildup is not checked, the entire disk space will eventually be eaten up. The administrator must regularly scan the disk and locate files that have outlived their utility. He needs the **df** and **du** commands for this task as well as **find** that has already been discussed *(11.7)*. All three commands can also be issued by any user.

15.6.1 df: Reporting Free Space

You are aware that your operating system is supported by multiple file systems *(11.1)*. The **df** (disk free) command reports the amount of free space available for each file system separately:

```
# df
/                 (/dev/dsk/c0t0d0s0 ):  3491876 blocks     483932 files
/usr              (/dev/dsk/c0t0d0s4 ):  2434820 blocks     458466 files
/proc             (/proc             ):        0 blocks      15875 files
/dev/fd           (fd                ):        0 blocks          0 files
/etc/mnttab       (mnttab            ):        0 blocks          0 files
/var              (/dev/dsk/c0t0d0s1 ):  3881394 blocks     484212 files
/var/run          (swap              ):  2602128 blocks     109840 files
/users1           (/dev/dsk/c0t8d0s0 ):  8037576 blocks    1024196 files
/users2           (/dev/dsk/c0t9d0s0 ):  4920276 blocks     956432 files
/tmp              (swap              ):  2602128 blocks     109840 files
/export/home      (/dev/dsk/c0t0d0s7 ):  2187782 blocks     340677 files
```

There are several file systems on this Solaris machine, but you don't have control over all of them (like /proc and /etc/mnttab). The first column shows the directory where the file system is attached (mounted). The second column shows the device name of the file system. The last two columns show the number of 512-byte blocks available and the number of files that you can create.

The first line in the list refers to the root file system (/), which has 3,491,876 blocks of disk space free. It also has 483,932 inodes free, which means that up to that many additional files can be created on this file system. The system will continue to function until the free blocks or inodes are eaten away, whichever occurs earlier.

The -t (total) option includes the above output, as well as the total amount of disk space in the file system. We won't display its output, but we'll consider the informative -k option that reports in units of KB. This time, let's obtain the statistics for the / and /usr file systems:

```
$ df -k / /usr                                    Reports on / and /usr file systems
Filesystem              kbytes    used    avail capacity Mounted on
/dev/dsk/c0t0d0s0      1986439  240501 1686345   13%    /
/dev/dsk/c0t0d0s4      2025076  807666 1156658   42%    /usr
```

You probably won't need to know anything more than what this output offers. It shows the percentage utilization also. Once you have identified the file system that needs to be investigated thoroughly, you need the **du** command that is considered next.

LINUX: The default output itself is quite informative; it shows both the total as well as the available space, but in a format that resembles the -k option used by UNIX. The -h option makes it even more readable by reporting in larger units (like MB, GB, etc):

```
$ df -h / /download
Filesystem      Size  Used Avail Use% Mounted on
/dev/hda10      4.8G  2.6G  1.9G  57% /
/dev/hda13      5.6G  985M  4.3G  18% /download
```

The block size used for reporting is usually different in Linux. **find**, **df** and **du** report in 1024-byte blocks.

Note: When the space in one file system is totally consumed, the file system can't borrow space from another file system.

15.6.2 du: Disk Usage

You'll often need to find out the consumption of a specific directory tree rather than an entire file system. **du** (disk usage) is the command you need as it reports usage by a recursive examination of the directory tree. This is how **du** lists the usage of /home/sales/tml:

```
# du /home/sales/tml
11554     /home/sales/tml/forms
12820     /home/sales/tml/data
638       /home/sales/tml/database
.....
25170     /home/sales/tml                Also reports a summary at end
```

By default, **du** lists the usage of each subdirectory of its argument, and finally produces a summary. The list can often be quite large, and more often than not, you may be interested only in a summary. For this, the -s (summary) option is quite convenient:

```
# du -s /home/sales/tml
25170     /home/sales/tml
```

Assessing Space Consumed by Users   Most of the dynamic space in a system is consumed by users' home directories and data files. You should use **du -s** to report on each user's home directory. The output is brief and yet quite informative:

```
# du -s /home/*
144208    /home/henry
98290     /home/image
```

```
13834    /home/local
28346    /home/sales
```

du can also report on each file in a directory (-a option), but the list would be too big to be of any use. You may instead look for some of the notorious disk eaters, and exceptional reporting is what you probably need. The **find** command can do this job.

Note: You have used **find** before *(11.7)*; the command uses the -size option to locate large files. Multiple selection criteria can also be specified:

```
find /home -size +2048 -print            Files above 1 MB
find /home -size +2048 -size -8192 -print   Above 1 MB and below 4 MB
```

You need to halve these figures when using Linux as **find** there uses 1024-byte blocks.

15.7 DEVICE FILES

Devices are also files, and you have seen some of these filenames in the **df** output. You open a device, read and write to it, and then close it like you do to any file. The functions for doing all this are built into the kernel for each and every device of the system. The same device can often be accessed with several different filenames. This has sometimes been done for backward compatibility and sometimes for associating a separate device with a specific function.

All device files are stored in /dev or in its subdirectories. The device names seen on one UNIX system and Linux are shown in Table 15.1. Though the device names in Linux have been known to be remarkably invariant, the same can't be said of the System V devices. If you are using Solaris or HP-UX, the names will be different. Here's a concise listing of these devices for a system running System V:

```
# ls -l /dev
total 52
brw-rw-rw-  1 root     sys       51,  0 Aug 31 07:28 cd0       CD-ROM
brw-rw-rw-  2 bin      bin        2, 64 Feb 23  1997 fd0       Default floppy drive
brw-------  1 sysinfo  sysinfo    1,  0 May  7  1996 hd00      First hard disk
crw-------  2 bin      bin        6,  0 Dec  5 14:12 lp0       Printer
cr--r--r--  1 root     root      50,  0 Aug 31 07:28 rcdt0     Tape drive
crw-------  1 henry    terminal   0,  0 Oct 15 10:23 tty01     Terminal
crw-rw-rw-  2 bin      bin        5,  0 May  7  1996 tty1a     Serial port 1
```

SVR4 also has two additional directories—/dev/dsk and /dev/rdsk containing some more files. The files in those directories sometimes have equivalents (or even links) in /dev. The lists in real life are much larger than this and includes every possible device on your system—including even the main memory of your computer. This listing reveals two vital points:

- Device files can be grouped into mainly two categories depending on the first character of the permissions field (b or c).
- The fifth field—normally representing the size for other files—consists of a pair of numbers. A device file contains no data.

Device files also have permissions with the same significance. To send output to a terminal, you need to have write permission for the device, and to read a floppy, you must have read permission for the device file. The significance of the device attributes is taken up next.

15.7.1 Block and Character Devices

First, a word about disk reading and writing. When you issue an instruction to save a file, the write operation takes place in chunks or blocks. Each block here represents an integral number of disk sectors (of 512 bytes each). The data is first transferred to a **buffer cache** (a pool of buffers) which the kernel later writes to disk. When you read from disk, the buffer cache is first accessed containing the most recently used data. If the data is found there, disk access is avoided. You may also decide to ignore this facility and access the device directly. Many devices allow you to do that, and the access method is determined by the name of the device that is called up.

Note that generally the first character in the permissions field is c or b. The floppy drive, CD-ROM and hard disk have b prefixed to their permissions. All data are read and written to these devices in blocks and use the buffer cache. That's why they are referred to as **block special** devices. On the other hand, the terminal, tape drive and printer are **character special** or raw devices, indicated by the letter **c**. For the latter, the read/write operations ignore the buffer cache and access the device directly.

Many devices have both a raw and a block counterpart in System V. Hard disks, floppy drives and CD-ROMs are both block and character devices. Generally, an r prefixed to a block device name makes it a character device. Block devices are also found separately in /dev/dsk and character devices in /dev/rdsk.

15.7.2 Major and Minor Numbers

The set of routines needed to operate a specific device is known as the **device driver**. When a particular device is accessed, the kernel calls the right device driver and passes some parameters for it to act properly. The kernel must know not only the type of device but also certain details about the device—like the density of a floppy or the partition number of the disk.

The fifth column of the previous listing doesn't show the file size in bytes, but rather a pair of two numbers separated by a comma. These numbers are called the **major** and **minor device numbers**, respectively. The major number represents the device driver; this is actually the type of device. All hard disks will have the same major number if they are attached to the same controller.

The minor number is indicative of the parameters that the kernel passes to the device driver. Often, it indicates the special characteristics of the device. For example, fd0h1440 and fd1h1440 represent two floppy devices attached to a particular controller. So both of them have the same major number but different minor numbers.

You'll see a lot of 0s, 1s and other digits in the device names. Often, you'll be able to identify a device from its filename. System V device files are resident in /dev/dsk (and /dev/rdsk for raw devices). The name /dev/dsk/f0q18dt represents a 3.5" floppy (block) device. It is bootable (0), of quad density and has 18 sectors/track—a 1.44 MB diskette. There is also a default name for many devices; the floppy drive can be accessed by /dev/fd0.

Note: Unlike ordinary and directory files, device files don't contain any data. They merely point to the location of the device driver routines that actually operate the device.

Table 15.1 Typical Device Names (Directory: /dev)

SVR4 Device	*Linux Device*	*Significance*
cd0 or dsk/c0t6d0s2	cdrom	CD-ROM
fd0 or diskette	fd0	Default floppy drive
dsk/f0q18dt	fd0H1440	1.44 MB floppy
rdsk/f0q18dt	fd0H1440	1.44 MB raw floppy
hd00 or dsk/c0t0d0s2	hda	First hard disk
hd10 or dsk/c1t3d0s2	hdb	Second hard disk
lp0	lp0	Printer
rcdt0 or rmt/0	st0	Tape drive
term/1	tty1	Terminal
tty1a	cua0	Serial port 1
tty2A	ttyS1	Modem port 2

15.8 HANDLING FLOPPY DISKETTES

Although the tape is the most common backup device, the floppy diskette represents the most convenient means of exchanging files between machines at work and home. For our examples, we'll be using the 3.5", 1.44 MB diskette.

15.8.1 `format` and `fdformat`: Formatting Diskettes

Before you use a floppy for backup purposes, you need to format it. This is done with the **format** or **fdformat** commands (whichever is available on your system):

```
# fdformat                                        On Solaris
Press return to start formatting floppy.
```

The -d option uses the DOS format.

This command formats and verifies a 1.44 MB floppy. Other systems may require you to specify the raw device name as argument:

```
format /dev/rdsk/f0q18dt          On another UNIX system running System V
```

LINUX: Linux too uses the **fdformat** command for formatting a floppy. Device names in Linux generally don't vary across the different flavors; a floppy usually has the name /dev/fd0 or /dev/fd0h1440, so you should use **fdformat /dev/fd0** (or the other device name).

15.8.2 dd: Copying Diskettes

dd (disk dump) is a versatile command that can be used to perform a variety of tasks. It is somewhat dated as some of its filtering functions have been taken over by other UNIX tools. It can be invoked by any user but is really the administrator's tool. It has a strange command line having a series of options in the form *option=value*.

dd was extensively used in copying file systems, but today its role is mainly restricted to copying media—like floppies and tapes. It is not interactive (in fact, a filter), and a pair of **dd** commands is needed to complete the operation.

We'll now use **dd** to make a copy of a 1.44 MB floppy diskette. The first step is to create the image of the floppy on disk:

```
# dd if=/dev/rdsk/f0q18dt of=$$ bs=147456
10+0 records in
10+0 records out
```

The keywords are if= (input filename), of= (output filename) and bs= (block size). The above command copies the raw contents of a 1.44 MB floppy to a temporary file, $$, using a block size of 147456—exactly one-tenth the capacity of a 1.44 MB diskette.

Next, take out the source floppy from the drive and insert a formatted target floppy. A second reversed **dd** command copies this temporary file to the diskette:

```
# dd if=$$ of=/dev/rdsk/f0q18dt bs=147456 ; rm $$
10+0 records in
10+0 records out
```

You should copy your boot floppies in this way. In the same manner, you can copy a tape, but if there are two tape drives, a single **dd** command can do the job:

```
dd if=/dev/rct0 of=/dev/rct1 bs=9k
```

dd uses only raw devices—those in /dev/rdsk or the ones in /dev beginning with an r—like /dev/rdiskette or /dev/rct0. Linux doesn't have separate devices for the two modes but selects the right mode automatically.

15.8.3 Handling DOS Diskettes

It is now quite common to see both Windows and UNIX systems on the desktop. UNIX today provides a family of commands (Table 15.2) that can read and write DOS floppy diskettes. These command names begin with the string dos in SVR4. They are modeled after UNIX commands performing similar functions.

The command required most is **doscp**, which copies files between disk and diskette:

```
doscp emp.lst /dev/dsk/f0q18dt:/per.lst
```

There are two components in the target specification—the device name (1.44 MB floppy drive) and the filename (/per.lst), with the : used as delimiter. As in **cp**, multiple file copying is also possible:

```
doscp emp[123].lst /dev/dsk/f0q18dt
```

doscat performs a simple "cat" of its arguments in the command line. When more than one filename is specified, the standard output for each is concatenated:

```
doscat /dev/dsk/f0q18dt:/CHAP01 /dev/dsk/f0q18dt:/CHAP02 > newchap
```

These commands make the newline conversions automatically *(5.13)*, but they also work with the -r option, in which case the files are copied or concatenated without newline conversions.

Table 15.2 shows the use of these commands with varying device names. One of them should work on your system. If a: and b: don't work, then use the appropriate filename in /dev or /dev/dsk.

LINUX: The Linux "DOS" commands begin with the string m, and use the corresponding DOS command as the rest of the string. Here are some examples:

```
mcopy emp.lst a:
mcopy a:* .
mdir a:
mdel a:*.txt
```

Note that Linux uses the DOS drive name. All of these commands belong to the "mtools" collection. For details, use **man mtools**.

Table 15.2 The Family of DOS Commands (Linux command name in parentheses)

Command	Action
doscp /dev/fd0135ds18:/tags .	Copies tags from DOS diskette (mcopy)
doscat a:readme a:setup.txt	Concatenates files readme and setup.txt in DOS diskette (mtype)
dosdir /dev/dsk/f0q18dt	Lists files in DOS diskette in DOS-style (mdir)
dosls /dev/dsk/f0q18dt	Lists files in UNIX ls-style
dosmkdir a:bin	Creates directory bin on DOS diskette (mmd)
dosrmdir a:bin	Removes directory bin on DOS diskette (mrd)
dosrm /dev/dsk/f0q18dt:setup.inf	Deletes file setup.inf on DOS diskette (mdel)
dosformat b:	Formats diskette in nonbootable drive for use on DOS systems (mformat)

15.9 cpio: A BACKUP PROGRAM

The importance of performing regular backups isn't usually appreciated until a crash has occurred and a lot of data has been lost. As administrator, you are partly responsible for the safety of the data that resides on the system. It is part of your duties to decide which files should be backed up and also to determine the periodicity of such backups. The effectiveness of the backup is determined by your ability to easily restore lost or corrupted data files. For reasons of security, backup media of sensitive data are often kept at distant locations.

We'll consider two backup programs in this chapter—**cpio** and **tar**. Both combine a group of files into an archive *(5.14)*, with suitable headers preceding the contents of each file. The backup device can be a magnetic or a cartridge tape, a floppy diskette, or even a disk file. Small systems, especially workstations, may not have the tape facility, so the floppy drive will be used here to illustrate the features of both commands.

The **cpio** command (copy input-output) copies files to and from a backup device. It uses standard input to take the list of filenames. It then copies them with their contents and headers to the standard output which can be redirected to a file or a device. This means that **cpio** can be (and is) used with redirection and piping.

cpio uses two *key* options, -o (output) and -i (input), either of which (but not both) must be there in the command line. All other options have to be used with either of these key options. The **cpio** options are shown in Table 15.3. The examples in this section and the next use System V device names. Linux users should use /dev/fd0h1440, and Solaris users should use /dev/rdiskette as the device names.

15.9.1 Backing Up Files (-o)

Since **cpio** uses only standard input, you can use **ls** to generate a list of filenames to serve as its input. The -o key option creates the archive on the standard output, which you need to redirect to a device file. This is how you copy files in the current directory to a 1.44 MB floppy:

```
# ls | cpio -ov > /dev/rdsk/f0q18dt          Use /dev/fd0 in Linux
array.pl
calendar
cent2fah.pl
convert.sh
xinitrc.sam
276 blocks                                   Total size of the archive
```

The -v (verbose) option displays each filename on the terminal while it's being copied. **cpio** needs as input a list of files, and if this list is available in a file, redirection can be used too:

```
cpio -o >/dev/rdsk/f0q18dt < flist
```

Incremental Backups   **find** can also produce a file list, so any files that satisfy its selection criteria can also be backed up. You'll frequently need to use **find** and **cpio** in combination to back up selected files—for instance, those that have been modified in the last two days:

```
find . -type f -mtime -2 -print | cpio -ovB >/dev/rdsk/f0q18dt
```

Since the path list of **find** is a dot, the files are backed up with their relative pathnames. However, if it is a /, **find** will use absolute pathnames.

The -B option sets the block size to 5120 bytes for input and output, which is 10 times the default size. For higher (or lower) sizes, the -C option has to be used:

```
ls *.pl | cpio -ovC51200 >/dev/rdsk/f0q18dt          100 times the default
```

Multivolume Backups   When the created archive in the backup device is larger than the capacity of the device, **cpio** prompts for inserting a new diskette into the drive:

```
# find . -type f -print | cpio -ocB >/dev/rdsk/f0q18dt
Reached end of medium on output.
If you want to go on, type device/filename when ready
/dev/fd0                                          Device name entered
3672 blocks
```

Enter the device name when **cpio** pauses to take input. In this way, an archive can be split into several extents (volumes).

15.9.2 Restoring Files (-i)

A complete archive or selected files can be restored with the -i key option. To restore files, use redirection to take input from the device:

```
# cpio -iv < /dev/rdsk/f0q18dt
array.pl
calendar
cent2fah.pl
convert.sh
xinitrc.sam
276 blocks
```

When restoring subdirectories, **cpio** assumes that the subdirectory structures are also maintained on the hard disk; it can't create them in case they are not. However, the -d (directory) option overrides that.

cpio also accepts a quoted wild-card pattern, so multiple files fitting the pattern can be restored. Restoring only the shell scripts becomes quite easy:

```
cpio -i "*.sh" < /dev/rdsk/f0q18dt
```

Tip: A file is restored in that directory that matches its pathname. In other words, if a file has been backed up with the absolute pathname (e.g., /home/romeo/unit13), then it will be restored in the same directory (/home/romeo). However, when relative pathnames are used, files can be restored anywhere. The "relative filename" method is normally recommended because the administrator often likes to back up files from one directory and restore them in another. Make sure you use **find** with a dot, rather than a /, to specify the path list when you are using it with **cpio**. This applies to the **tar** command also.

Handling Modification Times (-m)   By default, when a file is extracted, its modification time is set to the time of extraction. This could lead to problems as this file will participate in future incremental backups even though it has actually not been modified after restoration. Instead of using **touch** *(11.6.1)* to change the modification times (an impractical solution), you can use the -m option to tell cpio that the modification time has to be retained.

cpio compares the modification time of a file on the media with the one on disk (if any). If the disk file is newer than the copy, or of the same age, then it won't be restored; **cpio** then echoes this message:

```
"current <unit14> newer"
```

This is a useful built-in protection feature that safeguards the latest version of a file. (**tar** doesn't have this feature.) However, this can be overridden with the -u (unconditional) option.

Tip: If you are often moving files from one machine to another, use **cpio** instead of **tar**. You are then assured that a newer file on one machine is not overwritten by an older one from another.

15.9.3 Displaying the Archive (-it)

The -t option displays the contents of the device without restoring the files. This option must be combined with the -i key option:

```
# cpio -itv </dev/rdsk/f0q18dt
100755 henry        605  Oct 18 23:34:07 1997  cent2fah.pl
100755 henry        273  Oct 18 23:34:07 1997  check_number.pl
100755 henry        531  Oct 18 23:34:08 1997  dec2bin.pl
100755 henry        214  Oct 18 23:34:08 1997  get_home.pl
```

The files are displayed in a format resembling the listing. (Linux and Solaris output are identical to the listing.) This format shows the octal representation of the file type (10) and the permissions (0755) as well as the modification time of the file (to the nearest second!). Both file type and permissions are stored in the inode as an integral unit, and in Chapter 23 you'll learn to separate them.

Table 15.3   cpio Nonkey Options (used with -i or -o as relevant)

Option	Significance
-d	Creates directories as and when needed
-c	Writes header information in ASCII character form for portability
-r	Renames files in interactive manner
-t	Lists files in archive (only with -i option)
-u	Overwrites newer file with older version
-v	Verbose option; prints list of files that are being copied
-m	Retains original file modification time
-f *exp*	Copies all files except those in *exp*
-C*size*	Sets input-output block size to *size* bytes
-A -O *device*	Appends files to *device* (Solaris and Linux only)
-H tar	Creates or reads a tar header format (Solaris and Linux only)
-E *file*	Extracts only those files listed in *file* (Solaris and Linux only)

15.9.4 Other Options

There are two important options that can be used with the -o and -i options:

• The -r (rename) option lets you rename each file before starting the copying process. The system presents each filename and prompts you for a response. If you enter a filename, copying is done to that file; a null response leaves the file uncopied.

- The -f option, followed by an expression, causes **cpio** to select all files *except* those in the expression:

```
cpio -ivf "*.c" </dev/rdsk/f0q18dt          Restores all except C programs.
```

cpio relies on another command (usually **find**) or a file to provide its file list. It can't accept filename arguments in the command line. A **cpio** archive is also overwritten with every invocation of the command. This is where **tar** comes in.

15.10 tar: THE "TAPE" ARCHIVE PROGRAM

The **tar** (tape archive) command has been in existence since before the emergence of **cpio**. Today, it not only creates archives on tapes but supports floppies as well. Unlike **cpio**, **tar** doesn't normally write to the standard output (though it can be made to), but creates an archive in the media. It is a versatile command with certain exclusive features not found in **cpio**:

- It doesn't use standard input to obtain its file list. **tar** accepts file and directory names as arguments.
- It copies one or more entire directory trees; i.e., it operates recursively by default.
- It can append to an archive without overwriting the entire archive (**cpio** in Solaris and Linux also).

You have already used **tar** with its key options *(5.16)* to handle disk archives. The common key options are -c (copy), -x (extract) and -t (table of contents). The -f option additionally has to be used for specifying the device name. The **tar** options are listed in Table 15.4.

15.10.1 Backing Up Files (-c)

tar accepts directory and filenames directly on the command line. The -c key option is used to copy files to the backup device. The verbose option (-v) shows the progress of backup:

```
# tar -cvf /dev/rdsk/f0q18dt /home/sales/SQL/*.sql
a /home/sales/SQL/invoice_do_all.sql 1 tape blocks
a /home/sales/SQL/load2invoice_do_all.sql 1 tape blocks
a /home/sales/SQL/remove_duplicate.sql 1 tape blocks
a /home/sales/SQL/t_mr_alloc.sql 10 tape blocks
```

The a before each pathname indicates that the file is appended. The command backs up all SQL scripts with their absolute pathnames. The same restrictions apply; they can only be restored in the same directory. However, if you choose to keep the option open of installing the files in a different directory, you should first "cd" to /home/sales/SQL and then use a relative pathname:

```
cd /home/sales/SQL
tar -cvf /dev/rdsk/f0q18dt ./*.sql          Using the ./
```

The advantage of **tar** lies in that it can copy an entire directory tree with all its subdirectories. The current directory can be backed up with or without the hidden files:

```
tar -cvfb /dev/rdsk/f0q18dt 18 *            Doesn't back up hidden files
tar -cvfb /dev/fd0 18 .                     Backs up hidden files also
```

The files here are backed up with their relative pathnames, assuming they all fit in one diskette. If they don't, **tar** in System V may accommodate them as much as possible and then quit the program without warning.

Tip: If you have backed up your files with absolute pathnames and now want to restore them in another directory, then use the -C option.

The command will also execute faster if used with a block size of 18 (i.e., 18X2X512 bytes):

```
tar -cvfb /dev/rdsk/f0q18dt 18 *.sql            ./ prefix not required
```

Since both -f and -b have to be followed by an argument, the first word (/dev/rdsk/f0q18dt) after the option string -cvfb denotes the argument f or -f, and the second word (18) will line up with -b.

Note: tar is quite liberal in its handling of options. **tar cvf** is the same as **tar -cvf**. The - symbol is not required at all! However, future versions of **tar** will not support this.

Multivolume Backup (-k)   For multivolume diskette backups, **tar** in Solaris (and SCO UNIX) uses a special option (-k), followed by the volume size in kilobytes. This is how the file index is backed up in SCO UNIX:

```
# tar -cvfkb /dev/rdsk/f0q18dt 1440 18 index
Volume ends at 1439K, blocking factor = 18
tar: large file index needs 2 extents.
tar: current device seek position = OK
+++ a index 1439K [extent #1 of 2]
```

tar estimates that two 1440 KB (the argument to -k) diskettes will be required. After the first volume is full, **tar** prompts for a new volume:

```
tar: please insert new volume, then press RETURN.
```

At the time of restoration, the same option has to be used.

15.10.2 Restoring Files (-x)

Files are restored with the -x (extract) key option. When no file or directory name is specified, it restores all files from the backup device. The following command restores the files just backed up:

```
# tar -xvfb /dev/rdsk/f0q18dt 18
x /home/sales/SQL/invoice_do_all.sql, 169 bytes, 1 tape blocks
x /home/sales/SQL/load2invoice_do_all.sql, 456 bytes, 1 tape blocks
x /home/sales/SQL/remove_duplicate.sql, 237 bytes, 1 tape blocks
x /home/sales/SQL/t_mr_alloc.sql, 4855 bytes, 10 tape blocks
```

Selective extraction is also possible by providing one or more directory or filenames:

```
tar -xvf /dev/rdsk/f0q18dt /home/sales/SQL/t_mr_alloc.sql
```

Unlike **cpio**, when files are extracted, the modification times of the files also remain unchanged. This can be overridden by the **-m** option to reflect the system time at the time of extraction.

Note: Unlike **cpio**, some versions of **tar** (like in Solaris) don't read wild-card patterns. If you use **tar -xvf /dev/fd0 *.pl**, it's the shell that tries to expand the pattern, which means that the files have to reside in the current directory. However, some versions of **tar** (like in Linux) do permit the use of the wild-cards; it doesn't matter whether the files exist at all in the disk.

15.10.3 Displaying the Archive (-t)

Like in **cpio**, the **-t** key option displays the contents of the device in a long format similar to the listing:

```
# tar -tvf /dev/rdsk/f0q18dt
rwxr-xr-x203/50      472 Jun  4 09:35 1991 ./dentry1.sh
rwxr-xr-x203/50      554 Jun  4 09:52 1991 ./dentry2.sh
rwxr-xr-x203/50     2299 Jun  4 13:59 1991 ./func.sh
```

There's something here that you ought to pay attention to: The files have been backed up with relative pathnames. Each filename here is preceded by ./. If you don't remember this but want to extract the file func.sh from the diskette, you'll obviously first try this:

```
# tar -xvf /dev/rdsk/f0q18dt func.sh
tar: func.sh: Not found in archive
```

tar failed to find the file because it existed there as ./func.sh and not func.sh. Put the ./ before the filename, and get it this time. Remember this whenever you encounter extraction errors as above.

15.10.4 Other Options

There are a number of other options of **tar** that are worth considering:

- The **-r** key option is used to append a file to an archive. This implies that an archive can contain several versions of the same file!
- The **-u** key option also adds a file to an archive but only if the file is not already there or is being replaced with a newer version.
- The **-w** option permits interactive copying and restoration. It prints the name of the file and prompts for the action to be taken (y or n).
- Some versions of **tar** use a special option to pick up filenames from a file. You might want to use this facility when you have a list of over a hundred files, which is impractical (and sometimes, impossible) to enter in the command line. Unfortunately, this option is not standard; Solaris uses -I and Linux uses -T.

LINUX: The GNU **tar** command is more powerful than its System V counterpart and supports a host of exclusive options. Unfortunately, there is sometimes a mismatch with the options used by System V. The -M option is used for a multivolume backup (e.g. **tar -cvf /dev/fd0H1440 -M ***). There's one option (-z) related to compression that we have already discussed *(5.16.3—LINUX)*.

Table 15.4 **tar** Options

Key Options *(only one to be used)*

Option	Significance
-c	Creates a new archive
-x	Extracts files from archive
-t	Lists contents of archive
-r	Appends files at end of archive
-u	Like r, but only if files are newer than those in archive

Nonkey Options

Option	Significance
-f *device*	Uses pathname *device* as name of device instead of the default
-v	Verbose option—lists files in long format
-w	Confirms from user about action to be taken
-b *n*	Uses blocking factor *n*, where *n* is restricted to 20
-m	Changes modification time of file to time of extraction
-I *file*	Takes filenames from *file* (Solaris only)
-T *file*	Takes filenames from *file* (Linux only)
-X *file*	Excludes filenames in *file* (Solaris and Linux only)
-k *num*	Multivolume backup—sets size of volume to *num* kilobytes (Solaris only)
-M	Multivolume backup (Linux only)
-z	Compresses/uncompresses with gzip (Linux only)
--bzip2	Compresses/uncompresses with bzip2 *(Linux only)*

15.11 CONCLUSION

We discussed the routine administrative features and tools that you need to use everyday. This chapter didn't provide the forum to discuss what to do when things go wrong. That requires from the administrator an in-depth knowledge of the different components of the system. At a deeper level, system administration involves fixing file systems, controlling the system's services and configuring the network. With people increasingly owning machines that run Linux, it's much easier today for every user to try out these advanced features than previously. For this reason, system administration is worth a second visit, which we make in Part II of this text.

WRAP UP

The system administrator or *superuser* uses the root user account, though any user can also invoke the **su** command to acquire superuser powers. Most administrative commands are resident in /sbin and /usr/sbin. The current directory doesn't feature in the superuser's PATH.

The administrator can change the attributes of any file and kill any process. The administrator also controls user access to many services like **at**, **cron**, FTP and SSH.

For enforcing security, the superuser can change any user's password. The *set-user-id* (SUID) bit of a program makes its process run with the powers of the program's owner and not the user's. The *sticky bit* set on a directory allows users to create and remove files owned by them in that directory, but not remove or edit files belonging to others.

A user is identified by her UID and GID. A user can be added (**useradd**), modified (**usermod**) and removed from the system (**userdel**). User details are maintained in /etc/passwd and /etc/group. The password is stored in an encrypted manner in /etc/shadow.

During system startup, the **init** process takes the system to multiuser state, and spawns many processes that *mounts* (attaches) file systems and starts the system's daemons. **init** eventually becomes the parent of all login shells. **shutdown** kills all processes, *unmounts* file systems and writes file system information to disk before powering down the machine.

The administrator has to monitor disk usage and ensure that adequate free space is available. **df** displays the free disk space for each file system. **du** lists the detailed usage of each file or directory. The administrator also uses **find** to locate large files (-size).

All device files are stored in /dev. Devices can be *block special* (which use the buffer cache) or *character special* (which don't). A device file is also represented by a *major number* which represents the device driver, and *minor number* which signifies the parameters passed to the device driver. The same device can often be accessed with different filenames.

Floppy diskettes have to be formatted (**format** or **fdformat**) before they can be used. **dd** uses a character device to copy diskettes and tapes. UNIX provides an entire group of commands to handle DOS diskettes. Their names begin with the string dos (SVR4) or m (Linux).

cpio and **tar** are two commonly used backup tools. **cpio** takes a list of files from the standard input and it often depends on **find** to provide the list or for performing incremental backups.

tar is more suitable for backing up a directory tree. It can append to an archive and also keep several versions of the same file. GNU **tar** adds compression to the archiving activity.

Test Your Understanding

15.1 Where are the administrator's commands mainly located? Which directory is not found in the administrator's PATH even though nonprivileged users have it in theirs?

15.2 How does the behavior of the **passwd** command change when invoked by the superuser?

15.3 The letters s and t were seen in the permissions field of a listing. What do they indicate?

15.4 Why was the password encryption moved from /etc/passwd to /etc/shadow?

15.5 Two shell variables are assigned by the **login** program after reading /etc/passwd. What are they?

15.6 Specify the command line that changes romeo's shell from **/bin/csh** to **/bin/bash**.

15.7 Explain how **ls -l** displays the name of the owner and group.

15.8 Name some services that are not available when the machine is in the single-user mode.

15.9 What is the difference between the **find** options -perm 1000 and -perm -1000?

15.10 How will you use **shutdown** to bring down the system immediately? What shortcut does Linux offer?

15.11 How can the system administrator arrange to monitor the free disk space every hour on a working day between 9 a.m. and 10 p.m.?

15.12 How will you find out the total disk usage of the current directory tree?

15.13 How do you copy all HTML files to a DOS floppy in (i) SVR4, (ii) Linux?

Flex Your Brain

15.1 Why is the **su** command terminated with **exit**? What is the difference between **su** and **su - romeo**?

15.2 Name five administrative functions that can't be performed by a nonprivileged user.

15.3 If the administrator doesn't want romeo to use the **at** command but allows juliet to use **cron**, what does he need to do?

15.4 A program can be made to run with the privileges of its owner. Explain the feature that allows this and how you can use it make a program run with the privileges of root.

15.5 Explain what these commands do:

    (i) **find / -perm -4000 -print**
    (ii) **find / -type d -perm -1000 -exec ls -ld {} \;**
    (iii) **find / -type f -size +2046 -mtime +365 -print**

15.6 How will you arrange for a group of users to write to the same directory and yet not be able to remove one another's files?

15.7 How will you create a user guru with UID 212 and GID dialout (a new group)? guru will use Bash as his shell and be placed in the /home directory. How can you later change guru's shell to Korn without editing /etc/passwd?

15.8 A user romeo belongs to the student group, and yet /etc/group doesn't show his name beside the group name. How can that happen?

15.9 How do you display the run level for your system? What is the difference between run levels 0 and 6?

15.10 Explain the difference between (i) block and character devices, (ii) major and minor numbers. Can two devices have the same major and minor numbers?

15.11 Write a shell script to copy a floppy diskette.

15.12 Specify the **tar** and **cpio** command lines that will (i) prevent files from being overwritten during restoration, (ii) rename each file interactively during restoration, (iii) append to an existing archive during copying.

15.13 The command tar **xvf /dev/fd0 *.c** displays an error message even though the diskette contains a number of .c files. Name two reasons that can make this happen.

Part II

For the Advanced User ...

The X Window System

The command line and dumb terminal have for long dominated the user interface of UNIX systems. But terminals can't produce the high-quality graphics required by advanced scientific and engineering applications. Apple and Microsoft made the graphical user interface (GUI) popular, and users were also getting tired of complex command line syntaxes. This was the scene in the UNIX arena when a group of graduates at the Massachusetts Institute of Technology (MIT) came up with the X Window system.

Once snubbed as "the Vietnam of UNIX," X (i.e., X Window), has now been adopted as the standard windowing system by all UNIX vendors. It is controlled and maintained by X.Org, an organization of the Open Group. In this chapter, we'll take a look at the X Window system (not X Windows, as most mistakenly refer to it)—the X *server* and *clients* (the tools) that are usually shipped with it. We'll examine two sides of X. First, we'll learn to handle X the way we handle any GUI, using the mouse as the navigation tool. We'll also see how X is designed and ideally suited for running in a network.

WHAT YOU WILL LEARN

- Understand the X architecture and the role of the *server* and *client*.

- How a special client, the *window manager*, determines the look and feel of all X clients.

- Learn to start X and quit an X session.

- The features of a terminal emulator program like **xterm**.

- Copy data across different windows using the mouse and **xclipboard**.

- Learn the general command line options used with X programs.

- Use some common clients like the file manager, **xclock**, **xcalc**, **xkill** and **xload**.

- Configure the file, ~/.xinitrc, the startup file used by **xinit**.

- Specify X *resources* and override them with **xrdb** and the -xrm option.

TOPICS OF SPECIAL INTEREST

- Examine the features of the *Common Desktop Environment* (CDE) that is now common to all UNIX machines.
- Use the networked features of X to run a client on a remote machine and have the display on the local one.

16.1 X BASICS

When MIT started work on the project, they had a serious problem in their hands. People were already working with several types of graphic displays, each having its own methods for drawing lines and shapes on the screen. If an application were to write to all of these displays, then there had to be several versions of the application—one for each type of display. That would be absurd, so they reasoned that a separate program should handle the display. The application would send its output to this display-handling program. This led to a very important splitting of the application itself into two components—**client** and **server**.

Client-server computing, as we know it today, is the division of labor between two computers in a network. It means somewhat different things depending on the context to which it is applied. A network application like FTP is split up into a server and a client component—two separate programs by themselves. The database application server acts as a repository of data and business rules, while the client (the frontend) formats the data that it obtains from the server. This frontend is installed on the user's own workstation, normally a PC. The PC's display is handled by the client running on the PC and not the server.

X reverses this paradigm, and its architecture places the responsibility of handling the display on the *server*, while the application itself runs as a *client*. X programs are thus quite portable, being free of the complexities involved in handling the terminal. To run an X client on a different terminal, all one has to do is to write the server component of X for that terminal. Future X programs can then write to this new server program.

The X server program must be able to handle not only the application's output but its input as well. If you run an X calculator program that displays on a remote machine, it is obvious that the remote user should be able to use it for doing her calculations. The server thus comprises not only the display screen but also the mouse and keyboard. An X display can also comprise multiple screens on multiple monitors. In fact, many UNIX systems offer support for multiple screens.

X clients display their output on separate windows on the display. But these windows have no frames around them, so you can't move or resize them. A separate client program manages these windows. We'll be discussing the role of the window manager very shortly.

X was primarily designed to run in a network. The separation of the display handling component from the application also means that you can run an X client on one machine and have the display on another. This is the most important feature of X.

Fig. 16.1 The **dtwm** Window Manager on an X Client (**dtterm**)

16.1.1 The Window Manager

X on its own doesn't offer any window management facilities that would control the windows created by clients. Though the MIT shipment includes buttons and scrollbars, the windows wear a plain look and have no frames or menus. Left to themselves, these windows can't be moved around, resized, or positioned up or down in the window stack. The specific look and feel of X programs is determined not by the X server, but by the GUI, which is a separate product (another client) by itself. The GUI in X is known as the **window manager**.

The window manager is a special client that is built on top of other X client programs. It ensures that all clients have the same look and feel irrespective of the vendor they come from. We have seen many window managers come and go, starting with Open Look (from AT&T and Sun), and then a period of relative stability with Motif (from OSF). The window manager used by Motif is **mwm**, which may still be available on your system.

X has a complex startup sequence, and it reads one or more startup scripts which specify the window manager that is to be called. The window manager is run only once in a single session. It can also be run manually in case the startup script doesn't specify it:

```
mwm &
```
Sometimes found in `$HOME/.xinitrc`

The window manager that is now standard on most UNIX systems is **dtwm** (desktop window manager). An X client that has its frames and borders drawn by **dtwm** is shown in Fig. 16.1. **dtwm** features a button on the top-left and two on the right. The right button represented by a circle is used to *minimize* a window, i.e., convert it into an icon. The other right button shown by a "raised" rectangle (initially) is used to maximize a window. Once it is blown up full-screen, the rectangle appears depressed.

Once a window manager is in place, every window can be moved by dragging the window by its *title bar*, and resized by dragging any of the four corners. A window is brought to *focus* by simply clicking on it. No matter where an application is placed in the stack of overlapping windows, clicking on it always brings it to the top. You may also be able to use the Microsoft Windows technique—[Alt][Tab]—to select windows in a circular manner. The active window can easily be identified by the different color of its title bar.

There is a menu in **dtwm**, the Window Menu, that pops up when you click on the left button. Many of the window management functions mentioned above can also be handled by this Window Menu.

Tip: There is a feature of **mwm** and **dtwm** in that you can move a window without selecting it. Just press the [Alt] key, click on the title bar of any window and move it. The window doesn't get highlighted and yet gets moved!

16.2 THE COMMON DESKTOP ENVIRONMENT (CDE)

In the past, even if Motif was adopted by most vendors as the standard window manager, implementations of X still differed across vendors. The desktop appearance was not uniform, nor was the method of using the applications. This made it difficult for a user to feel at home when she encountered a different X version, even though both implementations used Motif. Motif remained a standard of sorts for some time before the "desktop environment" wave changed the appearance of the entire desktop (the entire screen)—and not merely the window manager.

Basing their initiative on Motif, industry leaders IBM, HP, Sunsoft and Novell started the COSE (Common Open Software Environment) movement in 1993. They introduced the *Common Desktop Environment* (CDE)—a standard desktop that made sure once and for all that all vendors' implementations of X not only had the same look and feel for all windows, but for the entire desktop as well.

CDE uses **dtwm** as its window manager. It is similar to Motif, so if you are comfortable with Motif, you'll find little difficulty in handling CDE. The window manager has an enhanced role to play in this environment. In addition to handling windows, **dtwm** features a Front Panel, a virtual Workspace Switch, a File Manager and a Trash Can (Fig. 16.2).

From the Front Panel, you can launch subpanels by clicking on the triangular symbols on the top. The most exhaustive option list is provided by the subpanel, Programs, and you can start many X clients from here. The most commonly used clients are also provided as icons in the Front Panel itself. You can start the clock, a calendar scheduling service or the File Manager directly by clicking on their icons.

At the center of the Front Panel is the Workspace Switch. This is a set of four buttons that let you create multiple "desktops" on your machine. You can have a set of windows on one desktop, a second set on another desktop, and you can select your desktop by clicking on the respective workspace button. With four buttons, you can have up to four such desktops. It's like having a screen four times as large.

Fig. 16.2 The Common Desktop Environment

A menu comes up when you click one of the mouse buttons on the desktop (also known as the *root window*)—sometimes at one of the edges. Called the *Root Menu*, it offers important X applications like calendar and mail, the Web browser, terminals or the option to exit the X session.

Further discussion on CDE is beyond the purview of this text. What follows is a generic presentation of the features of X. Remember that the appearance of the windows and desktop on your systems can be different if you use a different window manager or a different desktop environment.

LINUX: Not to be left behind, Linux too is part of the "desktop" movement, and now has two products—KDE and GNOME (from GNU). Both KDE and GNOME feature many of the essential components that you see on the CDE. Linux vendors (like Red Hat and SuSE) offer both environments, and we aren't sure which one will eventually become the standard (if at all).

16.3 STARTING AND QUITTING X

Your UNIX system boots to a specific run level *(25.8)*, and this run level is selected at the time of installing the system. However, it can also be changed by modifying an entry in the file /etc/inittab *(25.8.2)*. Depending on your system, X will start automatically for a certain run level (3 in Solaris and 5 in Linux). This startup uses the **xdm** (X display manager) to display a graphical screen that requires you to authenticate yourself by entering your username and password. **xdm** can otherwise be run only by the root user.

If X doesn't start at boot time, you can start it manually by using this command from the shell prompt:

```
startx
```

The command starts the X server, and *could* invoke **xinit** to load a set of common utilities onto the desktop. If X uses **xinit**, then **xinit** will read the file $HOME/.xinitrc. This is a shell script where you can place commands to load all your clients during startup. Common clients that you may like to have on your desktop are **xbiff** (for watching your mail), Netscape/Mozilla (the Web browser) and a terminal emulation program. They can all be seen in Fig. 16.2.

The terminal emulation program appears as a window that's running a shell. You can fire all UNIX commands from this window—even the ones that feature as separate icons or menu items on your desktop. **xterm** is the original emulation program you'll find on all systems, but today we have better programs. We'll be considering this important X client in a separate section.

There's no standard way of quitting X. On systems where X runs as CDE (or where it is started manually), clicking the right mouse button anywhere in the desktop brings up a menu (Workspace Menu in Solaris). This menu invariably features an item named *Log out*. On Linux systems running KDE or GNOME, click on the left-most icon on the panel at the bottom to see a similar option. You may either be returned a shell prompt or the graphic authentication screen to allow you to log in again.

Note: X has separate functions for three mouse buttons, but if you are using a two-button mouse, then press the two buttons simultaneously to simulate the action of the middle button.

16.4 THE TERMINAL EMULATOR

The terminal emulator is the client that you'll probably be using the most. MIT shipped X with the **xterm** program, but today we have a host of emulators available. Any emulator program (like **xterm**) simply runs a shell in a window. This makes it possible to run any UNIX command. UNIX commands use a character-based display, but you can also invoke any graphical X client from the emulator's shell. This is how you run Mozilla:

```
mozilla &
```
                                                                Run all X clients in the background

Since **xterm** itself is an X client, you can create one **xterm** from another **xterm**:

```
xterm &
```

Generally, a user has a number of such overlapping **xterm** windows, each running a separate application. She gets the feeling of working on several machines at a time. On one window, she may use the **vi** editor to edit a program; on the other, she may compile the program. On yet another **xterm**, she may query a database. However, input to an **xterm** is only possible when the user clicks on it or selects it by other means. The **exit** command in an **xterm** kills the shell and window associated with it.

Systems running CDE, KDE or GNOME have their own terminal emulators, though they all offer **xterm**. CDE uses **dtterm**, KDE uses **konsole** and GNOME uses **gnome-terminal**. You could see one of these emulator programs on your desktop when you log in. This client can often be invoked by clicking on some icon in the panel. **xterm** doesn't feature any menus in its title bar except the standard one provided by the window manager at the top-left corner. In contrast, the other emulators feature a number of menus in the title bar.

Using **xterm**   There are three menus in **xterm** which pop up when you hold down the *[Ctrl]* key and click a mouse button. Every option has a toggling effect; a check mark appears or disappears depending on whether the option is activated or unset. The *Main Options* menu is invoked by pressing *[Ctrl]* and the left button. You can terminate the window (*Send KILL signal*) or display the window in reverse video. The *VT Fonts* Menu appears when you use *[Ctrl]* with the right mouse button. It lets you select the size of the font.

The *Enable Scrollbar* option in the *VT Options* menu (*[Ctrl]* and the middle button) places a scrollbar on the left of the window. This scrollbar contains a grayed-out *thumb* which initially occupies the entire column, but reduces in size as commands are entered. Previous commands entered at this window can be recalled by dragging the thumb with the middle button. Note that the middle button is emulated by pressing both left and right buttons in a two-button mouse.

xterm doesn't offer any special techniques to copy and paste text. There's a standard technique available that applies to all X clients, and is discussed shortly. Other emulators have an *Edit* menu that can perform these functions.

Using **dtterm**   The **dtterm** emulator shown in Fig. 16.1 (located in /usr/dt/bin on Solaris) has three menu options. The *Edit* menu lets you copy and paste text. The *Options* menu lets you change the size of the window from 80 X 24 to 132 X 24. You can also change the size of the fonts. Another option enables you to use a scrollbar on the right (on by default).

Caution: If you don't affix the & to an X client command, the issued command becomes the child of the **xterm** window that created it. If you kill this parent window, the child window then gets terminated as well. This is not what you would want normally, so all X clients should be run asynchronously, i.e., in the background.

16.5 CUT-AND-PASTE OPERATIONS

Apart from the *Edit* menu that some X clients offer for copy-and-paste operations, X offers two techniques for this work. One uses only the mouse buttons, and the other is the **xclipboard** client—one of the native X clients that are shipped with every X system.

16.5.1 Using the Mouse Buttons

To copy text, highlight it by dragging it in the usual manner with the left mouse button; *the text automatically gets copied to a buffer.* Then, click on the other window with the left button, move the cursor to the point where you want to paste it, and click the middle button. The copied text is then pasted on this window. Using this technique, you can copy text from one window to another—perhaps for reexecuting a long command line in another window or placing text in another **vi** session. Make sure you are in **vi**'s Input Mode before pasting text.

Instead of dragging, you can also select text by clicking multiple times on the text. Double-clicking selects a word, the triple click selects the entire line. The former is equally applicable in the Windows environment, but X selection techniques go further. For selecting a block of text in one screen, click with the left button at the starting point of text, and right click at the end of the text; the entire text gets selected. To extend the selection on either side, right-click at the respective text boundary. This technique may not work on all non-**xterm** emulators.

16.5.2 xclipboard: Advanced Cut and Paste

The standard copy and paste features has its limitations. You can copy only single sections of text at a time; you can't copy multiple sections in one shot for later pasting. This is also a problem with software running Microsoft Windows, where a user has to repeatedly switch between two files for performing this dual operation. X solves the problem with the **xclipboard** program.

xclipboard (Fig. 16.3) is a typical MIT X application. There are six buttons at the top of the window; the last two are grayed out initially. To use this tool, copy text from one window in the usual manner, and then paste it in the blank space on **xclipboard**. The counter at the right, which initially showed 1, continues to do so. If the text is too large to fit in the window, the scrollbars appear, and you can then drag the thumb *(16.4)* of the scrollbar with the middle button.

Fig. 16.3 xclipboard

To repeat the copying operation with another text segment, you have to press *New* first. This clears the `xclipboard` display and advances the counter to 2. You can now paste the text that you have copied to this region. In this way, you can have multiple text sections stored in the clipboard. You can step through the various clipboard buffers by using *Next* and *Previous*. The important thing is that *once you have a text section on display on the clipboard window, that section is deemed to be copied*. You can then paste it at any place you want by using the middle button. You can delete a clipboard section (*Delete*) and even store it (*Save*) in a file. Nothing in Microsoft Windows can match this method of copying and pasting text.

16.6 RUNNING X CLIENTS REMOTELY

X was built primarily to run in a network, and in this respect, it is simply amazing. On single-user systems, the server and client run on the same machine, and you don't have to bother about controlling the display. But the beauty of X lies in running an X client on one machine and having its display on another! The X display has a very important role to play here, so let's understand it first.

16.6.1 The Display

You may decide to run a client on a remote machine, possibly because of its superior computing power, or because it's not available on your machine. As an example, consider that you want to run the `xcalc` program which is only available on a remote machine (*uranus*). However, the display of the program must appear on your local machine (*saturn*), so you can input data from your keyboard. There are two things that you have to ensure before you can make that happen:

- The server (on your machine, *saturn*) must enable others to write to its display. This is done by using the `xhost` command on the local machine.
- The client program must be directed to write its output to another display. This is achieved by setting either the `DISPLAY` variable or by using the `-display` option with the client.

We'll first use `xhost` on our local machine to enable any user on *uranus* to write to our display:

```
$ xhost +uranus
uranus being added to access control list
```

You can turn off the `xhost` setting with the - symbol or enable your display for all machines with +:

```
$ xhost -                                          Disables display for others
access control enabled, only authorized clients can connect
$ xhost +                                          Enables display for others
access control disabled, clients can connect from any host
```

You now have to run the `xcalc` program on *uranus*, the remote machine. A simple way of doing that is to log on to it using **telnet** or **ssh**. These networking tools are discussed in the next chapter, but you could be using it already to work on a remote host where you have an account. There are basically two ways of running an X client remotely, and they are considered next.

16.6.2 Using the DISPLAY variable

DISPLAY is a shell variable used by X to determine where the output of an X client should be displayed. After you have logged on to *uranus*, define and export the DISPLAY variable at the shell prompt of a terminal emulator:

```
DISPLAY=saturn:0.0                uranus must be able to access saturn
export DISPLAY                    by name; else use the IP address
```

The value assigned to DISPLAY is of the form *hostname:server.screen*. *saturn* is the hostname, :0 is the instance of the X server program and .0 is the screen number of the display. Both server and screen are usually 0 for single-user systems, and the screen number (.0) may be omitted. If X is running in a TCP/IP network, the hostname should either be present in /etc/hosts *(17.2.1)* or be accessible using DNS *(17.10)*. If it is not, you have to use the IP address *(17.1.3)* in place of the hostname.

The above setting signifies that *any* X client that will subsequently be run on *uranus* will use the display of *saturn* rather than its own. Now you can run the program **xcalc** on *uranus*:

```
xcalc &
```

Just notice what you have done here. You executed **xcalc** on a remote machine and the calculator pops up on your local machine! X allows the use of the local keyboard with a remote client simply because the keyboard is a component of the server definition, and this server runs locally.

16.6.3 Using the -display Option

The other technique is to use the -display option offered by every X client. The parameter to this option is the complete display name—the same value assigned to DISPLAY:

```
xcalc -display saturn:0.0 &
```

Depending on the system you are using, the -display option may override any previous DISPLAY setting. If that happens on your system (as in Linux), you don't need to use the -display option any more to run client programs from this emulator.

The above techniques assume that the TELNET service is enabled on the remote system; otherwise, you won't be able to log in at all. If it is not, you can use the **ssh** command to run a program remotely, provided it is also enabled and configured properly. **ssh** is discussed in Section 17.9 and its configuration in Section 17.8.

Tip: If you have a number of clients to run on a remote machine with the display on your local one, it is preferable to use DISPLAY, which needs to be set only once. If DISPLAY is not set, you'll have to use the -display option with every X client. Many Linux systems set DISPLAY automatically when you log in, so you don't need to use either feature at all!

16.7 COMMAND LINE OPTIONS

Most X client programs are built to handle a large number of options. Many of these options (Table 16.1) are common to practically all commands. They often take on abbreviations, which are shown in parentheses in the table. We'll discuss their significance briefly.

16.7.1 Window Position and Size (-geometry)

To run a number of client programs, it is necessary to size and place them properly so they can be easily selected. All X clients offer the -geometry option to determine the location and size of the client. The option is followed by a two-part component—the size of the window and the location of one of its corners from the respective edge of the screen.

For **xterm**, the size of the window has to be specified in characters, and the location (or offset) in pixels. The following command line sets up an **xterm** with a window size of 40 by 12 characters, with its top-left corner offset by 10 pixels from the left side of the display and 20 pixels from the top:

```
xterm -g 40x12+10+20 &
```

For other clients, 40x12 would mean 40 pixels by 12 pixels—a very small window to be of any use. By default, **xterm** windows have the size 80 by 24 characters. You can have multiple **xterm**s at different areas of the screen; the size can also be omitted:

```
xterm -g -10-20 &          Offset from lower-right corner of display
xterm -g +10-20 &          Offset from lower-left corner
xterm -g -10+20 &          Offset from upper-right corner
```

It should be quite obvious that when both numbers are zeros, the window is placed at the corner of the display.

16.7.2 Setting Colors (-fg, -bg and -rv)

The -foreground (-fg) and -background (-bg) options determine the respective colors of the client. You can set these colors for your terminal emulator window in this manner:

```
xterm -fg darkslategrey -bg lightblue &
```

X maintains this database of colors in the text file /usr/lib/X11/rgb.txt (/openwin/lib/X11/rgb.txt on Solaris). This file contains several hundred color descriptions, with each line containing three numbers representing the amount of red, green and blue (the RGB values). The file also contains variations in these spellings—often with spaces between the words. Here are some typical entries in this file:

```
255 255 240        ivory
 47  79  79        dark slate gray
 47  79  79        DarkSlateGray
  0   0 128        navy blue
135 206 235        sky blue
```

The foreground and background colors can be reversed with the -reverse (-rv) option. This option comes in handy when you need to have a distinctly different appearance for a window, say the parent **xterm**.

16.7.3 Other Options

You can start any X client, but in an iconic form, with the -iconic option. This option is required specially when there isn't sufficient space on your desktop to accommodate all of them. You can keep your parent **xterm** window permanently iconified so that you don't kill it by mistake.

You can provide a title (-title) to be displayed in the title bar at the top. When running multiple instances of **xterm**, it's better that you have separate names for them, perhaps named after the applications or the machines they are running on:

```
xterm -fg red -bg lightblue -title "Compilation"
```

The -name option lets you provide a name which can be identified by the server, and you'll see the name both in the title bar as well as in the icon label. *X resources understand the string provided with* -name . For this reason, it is often preferable to use this option rather than the -title option.

We'll discuss the significance of the -xrm option when we come to X resources (*16.10*).

Table 16.1 Common Command Line Options Used by X Clients

Option	Significance
-foreground	Window foreground color (-fg)
-background	Window background color (-bg)
-display	The display specification of the host that will be written by the client
-geometry	Size and location of window (-g)
-iconic	Starts client in minimized form
-title	Name of window to be displayed in title bar
-name	The name of the application
-xrm	Resource specification that overrides settings of resource files
-reverse	Reverses foreground and background colors (-rv)

16.8 SOME STANDARD X CLIENTS

MIT ships X with over 50 clients, ranging from desktop accessories, font and graphic utilities to special tools related to window and resource management. Many of them have superior counterparts in the form of desktop clients. For instance, **xfm** is the original MIT file manager, but CDE provides a superior client in **dtfile**. Both KDE and GNOME offer many more clients. We can't possibly discuss most of them, so we present below the ones that are commonly used. Many of them can be seen on the CDE desktop in Fig. 16.2. Only one, **dtfile**, is a CDE client; the rest are all original MIT clients.

Fig. 16.4 Two Views of the **dtfile** File Manager used on CDE

16.8.1 dtfile: The File Manager

We use files all the time; we copy, move and delete them several times in a day. It's no wonder that a file manager is considered by most to be the most useful X client. Windows also has a similar application, Windows Explorer, which is used by many users not only to perform the basic file-handling functions, but even to launch programs. On the CDE, the **dtfile** file manager performs similar functions (Fig. 16.4).

16.8.2 xclock: The Analog Clock

All X distributions come with the analog clock, **xclock** (Fig. 16.5). This client has a couple of useful options as the following command lines show:

```
xclock -chime &        Chime sounds once for every half-hour and twice every hour
xclock -digital &      Prints date and time in character format
xclock -update 5 &     Shows seconds dial which updates every 5 seconds
```

Besides these options, there are other options to set the color of the hands of the clock.

16.8.3 xcalc: The Calculator

X also features a calculator, the **xcalc** client (Fig. 16.6). You can run it in two modes—the Texas Instruments TI-30 mode or Hewlett-Packard 10C mode. The first mode is emulated by using **xcalc** without arguments. There is nothing special about this calculator except that its **-rpn** option lets you use *reverse polish notation* (i.e., the HP-10C mode).

Fig. 16.5 xclock

Fig. 16.6 xcalc

16.8.4 xbiff: Mail Intimation

This is a client that you would like to have on your desktop all the time (Fig. 16.7). **xbiff** monitors the arrival of mail by noting the modification time of the user's mailbox. The mailbox file is defined by the MAIL variable, which is often located in /var/mail or /var/spool/mail. xbiff is typically invoked like this:

```
xbiff -g -0+0 -file /home/sumit/nsmail/Inbox -update 60
```

Inbox is the mailbox used by Netscape/Mozilla (which doesn't read MAIL), but the location could differ on your system. The command places a picture of the mailbox on the top-right corner of the screen. It checks the modification file of Inbox every 60 seconds (-update 60). When it finds that the time has changed on arrival of a new message, it hoists the flag and darkens the window. A click on the window restores its original status (with the flag down).

16.8.5 xload: Displaying the System Load

xload displays a histogram of the system load average (Fig. 16.8). This is a useful program which you can run on multiple remote machines and have their histograms on your local machine. You can then run your next program on the machine with the lowest load, other things being equal (the processing power, for instance). The command should be used with two useful options— -update and -jumpscroll:

```
xload -update 15 -jumpscroll 1 &
```

By default, **xload** pools the machine every 5 seconds (10 in Linux). The -update option sets this time to 15 seconds. The -jumpscroll option ensures that the graph shifts to the left by 1 pixel when the histogram reaches the end on the right. This ensures smooth scrolling of the display. Because

Fig. 16.7 **xbiff**

Fig. 16.8 **xload**

the command is most often used to run on multiple machines, the window always shows the domain name of the host (or its alias) at the top.

16.8.6 xkill: Killing a Window

xterm windows are terminated by using *[Ctrl-d]* or **exit** at the shell prompt. You can also use **xkill** to kill a single window or all windows together. When used without arguments, X displays this message:

```
Select the window whose client you wish to kill with button 1....
```

You now have to move the cursor to the window and do exactly as told. However, if this window is the parent of a number of child windows, this action will kill the child windows as well. The **-all** option lets you kill all root-level windows in one shot, except that X makes you select the root window three times, once with each button. This gives you a number of chances to change your mind.

16.9 THE STARTUP FILES

X can be customized to present a specific look and feel upon startup. The techniques depend on whether you are using CDE or not. On a system which uses **xinit** to start X (through the **startx** route), **xinit** looks first in $HOME/.xinitrc, failing which it starts the X server and loads a single **xterm** window with or without the window manager. From that window, you'll have to invoke other X clients to continue your session.

Generally, if you want your desktop to be loaded with a number of **xterm** windows and other X clients upon startup with **xinit**, you have to place the command sequences in .xinitrc. This is a Bourne shell script where every command except the last is placed in the background. A sample .xinitrc is shown below:

```
$ cat $HOME/.xinitrc
xload -load $HOME/.Xdefaults
mwm &
xclock -g 100x100-0+0 -bg tomato3 -fg white -update 1 -chime &
```

```
xterm -g -80-55 -sb -sl 300 -bg darkslategrey -fg ivory -rv -iconic &
xterm -g -0-0 -sb -sl 3000 -bg darkslategrey -fg ivory &
xterm -g +0+0 -sb -sl 3000 -bg darkslategrey -fg ivory
```

Make sure that you start the **mwm** client, otherwise you won't be able to move or resize any of the windows.

16.10 X RESOURCES

Every X client is composed of a number of objects (*widgets*) like scrollbars, buttons etc. There are attributes (*resources*) that are associated with both a class of objects as well as individual instances of these objects. For instance, every application button has a foreground color, which is termed as the *resource* for the button. Every possible resource of every object of an application can be customized so you need not invoke the client with complex options.

The sample file, .xinitrc, shown previously shows xterm invoked with the same set of background and foreground colors (darkslategrey and ivory), and with a scrollbar. Now, if that is how you want xterm to always appear, you can set these attributes in a special file, $HOME/.Xdefaults. This file is read by X when it is started, but can also be made to be reread when you make changes to it in the middle of a session. To customize **xterm** as above, you have to place the following entries in this file:

```
XTerm*ScrollBar: True
XTerm*saveLines: 10000
XTerm*background: darkslategrey
XTerm*foreground: ivory
```

The resource definition always begins with the name of the client (the class), which may be followed by either the widget hierarchy (a series of objects separated by dots) or an asterisk which matches all objects at that location. In either case, the resource attribute follows, terminated by a :, and then the value of the attribute. These values can be boolean (True or False), a string (ivory), or a number (10000). Henceforth, you need not use the -sb, -sl, -fg and -bg options with **xterm** if you want it to always appear with these attributes. However, you would certainly want to leave the -geometry option out of this, being the only variable part of the **xterm** command line.

16.10.1 xrdb: Loading the Resources

You need not quit and restart X if you have made changes to .Xdefaults during your session. You can simply use the **xrdb** command to signal to X that it has to reread the configuration file:

```
xrdb $HOME/.Xdefaults
```

X starts with a number of defaults for these resources, some of which are specified in the application itself. There are yet others which are set in a systemwide configuration file, /usr/dt/app-defaults, on Solaris (/usr/X11R6/lib/X11/app-defaults in Linux). There could be a file named after each client in this directory. If a user has no .Xdefaults in her home directory, the specifications of the systemwide file are applicable when X is started. If you have created a customized .Xdefaults, then you should also put the **xrdb** statement in .xinitrc so clients are invoked with the right resource values.

16.10.2 The -xrm Option: Overriding the Resources

There are situations when you need not only to ignore the systemwide default settings but also the ones you have put in your .Xdefaults. A specific instance of an application may also require a different setting. You can sometimes override these settings by invoking the command with suitable options. However, not all resources have corresponding option equivalents, but a special option -xrm can let you specify any resource value. For example, you can change the background color of **xclock** with the -bg option. But you can also use the resource specification for the class:

```
xclock -xrm 'xclock*background: lightblue' &
```

Besides these simple resources, there are other settings related to the translation of events. A typical event could be the interpretation of mouse clicks or movements. They are not at all intuitive and a discussion on them is beyond the scope of this text.

16.11 CONCLUSION

Even if you are a habitual command line user, you'll often need to use X to view PDF and Postscript documents. This chapter covered X briefly simply because it is not central to the UNIX philosophy. We discussed just as much of X as is needed to use the file manager, view the documentation, handle multimedia mail attachments and browse the World Wide Web. We would be discussing the last two functions in Chapter 17.

> **WRAP UP**
>
> The X Window system splits an application into two components—*client* and *server*. The server program controls the monitor, keyboard and mouse, while the application itself runs as the client.
>
> A special client, the window manager, is invoked at the start of the session to make window management functions available. The standard window manager for UNIX has been Motif (**mwm**), but it is now being replaced by **dtwm** of CDE.
>
> The *Common Desktop Environment* (CDE) provides a standard look for both the desktop and window manager. It features a Front Panel from where you can launch many applications.
>
> X is started with the **startx** or **xinit** commands. X can also be invoked by the root user with the **xdm** command.
>
> The most important X client is **xterm**, which displays a simple terminal window that runs a shell. Further commands can be invoked at the shell prompt of this window. CDE and other desktop environments use better terminal emulation programs.
>
> You can copy text from any window by merely selecting it with the mouse button. The copied text is pasted back by clicking the middle button. Multiple sections of copied text can be stored in the **xclipboard** client from where it can be pasted anywhere.
>
> X normally runs on a network, and it is possible for a client to run on one machine and have its display on another. **xhosts** controls access to the server, while the environment variable, DISPLAY, determines where the client should display its output. The -display option overrides and resets the DISPLAY setting.

X programs run with a number of common options. You can position and specify the size and position of a window (-geometry) and its foreground and background colors (-fg and -bg). You can start a program as an icon (-icon) and provide a name (-name) or title (-title).

There are several clients available in X. The most commonly used client is the file manager that functions like Microsoft Windows Explorer. X offers a clock (**xclock**) and a calculator (**xcalc**). **xload** displays the system load and is often used with remote machines. **xkill** kills a window.

X can be easily customized. You can start X clients from ~/.xinitrc, the startup file used by xinit. X resources enable you to change practically any X feature. These features can be stored in ~/.Xdefaults, and **xrdb** can be used any time to read this file. These settings can also be overridden with the -xrm option available in every X client.

Test Your Understanding

16.1   What does an X display comprise?

16.2   Who places the frames, borders and buttons on the windows? Is it a server or a client?

16.3   Can an X client like **xterm** running on a Solaris machine display its output on a HP-UX machine?

16.4   How is text copied in an **xterm** window?

16.5   What is the function of the **xhost** command? What does **xhost** + signify?

16.6   What circumstances led to the development of the CDE?

16.7   What is the function of the four rectangles that you see on the Front Panel at the center of Fig. 16.2?

16.8   What happens if all the commands in .xinitrc are placed in the background?

16.9   How will you override a resource setting when invoking a client?

Flex Your Brain

16.1   How does X solve the problem of running the same program on displays having different characteristics?

16.2   How is the client-server mechanism in X different from others?

16.3   Explain the role of the window manager in X. Can you work without it?

16.4   Describe how text is copied using (i) the general features of X, (ii) **xclipboard**.

16.5   How can romeo running Netscape on his machine *saturn* write its output to juliet's display on a remote machine *uranus*? Do both users need to run X?

16.6   How is the DISPLAY variable more convenient to use than the -display option?

17

Networking Tools

The realization that standalone computers made no sense made the network possible. When there were too many of them, people realized that standalone networks made little sense either, and that they also needed to talk to one another. UNIX has played a predominant role in the development of TCP/IP as a communications technology. Network communication became so pervasive that the technology was ultimately made available to all operating systems and eventually led to the formation of the Internet. The Net is running on TCP/IP since 1983.

This chapter discusses the tools used in a TCP/IP network. Some of these tools, like **telnet** and **ftp**, belong to the original DARPA set which we cover only briefly. Rather, we'll examine the basics of cryptography, and how its principles are incorporated into the secure shell (SSH). We also need to study the mechanism behind email and the Web service, and how both applications have benefited from MIME technology.

WHAT YOU WILL LEARN

- The basics of TCP/IP and the way it splits data into packets before reassembling them.
- Understand how a host is addressed by the *hostname* and *IP address*.
- The function of /etc/hosts in resolving hostnames to IP addresses.
- Use **telnet** and **ftp** for remote login and file transfer.
- The concept of *domains* and the Internet domain hierarchy.
- The role of *name servers*, *resolvers* and a distributed database in performing hostname-IP address mappings.
- The role of *hypertext*, *URL* and *HTML* in the HTTP protocol.

TOPICS OF SPECIAL INTEREST

- The basics of *cryptography*.
- The use of *symmetric* and *asymmetric* keys for encryption and decryption.
- The mechanism behind SSH (the secure shell) and the tools **ssh**, **slogin**, **sftp** and **scp**.
- The significance of *daemons* and *ports* in the client-server scheme.

- The cooperative efforts of the *MUA*, *MTA* and *MDA* in transporting mail on the Internet.
- The *Multipurpose Internet Mail Extensions* (MIME) standard in handling mail attachments and different media types on the Web.

17.1 TCP/IP BASICS

You need to know some networking jargon to understand TCP/IP. In a network, a computer is known as a **host**, sometimes a **node**. Every host has a **hostname** which is unique throughout the network. To know your machine's hostname, use the **hostname** command:

```
$ hostname
saturn.heavens.com
```

This multiword name is of the type used by hosts on the Internet, where the first word (here, saturn) actually signifies the name of the host. *heavens.com* is the name of the *domain* to which the host belongs; we'll be taking up domains later. Some systems omit the domain name from the output of the **hostname** command.

When two or more TCP/IP networks are connected together, we have an **internet**, popularly known as an **intranet**. Note that an internet is different from *the* Internet (spelled with an uppercase I), which is the supernetwork of all networks. A local internet or intranet may easily be connected to the Internet which also uses the same protocol.

17.1.1 How TCP/IP Works

Unlike our telephone system, TCP/IP is a **packet-switching** system. In a packet-switched network, there is no dedicated connection between sender and receiver. Rather, the data is broken into packets and each packet is provided with a header. This header contains the sequence number and a *checksum*, which is a simple number determining the exact information in the packet. These packets are put inside envelopes, the sender's and recipient's addresses are written on them, and the packets are sent on their way.

As the packets travel along a vast network like the Internet, they encounter **routers** everywhere. These are special computers or intelligent devices that look at the envelope addresses and then determine the most efficient route each packet has to take to move closer to its destination. Because the load on the network varies constantly, packets may move along different routes and arrive out of order. The packets are reassembled in the correct order from the information provided in them.

Before assembly, the checksum of each packet is calculated and checked with the number that has been sent in the packet. If the checksums don't match, the packet is corrupted and has to be resent. When all clean packets are received, they are assembled, their headers discarded and data fed to the application in their original form.

17.1.2 TCP/IP Features

A **protocol** in TCP/IP context simply means a set of rules that are used by two or more machines to talk to one another. The term *TCP/IP* expands to Transmission Control Protocol/Internet Protocol, but that's not its real meaning. In fact, it's a collection of several protocols (of which TCP and IP are the most important ones). These protocols or rules are built into the kernel and have the following key features:

- Independence of vendor, type of machine and operating system.
- Delivery of data in multiple packets.
- One-hundred percent reliability of transmission with facilities for full error control.
- Ability to divert data immediately through other routes if one or more parts of the network went down.
- Facility to connect new subnetworks without significant disruption of services

TCP/IP is also characterized by the absence of any formal specification. All TCP/IP specifications are available in the form of **RFCs (Request for Comments)**—documents that are available widely on the Internet. You can download them using *anonymous FTP (17.6.3)* from *rs.internic.net*.

17.1.3 IP Addresses

Apart from the hostname, every host in the network has an address called the **IP address** which is used by other machines to communicate with it. This address is a series of four dot-delimited numbers (called octets), which could typically look like this:

```
192.168.0.1
```

The maximum value of each octet is 255. The IP address of a host is also independent of the networking hardware and is set at the time of booting by the system's startup scripts. TCP/IP applications can address a host by its hostname as well as its IP address:

```
telnet saturn
ftp 192.168.0.1
```

The network administrator sets the IP address of a host to make it unique not only within the network, but also in all connected networks. And if the network is connected to the Internet, it must be unique throughout the world.

17.1.4 Daemons and Ports

TCP/IP and the Internet operate on the client-server principle—the division of labor between two computers connected in a network. An FTP application is split into a server and a client component—two separate programs by themselves. The Web server's job is to send an HTML document, which the client software (the browser) formats on the user's screen.

The server programs are called **daemons** in UNIX, and you have seen many of them in the output of the **ps** command *(9.3)*. They are not associated with any terminal and always run in the background, *listening* for input from the clients. The **httpd** daemon listens for a Web page request. The **sendmail** daemon handles your mail.

How does an FTP packet know that it has to connect to another FTP application at the other end and not to a Web browser? Specifying the IP address in an FTP packet is not enough; a separate **port number** has to be included as well. This number is always associated with the FTP service, so the packet reaches the FTP server. Port numbers are like telephone extension numbers in an office. Specifying the office telephone number is not enough; one must know the extension number also to reach the right person.

Daemons listen for requests at certain specific port numbers assigned to them. **sendmail** listens on port 25, FTP on 21 and TELNET on 23. *However, their client counterparts use random port numbers at their ends.* For instance, the **ftp** client (the command named **ftp** on your machine) will open a connection using some random number at its end, but the FTP daemon will use port number 21 at the server end.

17.2 RESOLVING IP ADDRESSES

IP addresses are used by many utilities like **telnet** and **ftp**. For instance, to connect to a remote site with the IP address 202.54.37.108, you can use these applications in these ways:

```
ftp 202.54.37.108
telnet 202.54.37.108
```

Users find numbers difficult to remember, while network software understands only numbers. All machines in a network have names, and applications usually access these machines by their hostnames rather than their IP addresses. A set of routines linked to the application, called the **resolver**, translates the name into its corresponding IP address. These names take two forms:

- A simple hostname (like *saturn*) which can be used by hosts to communicate among themselves in a small network. In such networks, you can connect to a host *saturn* using commands like these:

  ```
  ftp saturn
  telnet saturn
  ```

  The resolver will look up /etc/hosts (called the *hosts* file) to find out the IP address, and the command will then use it to connect to the host.

- A *fully qualified domain name* (FQDN) where the hostname is a component. *ftp.download.com* is an FQDN, where *com* is a domain, *download* is a subdomain and *ftp* is the hostname. The Internet uses only FQDNs. You can download software from the Internet using the **ftp** command like this:

  > ftp ftp.download.com   *The second "ftp" is the hostname*

  The resolver in this case will look up a decentralized database to determine the IP address of this FQDN. This database belongs to the *Domain Name System*, and is normally maintained on separate machines that could be spread across the globe.

Irrespective of the form used in hostnames, the resolver translates the hostname or FQDN into its corresponding IP address. The application can only run when this resolution has been performed. We consider the hosts file in the next section and DNS in Section 17.10.

17.2.1 /etc/hosts: The Hosts File

In a small network, the name-address mappings are placed in /etc/hosts in each and every host of the network. This file is often called the **hosts** file. This database allows applications to look up a name and find out its corresponding IP address and vice versa. A look at a sample file reveals its flexible structure:

```
$ cat /etc/hosts
# Internet host table
#
127.0.0.1          localhost
192.168.35.11      jupiter
192.168.35.12      saturn     s2         Aliases permitted
192.168.35.13      mercury
```

For each machine in the network, this table contains a line mapping the IP address to its respective hostname. It contains at least two fields for each line—one for each address. The line for *saturn* shows that TCP/IP also permits the use of aliases. This makes addressing even simpler as you can now use **telnet saturn** instead of **telnet 192.168.35.12**. And if that seems a lot of work, you can use **telnet s2** too!

The network administrator needs to maintain /etc/hosts on *all* machines in the network. Once that is done, any user can choose either the IP address, the hostname or an alias to access a host. The problem arises when a machine is added to the network. In that case, the hosts file has to be changed on all machines. This could be manageable in a small network, but becomes tedious in a large one, and absolutely impossible on the Internet. The Internet uses DNS which is considered later in the chapter.

Note: You'll find the line relating to *localhost* in every hosts file. It's characteristic of TCP/IP that every host has a special address 127.0.0.1 and a special hostname, *localhost*. To test **telnet** or **ftp** on your host without being connected to a network, you can use **ftp localhost** or **telnet 127.0.0.1**.

17.3 THE APPLICATIONS

TCP/IP originally began by the development of a collection of programs called the **DARPA set**. Later, Berkeley developed an entire suite of tools known as the **r-utilities** because all their command names are prefixed with an r. The DARPA set comprise the **telnet** and **ftp** commands which use the login-password route to connect to the server. The Berkeley suite comprising **rlogin**, **rcp** and **rsh** offer password-free authentication instead. Both systems are inherently insecure.

DARPA tools send the password across the network in clear text. This allows network sniffers to intercept the password and gain illegal access to the system. Berkeley tools assume that the IP address of the remote host is the correct one, but it's possible to subvert DNS and provide a wrong IP address. These tools also transmit data in clear text, which could be intercepted and altered in transit.

We'll not discuss the Berkeley tools in this edition and the DARPA set only briefly. Rather, we'll spend some time on SSH (the secure shell), where the entire communication is encrypted.

Note: For applications like **ftp** and **ssh** to work, their corresponding server component must be running at the other end. For instance, you can't use **ftp** on your local host if the FTP server is not running remotely. You could see something like this if you try to do so:

```
ftp: connect: Connection refused
```

17.4 ping: CHECKING THE NETWORK

To operate in a network, a host must be equipped with a network interface card (NIC) that is configured and assigned an IP address. You can then use **ping** to send packets to a machine known to be working in the network. The command sends 56-byte packets to a remote destination which answers back on receipt:

```
# ping -s earth                                Solaris; Linux doesn't need -s option
PING earth: 56 data bytes
64 bytes from earth.pdsit.becs.ac.in (192.168.35.140): icmp_seq=0. time=0. ms
64 bytes from earth.pdsit.becs.ac.in (192.168.35.140): icmp_seq=1. time=0. ms
64 bytes from earth.pdsit.becs.ac.in (192.168.35.140): icmp_seq=2. time=0. ms
64 bytes from earth.pdsit.becs.ac.in (192.168.35.140): icmp_seq=3. time=0. ms
[Ctrl-c]                                    Display interrupted by pressing this key
----earth PING Statistics----
4 packets transmitted, 4 packets received, 0% packet loss
round-trip (ms)  min/avg/max = 0/0/0
```

That there has been no "packet loss" only confirms the connectivity between the local and remote hosts. "Pinging" a host doesn't require any server process to run at the other end. For instance, if **inetd** is not started up on the remote machine, neither **ftp** nor **telnet** will work even if **ping** reports success.

17.5 telnet: REMOTE LOGIN

The **telnet** command, belonging to the DARPA command set, allows you to log on to a remote machine. If you have an account on a host in a local network (or on the Internet), you can use **telnet** with the hostname or IP address as argument:

```
$ telnet 192.168.35.12
Trying 192.168.35.12...
Connected to 192.168.35.12.
Escape character is '^]'.

SunOS 5.8
login:
```

You now have to enter your login name at this prompt, and then the password to gain access to the remote machine. As long as you are logged in, anything you type is sent to the remote machine, and your machine just acts as a dumb terminal. Any files you use or commands that you run will always be on the remote machine. After you have finished, you can press *[Ctrl-d]* or type **exit** to log out and return to your local shell.

The "Escape character" lets you make a temporary escape to the `telnet>` prompt so you can execute a command on your local machine. To invoke it, press *[Ctrl-]]* (*[Ctrl]* and the]). You can then use the ! with a UNIX command, say **ls**, to list files on the *local* machine:

```
$ [Ctrl-]]
telnet> !ls -l *.sam
```

A TELNET session is closed in the same way as any login session. Use *[Ctrl-d]* or the command appropriate to the shell. If you are at the `telnet>` prompt, use **quit**, an internal command of **telnet**. Use **help** to view **telnet**'s internal commands.

Tip: It is sometimes difficult to find out which machine you are logged on to, especially when both machines use identical versions of UNIX. That's why the facility available in Bash to use the hostname in the prompt *(10.3.1)* becomes quite useful when using **telnet**.

Note: The reason why this service has been disabled on many hosts is that the password is transmitted in clear text to the server. Also, the entire session can be intercepted and altered. Modern setups use SSH for remote login. SSH is discussed in Section 17.8.

17.6 ftp: FILE TRANSFER PROTOCOL

DARPA's **ftp** command is used to transfer files between hosts. It offers a number of UNIX-like directory-oriented services, and many of its commands have similar names. Like **telnet**, **ftp** can also be invoked with or without the address. This time, we'll use the hostname:

```
$ ftp saturn
Connected to saturn.
220 saturn FTP server (Version wu-2.6.1-18) ready.
Name (saturn:henry): charlie          henry logs in as charlie
331 Password required for charlie.
Password: ********                     Enter the password
230 User charlie logged in.
Remote system type is UNIX.
Using binary mode to transfer files.
ftp> _                                 The ftp prompt
```

After establishing a connection with *saturn*, **ftp** prompts for the username and password. The local username is prompted as default (henry), and if you had pressed *[Enter]*, the system would have logged you in as henry. To quit **ftp**, break the connection with **close**, and then enter **bye** or **quit**:

```
ftp> close                             You can skip this if you want
221 Goodbye.
ftp> bye                               You can use quit also
$ _
```

We have to log on to the FTP server yet again to try out **ftp**'s internal commands that are featured in the forthcoming paragraphs. For a complete list, use the **help** command at the `ftp>` prompt.

17.6.1 Basic File and Directory Handling

ftp has all of the basic facilities needed to handle files and directories on the remote machine—like **pwd**, **ls**, **cd**, **mkdir**, **rmdir** and **chmod**. You can delete a single file (**delete**), multiple files (**mdelete**) or rename a file (**rename**). However, remember that all these commands apply only to the *remote* machine and not to the local machine.

If you have to use the operating system commands on the *local* machine, use the ! in the usual manner. Since the ! doesn't work with the **cd** command, **ftp** offers the **lcd** (local cd) command to do the job. The following session tells most of the story:

```
ftp> verbose                                Turns off some ftp messages
Verbose mode off.
ftp> pwd
257 "/home/sales" is current directory.
ftp> ls
-rw-r--r--    1 sales    group         1498 Jul 25 18:34 exrc
-rw-r--r--    1 sales    group           20 Jul 25 18:37 login.sql
-rwxr-xr-x    1 sales    group       289312 Jul 25 18:22 perl
-rw-r--r--    1 sales    group      1457664 Jul 25 18:43 vb4cab.2
.....
ftp> mkdir reports
ftp> cd reports
ftp> pwd
257 "/home/sales/reports" is current directory.
ftp> cdup                                   Equivalent to cd ..
ftp> pwd                                     This is on the remote machine
257 "/home/sales" is current directory.
ftp> !pwd                                    This is on the local machine
/home/henry/project3
ftp> delete exrc
ftp> mdelete login.sql perl vb4*            * is interpreted on remote machine
mdelete login.sql? y
mdelete perl? y
mdelete vb4cab.2? y
```

Observe that **mdelete** prompts for each filename. This default behavior is also displayed by the **mget** and **mput** commands which are also meant to be used with multiple files.

Tip: For clean output, set the **verbose** mode to off by using the command once or twice. The command is a toggle switch, i.e. it alternates between the two modes. By default, it is set on most systems.

17.6.2 Transferring Files

For the purpose of transfer, files can be seen as belonging to two types—*ascii* (text) and *binary*. All executables, graphics, word processing and multimedia files belong to the binary type. These files need special attention, so you should set the transfer mode to binary before initiating file transfer.

*Uploading (*put *and* mput*)*   If you are a Web site developer, you'll frequently need to upload your Web pages and graphic files to your Web site. The **put** command sends (uploads) a single file, **penguin.gif**, to the remote machine:

```
ftp> binary
200 Type set to I.
ftp> put penguin.gif                                     Copied under same name
local: penguin.gif remote: penguin.gif
200 PORT command successful.
150 Opening BINARY mode data connection for penguin.gif.
226 Transfer complete.
6152 bytes sent in 0.04 seconds (150.20 Kbytes/s)
```

You can change your destination filename, and you can also copy multiple files with **mput**:

```
put penguin.gif pelican.gif
mput t*.sql                                              * interpreted on local machine
```

By default, **mput** behaves interactively and seeks confirmation for every file that has to be transferred. To make **mput** behave noninteractively, run the **prompt** command before using **mput**. You'll see the message Interactive mode off. **prompt** is a toggle switch; the next invocation reverses the previous mode.

Downloading (get *and* mget)   To download files from the remote machine, use the **get** and **mget** commands in a similar manner as their "put" counterparts. This time, we'll turn off all messages with **verbose**:

```
ftp> verbose                                             Turns off noise
ftp> ls
drwxr-xr-x    14 888         999           4096 Jun 15 16:46 communicator
drwxr-xr-x     2 888         999             26 May 14 00:47 communicator_for_france
-rw-r--r--     1 888         999         323393 Sep  7 17:22 ls-lR
-rw-r--r--     1 888         999          28360 Sep  7 17:22 ls-lR.gz
.....
ftp> binary                                              Default on most systems
ftp> get ls-lR.gz
ftp> _                                                   No statistics this time—file copied
```

Like with **put**, you can change your destination filename, and you can also copy multiple files with **mget**:

```
get ls-lR.gz netscape_filelist
mget t*.sql                                              * interpreted on remote machine
```

The **prompt** setting that works with **mput** also works with **mget** in the same way.

Why does **ftp** have two transfer modes? When files are transferred in the ASCII mode, newline conversions take place automatically. That is, if you use the **ftp** command on Windows to transfer a file from a UNIX machine in the ASCII mode, all LF will be replaced with CR-LF (5.13). This replacement is desirable for text files but not for binary files where alteration makes them unusable.

Tip: If you want to monitor the downloading of a large file, use **ftp**'s **hash** command before you use **get** or **mget**. A # will be printed after every block (8192 bytes in Solaris and Linux) of data is transferred.

17.6.3 Anonymous FTP

On the Internet, there are several **anonymous FTP** sites which offer trial and public domain software for downloading. You can log on to such a site using the account, "anonymous", and your email address as password. You can only download files from an anonymous FTP site. This is how you connect to the anonymous FTP site of Netscape Corporation:

```
$ ftp ftp.netscape.com
Connected to ftp.netscape.com (64.12.168.249).
220 ftpnscp.newaol.com FTP server (SunOS 5.8) ready.
Name (ftp.netscape.com:sumit): anonymous
331 Guest login ok, send your complete e-mail address as password.
Password: sumit204@ebay.com                        Not echoed on screen
230 Guest login ok, access restrictions apply.
Remote system type is UNIX.
Using binary mode to transfer files.
```

This time we used **ftp** with an FQDN (*ftp.netscape.com*) that represents an Internet host. Once you are in, you can use the **get** and **mget** commands to download the software you want. Note that these sites won't let you upload files to these directories or remove them.

LINUX: On the Internet, file transfers sometimes get aborted, and **ftp** in Linux allows you to resume the transfer with the **reget** command. If the line drops with a file **foo** partially downloaded, you should use **reget foo** to continue the transfer from the point of failure.

How to Use `ftp` Noninteractively

You always use the same username and password for anonymous FTP sites. So why enter them every time and not take them from a file instead? **ftp** provides the file $HOME/.netrc for this purpose. Two of the three entries in .netrc shown below are for hosts *jupiter* and *neptune*. The other is for all anonymous FTP sites:

```
machine jupiter login sasol password l1u2dw3ig
machine neptune login romeo password b1e6e37nn
default login anonymous password sumit204@ebay.com
```

The first two lines apply to "private" FTP sites where the user has individual accounts. machine, login and password are keywords, and each keyword is followed by its corresponding parameter. The last line contains the keyword default and generally applies to all other sites. Here, it is used for anonymous FTP sites. This line has one word less than the previous ones.

Since the file contains the clear-text password, it must be made unreadable to group and others (with chmod 600 .netrc). You can now use **ftp** to log on to *jupiter*, *neptune* and anonymous FTP sites without keying in the authentication parameters.

17.7 CRYPTOGRAPHY BASICS

Before we take up SSH, the secure shell, we need to understand some principles of cryptography and its techniques. **Cryptography** is the science of protecting information. This protection is achieved by using mathematical techniques to transform information to an unintelligible form by a process known as **encryption**. The unscrambling of the data to its original form is called **decryption**. Both encryption and decryption are achieved by using one or more **keys**. It is practically impossible to retrieve the original data without knowledge of the key.

Cryptography is used for *authentication*, *confidentiality* and *message integrity*. When A sends a message to B, B needs to satisfy itself that the message is indeed from A (authentication). A also needs to make sure that only B can read the message (confidentiality). Both need to make sure that the message has not been altered in transit (message integrity). These principles form the basis of the secure shell, so let's look at the standard techniques that achieve these basic cryptographic goals.

There are many algorithms that determine the way data is encrypted and decrypted, and how keys are generated. Generally, we divide these algorithms as belonging to these types:

- *Symmetric key* algorithms that use a single key.
- *Asymmetric key* algorithms that use two keys.

Since the encrypted pattern is largely defined by the key used, the security of the data depends both on the strength of the algorithm and length of the key. Though it is practically impossible to decrypt data without knowledge of the key, a **brute force attack** (one that tries all possible keys) can theoretically retrieve data. However, by one estimate, if the key length is 128 bits, a brute force attack using a billion computers with each able to search a billion keys a second would still require over 10,000 billion years to search all keys. This is more than the residual life of our solar system (four billion years).

Both symmetric and asymmetric systems have their advantages and disadvantages, and SSH makes use of both technologies to provide a completely encrypted session between two ends. We'll now examine the basics of these two algorithms.

17.7.1 Symmetric Key Algorithms

Symmetric key algorithms make use of a single key for encryption and decryption of data. Both sender and recipient must have knowledge of the key. These algorithms enable very fast encryption and decryption and are thus widely used for bulk data. If you have a large document to send, then in all probability, you'll use a symmetric key to protect it. The most common symmetric algorithms in use are DES, 3DES, Blowfish and IDEA.

Symmetric algorithms have one problem, however—key distribution. If two individuals who trust each other decide to exchange data, then this isn't much of a problem. However, on the Internet, if 10 users agree to exchange data with one another, they would need to exchange 90 keys. Also, they would all need to trust one another. The solution is to use a symmetric key for encryption and asymmetric cryptography for key distribution.

17.7.2 Asymmetric Key Algorithms

Asymmetric key algorithms, also known as **public/private key algorithms**, make use of two keys—public and private. Data encrypted by one key can only be decrypted by the other key. The two keys are related to each other though it is "computationally infeasible" to derive one key from knowledge of the other. It's the public key that is distributed to all; the private key never leaves the machine.

When A needs to send an encrypted message to B using an asymmetric key algorithm, there are two options available to A:

- Encrypt the message with A's private key so B can decrypt it with A's public key. This achieves the goal of authentication. B is sure that message has indeed come from A.
- Encrypt with B's public key so that B can decrypt it with B's private key. The goal of confidentiality is achieved as A is assured that only B can read the message.

In real-life, however, the principles described above are used in a somewhat different manner. Symmetric key algorithms are slow (often, about a thousand times slower than asymmetric ones) and are thus totally unsuitable for encrypting bulk data. SSH uses the best of both worlds. It uses a symmetric algorithm to encrypt data but an asymmetric one to distribute the key. SSH uses RSA, DSA and Diffie-Hellman as public key systems for key distribution.

17.8 SSH: THE SECURE SHELL

To understand why the TELNET and FTP services are increasingly being disabled, let's walk through the steps that typically characterize an FTP session. The insecurity associated with each step will help us understand why cryptography was adopted in SSH design:

- The client connects to the server. Neither the server nor the client has any means to authenticate each other. An impostor can manipulate the DNS of the network to provide an IP address that actually belongs to a different server.
- The client logs on to the server using a username and password, both of which are sent in clear text. It's easy to intercept this data.
- The client requests a file to be transferred. The entire file is also sent unencrypted, so it can be read by an outsider (violating confidentiality) and also altered (violating integrity).

SSH addresses all three issues. It uses a symmetric key to encrypt an entire session, but also uses the public/private key mechanism to authenticate hosts and users. There are currently two SSH protocols in use, and the exact techniques differ in SSH-1 and SSH-2. We'll present the features of SSH-2 and note in an inset the changes you need to make when an SSH-2 client connects to an SSH-1 server. We use OpenSSH, a free implementation of SSH made by Berkeley, to run SSH-2.

17.8.1 Host Authentication

SSH uses public key algorithms to generate a public-private key pair not only for users but also for hosts. When the **sshd** daemon is first started, it generates the **host key** pair for that host. When you use an SSH client, say, **ssh** itself, to connect to a server running **sshd**, this is what you see:

```
$ ssh mercury
The authenticity of host 'mercury (192.168.35.1)' can't be established.
RSA key fingerprint is 89:7f:65:bd:dd:af:01:e2:30:51:41:1a:fa:51:64:81.
Are you sure you want to continue connecting (yes/no)? yes
```

```
Warning: Permanently added 'mercury,192.168.35.1' (RSA) to the list of known hos
ts.
sumit@mercury's password: **********
Last login: Fri Nov 28 10:19:03 2003 from saturn.heavens.com
$ _
```

SSH here points out that it is connecting to *mercury* for the first time, and that it has been provided with the public key of *mercury* (the host key, referred to as "fingerprint"). If you find nothing wrong with that, then *mercury*'s public key is added to ~/.ssh/known_hosts on the client host.

Once you decide to go ahead, the client generates a random and symmetric **session key**. The client encrypts this key with the server's public key and sends it to the server. Henceforth, all communication between server and client will be encrypted using this session key. The user is logged in using password authentication but this is not how we intend to use SSH.

17.8.2 The rhosts/shosts Authentication Scheme

The Berkeley r-utilities (comprising the **rsh**, **rlogin** and **rcp** commands) introduced the concept of **trusted hosts** to perform password-free authentication. A host either maintained a systemwide file, /etc/hosts.equiv, that listed those hosts (one per line) who are allowed to connect to this host. Alternatively, a user could also maintain the file ~/.rhosts with similar entries. We do not cover the r-utilities in this edition (look up the Web site), but we need to know the concepts because SSH may "fall back" to this scheme if everything else fails.

Consider that user romeo on host *saturn* has the entry mercury in ~/.rhosts. This implies that romeo on *mercury* can use rsh and rlogin to log on to his like-to-like account on *saturn* without using a password. However, if .rhosts contains the entry pluto juliet, it means that user juliet on *pluto* can also log on to romeo's account without using a password. If these conditions are not met, then a password would be prompted for.

This scheme has drawbacks. The r-utilities use DNS to verify the authenticity of a host and DNS is vulnerable to spoofing attacks. However, SSH also supports a variation of the above mechanism. It uses /etc/shosts.equiv and ~/.shosts for authentication, failing which it uses /etc/hosts.equiv and ~/.rhosts. The entries in both sets are of the same form, and password-free access is granted if equivalence can be established. If all's not well, SSH prompts for a password with the difference that the password is sent encrypted to the server.

We won't discuss this scheme any further because it may be disabled in favor of a public/private key-based user authentication system that is discussed next. To use this scheme, make sure that you delete both ~/.rhosts and ~/.shosts, both in the server and client. It's expected that the administrator won't also maintain /etc/hosts.equiv and /etc/shosts.equiv.

17.8.3 User Authentication with Symmetric Algorithms

Host authentication is followed by user authentication using public key encryption, provided the client is set up to work that way. The program **ssh-keygen** generates the public-private key pair for a user and stores them in two separate files. As an added precaution, SSH allows you to encrypt the private key using a **passphrase** which is prompted for at the time of key generation:

```
$ ssh-keygen -t rsa                                          Generating RSA keys
Generating public/private rsa key pair.
Enter file in which to save the key (/home/sumit/.ssh/id_rsa): [Enter]
Enter passphrase (empty for no passphrase): ************************
Enter same passphrase again: ************************
Your identification has been saved in /home/sumit/.ssh/id_rsa.
Your public key has been saved in /home/sumit/.ssh/id_rsa.pub.
The key fingerprint is:
29:75:68:49:30:e8:8b:e1:5c:db:13:97:01:d6:bc:15  sumit@saturn.planets
```

We opted for RSA-based authentication (-t rsa), but SSH-2 also supports DSA. A passphrase is similar to a password except that spaces are allowed. The default locations for the private and public RSA keys are ~/.ssh/id_rsa and ~/.ssh/id_rsa.pub, respectively. Expectedly, the private key file is a little more secure that the other:

```
$ cd ~/.ssh ; ls -l id_rsa*
-rw-------    1 sumit    users           951 2003-11-27 13:10 id_rsa
-rw-r--r--    1 sumit    users           223 2003-11-27 13:10 id_rsa.pub
```

Your private key is stored in encrypted form (using the passphrase you provided) in the first file. To use RSA-based public/private key authentication, you need to copy the file containing your public key (id_rsa.pub) to all hosts to which you need to connect by SSH. You could use **ftp** to do this job, but the service could be disabled, so use **scp**, a command of the SSH suite:

```
$ cd ~/.ssh
$ scp id_rsa.pub sumit@mercury:.                             On the client machine
sumit@mercury's password: **********
id_rsa.pub            100% |****************************|     230          00:00
```

scp still prompts for the password because RSA-based user authentication has not been set up yet. Now log on to the server (here, *mercury*) and append this file to ~/.ssh/authorized_keys on the remote host. This file contains the public keys for this user who connects from different hosts:

```
$ ssh mercury
sumit@mercury's password: ************
Last login: Fri Nov 28 10:25:49 2003 from saturn.heavens.com
$ cat id_rsa.pub >> ~/.ssh/authorized_keys
$ exit                                                       Back to client
Connection to mercury closed.
```

If everything has been set up properly, then when you use **ssh** or any of the tools of the SSH suite (**scp**, **sftp** or **slogin**) to connect to *mercury*, the program prompts for the passphrase of your private key:

```
$ ssh mercury
Enter passphrase for key '/home/sumit/.ssh/id_rsa':
Last login: Fri Nov 28 10:27:24 2003 from saturn.heavens.com
$ _
```

Note that SSH doesn't prompt for the password this time, but simply the passphrase used to encrypt the private key. The server verifies the authenticity of the user by sending the client a **challenge**—a randomly selected string encrypted with the user's public key. The client decrypts the string and sends back the challenge string thus proving that it possesses the private key. The user is then logged in. There could be a variation of this procedure, but the underlying idea of using public key cryptography for key distribution and authentication is evident.

Caution: If SSH has not been set up properly, it will fall back on the rhosts/shosts form of authentication and prompt for your password as stored on the remote host. If SSH is simply unable to establish a secure connection, then it may even transmit the password in an unencrypted manner, but only after warning you!

17.8.4 Using the SSH Agent for Noninteractive Logins

If you connect to a remote host regularly, typing a passphrase repeatedly can be quite annoying. We can use the SSH authentication agent program, **ssh-agent**, to cache the unencrypted private key in memory. Once you hand over this key to **ssh-agent**, all future connections will be both password- and passphrase-free.

ssh-agent needs two variables to be set. The default output shows their assignment in the form *variable=value*:

```
$ ssh-agent
SSH_AUTH_SOCK=/tmp/ssh-XXFh8izh/agent.1655;, export SSH_AUTH_SOCK;
SSH_AGENT_PID=1656; export SSH_AGENT_PID;
echo Agent pid 1656;
```

We haven't run the agent yet, but using the services of **eval** *(21.11)*, we can make these assignments and invoke the agent in a single invocation:

```
$ eval `ssh-agent -s`
Agent pid 1251
```
                                                              Use -c for C shell

The agent is now running with 1251 as the PID. You now have to hand over your private key with **ssh-add**:

```
$ ssh-add ~/.ssh/id_rsa
Need passphrase for /home/sumit/.ssh/id_rsa
Enter passphrase for /home/sumit/.ssh/id_rsa: ********************
Identity added: /home/sumit/.ssh/id_rsa (/home/sumit/.ssh/id_rsa)
```

The private key will remain cached in memory as long as you are logged in. You can display all keys registered with **ssh-agent** with the -l option, and delete a key with -d. Now you no longer need a passphrase to connect to the server:

```
$ ssh mercury
Last login: Fri Nov 28 10:28:17 2003 from saturn.heavens.com
$ _
```

Noninteractive login at last! You have a secure communication channel, and every character passing through this channel is encrypted using a symmetric key algorithm. You can now use any of the SSH tools (discussed next) in a noninteractive manner.

When an SSH-2 Client Connects to an SSH-1 Server

You may have the latest version of OpenSSH on your machine running SSH-2, but your server could still be running SSH-1. In that case, let's walk through all the configuration steps and note the differences:

- When you first connect to a remote host to obtain its public key, use **ssh -1 mercury**. The -1 option ensures that the **ssh** client uses SSH-1.
- Generate your private/public key pair with **ssh-keygen -t rsa1**. Previously, we used -t rsa which represented the RSA keys for SSH-2. RSA keys in SSH-1 have different formats and are stored in the files ~/.ssh/identity (for private) and ~/.ssh/identity.pub (for public).
- Copy the .pub file as usual to the server but make sure that the permissions of ~/.ssh/authorized_keys are set to 600. SSH-2 is indifferent to the permissions used as long as the file is readable.
- Now connect to the SSH-1 server using the -1 option with **ssh**, **slogin** and **sftp**, and -oProtocol=1 with **scp**.

If you still have any problems, then use **ssh -v** for a verbose output that shows the entire handshaking process. You should be able to locate the error in this output.

17.9 THE SSH TOOLS

The SSH suite comprises tools that emulate the behavior of both the DARPA set and Berkeley r-utilities. These tools also have similar names:

- **slogin** for remote login.
- **ssh** for remote login and command execution.
- **scp** and **sftp** for file transfer.

Note that the **ssh** command itself can be used both for remote login and command execution. Unlike the conventional tools, however, all SSH tools are secure (if configured properly); all communication between server and client is encrypted. We'll now discuss these tools.

17.9.1 ssh and slogin: Remote Login and Command Execution

SSH features two commands, **ssh** and **slogin**, both derived from the Berkeley tools (**rsh** and **rlogin**) for remote login. If you have previously run **ssh-agent** and **ssh-add** to save your private key in memory, then you can log in without supplying a passphrase:

```
$ ssh mercury
Last login: Fri Nov 28 10:45:23 2003 from saturn.heavens.com
$ _
```

However, if you have not used **ssh-agent** and **ssh-add**, then **ssh** will prompt for the passphrase:

```
$ ssh mercury
Enter passphrase for key '/home/sumit/.ssh/id_rsa':
```

Using the -1 option, you can also log in using a different user-id, provided the other user has permitted you to do so by saving your public key in ~/.ssh/authorized_keys on the server:

```
ssh -1 charlie mercury
```

The **slogin** command behaves similarly and also supports the -1 option.

Sometimes, you may like to run a remote command without logging in. **ssh** can do that too. Simply use the hostname and command name as arguments:

```
ssh saturn ls -1                                 ls -1 executed on host saturn
```

Though **ls** is run remotely, the output is seen on your terminal. To save this output in the remote machine as well, escape the >:

```
ssh saturn ls -1 \> dir.lst                      > interpreted remotely
```

If you use wild-cards that have to be interpreted remotely, you need to quote or escape them too so that your local shell doesn't interfere.

17.9.2 sftp and scp: Secure File Transfer

The **sftp** command is similar to **ftp** except that it has a restricted set of internal commands. Log in with or without a passphrase:

```
$ sftp mercury
Connecting to mercury...
sftp> _                                          The sftp prompt
```

Invoke **help** and you'll find that it uses an l prefix to run a command on the local machine. This prefix was seen only in the **lcd** command in **ftp**, but here you have to use **lpwd**, **lls** and **lmkdir** to run **pwd**, **ls** and **mkdir** on the local machine. Here's how you use **sftp** to upload a file:

```
sftp> cd workc
sftp> pwd
Remote working directory: /home/sumit/workc
sftp> lpwd
Local working directory: /home/sumit
sftp> lcd personal/workc
sftp> lpwd
Local working directory: /home/sumit/personal/workc
sftp> put shell.c
Uploading shell.c to /home/sumit/workc/shell.c
sftp> quit
```

Even though the feature is not documented, you can use the **mput** and **mget** commands in the same way they are used in **ftp**.

scp has one advantage over both **ftp** and **sftp**: It can copy subdirectory structures. **scp** accesses a remote file as *hostname:filename*. This is how a file is copied in both directions:

```
scp saturn:/home/henry/shell.c shell.c          From remote to local
scp shell.c saturn:/home/henry/                 From local to remote
```

If the file has to be copied from the user's home directory, then you can shorten the command line further. You can also use wild-cards to retrieve multiple files:

```
scp henry@saturn:shell.c .
scp henry@saturn:"*".c .
```

For copying a directory structure, use the -r option. Both the following commands copy henry's home directory tree from *saturn* to the local machine:

```
scp -r saturn:/home/henry .
scp -r henry@saturn:. .                          Two dots
```

Shell programmers can now use the **scp** command in shell scripts.

17.10 THE DOMAIN NAME SYSTEM (DNS)

Because of the innumerable number of hosts on the Internet, you can't use hosts files (/etc/hosts) there. The Internet (or, rather the ARPANET, its ancestor) did have a centralized file in its teens, but its maintenance became so painful that Berkeley had to step in with the **Domain Name System (DNS)**. DNS is a distributed system that is scalable easily. It introduces three key concepts:

- A hierarchical organization of hostnames.

- A distributed database for performing the name-address mappings.

- Delegation of authority to individual levels of the hierarchy.

In the Internet namespace, hosts belong to **domains**, which in turn could belong to subdomains, and so forth. Like in the file system, these domains and subdomains form a hierarchy with the *root* domain as the top, signified by a . (dot) (Fig. 17.1). The root domain has immediately below it a number of **top-level domains (TLDs)** or **generic domains**, like *edu* and *com*. These in turn have subdomains or second-level domains under them in the same way a directory has subdirectories under it. You can have further subdomains under these subdomains, and this nesting can descend several levels.

For instance, if *binghamton* is a subdomain under *edu*, and *cs* a subdomain under *binghamton*, then the host *ralph* could be uniquely described as

   ralph.cs.binghamton.edu.

In the hierarchy related to these dot-separated strings, *edu* is above binghamton, which in turn is above *cs*. *ralph.cs.binghamton.edu* represents a **fully qualified domain name (FQDN)** of the host *ralph*—something like the absolute pathname of a file. Another *site* (a collection of hosts of a single organization) can also have the hostname *ralph*, or the subdomain name *cs*, but the FQDN will be unique throughout the Internet.

The Net originally had eight three-character TLDs (top-level domains) allocated to organizations based on the nature of their activities. MIT is represented in the *edu* domain, but Sun Microsystems (*com*) and GNU (*org*) belong to different TLDs. Moreover, every country listed in the ISO-3166-1 specification is also represented by a two-letter **country-code top-level domain (ccTLD)** (India—*in*, Germany—*de*, France—*fr*, etc.). In late 2000, seven more TLDs have been added (*aero*, *museum*, *name*, etc.) as shown in Table 17.1.

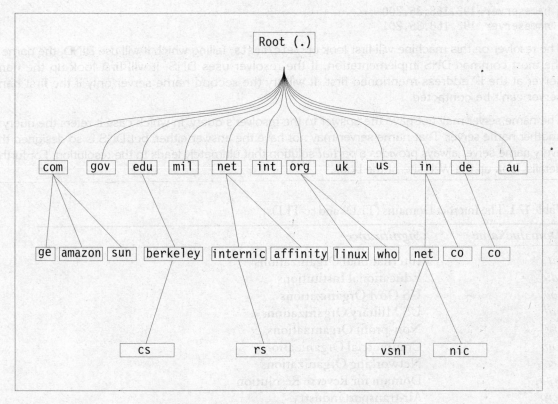

Fig. 17.1 The Internet Domain Hierarchy

Agencies spread across the globe allocate domains (like *binghamton*) without creating conflict. *However, the responsibility for maintaining all information related to the binghamton domain now rests with the authorities at binghamton.* This responsibility includes, apart from the allocation of further subdomains, also the maintenance of the relevant portion of the DNS database in one or more **name servers**. A name server contains hostname-IP address mappings but in a more elaborate form than /etc/hosts. The resolver *(17.2)* queries the name servers on behalf of the application to obtain the IP address of a host.

Note: FQDNs are case-insensitive; you can use *JACK.HILL.COM* in the same way you can use *jACk.HiLL.coM*. An FQDN should identify the organization easily.

HOW IT WORKS: How DNS Works

When a hostname or an FQDN is used with an application, the resolver first has to determine the mechanism of resolution that it has to adopt. It looks up its own configuration file, /etc/resolv.conf, for entries like these:

```
order hosts, bind
```

```
nameserver 192.168.35.200
nameserver 192.168.35.201
```

The resolver on this machine will first look up /etc/hosts, failing which it will use BIND, the name of the most common DNS implementation. If the resolver uses DNS, it will first look up the name server at the IP address mentioned first. It will try the second name server only if the first name server can't be contacted.

The name server may not have the answer to the resolver's query, in which case it refers the query to another name server. That name server may not have the answer either, but DNS is so designed that every name server always provides a *partial* solution that ultimately leads to the resolution. For further details, look up the Web site of the book.

Table 17.1 The Internet Domains (TLDs and cc-TLDs)

Domain Name	Significance
int	International Organizations
edu	Educational Institutions
gov	US Govt Organizations
mil	US Military Organizations
org	Non-profit Organizations
com	Commercial Organizations
net	Networking Organizations
arpa	Domain for Reverse Resolution
aero	Air-transport industry
biz	Businesses
museum	Accredited museums
name	Individuals; possible to have *henry.blofeld.name*
pro	Professionals
coop	Cooperatives
info	For all uses
in	A ccTLD; India
uk, ch, us, etc.	Other ccTLDs; United Kingdom, Switzerland, USA, etc.

17.11 INTERNET MAIL

Electronic mail was first discussed in Section 3.7 and the **mailx** command was used to move mail between users on the same host. The mail programs generally need no special configuration to deliver mail in these single-host situations. However, the mechanism used to move mail on the Internet is a little complex. Unlike TELNET and SSH, which work within a simple client-server framework, Internet mail handling requires the work of at least three agencies:

- *Mail user agent (MUA)*—For reading the mailbox and sending mail.
- *Mail transport agent (MTA)*—For transporting mail between machines.
- *Mail delivery agent (MDA)*—For delivering mail to the recipients' mailboxes.

In this three-tier arrangement, the **mail user agent (MUA)** like `mailx` or `pine` acts as the user's frontend. The MUA reads incoming mail from the mailbox and hands over outgoing mail to the **mail transport agent (MTA)**.

The MTA also has two functions: it both sends and receives mail. At the sending end, the MTA identifies the recipient's address and delivers the message *directly* to the MTA at the other end. At the receiving end, the MTA passes on mail to the **Mail Delivery Agent (MDA)**. Both these functions are handled universally by the *Simple Mail Transfer Protocol* (SMTP).

The MTA is not responsible for ultimate delivery of the message. It is the MDA that accepts mail from the receiving MTA and delivers it to the actual user's mailbox. This is handled by separate programs like **/usr/lib/mail.local** on Solaris and **procmail** on Linux.

A fourth tier comes in when the MTA is unable to deliver mail to the MDA. This is true for dialup lines where the user's host connects to the network intermittently. In this arrangement, users typically use their ISP's facilities to handle both incoming and outgoing mail. The ISP stores the user's mail on their server, and the user fetches the mail using a separate program. There are two protocols in use today for fetching mail—*Post Office Protocol* (POP3) and *Internet Message Access Protocol* (IMAP).

The simple character-based clients like **mailx** and **pine** can only view mail that has been delivered to the host on which they are running; they can't retrieve mail from a POP/IMAP server. However, if you compose and receive mail on your own workstation using a GUI client like Netscape Messenger or Mozilla Mail, then you need to specify the following parameters as part of your client's setup:

- The outgoing SMTP server.
- The incoming server that may use the POP3 or IMAP protocol.
- Your user-id on these servers.

If your own workstation is set up to act as a mail server, then you can use the generic name *localhost* to signify your own hostname or 127.0.0.1 if you prefer to specify the IP address.

HOW IT WORKS: The Role of DNS in Identifying the Mail Server

Apart from performing FQDN-address resolution, DNS also specifies the mail servers (called *mail exchangers*) meant to handle mail for that domain. When a message is addressed to *juliet floyd <juliet@heavens.com>*, the resolver of the sending host contacts its own DNS server to obtain the IP address of the mail server for *heavens.com* (which could be, say, *mail.heavens.com*). The MTA of the sending host then transfers the mail to the MTA of *mail.heavens.com*.

17.11.1 ~/.signature and ~/.forward: Two Important Files

Most mailers make use of the *signature* facility to append some static text to every outgoing message. This text is often the sender's personal details that are saved in $HOME/.signature. The contents of this file are attached to the user's outgoing messages provided the MUA is configured properly. Some mailers like Netscape also use the .signature file but it is located differently.

When you travel, you can consider the automatic *forwarding* facility to redirect all your incoming messages to another address. Simply place the address where you want all mail to be forwarded to in $HOME/.forward. If romeo's .forward contains an entry like this:

```
romeo@yahoo.com
```

the local MTA forwards the mail to the mail server of *yahoo.com* without delivering it to romeo's local mailbox. No mailer needs to be configured to use this facility because forwarding through .forward is a feature of **sendmail**—the program that uses SMTP and delivers most of our mail on the Internet.

17.12 MIME: HANDLING BINARY ATTACHMENTS IN MAIL

Every mail message consists of several lines of header information. Some of them are inserted by the MUA and the others by the MTA. A typical message shows at least the first four fields shown below:

```
Subject: creating animations in macromedia director from GIF89a images
Date: Fri, 08 Nov 2002 15:42:38 +0530
From: joe winter <winterj@sasol.com>
To: heinz@xs4all.nl
Cc: psaha@earthlink.net
```

The message body follows next, preceded by a blank line. The body contains mostly text, but it can also contain attachments which are held as a single *multipart* message. The original SMTP protocol had two limitations that disallowed the mailing of binary attachments:

- Only 7-bit ASCII characters could form a mail message.
- The line length could not exceed 1000 characters.

As mail usage increased, the requirement to include 8-bit binary files with arbitrary line lengths was being increasingly felt. RFC 822 had to be extended by another standard, **Multipurpose Internet Mail Extensions (MIME)**, that addresses these issues.

MIME extends the definition of mail to include binary files and multiple data formats in a *single* message. While RFC 822 was concerned with message headers, MIME is concerned with the format of the *content*. It also imposes no restriction on line length. Attachments containing binary data have to be encoded but the MIME standard requires two additional headers to be sent with the message:

```
Content-Type: application/pdf; name="interior.pdf"
Content-Transfer-Encoding: base64
```

The Content-Type: header defines the *type/subtype* of the data following the header. Here, pdf is a subtype of application. The Content-Transfer-Encoding: header defines the encoding techniques used on the data. We have here a PDF document as an attachment having application/pdf as its content type and encoded using the *base64* technique.

These two headers provide the necessary information that enable a MIME-compliant mail application at the other end to decode the content. Two configuration files play a vital role here:

`mime.types` on the sender's side and `mailcap` on the receiver's side. When you attach a PDF document to an outgoing message, your MUA looks up the file's extension in `mime.types` to determine the Content-Type header. Here's a sample entry for a PDF file (extension: `.pdf`):

```
application/pdf          pdf
```

The MUA sets the content type for the PDF portion of the message to `application/pdf`. At the receiving end, the MUA may not have the capability to handle this content type. It then looks up the file `mailcap` for the **helper application** (an external program) that is specified for this content type. Here's an entry from this file:

```
application/pdf; acroread %s                    Note the delimiter is ;
```

This entry directs the MUA to call up the Acrobat Reader to view the PDF document. Many UNIX systems maintain a systemwide `mailcap` database in `/etc`, but many MUAs (like Netscape Messenger) maintain their own. If `mailcap` doesn't specify a helper application for a content type, then the MUA would seek your approval for saving the file to disk.

Even though MIME was designed to make it possible to deliver multimedia attachments with mail messages, the standard applies equally well to newsgroup messages and Web resources. We'll revisit MIME when we discuss HTTP.

17.13 THE WORLD WIDE WEB

The World Wide Web is the Internet's latest and finest service yet. It was originally conceived by Tim Berners-Lee at CERN, Switzerland as a simple mechanism for interconnecting documents spread across the globe. It quickly went beyond the original vision of its creator, and today functions as a "one-stop shop" for practically everything that's discussed in this chapter. The Web kept the traditional Internet services (email, anonymous FTP and Net News) alive, but completely obsoleted its immediate ancestors, Archie and Gopher.

Even though the Web appears to be a conglomeration of multiple services, it works within the framework of the simple client-server model. Web service uses the **Hyper Text Transfer Protocol (HTTP)**, and Web servers, also known as *HTTP servers* listen for requests at port 80. The Web's access (client) tool is called the **browser**. A Web browser fetches a document (or any *resource*) residing on Web servers and formats it using the formatting instructions provided in the document itself. It also displays pictures if they are in GIF, JPEG or PNG formats. If there's a format it can't understand, it will call up a *plugin* or a *helper application* to handle it.

The World Wide Web is indeed a "web"—a vast collection of linked **hypertext** documents. This linkage is based on the understanding that if a resource is available on one server, it makes no sense to have it on another. These links are specified by *Uniform Resource Locators* (URLs). In this way, the user "wanders and roams" without needing to know where she is, and initiates a new connection with a simple keystroke or mouse click.

Web documents are written in the **Hyper Text Markup Language (HTML)**, a text-based portable language. HTML can highlight any portion of text to be displayed with some attributes (like bold, red in color, etc.). However, HTML's real power lies in its hypertext capability. HTML text contains hypertext links (or hyperlinks) to other Web pages. Activating a link can take you to another place in the same document, another document on the same server, or any page anywhere on the Internet. Text can also link to pictures, and what's more, even pictures themselves can contain links to other pictures.

17.13.1 The Uniform Resource Locator (URL)

A resource is described by a **Uniform Resource Locator (URL)**—a form of addressing that combines the FQDN of the site and the pathname of the resource. The simplest URL is one that specifies only the FQDN of the server, and is entered through the URL window of the browser:

http://java.sun.com   *Press [Enter]*

This displays the *home page* of Sun's Java site. Web servers are often configured to send the file index.html when you specify the FQDN as above. The home page will also show a number of hyperlinks in the form of underlined text. Clicking on a link fetches a different page, and your URL could change to something like this:

http://java.sun.com/docs/books/tutorial/information/FAQ.html

URL syntax ranges from the simple to the complex, but in general, a URL is a combination of three or four things:

- The protocol (usually http://) used in transferring the resource. A Web browser supports other protocols, so you can use ftp:// to transfer a file. You may drop the http:// prefix when fetching a Web page because that's the default used by all browsers.

- The port number, which is not usually specified if the server uses the default port 80. The above URL is equivalent to *http://java.sun.com:80/docs/books/tutorial/information/FAQ.html*. Note the colon before the port number.

- The FQDN of the host (here, *java.sun.com*).

- The pathname of the resource (here, docs/books/tutorial/information/FAQ.html). This need not always be a resource to fetch, but could be a program to run on the server.

The Web has a strong UNIX tradition, so frontslashes are the rule. Like FTP servers, Web servers also have their own root directory, which is distinctly different from the file system's root. In other words /docs is not under the system's root.

Note: The URL string is not *fully* case-insensitive. As discussed before, the FQDN is case-insensitive; *JAVA.SUN.COM* is the same as *java.sun.com*. But whether the pathname is case-insensitive or not depends on the operating system used by the server. Most Web servers use UNIX, and UNIX is case-sensitive. If you have seen the pathname /Docs/index.html, then enter it just that way.

17.13.2 HTTP: The Protocol of the Web

Like the other Internet services, HTTP has separate client and server components. A Web page typically contains links to many resources that may be distributed across multiple servers. The client requests the server for a document, and the server responds by sending it. The client then extracts the URLs of other resources from the document and then makes separate requests for each resource that has to be fetched to complete the page display. The life-cycle of a connection using HTTP/1.1 is as below:

- The client contacts the server and opens a connection at port number 80.
- The client requests the Web server for some service. This service may be to ask for a document or to post some form data back to the server. The request consists of a request header followed by data sent by the client.
- The server now sends a response which consists of a response header, followed by data.
- The server waits for more requests and finally closes the connection. On older HTTP/1.0 servers, the server would close the connection after each request.

Most Web servers today use HTTP/1.1 and its **Keep-Alive** feature which makes connections **persistent**. This implies that if a Web page contains five graphic files, a single connection can fetch them using Keep-Alive and not six, as was required earlier. The protocol is also **stateless** in that each connection is unaware of the other, even though they took place sequentially.

If the client requests a document, the request header contains the URL of the document. It could also contain form data that has to be processed on the server end. The server's response header describes the type of data sent from the server. HTTP uses the MIME feature that was first used in email of specifying the content type of the data that is to follow. For HTML documents, this is `text/html`.

17.13.3 Running External Programs

The previous URL specifications referred to static resources—files that reside on a Web server. However, a lot of content on the Web is generated dynamically, i.e., they don't exist as files on the server. Take for instance this URL which specifies a search for the string `unix system calls` on the Teoma site:

http://s.teoma.com/search?q=unix+system+calls&qcat=1&qsrc=1

Here, the string `search` following the FQDN is not the filename of a Web page, but of a *program* to be run on the server. The remaining string following the ? symbol comprise the arguments to this program, suitably encoded to avoid conflict with the characters used in the rest of the URL string. A Web server has no capacity to run these programs.

The server passes on the request to a **Common Gateway Interface** (CGI), which makes arrangements to execute the program and returns its standard output to the Web server for onward transmission back to the client. We call them **CGI programs**, and such programs could be written in any language. **perl** is the language of choice for CGI because of its parsing capabilities using regular expressions. However, Java servlets are being increasingly used in this domain.

17.13.4 HTML: The Language of Web Pages

Web pages are written in HTML. Even though the HTML acronym expands to Hyper Text Markup Language, it's not really a programming language like C, which produces binary executables from text sources. Rather, HTML uses tags to "mark up" text. It owes its origin to the **nroff/troff** suite of UNIX systems that used some of these tags several years before the Web was born. A few sample lines from a Web page show the use of these tags:

```
<BODY>
    <H1> Perl: Larry Wall's Brainchild </H1>
    <STRONG>perl</STRONG> is an interpretive language and is probably the
    best     language yet          available for text manipulation.
    <IMG SRC="perl.gif" ALIGN=LEFT VSPACE=10 HSPACE=10>
    It was created by Larry Wall, and made freely available to the world.
    <EM><STRONG> You don't have to pay for using perl</STRONG></EM>,
    It's     distributed      under the GNU General Public License,
    which means that no one can impose any restrictions on its distribution.

    You can know more about <STRONG>perl</STRONG> by visiting
    <A HREF="http://www.perl.org"> the Perl site</A>.
</BODY>
```

Each tag begins with a < and ends with a >, and most tags have some formatting capability. For instance, <STRONG> and its closing counterpart, </STRONG>, serve to boldface text. In the HTML source shown above, the word perl appears twice in boldface as shown in Fig. 17.2. The browser ignores extra spaces and blank lines, and combines multiple adjacent spaces to a single space.

Two tags provide the actual hyptertext capability—<IMG> and <A>. Both of them take on *attributes* in the form *attribute=value*. The <IMG> tag and its SRC attribute is used to specify a URL of a graphic. The browser fetches the graphic file from the server (which could be a different one) and displays it inline within the Web page. Here, the tag places the picture of a pearl on the page.

The anchor tag, <A>, and the HREF attribute behave in a similar manner except that they allow you to click on a section of text or an image to fetch another resource. Here, the words the Perl site appear underlined, indicating a hyperlink. Clicking on it replaces the current page with the home page of *www.perl.org*.

Because HTML documents are text files, they are portable, and you can view them on *any* browser on *any* machine running *any* operating system. They are also small in size and thus are ideally suited for use on the Web where network bandwidth is often a severe constraint.

17.13.5 The Web Browser

The Web browser is the HTTP client. It accepts a URL either from the URL window or from a bookmark, and fetches the resource from the server. If the document contains <IMG SRC> tags, the

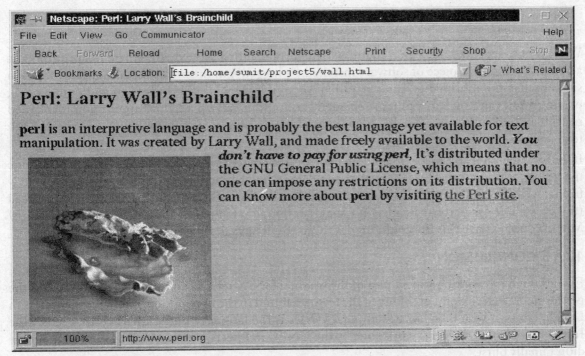

Fig. 17.2 An HTML Document Viewed with Netscape

browser fetches the images the tags link to—using a single Keep-Alive connection, wherever possible. Every browser is also expected to offer these features:

- Step back and forth through documents viewed in a session.
- Save HTML files (and graphics) to the local machine.
- Bookmark important URLs so they can be fetched later without actually entering the URL.
- Support other application protocols like FTP and TELNET.
- Automatically invoke helper applications and special software (plugins) when encountering a file format it can't handle.

Like email clients, the earliest Web browsers were character-based, and the **lynx** browser remained popular until the advent of graphics. Netscape Navigator/Mozilla is the standard graphic browser for UNIX and Linux systems today.

17.14 MULTIMEDIA ON THE WEB: MIME REVISITED

Web documents today feature a variety of multimedia objects like Java applets, RealAudio, RealVideo and Shockwave technology. MIME technology *(17.12)* also applies to multimedia files on the Web. However, these files are sent by Web servers not as multipart messages but as independent files. The server sends the content type to the client before it sends the file by looking up the file mime.types that associates the content type with the file's extension, as shown below for a PDF document:

```
type=application/acrobat   exts=pdf                    Solaris
application/pdf            pdf                         Linux
```

When a browser encounters an unfamiliar data format, it first sees whether there is a **plugin** in its arsenal. A plugin is a piece of software installed ("plugged") in the browser. It is normally small in size and has the minimal features required for simple viewing (or, in case of audio and video, playing). You can't invoke a plugin separately as you can call up a helper application (explained next) like Acrobat Reader. When a file is viewed with a plugin, it appears inline with the HTML text, and not in a separate window.

If the browser is not able to locate a plugin for a specific content type, it looks up mailcap to determine the **helper application**. This is a separate standalone application that can also be invoked separately from the UNIX command line. We saw one entry in this file in Section 17.12 that specified acroread (the executable for Acrobat Reader) for application/pdf. Unlike in Windows, UNIX Netscape/Mozilla doesn't have this file configured well, so you'll have to fill it up yourself.

17.15 CONCLUSION

Even though networking wasn't part of the original UNIX scheme of things, UNIX provided the platform for its development. Many of the features found in the networking tools have their roots in UNIX. Thus, it would be fair to state that UNIX is the language of the Internet. In a sense, the Internet continued the good work done by the UNIX architects, one reason why this giant bubble didn't finally burst.

WRAP UP

TCP/IP splits data into packets and ensures reliable transmission with full error control. Packets are *routed* between hosts of two networks using a *router* which is part of both networks.

Every host in a network is represented by a unique *hostname* and a unique *IP address*. An IP address consists of four dot-separated octets. The name-address mappings are kept in /etc/hosts on *all* machines of a small network.

TCP/IP works in the *client-server* model. Server programs are known as *daemons*, which run in the background and listen for request at certain *ports*. Servers use fixed port numbers for a service, but clients use random port numbers at their end.

The DARPA set of TCP/IP applications comprise **telnet** and **ftp**. **telnet** is used to run commands on a remote machine and have the display on the local machine. **ftp** is meant for file transfer. You can upload one or more files (**put** and **mput**) or download them (**get** and **mget**).

The *secure shell* is more secure than **telnet** and **ftp** as it encrypts the entire session including the password. It uses a *symmetric key* for encryption of bulk data, but uses *asymmetric keys* (public and private) for host and user authentication and key distribution. You can login in a secure manner (**ssh** and **slogin**), transfer files (**scp** and **sftp**) and run a command remotely (**ssh**).

Large networks and the Internet use the *Domain Name System* (DNS) where each host is represented by its *fully qualified domain name* (FQDN). The FQDN-IP address mappings are maintained across a number of *name servers* which are queried by a *resolver* to obtain the IP address of a host.

Internet mail is handled by three agencies. The *Mail User Agent* (MUA) reads and composes mail. The Mail Transport Agent (MTA) transports mail to the MTA at the receiving end. The *Mail Delivery Agent* (MDA) delivers mail to the user's mailbox.

The Web works on the *Hyper Text Transfer Protocol* (HTTP) at port 80. Web documents written in the *Hyper Text Markup Language* use *hypertext* to link one document with another resource. An HTML document is cross-platform and can be viewed in any environment.

The *Uniform Resource Locator* (URL) combines the FQDN of the site with a pathname. It can point to a static resource like a file or a program to be run using the *Common Gateway Interface* (CGI). **perl** is the language of choice for CGI programming.

Multipurpose Internet Mail Extensions (MIME) enables transmission of binary data using both email and HTTP. The Content-Type: and Content-Transfer-Encoding: headers together define the type of data and encoding techniques used. mime.types associates the content type with a file's extension and mailcap specifies the helper application that will handle a specific content type.

Test Your Understanding

17.1 Why is TCP termed a *reliable* protocol?

17.2 What is the significance of the *loopback address*?

17.3 What is the significance of the port number?

17.4 How can you be sure whether you are working on the local machine or have used **telnet** or **ssh** to log on to a remote machine?

17.5 You copied a graphics file with **ftp** and the file appears to be corrupted. What could be the possible reason?

17.6 With which command do you upload files to an anonymous FTP site?

17.7 Why are the TELNET and FTP services increasingly being disabled on most networks? What are they being replaced with?

17.8 What is a *brute force attack*? Why does the security of data mainly depend on the size of the key?

17.9 To send a large volume of data securely over a network connection, what form of encryption would you adopt?

17.10 What is the difference between a *password* and a *passphrase*? Why is it necessary to have a passphrase?

17.11 When will you be compelled to use **scp** in preference to **ftp**?

17.12 Name three top-level domains that have been added to the Internet namespace in the year 2000.

17.13 What is the problem with /etc/hosts?

17.14 Explain the significance of the MUA and MTA. Whom does the MTA hand over mail to?

17.15 How are binary files included in mail messages even though SMTP handles only 7-bit data? Name the two mail headers that play an important role here.

17.16 What is *hypertext*? Is it confined to text only?

17.17 What are *CGI programs*? How are they invoked?

Flex Your Brain

17.1 How is a TCP/IP network different from a telephone network?

17.2 Name the sequence of commands to be executed to download *noninteractively* all PDF files from the directory /home/romeo/docs on host *pluto* to the directory /home/kumar/docs on the local machine.

17.3 When you change your local directory from inside **ftp**, will the changed directory still be in place after you quit **ftp**, and why?

17.4 When A sends data to B over a network connection using public key cryptography, how does A achieve the goals of (i) authentication, (ii) confidentiality?

17.5 Public key cryptography is more suitable for key distribution than bulk data encryption. Explain how you can use this mechanism to distribute a symmetric key.

17.6 For using SSH, why does a host also need to have a public and private key?

17.7 Cite two reasons why **scp** is preferable to **ftp**.

17.8 What does this command do? `ssh jupiter date \> .date`

17.9 What is an *FQDN*? Why are hostnames not used on the Internet, but only FQDNs?

17.10 Describe the role of the resolver when handling (i) simple hostnames, (ii) fully qualified domain names.

17.11 Name the three important features of DNS. What advantages does DNS have over the hosts file?

17.12 Explain the significance of each word in the acronym *URL*. What happens if you leave out the port number in the URL?

17.13 Why is HTTP called a *stateless* protocol? What is meant by the *Keep-Alive* feature?

17.14 Why is HTML particularly suitable for use on the Web compared to Word documents?

17.15 Can you use *WWW.PLANETS.COM/CATALOG.HTML* instead of *www.planets.com/catalog.html* as the URL?

17.16 What is a *helper application*? Explain the role of the file `mailcap` when using a helper application.

awk—An Advanced Filter

18

The **awk** command made a late entry into the UNIX system in 1977 to augment the tool kit with suitable report formatting capabilities. Named after its authors, Aho, Weinberger and Kernighan, **awk**, until the advent of **perl**, was the most powerful utility for text manipulation. Like **sed**, it combines features of several filters, though its report writing capability is the most useful. **awk** appears as **gawk** (GNU awk) in Linux.

awk doesn't belong to the do-one-thing-well family of UNIX commands. In fact, it can do several things—and some of them quite well. Unlike other filters, it operates at the *field* level and can easily access, transform and format individual fields in a line. It also accepts extended regular expressions (EREs) for pattern matching, has C-type programming constructs, variables and several built-in functions. Knowing **awk** will help you understand **perl**, which uses most of the **awk** constructs, sometimes in identical manner.

What You Will Learn

- Understand **awk**'s unusual syntax with its *selection criteria* and *action* components.
- Split a line into *fields* and format the output with **printf**.
- Understand the special properties of **awk** variables and expressions.
- Use the comparison operators to select lines on practically any condition.
- Use the ~ and !~ operators with extended regular expressions (EREs) for pattern matching.
- Handle decimal numbers and use them for computation.
- Use variables without declaring or initializing them.
- Do some pre- and post-processing with the BEGIN and END sections.
- Examine **awk**'s built-in variables.
- Use the built-in functions for performing string handling tasks.
- Make decisions with the **if** statement.
- Use the **for** and **while** loops to perform tasks repeatedly.

Topics of Special Interest

- Use arrays and access an array element with a nonnumeric subscript.

18.1 SIMPLE awk FILTERING

awk is a little awkward to use at first, but if you feel comfortable with **find** and **sed**, then you'll find a friend in **awk**. Even though it is a filter, **awk** resembles **find** in its syntax:

  awk *options* 'selection_criteria {action}' *file(s)*

The *selection_criteria* (a form of addressing) filters input and selects lines for the *action* component to act upon. This component is enclosed within curly braces. The *selection_criteria* and *action* constitute an **awk** program that is surrounded by a set of single quotes. These programs are often one line long though they can span several lines as well.

The selection criteria in **awk** have wider scope than in **sed**. Like there, they can be patterns like /negroponte/ or line addresses that use **awk**'s built-in variable, NR. Further, they can also be conditional expressions using the && and || operators as used in the shell. You can select lines practically on any condition.

A typically complete **awk** command specifies the selection criteria and action. The following command selects the directors from emp.lst:

```
$ awk '/director/ { print }' emp.lst
9876|jai sharma        |director |production|12/03/50|7000
2365|barun sengupta    |director |personnel |11/05/47|7800
1006|chanchal singhvi  |director |sales     |03/09/38|6700
6521|lalit chowdury    |director |marketing |26/09/45|8200
```

The *selection_criteria* section (/director/) selects lines that are processed in the *action* section ({ print }). If *selection_criteria* is missing, then *action* applies to all lines. If *action* is missing, the entire line is printed. Either of the two (but not both) is optional, but they must be enclosed within a pair of single (not double) quotes.

The **print** statement, when used without any field specifiers, prints the entire line. Moreover, since printing is the default action of **awk**; all the following three forms could be considered equivalent:

```
awk '/director/' emp.lst              Printing is the default action
awk '/director/{ print }' emp.lst     Whitespace permitted
awk '/director/ { print $0}' emp.lst  $0 is the complete line
```

For pattern matching, **awk** uses regular expressions in **sed**-style:

```
$ awk -F"|" '/sa[kx]s*ena/' emp.lst
3212|shyam saksena     |d.g.m.   |accounts  |12/12/55|6000
2345|j.b. saxena       |g.m.     |marketing |12/03/45|8000
```

The regular expressions used by **awk** belong to the basic BRE (but not the IRE and TRE) and ERE variety that's used by **grep -E** *(13.3)* or **egrep**. This means that you can also use multiple patterns by delimiting each pattern with a |.

Note: An **awk** program must have either the selection criteria or the action, or both, but within single quotes. Double quotes will create problems unless used judiciously.

18.2 SPLITTING A LINE INTO FIELDS

awk uses the special parameter, $0, to indicate the entire line. It also identifies fields by $1, $2, $3. Since these parameters also have a special meaning to the shell, single-quoting an **awk** program protects them from interpretation by the shell.

Unlike the other UNIX filters which operate on fields, **awk** uses a contiguous sequence of spaces and tabs as a *single* delimiter. But the sample database *(12.1)* uses the |, so we must use the -F option to specify it in our programs. You can use **awk** to print the name, designation, department and salary of all the sales people:

```
$ awk -F"|" '/sales/ { print $2,$3,$4,$6 }' emp.1st
a.k. shukla       g.m.      sales     6000
chanchal singhvi  director  sales     6700
s.n. dasgupta     manager   sales     5600
anil aggarwal     manager   sales     5000
```

Notice that a , (comma) has been used to delimit the field specifications. This ensures that each field is separated from the other by a space. If you don't put the comma, the fields will be glued together.

So far, the programs have produced readable output, but that is because the file emp.1st contains fixed-length lines. Henceforth, the input for most **awk** programs used in this chapter will come from the file empn.1st which we created with **sed** in Section 13.10. This file is similar to emp.1st except that the lines are of variable length. A few lines of the file show the total absence of spaces around the |:

```
$ head -n 2 empn.1st
3212|shyam saksena|d.g.m.|accounts|12/12/55|6000|6213
6213|karuna ganguly|g.m.|accounts|05/06/62|6300|6213
```

With this file as input, we'll use **awk** with a line address (single or double) to select lines. If you want to select lines 3 to 6, all you have to do is use the built-in variable NR to specify the line numbers:

```
$ awk -F"|" 'NR == 3, NR == 6 { print NR, $2,$3,$6 }' empn.1st
3 n.k. gupta chairman 5400
4 v.k. agrawal g.m. 9000
5 j.b. saxena g.m. 8000
6 sumit chakrobarty d.g.m. 6000
```

This is **awk**'s way of implementing the **sed** instruction **3,6p**. The statement NR == 3 is really a condition that is being tested, rather than an assignment; this should appear obvious to C programmers. NR is one of those built-in variables used in **awk** programs, and == is one of the many operators employed in comparison tests.

Note: awk is the only filter that uses whitespace as the default delimiter instead of a single space or tab.

18.3 `printf`: FORMATTING OUTPUT

The above output is unformatted, but with the C-like **printf** statement, you can use **awk** as a stream formatter. **awk** accepts most of the formats used by the **printf** function used in C, but in this chapter, the %s format will be used for string data, and %d for numeric. You can now produce a list of all the agarwals:

```
$ awk -F"|" '/[aA]gg?[ar]+wal/ {
> printf "%3d %-20s %-12s %d\n",NR,$2,$3,$6 }' empn.lst
   4 v.k. agrawal        g.m.          9000
   9 sudhir Agarwal      executive     7500
  15 anil aggarwal       manager       5000
```

Like in **sed**, an **awk** command is considered complete only when the quote is closed. The name and designation have been printed in spaces 20 and 12 characters wide, respectively; the - symbol left-justifies the output. The line number is three characters wide, right-justified. Note that **printf** requires \n to print a newline after each line. Using the various formats in an **awk** program, you can have complete control over the way the output is presented.

18.3.1 Redirecting Standard Output

Every **print** and **printf** statement can be separately redirected with the > and | symbols. However, make sure the filename or command that follows these symbols is enclosed within double quotes. For example, the following statement sorts the output of the **printf** statement:

```
printf "%s %-10s %-12s %-8s\n", $1, $3, $4, $6 | "sort"
```

If you use redirection instead, the filename should be enclosed in quotes in a similar manner:

```
printf "%s %-10s %-12s %-8s\n", $1, $3, $4, $6 > "mslist"
```

awk thus provides the flexibility of separately manipulating the different output streams. But don't forget the quotes!

18.4 VARIABLES AND EXPRESSIONS

Throughout this chapter, we'll be using variables and expressions with **awk**. Expressions comprise strings, numbers, variables and entities that are built by combining them with operators. (x + 5)*12 is an expression. Unlike in programming languages, awk doesn't have char, int, long, double and so forth as primitive data types. Every expression can be interpreted either as a string or a number, and **awk** makes the necessary conversion according to context.

awk also allows the use of user-defined variables but without declaring them. Variables are case-sensitive; x is different from X. A variable is deemed to be declared the first time it is used. Unlike shell variables, **awk** variables don't use the $ either in assignment or in evaluation:

```
x = "5"
print x
```

A user-defined variable needs no initialization. It is implicitly initialized to zero or a null string. As mentioned before, **awk** has a mechanism of identifying the type and initial value of a variable from its context.

Strings in **awk** are always double-quoted and can contain any character. Like **echo**, **awk** strings can include escape sequences and octal values, but strings can also include hex values. There's one difference however; octal and hex values are preceded by only \ and \x, respectively:

```
x ="\t\tBELL\7"
print x                                     Prints two tabs, the string BELL and sounds a beep
```

awk provides no operator for concatenating strings. Strings are concatenated by simply placing them side-by-side:

```
x = "sun" ; y = "com"
print x y                                   Prints suncom
print x "." y                               Prints sun.com
```

Concatenation is not affected by the type of variable. A numeric and string value can be concatenated just as easily. The following examples demonstrate how **awk** makes automatic conversions when concatenating and adding variables:

```
x = "5" ; y = 6 ; z = "A"
print x y                                   y converted to string; prints 56
print x + y                                 x converted to number; prints 11
print y + z                                 z converted to numeric 0; prints 6
```

Even though we assigned "5" (a string) to x, we could use it for numeric computation. Also observe that when a number is added to a string, **awk** converts the string to zero since it doesn't have numerals.

Expressions also have true and false values associated with them. Any nonempty string is true; so is any positive number. The statement

```
if (x)
```

is true if x is a nonnull string or positive number.

Note: Variables are neither declared nor their type specified. **awk** identifies their type and initializes them to zero or null strings. String variables are always double-quoted, but can contain escape sequences. Nonprintable characters can be represented by their octal or hex values.

18.5 THE COMPARISON OPERATORS

How do you print the three fields for the directors and the chairman? Since the designation field is $3, you have to use it in the selection criteria:

```
$ awk -F"|" '$3 == "director" || $3 == "chairman" {
> printf "%-20s %-12s %d\n", $2,$3,$6 }' empn.lst
n.k. gupta          chairman     5400
lalit chowdury      director     8200
```

```
barun sengupta        director      7800
jai sharma            director      7000
chanchal singhvi      director      6700
```

This is the first time we matched a pattern with a field. In fact, field matching is possible only in **awk** and **perl**. Here, **awk** uses the || and && logical operators in the same sense as used by C and the UNIX shell. This command looks for two strings only in the third field ($3). The second match is attempted only if (||) the first match fails.

For negating the above condition, you should use the != and && operators instead:

```
$3 != "director" && $3 != "chairman"
```

The selection criteria here translates to this: "Select those lines where the third field doesn't (!=) completely match the string director and (&&) also doesn't (!=) completely match the string chairman. Note that the match is made for the *entire* field, rather than a string embedded in the field space. We couldn't verify this because empn.1st has all trailing spaces trimmed. But will a similar **awk** program work on emp.1st which has trailing spaces attached to the strings?

```
$ awk -F"|" '$3 == "director" || $3 == "chairman"' emp.1st
$ _
```

No, it won't; the third field contains trailing whitespace, so a perfect match wasn't found. Field matching is better done with regular expressions as you'll see in the next topic.

18.5.1 ~ and !~: The Regular Expression Operators

How does one match regular expressions? Previously we had used **awk** with regular expressions in this manner:

```
awk -F"|" '/sa[kx]s*ena/' emp.1st
```

This matches the pattern saxena and saksena anywhere in the line and not in a specific field. For matching a regular expression with a field, **awk** offers the ~ and !~ operators to match and negate a match, respectively. With these operators, matching becomes more specific as seen in the following examples:

```
$2 ~ /[cC]ho[wu]dh?ury/ || $2 ~ /sa[xk]s?ena/       Matches second field
$2 ~ /[cC]ho[wu]dh?ury|sa[xk]s?ena/                 Same as above
$3 !~ /director|chairman/                           Neither director nor chairman
```

Remember that the operators ~ and !~ work only with field specifiers ($1, $2 etc.). The delimiting of patterns with the | is an ERE feature, and **awk** uses extended regular expressions. However, **awk** doesn't accept the IRE and TRE used by **grep** and **sed**.

Tip: To match a string embedded in a field, you must use ~ instead of ==. Similarly, to negate a match, use !~ instead of !=.

To locate only the *g.m.*s, you just can't use this:

```
awk -F"|" '$3 ~ /g.m./ { printf " .....
```

Because g.m. is embedded in d.g.m., locating just the *g.m.*s requires use of the ^ and $. These characters have slightly different meanings when used by **awk**. Rather than match lines, they are used to indicate the beginning and end of a *field*, respectively (unless you use them with $0). So, if you use the condition

```
awk -F"|" '$3 ~ /^g.m./ { printf " .....
```

you'll locate only the *g.m.*s and discard the *d.g.m.*s.

Tip: To match a string at the beginning of the field, precede the search pattern by a ^. Similarly, use a $ for matching a pattern at the end of a field.

18.5.2 Number Comparison

awk can also handle numbers— both integer and floating type—and make relational tests on them. Using operators from the set shown in Table 18.1, you can now print pay-slips for those people whose basic pay exceeds 7500:

```
$ awk -F"|" '$6 > 7500 {
> printf "%-20s %-12s %d\n", $2,$3,$6 }' empn.1st
v.k. agrawal         g.m.         9000
j.b. saxena          g.m.         8000
lalit chowdury       director     8200
barun sengupta       director     7800
```

You can also combine regular expression matching with numeric comparison to locate those, either born in 1955 or drawing a basic pay greater than 8000:

```
$ awk -F"|" '$6 > 8000 || $5 ~/45$/' empn.1st
0110|v.k. agrawal|g.m.|marketing|31/12/40|9000|6521
2345|j.b. saxena|g.m.|marketing|12/03/45|8000|6521
6521|lalit chowdury|director|marketing|26/09/45|8200|6521
```

Recall that the context address /45$/ matches the string 45 at the end ($) of the field. With these operators, you can now select lines by locating a pattern as a simple string or a regular expression, as well as by a relational test on a number.

Table 18.1 The Comparison and Regular Expression Matching Operators

Operator	Significance
<	Less than
<=	Less than or equal to
==	Equal to
!=	Not equal to
>=	Greater than or equal to
>	Greater than
~	Matches a regular expression
!~	Doesn't match a regular expression

18.6 NUMBER PROCESSING

awk can perform computations on numbers using the arithmetic operators +, -, *, / and % (modulus). It also overcomes one of the most major limitations of the shell—the inability to handle decimal numbers.

In any environment maintaining data for the payroll application, it's common practice to store only the basic pay in the file. This is acceptable because normally the other elements of pay can be derived from this basic pay. For the purpose of using **awk**, the sixth field will now signify the basic pay, rather than the salary. Assume that the total salary consists of basic pay, dearness allowance (@40 % of basic pay) and house rent (@15 % of basic pay). You can use **awk** to print a rudimentary pay-slip for the directors:

```
$ awk -F"|" '$3 == "director" {
> printf  "%-20s %-12s %d %d %d\n",$2,$3,$6,$6*0.4,$6*0.15}' empn.lst
lalit chowdury        director      8200 3280 1230
barun sengupta        director      7800 3120 1170
jai sharma            director      7000 2800 1050
chanchal singhvi      director      6700 2680 1005
```

18.7 VARIABLES

While **awk** has certain built-in variables, like NR and $0, it also permits the user to use variables of her choice. You can now print a serial number, using the variable kount, and apply it to those directors drawing a salary exceeding 6700:

```
$ awk -F"|" '$3 == "director" && $6 > 6700 {
> kount = kount + 1
> printf "%3d %-20s %-12s %d\n", kount,$2,$3,$6 }' empn.lst
  1 lalit chowdury        director      8200
  2 barun sengupta        director      7800
  3 jai sharma            director      7000
```

The initial value of kount was 0 (by default). That's why the first line is correctly assigned the number 1. **awk** also accepts the C-style incrementing forms:

kount++	*Same as* kount = kount + 1
kount += 2	*Same as* kount = kount + 2
printf "%3d\n", ++kount	*Increments* kount *before printing*

18.8 THE -f OPTION: STORING awk PROGRAMS IN A FILE

You should hold large **awk** programs in separate files and provide them with the .awk extension for easier identification. Let's first store the previous program in the file **empawk.awk**:

```
$ cat empawk.awk
$3 == "director" && $6 > 6700 {
printf "%3d %-20s %-12s %d\n", ++kount,$2,$3,$6 }
```

Observe that this time we haven't used quotes to enclose the **awk** program. You can now use **awk** with the -f *filename* option to obtain the same output:

```
awk -F"|" -f empawk.awk empn.lst
```

Note: If you use **awk** with the -f option, make sure the program stored in the file is not enclosed within quotes. **awk** uses single quotes when the program is specified in the command line or when the entire **awk** command line is placed in a shell script.

18.9 THE BEGIN AND END SECTIONS

awk statements are usually applied to all lines selected by the address, and if there are no addresses, then they are applied to every line of input. But, if you have to print something before processing the first line, for example, a heading, then the BEGIN section can be used quite gainfully. Similarly, the END section is useful in printing some totals after processing is over.

The BEGIN and END sections are optional and take the form

```
BEGIN { action }                          Both require curly braces
END { action }
```

These two sections, when present, are delimited by the body of the **awk** program. You can use them to print a suitable heading at the beginning and the average salary at the end. Store this **awk** program, in a separate file **empawk2.awk** (Fig. 18.1).

Like the shell, **awk** also uses the # for providing comments. The BEGIN section here prints a suitable heading, offset by two tabs (\t\t), while the END section prints the average pay (tot/kount) for the selected lines. To execute this program, use the -f option:

```
$ awk -F"|" -f empawk2.awk empn.lst

        Employee abstract

1 v.k. agrawal          g.m.          9000
2 j.b. saxena           g.m.          8000
```

```
BEGIN {
    printf "\t\tEmployee abstract\n\n"
} $6 > 7500 {       # Increment the variables for the serial number and the pay
    kount++ ; tot+= $6    # Multiple assignments in one line
    printf "%3d %-20s %-12s %d\n", kount,$2,$3,$6
}
END {
    printf "\n\tThe average basic pay is %6d\n", tot/kount
}
```

Fig. 18.1 empawk2.awk

```
3 lalit chowdury      director      8200
4 barun sengupta      director      7800

  The average basic pay is    8250
```

Like all filters, **awk** reads standard input when the filename is omitted. We can make **awk** behave like a simple scripting language by doing all work in the BEGIN section. This is how you perform floating point arithmetic:

```
$ awk 'BEGIN { printf "%f\n", 22/7 }'
3.142857
```

This is something that you can't do with **expr** *(14.9.1)*. Depending on your version of **awk**, the prompt may or may not be returned, which means that **awk** may still be reading standard input. Use *[Ctrl-d]* to return the prompt.

Caution: Always start the opening brace in the same line the section (BEGIN or END) begins. If you don't do that, **awk** will generate some strange messages!

18.10 BUILT-IN VARIABLES

awk has several built-in variables (Table 18.2). They are all assigned automatically, though it is also possible for a user to reassign some of them. You have already used NR, which signifies the record number of the current line. We'll now have a brief look at some of the other variables.

The FS Variable   As stated elsewhere, **awk** uses a contiguous string of spaces as the default field delimiter. FS redefines this field separator, which in the sample database happens to be the |. When used at all, it must occur in the BEGIN section so that the body of the program knows its value before it starts processing:

```
BEGIN { FS="|" }
```

This is an alternative to the -F option which does the same thing.

The OFS Variable   When you used the **print** statement with comma-separated arguments, each argument was separated from the other by a space. This is **awk**'s default output field separator, and can be reassigned using the variable OFS in the BEGIN section:

```
BEGIN { OFS="~" }
```

When you reassign this variable with a ~ (tilde), **awk** will use this character for delimiting the **print** arguments. This is a useful variable for creating lines with delimited fields.

The NF Variable   NF comes in quite handy for cleaning up a database of lines that don't contain the right number of fields. By using it on a file, say empx.1st, you can locate those lines not having six fields, and which have crept in due to faulty data entry:

```
$ awk  'BEGIN { FS = "|" }
> NF != 6 {
> print "Record No ", NR, "has ", NF, " fields"}' empx.1st
```

```
Record No 6 has 4 fields
Record No 17 has 5 fields
```

The FILENAME *variable*   FILENAME stores the name of the current file being processed. Like **grep** and **sed**, **awk** can also handle multiple filenames in the command line. By default, **awk** doesn't print the filename, but you can instruct it to do so:

```
'$6 < 4000 { print FILENAME, $0 }'
```

With FILENAME, you can devise logic that does different things depending on the file that is processed.

Table 18.2 Built-in Variables Used by **awk**

Variable	Function
NR	Cumulative number of lines read
FS	Input field separator
OFS	Output field separator
NF	Number of fields in current line
FILENAME	Current input file
ARGC	Number of arguments in command line
ARGV	List of arguments

18.11 ARRAYS

An **array** is also a variable except that this variable can store a set of values or elements. Each element is accessed by a subscript called the **index**. **awk** arrays are different from the ones used in other programming languages in many respects:

- They are not formally defined. An array is considered declared the moment it is used.
- Array elements are initialized to zero or an empty string unless initialized explicitly.
- Arrays expand automatically.
- The index can be virtually anything; it can even be a string.

In the program **empawk3.awk** (Fig. 18.2), we use arrays to store the totals of the basic pay, da, hra and gross pay of the sales and marketing people. Assume that the da is 25%, and hra 50% of basic pay. Use the tot[ ] array to store the totals of each element of pay, and also the gross pay:

Note that this time we didn't match the patterns sales and marketing specifically in a field. We could afford to do that because the patterns occur only in the fourth field, and there's no scope here for ambiguity. When you run the program, it outputs the averages of the two elements of pay:

```
$ awk -f empawk3.awk empn.1st
              Basic   Da   Hra Gross
     Average  6812  1703  3406 11921
```

C programmers will find the syntax quite comfortable to work with except that **awk** simplifies a number of things that require explicit specification in C. There are no type declarations, no initializations and no statement terminators.

```
BEGIN {
    FS = "|"
    printf "%46s\n", "Basic    Da    Hra Gross"
} /sales|marketing/ {
    # Calculate the da, hra and the gross pay
    da = 0.25*$6 ; hra = 0.50*$6 ; gp = $6+hra+da

    # Store the aggregates in separate arrays
    tot[1] += $6 ; tot[2] += da ; tot[3] += hra ; tot[4] += gp
    kount++
}
END { # Print the averages
    printf "\t      Average    %5d %5d %5d %5d\n", \
    tot[1]/kount, tot[2]/kount, tot[3]/kount, tot[4]/kount
}
```

Fig. 18.2 empawk3.awk

18.11.1 Associative (Hash) Arrays

Even though we used integers as subscripts in the tot [ ] array, **awk** doesn't treat array indexes as integers. **awk** arrays are **associative**, where information is held as *key-value* pairs. The index is the key that is saved internally as a string. When we set an array element using mon[1] = "mon", **awk** converts the number 1 to a string. There's no specified order in which the array elements are stored. As the following example suggests, the index "1" is different from "01":

```
$ awk 'BEGIN {
>    direction["N"] = "North" ; direction["S"] = "South" ;
>    direction["E"] = "East" ; direction["W"] = "West" ;
>    printf("N is %s and W is %s\n", direction["N"], direction["W"]) ;
>
>    mon[1] = "jan" ; mon["1"] = "january" ; mon["01"] = "JAN" ;
>    printf("mon[1] is %s\n", mon[1]) ;
>    printf("mon[01] is also %s\n", mon[01]) ;
>    printf("mon[\"1\"] is also %s\n", mon["1"]) ;
>    printf("But mon[\"01\"] is %s\n", mon["01"]) ;
> }'
N is North and W is West
mon[1] is january
mon[01] is also january
mon["1"] is also january
But mon["01"] is JAN
```

There are two important things to be learned from this output. First, the setting with index "1" overwrites the setting made with index 1. Accessing an array element with subscripts 1 and 01 actually locates the element with subscript "1". Also note that mon["1"] is different from mon["01"].

18.11.2 ENVIRON[]: The Environment Array

You may sometimes need to know the name of the user running the program or the home directory. **awk** maintains the associative array, ENVIRON[], to store all environment variables. This POSIX requirement is met by recent versions of **awk** including **nawk** and **gawk**. This is how we access the shell variables, HOME and PATH, from inside an **awk** program:

```
$ nawk 'BEGIN {
> print "HOME" "=" ENVIRON["HOME"]
> print "PATH" "=" ENVIRON["PATH"]
> }'
HOME=/users1/home/staff/sumit
PATH=/usr/bin::/usr/local/bin:/usr/ccs/bin
```

In Section 18.4.1, we'll use a special form of a **for** loop to print all environment variables.

18.12 FUNCTIONS

awk has several built-in functions, performing both arithmetic and string operations (Table 18.3). The arguments are passed to a function in C-style, delimited by commas and enclosed by a matched pair of parentheses. Even though **awk** allows use of functions with and without parentheses (like **printf** and **printf()**), POSIX discourages use of functions without parentheses.

Some of these functions take a variable number of arguments, and one (**length**) uses no argument as a variant form. The functions are adequately explained here so you can confidently use them in **perl** which often uses identical syntaxes.

There are two arithmetic functions which a programmer will expect **awk** to offer. **int** calculates the integral portion of a number (without rounding off), while **sqrt** calculates the square root of a number. **awk** also has some of the common string handling functions you can hope to find in any language. We'll review them briefly.

length   **length** determines the length of its argument, and if no argument is present, the entire line is assumed to be the argument. You can use length (without any argument) to locate lines whose length exceeds 1024 characters:

```
awk -F"|" 'length > 1024' empn.lst
```

You can use length with a field as well. The following program selects those people who have short names:

```
awk -F"|" 'length($2) < 11' empn.lst
```

index   **index(*s1, s2*)** determines the position of a string *s2* within a larger string *s1*. This function is especially useful in validating single character fields. If a field takes the values a, b, c, d or e, you can use this function to find out whether this single character field can be located within the string abcde:

```
x = index("abcde","b")
```

This returns the value 2.

substr   The **substr**(*stg, m, n*) function extracts a substring from a string *stg*. *m* represents the starting point of extraction and *n* indicates the number of characters to be extracted. Because string values can also be used for computation, the returned string from this function can be used to select those born between 1946 and 1951:

```
$ awk -F"|" 'substr($5,7,2) > 45 && substr($5,7,2) < 52' empn.1st
2365|barun sengupta|director|personnel|11/05/47|7800|2365
3564|sudhir Agarwal|executive|personnel|06/07/47|7500|2365
4290|jayant Choudhury|executive|production|07/09/50|6000|9876
9876|jai sharma|director|production|12/03/50|7000|9876
```

You can never get this output with either **sed** or **grep** because regular expressions can never match the numbers between 46 and 51. Note that **awk** does indeed possess a mechanism of identifying the type of expression from its context. It identified the date field as a string for using **substr** and then converted it to a number for making a numeric comparison.

Note: **awk** makes no distinction between numeric and string variables. You can use a string for numeric computations as well.

---

split   **split**(*stg, arr, ch*) breaks up a string *stg* on the delimiter *ch* and stores the fields in an array *arr*[ ]. Here's how you can convert the date field to the format *YYYYMMDD*:

```
$ awk -F\| '{split($5,ar,"/") ; print "19"ar[3]ar[2]ar[1]}' empn.1st
19521212
19501203
19431904
.....
```

You can also do this with **sed**, but this method is superior because it explicitly picks up the fifth field, whereas **sed** would transform the only date field that it finds.

system   You may want to print the system date at the beginning of the report. For running a UNIX command within **awk**, you'll have to use the **system** function. Here are two examples:

```
BEGIN {
    system("tput clear")            Clears the screen
    system("date") }                Executes the UNIX date command
```

You should be familiar with all the functions discussed in this section as they are used in a wide variety of situations. We'll use them again in **perl**. **awk** features some more built-in variables and functions and also allows the user to define her own functions.

18.13 CONTROL FLOW—THE if STATEMENT

awk has practically all the features of a modern programming language. It has conditional structures (the **if** statement) and loops (**while** and **for**). They all execute a body of statements depending on the success or failure of the *control command*. This is simply a condition that is specified in the first line of the construct. Since you have already been introduced to similar structures in the shell, they will be described briefly in these sections.

Table 18.3 Built-in Functions in **awk**

Function	Description
int(x)	Returns integer value of x
sqrt(x)	Returns square root of x
length	Returns length of complete line
length(x)	Returns length of x
substr(stg,m,n)	Returns portion of string of length n, starting from position m in string stg
index(s1,s2)	Returns position of string s2 in string s1
split(stg,arr, ch)	Splits string stg into array arr using ch as delimiter; returns number of fields
system("cmd")	Runs UNIX command cmd and returns its exit status

The **if** statement can be used when the && and || are found to be inadequate for certain tasks. Its behavior is well known to all programmers, and has also been elaborated in Section 14.6. The statement here takes the form

```
if ( condition is true ) {
    statements
} else {                          else is optional
    statements
}
```

Like in C, none of the control flow constructs need to use curly braces if there's only one *statement* to be executed. But when there are multiple actions to take, the statements must be enclosed within a pair of curly braces. Moreover, the control command must be enclosed in parentheses.

Most of the addresses that have been used so far reflect the logic normally used in the **if** statement. In a previous example, you had selected lines where the basic pay exceeded 7500, by using the condition as the selection criteria:

```
$6 > 7500 {
```

An alternative form of this logic places the condition inside the action component rather than the selection criteria. But this form requires the **if** statement:

```
awk -F"|" '{ if ($6 > 7500) printf  .....
```

if can be used with the comparison operators and the special symbols ~ and !~ to match a regular expression. When used in combination with the logical operators || and &&, **awk** programming becomes quite easy and powerful. Some of the earlier pattern matching expressions are rephrased in the following, this time in the form used by **if**:

```
if ( NR >= 3 && NR <= 6 )
if ( $3 == "director" || $3 == "chairman" )
if ( $3 ~ /^g.m/ )
if ( $2 !~ /[aA]gg?[ar]+wal/ )
if ( $2 ~ /[cC]ho[wu]dh?ury|sa[xk]s?ena/ )
```

To illustrate the use of the optional **else** statement, let's assume that the dearness allowance is 25% of basic pay when the latter is less than 600, and 1000 otherwise. The **if-else** structure that implements this logic looks like this:

```
if ( $6 < 6000 )
    da = 0.25*$6
else
    da  = 1000
```

You can even replace the above **if** construct with a compact conditional structure:

```
$6 < 6000 ? da = 0.25*$6 : da = 1000
```

This is the form that C and **perl** use to implement the logic of a simple if-else construct. The ? and : act as separators of the two actions.

When you have more than one statement to be executed, they must be bounded by a pair of curly braces (as in C). For example, if the factors determining the hra and da are in turn dependent on the basic pay itself, then you need to use terminators:

```
if ( $6 < 6000 ) {
    hra = 0.50*$6
    da = 0.25*$6
} else {
    hra = 0.40*$6
    da  = 1000
}
```

Note: There's no **endif** or **fi** terminator for the **if** statement used in **awk**. **awk** uses the { and } to define a block of code.

18.14 LOOPING WITH for

awk supports two loops—**for** and **while**. They both execute the loop body as long as the control command returns a true value. **for** has two forms. The easier one resembles its C counterpart. A simple example illustrates the first form:

```
for ( K=1 ; K<=9 ; K+= 2 )
```

This form also consists of three components; the first component initializes the value of K, the second checks the condition with every iteration, while the third sets the increment used for every iteration. **for** is useful for centering text, and the following example uses **awk** with **echo** in a pipeline to do that:

```
$ echo "
> Income statement\nfor\nthe month of August, 2002\nDepartment : Sales" |
> awk '{ for (k = 1 ; k < (55 - length($0)) / 2 ; k++)
> printf "%s"," "
> print $0 }'
```

```
          Income statement
                for
       the month of August, 2002
          Department : Sales
```

The loop here uses the first **printf** statement to print the required number of spaces (page width assumed to be 55). The line is then printed with the second **printf** statement, which falls outside the loop. This is a useful routine which can be used to center some titles that normally appear at the beginning of a report.

18.14.1 Using for with an Associative Array

The second form of the **for** loop exploits the associative feature of **awk**'s arrays. This form is also seen in **perl** but not in the commonly used languages like C and Java. The loop selects each index of an array:

```
for ( k in array )
    commands
```

Here, k is the subscript of the array *arr*. Because k can also be a string, we can use this loop to print all environment variables. We simply have to pick up each subscript of the ENVIRON array:

```
$ nawk 'BEGIN {
>    for (key in ENVIRON)
>       print key "=" ENVIRON[key]
> }'
LOGNAME=sumit
MAIL=/var/mail/sumit
PATH=/usr/bin::/usr/local/bin:/usr/ccs/bin
TERM=xterm
HOME=/home/sumit
SHELL=/bin/bash
   ......
```

Because the index is actually a string, we can use any field as the index. We can even use elements of the array as counters. Using our sample database, we can display a count of the employees, grouped according to designation (the third field). You can use the string value of $3 as the subscript of the array kount[]:

```
$ awk -F"|" '{ kount[$3]++ }
> END { for ( desig in kount)
> print desig, kount[desig] }' empn.1st
g.m.       4
chairman   1
executive  2
director   4
manager    2
d.g.m.     2
```

The program here analyzes the database to reveal the break-up of employees, grouped on their designation. The array kount[ ] takes as its subscript nonnumeric values like g.m., chairman, executive, etc. **for** is invoked in the END section to print the subscript (desig) and the number of occurrences of the subscript (kount[desig]). Note that you don't need to sort the input file to print this report!

Note: The same SQL-style logic has already been implemented by using three commands in a pipeline—**cut**, **sort** and **uniq** *(12.8.1)*. That one used only a single line of code!

18.15 LOOPING WITH while

The **while** loop has a similar role to play; it repeatedly iterates the loop until the control command succeeds. For example, the previous **for** loop used for centering text can be easily replaced with a **while** construct:

```
k = 0                                          k first initialized
while (k < (55 - length($0))/2) {
     printf "%s", " "
     k++
}
print $0
```

The loop here prints a space and increments the value of k with every iteration. The condition (k < (55 - length($0))/2) is tested at the beginning of every iteration, and the loop body performed only if the test succeeds. In this way, the entire line is filled with a string of spaces before the actual text is printed with **print $0**.

Note that the **length** function has been used with an argument ($0). This **awk** understands to be the entire line. Since **length**, in the absence of an argument, uses the entire line anyway, $0 can be omitted. Similarly, **print $0** may also be replaced by simply **print**.

18.16 CONCLUSION

awk, like **sed**, violates the do-one-thing-well philosophy that generally characterizes UNIX tools. Although presented in this chapter as a utility filter, it's more of a scripting language. An **awk** program is often a fraction of the size of its C counterpart. However, **awk** has been completely overwhelmed in sheer power by **perl**—the latest and most notable addition to the UNIX tool kit for several years. **perl** is even more compact, is faster, and in every sense better than **awk**. **perl** is taken up in Chapter 19.

WRAP UP

The **awk** filter combines features of several filters. **awk** can manipulate individual fields ($1, $2, etc.) in a line ($0). It uses **sed**-type addresses and the built-in variable NR to determine line numbers. Each **print** or **printf** statement can be used with the shell's operators for redirection and piping.

awk identifies the type of a variable from its context and makes the necessary string or numeric conversions when performing computation or string handling. **awk** overcomes a shell limitation by handling decimal numbers.

awk uses the special operators ~ and !~ to match regular expressions. The ^ and $ are used to anchor a pattern at the beginning or end of a *field* rather than the line.

awk can take instructions from an external file (-f). The BEGIN and END sections are used to do some pre- and post-processing work.

awk built-in variables can be used to specify the field delimiter (FS), number of fields (NF) and filename (FILENAME). awk uses one-dimensional arrays where the array subscript can be a string as well.

awk has a number of built-in functions. You can find the length (**length**), extract a substring (**substr**) and find the location (**index**) of a string within a larger string. The **system** function executes a UNIX command.

The **if** statement uses the return value of its control command to determine program flow. A special form of the **for** loop uses an array with a nonnumeric subscript. The **while** loop repeats a set of instructions as long as its control command returns a true value.

perl is better than **awk**.

Test Your Understanding

18.1 What is the difference between **print** and **print $0**? Is the **print** statement necessary for printing a line?

18.2 Implement the following commands in **awk**: (i) **head -n 5 foo** (ii) **sed -n '5,10p' foo** (iii) **tail +20 foo** (iv) **grep negroponte foo**

18.3 Print only the odd-numbered lines of a file.

18.4 How do you delete all blank lines (including those that contain whitespace) from a file?

18.5 Use **awk** to locate lines longer than 100 and smaller than 150 characters.

18.6 How do you print the last field without knowing the number of fields in a line?

18.7 Split empn.1st so that lines are saved in two separate files depending on whether the salary exceeds 6000.

18.8 Find out recursively the files in your home directory that have been last modified on January 6 of the current year at the 11th hour.

18.9 Find out the total space usage of ordinary files in the current directory.

18.10 Use a **for** loop to center the output of the command **echo "DOCUMENT LIST"**, where the page width is 55 characters.

18.11 Repeat the previous exercise with a **while** loop.

18.12 Write a shell script that uses **awk** to find the total size of all ordinary files owned by a user (which could be anywhere in the system), whose name is specified as argument. First check whether the user is available in /etc/passwd.

18.13 Write an **awk** program to provide extra spaces at the end of a line (if required) so that the line length is maintained at 127.

18.14 A file contains a fixed number of fields in the form of space-delimited numbers. Write an **awk** program to print the lines as well as a total of its rows and columns. The program doesn't need to know the number of fields in each line.

Flex Your Brain

18.1 Display from /etc/passwd a list of users and their shells for those using the Korn shell or Bash. Order the output by the absolute pathname of the shell used.

18.2 Find out the next available UID in /etc/passwd after ignoring all system users placed at the beginning and up to the occurrence of the user nobody.

18.3 The **tar** command on one system can't accept absolute pathnames longer than 100 characters. How can you generate a list of such files?

18.4 Devise a sequence to examine recursively all ordinary files in the current directory and display their total space usage. Hard-linked files will be counted only once.

18.5 Invert the name of the individual in emp.1st (12.1) so that the last name occurs first.

18.6 Devise a shell script that kills a process by specifying its name rather than the PID.

18.7 From a **tar** archive print only the pathnames of directories. Directory pathnames end with a / but the **tar** output may contain a variable number of fields.

18.8 How do you list the users currently using the system along with a count of the number of times they have logged in?

18.9 Develop an **awk** program to summarize from the list of all processes, a count of processes run by every user (including root).

18.10 Write an **awk** sequence in a shell script which accepts input from the standard input. The program should print the total of any column specified as script argument. For instance, prog1 | awk_prog 3 should print the total of the third column in the output of prog1.

18.11 A stamp dealer maintains a price list that displays the country, the Scott catalog number, year of issue, description and price:

```
Kenya 288-92 1984 Heron Plover Thrush Gonolek Apalis $6.60
Surinam 643-54 1983 Butterflies $7.50
Seychelles 831-34 2002 WWF Frogs set of 4 $1.40
Togo 1722-25 1996 Cheetah, Zebra, Antelope $5.70
```

Write an **awk** program to print a formatted report of the data as well as the total price. Note that the description contains a variable number of words.

18.12 Develop a control-break **awk** program that reads empn.1st and prints a report that groups employees of the same department. For each department, the report should print

  (i) the department name at the top.
  (ii) the remaining details of every person in the department.
  (iii) total salary bill for that department.

Do you need to process the input before it is read by **awk**?

perl—The Master Manipulator

perl is UNIX's latest major acquisition and one of its finest. Developed by Larry Wall, this Practical Extraction and Report Language is often hailed as the "Swiss Army Officer's Knife" of the UNIX system. In **perl**, Wall invented a general-purpose tool which is at once a programming language and the mother of all filters. **perl** is standard on Linux and also offered on Solaris 8. However, it is free and executables are available for all UNIX flavors (*http://www.perl.com*).

perl combines the power of some of the most powerful UNIX tools—the shell, **grep**, **tr**, **sed** and **awk**. In fact, there's nothing these tools can do, which **perl** can't. It has all the control structures that you could possibly have seen anywhere. **perl** can handle files, directories and processes and also understands all the regular expressions that we have discussed so far. In spite of offering so much, **perl** is faster than the shell and **awk**.

WHAT YOU WILL LEARN

- Gain an overview of a sample **perl** program.
- Use **chop** to remove the last character of a line or variable.
- Use the escape sequences and concatenation operators.
- Use the superior string handling features.
- Specify loops both in the command line and inside a script for reading files.
- Use the **foreach** loop for working with a list.
- Use *lists* and *scalar* arrays and their operators.
- Split and join a line with **split** and **join**.
- Use **grep** to search an array.
- Handle *associative arrays* with a nonnumeric subscript.
- Handle substitution with regular expressions, the **s** and **tr** commands.
- Use *filehandles* to access a file or stream.
- Test the file attributes.
- Develop *subroutines* for repeated use.

TOPICS OF SPECIAL INTEREST

- The significance of the default variable, $_, and how its presence can be felt everywhere.
- The special regular expression characters and escape sequences that **perl** uses for pattern matching.

19.1 perl PRELIMINARIES

A **perl** program runs in a special interpretive mode; the entire script is compiled internally in memory before being executed. Unlike other interpreted languages like the shell and **awk**, script errors are generated before execution itself. With this simple one-liner you can test whether **perl** is in your PATH:

```
$ perl -e 'print("GNUs Not Unix\n") ;'
GNUs Not Unix
```

perl doesn't behave like a filter here in printing the GNU acronym, but more like **echo**. Unlike **awk**, printing isn't **perl**'s default action, so you have to specify it explicitly. Like in C, all **perl** statements end with a semicolon.

perl can do a lot of useful things from the command line when used with the -e option. However, most **perl** programs are big—often very big—and are better placed in .pl files. The program, **sample.pl** (Fig. 19.1), shows the use of variables and computation.

We used the interpreter line as the first line in all of our shell scripts (14.1); we'll use a similar line for all of our **perl** scripts as well. **perl** variables need the $ prefix both in the definition ($name = <STDIN>), as well as in evaluation (The temperature, $name .....). <STDIN> is a *filehandle* (a logical name for a file) representing standard input. Note that the last **print** function doesn't use parentheses. *In general, functions in* **perl** *require parentheses only when their omission leads to ambiguity.* Handling decimal numbers also appears to be no problem.

Let's execute this program in the same way we execute a shell script. This means we need to use **chmod** to make the script executable first. We'll also enter a lot of spaces before keying in the actual input:

```
#!/usr/bin/perl
# Script: sample.pl - Shows use of variables
#
print("Enter your name: ") ;
$name = <STDIN> ;                              # Input from the keyboard
print("Enter a temperature in Centigrade: ") ;
$centigrade=<STDIN> ;                          # Whitespace unimportant
$fahrenheit=$centigrade*9/5 + 32 ;             # Here too
print "The temperature $name in Fahrenheit is $fahrenheit\n" ;
```

Fig. 19.1 **sample.pl**

```
$ chmod +x sample.pl ; sample.pl
Enter your name:                        stallman
Enter a temperature in Centigrade:                 40.5
The temperature                        stallman
in Fahrenheit is 104.9
```

Note that **perl** reads the spaces provided before stallman but not those entered before 40.5 (a number).

Note: You can also execute a **perl** script using **perl** *scriptname*. In that case, you don't need to provide the interpreter line in the first line of the script.

Tip: You can run your **perl** and shell scripts from within the **vi** editor. The technique of doing that is detailed in the Tip of Section 20.8.2.

19.2 THE chop FUNCTION: REMOVING THE LAST CHARACTER

Why did **perl** show the output in two lines? That's because it included the newline generated by *[Enter]* as part of $name. (The shell's **read** statement doesn't do that.) So $name is now actually stallman\n (ignoring the spaces at the front). In many instances, we need to remove the last character—especially when it's a newline. This is done by the **chop** function which is used in the program, **name.pl** (Fig. 19.2).

The **if** conditional here differs from its namesake in C and **awk** in that the curly braces are *always* required—whether it's one or multiple statements to be executed. **chop** removes the last character all right, but here it also assigns the "chopped" value to the same variable. This time, you'll find the output in a single line:

```
$ name.pl
Enter your name: larry wall
larry wall, have a nice day
```

```
#!/usr/bin/perl
# Script: name.pl - Demonstrates use of chop
#
print("Enter your name: ") ;
$name = <STDIN> ;
chop($name) ;                          # Removes newline character from $name
if ( $name ne "" ) {
    print("$name, have a nice day\n") ;
} else {
    print("You have not entered your name\n") ;
}
```

Fig. 19.2 name.pl

There are other ways of using **chop**:

```
chop($name = <STDIN>) ;
$lname = chop($name) ;
```
Reading and assigning together
lname stores last character chopped

The first statement combines, in C-style, both reading and chopping in a single statement. The second one is a special case of the **substr** function for extracting the last character of a string.

Tip: You should remember to use **chop** whenever you read a line from the keyboard or a file unless you deliberately want to retain the newline character.

19.3 VARIABLES AND OPERATORS

As you would have already seen, **perl** variables have no type and need no initialization. Strings and numbers can be as large as the machine permits. These are some of the variable attributes that one should remember:

- When a string is used for numeric computation or comparison, **perl** immediately converts it into a number.

- If a variable is undefined, it is assumed to be a null string and a null string is numerically zero. Incrementing an uninitialized variable returns 1:

```
$ perl -e '$x++ ; print("$x\n");'
1
```

- If the first character of a string is not numeric, the entire string becomes numerically equivalent to zero.

perl uses the same set of operators as **awk** for numeric comparison *(18.5.2)* with ==, !=, >, <, >= and <=. For string comparison, you'll have to use similar operators the shell uses—eq, ne, gt, lt, ge and le (but without the hyphen).

When **perl** compares strings, it has to match the ASCII value of each character starting from the left. Thus, b is greater than aa1234 because the first character, b, is greater than a in the ASCII collating sequence. Similarly, a is greater than Z.

Like the shell but unlike **awk**, **perl** supports both unquoted, single- and double-quoted strings. Unquoted strings can't contain a special character. Every character in a single-quoted string is treated literally (including the newline); this lets us protect spaces and the \. Double-quotes allow the inclusion of escape sequences and variables:

```
$x = $y = $z = 5 ;
$name = "larry\t\twall\n" ;
$y = "A" ;    $y++ ;
$z = "P01" ; $z++ ;
$todays_date = `date` ;
$name = 'steve jobs' ;
$result = "\U$name\E" ;
$result = "\u$name\E" ;
```
Multiple assignments
Two tabs and newline
This becomes B
This becomes P02!
Uses command substitution

$result *is* STEVE JOBS
$result *is* Steve jobs

There are some unusual things to observe here. The escape sequences \U and \u convert to uppercase the entire string and the first character, respectively. The end of the affected area is marked by \E.

perl also offers the C and **awk** feature of conditional assignment, using the ? and :. The following assignment determines whether February has 28 or 29 days:

```
$feb_days = $year % 4 == 0 ? 29 : 28 ;
```

Every expression or comparison in **perl** returns a value, and you can set this value to a variable. **perl** emulates C by using 1 to signify the true value of an expression or comparison. The following comparison sets $x:

```
$x = $y == $z ;
```

Here, $x has the value 1 if $y and $z are equal; otherwise it has the value 0.

19.3.1 The Concatenation Operators . and x

Unlike in the shell, the expression xy (or ${x}${y}) isn't interpreted as variable concatenation. Rather, **perl** uses the . (dot) operator for concatenating variables:

```
$ perl -e '$x=maruti ; $y=".com" ; print($x . $y . "\n") ;'
maruti.com
```

Note that $y itself contains a dot, so it had to be placed within quotes. For the sake of readability, it's preferable to have whitespace on either side of the dot operator.

perl uses the x operator to repeat a string. The following statement prints 40 asterisks on the screen:

```
$ perl -e 'print "*" x 40 ;'
****************************************
```

The string to print isn't restricted to a single character; it can even be an expression. This operator is most useful in printing rulers for reports.

19.4 THE STRING HANDLING FUNCTIONS

perl has all of the string functions that you can think of. Some of them were seen in **awk** and the others are supported by compiled languages. Two important functions, **split** and **join**, deserve discussion in separate sections. In most cases, we are interested in the return values of these functions, but sometimes we use them for their side effect.

length and **index** play their usual role (*18.12*), but the **substr** function is quite versatile. The following examples tell the story:

```
$x = "abcdijklm" ;
print length($x) ;                 This is 9
print index($x,j) ;                This is 5
substr($x,4,0) = "efgh" ;          Stuffs $x with efgh
print "$x" ;                       $x is now abcdefghijklm
```

```
$y = substr($x,-3,2) ;                              Extracts from right
print "$y" ;                                         $y is kl
```

The **reverse** function, which can also operate on an array, reverses the characters in *str* and returns the reversed string:

```
$x = "abcd" ;
print reverse($x) ;                                  Prints dcba
```

substr can do more than what it is normally expected to do; it can extract characters from the *right* of the string, and insert or replace a string. Here, **substr($x,4,0)** stuffs the string $x with efgh without replacing any characters; 0 denotes nonreplacement. **substr($x,-3,2)** extracts two characters from the third position on the *right*.

There are four functions for changing case of text. **uc** converts to uppercase its entire argument, while **ucfirst** converts only the first character to uppercase:

```
$name = "larry wall" ;
$result = uc($name);                                  $result is LARRY WALL
$result = ucfirst($name);                             $result is Larry Wall
```

The functions **lc** and **lcfirst** perform opposite functions of their "uc" counterparts. Apart from converting case, **perl** can filter the contents of variables in the same way UNIX filters manipulate text. We'll be discussing the **tr** and **s** functions later—two important functions that **perl** uses for substitution.

19.5 SPECIFYING FILENAMES IN COMMAND LINE

Unlike **awk**, **perl** provides specific functions to open a file and then perform I/O operations on it. However, using special symbols, these actions can occur "beneath the hood." The diamond operator, <>, is used for reading lines from a file. For example, <STDIN> reads a line from standard input, and <> reads a line from the filename specified as argument. Here are two ways of reading dept.lst:

```
perl -e 'print while (<>)' dept.lst                  File opening implied
perl -e 'print <>' dept.lst                          As above but loop also implied
```

The context of the <> operator is different in these two examples. The first is interpreted in *scalar* context which signifies reading one line. The second is interpreted in *list* context where it represents all lines. You can use **while (<>)** to read multiple files:

```
perl -e 'print while (<>)' foo1 foo2 foo3
```

perl also supports the -n option which implies this loop. Make sure that -n precedes -e when using this feature.

```
perl -ne 'print' dept.lst                            -en won't work here!
```

The advantage of this form is that you can use simple one-line conditionals in the command line itself. Here is a bare-bones **grep** command at work:

```
$ perl -ne 'print if /\bgupta/' emp.lst
5423|n.k. gupta        |chairman |admin        |30/08/56|5400
```

This one-line conditional uses the regular expression /\bgupta. **perl** uses an enlarged regular expression set (Table 19.1), where \b is used to match on a word boundary. This eliminated sengupta and dasgupta from the output. We'll see more of **perl** regular expressions later.

19.5.1 Reading Files in a Script

The previous **perl** statement could have been placed in a script. This time, a loop is implied, so we have to use **perl** with the -n option in the interpreter line:

```
#!/usr/bin/perl -n
print if /\bgupta/ ;
```

We often need to do some processing outside the loop—like printing a heading or a total. The -n option doesn't allow that, so we have to set up the **while** loop inside the script:

```
#!/usr/bin/perl
printf("%30s", "LIST OF EMPLOYEES\n") ;
while (<>) {
    print if /\bgupta|ag+[ar][ar]wal/ ;          Using an extended RE
}
print "\nREPORT COMPLETE\n" ;
```

What you see above is something that we do many a time: print a heading before the detail and then something after the detail.

Tip: For pure filtering, use **perl -n** as the interpreter name at the beginning of the script. No explicit **while** loop is then required. If you have headers and footers to print, then drop the -n option and set up a **while** loop inside the script.

19.6 $_: THE DEFAULT VARIABLE

The previous programs used **print** without specifying what to print; **perl** automatically understood it to be the entire line. **perl** assigns the line read from input to a special variable, $_; often called the **default variable**. This is an extremely important variable, and you must understand its magical properties if you want to write compact code.

Suppose you have to prefix a line number to every line. This is where you need $_ to explicitly specify the line. The comments in the script, **grep1.pl** (Fig. 19.3) show what **perl** does internally with $_.

chop, <> and pattern matching operate on $_ by default, the reason why it isn't explicitly specified anywhere except in the **print** statement. Though its function is difficult to define exactly, $_ often represents the last line read or last pattern matched. We used it with the **print** statement only because it had to be concatenated with $slno; otherwise **print** also operates on $_ by default. The program locates the email addresses of all senders from the *velvet.com* domain:

```
$ grep1.pl $HOME/mbox
1  From: "Caesar, Julius" <Julius_Caesar@velvet.com>
2  From: "Goddard, John" <John_Goddard@velvet.com>
3  From: "Barnack, Oscar" <Oscar_Barnack@velvet.com>
```

```
#!/usr/bin/perl
# grep1.pl: Extracts the From: headers from the mailbox
#
while (<>) {                                    # Actually ($_ = <>)
    chop() ;                                    # chop($_)
    if (/From:.*\@velvet.com/) {                # if ($_ =~ /From:.*\@velvet ...)
        $slno++ ;
        print($slno . "   " . $_ . "\n") ;
    }
}
```

Fig. 19.3 grep1.pl

You can reassign the value of $_. Since many **perl** functions operate on $_ by default, you may often want to set $_ to the expression you are working with. This allows you to use these functions without specifying either $_ or any variable name as argument.

19.7 CURRENT LINE NUMBER ($.) AND THE RANGE OPERATOR (..)

We'll now learn the use of two special operators for addressing lines by their numbers. **perl** stores the current line number in another special variable, $. ($ followed by a dot). You can use it to represent a line address and select lines from anywhere:

```
perl -ne 'print if ($. < 4)' foo                            Like head -n 3
perl -ne 'print if ($. > 7 && $. < 11)' foo                 Like sed -n '8,10p'
```

perl has a host of built-in variables, and $. is **perl**'s counterpart of **awk**'s NR variable. But **perl** has shortcuts to these comparisons too. Use its range operator, .. (2 dots):

```
perl -ne 'print if (1..3)' foo
perl -ne 'print if (8..10)' foo
```

For selecting multiple segments from a file, you can use multiple **print** statements or you can use compound conditions:

```
if ((1..2) || (13..15)) { print ; }
```

Unlike $_ which can be reassigned, $. always retains the current line number. If all input lines are passed through, you can use $. to number lines; a separate variable like $slno is not required.

19.8 LISTS AND ARRAYS

Lists and arrays lie at the very heart and soul of **perl**. **perl** has a large number of functions that can manipulate them. The following is an example of a list:

```
( "Jan", 123, "How are you", -34.56, Dec )
```

A list need not contain data of the same type. For this list to be usable, it needs to be assigned to a set of variables:

```
($mon, $num, $stg, $neg, $mon2) = ( "Jan", 123, "How are you", -34.56, Dec );
```

When the size of a list can be determined only at runtime, we need an array to hold the list. These arrays are of two types—*scalar lists* and *associative arrays*. We'll be looking at scalar lists in this section. Let's assign the following list to a three-element array, @month:

```
@month = ("Jan", "Feb", "Mar") ;                    $month[0] is Jan
```

These are quoted strings, and **perl** supports the **qw** function that can make short work of this assignment:

```
@month = qw/Jan Feb Mar/;                    No commas and no quotes
print $month[1] ;                            Prints Feb
```

Arrays in **perl** are not of fixed size; they grow and shrink dynamically as elements are added and deleted. Each element of the array is accessed using $mon[$n$], where n is the index, which starts from zero. In the previous example, $month[0] evaluates to the string Jan and $month[3] is undefined.

Array assignment is also quite flexible in **perl**. You can use the range operator or even assign values selectively in a single statement:

```
@x = (1..12) ;                                          Assigns first twelve integers
@month[1,3..5,12] = ("Jan", "Mar", "Apr", "May", "Dec") ;
@month[1,3..5,12] = qw/Jan Mar Apr May Dec/ ;           Same
```

In the second example, note that $month[4] is Apr and $month[0] and $month[2] are null if they weren't defined previously.

Like <>, the array @month can be interpreted in both scalar and list context. When used as the *rvalue* of an assignment, @month evaluates to the length of the array:

```
$length = @month;                            Length of the array
```

The $# prefix to an array name signifies the last index of the array. It's always one less than the size of the array:

```
$last_index = $#month;
```

The $# mechanism can also be used to set the array to a specific size or delete all its elements. Previously defined array elements that fall outside the new index are deleted:

```
$#month = 10;                                Array size now 11
$#month = -1;                                No elements
```

Reading a File into an Array   An array can also be populated by the <> operator. Each line then becomes an element of the array:

```
@line = <> ;                                 Reads entire file from command line
print @line ;                                Prints entire file
```

The entire file is read with a single statement (@line = <>), and each element of the array, @line, contains a line of the file (including the newline).

Note: When you read a file into an array, every element will have newline as the last character. The **chop** function, when applied to arrays, removes the newline from each and every element of the array, and not just the last element.

Before we use the array handling functions, let's examine the script, **ar_in_ar.pl** (Fig. 19.4 that illustrates some features of **perl** arrays.

The array is populated in three stages, and the final filling is done with the **qw** function. Observe that **perl** permits a second array (@days_between) to form part of another array @days. The length of the array is directly available in $length and indirectly in $#days before it is reassigned to 5. Because the index of an array starts from 0, $length is one greater than $#days:

```
$ ar_in_ar.pl
The third day of the week is Wed
The days of the week are Mon Tue Wed Thu Fri Sat Sun
The number of elements in the array is 7
The last subscript of the array is 6
$days[6] is now
```

Note that after resizing the array (with $#days = 5), $days[6] is now a null string.

19.8.1 ARGV[]: Command Line Arguments

perl also uses command line arguments which are stored in the system array @ARGV[]; the first argument is $ARGV[0]. Note that the command name itself *isn't* stored in this element; it is held in another system variable, $0. The next program, **leap_year.pl** (Fig. 19.5), expects a year as the argument string and determines whether it's a leap year or not.

We used the **die** function to simply print its argument and exit a script. **die** is most often used to handle errors in opening a file or in discarding erroneous user input. Note that the value of @ARGV

```perl
#!/usr/bin/perl
# ar_in_ar.pl - Shows use of arrays
#
@days_between = ("Wed", "Thu") ;
@days = (Mon, Tue, @days_between, Fri) ;
@days[5,6] = qw/Sat Sun/ ;
$length = @days ;                           # @days in scalar context
#
print("The third day of the week is $days[2]\n") ;
print("The days of the week are @days\n") ;
print("The number of elements in the array is $length\n") ;
print("The last subscript of the array is $#days\n") ;
$#days = 5;                                  #Resize the array
print("\$days[6] is now $days[6]\n") ;
```

Fig. 19.4 ar_in_ar.pl

```
#!/usr/bin/perl
# Script: leap_year.pl - Determines whether a year is a leap year or not
#
die("You have not entered the year\n") if (@ARGV == 0 ) ;
$year = $ARGV[0] ;                              # The first argument
$last2digits = substr($year, -2, 2) ;           # Extract from the right
if ($last2digits eq "00") {
    $yesorno = ($year % 400 == 0 ? "certainly" : "not" ) ;
}
else {
    $yesorno = ($year % 4 == 0 ? "certainly" : "not" ) ;
}
print("$year is " . $yesorno . " a leap year\n") ;
```

Fig. 19.5 leap_year.pl

(without the subscripts) equates to the length of the array. You also see here a rather unusual use of the **substr** function. Let's run the program:

```
$ leap_year.pl
You have not entered the year
$ leap_year.pl 2004
2004 is certainly a leap year
$ leap_year.pl 1997
1997 is not a leap year
```

There is one drawback with the above script; you have to invoke the program five times if you want to subject five numbers to leap year checks. This can be taken care of by the **foreach** loop which is taken up soon.

19.8.2 Modifying Array Contents

perl has a number of functions for manipulating the contents of an array. A few string handling functions (like, **chop** and **reverse**) also apply to an array. **perl** supports operations both at the left and right of an array. In that sense, we can treat the array both as a stack and a queue.

For deleting elements at the beginning or end, **perl** uses the **shift** and **pop** functions:

```
@list = (3..5, 9) ;                   This is 3 4 5 9
shift(@list) ;                        The 3 goes away, becomes 4 5 9
pop(@list) ;                          Removes last element, becomes 4 5
```

The **unshift** and **push** functions add elements to an array. Let's apply them to the residual value of @list at the end of the previous example:

```
unshift(@list, 1..3) ;                Adds 1, 2 and 3—1 2 3 4 5
push(@list, 9) ;                      Pushes 9 at end—1 2 3 4 5 9
```

The **splice** function can do everything these four functions can do. Additionally, it uses up to four arguments to add or remove elements at any location of the array. The second argument is the offset from where the insertion or removal should begin. The third argument represents the number of elements to be removed. If it is 0, elements have to be added. The new replaced list is specified by the fourth argument (if present):

```
splice(@list, 5, 0, 6..8) ;              Adds at 6th location—1 2 3 4 5 6 7 8 9
splice(@list, 0, 2) ;                    Removes from beginning—3 4 5 6 7 8 9
```

We'll be using some of these functions later in another script after we have examined the **foreach** loop and the **join** function.

19.9 foreach: LOOPING THROUGH A LIST

perl provides an extremely useful **foreach** construct to loop through a list. The construct borrowed from the C shell has a very simple syntax:

```
foreach $var (@arr) {
   statements
}
```

Functionally, **foreach** works like the **for** loop of the shell. Each element of the array @arr is picked up and assigned to the variable $var. The iteration is continued as many times as there are items in the list. The program, **square_root.pl** (Fig. 19.6), uses **foreach** to calculate the square root of some numbers.

Every element in the array @ARGV is assigned to the variable $number. You can now supply as many arguments to the script as you like:

```
$ square_root.pl 123 456 25
The program you are running is ./square_root.pl
The square root of 123 is 11.0905365064094
The square root of 456 is 21.3541565040626
The square root of 25 is 5
```

We have previously noted $_ making its presence felt everywhere, and this is no exception. In the above example, you need not use $number at all. **foreach** stores each item in $_, and **sqrt** works on it as well:

```
foreach (@ARGV) {                        $_ is the default variable
   print("The square root of $_ is " . sqrt() . "\n") ;
```

```
#!/usr/bin/perl
# square_root.pl - Finds the square root of each command line argument
#
print("The program you are running is $0\n") ;
foreach $number (@ARGV) {                # Each element of @ARGV goes to $number
    print("The square root of $number is " . sqrt($number) . "\n") ;
}
```

Fig. 19.6 square_root.pl

It's not that **foreach** is used with named arrays only. It can be used with lists generated by UNIX commands as well. You can use command substitution to generate the list:

```
foreach $file (`ls`) {
```

This loop construct picks up each file in the current directory and assigns it to the variable $file. We'll use this feature later in the chapter.

Note: perl has a **for** loop as well. The following construct performs its enclosing code block three times: **for ($i=0 ; $i<3 ; $i++) {**

19.10 split: SPLITTING INTO A LIST OR ARRAY

CGI programmers using **perl** need to understand two important array handling functions—**split** and **join**. **split** breaks up a line or expression into fields. These fields are assigned either to variables or an array. Here are the two syntaxes:

```
($var1, $var2, $var3..... ) = split(/sep/,stg) ;
@arr = split(/sep/,stg) ;
```

split takes up to three arguments but is usually used with two. It splits the string *stg* on *sep*, but here *sep* can be a literal character or a regular expression (which could expand to multiple characters). *stg* is optional, and in its absence, $_ is used as default. The fields resulting from the split are assigned either to the variables $*var1*, $*var2* and so on, or to the array @*arr*.

19.10.1 Splitting into Variables

We'll now use the first syntactical form in our next program, **3_numbers.pl** (Fig. 19.7), to assign three numbers, taken from the keyboard, to a set of variables.

To understand how **split** breaks up the variable $numstring and assigns three new variables, let's run this program twice:

```
$ 3_numbers.pl
Enter three numbers: [Enter]              Nothing entered
Nothing entered
```

```
#!/usr/bin/perl
# Script: 3_numbers.pl - Splits a string on whitespace
#
print("Enter three numbers: " ) ;
chop($numstring = <STDIN>) ;
die("Nothing entered\n") if ($numstring eq "") ;
($f_number, $s_number, $l_number) = split(/ /, $numstring) ;
print("The last, second and first numbers are ") ; .
print("$l_number, $s_number and $f_number.\n" ) ;
```

Fig. 19.7 3_numbers.pl

```
$ 3_numbers.pl
Enter three numbers: 123 345 567
The last, second and first numbers are 567, 345 and 123.
```

When the three numbers are entered, $numstring acquires the value 123 345 567\n, from where the newline is subsequently chopped off. **split** acts on this string using a *single* space as delimiter, and breaks it up into three variables.

19.10.2 Splitting into an Array

What do you do when a line contains a large number of fields? In that case, it's better to split it into an array rather than variables. The following statement fills up the array @thislist:

```
@thislist = split(/:/, $string) ;
```

$string is often the last line read, in which case we can replace it with $_, or rather, drop it altogether:

```
@thislist = split(/:/) ;                          split uses $_ by default
```

In the next program, **rep1.pl** (Fig. 19.8), we print some specific fields from the sample database with the last name shown before the first name. We need to use **split** twice—first on the | delimiter and then again on the space that separates the first and last names. The program selects the first four lines and prints a total of the salary field for the selected lines.

The second **split** was used to enable the reversal of the first and last names, with a comma between them. We also use the range operator (..) to print only the first four lines, and $. to print the current line number as serial number:

```
$ rep1.pl emp.lst
    1 shukla, a.k.          sales           6000
    2 sharma, jai           production      7000
```

```
#!/usr/bin/perl
# Script: rep1.pl - Uses split twice; prints with first and last name reversed
#
while (<>) {
    chop;
    @field = split (/\|/) ;    # $_ is used by default
    if (1..4) {                # Lines 1 to 4
        $dept = $field[3] ; $name = $field[1] ; $salary = $field[5] ;
        ($f_name, $l_name) = split(/ +/, $name);
        $name = $l_name . ", " . $f_name ;       # Reusing $name
        $totsal += $salary ;
        printf( "%3d %-20s %-11s %4d\n", $., $name, $dept, $salary) ;
    }
}
printf("%35s %5d\n", "Total Salary: ", $totsal) ;
```

Fig. 19.8 rep1.pl

```
3 chakrobarty, sumit   marketing   6000
4 sengupta, barun      personnel   7800
          Total Salary:  26800
```

split can also be used without an explicit assignment, in which case it populates the built-in array, @_:

```
split (/:/) ;
```
Fills up the array @_

split gets shortened further. The array @_ has the elements $_[0], $_[1] and so forth. You should get used to this form also as you'll see it used in many programs.

Note: When the return value of **split** is not *explicitly* assigned to variables or an array, the built-in array, @_, is automatically assigned. Also, when **split** is used with the null string (//) as delimiter, @_ stores *each* character of the string as a separate element.

19.11 join: JOINING A LIST

The **join** function acts in an opposite manner to **split**. It combines its arguments into a single string and uses the delimiter as the first argument. The remaining arguments could be either an array name or a list of variables or strings to be joined. This is how you provide a space after each day:

```
$weekstring = join(" ", @week_array) ;
$weekstring = join(" ", "Mon", "Tue", "Wed", "Thu", "Fri", "Sat", "Sun") ;
print $weekstring ;
```

Either statement should produce this output:

```
Mon Tue Wed Thu Fri Sat Sun
```

split and **join** often go together. The next program, **rep2.pl** (Fig. 19.9), splits each line of our sample database on the |, adds a century prefix to the date and then joins all fields back. The script is well documented to need elaboration.

Let's now print the first two lines of our transformed database by running the program:

```
$ rep2.pl emp.1st | head -n 2
2233|a.k. shukla    |g.m.     |sales     |12/12/1952|6000
9876|jai sharma      |director |production|12/03/1950|7000
```

```
#!/usr/bin/perl -n
# Script: rep2.pl - Uppercases the name and adds century prefix to the date
#
@line = split(/\|/) ;                             # $_ is assumed
($day, $month, $year) = split(/\//, $line[4]);    # Splits date field
$year = "19" . $year ;                            # Adds century prefix
$line[4] = join("/", $day, $month, $year);        # Rebuilds date field
$line = join("\|", @line);                        # Rebuilds line
print $line;
```

Fig. 19.9 rep2.pl

Joining on a specified delimiter has common applications in everyday programming. Even though we used **join** on a specific delimiter in our examples, the next section uses **join** without any delimiter to perform a very useful task.

19.12 dec2bin.pl: CONVERTING A DECIMAL NUMBER TO BINARY

We'll now consolidate our knowledge of array-handling functions by developing a script, **dec2bin.pl** (Fig. 19.10). This script accepts a decimal number as argument and converts it to binary. You are probably aware that, to do that you have to repeatedly divide a number (rather the quotient) by 2, and then reverse all the collected remainders. We need the **unshift** function here to perform this reversal by filling up an array with the remainder bit that arises from every division.

Like the shell, **perl** also uses the **until** loop with the same meaning. The **join** function is used simply to concatenate all digit strings (0 or 1) that are stored in the array, **@bit_arr**, without using a delimiter at all! The **foreach** loop lets you supply as many numbers as you want in a single invocation of the script:

```
$ dec2bin.pl 2 7 65 191 255
The binary number of 2 is 10
The binary number of 7 is 111
The binary number of 65 is 1000001
The binary number of 191 is 10111111
The binary number of 255 is 11111111
```

You can use this program for determining whether two hosts are in the same subnet (not discussed in this edition) by converting their network addresses to binary.

19.13 grep: SEARCHING AN ARRAY FOR A PATTERN

perl has a **grep** function, and you can guess what it does; it searches an array for a pattern. **grep** also returns an array which stores the found array elements in another array. This is how you search the array, **@dept_arr**, for the pattern marketing:

```
#!/usr/bin/perl
# Script: dec2bin.pl - Converts decimal numbers to binary
#
foreach $number (@ARGV) {
    $original_number = $number ;
    until ($number == 0 ) {
        $bit = $number % 2  ;                      # Find the remainder bit
        unshift (@bit_arr, $bit) ;                 # Insert bit at beginning
        $number = int($number / 2 ) ;
    }
    $binary_number = join ("", @bit_arr) ;         # Join on nothing!
    print("The binary number of $original_number is $binary_number\n") ;
    $#bit_arr = -1 ;                               # Deletes all array elements
}
```

Fig. 19.10 **dec2bin.pl**

```
@found_arr = grep(/marketing/, @dept_arr) ;
```

If **grep** succeeds, the matched lines will be stored as separate elements in @found_arr. You can then check the variable $#found_arr for success or failure. This expression, you'll recall, stores the last index of the array. By definition, this is -1 if the array is null. Using this principle, our next script, **search_array.pl** (Fig. 19.11), accepts a pattern from the user and searches an array that was previously populated by reading the file dept.1st.

We split the first array element of @found_arr to extract the code and description separately. The **for** loop ensures that the program prompts for the code only thrice. It then prints the code description if it finds a match:

```
$ search_array.pl dept.1st
Enter a code to look up: 05
Code = 05    Description = production
Enter a code to look up: 99
Code does not exist
Enter a code to look up: 02
Code = 02    Description = admin
```

It makes a lot of sense to store a table in an array rather than access its disk file repeatedly. **grep** enables table lookups, and is extremely useful for report writing purposes. Like its UNIX counterpart, **grep** also accepts regular expressions for pattern matches, but more of these expressions later.

19.14 ASSOCIATIVE ARRAYS

Like **awk**, **perl** also supports a **hash** or **associative array**. It alternates the array subscripts (called **keys**) and values in a series of strings. When declaring the array, these strings are delimited by commas or the more-friendly => notation:

```
%region = ("N", "North", "S", "South", "E", "East", "W", "West") ;
%region = ("N" => "North", "S" => "South", "E" => "East", "W" => "West") ;
```

```
#!/usr/bin/perl
# Script: search_array.pl - Searches array for a string or regular expression
#
@dept_arr = <> ;                         # Read file into array
for ($i=0 ; $i<3 ; $i++) {               # Can use only three times
    print("Enter a code to look up: ") ;
    chop($code = <STDIN>) ;
    @found_arr = grep (/^$code/, @dept_arr) ;          # Search at beginning
    if ($#found_arr == -1 || $code eq "") {            # -1 means null array
        print("Code does not exist\n") ;
        next ;                           # Go to beginning of loop
    }
    split(/\|/, $found_arr[0]) ;         # Split first element only
    print("Code = $code    Description = $_[1]\n") ;
}
```

Fig. 19.11 search_array.pl

This array uses the % symbol to prefix the array name. This assignment creates an array of four elements where the subscript precedes the value in the array definition. The array subscript, which can also be a string, is enclosed within a pair of curly braces rather than [ ]. For instance, $region{"N"} produces North. CGI programmers must feel totally at home with associative arrays.

We use an associative array, %region, in the program, **region.pl** (Fig. 19.12) to expand region codes. The program shows how to use two associative array functions, **keys** and **values**.

keys stores the list of subscripts in a separate array (here, @key_list), while **values** holds the value of each element in yet another array (here, @value_list). Let's test the script by supplying a couple of single-character strings:

```
$ region.pl S W
The letter S stands for South
The letter W stands for West
The subscripts are S E N W
The values are South East North West
```

There are important implications here. You can separately extract both the keys and their values from an associative array. You can also present these values in the same way the **env** statement shows all environment variables:

```
foreach $key (keys %region) {
    print "$key" . "=" . "$region{$key}\n" ;
}
```

We found out the value of each key and stored it in turn in the variable $key. It's then a simple matter to use it as the subscript of %region. The element $region{$key} stores the value of each key as shown by this output:

```
S=South
E=East
N=North
W=West
```

```
#!/usr/bin/perl
# Script: region.pl - Uses an associative array
#
%region = ("N", "North", "S", "South", "E", "East", "W", "West") ;
foreach $letter (@ARGV) {
    print("The letter $letter stands for $region{$letter}" . "\n" );
}
@key_list = keys(%region) ;                          # List of subscripts
print("The subscripts are @key_list\n") ;
@value_list = values %region  ;                      # List of values
print("The values are @value_list\n") ;
```

Fig. 19.12 region.pl

Normally, **keys** returns the key strings in a random sequence. To order the list alphabetically, you'll often find the **sort** function used with **keys**. You can have both a normal and a reverse sort:

```
foreach $key (sort(keys %region)) {
@key_list = reverse sort keys %region  ;          No ()—OK
```

Note: The built-in array, %ENV, stores all of the shell's environment variables. For instance, $ENV{'PATH'} contains the value of the shell's PATH. You can easily access these variables using the techniques discussed here.

19.14.1 Counting Number of Occurrences

Associative arrays are extremely useful in counting the number of occurrences of an item. From the sample database, you can create a report showing the number of people in each department. We tried a similar exercise before with **awk** *(18.14.1)*, and we'll do it again with **perl**. For a programming language, this is quite some work, but a small **perl** program, **count.pl** (Fig. 19.13), does the job.

The program is divided into two parts. The **while** construct first filters out the values of $dept for each line read, and increments the counter of the respective element of the array %deptlist. After all input has been read, the **foreach** construct assigns each value of the key from %deptlist to the variable $dept. $deptlist{$dept} now contains the accumulated total for each key. This sorted output shows the power of **perl**:

```
$ count.pl emp.lst
accounts   : 2
admin      : 1
marketing  : 4
personnel  : 2
production : 2
sales      : 4
```

With only a few lines of **perl** code you have been able to print the department-wise distribution of people.

```
#!/usr/bin/perl
# Script: count.pl - Counts frequency of occurrence of an item
#
while (<>) {
    split(/\|/) ;                    # | has to be escaped
    $dept = $_[3] ;                  # Department is fourth field
    $deptlist{$dept} += 1 ;          # Same as ++
}
foreach $dept (sort (keys %deptlist)) {
    print("$dept: $deptlist{$dept}\n") ;
}
```

Fig. 19.13 count.pl

19.15 REGULAR EXPRESSIONS AND SUBSTITUTION

perl offers a grand superset of *all* possible regular expressions found in the UNIX system (except the special ones specified by POSIX). You have already used some of them for pattern matching. **perl** understands both basic and extended regular expressions (BRE and ERE) and has some of its own too. You must know well regular expressions and the **sed** and **tr** commands before you can appreciate the material presented in this section.

19.15.1 The s and tr Functions

The **s** and **tr** functions handle all substitution in **perl**. The **s** function is used in the same way as the **s** command in **sed**. **tr** translates characters in just the same way the UNIX **tr** command does, but with a slightly different syntax. This is how we use them:

```
s/:/-/g ;                          Sets $_ when used this way
tr/a-z/A-Z/ ;                      In UNIX, you use tr '[a-z]' '[A-Z]'
```

In either case, you set the system variable, $_. Often, you'll split a line into fields and then use one of these functions for transforming the fields. In that case, you'll have to use the operator, =~, for performing a match and !~ for negating it:

```
$line =~ s/:/-/g ;                 $line is reassigned
$name =~ tr/a-z/A-Z/ ;             Here too
```

s and **tr** also accept flags. **s** accepts the g flag (shown above) for global substitution, and yet another (e) for indicating that the replaced pattern is to be evaluated as an expression. **tr** uses all of the UNIX **tr** options as flags—s squeezes multiple occurrences, c complements and d deletes the character *(12.9.1)*.

The next program, **rep3.pl** (Fig. 19.14), takes the last two digits of the year as user input, and then selects those lines where the year of birth (embedded in the fifth field) matches this input. It then performs some transformation on the selected lines before printing them.

We split the sample database as usual, and then again split the date field to extract the two-digit year. This year string is compared with user input for every line read. If the match succeeds, two changes are made at field level and two more at global level. At the field level, the name is converted to uppercase, and the prefix 9 is added to the emp_id. Both require the use of the regular expression matching operator, =~. The fields are joined before the global changes are carried out. We also change the delimiter to a colon when joining.

To use the **s** and **tr** functions on the entire line (globally), we need to make sure that $_ is properly set. The **join** function cleverly achieves this by assigning its return value to $_. The **s** function first removes all spaces before the delimiter, which has now become a : on account of the previous join. The next **s** function changes every / in the line to a -. This affects only the date field, and rather than place a \ before the /, it's better to change the delimiter used by **s** to a #. The statement is more readable too.

We'll run the script with two inputs—one that exists and one that doesn't exist:

```
#!/usr/bin/perl
# Source: rep3.pl - Uses the s and tr functions for substitution
#
print("Last two digits of date of birth: ");
$yearin = <STDIN> ;
chop($yearin);                      # Remove \n else comparison will fail later

$found = 0;
while (<>) {
    @line = split(/\|/) ;
    $name = $line[1] ; $emp_id = $line[0] ;
    split(/\//, $line[4]);          # Splits date field
    $year =  $_[2] ;                # 2-digit year extracted ...

    if ($year eq $yearin)  {        # .. and compared with user input
        $found = 1;
        $name =~ tr/a-z/A-Z/ ;      # Name field changed to uppercase
        $emp_id =~ s/^/9/ ;         # Adds a "9" prefix to the first field
        $line[0] = $emp_id ;        # Reassign elements of @line with
        $line[1] = $name;           # the two changes made by tr and s
        $_ = join(":", @line) ;     # Assigning to $_ allows use of next
                                    # two s functions without using =~
        s/\s+:/:/g ;                # Removes whitespace before delimiter
        s#/#-#g ;                   # Delimiter in date is now the -
        print ;                     # Print $_
    }
}
print("Year 19" . $yearin . " not found\n") if $found eq 0 ;
```

Fig. 19.14 rep3.pl

```
$ rep3.pl emp.lst
Last two digits of date of birth: 45
96521:LALIT  CHOWDURY:director:marketing:26-09-45:8200
92345:J.B.  SAXENA:g.m.:marketing:12-03-45:8000
$ rep3.pl emp.lst
Last two digits of date of birth: 60
Year 1960 not found
```

19.15.2 Identifying Whitespace, Digits and Words

perl also offers some escaped characters to represent whitespace, digits and word boundaries (Table 19.1). Here are three commonly-used ones:

\s — A whitespace character

\d — A digit

\w — A word character

All of these escaped characters also have uppercase counterparts that negate their lowercase ones. Thus, \D is a nondigit character. We have already used the anchoring sequence \b for matching a pattern on a word boundary *(19.5)*, and the \s in the previous program to match whitespace.

The following statement uses the anchoring characters, ^ and $, to check whether $stg consists only of word characters :

```
if ($stg =~ /^\w+$/) {                          Same as ($stg =~ /^[a-zA-Z0-9_]+$/)
```

The following statement locates all lines that contain IP addresses. Since dots separate the octets, we need to escape the dots too for perfect matching:

```
if (/\d+\.\d+\.\d+\.\d+/) {
```

You can often compact regular expressions by using these characters. In the next example, we'll be using some of these escape sequences.

Table 19.1 Additional Regular Expression Sequences Used by **perl**

Symbols	Significance
\w	Matches a word character (same as [a-zA-Z0-9_])
\W	Doesn't match a word character (same as [^a-zA-Z0-9_])
\d	Matches a digit (Same as [0-9])
\D	Doesn't match a digit (Same as [^0-9])
\s	Matches a whitespace character
\S	Doesn't match a whitespace character
\b	Matches on word boundary
\B	Doesn't match on word boundary

19.15.3 The IRE and TRE Features

perl accepts the IRE and TRE used by **grep** and **sed** *(13.11)*, except that the curly braces and parentheses are not escaped. For instance, this is how you use an IRE to locate lines longer than 512 characters:

```
perl -ne 'print if /.{513,}/' foo                          No \ before { and }
```

You can enclose part of a pattern within parentheses and use them anywhere in the program with $1, $2, etc. This is **sed**'s TRE *(13.11.3)* implemented in **perl**. The repeated pattern could be \1 if it is specified in a pattern search with 2 /s, or $1 if the ~= operator is used.

The next example, **rep4.pl** (Fig. 19.15), changes the form of reporting for the date format of the sample database. It uses a TRE to report in the form *dd-mon-yyyy* format where *mon* is a three-character month name.

We split the database yet again, and store the split fields in the default array, @_. Each of the three components of the date field can be represented by the TRE (\d+), which signifies one or more

```
#!/usr/bin/perl -n
# Script: rep4.pl - Reports a date in format dd-mon-yyyy using a TRE
#
@month[1..12] = ("Jan", "Feb", "Mar", "Apr", "May", "Jun",
                 "Jul", "Aug", "Sep", "Oct", "Nov", "Dec") ;
split (/\|/) ;              #
$_[4] =~ /(\d+).(\d+).(\d+)/ ;   # Splits up into $1, $2 and $3
$_[4] = join ("-", $1, $month[$2], "19$3") ;
$_ = join(":", @_);
print ;
```

Fig. 19.15 rep4.pl

occurrences of a digit. **perl** TREs are more readable than their UNIX counterparts; they don't use the \s before the (and). The three groups get the tags $1, $2 and $3. Using $2, we extract the month name from the array @month. Finally, we join the elements of the @_ array on the : delimiter. Here are the first three lines of output:

```
$ rep4.pl emp.lst | head -n 3
2233:a.k. shukla         :g.m.      :sales      :12-Dec-1952:6000
9876:jai sharma          :director  :production:12-Mar-1950:7000
5678:sumit chakrobarty:d.g.m.       :marketing  :19-Apr-1943:6000
```

Look at the fifth field showing a date format that is also used by Oracle. The TRE in **perl** is unique in another way; **perl** stores these groupings ($1, etc.) in memory until the next grouping is done.

19.15.4 Editing Files In-Place

Instead of writing to the standard output or to a separate file, **perl** can edit and *rewrite* the input file itself. With **sed**, you would have redirected the output to a temporary file and then renamed it back to the original file. For a group of files, you would have used a **for** loop as well. Not so for **perl**; the -i option can edit multiple files in-place:

```
perl -p -i -e "s/<B>/<STRONG>/g" *.html *.htm
```

This changes all instances of <B> in all HTML files to <STRONG>. The files themselves are rewritten with the new output. If in-place editing seems a risky thing to do, you can back the files up before undertaking the operation:

```
perl -p -i.bak -e "tr/a-z/A-Z/" foo[1-4]
```

This first backs up foo1 to foo1.bak, foo2 to foo2.bak, and so forth, before converting all lowercase letters in each file to uppercase.

19.16 FILE HANDLING

So far, we have specified input filenames from the command line. **perl** also provides low-level file handling functions that let you hard-code the source and destination of the data stream in the script itself. A file is opened for reading like this:

```
open(INFILE, "/home/henry/mbox") ;
```
                                                        Don't forget the quotes!

INFILE here is a **filehandle** (an identifier) of the file mbox (file presumed to be in current directory if a pathname is not used). Once a file has been opened, functions that read and write the file will use the filehandle to access the file. A filehandle is similar to a file descriptor.

A file is opened for writing with the shell-like operators, > and >>, having their usual meanings:

```
open(OUTFILE, ">rep_out.lst") ;
open(OUTFILE, ">>rep_out.lst") ;
```

perl's filehandles can be associated with pipelines also. To shell programmers, the meanings of these statements should be quite obvious:

```
open(INFILE, "sort emp.lst |" ) ;
open(OUTFILE, "| lp" ) ;
```
                                                        Input from sort *output*
                                                        Output to print spooler

The next script, **rw.pl** (Fig. 19.16), uses **open** to obtain two filehandles to read one file and write another. It also uses the **print** statement with a filehandle as argument to write output to a file without using redirection. Both files are explicitly closed at the end with **close**.

The statement **while (<FILEIN>)** reads a line at a time from the file represented by the FILEIN filehandle, and stores it in $_. Every time the <FILEIN> statement is executed, the next line is read. You can read and print a single line in this way:

```
$_ = <FILEIN> ;
print ;
```
                                                        Assign to $_
                                                        print uses $_ *by default*

Even if you don't close the files before terminating the script, **perl** closes them on its own. When we run the script without arguments, the output doesn't come to the terminal this time, but goes to the file desig_out.lst.

Tip: If a number of **print** statements have to write to the same filehandle (say, FILEOUT), you can assign this filehandle as the default using **select (FILEOUT)** ;. Subsequent **print** statements don't need to use the FILEOUT argument in that case.

```
#!/usr/bin/perl
# Script: rw.pl - Shows use of low-level I/O available in perl
#
open(FILEIN, "desig.lst") || die("Cannot open file") ;
open(FILEOUT, ">desig_out.lst") ;
while (<FILEIN>) {                       # As long there are lines in the file
    print FILEOUT if (1..3) ;            # Can also use if ($. < 4 )
}
close(FILEIN) ;
close(FILEOUT) ;
```

Fig. 19.16 rw.pl

19.17 FILE TESTS

perl has an elaborate system of file tests. It overshadows the capabilities of the Bourne shell—and even the **find** command in some ways. The following statements test some of the common file attributes:

```
$x = "rdbnew.lst" ;
print "File $x is readable\n" if -r $x ;
print "File $x is executable\n" if -x $x ;
print "File $x has non-zero size\n" if -s $x ;
print "File $x exists\n" if -e $x ;
print "File $x is a text file\n" if -T $x ;
print "File $x is a binary file\n" if -B $y ;
```

perl file tests go further; it can tell you a file's modification and access times very accurately. The script, **when_last.pl** (Fig. 19.17), uses the C- and **awk**-like **printf** statement with its standard formats. It detects files which were modified less than 2.4 hours ago.

-M $file returns the time elapsed in hours since $file was last modified. It's a general **perl** feature (an idea borrowed from C) that you can make a test (< 0.1) and assignment ($m_age = ...) at the same time. Let's observe the output:

```
$ when_last.pl
File bf2o.sh was last modified 0.063 days back
File profile.sam was last modified 0.082 days back
File when_last.pl was last modified 0.000 days back
```

Three decimal places are not enough it seems for the last file that has just been modified. You have to increase the length of the **printf** format if you need to know the exact time.

Apart from testing file attributes, **perl** can manipulate files and directories very easily. It uses **chmod, chown, chgrp, chdir** (like **cd**), **mkdir, rmdir, rename** (like **mv**), **link, unlink** (like **rm**) and **umask** in the same way. It can also open directories with directory filehandles. The UNIX system call library also uses functions having these names, as you'll discover in Chapter 23.

```
#!/usr/bin/perl
# Script: when_last.pl - Finds files that are less than 2.4 hours old
#
foreach $file (`ls`)  {
  chop($file) ;
  if (($m_age = -M $file) < 0.1) {            # tenth of a day i.e., 2.4 hours
     printf "File %s was last modified %0.3f days back \n", $file, $m_age ;
  }
}
```

Fig. 19.17 when_last.pl

19.18 SUBROUTINES

perl supports functions but calls them **subroutines**. A subroutine is called by the & symbol followed by the subroutine name. If the subroutine is defined without any formal parameters, **perl** uses the array @_ as the default. Variables inside the subroutine should be declared with **my** to make them invisible in the calling program.

Many applications require the user to supply a username and password. Since this involves executing the same amount of code twice, it becomes an ideal candidate for a subroutine. The program, **input.pl** (Fig. 19.18), uses the subroutine **take_input**, which accepts the prompt string as argument, validates the input for word characters and returns the value that was input.

The subroutine arguments are accepted into the system array, @_, and then reassigned to two local variables, $prompt and $flag. What is checked in the subroutine is only the number of arguments passed (@_ == 2). When you pass two arguments to it, the UNIX **stty** command blanks out the display during password entry.

last is **perl**'s equivalent of the shell's **break** statement that exits a loop. (**perl** also uses **next** instead of **continue**.) Here, control breaks out of the loop when there is at least one word character in the input. This is how you can ensure that the password is not displayed:

```
$ input.pl
Oracle user-id: !@#$%^&*          Nonword characters
Oracle user-id: scott
Oracle password: *****            Password not echoed
The username and password are scott and tiger
```

```perl
#!/usr/bin/perl
# Script: input.pl - Shows use of subroutines
#
system("tput clear") ;                          # Executes the UNIX command
$username = &take_input("Oracle user-id: ") ;
$password = &take_input("Oracle password: ", "noecho") ;
print "\nThe username and password are $username and $password\n" ;

sub take_input {
   my ($prompt, $flag) = @_ ;            # @_ stores arguments of subroutine
   while (1) {                           # (1) is always true
      print("$prompt") ;
      system("stty -echo") if (@_ == 2 ) ;              # Echo mode off
      chop($name = <STDIN>) ;
      system("stty echo") if (@_ == 2 ) ;               # Echo mode on
      last if $name =~ /\w/ ;            # Quit the loop if $name has at
   }                                     # least one word character
   $name ;                               # return $name will also do
}
```

Fig. 19.18 input.pl

The last statement in the program ($name ;) is typically **perl**'s way of returning a value. You should store frequently used subroutines in separate files. Instruct the calling program to read a file containing a subroutine by placing the **require** statement at the beginning. If you save the **ake_input** subroutine in the file **oracle_lib.pl**, you should do these two things:

- Insert the statement **require "oracle_lib.pl" ;** in the calling program immediately after the line specifying the **perl** interpreter.

- Place the statement **1;** at the end of the file containing one or more subroutines. The **perl** documentation requires every "required" file to end with a true value. Any nonzero value is a true value in **perl**, so **1;** returns true.

n the above example, you can use $_[0] instead of $prompt and $_[1] in place of $flag. You can also drop the word **my** when assigning the subroutine arguments in case you want the variables to be visible outside the subroutine.

19.19 CONCLUSION

perl has specific functions for inter-process communication which have not been skimmed at all here. Its object-oriented tools and networking functions have been ignored. It has several options and many more functions that let you do things with minimal amount of code. **perl** is a real gold mine of techniques. The UNIX spirit lives in **perl**. Think of a strong UNIX feature; it is there in **perl**. Browse the Web; you are most likely invoking a CGI program written in **perl**. **perl** is the pride of UNIX.

WRAP UP

perl is a superset of **grep**, **tr**, **sed**, **awk** and the shell.

perl reads all characters, including spaces and newline that are keyed in, by assigning <STDIN> to a variable. The last character of a line is removed by **chop**.

Variables need the $ both for assignment and evaluation and need no type declarations. Variable values can include escape sequences. You can capitalize the first character of a string (\u) or the entire string (\U).

The . is used for string concatenation. x is used for repetition. **substr** extracts a string both from right and left, and also inserts a string. **uc** and **ucfirst** convert into uppercase the entire argument and the first character, respectively.

perl uses the -n option to set up an implicit loop for reading files. An explicit loop can also be set up with the symbols <>—representing the filenames specified in the command line.

$. stores the current line number, and the range operator (..) specifies a group of lines.

$_ is the *default variable* used by many **perl** functions. It stores the last line read or last pattern matched. **print**, **chop**, **split**, pattern matching and substitution operate on $_ by default.

perl uses *lists* and arrays extensively. @arr, when assigned to a variable, represents the length of the array. $#arr stores the last subscript of the array. @ARGV[] stores all command line arguments, but the command name is available as $0.

The **foreach** construct loops through an array and assigns each element in turn to a variable.

split breaks up a list into variables or an array. @_ is the default array, and whitespace the default delimiter. Elements of a split line can be glued together with **join**. Elements can be deleted from an array (**shift** and **pop**) or inserted (**unshift** and **push**). **splice** can do everything at any array location.

The *associative array* uses the % symbol and alternates the array subscript and value in a series of comma-delimited values. The **keys** function extracts these subscripts, and **values** filters out the values.

perl accepts all regular expressions used by all UNIX commands, and has some of its own. Now you can match a digit (\d), a word character (\w), the beginning of a word (\b) and a whitespace character (\s).

The **s** and **tr** functions are used for substitution and character translation in the same way done in **sed** and **tr**. The operators =~ and !~ are used to match regular expressions with variables. Files can be edited "in-place" with the -i option.

The IRE and TRE work in the same way as before except that the \ is not required before the () and {} characters. A grouped pattern can also be reproduced elsewhere with $1, $2 and so on, until the next grouping is done.

perl uses a *filehandle* to access a file. A filehandle can represent a pipeline as well. The **select** *filehandle* statement makes **print** use that filehandle as the default.

Subroutines are invoked with an &, and its arguments are stored in the array, @_. Subroutines can be held in an external file but must have the statement **1;** placed at the end of the file. The calling program "includes" subroutines placed in an external file with the **require** statement.

Test Your Understanding

19.1   Write one-liners to execute the following **perl** commands and explain your observations: (i) **print '\t'** (ii) **print "\t"** (iii) **print "romeo@heavens.com"**

19.2   Write a one-liner that prints all lines of a file, preceded by its line number and with the tab as delimiter.

19.3   Write a one-liner to print the string UNIX 20 times without using a loop.

19.4   Write a program that accepts three integers as arguments and prints the maximum value entered.

19.5   How do you list the line in /etc/passwd that has 1 as the UID?

19.6   Write a program to prefix all lines of a file with the letters A., B., C. and so on. What do you see after Z.?

19.7   How will you print *only* the first occurrence of a string in a file?

19.8   Use **perl** to show all lines containing the string director and the next line.

19.9   Ask the user repeatedly to enter a number, and when the user enters 0, print the total of all numbers entered so far.

19.10 How will you convert all characters in a file to uppercase without using shell redirection?

19.11 Write a program that prompts a user to input a string and a number, and prints the string that many times,   ach string on a separate line.

19.12 Write a one-liner to print the uppercase letters of the English alphabet as a contiguous string using a loop.

19.13 By default, file reading, chopping and pattern matching operate on (i) $. (ii) $_ (iii) @_ (iv) None of these.

19.14 Write a program that prompts for an integer not exceeding 255, and then prints A if the number is below 127, B if it is below 224, and C otherwise.

19.15 Write a program that uses a loop to print from an array all the 12 months in the form 1. Jan .....

19.16 Using a regular expression, write a one-liner to display the contents of a file after capitalizing every word.

19.17 Write a one-liner to convert all characters in a file to uppercase and write the changes back to the same file without using redirection.

19.18 Write a program that accepts a filename (say, foo) as argument and then writes the first 10 lines to foo.1, the next 10 to foo.2 and so forth. Does it make any difference if any of these files exist?

19.19 Write a program that takes a filename as argument, checks whether the file exists and prints binary if the file is binary.

Flex Your Brain

19.1   Detect the errors in the following program (line numbers on left):

```
1        # foo.pl -- Checking file system block size
2        #/usr/bin/perl
3        print "Enter the block size of your file system: "
4        bs = <STDIN> ;
5        chop ($bs) ;
6        if ( $bs > 8192 )
7          print "Lot of wasted space /n" ;
8        } else {
9          print "Reasonable size" ;
10       }
```

19.2   Write a one-liner to print double-spaced lines from a file.

19.3   Write a program to convert a binary number specified as argument to decimal. (HINT: Use the **reverse** function.)

19.4   Write a program that looks up /etc/passwd and /etc/group and prints (i) the highest UID, (ii) the login name, real name and GID (both number and name) of that user.

19.5   Devise a script which lists the usage of words (in the form word: count) in its argument files.

19.6   Write a program that populates an array named weekday from the string SunMonTueWedThuFriSat, and then prints each day in uppercase.

19.7   How will you use **find** and **perl** to delete all ordinary files modified more than a year back? What is the advantage of using this method compared to using **find** with -exec rm?

19.8   (i) Write a one-liner to change the interpreter line to `#!/usr/local/bin/perl` in all `.pl` files in the current directory. (ii) Enlarge the scope to add the interpreter line if it doesn't exist. Also, don't make any substitution if a proper interpreter line is already in place.

19.9   A closing HTML tag starts with /. For instance, `<b>` is closed with `</b>`. Convert all these tags comprising single words (without attributes) to uppercase. (Tags like `<img src= ....` must not get converted.)

19.10 A file contains a set of numbers and strings as shown by these sample entries:

```
1
5
3
botswana
namibia
swaziland
```

Devise a *generalized* program that prints 1. botswana on the first line, 5. namibia in the second line, and so forth. It does not matter how many sets of entries there are in the file, as long as the set of numbers is followed by an equal number of country names.

19.11 Refer to the stamp dealer problem in Exercise 18.11 and implement it in **perl**.

Advanced vi

In this chapter, we consider some of the advanced features of the **vi** editor. After having worked with **vi** for some time, you'll find it helpful to know these features. Many of them aren't available in other editors with the possible exception of **emacs**. Editing can be very productive if you customize your editor to suit your requirements, and we'll do that in this chapter. With **vi** you can move mountains with only a few keystrokes, but only if you have gone through Chapter 7 thoroughly.

WHAT YOU WILL LEARN

- The use of *operator-command* combinations to delete, move and copy text.
- Change screen text by running (filtering) a UNIX command on it.
- Edit multiple files and switch from one file to another.
- Split the window in **vim**.
- Recover up to nine complete line deletions using *numbered buffers*.
- Use *[Ctrl-v]* to enter any control character and *[Esc]*.
- Place the cursor on or near any character.
- Mark text and access any mark. Toggle between two marked locations.
- Customize the editor's environment by defining abbreviations, key maps and setting variables.

TOPICS OF SPECIAL INTEREST

- Copy or delete multiple text sections to 26 separate *named buffers* and restore them in another file.
- Use the mapping feature to compile programs and execute shell and **perl** scripts without leaving the editor.

20.1 OPERATORS

Most of the useful functions in the Command Mode are derived from a combination of an **operator** and a command. This is probably **vi**'s strongest feature, and it opens up a new domain of commands for you to work with. With operators, you can frame a command to handle practically any situation. There are only a few operators and you must know at least the following ones:

d —Delete

c —Change

y —Yank (copy)

! —Filter to act on text

An operator alone can't perform any function unless it is combined with a command or itself. When used with itself (i.e., twice), it can handle a very specialized function. In Chapter 7, you've seen how these specialized functions were performed by using **dd** and **yy** to delete and copy a line, respectively. All of these operators also take a repeat factor which greatly enhances their power.

Note: An operator, when doubled by itself, (like **dd**, **cc**, **yy** and **!!**), acts only on the current line.

20.1.1 Deleting and Moving Text (d, p and P)

You know how to delete characters and lines with **x**, **X** and **dd** *(7.5.1)*. **dd** is really a combination of the **d** operator with itself. **vi** can perform some complex deletion when this operator is combined with a command of the Command Mode.

Consider that you have to delete text from the present cursor position to the end of line. You can frame the command yourself if you recall the primary commands that are used in the Command Mode. Since the command to move to the end of line is **$**, you can combine the **d** operator with **$** to delete from the cursor position to the end of line:

d$ *Deletes rest of line*

Note how a specialized function could be devised by following a simple set of rules. Taking the cue from here, the command to delete a word should be equally simple—**dw. dG** should delete text from current position to the end of file. A repeat factor applies here too; **3dw** deletes three words, and **5dd** deletes five lines including the current line.

For using operators to move text, there are no special considerations involved. We have deleted text using the **dd**, **x** and **X** commands and then placed the deleted text at a different location with the **p** and **P** commands. Recall that **p** and **P** behave differently depending on whether the deletion affects entire lines or parts of lines *(7.5.2)*. When working with entire lines, **p** puts text *below* the cursor and **P** places it *above*. However, when you delete a word with **dw**, you can put the deleted word only to the *left* (with **p**) or *right* (with **P**) of the cursor position, and not above or below the current line.

20.1.2 Yanking Text (y)

The **y** operator yanks (or copies) text. It is used in the same way the **d** operator is combined with another command or by itself. With this operator, you can yank a word, a group of words, line segments, or even entire lines. Moreover, the **p** and **P** commands act in the same way for putting the copied text at its destination.

For instance, to yank five lines of text, move the cursor to the first of these lines and press

5yy

Next, move the cursor to the new location, and press

   p *or* P

to place the copied text below or above the current line, respectively. When you yank words, **p** and **P** have the same significance as with the **d** operator; **p** puts text on the right of the cursor location, while **P** puts it on the left.

20.1.3 Changing Text (c)

Text is changed with the **c** (change) operator. This operator is also combined with a command to indicate the boundaries of replacement. If **dw** deletes a word, **cw** changes it. This is the only operator which functions in the Input Mode. The change operation thus has to be terminated with *[Esc]*.

When you use **c** with a Command Mode command, you are taken to the Input Mode. But this time the boundary limiting your area of operation could be indicated by a $. If you change three words with **3cw**, a $ should appear at the end of the third word (Linux excepted). The inserted text overwrites the characters delimited by the $ that temporarily appears on the screen. If the replaced text is larger, then once the cursor moves up to the $ marker, further insertion shifts existing text to the right.

To change text from the present cursor position up to the end of a line, use

   c$ *or* C

To change entire lines, use

   cc

How can you frame a command to change text from the current position to the first occurrence of a pattern? For instance, you may like to change the contents of the rest of this section, i.e., until the heading of the next section (entitled Filtering Text). Since searching is done with the */pattern* sequence, combine this sequence with the operator and it does the job:

   c/Filtering Text/*[Enter]*

When you use this command, all text starting from the current cursor position, up to, but not on to, the string Filtering Text will be deleted, and **vi** will switch to the Input Mode. Enter the changed text and press *[Esc]*. Some systems don't show the $ but simply remove the defined text the moment the change command is entered.

20.1.4 Filtering Text (!)

vi has a marvelous feature of allowing a UNIX filter to act on text that's on display at your terminal. Can you sort the contents of your editing window without leaving the editor? Yes, that is possible with the **!** operator and the UNIX **sort** command. In general, filtering text on the screen requires three steps:

1. Move to the beginning of the text to be acted upon and type **!**.
2. Move to the other end of the text using any navigation command like **G**.
3. Enter the UNIX command to act on the text. The text on the screen should change immediately.

For instance, to sort lines 21 to 40 of a file, move the cursor to the first character of line 21 (with **21G**), and then press the following sequence:

!40Gsort*[Enter]*

Nothing appears on the screen until the second address (**40G**) is entered. After you enter the word **sort**, the last line could look like this:

:21,40!sort   *You executed an ex Mode command!*

After you press *[Enter]*, the 20 specified lines are sorted and the output replaces the current contents. You have just executed the ex Mode command **:21,40!sort** without knowing it. You can enter this command directly as well. You can save the change or undo it (with **u**) if it didn't do exactly what you wanted.

Like the other operators, the **!**, when doubled, uses the command following it to operate on the current line. This is how you use **tr** to change the case of text of the current line to upper:

!!tr '[a-z]' '[A-Z]'

To make editing work very productive and satisfying, you must have thorough knowledge of the commands that are used to control cursor positioning. After that, it's easy to perform any text manipulation by using the right operator-command combination, employing a repeat factor wherever necessary. Now you shouldn't find it difficult to understand the significance of these combinations listed in Table 20.1.

Table 20.1 A Few Specimen Operator-Command Combinations

Command	*Function*
d$ or D	Deletes from cursor to end of line
5dd	Deletes 5 lines
d/}	Deletes from cursor up to first occurrence of }
d30G	Deletes from cursor up to line number 30
df.	Deletes from cursor to first occurrence of a dot
y$ or Y	Yanks from cursor to end of line
3yw or y3w	Yanks three words from cursor position
5yy	Yanks five lines
yG	Yanks from cursor to end of file
y?case	Yanks from cursor up to first occurrence of string case in reverse direction
c0	Changes from cursor to beginning of line
c$ or C	Changes from cursor to end of line
3cw or c3w	Changes three words
cc	Changes current line
!Gsort	Sorts all lines from current cursor position to end of file
!!tr '[a-z]' '[A-Z]'	Converts current line to uppercase

Note: Doubling an operator (like **dd**, **yy** and **cc**) constitutes a special command, which always acts on the current line. Three operator-command combinations also have synonyms—**D** (**d$**), **Y** (**y$**) and **C** (**c$**). They act on text from the current position to the end of line.

20.2 THE ex MODE: HANDLING MULTIPLE FILES

This mode offers some facilities not seen in the Command Mode, especially those related to handling multiple files. You can work with multiple files and easily switch from one file to another. As a programmer, you need to know multiple file-handling techniques since you'll often need to move or copy text from one program to another. The basic file handling commands are already known to you *(7.3)*; the advanced ones (Table 20.2) are discussed in this section.

20.2.1 Switching Files

You may sometimes need to ignore all the unsaved changes you made. Instead of quitting **vi** and then invoking it once again, you can reload the last saved version of the file with

    :e!   *Like Revert in Microsoft Windows*

You can also edit multiple files without leaving the editor. While editing one file, you can easily switch to another by using its **:e** command:

    :e note2

You can return to the original file by using one of these sequences:

    [Ctrl-^]   *Toggle between current and previous file*
    :e#   *Same*

This has a toggling effect; the next time you use either of these sequences, you'll switch to the previous file again. The first sequence is easier to execute and you should use it.

Using vi *with Multiple Filenames*   When **vi** is used with multiple filenames, say with **vi note[1-4]**, it throws out a message 4 files to edit, and loads the first file (note1) into the buffer. You can switch to the next file, viz. note2, by using

    :n   *Next file in command line*

You can go on in this manner and without leaving the editor until you have encountered the last file. At any stage, you can move back to the first file specified in the command line by "rewinding" the file list:

    :rew   *Back to first file in command line*

When you switch from one file to another, there is a protection mechanism which prevents the switch if changes have been made to the file. The system displays a terse message:

    No write since last change (:edit! overrides)

Just as the command **:q!** quits the editor after discarding all changes, the **:e! #** command similarly switches to the last edited file after discarding the changes made to the current file. You can also use **:n!** or **:rew!** in the same vein.

20.2.2 Inserting File and Command Output

With most Windows text editors, there's no easy way of inserting the contents of one file at a certain location in another file. You have to open the file, use something like *Select All* from the *Edit* menu, copy the entire text with *[Ctrl-c]*, switch to the original file, and then paste the contents with *[Ctrl-v]*. That involves a great deal of work by UNIX standards.

With **vi**, you don't have to visit the other file at all. Just insert its contents at the present cursor location:

    :r note1   *Inserts file* note1

You can also place the output of a command in your file. Use **:r** like before, but instead of specifying the filename, enter the command name preceded by **!**:

    :r !date   *Inserts output of* date *command*

This is a very useful feature for documentation authors, who need to feature command output in their text. There's no need to save this output in a file and then read in the file.

Tip: There is a useful shortcut available in the Command Mode to toggle between two files; use *[Ctrl-^]* (Control-caret). For this to work at all times, make the ex Mode setting **:set autowrite** or **:set aw**. This ensures that the file is saved automatically before the switch occurs.

LINUX: Splitting the Window

You can split the screen into multiple windows in **vim**. The window can be empty or it can contain a file—even a copy of the same file. To view the same file in two separate windows, use the **:sp** (split) command in the ex Mode:

    :sp   *Splits existing window in two*

In this situation, changes made to the buffer in one window are also seen in the other window. You can also create a new window not associated with any file:

    :new   *New blank window*

In either case, you'll see the screen split into two. You can move between the two windows by using this command:

    [Ctrl-w][Ctrl-w]   *Cycles through windows*

In any window (empty or otherwise), you can open a new file by using **:e** *filename*. You can also increase or decrease the vertical size of a window:

    [Ctrl-w]+   *Increases size of current window*
    [Ctrl-w]-   *Reduces size of current window*

To make the current window the only window on the screen and close all other windows, use

    :on   *Removes all other windows*

You can kill the current window and move to the other window (if any):

`:q`

Note that when you have multiple windows on, `:q` will quit editing from the current window and close it. To apply the save, quit and exit commands to all windows in **vim**, you have to append an **a** to the existing commands. To quit all windows without saving, use `:qa`. To save all buffers and quit, use `:xa`.

Table 20.2 ex Mode Commands for File Handling

Command	Function
`:r note`	Reads file `note` below current line
`:r !head -n 3 dec2.pl`	Reads first three lines of `dec2.pl` below current line
`:w >> note1`	Appends buffer contents to file `note1`
`:e note1`	Stops editing current file and edits file `note1`
`:e! note1`	As above, but after abandoning changes made to current file
`:e!`	Loads last saved edition of current file (Like *Revert* in Windows)
`:e#`	Returns to editing most recently edited file
`:n`	Edits next file (if **vi** is invoked with more than one filename)
`:rew`	Rewinds file list to start editing from first file in command line

20.3 NAMED BUFFERS: STORING MULTIPLE TEXT SECTIONS

So far, we have moved a single section of text by deleting it from the original location and putting it in the new one. **vi** actually stores the deleted text in an unnamed buffer. This technique has two limitations. First, you can use only one buffer at a time. Second, when moving text from one file to another (using `:e` *filename*), the contents of this special buffer are lost (Linux excepted).

Actually, **vi** has 26 special **named buffers**, but by default we don't use them. These buffers are named after the letters of the alphabet, and their use is fairly straightforward. Just precede the editing operation (deletion or yank) with a " (double quote) and the buffer name, say a. Thus, to yank four lines into this buffer named a, you should simply use

`"a4yy`   *Copies 4 lines into buffer* a

Now navigate to the desired location, press ", the buffer name (a) and **p** or **P** to put back the text:

`"ap`   *Use* P *to put text above*

You can delete or copy another section of text into another buffer, say b, and restore the same with **"bp** (or **"bP**). In this way, you have access to 26 buffers to hold 26 sections of text. Windows and the mouse can't do this! However, the X Window System and its **xclipboard** client *(16.5.2)* can do even better than this. If you have to switch files, note that you can toggle between two files using *[Ctrl-^]* or `:e#`.

20.3.1 Moving Text from One File to Another

Using this feature of named buffers, you can now copy and move text freely across a file, and even from one file to another. This is how you copy text across two files:

`"a10yy`	*Copy 10 lines into buffer* a
`:e bin2dec.pl`	*Switch to file* bin2dec.pl
`30G`	*Move to line 30*
`"ap`	*Put the 10 lines after line 30*

The only precaution you need to take here is that, on no account, should you exit **vi** to open a second file. The buffer contents are lost when you leave **vi**.

Note: If you perform an operation on a named buffer which already contains some text, the contents of the buffer are overwritten. **vi** uses the uppercase letters to append to these buffers—**"Ayy** instead of **"ayy**.

20.4 NUMBERED BUFFERS: UNDOING MULTIPLE LINE DELETIONS

Even though the **u** command can undo only the last editing action, we often need to restore a number of recent deletions. **vi** makes it possible to restore up to the last nine *complete* line deletions using its **numbered buffers**. These buffers are numbered 1 to 9. The most recent deletion is stored in the buffer numbered 1, the next-most in the buffer numbered 2, and so forth. These buffers are accessed by prefixing the buffer number with a **"**. *Entire lines, when deleted, are stored in these buffers; parts of lines can't be stored.*

To restore the most recently deleted group of lines, move the cursor to your desired location and use

`"1p`	*Restores most recent deletion*

And if that's not the text you expected to restore, you can undo the last restoration with **u**, and then use **"2p** to see whether the desired text is stored in the buffer numbered 2. You can go on like this, using the nine numerals available and undo up to nine deletions.

LINUX: Even though Linux can undo and redo *all* editing actions, this feature is still useful in that environment.

20.4.1 The Dot (.) Command

The above technique of undoing deletions can be quite tedious, especially when you are doing a mass restoration. As a shortcut, **vi** offers the **.** command to restore the contents of any buffer. The command generally repeats the last editing instruction *(7.7)*, but behaves differently when used on a numbered buffer. Every time it is pressed, it steps through the buffer set to restore the contents of the *next* buffer.

To use this command here, you have to first restore at least one deletion using, say **"1p**. If that's not the block you are looking for, you can undo the restoration with **u**, and then press to restore the contents of the next numbered buffer, i.e., the one numbered 2. You can issue a series of dots to step through the various buffers, each dot followed by **u**, until you spot the one you have been looking for. For instance, if the desired text to be undeleted resides in the buffer numbered 4, you can start with buffer number 1, and then issue the following sequence of commands:

```
"1pu.u.u.
```

This feature lets you retrieve entire groups of deleted lines, which you may like to restore after you have changed your mind.

Note: This facility to restore line deletions from numbered buffers applies only to *entire* lines. You can't hope to restore three words deleted with **3dw** unless it was the last editing action performed.

20.5 ENTERING CONTROL CHARACTERS (*[Ctrl-v]*)

If you write shell scripts to send some escape sequences to your printer or terminal, then you would need to enter control characters. In **vi**, some of these characters are directly enterable, but generally a control character has to be preceded by another control character for it to be interpreted properly.

vi uses *[Ctrl-v]* to precede any control character. For instance, to enter *[Ctrl-h]*, you have to first press *[Ctrl-v]* and then *[Ctrl-h]*. You'll then see this on the screen:

    ^H   *Just one character here*

Even though you feel you are seeing a ^ (caret) and an H, there's only a single character out there. You can position the cursor only on the ^ and not on the H; that's how you identify control characters anyway.

The same technique can be adopted for entering the *[Esc]* character. Press *[Ctrl-v][Esc]*, and you'll see the *[Esc]* character looking like this:

    ^[*Just one character here*

This too is a single character; you can place your cursor only on the ^. If your version of **vi** doesn't let you enter the *[Esc]* character as advised above, then you can use this: *[Ctrl-v][Ctrl-[]* (Control with []). The *[Esc]* character may need special treatment in **vi** since it is the terminator of the Input Mode.

20.6 SEARCHING FOR A CHARACTER

There's a special facility to take the cursor *near* or to a specific character in the current line. This is done with the **f** and **t** commands, with either command followed by the character to be searched for. To move the cursor forward to the first occurrence of the character, use

    f

followed by the character. For instance, **f.** moves the cursor to the first period following the current cursor position. This is a convenient way of moving to the end of a sentence when editing a document. **t** also acts in a similar fashion except that the cursor is positioned a single character *before* the occurrence.

F and T perform the respective functions as their lowercase counterparts, but in the reverse direction. The repeat factor works with all of these characters. For example, **2f}** places the cursor on the second occurrence of the } in the line. However, all these characters restrict their activities to the current line only.

The character search is repeated by using the **;** (semi-colon) and **,** (comma) characters. Table 20.3 lists the character search and repeat commands.

Table 20.3 The Character Search and Repeat Commands in Current Line

Command	Action
f*ch*	Moves cursor forward to first occurrence of character *ch*
t*ch*	Moves cursor forward onto but before first occurrence of character *ch*
;	Repeats search in same direction along which previous search was made with f or t
,	Repeats search in a direction opposite to that along which previous search was made with f or t

20.7 MARKING TEXT

You can mark up to 26 positions (labeled a to z) in the file, and later locate them. The **m** command is used for marking lines, while the **'** (single quote) command locates a marked line. Any alphabetic character can be used in combination with **m** and **'** for marking and locating different portions of text.

To mark any portion of a file with the label a, move the cursor to the required location and press

    ma

An invisible mark is left at the corresponding point in the file. You can move back to this mark from any point in the file simply by using a **'** in combination with the character used to mark that location, in this case, a:

    'a   *Moves to mark* a

The **'** when doubled by itself toggles the motion of the cursor between its present and immediately previous locations. If you had first moved to a mark a with **'a** and then to mark b with **'b**, you can return to the mark a with **''** (two single quotes) and then again move back to mark b with the same command.

This also applies to those situations where the cursor is not explicitly moved away from a line. If you have moved to a line with **30G** and then to the end of the file with **G**, you can alternate between these two locations by using **''** (two single quotes).

20.8 CUSTOMIZING vi

vi can be tailored to behave in the way you want. For instance, you may like to define (or redefine) some of the keys to represent a command sequence which you may be using often, or abbreviate frequently used words or phrases into short strings. There are three ex Mode commands—**set**, **map** and **abbr**—which let you do all that.

vi reads the file ~/.exrc only once, upon startup, and its behavior is determined by statements placed in that file. We have used some of these commands already (like :set showmode, :set aw, etc.). In the following paragraphs, we'll learn to place some more commands in this file. Keep in mind that you have to restart **vi** whenever you make changes to .exrc. Linux users using **vim** may need to edit ~/.vimrc instead.

20.8.1 The set Command

The general **vi** environment is determined by its variable settings. These variables are controlled by the :set command. We have met this command already in this chapter and in Chapter 7 on two occasions:

```
:set showmode
:set autowrite                         Or :set aw
```

set is used with a variable name (like showmode). The variable in the second example takes on an abbreviation, which means that you can also use :set aw. Many of these variables can have the string no prefixed to their name, in which case the setting is deactivated. For instance, noautowrite (or noaw) negates autowrite (or aw). Other variables are of the form *variable=value*. Let's take a look at some of these variables.

*Automatic indentation (*autoindent*)* Programmers need to provide indentation to their code for easier readability. Nested **if** statements along with their corresponding **fi**s should appear at the right indentation. This aspect is taken care of when you use the following **set** statement:

```
:set autoindent                        Or :set ai
```

When this option is set, an *[Enter]* in the Input Mode places the cursor in the next line at the current indentation.

*Numbering Lines (*number*)* The number setting shows all lines duly numbered. This makes it easier to debug programs. However, the line numbers are not preserved when the file is saved. To reverse this setting (i.e., switching back to the nonumber option), you simply have to prefix the string no to the option:

```
:set nonumber
```

*Ignoring Case in Pattern Searches (*ignorecase*)* The search commands (not the substitution ones) may or may not pursue a case-insensitive search. That depends on the ignorecase setting. By default, this is generally off, but you can turn it on with :set ignorecase.

*No Regular Expressions in Search (*nomagic*)* You may sometimes need to despecialize the regular expression characters when searching for a pattern. In that case you should use this setting:

```
:set nomagic                           Searching with /g* will now show g*
```

By default, the setting is magic, i.e., the characters *, ., etc. retain their special meanings.

*See Matching } or) (*showmatch*)* Another option, especially useful for C and **perl** programmers, enables the programmer to see momentarily the matching bracket to a) or }. The showmatch option helps you locate matching brackets:

```
:set showmatch
```

When text is entered in the Input Mode, the moment a) or } is entered, the cursor will jump to its matching counterpart, and stay there for a fraction of a second before returning to its current location. If a match is not found, it responds with a beep.

Setting Tab Stops (tabstop=*n*)   Too many nested programming constructs often cause a line to wrap around. To some extent, this can be alleviated by changing the default tab setting (8 spaces). You can reduce this value, say to 4, with **:set tabstop=4**.

Most options can be reversed as discussed (except the ones that take a parameters like tabstop), using the option prefix no. All settings made with set are displayed with the **:set all** command. Some of the important **set** options are shown in Table 20.4.

Table 20.4   set Options

Option	Abbreviation	Significance
autoindent	ai	Next line starts at previous indented level
autowrite	aw	Writes current file automatically whenever switching files with :n or :e
ignorecase	ic	Ignores case when searching for patterns
magic		Treats regular expression characters as special when searching for patterns
number	nu	Displays line numbers on screen
showmatch	sm	Shows momentarily match to a) and }
showmode		Displays a message when vi is in Input Mode
tabstop	ts	Sets tabs for display (default: 8 spaces)
wrapscan	ws	Continues pattern search by moving to other end of a file so that entire file is scanned

20.8.2 map: Mapping Keys of Keyboard

The **map** command lets you assign the undefined keys or reassign the defined ones so that when such a key is pressed, it expands to a command sequence. It's particularly useful to convert a sequence of keystrokes into a macro. The command **:map** is followed by the key which needs mapping and the key sequence which is mapped.

You may, for instance, like to have the writing of the buffer achieved with a single keystroke. This is normally done with **:w**[*Enter*], but you can use the **map** command to condense this sequence to the character **g** by using the following command:

```
:map g :w^M                                     ^M signifies the [Enter] key
```

This mapping also includes the *[Enter]* key, which **vi** understands as *[Ctrl-m]* (shown as ^M). This character is entered by first pressing *[Ctrl-v]* and then *[Ctrl-m]* (20.5). Once **g** is mapped, when you press it in the Command Mode, the buffer is written.

There are other useful mappings you can create for yourself. If you have been working with **vi** for a long time, then by now you probably know that the letters g, q, v, K, V and Z are undefined. You can map v to write the current line into the buffer named a. You can also use V to restore it:

```
:map v "ayy
:map V "ap
```
                        Copies current line into buffer a
                        Restores the line when pressing V

You can map keys in the Input Mode also, in which case, you can press the mapped key while entering or changing text itself. You can use one of the function keys, say *[F2]*, and map it to the function. For instance, this mapping

```
:map! #2 ^[:w^M
```
                        Function key [F2] is #2

lets you save the file in the Input Mode. The string ^[is actually the *[Esc]* character.

The **:map** command displays the mapped environment. **:unmap** cancels a Command Mode map and **:unmap!** cancels an Input Mode map.

Tip: Did you know that you can compile your C program or execute a shell or **perl** script from inside the editor with a single keystroke? **vi** understands the current file as %, so **:!cc** % compiles the current file. Let's map the function key *[F3]* to invoke this function:

```
:map #3 :!cc %^M
```
                        [F3] now compiles current C program

The symbols **:!** invoke a temporary shell escape which is used to run **cc** (the C compiler). To invoke a shell or **perl** script, make this mapping of the function key *[F4]*:

```
:map #4 :!%^M
```
                        [F4] now executes current script

These are two important mappings used by the author. Note that scripts need to have execute permission, so you should first use **:!chmod 755 %** to assign this permission. You don't have to leave **vi** for this task either.

20.8.3 abbr: Abbreviating Text Input

The **abbreviate** command (itself abbreviated to **ab**) is used to expand short strings to long words. The syntax is similar to **map** except that the string that is mapped can consist of more than one character. While writing this text, the following abbreviations were used:

```
:ab re regular expression
:ab me metacharacter
```

This indicates that when you enter the word re followed by a key which is neither alphanumeric nor the _ (underscore) character, you'll see re expanded to regular expression.

Tip: Store all sets, maps and abbreviations in the file $HOME/.exrc ($HOME/.vimrc for vim). **vi** reads this file on startup and executes its instructions as ex Mode commands to set the environment for the session. Carry this file with you wherever you go; it could be your most precious possession.

20.9 CONCLUSION

In this chapter, we had a second look at the **vi** editor to discover some of its advanced features. We saw how operators serve both to select text and pass commands to act on the selection. C programmers will also find the features of copying or moving multiple sections of text from one file to another quite useful. But you still need to customize the editor and it won't be long before you realize that there's one file that you should never fail to back up—the .exrc (or .vimrc).

WRAP UP

vi's power lies in its operators. By combining an operator with a Command Mode command, you can delete (**d**), yank (**y**), change (**c**) and filter (**!**) text in practically any manner. When the operator is used doubly, the operation affects the current line only.

Using the ex Mode, you can switch to an alternate file (**:e**), return to the last edited file (**:e#**) and revert to the last saved version (**:e!**). You can also invoke **vi** with multiple filenames, edit each file in turn (**:n**), and rewind the file list (**:rew**) to start from the beginning. **vi** normally doesn't allow a change of file if changes made to the current file are not saved unless the **!** suffix is used.

vim in Linux can split the window (**:sp**) in two (or more) so you can display two different (or same) files on them. Any ex Mode command (like **:q**) applies to the current window unless suffixed with a, when it applies to all windows (like **:qa**).

You can use up to 26 buffers to store text, using the **"** to precede the buffer name. The stored text can be placed—even in another file—with **"**, the buffer name and **p**.

You can also undo up to nine sets of deletions of *complete* lines using the numerals 1 to 9. The **.** here steps through the buffer and restores the previous line deletion.

You can enter control characters (using *[Ctrl-v]* first) and then the character. The *[Esc]* character is inserted using *[Ctrl-v][Ctrl-[]*.

The cursor can placed on (**f**) or near (**t**) a character in the current line. Up to 26 areas in a text can be marked using **m** and a letter. The **'** and the letter is used to access any marked portion.

You can abbreviate (**:ab**) long strings to short ones so they are automatically expanded when they are input. You can map a frequently used command sequence to a single key, both in the Command Mode (**:map**) and Input Mode (**:map!**). Use *[Ctrl-m]* to signify *[Enter]*.

With the **:set** command, you can ensure that a file is saved before switching (autowrite). You can make searches case-insensitive (ignorecase) and turn off the significance of regular expressions (nomagic). The no prefix reverses a setting.

All **:ab**, **:map** and **:set** commands should be placed in $HOME/.exrc (or .vimrc for vim) so they are always available on startup.

Test Your Understanding

20.1   What is the difference between the commands /* and **f***?

20.2   Frame a command to delete the first two sentences of a line. How will you do that for subsequent lines?

20.3 How can you edit a second file without leaving **vi**, and then toggle between the two files?

20.4 How will you ensure that **vi** automatically saves a file when moving from one file to another?

20.5 How are **d** and **y** different from Command Mode commands?

20.6 How will you copy 5 lines of text from one file to another?

20.7 You copied 20 lines in one file, then switched to another file with **:e foo**, but when you tried to paste these lines back with **p**, it didn't work. Why?

20.8 How do you (i) revert to the last-saved version of a file, (ii) read in the entire contents of another file at the beginning of the current file?

20.9 How will you compile a C program without leaving the editor?

20.10 You defined an abbreviation re to expand to regular expression, and when you try to input the word re-rating, you find the expansion getting in the way. What do you do?

20.11 Write a map to define the first function key to search for loop, and copy into the buffer a all subsequent text up to but not including the string end loop.

Flex Your Brain

20.1 How do you copy from the current cursor position to the following? (i) the character under the cursor, (ii) the beginning of line, (iii) 10 words, (iv) the current sentence and the next.

20.2 How will you delete the following? (i) text from the current cursor position to the end of the file, (ii) the entire contents of the file.

20.3 How do you move to the 100th line and then write the remaining lines (including that line) to a separate file?

20.4 How do you do the following? (i) invert the case of all characters in the current line, (ii) convert to uppercase the entire line, (iii) convert to uppercase all text up to the end of file.

20.5 How will you copy two groups of ten and five lines each from one file to another?

20.6 You have inadvertently deleted three groups of lines with **10dd**, **5dd** and **dd** (in that order). How will you restore the 10 deleted lines?

20.7 What are the two functions of the dot command?

20.8 Write a map which removes all trailing spaces in a line.

20.9 Use one of the unused keys to create a map that locates the next blank line (which may or not contain spaces) and deletes it.

20.10 Explain the significance of the following **set** options: (i) autoindent (ii) showmode (iii) magic.

20.11 How can you number all lines which are (i) saved, (ii) not saved, when saving the file?

21

Advanced Shell Programming

You have already discovered the basic features of the shell—both as an interpreter and as a scripting language. But the shell is more than just an interpreter or a language. It is also a process, an environment which makes itself available to programs. It is necessary that you understand the environmental changes that take place when the shell executes a program, especially a shell script. You should also know how to change these environmental parameters.

Advanced knowledge of shell programming is needed by the system administrator who has to constantly devise scripts that monitor and correct system functioning. A detailed knowledge of the shell's subtle features is also necessary if you aspire to be an expert script writer. The following discussions mostly assume the Bourne shell, but the special features of the Korn and Bash shells are also examined here.

WHAT YOU WILL LEARN

- How the shell uses a second shell to execute a shell script.
- When and how commands are executed in the current shell and a sub-shell.
- Make variables visible in sub-shells with **export**.
- Use **let** and **(( ))** for computation in the Korn shell and Bash.
- Use arrays supported by the Korn shell and Bash.
- Handle strings with the built-in facilities of the Korn shell and Bash.
- Evaluate variables in different ways depending on whether they are set or not.
- Merge the standard output and standard error streams with the symbols 1>&2 and 2>&1.
- Understand how *shell functions* are superior to aliases.
- Use **eval** to evaluate a command line twice and produce generalized prompts and variables.
- Overlay the current program with another and handle multiple streams with **exec**.

TOPICS OF SPECIAL INTEREST

- The situations that demand execution of a command in the current shell. Use of the dot command for this purpose.

- Devise useful shell functions required for everyday use.
- Use **exec** to access files with file descriptors in the same way system calls access them.

21.1 SHELLS AND SUB-SHELLS

When the shell executes a shell script, it first spawns a sub-shell, which in turn executes the commands in the script. When script execution is complete, the child shell withers away and returns control to the parent shell. You can also *explicitly* invoke a sub-shell to execute a shell script. The command representing the shell itself (**sh**, **ksh** or **bash**) can be used to read the statements in **join.sh**:

```
sh join.sh                    Shell also accepts script name as argument
sh < join.sh                  Its standard input can also be redirected
```

Thus a shell script run with **sh**, **ksh** or **bash** need not have execute permission. This technique, however, is applicable for executing only shell scripts and not executables. You certainly can't use **sh < a.out**.

Even though the shell accepts a script name as argument, we generally don't run shell scripts in the way shown above. We simply key in the script name from the shell prompt and run it as an executable. In this case, the current shell uses a sub-shell of the same type to execute it. However, if the script contains the interpreter line in this form:

```
#!/usr/bin/ksh
```

then, even though the login shell may be Bourne, it will use the Korn shell to execute the script. Specification of the interpreter line also helps us identify the shell the script is meant to use. We have specified the interpreter line in every script used in Chapter 14; we'll continue this practice in this chapter also.

21.2 () AND {}: SUB-SHELL OR CURRENT SHELL?

The shell uses two types of operators to group commands. You must understand clearly the consequences of using one group in preference to the other:

- The () Statements enclosed within parentheses are executed in a sub-shell.
- The {} Statements enclosed within curly braces are executed in the current shell only.

You have used the first type *(8.5.2)* to collectively redirect the standard output of two commands with a single redirection symbol in a manner similar to this:

```
( a.sh ; b.sh ; c.sh ) > d.sh
```

Sub-shell considerations are not important here, so we can use either form, but some applications require a set of commands to be run *without* spawning a child shell. To consider an example, let's use both grouping operators with the **cd** and **pwd** commands. Check your current directory and then change it with **cd**:

```
$ pwd
/home/kumar
```

```
$ ( cd progs ; pwd )
/home/kumar/progs
$ pwd
/home/kumar                                         Back to original directory
```

Working from a sub-shell, **cd** changed the working directory (one of the environmental parameters) to /home/kumar/progs. The parent (login shell) can't adopt this change, so the original directory is back in place. The same command group—this time using the {} operators—tells a different story:

```
$ pwd
/home/kumar
$ { cd progs ; pwd ; }
/home/kumar/progs
$ pwd
/home/kumar/progs                                   Directory change is now permanent
```

The two commands have now been executed without spawning a shell; no separate environment was created, and the change of directory became permanent even after the execution of the command group. Note that we need to precede the closing brace with a ; if both { and } appear in the same line.

An often-used sequence used in many shell scripts checks the number of command line arguments and terminates the script with **exit** if the test fails. For instance, a sequence like this:

```
if [ $# -ne 3 ] ; then
    echo "You have not keyed in 3 arguments"
    exit 3
fi
```

can be easily replaced with this sequence using curly braces:

```
[ $# -ne 3 ] && { echo "You have not keyed in 3 arguments" ; exit 3 ; }
```

Why can't we use () instead of {} here? The **exit** statement can terminate a script only if it runs in the same shell that's running the script. This is the case when **exit** runs inside the {}, but not when it runs inside (). An **exit** inside () will stop executing the remaining statements in the group, but that won't automatically terminate a script.

21.3 export: EXPORTING SHELL VARIABLES

By default, the values stored in shell variables are local to the shell and are not passed on to a child shell. But the shell can also **export** these variables (with the **export** statement) recursively to all child processes so that, once defined, they are available globally. You have used this statement before, but now you should understand why you have done so.

Consider a simple script which displays the value of a variable x, assigns a new value to it and then displays the new value again:

```
$ cat var.sh
echo The value of x is $x
x=20                                      # Now change the value of x
echo The new value of x is $x
```

First assign 10 to x at the prompt and then execute the script:

```
$ x=10 ; var.sh
The value of x is                              Value of x not visible in a sub-shell
The new value of x is 20
$ echo $x                                      Value set inside the script doesn't
10                                             affect value outside script
```

Because x is a local variable in the login shell, its value can't be accessed by **echo** in the script, which is run in a sub-shell. To make x available globally, you need to use the **export** statement before the script is executed:

```
$ x=10 ; export x
$ var.sh
The value of x is 10                           Value in parent shell now visible here
The new value of x is 20
$ echo $x                                      Value reset inside script (child shell)
10                                             is not available outside it (parent shell)
```

When x is exported, its assigned value (10) is available in the script. But when you export a variable, it has another important consequence; a reassignment (x=20) made in the script (a sub-shell) is not seen in the parent shell which executed the script.

You must export the variables you define unless you have strong reasons not to let sub-shells inherit their values. To know whether you have already done so, use **export** without arguments. It lists all environment variables (which are already exported) and user-defined variables (like x) that you have exported. The **env** command also lists exported variables.

Note: A variable defined in a process is only local to the process in which it is defined, and is not available in a child process. But when it is exported, it is available recursively to all child processes. However, when the child alters the value of the variable, the change is not seen in the parent.

21.4 RUNNING A SCRIPT IN THE CURRENT SHELL: THE . COMMAND

Variable assignments made in the shell's startup file (.profile or .bash_profile) are *always* seen in the login shell. It's obvious that the profile is executed by the login shell without creating a sub-shell. But how? If you thought that the .profile was executed by grouping it with the curly braces:

```
{ .profile ; }
```

then you'll be disappointed to see that there is no execute permission for the file:

```
$ ls -l .profile
-rw-r--r--  1 kumar    group       727 Feb 27 23:02 .profile
```

There's a special command used to execute a shell script without creating a sub-shell—the . (dot) command. You can make changes to .profile and execute it with the . command *without requiring to log out and log in again*:

```
. .profile
```

Most users have the impression that you must log out and log in if you have made a change to the .profile. You actually don't need to do that; simply execute the edited file with the . command. You'll need this facility later to execute files containing shell functions.

Note: The dot command executes a script without using a sub-shell. It also doesn't require the script to have execute permission.

21.5 let: COMPUTATION—A SECOND LOOK (KORN AND BASH)

Korn and Bash come with a built-in integer handling facility that totally dispenses with the need to use **expr**. You can compute with the **let** statement which is used here both with and without quotes:

```
$ let sum=256+128                          No whitespace after variable
$ let sum="256 + 128"                      No whitespace after variable
```

If you use whitespace for imparting better readability, then quote the expression. In either case, sum is assigned the result of the expression:

```
$ echo $sum
384
```

Let's see how **let** handles variables. First define three variables; a single **let** does it:

```
$ let x=12 y=18 z=5
$ let z=x+y+$z                             $ not required by let
$ echo $z
35
```

let permits you to get rid of the $ altogether when making an assignment. Since this computational feature is built in, scripts run much faster than when used with **expr**. Later, we'll be using **let** in place of **expr** in one of our scripts.

A Second Form of Computing with ((*and*))   The Korn shell and Bash use the (( )) operators that replace the **let** statement itself:

```
$ x=22 y=28 z=5
$ z=$((x+y + z))                           Whitespace is unimportant
$ echo $z
55
$ z=$((z+1))
$ echo $z
56
```

POSIX recommends the use of ((and)) rather than **let**, and this form is likely to become a standard feature. It's easier to use too because a single dollar can replace multiple ones.

21.6 ARRAYS (KORN AND BASH)

Korn and Bash support one-dimensional arrays where the first element has the index 0. Here's how you set and evaluate the value of the third element of the array prompt:

```
$ prompt[2]="Enter your name: "
$ echo ${prompt[2]}
Enter your name:
```

Note that evaluation is done with curly braces, and prompt[2] is treated just like a variable. It, however, doesn't conflict with a variable prompt that you may also define in the same shell. For assigning a group of elements, use a space-delimited list having either of these two forms:

```
set -A month_arr 0 31 29 31 30 31 30 31 31 30 31 30 31        Korn only
month_arr=(0 31 29 31 30 31 30 31 31 30 31 30 31)             Bash only
```

In either case, the array stores the number of days available in each of the 12 months. The first element had to be deliberately assigned to zero for obvious reasons. Finding out the number of days in June is simple:

```
$ echo ${month_arr[6]}
30
```

Using the @ or * as subscript, you can display all elements of the array as well as the number of elements. The forms are similar except for the presence of the # in one:

```
$ echo ${month_arr[@]}
0 31 29 31 30 31 30 31 31 30 31 30 31
$ echo ${#month_arr[@]}                      Length of the array
13
```

Can we use arrays to validate an entered date? The next script, **dateval.sh** (Fig. 21.1), does just that. It takes into account the leap year changes (except the one that takes place at the turn of every fourth century).

The first option of the outer **case** construct checks for a null response. The second option uses the expression $n/$n/$n to check for an eight-character string in the form *dd/mm/yy*. Using a changed value of IFS, the components of the date are set to three positional parameters and checked for valid months. The second **case** construct makes the leap year check and then uses an array to validate the day. The **continue** statements take you to the beginning of the loop whenever the test fails the validity check. Let's test the script:

```
$ dateval.sh
Enter a date: [Enter]
No date entered
Enter a date: 28/13/00
Illegal month
Enter a date: 31/04/00
Illegal day
Enter a date: 29/02/01
2001 is not a leap year
Enter a date: 29/02/00
29/02/00 is a valid date
[Ctrl-c]
```

Since the script has no exit path, we had to use the interrupt key to terminate execution.

```
#!/usr/bin/ksh
# Script: dateval.sh - Validates a date field using an array
IFS="/"
n="[0-9][0-9]"
set -A month_arr 0 31 29 31 30 31 30 31 31 30 31 30 31
while echo "Enter a date: \c" ; do
   read value
   case "$value" in
           "") echo "No date entered" ; continue ;;
    $n/$n/$n) set $value
           let rem="$3 % 4"
           if [ $2 -gt 12 -o $2 -eq 0 ] ; then
               echo "Illegal month" ; continue
           else
               case "$value" in
          29/02/??) [ $rem -gt 0 ] &&
                     { echo "20$3 is not a leap year" ; continue ; } ;;
                 *) [ $1 -gt ${month_arr[$2]} -o $1 -eq 0 ] &&
                     { echo "Illegal day" ; continue ; } ;;
               esac
           fi;;
          *) echo "Invalid date" ; continue ;;
   esac
   echo "$1/$2/$3" is a valid date
done
```

Fig. 21.1 `dateval.sh`

21.7 STRING HANDLING (KORN AND BASH)

Korn and Bash don't need **expr** as they have adequate string handling features themselves. Unlike **expr**, they use wild-cards but not regular expressions. All forms of usage require curly braces to enclose the variable name along with some special symbols. The subtle variations in their forms make them difficult to remember and sometimes uncomfortable to work with.

21.7.1 Length of a String

The length of a string is easily found by preceding the variable name with a #. Consider this example:

```
$ name="vinton cerf"
$ echo ${#name}
11
```

You can now use this expression with an **if** statement to check the length of a string. This built-in feature is not only easier to use than its corresponding **expr** version *(14.9.2)* but is also comparatively faster:

```
if [ ${#name} -gt 20 ] ; then
```
Korn and Bash

This form should appear familiar to you as **perl** uses a similar form to evaluate the length of an array *(19.8)*.

21.7.2 Extracting a String by Pattern Matching

You can extract a substring using a special pattern matching feature. These functions make use of two characters—# and %. Their selection seems to have been based on mnemonic considerations. # is used to match at the beginning and % at the end, and both are used inside curly braces when evaluating a variable.

To remove the extension from a filename, previously you had to use an external command—**basename** *(14.12.2)*. This time, you can use a variable's ${*variable%pattern*} format to do that:

```
$ filename=quotation.txt
$ echo ${filename%txt}
quotation.                                          txt stripped off
```

The % symbol after the variable name deletes the *shortest* string that matches the variable's contents at the *end*. Had there been two %s instead of one, the expression would have matched the longest one. Let's now use %% with wild-cards to extract the hostname from an FQDN:

```
$ fqdn=java.sun.com
$ echo ${fqdn%%.*}
java
```

You'll recall that **basename** can also extract the base filename from a pathname. This means deleting the longest string that matches the pattern */, but at the beginning:

```
$ filename="/var/mail/henry"
$ echo ${filename##*/}
henry
```

This deletes the segment, /var/mail—the longest pattern that matches the pattern */ at the beginning. The pattern matching forms of Korn and Bash are listed in Table 21.1.

Table 21.1 Pattern Matching Operators Used by Korn and Bash

Form	Evaluates to segment remaining after deleting
${*var#pat*}	Shortest segment that matches *pat* at beginning of $*var*
${*var##pat*}	Longest segment that matches *pat* at beginning of $*var*
${*var%pat*}	Shortest segment that matches *pat* at end of $*var*
${*var%%pat*}	Longest segment that matches *pat* at end of $*var*

21.8 CONDITIONAL PARAMETER SUBSTITUTION

To continue on the subject of variable evaluation, you can evaluate a variable depending on whether it has a null or defined value. This feature is known as **parameter substitution**, and is available in the Bourne shell also. It takes this general form:

${ <*var*> : <*opt*> <*stg*> }

This time, the variable <*var*> is followed by a colon and any of the symbols +, -, = or ? as <*opt*>. The symbol is followed by the string <*stg*>. In all cases barring one, this doesn't alter the value of the variable, but only determines the way it is *evaluated*. This evaluation can be done in four ways.

The + Option   Here, *var* evaluates to *stg* if it is defined and assigned a nonnull string. This feature can be used to set a variable to the output of a command and echo a message if the variable is nonnull:

```
found=`ls`
echo ${found:+"This directory is not empty"}
```

`ls` displays nothing if it finds no files, in which case the variable found is set to a null string. However, the message is echoed if `ls` finds at least one file.

The - Option   Here, *var* is evaluated to *stg* if it is undefined or assigned a null string (the opposite of the + option). You can use this feature in a program which prompts for a filename, and then uses a default value when the user simply presses *[Enter]*:

```
echo "Enter the filename : \c"
read flname
fname=${flname:-emp.lst}                       Instead of using if [ -z $flname ]
```

If flname is null or is not set, it *evaluates* to the string emp.lst. The value of flname, however, still remains null. This compact assignment dispenses with the need for an **if** conditional.

The = Option   This also works similarly except that it goes a step further and *makes the assignment* to the variable that is evaluated. With the = option, you can use parameter substitution with a command without making the intermediate assignment:

```
echo "Enter the filename : \c"
read flname
grep $pattern ${flname:=emp.lst}                      flname is now assigned
```

Note that in the last statement, the variable flname itself got assigned (provided it was either unset or set to a null string). This feature is also useful in initializing a variable that is used in the control command of a loop. The following statements

```
x=1 ; while [ $x -le 10 ]
```

can now be combined in one:

```
while [ ${x:=1} -le 10 ]
```

The ? Option   It evaluates the parameter if the variable is assigned and nonnull. Otherwise, it echoes a string and kills the shell. This is quite useful in terminating a script if the user fails to respond properly to shell directives:

```
echo "Enter the filename : \c"
read flname
grep $pattern ${flname:?"No filename entered"}
```

If no filename is entered here, the message No filename entered is displayed. The script is also aborted without the use of an explicit **exit** command.

Apart from the = operator, the other operators can also be used with positional parameters. You can now easily set a variable to some default if the script is invoked without an argument:

```
flname=${1:-emp.lst}                    $1 is null if script invoked without arguments
```

You can now compress some of the earlier scripts to even shorter command sequences. You'll see some of these applications later in the chapter.

Note: Only the = option actually assigns a value to a variable; the others merely control the way the variable is evaluated.

21.9 MERGING STREAMS

You have seen the utility of redirecting a loop at the **done** keyword *(14.11)*. This also meant redirecting individual statements inside the loop to /dev/tty when these statements needed to send output to the terminal. When there are a large number of such terminal-destined statements, separately using >/dev/tty with each one of them can be quite tedious. The shell offers a simple solution to this problem.

Though the standard output and standard error are two separate streams, the shell lets you merge the two so that they can be collectively manipulated. Once you do that, you effectively have a single stream, which you can subsequently use with any of the shell's redirection and piping symbols. This is done with the & operator following the redirection symbol. When the **echo** statement is placed in a script in this way:

```
echo "None of the patterns found" 1>&2
```

it's like saying: "Send the standard output to the destination of standard error". Since the default file descriptor for standard output is 1, you can also use >&2.

The notation 1>&2 merges standard output with standard error, which, in the absence of further redirection, is connected to the terminal. However, when you redirect the standard error of the entire script in this way:

```
emp8.sh > sclist 2> errlist
```

all script statements having the symbols 1>&2 affixed, will actually write to errlist. The rest of the script output will, however, be saved in sclist.

For the reverse situation, i.e., sending the standard error to the destination of the standard output, the notation becomes 2>&1. You may need this to be done on many occasions, especially when a job is run in the background and you still want the error messages to be held in the same file that contains the actual output.

21.10 SHELL FUNCTIONS

A **shell function** is like any other function; it executes a group of statements as a bunch. Optionally, it also returns a value. This construct is available in most modern shells where you can use them to condense important routines to short sequences. The syntax is simple:

```
function_name() {
    statements
    return value            Optional
}
```

The function definition is followed by (), and the body is enclosed within curly braces. On invocation, the function executes all *statements* in the body. The **return** statement, when present, returns a value representing the success or failure of the function (and not a string value).

Let's consider a simple application. When viewing the listing of a large number of files in a directory, you are often compelled to use **ls -l | more**. This command sequence is an ideal candidate for a shell function, which we'll name **ll**:

```
$ ll() {
> ls -l $* | more            Function defined in the command line
> }                          is available in current shell only
```

Like shell scripts, shell functions also use command line arguments (like $1, $2, etc.). $*, "$@" and $# also retain their usual significance in functions. Even though you need the () in the function definition, you must not use them when invoking the function with or without arguments:

```
ll                           Executes ls -l | more
ll ux3rd??                   Executes ls -l ux3rd?? | more
```

We have used the **ll** function more like a procedure, but a shell function can also return its exit status with the **return** statement. This exit status can be gathered from the shell parameter, $?.

Shell functions can be defined at a number of places:

- At the beginning of every script using them. Since shell statements are executed in the interpretive mode, a shell function must precede the statements that call it.
- In the .profile so they are available in the current session.
- In a separate "library" file so other applications can also use them.

Since the above function is often required, it's better you create a file **mainfunc.sh** to hold it. You then have to place the following entry at the beginning of every shell script that uses the function:

```
. mainfunc.sh                Functions available in the current shell
```

Caution: The positional parameters made available to shell scripts externally are not available *directly* to a shell function. To make them available, store these parameters in shell variables first and then invoke the function with these variables as arguments.

21.10.1 Generating a Filename from the System Date

As system administrator, you'll often need to maintain separate files for each day of a specific activity. These filenames can be derived from the system date, so you can easily identify a file pertaining to a certain day. It's a good idea to have this value echoed by a shell function **dated_fname**, which in turn gets it from the **date** output:

```
dated_fname() {
    set -- `date`
    year=`expr $6 : '..\(..\)'`                 Picks up last two characters from year
    echo "$2$3_$year"
}
```

When you invoke the function, **echo** displays a string derived from the current date:

```
$ dated_fname
Jan28_03
```

This string can be used to generate one filename a day. Oracle users can easily use this function to have a system-generated dump filename for the **exp** command:

```
exp scott/tiger file=`dated_fname`
```

This will generate the export dump file Jan28_03.dmp. Create a library file **mainfunc.sh** and place this function definition there. We'll use this file later—after we have added two more functions to it.

21.10.2 To Continue or Not to Continue

We'll now consider a shell function which actually returns a value. Recall the sequence used at the end of the script, **dentry1.sh** *(14.17.2)*, which prompts the user for a y to continue, or an n to terminate the outermost loop. This routine is very often used inside shell scripts, and it's a good idea to convert this into a function, **anymore**:

```
anymore() {
    echo "\n$1 ?(y/n) : \c" 1>&2            Prompt supplied as argument
    read response
    case "$response" in
      y|Y) echo  1>&2 ; return 0 ;;
        *) return 1 ;;
    esac
}
```

The function uses its argument $1 to determine what the prompt will look like. When this function is invoked with the string Wish to continue, you are prompted for a response:

```
$ anymore "Wish to continue"

Wish to continue ?(y/n) : n
$ echo $?
1                                       Same value as specified in return statement
```

We'll make use of the return value of this function later in the chapter.

21.10.3 Validating Data Entry

Consider the script, **dentry1.sh** *(14.17.2)*, where you used a **while** loop to repeatedly prompt the user for a valid entry. This sequence can also be easily converted into a shell function, **valid_string**. We expect the function to check two things—first that something is entered at all, and whether it exceeds a certain length:

```
valid_string() {
    while echo "$1 \c"  1>&2 ; do
        read name
        case $name in
            "") echo "Nothing entered" 1>&2 ; continue ;;
            *) if [ `expr "$name" : '.*'` -gt $2 ] ; then
                   echo "Maximum $2 characters permitted" 1>&2
               else
                   break
               fi ;;
        esac
    done
    echo $name
}
```

The function takes two arguments—the prompt string and the maximum number of characters permitted. We'll place this function in our library file, **mainfunc.sh**, and call it from the script **user_passwd.sh** (Fig. 21.2).

This small script accepts the user's name and password, which can't exceed 16 and 5 characters in length, respectively. A sample session shows how shell functions can reduce script size:

```
$ user_passwd.sh
Enter your user-id : robert louis stevenson
Maximum 16 characters permitted
Enter your user-id : scott
Enter your password:
Nothing entered
Enter your password: *****                         Doesn't show on screen
Your user-id is scott and your password is tiger
```

```
#!/bin/sh
# Script: user_passwd.sh - Uses a shell function
#
. mainfunc.sh                      # Script containing valid_string function

user=`valid_string "Enter your user-id :" 16`
stty -echo                                  # Password not to be echoed
password=`valid_string "Enter your password:" 5`
stty echo                                   # Turns on echoing facility
echo "\nYour user-id is $user and your password is $password"
```

Fig. 21.2 user_passwd.sh

Invocation of a shell function reduces disk I/O since the function is resident in memory. On the other hand, when you execute a shell script, the shell first scans the disk for the script file. However, you must take care to see that you don't keep a lot of functions in memory as that would eat up CPU resources. Shell functions are better than aliases in every way, and they work in the Bourne shell also.

Tip: If a number of shell functions are used by multiple programs, you should place all of them in a single "library" file, and store the file at a convenient location. At the beginning of every script which requires these functions, provide a statement that executes the library file with the dot command.

21.11 eval: EVALUATING TWICE

The previous script requires that you set the variable names ($user and $password) for reading each input. In some situations, we would prefer to have the variable name generated on the fly. We could store the prompts as "generalized variables" and read the input as "numbered variables".

First define a couple of prompts at the prompt and then attempt to issue the first prompt with a numbered variable:

```
$ prompt1="Employee id : " ; prompt2="Name : " ; prompt3="Designation : "
$ x=1
$ echo $prompt$x
1
```

Instead of echoing Employee id : , it simply echoes the value 1, viz. the value of x. This happens because the shell evaluates the command line from left to right. It first encounters the $ and evaluates $prompt; obviously $prompt is undefined. The shell then evaluates $x, which has the value 1.

The shell's **eval** statement evaluates a command line twice. It suppresses *some* evaluation in the first pass and performs it only in the second pass. This is exactly what we need the shell to do in our previous example. If we escape the first $ (like \$prompt$x), the first pass evaluates only $x, so we have prompt1. The second pass evaluates $prompt1. This is done by prefixing the **echo** command with **eval**:

```
$ x=1 ; eval echo \$prompt$x
Employee id :
```

We have a numbered prompt; we now need to use a numbered variable to read the input. For instance, the responses against numbered prompts can also be held in variables value1, value2, value3, etc. The following sequence does it for the second prompt:

```
$ { x=2
>     eval echo \$prompt$x '\\c'
>     read value$x                          This has no problems
>     eval echo \$value$x
> }
Name : rahul verma
rahul verma
```

Let's consider another application of **eval**. We can access a positional parameter with $1 or whatever, but can we access the last parameter directly? Since we have the value of $# available, we can use the services of **eval**:

```
$ tail -n 1 /etc/passwd
martha:x:605:100:martha mitchell:/home/martha:/bin/ksh
$ IFS=:
$ set `tail -n 1 /etc/passwd`    set -- not required here
$ eval echo \$$#
/bin/ksh
```

Using **eval**, we don't even have to know the number of fields in a line of /etc/passwd. In the next section, we'll use the services of **eval** both to generate prompts as well as to read user input.

21.11.1 A Generalized Data Entry Script with eval

We'll now use the **eval** feature to accept input into six fields with a generalized script, **dentry2.sh** (Fig. 21.3). There are six prompts defined at the beginning of the script as numbered variables, and an inner **while** loop issues all of them in turn. The values are read into the variables value1, value2, etc., and appended to the variable $rekord, using the | as delimiter each time.

Note how the use of shell functions has kept the script size small. Here's a sample interaction:

```
$ dentry2.sh
Enter the output filename : newlist

Employee id : 2244
Name : prakash kumar
Designation : director
Department : marketing
Date birth : 27/02/44
Basic pay : 6700

More entries to add ?(y/n) : y

Employee id : 4789
Name : v.k. singh
Designation : manager
Department : personnel
Date birth : 21/12/46
Basic pay : 6500

More entries to add ?(y/n) : n
```

When you see newlist, you'll find two lines with an extra | at the end of each:

```
$ cat newlist
2244|prakash kumar|director|marketing|27/02/44|6700|
4789|v.k. singh|manager|personnel|21/12/46|6500|
```

```
#!/bin/sh
# Script: dentry2.sh - Uses eval and shell functions
#
trap 'echo "Program interrupted"; exit' HUP INT TERM
. mainfunc.sh          # Invokes functions valid_string() and anymore ()

prompt1="Employee id : " ; prompt2="Name : " ; prompt3="Designation : "
prompt4="Department : " ; prompt5="Date birth : " ; prompt6="Basic pay : "
rekord=

flname=`valid_string "Enter the output filename: " 8`
while true ; do
    while [ ${x:=1} -le 6 ] ; do                    # x first set to 1
        eval echo \$prompt$x '\\c' 1>&2
        read value$x
        rekord="${rekord}`eval echo \\$value$x`|"
        x=`expr $x + 1`
    done
    echo "$rekord"
    anymore "More entries to add" 1>&2 || break
done > $flname
```

Fig. 21.3 `dentry2.sh`

This is amazing; thanks to **eval**, we have managed to read six user responses into six variables with a minuscule script!

21.12 THE exec STATEMENT

Your study of the mechanism of process creation (9.4) led you to the **exec** system function—one that overlays a forked process. This property has some importance to shell scripters who sometimes need to overwrite the current shell itself with the code of another program. This is something we haven't done yet, but if you precede any UNIX command with **exec**, the command overwrites the current process—often the shell. This has the effect of logging you out after the completion of the command:

$ exec date
Tue Jan 28 21:21:52 IST 2003   *Shell no longer exists!*
login:

Sometimes, you might want to let a user run a single program automatically on logging in and deny her an escape to the shell. You can place the command in the .profile, duly preceded by **exec**. The shell overlays itself with the code of the program to be executed, and when command execution is complete, the user is logged out (since there's no shell waiting for it).

21.12.1 Using exec to Create Additional File Descriptors

exec has another important property; it can redirect the standard streams for an entire script. If a script has several commands whose standard output go to a single file, then instead of using separate redirection symbols for each, you can use **exec** to reassign their default destination like this:

```
exec > foundfile
```
Can use >> also

What's the big deal you might say; one could redirect the script itself. But **exec** can create several streams apart from the standard three (0, 1 and 2), each with its own file descriptor. For instance, you can create a file descriptor 3 for directing all output and associate it with a physical file invalidfile:

```
exec 3>invalidfile
```

In system call parlance (23.2.1), you have *opened* this file to generate the file descriptor 3. Subsequent access to this file can be made by using this file descriptor. You can now write the file by merging the standard output stream with the file descriptor 3:

```
echo "This goes to invalidfile" 1>&3
```

With this powerful I/O handler, you should now be able to handle files in a simpler and more elegant way. Let's design a script which reads emp-ids from a file. It then searches emp.1st and saves in three separate files the following:

- The lines found.
- The emp-ids not found.
- Badly formed emp-ids.

First, here's the file that contains emp-ids. It contains two three-digit emp-ids which should be trapped by the script:

```
$ cat empid.1st
2233
9765
2476
789
3564
9877
0110
245
2954
```

The script, **countpat.sh** (Fig. 21.4), divides the standard output into three streams and redirects them to three separate files. It requires four arguments—the file containing the patterns and the files for the three streams.

The standard output streams are merged with the file descriptors 1, 3 and 4 using **exec**. Note that we have also set $1 as the source of all standard input. This means that the **read** statement in the loop will take input from $1—the file containing the patterns. Once all file writing is over, the standard output stream has to be reassigned to the terminal (**exec >/dev/tty**), otherwise the message Job Over will also be saved in the filename passed to $2.

This script is quite clean and has two statements using the merging symbols. The **grep** statement uses the standard output's file descriptor, so no merging is required. The script takes four arguments and diverts its output to three of them:

```
$ countpat.sh empid.lst foundfile notfoundfile invalidfile
Job Over
```

The message appears on the terminal instead of going to any of these files. Now, just have a look at the three files and see for yourself what has actually happened:

```
$ cat foundfile
2233|a.k. shukla     |g.m.      |sales     |12/12/52|6000
2476|anil aggarwal   |manager   |sales     |05/01/59|5000
3564|sudhir Agarwal  |executive |personnel |07/06/47|7500
0110|v.k. agrawal    |g.m.      |marketing |12/31/40|9000
$ cat notfoundfile
9765 not found in file
9877 not found in file
2954 not found in file
$ cat invalidfile
789 not a four-character string
245 not a four-character string
```

```
#!/bin/sh
# Script: countpat.sh -- Uses exec to handle multiple files
#
exec > $2                    # Open file 1 for storing selected lines
exec 3> $3                   # Open file 4 for storing patterns not found
exec 4> $4                   # Open file 5 for storing invalid patterns


[ $# -ne 4 ] && { echo "4 arguments required" ; exit 2 ; }

exec < $1                                # Redirecting input
while read pattern ; do
     case "$pattern" in
        ????) grep $pattern emp.lst ||
            echo $pattern not found in file 1>&3 ;;
        *) echo $pattern not a four-character string 1>&4 ;;
     esac
done
exec >/dev/tty               # Redirects standard output back to terminal
echo Job Over
```

Fig. 21.4 `countpat.sh`

This then is the power of **exec**. It can open several files and access each one in the same way **perl** uses filehandles and system calls use file descriptors. It is always preferable to use file descriptors instead of filenames because using **exec**, you can keep them open, and this makes I/O operations efficient.

21.13 CONCLUSION

We examined the shell's environment and discussed some of the useful features of the Korn and Bash shells. We also discussed two advanced features, **eval** and **exec**, that are available in the Bourne shell also. Like with **sed**, it takes time to master these features, but they are extremely useful tools. The **eval** feature is indeed unique, but knowing **exec** will help you understand how file I/O actually takes place. In Chapter 24 we take up this topic in our study of the UNIX system calls.

We have finally come to the end of our journey with the shell. Along with **awk** and **perl**, the shell too has to be taken seriously if the power of the UNIX system is to be exploited to the hilt.

WRAP UP

A shell script is executed in a sub-shell which inherits a number of environmental parameters from its parent. Variables defined in the parent shell are inaccessible in the child unless they are exported. However, when the child alters the value of a variable, the changed value is not seen by the parent.

The grouping operators () run a group of commands in a sub-shell but the {} don't spawn one. The . command executes a shell script without using a second shell.

Shell variables can be evaluated in a conditional manner, depending on whether they are assigned a nonempty value. The = operator additionally assigns a value to the variable, while ? prints an error message and exits the shell.

The shell has a mechanism for merging the standard output and standard error streams using the symbols 1>&2 and 2>&1. Using this mechanism, it is possible to treat standard output as standard error, and vice versa.

Shell functions let you condense important and repetitive sequences so they are available everywhere. Unlike aliases, they accept command line arguments and also return a true or false value.

eval is used to process a command line twice. This makes it possible to simulate arrays and execute variables. **exec** overlays the current shell when prefixed to a command. It is also used to associate file descriptors with filenames.

Test Your Understanding

21.1   If you define a variable at the command prompt, how can you make its value available in a shell script?

21.2   Invoke the **script** command and define a variable at the prompt. Now quit **script** with **exit** and echo the value of this variable. What do you see and why?

21.3   If a directory change is made inside a shell script, why is the original directory restored after the completion of the script? How can you overcome this problem?

21.4   Write a shell function, **size()**, which lists *only* the total size of the files supplied as arguments (all files without arguments).

21.5   Why can't you use the **exit** statement inside a function to return control to the calling program?

21.6   What will this statement do? `flname=${1:-emp.lst}`

21.7   Write a shell function for **rm** which goes to the interactive mode whenever you use it with more than one filename.

21.8   Write a shell function that removes the current directory by invoking the function from there.

21.9   How will you make sure that a specific program is executed immediately on logging in, and the user is logged out when the program finishes?

Flex Your Brain

21.1   Write a script which accepts an anonymous FTP site (like *ftp.heavens.com*) and any number of **ftp** commands (like **"cd pub"**, **"get cp32.tar.gz"**) as arguments. It should then connect to the site, log in automatically, and execute the **ftp** commands.

21.2   Why won't the **exit** command, when placed in a shell script like this, terminate the script? How do you get over this? **(** *statements* **; exit)**

21.3   Invoke the **su** command (if you know the root password), and then run **ps -t** with the terminal name. What conclusion would you draw?

21.4   Write a shell function that locates a directory supplied as argument, in the home directory tree and switches to it. Will the same code work if placed in a shell script?

21.5   What is wrong with this statement? How do you modify it to execute correctly?
        `[ $# -ne 2 ] && echo "Usage: $0 min_guid max_guid" ; exit`

21.6   You have to run a job at night and need to have both the output and error messages in the same file. How will you run the script?

21.7   How can you extract the last command line argument to a script using (i) arrays, (ii) **eval**?

21.8   Write a script to copy files to a directory only when they don't exist there. The filenames are supplied as arguments and the last argument is the directory. You are allowed to use only one external command (**cp**) and exploit the features of the Korn and Bash shells. (HINT: Use the **eval** statement to identify the directory name.)

Program Development Tools

UNIX systems today support a host of programming and scripting languages, but the C language has a special place in the system. UNIX was written in C, and until recently, the C compiler was shipped as standard with every UNIX system. Apart from its text manipulation skills, UNIX also excels in the management of C programs—both in their text and binary form. In this chapter, we take a look at some of the native programming tools available on most UNIX systems.

Large programming projects need the administration of program sources and binaries. We discuss the tools that help you keep track of changes made in program sources. We'll learn how to rebuild only the affected program sections and preserve all versions using a version control scheme that allows easy retrieval. We'll also build a library of object modules. For a C programmer, this chapter is compulsory reading.

WHAT YOU WILL LEARN

- Understand the three phases of the compilation process and how they apply to a multimodule C application.
- How **make** handles *dependencies* by recompiling only the changed sources.
- Understand the differences between *static* and *shared* libraries.
- How storing differences between successive versions form the basis of *version control*.
- Check files in and out with the *Source Code Control System (SCCS)* using the **admin**, **get** and **delta** commands.
- Use the *Revision Control System (RCS)* and the **ci** and **co** commands for the same purpose.

TOPICS OF SPECIAL INTEREST

- Build a *static library* of object files with **ar** and use **make** to automatically update entries in a library.

22.1 HANDLING MULTISOURCE C APPLICATIONS

The standard technique of using **cc foo.c** to create the **a.out** executable needs to be modified when working with multisource programs. Before we take up such an application, we need to examine the three phases a C program has to pass through before a standalone executable is created:

- **Compiling**   Even though we use the term *compiling* to signify all three phases, compilation actually converts the C source code (in the .c files) to assembly language (.s files).

- **Assembling**   The assembled code is transformed into object code by the *assembler*. A file containing object code has the .o extension. The machine understands this code, but it can't be executed directly as it is incomplete; it doesn't include the code of functions used in the program.

- **Linking**   The object code of the program is finally linked by the *linker* or *loader* with other object files and libraries that contain code used by functions. This phase produces a single executable file, which by default is named a.out.

The default action of the **cc** compiler (or GNU's **gcc**) is to combine the three phases. For instance, if the code is distributed across a number of files, the following command could generate a.out:

```
cc a.c b.c c.c                                    Creates a.out; no .o files
```

cc calls the assembler (a program named **as**) to create the .o files before it invokes the linker (a program named **ld**) to create a single executable. We can also invoke **ld** directly, but its syntax is a little awkward; we can leave this job to **cc**. After **ld** has created the executable (by default, a.out), **cc** removes the .o files.

Using the -c option, you can create only the object files and without creating a.out:

```
cc -c a.c b.c c.c                                 Creates only a.o, b.o and c.o
```

A mix of source and object files is also permitted. You can also use the -o option to specify your own executable name:

```
cc -o foo a.c b.o c.o                             Creates executable named foo
```

For single-source programs (where functions are stored in the same file as the main program itself), we normally don't need to look at these three phases separately. In fact, we don't even need the intermediate .o file. However, in a real-life scenario, we often need to do a *partial* compilation and maintain these .o files. To understand why, let's examine a multisource application.

22.2 A MULTISOURCE APPLICATION

Large applications are generally spread across multiple files. These files contain the source and object code of functions used by the main program (the program containing the **main** function). They also include the header files containing the prototypes of the functions. Dividing a task into functions has two advantages:

- Functions impart modularity to our code. They make programs comprehensible and thus help in debugging them.
- Enable their reuse. The same function can be used by another application.

We'll now develop a multisource application that computes the interest on a recurring deposit. The main program, **rec_deposit.c** (Fig. 22.1), accepts three arguments representing the principal, interest and term, and writes the maturity amount to the standard output. It invokes three functions:

```
#include <math.h>
#include "quit.h"
#include "arg_check.h"

float compute(float, float, float);              /* Declaring function prototype */

int main(int argc, char **argv) {
    float principal, interest, term, sum ;
    char *mesg = "Three arguments required\n" ;
    char *mesg2 = "All arguments must be positive\n" ;
    arg_check(4, argc, mesg, 1);                 /* Checks for three arguments */
    sscanf(argv[1], "%f", &principal);           /* Converting strings to float */
    sscanf(argv[2], "%f", &interest);
    sscanf(argv[3], "%f", &term);
    if (principal <= 0 || interest <= 0 || term <= 0)
        quit(mesg2, 2);                          /* Quits with 2 as $? on error */
    sum = compute(principal, interest, term);    /* Function declared here */
    printf("Maturity amount: %f\n", sum );
    exit(0);
}

float compute(float principal, float interest, float term) {
    int i;
    float maturity = 0;
    interest = 1 + interest / 100 ;
    for (i = 1 ; i <= term ; i++)
        maturity += principal * pow(interest, i) ;
    return maturity;
}
```

Fig. 22.1 `rec_deposit.c`

- **arg_check** This function checks whether the right number of arguments have been entered. It is defined in **arg_check.c** which includes **arg_check.h** (Fig. 22.2).

- **quit** This function prints a message and terminates the program. It is defined in **quit.c** and includes **quit.h** (Fig. 22.3).

- **compute** It computes the interest from the three arguments provided. This function is not placed in a separate file.

arg_check and **quit** are useful, reusable functions; they will be reused in the next two chapters. **compute** is maintained in the main file only to understand why this too should be moved to its own source file. The two header files contain—apart from the usual **#include** statements— the prototypes of their respective functions. These functions are used in **main**, so they need to be included in **rec_deposit.c** also.

```
$ cat arg_check.c
#include "arg_check.h"
void arg_check (int args, int argc, char *message, int exit_status) {
    if (argc != args) {
        fprintf(stderr, message);
        exit(exit_status);
    }
}

$ cat arg_check.h
#include <stdio.h>
void arg_check (int, int, char *, int);
```

Fig. 22.2 `arg_check.c` and `arg_check.h`

```
$ cat quit.c
#include "quit.h"
void quit (char *message, int exit_status) {
    fprintf(stderr, message);
    exit(exit_status);
}

$ cat quit.h
#include <stdio.h>
void quit (char *, int);
```

Fig. 22.3 `quit.c` and `quit.h`

Tip: There's a useful rule of thumb that determines whether or not a section of code is worthy of conversion to a function. If the code is used at least twice in the same program or by at least one other program, then it needs to maintained as a function. However, we also use functions to divide the job into discrete tasks even though the code may not be reused.

The main program, **rec_deposit.c**, invokes **arg_check** to check whether three arguments have been input. It invokes **sscanf** three times to convert the argument strings to floating point numbers. If any of the arguments is not positive, **quit** prints a user-specified message to the standard error and terminates the program with a specified exit status. If validation succeeds, **main** invokes **compute** to make the actual computation.

Note: Both **quit** and **arg_check** use **fprintf** to write to the standard error rather than standard output. It's like using 1>&2 in shell scripts, and recall that diverting diagnostic messages to the error stream allows us to redirect the program output *(21.9)*.

22.2.1 Compiling and Linking the Application

The functions **arg_check** and **quit** are general enough to be used by other programs also, so it makes sense to preserve their object files. The following invocation of **cc -c** creates three .o files:

```
$ rm *.o                                      First remove all object files
$ cc -c rec_deposit.c arg_check.c quit.c
$ ls *.o
arg_check.o      quit.o       rec_deposit.o      No .o file for compute
```

These object files have to be linked now to create the executable. We use the -o option to specify our own executable filename, but the linker complains of an "undefined reference":

```
$ cc -o rec_deposit rec_deposit.o arg_check.o quit.o
rec_deposit.o: In function `compute':
rec_deposit.o(.text+0x154): undefined reference to `pow'
collect2: ld returned 1 exit status
```

By default, the linker obtains the object code of commonly used functions like **printf**, **sscanf**, etc. from the library, libc.a (in /lib or /usr/lib). **pow** belongs to a separate library, libm.a, containing mathematical functions. The linker will look up this library only if specifically directed to do so with the -l option. This option assumes the library name has the lib prefix and .a suffix, and requires only the remaining portion of the filename to be specified. Thus to link libm.a that contains the code for **pow**, you need to use -lm:

```
$ cc -o rec_deposit rec_deposit.o arg_check.o quit.o -lm
$ _
```

Run the program a number of times in ways that test the user-defined functions:

```
$ rec_deposit
Three arguments required                      arg_check working
$ rec_deposit 100 5 0
All arguments must be positive                quit working
$ rec_deposit 100 5 2
Maturity amount: 215.249985                   compute working
```

The output shows 215.25 as the maturity value of 100 units invested every year for two years at 5% interest. Since the program is working fine, do we need to hold to the .o files? Read on.

22.2.2 Why We Need the .o Files

Even though object files can't be executed directly, they have three important functions, the reason why they are often retained even after the creation of the executable:

- If you decide to change the behavior of the **quit** function, you need to recreate **quit.o** and then relink the three .o files. You can't do that if you don't have these files, in which case you'll have to recreate all of them with **cc -c**—a job that could have been avoided.

- Because **quit.o** is created from **quit.c**, you can compare their last modification times to determine whether the source has changed after the object file was created. The **make** program handles this function.

- You can combine a set of .o files to form a library or archive so that you can specify one file rather than several .o files to generate the final executable. Library creation is the job of the **ar** command.

Note that we don't have a separate object file for **compute**; its code is embedded in **rec_deposit.o**. Other programs can use **quit** and **arg_check**, but they can't use **compute**. The lesson: Reusable functions should be placed in separate files.

22.3 make: KEEPING PROGRAMS UP-TO-DATE

Now let's see how the files in the sample application are related to one another. **quit.o** *depends* on **quit.c** and **quit.h**, and if either **quit.c** or **quit.h** is modified, then **quit.c** needs to be recompiled to recreate **quit.o**. But then **rec_deposit.o** also depends on **quit.o**, which means that it needs to be rebuilt as well. A similar line of reasoning applies to the **arg_check** module also.

Keeping track of these dependencies in a large application involving several dozen files is simply impossible without a tool to assist us. The **make** command handles this job well. It shortens program compilation time by recompiling only those sources (.c and .h files) that have changed. It looks up a **makefile** (a control file) that specifies two things:

- How a program or object file has dependencies on other files. For instance, **rec_deposit** is dependent on **rec_deposit.o**, **arg_check.o** and **quit.o**.
- The command to execute when a file, on which another file depends, changes. This could be to run the **cc** command to regenerate the object files.

make by default uses a file named makefile or Makefile in the user's current directory. The file contains a set of *rules* where each rule is of the following form:

> *target*: *dependency_list*
>   *command_list*   *Tab at beginning of line!*

Here, *target* is generally an executable or an object file which depends on files in *dependency_list*. If any of the files in this list change, then *target* has to be rebuilt using commands provided in *command_list*. The rule syntax is simple except that you need to keep in mind that *command_list* is preceded by a tab (spaces here won't do).

The **make** rule for **quit.o** is this:

```
quit.o: quit.c quit.h
    cc -c quit.c
```
The dependency
The command to execute—tab before cc

make monitors the modification time of all three files, and when it sees at least one file in *dependency_list* to be newer than *target*, it runs **cc -c quit.c** to recreate **quit.o**. Enter these two lines of code in a file named makefile in your current directory. Next use **touch** to change the modification time of **quit.c** and then run **make**:

```
$ touch quit.c
$ make
cc -c quit.c
```
Not necessary if quit.o *doesn't exist*

make runs cc

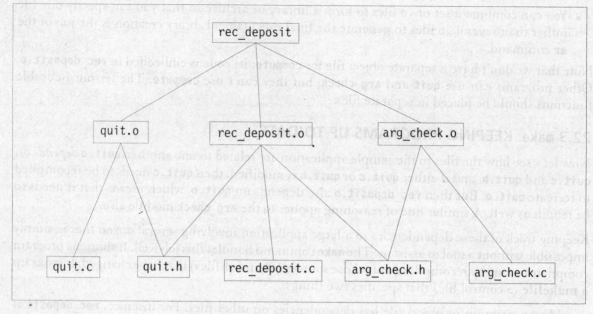

Fig. 22.4 The **make** Dependency Tree

Now examine the other modules of the sample application (Figs. 22.1 to 22.3) and you'll find a similar dependency in the **arg_check** function. Also, the main program depends on three .o files and two .h files. These dependencies are represented in the form of a dependency tree as depicted in Fig. 22.4.

Note that **quit.c** includes **quit.h**, and **arg_check.c** includes **arg_check.h**, but the main program includes them both. The dependency tree is implemented in the form of four rules placed in makefile, the default file used by **make**:

```
$ cat makefile
# Makefile containing redundancies
rec_deposit: rec_deposit.o arg_check.o quit.o          # Rule 1
    cc -o rec_deposit rec_deposit.o arg_check.o quit.o -lm

rec_deposit.o: rec_deposit.c quit.h arg_check.h        # Rule 2
    cc -c rec_deposit.c

quit.o: quit.c quit.h                                  # Rule 3
    cc -c quit.c

arg_check.o: arg_check.c arg_check.h                   # Rule 4
    cc -c arg_check.c
```

make uses # as the comment character and supports the use of the \ in splitting a line into two. Each rule is separated from the other by a blank line (not necessary on all systems).

The ultimate target (**rec_deposit**) is placed in the first rule which lists three object files as its dependencies. While scanning the makefile from top to bottom, **make** recursively treats each dependency as a target of its own. The three targets of the second tier also have their own dependencies and are shown as three separate rules. **make** then works back right to the top, issuing the necessary commands whenever it finds the modification time of any of the dependencies to be later that it associated target. If an object file doesn't exist, then **make** creates one.

Let's first remove all object files in this directory (if any), so **make** gets a chance to run all four commands:

```
$ rm *.o
$ make
cc -c rec_deposit.c
cc -c arg_check.c
cc -c quit.c
cc -o rec_deposit rec_deposit.o arg_check.o quit.o -lm
```

The object files can now be considered to be up-to-date. When you issue **make** again, you'll find that there's nothing left for it to do:

```
$ make
`rec_deposit' is up to date.
```

make is not restricted to handling only C programs. It can compile any program written in any language provided the compilation generates target files that can be compared to their sources. We can use **make** to run Fortran and C++ programs, but Java has the "make" feature built in. The **javac** compiler makes sure that all dependent source files are automatically compiled before it generates the .class file that is used by the **java** interpreter.

Tip: If **make** outputs a message like missing separator. Stop., it could mean that **make** didn't see the tab at the beginning of a line containing *command_list*. Use **cat -tv makefile** to view all tabs as ^I.

22.3.1 Removing Redundancies

The makefile that we just worked upon has a number of redundancies. **make** is provided with a fair amount of intelligence to make the following deductions:

- If the target and dependency have the same basename, then *command_list* need not be specified. In other words, if **quit.o** has **quit.c** as its dependency, then you don't need to specify **cc -c quit.c**. Simply this statement would do as Rule 3:

  ```
  quit.o: quit.c quit.h                    No command_list required
  ```

- If the source file itself is omitted in the dependency, **make** assumes that the base source filename is the same as the object file. The above line thus gets shortened further:

  ```
  quit.o: quit.h
  ```

make assumes that **quit.o** is created from **quit.c**. Before we view the next makefile that shows the changes, let's understand from the next section that **make** is not merely concerned with compiling programs.

22.3.2 Other Functions of make: Cleaning Up and Backup

make doesn't always need a dependency to work on; it can run a UNIX command depending on the command line argument. For instance, you can instruct **make** to remove all object files or even perform a backup with **tar**. Our next makefile incorporates these features and the two "intelligent" features discussed previously:

```
$ cat makefile2
# All redundancies removed
rec_deposit: rec_deposit.o arg_check.o quit.o
    cc -o rec_deposit rec_deposit.o arg_check.o quit.o -lm

rec_deposit.o: quit.h arg_check.h        # Rule 2

quit.o: quit.h                           # Rule 3

arg_check.o: arg_check.h                 # Rule 4

clean:                                   # No dependency list here
    rm *.o

tar:                                     # ... and here
    tar -cvf progs.tar *.c *.h
```

You can see **make**'s built-in rules implemented in Rules 2 to 4. To consider the second rule, **rec_deposit.o** depends on **rec_deposit.c** (assumed by **make** since there's no .c file specified), and if that file or any of the two .h files is modified, **make** will run **cc -c rec_deposit.c** to generate **rec_deposit.o**.

Now examine the last two rules. There are no dependencies associated with the "pseudo-targets", clean and tar. **make** this time has to be used with the target as argument. When **make** runs with clean as argument, it removes all .o files:

```
$ make -f makefile2 clean
rm *.o
$ make -f makefile2 tar
tar -cvf progs.tar *.c *.h
a arg_check.c 1K
a compute.c 1K
a rec_deposit.c 1K
a arg_check.h 1K
a quit.h 1K
```

The **make clean** command is often run at the beginning to remove all object files in the current directory. This is usually followed by a "regular" **make** to force compilation of all programs. Finally, a **make install** (not discussed) moves the executables to a system directory.

22.3.3 Macros

make supports **macros**, sometimes called *variables*, that are used to define repeatedly used strings. A macro is of the form *macroname = value* and is defined at the beginning of the makefile. A macro is invoked in a rule with $(*macroname*) or ${*macroname*}.

Even though we have used the **cc** compiler here, some systems may instead use GNU's **gcc**. To be able to run the same makefile on another system that uses **gcc** and without making major changes in the body of the makefile, we simply define a macro CC = gcc, and then use it in a rule as $(CC):

```
$ cat makefile3
CC = gcc
SOURCES = rec_deposit.c arg_check.c quit.c
OBJECTS = rec_deposit.o arg_check.o quit.o
HEADERS = arg_check.h quit.h

rec_deposit: $(OBJECTS)
    $(CC) -o rec_deposit $(OBJECTS) -lm

rec_deposit.o: $(HEADERS)

arg_check.o: arg_check.h

quit.o: quit.h

clean:
    rm $(OBJECTS)

tar:
    tar -cvf progs.tar $(SOURCES) $(HEADERS)
```

One of the four macros defines the compiler, and the other three group all files into three categories. Note that even though the compiler has changed here, we can still continue to omit the command list in three rules. This is because the CC macro is a **make** builtin, and by default, CC expands to cc. Here, it expands to gcc:

```
$ make -f makefile3 clean
rm rec_deposit.o arg_check.o quit.o
$ make -f makefile3
gcc    -c  rec_deposit.c
gcc    -c  arg_check.c
gcc    -c  quit.c
gcc -o rec_deposit rec_deposit.o arg_check.o quit.o -lm
```

Apart from CC, there are two macros that are built into **make**. CFLAGS lists the options that have to be additionally used in compilation. LDFLAGS determines the options to be used by the linker. We'll revisit **make** after we have learned to build a library file with **ar**.

22.4 ar: BUILDING A LIBRARY (ARCHIVE)

In real-life projects, specifying all object files in a makefile can be a tedious job. It's more convenient to group them into a **library** or **archive** with the **ar** command. **ar** can manipulate an archive in the same way **tar** does, except that an **ar** archive has the extension, .a. The command uses the following options:

-r   Adds a file if it is not present in the archive or replaces an existing one.

-q   Appends a file at the end of the archive.

-x   Extracts a file from the archive.

-d   Deletes a file in the archive.

-t   Displays the table of contents of the archive.

-v   Verbose Output

Though **ar** supports options without the hyphen, POSIX requires **ar** options to be hyphen-prefixed. Let's stick to the example files used in the section on **make** and create an archive named librec.a to initially contain two object files. The -r option creates the archive before adding the object files:

```
$ ar -rv librec.a quit.o arg_check.o
r - quit.o
r - arg_check.o
ar: writing librec.a
```

The library filename is specified first, followed by object filenames. We can add other object files with -q, and then check the table of contents with -t:

```
$ ar -qv librec.a compute.o                        Appending to archive
a - compute.o
ar: writing librec.a
$ ar -tv librec.a
rw-r--r-- 1027/    10    676 Dec 21 14:37 2003 quit.o
rw-r--r-- 1027/    10    724 Dec 21 14:37 2003 arg_check.o
rw-r--r-- 1027/    10    952 Dec 21 14:38 2003 compute.o
```

We can now safely delete all three object files from the directory. If required, we can extract a file from the archive using -x or remove it from the archive with -d:

```
$ ar -xv librec.a compute.o
x - compute.o
$ ar -dv librec.a compute.o
d - compute.o
ar: writing librec.a
$ ar -tv librec.a
rw-r--r-- 1027/    10    676 Dec 21 14:37 2003 quit.o
rw-r--r-- 1027/    10    724 Dec 21 14:37 2003 arg_check.o
```

By default, the -x option extracts all object files. We deleted **compute.o** from the archive because the sample application doesn't need it.

22.4.1 Using the Library

Now that we have a library that is ready for use, rather than specify all object files separately, we can specify instead the library name as an argument to **cc** (and the -lm option, of course):

```
cc rec_deposit.c librec.a -lm
```

We can also use the -l option with our library. Since our library name was chosen carefully (lib + rec + .a), the -lrec option is the correct specification, but we also need to use -L to specify the location of the library:

```
cc rec_deposit.c -lrec -L"." -lm
```

By default, the compiler looks in /lib and /usr/lib to locate all library files. Our library is not located there, so we need to use -L.

Tip: If you have built a number of libraries, store them in a separate directory in your own home directory tree, and then use the -L option to **cc** to point to this directory. If others are going to use your library, ensure that the directory has execute permission.

22.4.2 Maintaining an Archive with make

What happens when the sources for these object files are modified? Interactive use of **ar** to maintain an archive can still be quite painful. **make** is the answer yet again; it can both recompile the source files and replace the archive entries with their newer versions. For doing this, **make** identifies an archived object file in this form:

archive_name(object_file)

The object file is placed in parentheses and is preceded by the library name. The following makefile takes care of compiling and archiving:

```
$ cat makefile4
CC = gcc
rec_deposit: rec_deposit.o librec.a(quit.o) librec.a(arg_check.o)
    $(CC) -o rec_deposit rec_deposit.o librec.a -lm

rec_deposit.o: quit.h arg_check.h

librec.a(quit.o): quit.h

librec.a(arg_check.o): arg_check.h
```

Observe the changed specification of the object files. The makefile entries are a little longer this time, but **make** here has some additional work to do: it has to ensure that the archive is rebuilt:

```
$ touch quit.c                      Change modification time of this file
$ make -f makefile4
gcc   -c -o quit.o quit.c
ar rv librec.a quit.o
a - quit.o
ar: writing librec.a
rm -f quit.o
gcc -o rec_deposit rec_deposit.o librec.a -lm
```

Note that **make** invokes **ar** to replace the archive with the updated versions of **quit.o**.

22.5 STATIC AND SHARED LIBRARIES

In the previous section, we created a **static library**. When a program is compiled and linked to a static library, the object code of the library is included in the executable. Several programs may use the same function, which means that the same library code gets included in all these programs. This bloats the code size and eats into the disk space. This also means that if the code for the function changes, all programs that have the functions statically linked to them, have to be recompiled. Even though **make** can do this work for us, compilation of several hundred programs can still take a lot of time.

C also supports **shared libraries** (also called **shared objects**). In contrast to a static library, a program using a shared library loads the library code only during runtime. Once it is loaded, a single copy of the library code is kept in memory for other programs to use. Programs using shared libraries could be a little slower, but the executables are smaller since they don't include library code. Unlike with static libraries, a change in function code doesn't necessitate recompilation of those programs using the function (provided the signature is not altered).

Shared libraries usually have the extension .so, and the compiler has system-dependent options to create them. Look in /lib and /usr/lib, and you'll see a number of these .so files. Many of them are in fact symbolic links to the actual library. For instance, libbz2.so could be a symlink to libbz2.so.1.0.0, so named to include the version number. Shared libraries are increasingly being used by modern UNIX systems.

22.6 VERSION CONTROL WITH SCCS AND RCS

A software product is never perfect and has to maintained in two ways. One, bugs have to be rectified as and when they are reported. Second, applications have to be constantly enhanced by incorporation of new features. In most cases, both activities go on concurrently and programs thus experience version changes. For instance, development work could be going on for Release 2 when the customer reports a bug detected in Release 1.2.

When a bug is detected, the program developer needs to access the relevant version of the program to make modifications. Since all versions of the program have the same filename, how does one store them all without wasting disk space? If you recall what **diff** does *(5.12)*, you would be tempted to adopt a system that stores one version in full, and only its differences with the subsequent versions. You are on the right track; we are talking about *version control*.

Version control is widely used to maintain multiple versions of programs, shell scripts, configuration files and even documents that undergo revisions. Every UNIX system supports the **Source Code Control System (SCCS)**. Berkeley was responsible for the **Revision Control System (RCS)**, which is also available on Linux systems. Irrespective of the system you use, version control implies the following:

- When a program or document has multiple versions, only one of them is stored in its entirety. Subsequently, the differences of one version with its immediate ancestor need to be stored. The complete information is held in a single encoded file.
- You can **check out** (i.e., retrieve) any version from the encoded file for compilation or editing.
- After the changes have been carried out, they are **checked in** (put back) to the encoded file.
- The system must not allow two users to edit identical versions of a file even though they can be permitted to view their contents or compile them.
- Users can be allowed or denied checkout rights to one or more versions.

In a version control system, the set of changes made to a version is known as a **delta**. It's the delta that is saved in the special file rather than the complete version. Every version is allocated a version number, which in SCCS is known as the **SID (SCCS Id)**. An SID or version number comprises two or four components:

- By default, the system allocates a two-component SID of the form *release.level*. The first SID is 1.1, which represents release 1, level 1. Every time a version is created, the level number is incremented and the SID correspondingly changes to 1.2, 1.3, and so forth. The system won't change the release unless you specifically direct it to do so.

- When you need to change a version (say, one with SID 1.2) when a later version also exists (say, SID 1.3), the system creates intermediate versions, called **branch deltas**. The SID of a branch delta has four components, the two additional ones being called *branch* and *sequence*. In this case, the system will allocate SID 1.2.1.1 to the next version. Subsequent branch deltas would be 1.2.1.2, 1.2.1.3 and so forth.

Both SCCS and RCS implement these features with their own set of commands. Both use **diff** (or a derivative) to maintain these differences in a special encoded file but in reverse ways. SCCS saves the first version and applies the saved **diff** commands to retrieve subsequent versions. RCS saves the final version and retrieves earlier versions by working backwards. The systems are incompatible and have different file naming conventions and formats. POSIX includes SCCS but not RCS. We'll discuss the SCCS system in fair detail and the RCS system briefly.

Note: The term *delta* is used liberally in the SCCS system to refer to a set of changes, a version or the SID. There is also an SCCS command by that name. RCS documentation doesn't use this term as much as SCCS does; *revision* is their delta.

Caution: The encoded file contains mainly text but also includes control characters. Never edit this file directly to retrieve a version. Always use the appropriate commands that check out and check in a version (or delta).

22.7 AN SCCS SESSION

SCCS comprises a suite of programs which are often held in a separate directory (/usr/ccs/bin in Solaris), so make sure you have the directory in your PATH. These programs can be run in two ways:

- Individually, which we are going to do with the **admin**, **get**, **delta** and **unget** commands.
- Using the **sccs** command itself as a frontend to these tools. You can run both **get** and **sccs get**, but the **sccs** frontend has certain additional features which are not available in the standalone tools.

SCCS saves all versions of a program in a single encoded file that is often called the **SCCS file** or **SCCS history file**. This file is named with a **s.** prefix. The program **foo.c** is saved in the SCCS file, **s.foo.c**. SCCS will look up the SCCS directory for an SCCS file if it doesn't find it in the current directory. In the following sections, we'll use these tools:

- **admin**, initially for creating the SCCS file, and later for controlling user access.
- **get** to check out any version—read-only or editable.
- **delta** to save the changes (delta) in the SCCS file.
- **unget** to reverse the action of **get** when we discover that the checkout was not the right thing to do.
- **sact** and **prs** to report on the current state of editing activity and the state of SCCS files.

By default, checkout and checkin access is permitted to all users. We won't consider the access control features in this chapter. In this section, we'll create an SCCS file, check out a version, make changes to it and then check it in.

22.7.1 admin: Creating an SCCS File

For our discussions, we'll use the program, **quit.c**, a variant of which was used in the discussions on **make** and **ar**. So let's first have a look at the contents of the first version having the SID 1.1, i.e. release 1, level 1:

```
$ cat quit.c                                           SID 1.1
#include <stdio.h>
#include <errno.h>
void quit (void) {
    printf("Error number %d, quitting program\n", errno);
    exit(1);
}
```

This file now has to be checked in to its SCCS file, **s.quit.c**. This file doesn't yet exist, so we have to create it with the **admin** command. The -i option specifies the input filename:

```
$ admin -i quit.c s.quit.c
No id keywords (cm7)
$ ls -l s.quit.c                                cm7 is an SCCS keyword
-r--r--r--   1 sumit    staff        279 Dec 21 14:49 s.quit.c
$ rm quit.c
```

admin creates **s.quit.c**, which contains the contents of **quit.c** as well as control information like the owner of the file and time of creation. All future versions of **quit.c** must be checked in to this file. We no longer need to maintain **quit.c** separately.

To understand what SCCS understands by cm7, just use its **help** command with the keyword as argument, only to know that the message can be ignored:

```
$ /usr/ccs/bin/help
Enter the message number or SCCS command name: cm7
cm7:
"No id keywords"
No SCCS identification keywords were substituted for.
You may not have any keywords in the file,
in which case you can ignore this warning.
..........
```

The reason why we used the absolute pathname here is that this author uses the Bash shell, and **help** is a Bash builtin. We'll also be looking at some of the other keywords that SCCS displays, especially when things don't work properly.

22.7.2 get: Checking Out

We now have a single version of **quit.c** in the SCCS file, **s.quit.c**. The **get** command checks out a file, and depending on the options used, you can

- check out a read-only version or delta (the default).
- display the contents to the standard output with the -p option.
- check out an editable version using the -e option.
- check out a specific version using the -r option. The same option is also used to change the release number.

Sometimes, we need to check out a noneditable version for compilation, so let's use **get** to obtain a read-only version:

```
$ get s.quit.c
1.1                                              Current version number
7 lines                                          File contains 7 lines
No id keywords (cm7)
$ ls -l quit.c
-r--r--r--   1 sumit     staff          129 Dec 21 14:50 quit.c
```

SCCS notifies that delta 1.1 comprising 7 lines has been checked out. This file doesn't contain keywords, but we'll learn to place some useful keywords later. **get -e** checks out an editable version and also creates a lock file, **p.quit.c**:

```
$ get -e s.quit.c
1.1
new delta 1.2
7 lines
$ ls -l quit.c
-rw-r--r--   1 sumit     staff          129 Dec 21 14:51 quit.c
$ ls -l p.quit.c
-rw-r--r--   1 sumit     staff           32 Dec 21 14:51 p.quit.c
```

This time SCCS points out that unless you explicitly specify the SID, it will assign 1.2 to this delta when you return it. The lock file prevents the user to check out the file again:

```
$ get -e s.quit.c
ERROR [s.quit.c]: writable `quit.c' exists (ge4)
$ /usr/ccs/bin/help ge4
ge4:
"writable `...' exists"
For safety's sake, SCCS won't overwrite an existing g-file if it's writable.
If you don't need the g-file, remove it and rerun the get command.
```

The lock file maintains information related to the current session. It is used by the **sact** command to be discussed later. SCCS also understands the checked out file as a *g-file*, but we won't need to use this term again.

Note: When you use **get -e**, the SCCS file is locked for the delta that was checked out. No other user can check out this delta until it has been checked in. However, other users can check out editable versions of other deltas but the files have to reside in different directories since they all have the same name.

22.7.3 delta: Checking In

You can now edit the file that you just checked out, so let's change the **quit** function to accept the exit status as an argument. After editing, **quit.c** should look like this:

```
$ cat quit.c                                              SID 1.2
#include <stdio.h>
#include <errno.h>
void quit (int exit_status) {                             This line has changed
    printf("Error number %d, quitting program\n", errno);
    exit(exit_status);                                    ..... and this one
}
```

Two lines have changed. We'll now use the **delta** command to check this file in. **delta** pauses for a line of comment which is also recorded in the SCCS file:

```
$ delta s.quit.c
comments? Function modified to accept exit status as argument
No id keywords (cm7)
1.2
2 inserted
2 deleted
5 unchanged
$ ls -l quit.c
quit.c: No such file or directory
```

By default, SCCS assigns this version the same SID that was displayed by **get** (new delta 1.2) when it was checked out for editing. **delta** also removes **quit.c**, so you can't modify a version that is in SCCS custody until you "get" it first. Next time you retrieve a version with **get -e**, the next **delta** would check it in as 1.3.

You must document the changes at the comment? prompt. These comments are displayed by the **prs** command and help other programmers when they need to know why the changes were made in the first place. It will also help you when you look at your own program months later. It is characteristic of many commands of the SCCS suite that changes are reported in three parts—the number of lines inserted, deleted and unchanged.

Tip: Sometimes, you'll like to check in a delta because you don't want to lose the changes and still continue editing. In that case, use **delta -n** which leaves the file undeleted. But the SCCS file has recorded that the delta has been checked in and won't allow you to check in the changes you make to this file. You must rename it before you use **get -e** again, and then overwrite the checked-out version with the one you just edited. RCS handles this situation better; it allows you to "lock" the file and check it in.

22.7.4 unget: When You Change Your Mind

It's possible that you checked out a version for editing, then found that the changes weren't worthy of a new delta. You can undo your previous checkout by using the **unget** command:

```
$ get -e s.quit.c
1.2
new delta 1.3
7 lines
$ unget s.quit.c
1.3                                    New delta had you checked it in
```

Since SCCS keeps track of all editable checked-out versions, you can't check out the same delta again for editing unless you reverse the action of **get -e**. Note that **unget** has nothing to reverse when you check out a read-only version:

```
$ get s.quit.c
1.2
......
$ unget s.quit.c
ERROR [s.quit.c]: `p.quit.c' nonexistent (ut4)
```

We'll be using the **get** and **delta** commands again for retrieving multiple deltas and changing release numbers. Before that, we need to look at two tools that maintain state information.

22.8 ACTIVITY AND HISTORY INFORMATION

You won't always remember the exact form of the delta tree, nor will you always be able to recall the exact SID of a delta that you want to check out. SCCS offers the **prs** command to present the history of an SCCS file and **sact** to provide information on the state of editing activity.

22.8.1 sact: Displaying Activity Status

The **sact** command shows the status of editing activity of a file. When no editable version has been checked out, it reports an error:

```
$ sact s.quit.c
ERROR [s.quit.c]: No outstanding deltas
```

As you are aware, **get -e s.quit.c** creates the lock file **p.quit.c**. The same file also provides information about editing activity to **sact**. Here, **sact** reports that user sumit has checked out a version with SID 1.1, and note that the contents of the lock file are identical:

```
$ sact s.quit.c
1.1 1.2 sumit 03/12/21 14:51:09
$ cat p.quit.c
1.1 1.2 sumit 03/12/21 14:51:09
```

The current SID (1.1) is followed by the default SID (1.2) to be used for the next delta. The output also shows the user and date (in *yy/mm/dd* format) and time of checking out. **get -e** looks up this file and prevents a checkout if the SID of a requested delta is found to be present. When multiple deltas have been checked out, **sact** reports with multiline output:

```
$ sact s.quit.c
1.2 1.2.1.1 sumit 03/12/21 15:53:46
2.1 2.2 jpm 03/12/21 15:54:30
```

The second line shows that user jpm has checked out delta 2.1. When all users have checked in the changes, the lock file is deleted.

22.8.2 prs: Displaying the SCCS History

The **prs** command displays the history of an SCCS file. It helps you identify the delta you need by displaying the comments that you provided when you checked in a delta. By default, the command presents the complete history:

```
$ prs s.quit.c
s.quit.c:

D 1.2 03/12/21 14:53:41 sumit 2 1        00002/00002/00005
MRs:
COMMENTS:
Function modified to accept exit status as argument

D 1.1 03/12/21 14:49:39 sumit 1 0        00007/00000/00000
MRs:
COMMENTS:
date and time created 03/12/21 14:49:39 by sumit
```

Each delta is presented in a group of four lines with the most recent delta shown first. The first line replicates the information provided by **sact**, but it also shows three /-delimited numbers that represent the number of lines inserted, deleted and unchanged.

22.9 CONTINUING EDITING WITH SCCS

We have performed the basic editing and activity monitoring functions. The default SID allocation system and version locking should suffice for single-user SCCS sessions. However, SCCS also permits you to

- change the release number, using *branch deltas* as and when required.
- place identification keywords in an SCCS file.

In the following sections, we'll examine these features.

22.9.1 get -r: Changing the Default Numbering Sequence

By default, SCCS increments the level number every time you use **get -e** to check out a file, and **delta** to check it in after modification. At some point, you'll need to change this default numbering scheme:

- When the changes are significant, you may need to assign a new release number rather than increment the level number.
- When you make changes to a previous delta rather than the latest one. The previous delta develops into a *branch delta*.

Let's first consider the allocation of a new release number to our **quit.c** program. You'll first have to indicate to SCCS your *intention* of doing so when you check out the version with **get**. By default, SCCS displays the next delta in the **get** output, but you can override that by specifying your own release number with the -r option:

```
$ get -e -r2 s.quit.c                                    Last version
1.2
new delta 2.1
7 lines
```

Here, -r2 indicates to SCCS that the next delta would be 2.1, but observe that **get** checks out 1.2, the latest version. After editing, check in the file in the usual manner:

```
$ delta s.quit.c
comments? Function modified to accept the message as argument.
No id keywords (cm7)
2.1
2 inserted
4 deleted
3 unchanged
```

Now that you have SID 1.1, 1.2 and 2.1 in the SCCS file, you have to specify the -r option with **get** to retrieve a previous version. For instance, you need to use **get -r1.2 s.quit.c** to check out a read-only version of delta 1.2.

Branch Deltas   Consider this real-life situation where you need to check out an editable version of an older delta, say 1.2, for a client when delta 1.3 also exists in the SCCS file. What SID would you allocate to the revised version? SCCS the makes use of the four-level numbering scheme discussed earlier *(22.6)*. The checked-out version develops into a **branch delta** with SID 1.2.1.1, where the last two numbers represent the branch and sequence numbers:

```
$ get -e -r1.2 s.quit.c
1.2
new delta 1.2.1.1
7 lines
$ sact s.quit.c
1.2 1.2.1.1 sumit 03/12/21 15:00:35
```

The checkin is done in the usual manner with **delta**. Next time you need to revise this version to 1.2.1.2, you'll have to "get" it with -r1.2.1.

22.9.2 Using Identification Keywords

You can take advantage of SCCS **identification keywords** to place control information in the file itself. A keyword is of the form *%keyword%*, and some useful keywords are shown below:

%I%   SID of the checked-out file
%M%   Filename (without .s prefix)
%D%   Current date in *yy/mm/dd* format
%T%   Current time in *hh:mm:ss* format
%U%   Time of creation of delta in *hh:mm:ss* format

These keywords must be embedded in the comments used with /* and */. For instance, you can insert the following comment lines at the beginning of your source file:

```
/* Filename: %M%
   SID: %I%
   Time: %D% %T% */
```

These lines are left alone when you check out an editable version, but when you retrieve a read-only version or use **get -p**, SCCS expands the keywords:

```
$ get -p -r2.2 s.quit.c | head -n 3
2.2
9 lines
/* Filename: quit.c
   SID: 2.2
   Time: 03/12/21 15:23:46 */
```

These two lines are written to the standard error

It's convenient to maintain the SID and current date and time in the file itself. Note that this expansion is not performed on an editable delta, because subsequent deltas could be related to this delta. Saving the expanded form would pass on wrong information to the next related delta. RCS betters SCCS in the handling of these keywords.

SCCS also supports the **sccs** command that acts as a frontend to other *subcommands*. Many of these subcommands have the same names as the standalone commands that we have used (**get** and **sccs get**), but some **sccs** subcommands don't have standalone equivalents. Look up the **sccs** man page for further details.

22.10 THE REVISION CONTROL SYSTEM (RCS)

The Revision Control System (RCS) was created by Berkeley as an alternative to AT&T's SCCS. RCS is standard on all BSD UNIX systems and is also available on many UNIX systems. Linux supports the GNU implementation of RCS which is arguably simpler to use than SCCS. The basic functionality is achieved with just three commands: **ci**, **co** and **rcs**.

Unlike SCCS, RCS saves the latest file in entirety and reconstructs previous versions by working backwards. (SCCS saves the earliest version in full.) The encoded **RCS file** contains the information required to assemble all **revisions** (the name RCS uses for versions or deltas) along with status and activity information. It is not much different from an SCCS file in essence though. However, RCS maintains no separate lock file (like the one created by **get -e**). All locking information is kept in the RCS file itself.

An RCS file is named with a ,v suffix. Thus, **quit.c** is checked in to the RCS file, **quit.c,v**. The system looks in a directory named RCS for the RCS file, failing which it looks in the current directory. To avoid repetition, we'll briefly repeat the session (using **quit.c**) that we went through with SCCS, and note the differences that are also presented in Table 22.1. This time, we'll maintain the RCS file in the **RCS** directory.

22.10.1 Creating an RCS File with ci

Unlike in SCCS, there are two commands that can create an RCS file. The **rcs -i** command creates an initialized and empty file. Versions are subsequently checked in with the **ci** command.

Table 22.1

SCCS Command	RCS Command	Significance
admin -i foo.c s.foo.c	ci foo.c	Creates encoded file with SID 1.1
get s.foo.c	co foo.c	Checks out read-only version
get -e s.foo.c	co -l foo.c	Checks out editable version
delta s.foo.c	ci foo.c	Checks in current editable version
unget s.foo.c	rcs -u foo.c	Reverses the action of checkout
get -r *ver* s.foo.c	ci -r *ver* foo.c	Specifies release number *ver* for next checkin
prs s.foo.c	rlog foo.c	Prints version history
sact s.foo.c	rlog foo.c	Prints checked-out status

Alternatively, we can use **ci** itself for both tasks, and the first invocation creates version 1.1:

```
$ ci quit.c
RCS/quit.c,v  <--  quit.c
enter description, terminated with single '.' or end of file:
NOTE: This is NOT the log message!
>> RCS file created with version 1.1
>> .                                      Dot terminates standard input
initial revision: 1.1
done
$ ls -l RCS
total 4
-r--r--r--   1 sumit    users       342 2003-12-23 12:41 quit.c,v
```

ci creates this file with revision 1.1 checked in. We'll use the same command to check in editable versions. Unlike **admin -i** of SCCS, the default invocation of **ci** removes the original file.

Note: Unlike SCCS commands that use the SCCS filename as argument (like **s.quit.c**), RCS commands use the unencoded filename (like **quit.c**), the file that you actually work with.

22.10.2 co and ci: Checking Out and In

The **co** command checks out a file. Like **get**, it retrieves a read-only version of the latest version by default, and displays the retrieved data on the standard output with the -p option. It's the -l (lock) option that checks out an editable version:

```
$ co -l quit.c                            Like get -e s.quit.c
RCS/quit.c,v  -->  quit.c
revision 1.1 (locked)
done
$ ls -l quit.c
-rw-r--r--   1 sumit    users       129 2003-12-23 12:42 quit.c
```

Unlike SCCS, RCS doesn't create a lock file, but it locks a version from concurrent editing by placing an entry in the RCS file. If you attempt to check out again, **co** issues a warning and offers to remove the existing checked-out version:

```
$ co -l quit.c
RCS/quit.c,v  -->  quit.c
revision 1.1 (locked)
writable quit.c exists; remove it? [ny](n): n
co: checkout aborted
```

SCCS doesn't offer this feature, but we preferred not to take advantage of it by entering n at the prompt. You can now edit the file that you just checked out, and then use the **ci** command to check it in:

```
$ ci quit.c
RCS/quit.c,v  <--  quit.c
new revision: 1.2; previous revision: 1.1
enter log message, terminated with single '.' or end of file:
>> Function modified to accept exit status as argument
>> .
done
```

RCS assigns revision number 1.2 to this version. We'll soon use the -r option with both **ci** and **co** to explicitly specify the revision number.

Reversing the Action of co -l   If you have checked out a version for editing and now want to reverse the action, use the command **rcs -u quit.c** (**unget** in SCCS). The **rcs** command simply removes the entry specifying the lock in the RCS file.

Tip: You can't normally check in a version unless you have checked it out with a lock with **co -l**. In case you have used **chmod +w** on a read-only version, and edited the file, you need to lock this file first with **rcs -l** *filename* before you return it to the RCS file with **ci**.

22.10.3 Specifying Versions

Unlike in SCCS, the -r option in **co** can't be used to indicate what the next revision number would be. For instance, you can't use this command to indicate that you intend to check in the next revision as 2.1:

```
$ co -l -r2 quit.c
RCS/quit.c,v  -->  quit.c
co: RCS/quit.c,v: revision 2 absent
```

The -r option is used with **co** to check out an *existing* version only. Let's check out the latest version of the file:

```
co -l quit.c
```

After you have edited the file, you have to explicitly assign the version number when checking it in:

```
$ ci -r2 quit.c
RCS/quit.c,v  <--  quit.c
new revision: 2.1; previous revision: 1.2
enter log message, terminated with single '.' or end of file:
>> Function modified to accept the message as argument.
>> .
done
```

You can specify higher version numbers also, but the missing ones can't then be allocated.

Creating a Branch Delta   Like in SCCS, when you check out a version that is not the latest, you can check in that version only as a branch delta. RCS follows the same four-numbered component scheme used by SCCS:

```
$ co -l -r1.2 quit.c
RCS/quit.c,v --> quit.c
revision 1.2 (locked)
done
```

Unless you invoke the **rlog** command to find out the state of the revisions, you won't know at this stage what the next revision would be. You'll know that only when you check it in:

```
$ ci quit.c
RCS/quit.c,v <-- quit.c
new revision: 1.2.1.1; previous revision: 1.2
enter log message, terminated with single '.' or end of file:
>> Creating a branch delta
>> .
done
```

22.10.4 rlog: Status Information

rlog combines the **sact** and **prs** commands of SCCS in one; it reports both on the versions existing in the RCS file and the ones that are locked for editing. The output shows details of each revision in three or four lines, and also points out the one that has a branch. **rlog** also shows locking information. We are constrained to overlook these features in this text.

22.10.5 ident: Using Identification Keywords

Like SCCS, RCS also supports the use of identification keywords except that the keywords are both expanded and remain usable even after an editable version of the file has been checked out. Here are some of the keywords that you can use in the comments section of your C program:

```
/*
  $RCSfile$
  $Author$
  $Date$
  $Id$
  $Revision$
*/
```

After you have checked in and checked out the file, use the **ident** command to display this section:

```
$ ident quit.c
quit.c:
     $RCSfile: quit.c,v $
     $Author: sumit $
     $Date: 2003/12/24 08:13:55 $
     $Id: quit.c,v 1.7 2003/12/24 08:13:55 sumit Exp sumit $
     $Revision: 1.7 $
```

Note that RCS preserves the variable names even after expansion. The scheme is so well designed that all editable check-out versions also contain this information. This is not the case with SCCS.

22.11 CONCLUSION

As mentioned before, UNIX is a system developed for programmers, and this chapter bears testimony to the fact. Both **make** and version control were developed for easier maintenance of programs. There are a lot of other tools that we have not been able to discuss in this chapter for reasons of space. One of them, the UNIX debugger (**dbx** and **gdb**), is extermely useful fordetecting bugs in your programs. For details on the use of **dbx**, look up the Web site of the book. The next two chapters will help you program in UNIX using its system calls.

WRAP UP

A C program is *compiled* and *assembled* to create an object (.o) file, and *linked* to create the executable. Object files should be retained for multisource programs to avoid recompilation of unchanged sources. Functions should be placed in separate files to be reusable.

make monitors the last modification times of the executable, object, source and header files to determine the sources that need to be recompiled. It looks up a *makefile* for associating a *target* with a *dependency*, and then takes a defined action if the dependency is found to be newer than target.

The **ar** command combines a group of object files into a *static library* or *archive*. **make** can automatically recompile a module and replace it in the archive. A *shared library* or *shared object* is not linked to the executable but is loaded during runtime.

The *Source Code Control System (SCCS)* saves the first version in full and its differences with subsequent versions in an encoded *SCCS file*. A *delta* is checked out (**get**) and checked in (**delta**) after editing. Revision of intermediate versions creates a *branch delta*.

The *Revision Control System (RCS)* saves the latest *revision*. A revision is checked in with **ci** and checked out with **co**.

Test Your Understanding

22.1 Name the three phases that a program has to go through before an executable is created from it.

22.2 Name the two commands invoked by the **cc** command to create an executable.

22.3 Place the function definitions of **arg_check** and **quit** (22.2) in a single file, **foo.c**. Can the main program, **rec_deposit** (in **rec_deposit.c**) access them?

22.4 Why does a static library have the **lib** prefix? What suffix does it have? Where are the system's library and include files available?

22.5 The command **cc -c foo.c** compiles without error. Explain why **make** could generate an error with a makefile that contains the following entry:

```
foo.o: foo.c
    cc -c foo.c
```

22.6 How is **libc.a** different from other libraries?

22.7   Mention two advantages a shared library has over a static library.

22.8   Create a file foo containing a line of text. Mention the commands needed to (i) create the SCCS file for foo, (ii) check out an editable version of foo, (ii) check in foo after editing.

22.9   Why do we enter comments when using the **delta** command? How can you see them?

22.10 Explain when you need to create a branch delta. Is 1.2.1 a branch delta?

Flex Your Brain

22.1   How does an executable C program differ from its associated object files?

22.2   It makes no sense to save object files if other programs are not going to use them. Right or Wrong?

22.3   Explain the significance of the -c, -o and -l options of the C compiler.

22.4   Modify the application presented in Section 22.2 to implement the following:

(i) The **compute** function should be in a separate file, **compute.c**, and its **include** statement in **compute.h**.

(iii) All function prototypes should be defined in a single file, **prototype.h**.

Modify makefile2 discussed in Section 22.3.2 accordingly.

22.5   Look up the man page of **make** to find out how it can be invoked to display the command line that it would execute without actually executing it.

22.6   Explain how **make** may run without error with a makefile that contains only the following entry. What command will it run?

        foo:

22.7   A **make** rule doesn't always have a dependency and the target need not be a disk file. Explain with an example of a makefile entry.

22.8   Specify the commands that will (i) create an archive named foobar.a containing the object files **foo1.o** and **foo2.o**, (ii) delete **foo2.o** from the archive. Can this archive be used with the -l option to **cc**?

22.9   What does this entry in a makefile mean? What command does **make** run if **a.h** is modified?

        foo.a(a.o): a.h

22.10 SCCS and RCS basically use the same mechanism to store file versions except that they work in opposite directions. Explain. Which system do you think reconstructs a version faster?

22.11 You have three versions of a program named **foo1.c**, **foo2.c** and **foo3.c**. Mention the steps needed to check in all three versions to a single SCCS file.

22.12 Mention the set of commands that produce the deltas 1.1, 1.2, 1.3 and 1.2.1.1 of **foo.c**. Now use **get -r9 s.foo.c** and **get -e -r9 s.foo.c**. What do you observe?

22.13 Which file does **sact** obtain activity information from? When is the file created and deleted?

22.14 You checked out a delta with **get -e s.foo.c**, and then realized that you shouldn't have done so. What should you do now and why?

23

Systems Programming I —Files

Now that you know what the UNIX system has to offer, some questions should be playing in your mind already. How are files and processes handled by the kernel and shell? Since UNIX is written in C, can we use the same functions that are internally used by UNIX commands? The answers to these questions lie in the system call library that is available to a C programmer working in the UNIX environment. In this chapter and the following, we look at files and processes from the system programmer's point of view.

Because of the multiprogramming nature of UNIX, a single resource is often shared by multiple processes. As a UNIX programmer, you are required to use your existing knowledge of the C language to devise programs and applications that ensure that resources are shared in the way they are meant to, and without causing conflict. This chapter takes up file internals and their associated system calls; the next chapter does the same for processes. The knowledge you acquire from them will help you write new tools and improve the existing ones.

WHAT YOU WILL LEARN

- The basics of *system calls* and *library functions*.
- Perform file I/O with **open**, **read**, **write**, **lseek** and **close**, using a *file descriptor*.
- How system call errors are handled and reported with **perror** and **strerror**.
- Navigate a directory structure with **chdir** and **getcwd**.
- Read directory entries with **opendir** and **readdir**, and examine the **dirent** structure.
- The combined role of the **stat** structure and **stat** calls in retrieving inode information.
- Use S_IFMT and the S_IS*xxx* macros to determine the file type.
- How to use symbolic constants to test each permission bit of a file.
- Use **access** to test a file's access rights, and how the SUID bit affects file access.

TOPICS OF SPECIAL INTEREST

- Understand how **unlink** works and the consequences of using it with an open file.
- Why it is important to properly set the size of the buffer used by **read** and **write**.
- The three-table scheme that comes into play when a file is opened, and how the scheme changes when a file is accessed by multiple processes.

23.1 SYSTEM CALL BASICS

C was created by Dennis Ritchie to rewrite the UNIX operating system in that language. To access the services available in the operating system, all UNIX systems offer around 200 special functions called **system calls**. A system call is a routine built into the kernel and performs a very basic function that requires communication with the CPU, memory and devices. These calls are often written in assembly language but provide a C-like function interface so we can invoke them as functions from a C program running on UNIX.

When you execute a C program, the CPU runs in **user mode** until a system call is invoked. In this mode, the process has access to a limited section of the computer's memory, and can execute a restricted set of machine instructions. However, when the process invokes a system call, the CPU switches from user mode to a more privileged mode—the **kernel mode** (*supervisory mode* in operating system parlance). In this mode, it's the kernel that runs on behalf of the user, but it has access to any memory location and can execute any machine instruction. After the system call has returned, the CPU switches back to user mode.

As mentioned before, all UNIX and Linux systems have one thing in common; they use the same system calls. Thus, a programmer knowing ANSI C should have no difficulty in using system calls provided she knows well the UNIX commands that internally use these calls. Many commands and system calls share the same names; the **chmod** command invokes the **chmod** system call.

23.1.1 System Calls and Library Functions

If you are a C programmer and have not used system calls, then you have must have used the **standard library functions**. These are a set of functions available for all UNIX and non-UNIX systems in the standard library of the C compiler. On UNIX systems, these library functions are built on top of the system calls. The C standard library offers separate functions to read a block of data (**fread**), a line (**fgets**) and a single character (**fgetc**). All of these functions ultimately invoke the only system call available for reading input—**read**. The library functions provide convenient interfaces that take care of some things that we may not like to bother about.

Does all this mean that we use only library functions and not system calls? No. Library functions are specialized and often don't provide the finer control features offered by system calls. For instance, **fopen** can't set file permissions (in **chmod**-style) which **open** does easily. A library function can't tell you the size of a file which the **stat** system call does. Further, a process can be created only with the **fork** system call.

There are significant overheads associated with system calls and mode switches (user mode to kernel mode, and vice versa), so we'll have to use these calls judiciously. It's advantageous to direct the **read** system call to read a large block of data in a single invocation rather that read in small blocks with multiple invocations. This is sometimes difficult to achieve, so we'll also be using library functions whenever it's expedient to do so.

23.1.2 Anatomy of a System Call

Irrespective of the way they are implemented, for all practical purposes system calls behave like C functions. They accept arguments (generally, not exceeding five) of all types (int, char, struct, pointers, etc.) and return values as can be seen from the prototype declaration of this **write** call:

```
ssize_t write(int fd, const void *buf, size_t count);
```

The third argument is of type size_t and the return type is of ssize_t. Generally, C uses **typedef** to ultimately translate them to the primitive types. For instance, size_t and ssize_t could ultimately be typedef'd to unsigned int and int, respectively on your machine. On another machine, they could represent unsigned long and long, respectively. int itself could be 16 bits on one machine and 32 bits on another. By using the derived types, size_t and ssize_t, rather than the primitive types in our programs, we are assured that appropriate mapping will be performed by the compiler.

ANSI C introduced the concept of a generic data type named void, and many system calls (like **write**) use this data type. In the prototype for **write** shown above, void *buf represents a generic buffer which can be for char * buf, int *buf, etc. We don't need to cast this generic buffer to the type that we actually use in our program.

Unlike library functions that often return null on error, system calls generally return -1. On error, a system call also sets a static (global) variable, errno, to a numeric value representing the error. There's a text message associated with every error number, and we'll learn to identify the cause of the error and print these messages. Some system calls, however, never return an error and some never return at all.

23.1.3 Atomic Operations

When you program in this multiprogramming environment, there's one thing that you have to keep in mind at all times: Multiple processes can contend for a single resource—like a file. There can be serious consequences in using two system calls (**open** and **lseek**) to append to a file when one would have sufficed (**open**). It's possible that a process is taken out of the CPU after **open** and before **lseek**, and a second process could overwrite the file in this period.

Wherever possible, you need to take care that certain critical operations are performed in an *atomic* manner. An **atomic operation** comprises multiple actions that are either performed in their entirety or not at all. Using two system calls in succession can't be an atomic operation because that allows a second process to run in between. In this chapter and the next, we'll note the instances of atomic behavior as and when we encounter them.

Tip: The UNIX man documentation features system calls and library functions in Sections 2 and 3, respectively. Sometimes, the same name represents both a UNIX command and a system call (like **read**, **write** and **exec**), so calling **man** without the section number would wrongly display the man page for the command. (**man read** shows the man page for the shell's built-in **read** command.) You must use **man 2 read** (or **man -s2 read** on Solaris). The documentation is complete and very well-explained.

23.2 OPENING AND CLOSING A FILE

We begin our discussion on system calls with the ones related to file I/O. These comprise the **open**, **read**, **write**, **close** and **lseek** calls. Since UNIX treats even pipes and sockets as files, all of these calls (barring **lseek**) are used with these objects also.

23.2.1 open: Opening and Creating a File

You don't need to open a file to access its attributes, but you can't read or write a file unless you first open it. **open** has two forms; the first form assumes that the file exists, and the second one creates it if it doesn't. Both forms can be expressed by this syntax:

```
int open(const char *path, int oflag, ... );
```

open returns a **file descriptor** as an int. This is the lowest number available for allocation and is used as an argument by the other four calls. Since every program always finds the three standard files (having the descriptors 0, 1 and 2) open, we don't need to open these files from our programs (though we can close them). Normally, the first **open** in your program should return the file descriptor 3.

The first argument (*path*) is a pointer to a character string that represents the file's pathname (either absolute or relative). The second argument (*oflag*) is used to set the *mode* of opening (read, write or read-write), which is conveniently represented by three symbolic constants. When opening a file, only one of the following modes must be specified:

O_RDONLY	Opens file for reading.
O_WRONLY	Opens file for writing.
O_RDWR	Opens file for reading and writing.

These constants are defined in the file fcntl.h in /usr/include, so you need to place the statement **#include <fcntl.h>** at the top of your program. For added functionality, you'll often need to use one or more of the following *status flags* (also defined in fcntl.h) as components of *oflag*:

O_APPEND	Opens file in append mode (only if file opening mode is O_WRONLY or O_RDWR).
O_TRUNC	Truncates file to zero length (same conditions as above).
O_CREAT	Creates file if it doesn't exist.
O_EXCL	Generates an error if O_CREAT is also specified and the file also exists.
O_SYNC	Synchronizes read-write operations. Ensures that **write** doesn't return until the data is written to disk (explained later).

These status flags are used with the bit-wise OR operator, |, along with the mode of opening. Here are some ways you can use **open** with a file that exists:

```
int fd;
fd = open("/etc/passwd", O_RDONLY);
fd = open("foo.txt", O_WRONLY | O_APPEND) ;
fd = open("../foo.txt", O_WRONLY | O_TRUNC) ;
```

The file descriptor
Read only
Like the >> symbols
Similar to the > symbol

The first **open** call above sets the *file offset pointer* to the beginning of the file. This pointer determines where in the file the subsequent read or write will take place. In the second call, the file is opened for writing but only by appending (O_APPEND), which sets the offset pointer to EOF. A subsequent write call here doesn't overwrite this file but increases its size. The third call truncates a file's contents (O_TRUNC) and positions the offset pointer at the beginning.

If the file doesn't exist, then use the status flag, O_CREAT (and sometimes, O_EXCL also), to create the file. (Previously, the **creat** system call was used for this function.) In that case, you'll have to specify the absolute permissions of the file as the third argument. This argument can be specified as an octal number in the same way used by **chmod**, except that you'll have to prefix the number with a 0 (like 0644 instead of 644). However, you are advised to use the symbolic constants provided in sys/stat.h. They are displayed in a tabular form below:

Permission	User	Group	Others	All
Read	S_IRUSR	S_IRGRP	S_IROTH	S_IRWXU
Write	S_IWUSR	S_IWGRP	S_IWOTH	S_IRWXG
Execute	S_IXUSR	S_IXGRP	S_IXOTH	S_IRWXO

Since each permission is represented by a separate bit, you have to OR these constants (bit-wise) to obtain the desired permissions. For instance, 0644 is the same as

```
S_IRUSR | S_IWUSR | S_IRGRP | S_IROTH
```

To open a file for writing after truncation (O_TRUNC), while ensuring that the file is created if it doesn't exist (O_CREAT), specify the permissions as the third argument:

```
fd = open("foo.txt", O_WRONLY | O_CREAT | O_TRUNC,        Second argument is 01101
         S_IRUSR | S_IWUSR | S_IRGRP | S_IROTH) ;         Permissions are 0644
```

This is how the shell opens a file or overwrites one that exists when it sees the > symbol. Note that the bit-wise OR of the opening mode and status flags equates to octal 01101. We can't remember these numbers; that's why we must use symbolic constants.

The status flag, O_EXCL, provides protection from overwriting an existing file. If used at all, it must be combined with O_CREAT (O_CREAT | O_EXCL). With the two flags set in this way, **open** will return an error (-1) if the file exists. We can use this mechanism to test for the existence of a file.

Note: The file may not be created with the exact permissions you specify with **open** and the O_CREAT flag. The specified permissions get reduced by the umask value of the process. There's a separate system call named **umask** for handling this function and is discussed in Section 23.5.

Tip: The O_EXCL feature comes in handy when you devise a scheme to let two processes share a file, foo, in a cooperative manner. To make the scheme work as an *advisory* form of file locking, both programs must agree to first create a lock file (with the same name) before they write to foo, and then remove the lock file when they are done with foo. If all cooperating programs use the O_EXCL flag in their **open** calls that attempt to create the lock file, the first **open** will succeed and others will fail. Adherence to this agreement ensures that a file is not written simultaneously by two or more processes.

23.2.2 `close`: Closing a File

A program automatically closes all open files before termination, but it's good practice to close them explicitly when you no longer require them. The **close** system call closes a file:

```
int close(int fd);
```

close returns 0 if successful and -1 otherwise. It actually deallocates the file descriptor for that process and makes it available for the next **open** (if there is one). When the **unlink** call is invoked to delete a file, the kernel can actually delete it only when the file is closed. This is discussed in Section 23.10.3.

When the same file is opened by two processes A and B (or by two **open** calls in the same program), the kernel simply assigns two separate file descriptors for them. If you use **close** in process A, you would simply release the descriptor for process A; process B would still find the file open. How all this happens will be described soon with reference to three tables maintained by the kernel for every open file.

Note: You can close any of the standard files explicitly in your program. Yes, you can use **close(1);** to close the standard output file and then open a disk file to return 1 as the descriptor value. The implications of a file having descriptor values that are normally associated with the three standard streams will be examined in the next chapter.

23.3 USING THE I/O CALLS

The standard library offers a host a functions for reading (like **fread**, **fgets**, **fgetc** and **scanf**) and writing (like **fwrite**, **fputs**, **fputc** and **printf**), but only two system calls are actually at work here—**read** and **write**. These calls share a similar syntax that makes use of a user-defined buffer for reading and writing. We'll soon learn how the size of the buffer impacts disk I/O operations, so let's begin with **read**.

23.3.1 read: Reading a File

You need the **read** call to read a file using a file descriptor returned by a prior **open**. The prototype declaration for **read** is shown below:

```
ssize_t read(int fildes, void *buf, size_t nbyte);
```

read attempts to read *nbyte* characters from the file descriptor *filedes* into the buffer *buf*. *buf* represents a pointer to a generic buffer (which could be any of the primitive data types, often char). *nbyte* is generally the size of the buffer itself. The call returns the number of characters read.

If you have to process every character you read, then declare *buf* as a char variable and then pass its address to **read**:

```
int fd, n; char buf ;
while ((n = read(fd, &buf, 1)) > 0)                    fd obtained from a prior open
```

The number of characters read as returned by this call (here, n) is generally equal to the number requested (here, 1). However, in a general situation, the two will not match when **read** encounters EOF, in which case it returns the number of characters that it could *actually* read. Network congestion and signals can also affect the return value of **read**. For these reasons, we simply check the return value for a positive integer and run **read** in a loop until it encounters EOF.

Reading 100 characters with a single character buffer (as above) would require 100 system call invocations, which is rather expensive. If you don't need to process each character individually, then you should use an array. If it's a character array, then read into this array as many characters as its size:

```
#define BUFSIZE 100
int n; char buf[BUFSIZE];
while ((n = read(fd, buf, BUFSIZE)) > 0)
```

This **read** call is more efficient than the previous one as a single invocation reads in 100 characters in a *single* mode switch (user mode to kernel mode).

23.3.2 `write`: Writing a File

You need the **write** call to write a file that has previously been opened with **open**. The prototype declaration of **write** is virtually identical to that of **read**:

```
ssize_t write(int fildes, const void *buf, size_t nbyte);
```

Each invocation of **write** writes *nbyte* number of bytes from the generic buffer *buf* to the file descriptor *fildes*. **write** returns the number of characters written, which *must* be equal to the number requested. However, if the disk fills up while a **write** is in progress or if the file size exceeds the system's limit, **write** returns -1.

As in **read**, you can write one character at a time in which case you should declare buf as a char variable:

```
char buf ;
write(fd, &buf, 1));                          fd obtained from a prior open
```

For writing data in chunks of characters, say, 8192 bytes, buf should be declared as a character array for holding that many characters, and **write**'s third argument should represent the size of this array:

```
#define BUFSIZE 8192
int n; char buf[BUFSIZE];
n = write(fd, buf, BUFSIZE));
```

The determination of the buffer size for both **read** and **write** depends on the device written to (terminal, hard disk, etc.) and the size of the kernel buffer maintained in memory. We are coming to that soon.

Note: When reading and writing the standard streams, we should use the symbolic constants, STDIN_FILENO, STDOUT_FILENO and STDERR_FILENO as the file descriptors rather than the integers 0, 1 and 2 that they represent. These symbolic constants are defined in unistd.h.

23.3.3 ccp.c: COPYING A FILE

Our first program, **ccp.c** (Fig. 23.1), copies the file /etc/passwd to passwd.bak in the user's current directory. The source file is opened in the read-only mode (O_RDONLY). The destination file is opened in the write mode (O_WRONLY), is created if it doesn't exist (O_CREAT) and truncated if it does (O_TRUNC). Each **open** returns a file descriptor which should have the values 3 and 4 in this program.

For copying operations, both **read** and **write** need to use the same buffer. We set up a loop that attempts to read 1024 bytes into buf (an array of 1024 characters) from the descriptor fd1. The return value of **read** is next used by **write** to save the same buffer to disk using file descriptor fd2. The loop terminates when **read** returns 0 (on EOF). The descriptors are explicitly closed before exiting the program.

The program doesn't do any error checking and works only if ideal conditions prevail. Let's now compile this program with **cc** (or **gcc**) and then run the executable a.out. A byte-by-byte comparison of the two files with **cmp** confirms the faithfulness of the copy:

```
$ cc ccp.c
$ a.out
$ cmp /etc/passwd passwd.bak
$ _                                          Prompt returns—files identical
```

You need not always write data to disk; you can write to the standard output also. So if we replace fd2 in the **write** statement with 1 (rather, STDOUT_FILENO), we can use the program as a simple **cat** command. The second **open** and **close** calls won't then be required.

```
/* Program: ccp.c -- Copies a file with the read and write system calls */

#include <fcntl.h>              /* For O_RDONLY, O_WRONLY, O_CREAT etc. */
#include <sys/stat.h>           /* For S_IRUSR, S_IWUSR, S_IRGRP etc. */
#define BUFSIZE 1024            /* May not be the right size here */

int main(void) {
    int fd1, fd2;              /* File descriptors for read and write */
    int n;                     /* Number of characters returned by read */
    char buf[BUFSIZE];         /* BUFSIZE should be carefully chosen */
    fd1 = open("/etc/passwd", O_RDONLY);
    fd2 = open("passwd.bak", O_WRONLY | O_CREAT | O_TRUNC,
            S_IRUSR | S_IWUSR | S_IRGRP |S_IWGRP | S_IROTH);   /* Mode 664 */

    while ((n = read(fd1, buf, BUFSIZE)) > 0)    /* Return value of read is */
        write(fd2, buf, n) ;                      /* used by write as argument */

    close(fd1);
    close(fd2);
    exit(0);                   /* This would have closed all file descriptors */
}
```

Fig. 23.1 ccp.c

Note: The library function **fopen** doesn't return a file descriptor, but a pointer to a FILE structure. The other functions like **fread** and **fwrite** access the file through this pointer. Beneath the hood, these functions actually run the corresponding system calls, **open**, **read** and **write**, and the file descriptor is embedded in the FILE structure as a separate member.

23.3.4 lseek: Positioning the Offset Pointer

The **lseek** call moves the file offset pointer to a specified point. **lseek** doesn't do any physical I/O, but it determines the position in the file where the next I/O operation will take place. Here's its syntax:

```
off_t lseek(int fildes, off_t offset, int whence);
```

The *offset* and *whence* arguments together control the location of the file's offset pointer. *offset* signifies the position (positive or negative) of this pointer relative to *whence*, which can take one of three values:

SEEK_SET	Offset pointer set to beginning of file.
SEEK_END	Offset pointer set to end of file.
SEEK_CUR	Offset pointer remains at current location.

With some restrictions, *offset* can be a positive or negative integer, so it is represented by a signed data type. For instance,

```
lseek(fd, 10, SEEK_CUR)                          Descriptor fd obtained from prior open
```

moves the pointer forward by 10 characters from its current position, and

```
lseek(fd, -10, SEEK_END)                          Negative offset
```

sets the pointer 10 characters before EOF. You can't have a negative *offset* with *whence* set to SEEK_SET, but strangely enough you can have a positive *offset* with *whence* at SEEK_END. In this case, the pointer moves beyond EOF, thus creating a *sparse* file—also called a file with a "hole". Sparse files find use in database applications.

lseek returns the position of the pointer in bytes from the beginning of the file. The return value can be used to determine the file size:

```
size = lseek(fd, 0, SEEK_END);                          This returns the file size
```

Unlike **read** and **write**, which work with practically all file types, **lseek** works only with those files that are capable of seeking. It doesn't work with the terminal file or with a socket or pipe, and is mainly used for disk files.

Tip: There are two ways of appending data to a file. You can use **open** with the O_APPEND status flag which positions the file's offset pointer to EOF. Alternatively, you can use **open** (without the flag) followed by **lseek(fd, 0, SEEK_END)**. The former technique is an atomic operation (23.1.3) and is recommended for use, but the latter is not.

23.3.5 `reverse_read.c`: Reading a File in Reverse

You can't read a file from the end to the beginning using the standard UNIX utilities (except **perl**), but using **lseek** in a C program, **reverse_read.c** (Fig. 23.2), you can. You have to first move the file pointer to one character before EOF to allow the last character to be read. Subsequently, every time you read one character, you must move the pointer back by two positions. This action needs to be performed in a loop until the beginning of file is reached.

The program accepts the input filename as argument and writes to standard output. Observe that by moving the file offset pointer to one character before SEEK_END (EOF), we effectively captured the size of the file from **lseek**'s return value. size in the program is initially one less than the file size, a fact that is taken into account in the control command of the **while** loop.

Unlike in **ccp.c**, where we picked up data in chunks, this application demands that we read *one* character at a time. Hence, we use a single-character buffer with **read** and **write**. While **read** advances the pointer one byte forward, the next **lseek** takes it back by two bytes.

This program isn't logically correct; it does the job all right but terminates with an error. Let's run it on the file planets, which contains hostnames derived from our solar system. Finally, we'll check the exit status:

```
$ a.out planets
... A blank line ...          The terminating \n of the last line
retipuj                       This is jupiter
yrucrem                       mercury
htrae                         earth
nrutas                        saturn
```

```
/* Program: reverse_read.c -- Reads a file in reverse - uses lseek  */

#include <fcntl.h>                        /* For O_RDONLY */
#include <unistd.h>                       /* For STDOUT_FILENO */

int main(int argc, char **argv) {
    char buf;                             /* Single-character buffer; will make */
    int size, fd;                         /* I/O inefficient. See Section 23.4 */

    fd = open(argv[1], O_RDONLY);
    size = lseek(fd, -1, SEEK_END);       /* Pointer taken to EOF - 1 ... */
    while (size-- >= 0) {                  /* ... so size = file size - 1 */
        read(fd, &buf, 1);                /* Read one character at a time */
        write(STDOUT_FILENO, &buf, 1);    /* and write it immediately */
        lseek(fd, -2, SEEK_CUR);          /* Now move file pointer back */
    }                                     /* by two characters */
    /* exit(0); */                        /* Done deliberately */
}
```

Fig. 23.2 `reverse_read.c`

```
$ echo $?
132
```

Why did the program terminate with a non-zero exit value? Look at the **while** loop closely and you'll find that in the last iteration, **lseek** runs with a negative offset at the beginning of the file. The second argument to **lseek** then becomes invalid. We didn't see any error message because we didn't trap it. Later, we'll rewrite this program after incorporating error-handling features.

23.3.6 truncate and ftruncate: Truncating a File

The O_TRUNC flag used with **open** truncates a file to zero bytes, but needs to open the file too. The **truncate** and **ftruncate** calls can truncate a file to any length. They are used like this:

```
int truncate(const char *path, off_t length);
int ftruncate(int fildes, off_t length);
```

truncate needs the pathname (*path*) as argument but **ftruncate** works with the file descriptor (*fildes*) of an open file. Both truncate the file to *length* bytes. These calls are often used in combination with **lseek** to overwrite a certain segment of a file. You can truncate a file to any desired length and then use **lseek** to take the pointer to the location of truncation so you can start writing from there.

Note: Many of the system calls discussed in this chapter have two, and sometimes, three versions. There's a "normal" version (like **truncate**) that uses the pathname, and a "f"-prefixed version (like **ftruncate**) that uses the file descriptor as argument. You can use either version if the file is open, but only the normal version if the file is not open.

23.4 BUFFERED AND UNBUFFERED I/O

Before we move away from file I/O, we need to know something about the way disk I/O actually takes place. The **read** and **write** calls never access the disk directly. Rather, they read and write to a pool of buffers maintained by the kernel for this purpose, called the **buffer cache** *(15.7.1)*. If the kernel buffer is found to be empty during a read, the kernel instructs the disk controller to read data from disk and fill up the cache. The **read** call **blocks** (waits) while the disk is being read and even relinquishes control of the CPU.

To ensure that a single invocation of **read** gathers all bytes stored in the kernel buffer, the size of the latter should be set to the buffer size used by **read** (BUFSIZE in the previous example). Improper setting of the buffer size can make your program inefficient. So if each kernel buffer stores 8192 bytes, then BUFSIZE should also be set to 8192; there's no point choosing a figure larger than this.

write also uses the buffer cache, but it differs from **read** in one way; it returns *immediately* after the call is invoked, and doesn't wait for the actual writing to take place. The kernel writes the buffer to disk *later* at a convenient time. Database applications often can't accept this, in which case you should open a file with the O_SYNC status flag to ensure that **write** doesn't return until the kernel has finally written the buffer to disk.

Unlike the standard library functions, the **read** and **write** calls are unbuffered when they interact with the terminal. When you use **write** to output a string to the terminal, the string appears on your display as soon as the call is invoked. On the other hand, the standard library functions (like **printf**) are line-buffered when they access the terminal. That means a string is printed on the terminal when the newline character is encountered.

Note: The size of the kernel buffer is set at the time of installation of the operating system, and varies across systems. It's inconvenient to write programs that explicitly specify buffer sizes that are file system- and machine-dependent; we can't then have portable applications. This is where library functions come in. They use a buffer in the FILE structure and adjust its size *dynamically* during runtime using **malloc**.

23.5 umask: MODIFYING FILE PERMISSIONS DURING CREATION

The permissions that you specify with **open** (when used with the O_CREAT flag) are modified by the umask value that is set in your shell. This mask, you'll recall (*11.5*), reduces the default file and directory permissions (666 and 777, respectively) by the value of the mask. The **umask** system call kills two birds with one stone; it sets the mask to the value specified as argument, but it also returns the previous value of the mask:

```
mode_t umask(mode_t cmask);
```

Unlike the shell's **umask** statement, however, the **umask** call can't display the current value of the mask without changing it. To use a workaround, store the current mask by changing it to some arbitrary value, display the returned value and finally restore the saved mask. In our next program, **umask.c** (Fig. 23.3), we change the mask, print its old value and then create two files with two different settings of the mask.

In this program, we first set the mask to 0 and save its previous value in old_mode. After printing the previous value of the mask, we create a file with permissions 777. Next, we restore the old mask and then create another file with permissions 764. The output makes for some interesting reading:

```
/* Program: umask.c -- Changes umask twice and checks effect on permissions */

#include <stdio.h>
#include <fcntl.h>

int main(void) {
    mode_t old_mode, new_mode;

    old_mode = umask(0);                                /* No mask */
    printf("Previous umask value: %o\n", old_mode);

    open("foo1", O_RDONLY | O_CREAT, 0777);    /* Create file using new mask */
    umask(old_mode);                           /* Revert to previous mask */
    open("foo2", O_RDWR | O_CREAT, 0764);      /* Create file using old mask */
    exit(0);
}
```

Fig. 23.3 umask.c

```
$ a.out
Previous umask value: 22
$ ls -l foo?
-rwxrwxrwx   1 sumit    sumit        0 Dec  1 12:01 foo1
-rwxr--r--   1 sumit    sumit        0 Dec  1 12:01 foo2
```

Note that we could create a file foo1 with all permissions; this is something we can't do from the shell. The permissions of foo2 are 744, which isn't what you get when you subtract 022 from 764. A umask value of 022 indicates that a file will be created with the write permission bit absent for group and others. A simple arithmetic subtraction (764 - 022) would result in write permission for others—something that wasn't intended!

Note: The restrictions placed by **umask** in no way affect our ability to change the permissions later with the **chmod** system call. **chmod** is taken up in Section 23.13.1.

23.6 HANDLING ERRORS

We haven't checked for errors in any of our previous programs. But errors can occur for a host of reasons—a resource not available, the receipt of a signal, I/O operational failures or invalid call arguments. A system call returns -1 on error, so to create robust code, we should always check for this condition (unless we are certain that this check isn't really necessary).

When a system call returns -1, the kernel sets the static (global) variable, errno, to a positive integer. This integer is associated with an error message and is represented by a symbolic constant. For instance, ENOENT has the value 2 and signifies No such file or directory. The number of messages available on your system is available in the extern variable, sys_nerr. The message strings can be printed with the library functions, **strerror** and **perror**.

23.6.1 Using strerror

The library function, **strerror**, uses the error number as argument and returns a pointer to the string representing the error:

```
char *strerror(int errnum);
```

The program, **show_errors.c** (Fig. 23.4), uses **strerror** to print all error messages used by your system. A **for** loop iterates as many times as the value of sys_nerr, and strerror prints the message for each value of errno. The output obtained on a Solaris system is suitably edited to show the most common messages from the top of the list:

```
$ a.out
0: Error 0
1: Not owner
2: No such file or directory
3: No such process
4: Interrupted system call
5: I/O error
13: Permission denied
```

```
/* Program: show_errors.c -- Uses strerror to print all error messages */

#include <stdio.h>

int main(void) {
    int i;
    extern int sys_nerr;                  /* Total number of error messages */

    for (i =0; i < sys_nerr; i++)
        printf("%d: %s\n", i, strerror(i));
    printf("Number of errors available: %d\n", sys_nerr);
    exit(0);
}
```

Fig. 23.4 show_errors.c

```
17: File exists
22: Invalid argument
Number of errors available: 151
```

Solaris shows 151 possible error messages. To see how errno gets set, let's now modify the program in Fig. 23.2 by replacing the line containing the last occurrence of **lseek** with these two lines:

```
if (lseek(fd, -2, SEEK_CUR) == -1)
    fprintf(stderr, "\nerrno = %d, Message = %s\n", errno, strerror(errno));
```

When you now run the program on the same file, planets, you should additionally see this error message at the end of output:

```
errno = 22, Message = Invalid argument
```

lseek eventually was called with an "invalid argument", which set errno to 22.

23.6.2 Using perror

Let's take a cue from the previous output to write a program, **show_errno.c** (Fig. 23.5), that attempts to open a non-existent file (non_existent_file), an unreadable file (/etc/shadow) and create a file that exists (the current program file, **show_errno.c**). This time, we use **perror** to print the error messages. **perror** follows this syntax:

```
void perror(const char *s);
```

Unlike **strerror**, **perror** doesn't use errno as argument; so it can only print the message associated with the current value of errno. The function takes a character string, *s*, as argument, and prints the string, a colon, a space followed by the message associated with errno.

In this program, we check the return value of **open** every time we use it. The first **open** should fail because non_existent_file won't (hopefully) exist in your directory. The second **open** tries to open /etc/shadow, which is unreadable to all except root. The third **open** uses O_CREAT | O_EXCL to create this source file itself; obviously it will fail. Here's the output of this program:

```
/* Program: show_errno.c -- Displaying system call errors with perror */

#include <fcntl.h>

int main(int argc, char **argv) {
   int fd;
   char* filename = "non_existent_file";   /* This file must not exist */

   fd = open(filename, O_RDONLY);              /* File descriptor assigned first */
   if (fd == -1)                               /* and then checked */
      perror("non_existent_file");
   if ((fd = open("/etc/shadow", O_RDONLY)) == -1)   /* Both combined here */
      perror("shadow");
   if ((fd = open("show_errno.c", O_WRONLY | O_CREAT | O_EXCL, 0744)) == -1)
      perror("show_errno.c");
   exit(0);
}
```

Fig. 23.5 <code>show_errno.c</code>

```
$ a.out
non_existent_file: No such file or directory
shadow: Permission denied
show_errno.c: File exists
```

perror doesn't print errno, but you know their values from the output of the program prior to the previous one. These error numbers are associated with symbolic constants defined in <sys/errno.h>. A subset of these constants, their errno values and the message strings are shown in Table 23.1. Henceforth, we'll be using error checking in most of our programs, and sometimes check for specific error conditions.

Caution: You must check the value of errno *immediately* after a system call returns an error, and before you do anything else. The behavior of errno in the event of a successful call is undefined. Some systems leave it unchanged, but some don't. If necessary, save the value of errno in a separate variable if you need this value later in your program.

23.6.3 reverse_read2.c: Reverse Reading a File with Error Handling

Now let's use our knowledge of error handling to improve our previous program (Fig. 23.2) that reads a file in reverse order. The program, **reverse_read2.c** (Fig. 23.6), employs three types of error handling techniques and provides five exit points. It checks for possible error conditions in most of the system calls used, but lets some of them off only because there's hardly a way they could generate errors.

The first form of error handling uses **write** with a character string, but gives no indication of the nature of the error. The second form checks for a specific type of error (here, ENOENT), and is useful in situations where program flow depends on the nature of the error. But this form uses **fprintf**

Table 23.1 Significance of Symbolic Constants Associated with errno

Symbolic Constant	errno	Message
EPERM	1	Not super-user
ENOENT	2	No such file or directory
ESRCH	3	No such process
EINTR	4	Interrupted system call
EIO	5	I/O error
EACCES	13	Permission denied
EEXIST	17	File exists
ENOTDIR	20	Not a directory
EISDIR	21	Is a directory
ENOSPC	28	No space left on device
ESPIPE	29	Illegal seek
EROFS	30	Read only file system

and **strerror** to print the error message; it's inconvenient to use it this way. The third form uses the library functions, **perror** and **exit**, three times in a consistent manner which justifies their conversion to a function.

Observe that this time **lseek** takes the offset pointer beyond EOF before moving back from there. The program provides five abnormal exit points having different values of the exit status (1 to 5). If the program generates an error, you can know the exit route it took by examining the value of $?. So let's run it in a number of ways:

```
$ a.out ; echo $?
Not enough arguments
1
$ a.out /etc/shdaow ; echo $?
No such file or directory          Printed with strerror; this is ENOENT
2
$ a.out /etc/shadow ; echo $?
/etc/shadow: Permission denied     Printed with perror; this is EACCES
3
```

Note how the program returned three different exit values when the command line arguments to the program were either wrongly specified or the input file was unreadable. Let's use the right file now:

```
$ a.out planets              Displays same output as
... A blank line ...         program in Fig. 23.2.
retipuj
yrucrem
htrae
nrutas
$ echo $?
0                            Normal exit from program
```

```
/* Program: reverse_read2.c -- Reads a file in reverse - uses error handling  */

#include <fcntl.h>                    /* For O_RDONLY */
#include <unistd.h>                   /* For STDOUT_FILENO */
#include <errno.h>                    /* For ENOENT, errno, etc. */
#include <stdio.h>                    /* For ENOENT, errno, etc. */

int main(int argc, char **argv) {
    int size, fd;
    char buf;                                    /* Single-character buffer */
    char *mesg = "Not enough arguments\n";

    if (argc != 2) {                  /* Our own user-defined error message */
        write(STDERR_FILENO, mesg, strlen(mesg));  /* Crude form of error */
        exit(1);                                 /* handling using write */
    }                                            /* Use fprintf instead */

    if ((fd = open(argv[1], O_RDONLY)) == -1) {
        if (errno == ENOENT) {                   / *Checking for specific error*/
            fprintf(stderr, "%s\n", strerror(errno)); /* perror is better */
            exit(2);
        } else {
            perror(argv[1]);                     /* Using two library functions */
            exit(3);                             /* perror and exit. Often the */
        }                                        /* preferred way */
    }

    lseek(fd, 1, SEEK_END);                      /* Pointer taken to EOF + 1 first */
    while (lseek(fd, -2, SEEK_CUR) >= 0) { /* and then back by two bytes */
        if (read(fd, &buf, 1) != 1) {            /* A signal can create error here */
            perror("read");
            exit(4);
        }
        if (write(STDOUT_FILENO, &buf, 1) != 1) { /* Disk may run out of space */
            perror("write");
            exit(5);
        }
    }
    close(fd);                        /* Can have error here too */
    exit(0);                          /* exit doesn't return - hence no error */
}
```

Fig. 23.6 **reverse_read2.c**

It's often the case that when you use **perror**, you also quit the program immediately thereafter. Henceforth, we'll be using the **quit** function to handle most error conditions. Enter this definition for **quit** in a file, **quit.c**:

```
#include <stdio.h>
void quit(char *message, int exit_status) {
    perror(message);
    exit(exit_status);
}
```

quit uses **perror** to print the message associated with errno. The same message could be used by multiple **quit** invocations, so we additionally provide the exit status as the second argument. We can gather this exit status from the shell by examining $?. Create the object code, **quit.o**, for this function with **cc -c quit.c**.

23.7 FILE SHARING

Things start to get complex when we realize that UNIX is a multiprogramming system, which allows multiple processes to use the same file. It's also possible for a parent process to open a file and make its file descriptor available to the child. That's similar to the way the shell handles redirection, so we need to understand the structural changes that take place in memory when a file is opened.

The inode contains only static data about a file, but when a file is opened, the dynamic attributes come into play. These attributes comprise the mode of opening (like O_RDONLY), the status flags (like O_CREAT, O_APPEND, etc.), the file offset, and so forth. The kernel maintains three data structures in memory that contain all information about an open file that a process needs to access:

- The *file descriptor table*—This structure contains all allocated file descriptors for a process. Each entry points to the file table.
- The *file table* —It contains all parameters that are supplied at the time of opening a file. It also contains the file offset. This table points to the vnode table.
- The *vnode table*—This contains all inode information, and can be considered as an approximation of the inode in memory (in-core inode).

Even though the file descriptor table is a per-process structure (only one table per process), the other two tables are not. It's possible to have multiple file tables for the same file (with multiple **open**s) or for multiple processes to access the same file table and vnode table (by replicating file descriptors). Both tables maintain a *reference count* field that signifies the number of pointers to the table. In the following sections, we'll examine these tables and their relationship as depicted in Fig. 23.7. This knowledge is essential to our understanding of processes that is taken up in the next chapter.

23.7.1 The File Descriptor Table

The kernel returns a non-negative integer, the file descriptor, to the process that opens the file. This file descriptor is stored along with a flag in the **file descriptor table**. This table is maintained separately for every process that runs in the system. The shell's three standard files occupy the first three slots (0, 1 and 2) in the file descriptor table.

If you close, say, descriptor number 1, the kernel will allocate this number to the next file that is opened. We'll use this behavioral property in the next chapter to implement redirection. The flag, FD_CLOEXEC, is not used by **open**, but by a powerful system call named **fcntl** to determine whether

Fig. 23.7 File Sharing—The Three Tables

the descriptor will be closed when the process does an exec *(9.4)* to run a separate program. By default, a descriptor is not closed when the process does an exec.

23.7.2 The File Table

Every entry in the file descriptor table points to a **file table**. This table contains all data that are relevant to an opened file. More specifically, it contains

- The mode of opening (like O_RDONLY).
- The status flags (like O_CREAT, O_TRUNC, etc.).
- The offset pointer location that determines the byte position to be used by the next read or write operation.
- A reference count that indicates the number of processes or calls that point to this table.

Every symbolic constant used as the second argument to **open** is made available in the file table. Since the file descriptor table and file table appear to share a one-to-one relationship, you could ask this: Why can't the mode, flags and offset be kept in the file descriptor table rather than in the file table? The answer is that UNIX also allows two or more file descriptors to point to the same file table entry (many-to-one). This happens when you duplicate the file descriptor (with the **dup** and **dup2** system calls) and when you create a process (with **fork**). We'll consider the implications of this replication in the next chapter.

The file status flags (though not its mode) can be changed by the **fcntl** system call—the same call that controls the FD_CLOEXEC flag in the file descriptor table. The reference count field tracks the number of descriptors pointing to the file table (in a many-to-one situation). The kernel releases the table from memory only when there's no descriptor pointing to it, i.e. when the reference count has dropped to zero.

23.7.3 The Vnode Table

The file table contains a pointer to the **vnode table**, the third table in the scheme. Maurice Bach (*The Design of the UNIX Operating System*, Prentice Hall) calls this the *inode table*, but that is because the *vnode* originated after the book was written. That was when UNIX systems supported only a single type of file system. Today, we have multiple file system types on the same machine, so the vnode abstraction was created to make it possible to access the inode in a file-system independent way.

The vnode table contains all information present in the inode except that this structure is maintained in memory. It's often called the *in-core inode* (Bach). There's only a single copy of the vnode in memory. The inode on disk is updated from the information in the vnode by the kernel. If two processes open the same file, or the same program opens the same file twice, there would be separate entries in the file descriptor tables and two separate file table structures, but both structures would point to the same vnode table (Fig. 23.8).

Like the file table, the vnode table also maintains a reference count field that signifies the number of file table entries that point to this table. When a file is deleted, the kernel has to first check the reference count to see whether any process still has the file open. If the reference count is at least one, the kernel can't delete the file and release the inode *though it will delete the directory entry for the file*. This unusual action is discussed later (*23.10.3*).

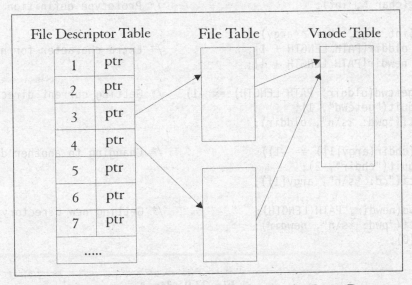

Fig. 23.8 When a File is Opened Twice in the Same Process

23.8 DIRECTORY NAVIGATION

There are two system calls that perform the action of the **cd** command. They are **chdir** and **fchdir**, which use a pathname and a file descriptor, respectively as argument:

```
int chdir(const char *path);
int fchdir(int fildes);
```

We'll be using **chdir** in our next example. The current directory is obtained by the **getcwd** library function. Some UNIX systems feature other functions (like **getwd**), but POSIX recommends the use of **getcwd** which must use this syntax only:

```
extern char *getcwd(char *buf, size_t size);
```

Here, *buf* is defined as a character array of *size* bytes. After invocation of **getcwd**, the pathname of the current directory is made available in *buf*.

The next program, **dir.c** (Fig. 23.9), uses **chdir** to switch to a directory. It also invokes **getcwd** to obtain the pathname of the current directory, both before and after the switch. The buffers that store the directory pathnames are provided with one extra slot for storing the null character.

The program makes use of the **quit** function that we just developed. We'll now have to link the object code for **quit.o** with this program using

```
/* Program: dir.c -- Directory navigation with chdir and getcwd */

#include <stdio.h>
#define PATH_LENGTH 200

void quit(char *, int);                         /* Prototype definition */

int main(int argc, char **argv) {
    char olddir[PATH_LENGTH + 1];               /* Extra character for null */
    char newdir[PATH_LENGTH + 1];

    if (getcwd(olddir, PATH_LENGTH) == -1)      /* Getting current directory */
        quit("getcwd", 1);
    printf("pwd: %s\n", olddir);

    if ((chdir(argv[1]) == -1))                 /* Changing to another directory */
        quit("chdir", 2);
    printf("cd: %s\n", argv[1]);

    getcwd(newdir, PATH_LENGTH);                /* Getting new directory */
    printf("pwd: %s\n", newdir);
    exit(0);
}
```

Fig. 23.9 dir.c

```
cc dir.c quit.o
```

Let's now use the generated executable, a.out, to switch to the directory /usr/include/sys. The program prints the current directory both before and after the switch:

```
$ a.out /usr/include/sys
pwd: /users1/home/staff/sumit
cd: /usr/include/sys
pwd: /usr/include/sys                           Change of directory inside program ...
$ pwd
/users1/home/staff/sumit                        ... is not available outside it
```

After completion of the program, we also ran the shell's **pwd** command. As explained previously *(9.4)*, a change of environment inside a program is not available outside it.

23.9 READING A DIRECTORY

Directories are also files, and they can be opened, read and written in the same way as regular files. The format of a directory is not consistent across file systems—and even across different flavors of UNIX. Using **open** and **read** to list directory entries can be a grueling task. UNIX offers these library functions to handle a directory:

```
DIR *opendir(const char *dirname);              Opens a directory
struct dirent *readdir(DIR *dirp);              Reads a directory
int closedir(DIR *dirp);                        Closes a directory
```

Note that we can't *directly* write a directory; only the kernel can do that. These three functions take on the role of the **open**, **read** and **close** system calls as applied to ordinary files except that a directory is identified by a structure of type DIR (whose structure need not bother us). **opendir** takes *dirname* as the pathname and returns a pointer to a DIR structure. The other two functions use the address of this structure as argument.

A directory maintains the inode number and filename for every file in its fold. Expectedly, these two entities are members of the dirent structure that is returned by **readdir**. Every invocation of **readdir** fills up this structure with information related to the next directory entry (i.e., the next filename). POSIX doesn't specify the internal format of a directory, but it requires the dirent structure (defined in <dirent.h>) to provide at least these two members:

```
struct dirent {
    ino_t   d_ino                               Inode number
    char    d_name[]                            Directory name
};
```

UNIX systems usually have the upper limit for d_name[] set to 256, so filenames can't exceed 255 characters (one element of the array to be reserved for the terminating null).

23.9.1 11s.c: Listing Filenames in a Directory

Let's now use the three functions and the dirent structure in out next program, **11s.c** (Fig. 23.10), to list for every file in a directory, its inode number and filename. This program also uses the **quit** function, so you should remember to link **quit.o** when you compile the program.

```
/* Program: lls.c -- Uses readdir to populate a dirent structure */

#include <dirent.h>
#include <stdio.h>

int main(int argc, char **argv) {
    DIR *dir;                               /* Returned by opendir */
    struct dirent *direntry;                /* Returned by readdir */

    if ((dir = opendir(argv[1])) == NULL)   /* Directory must exist and */
        quit("opendir", 1);                 /* have read permission */

    while ((direntry = readdir(dir)) != NULL)  /* Till there are entries */
        printf("%10d %s\n", direntry->d_ino, direntry->d_name);

    closedir(dir);
    exit(0);
}
```

Fig. 23.10   lls.c

We first define two pointers of type DIR and struct dirent. **opendir** returns the pointer dir of type DIR, and **readdir** uses this pointer to return another pointer direntry of type struct dirent. The members of this structure are accessed using the pointer notation ->. The partial output of the program shows the inode number and filename of all files in the root directory:

```
$ a.out /
         2 .                          Program shows hidden files also
         2 ..
      6784 usr
     13568 var
     20352 export
     54272 etc
     67840 dev
         5 lib
    407040 sbin
    ......
```

This is how **ls -ia** / displays the contents of the root directory.

Note: In the output of the previous program, both directories . and .. represent root, which has the inode number 2.

23.10 MODIFYING ENTRIES IN DIRECTORY

Even though we can't directly edit a directory, we can use functions to add, remove or modify entries in a directory. In this section, we take up the following system calls:

- **mkdir** and **rmdir**—These calls have the same significance as the commands of the same name.
- **link**, **symlink** and **unlink**—**link** behaves like the **ln** command, but only to create a hard link. **symlink** creates a symbolic link. **unlink** removes a directory entry which can be used to remove a file (or a link) and a symbolic link.
- **rename**—Like **mv**, this call is used to modify the name in a directory entry.

Every function in this group uses a syntax that is identical to the simplest form of its corresponding UNIX command. They are, therefore, considered briefly in the following paragraphs.

23.10.1 mkdir and rmdir: Creating and Removing Directories

Like a regular file, a directory also has an entry in its parent directory. The **mknod** system call can be used by the superuser to create a directory, but a nonprivileged user can use the **mkdir** and **rmdir** calls to create and remove a directory:

```
int mkdir(const char *path, mode_t mode);
int rmdir(const char *path);
```

The second argument to **mkdir** sets the permissions the directory will have on creation. (**open** also uses this *mode* as its third argument when invoked with the 0_CREAT flag.) The permissions are also modified by the umask setting. Note that the parent directory needs to have write permission for a directory to be created in it. The directory also needs to be empty to be removable with **rmdir**.

23.10.2 link and symlink: Creating a Hard and Symbolic Link

Unlike the **ln** command which creates both hard and symbolic links, the system call library has two separate functions, **link** and **symlink**, for these tasks. Both require two arguments:

```
int link(const char *path1, const char *path2);
int symlink(const char *path1, const char *path2);
```

Here, both **link** and **symlink** create a directory entry with the name *path2* for an existing file *path1*. **symlink** creates a new inode for *path2* also. **link** doesn't create an inode but simply updates the link count of the existing inode for *path1* by one.

23.10.3 unlink: Removing a Link

The **unlink** call reverses the action of **link** and **symlink**. It removes the directory entry for the file (the argument) and decrements the link count in its inode by one. The syntax is simple:

```
int unlink(const char *path);
```

Although **link** doesn't create a symbolic link, **unlink** removes one, but not the file it points to; that has to be done separately. A file is considered to be removed when its link count in the inode has dropped to zero. When that happens, the kernel frees the inode and the associated disk blocks for fresh allocation, *but provided the file is closed also*. We need to understand exactly how the kernel responds to an **unlink** call.

There's one important thing that you need to remember when you use **unlink** on a file which has a single link count: If the file has been opened by another program or by code in your own program, the kernel will remove the directory entry all right, but it won't delete the file as long as at least one file descriptor points to the file. So it's possible to issue an **unlink** command immediately after an **open** and then read the file like this:

```
fd = open("foo", O_RDONLY);
unlink("foo");
while ((n = read(fd, buf, BUFSIZE)) > 0)
```
Even after "removing" the file you can still read it!

Here, foo will be deleted only after it is closed or on termination of the program, which closes all open file descriptors. You can read the file even after issuing **unlink** since its descriptor still points to the file table, and ultimately to the vnode table. But the kernel has already removed the directory entry for the file, so another **open** on this file will fail. Because the file is open, both the file table and vnode table are available in memory, the reason why the file can be read even after the "unlink."

Tip: The facility to "unlink" a file immediately after opening it can be used gainfully in a program having multiple exit points. If your application requires doing I/O on a temporary file and then deleting it before program termination, then unlinking the file at an early stage makes sure your file is ultimately deleted. In the interim, this "unlinking" doesn't affect I/O operations on the file in any way.

23.10.4 rename: Renaming a File, Directory or Symbolic Link

The **rename** call is used for renaming any type of file. Like **mv**, it can work with the three types of files shown in the section header, and follows this syntax:

```
int rename(const char *old, const char *new);
```

Here, **rename** modifies the directory entry by replacing the filename *old* with *new*. When operated on regular files or symbolic links, the behavior of **rename** is identical to that of **mv**. However, **rename** differs from **mv** when it comes to handling directories:

- If *old* is a directory and *new* exists as a directory, **rename** simply removes *new* and moves *old* to *new*. **mv** makes *old* a subdirectory of *new*.
- If *old* is a regular file, *new* can't be a directory. **mv** doesn't operate with this constraint.

You'll recall how simply you used the command **mv *.c workc** to move all C source files to the **workc** directory. To emulate this function in your C program, you'll have to call **rename** as many times as there are C programs.

23.11 READING THE INODE: stat

We now move on to the vnode table to access the information available in the inode. The inode contains all file attributes (except the filename), and to get these attributes, we must access the stat structure. The information in this structure is obtained by a system call having the same name as the structure. Let's first examine the members of the stat structure as mandated by POSIX:

```
struct stat {
    ino_t    st_ino                        Inode number
    mode_t   st_mode                       Mode (type and permissions)
```

```
    nlink_t    st_nlink
    uid_t      st_uid
    gid_t      st_gid
    dev_t      st_rdev
    off_t      st_size
    time_t     st_atime
    time_t     st_mtime
    time_t     st_ctime
    blksize_t  st_blksize
    blkcnt_t   st_blocks
};
```

Number of hard links
UID (owner)
GID (group owner)
Device ID (for device files)
File size in bytes
Last access time
Last modification time
Last time of change of inode
Preferred block size for I/O
Number of blocks allocated

The **ls** command looks up this structure to gather the file attributes, and the dirent structure for the filename. You can do that too with the **stat** system call (or with its two derivatives, **fstat** and **lstat**). All three calls use an address to a stat structure as their second argument as shown below:

```
int stat(const char *path, struct stat *buf);
int fstat(int fildes, struct stat *buf);
int lstat(const char *path, struct stat *buf);
```

stat requires the pathname as the first argument, and **fstat** requires a file descriptor. **stat** follows symbolic links, so if a file foo is symbolically linked to a file bar (foo->bar), doing a "stat" on foo will actually populate the stat structure with the attributes of bar. **lstat** behaves exactly like **stat** for ordinary files and directories, but it doesn't follow symbolic links, so an "lstat" on foo actually extracts the attributes of foo. We'll be using **lstat**, rather than **stat**, for the examples in this book.

Some of the members of the stat structure need some processing before they can be displayed in a meaningful format. stat (the structure) stores the three time stamps in seconds elapsed since the Epoch (January 1, 1970), so we'll use the library function, ctime, to display the time stamps in the Internet format. We need to process the st_mode member too, but before we do that, let's first write a program that prints some of these members.

23.11.1 attributes.c: Displaying Some File Attributes

Our next program, **attributes.c** (Fig. 23.11), uses **lstat** to populate the statbuf variable of type struct stat. It uses the ctime function to format the time stamps by passing the address of the respective member (st_mtime or st_atime) as argument. The program shows how easy it is to display file attributes.

All numeric data are printed in decimal (with %d) except the file type and permissions, which are formatted in octal. When we run this program with the filename /etc/passwd as argument, we see all attributes that **ls** also shows us with its various options (except that you need separate invocations of **ls** to display each time stamp):

```
$ a.out /etc/passwd
File: /etc/passwd
Inode number: 54412
UID: 0    GID: 3
Type and Permissions: 100755
Number of links: 1
```

```
/* Program: attributes.c -- Uses lstat call and
                         struct stat to display file attributes*/
#include <stdio.h>
#include <sys/stat.h>

void quit(char *, int);

int main(int argc, char **argv) {
   struct stat statbuf;                  /* We'll use lstat to populate this */

   if (lstat(argv[1], &statbuf) == -1)
      quit("Couldn't stat file", 1);

   printf("File: %s\n", argv[1]);
   printf("Inode number: %d \n", statbuf.st_ino);
   printf("UID: %d    ", statbuf.st_uid);
   printf("GID: %d\n", statbuf.st_gid);
   printf("Type and Permissions: %o\n",  statbuf.st_mode);
   printf("Number of links: %d \n", statbuf.st_nlink);
   printf("Size in bytes: %d\n", statbuf.st_size);
   printf("Blocks allocated: %d\n", statbuf.st_blocks);
   printf("Last Modification Time: %s", ctime(&statbuf.st_mtime));
   printf("Last Access Time: %s\n", ctime(&statbuf.st_atime));
   exit(0);
}
```

Fig. 23.11 attributes.c

```
Size in bytes: 10803
Blocks allocated: 22
Last Modification Time: Tue Nov 19 16:29:13 2002
Last Access Time: Tue Nov 26 19:57:01 2002
```

Observe the line that displays the file type and permissions as a single number in octal (100755). Unfortunately, UNIX doesn't have separate members for them in stat, so we need to mask out one attribute to obtain the other. This is what we are going to do next.

23.11.2 S_IFMT: Manipulating the st_mode Member

The st_mode member of stat combines the file type with its permissions in a space of 16 bits. The organization of these bits is shown below:

Bits	File Attribute
1-4	Type
5-7	SUID, SGID and Sticky bit permissions
8-10	Owner permissions
11-13	Group permissions
14-16	Other permissions

The four most significant bits contain the file type. We need 12 bits (and not 9) to represent a file's permissions completely. Recall that 3 separate bits are needed to set the SUID, SGID and the sticky bit *(15.3.2)*. In the previous example, the file type is represented by the octal number 100000 and the permissions by 755.

To extract these components separately, we need to use the S_IFMT mask. When an AND operation is performed with st_mode and this mask, it returns the file type. An inverse AND operation (with ~) returns the permissions. This is how you'll be using S_IFMT in your programs:

```
mode_t file_type, file_perm;
file_type = statbuf.st_mode & S_IFMT;        Bits 1-4
file_perm = statbuf.st_mode & ~S_IFMT;       Bits 5-16
```

Once you are able to separate the two components with this mask, you can identify files of a specific type or ones having (or not having) a specific permission. Checking file types for numeric values is not very convenient, so UNIX provides a number of macros that make our task simpler.

23.11.3 Using the S_ISxxx Macros to Determine File Type

All UNIX systems provide a set of macros beginning with S_IF (often called the S_IFxxx macros) that simplify the work of checking for file types, but modern UNIX systems make this task even simpler with the S_ISxxx macros (Table 23.2). Each S_ISxxx macro uses the st_mode member as argument and returns true or false. For instance, S_ISREG checks for a regular file, and S_ISDIR checks for a directory. This is how you determine whether a file is a directory:

```
if (S_ISDIR(buf.st_mode)) printf("File is a directory\n");
```

These macros actually mask out the file type from st_mode with S_IFMT and then checks the residual value. We'll make use of the S_IFMT and S_ISDIR macros in our next program.

Table 23.2 The S_ISxxx Macros

Macro	Returns True if File Type is
S_ISREG	Regular
S_ISDIR	Directory
S_ISBLK	Block special
S_ISCHR	Character special
S_ISLNK	Symbolic link
S_ISFIFO	FIFO
S_ISSOCK	Socket

23.11.4 lsdir.c: Listing Only Directories

ls has no option to list only directories, but using the directory handling functions and the information in the stat structure, we can devise a program that does just that. This program, **lsdir.c** (Fig. 23.12), uses the S_IFMT mask and the S_ISDIR macro to display the file type, permissions and the name of every subdirectory of the directory name provided as argument. We are not recursively examining directories here.

```
/* Program: lsdir.c --
                    Lists only directories - Uses S_IFMT and S_ISDIR macros */
#include <sys/types.h>
#include <sys/stat.h>
#include <stdio.h>
#include <dirent.h>

int main(int argc, char *argv[]) {
    DIR *dir;
    struct dirent *direntry;                /* Returned by readdir() */
    struct stat statbuf;                    /* Address of statbuf used by lstat() */
    mode_t file_type, file_perm;

    if ((dir = opendir(argv[1])) == NULL)
        quit("Couldn't open directory", 1);
    if ((chdir(argv[1]) == -1))             /* Change to the directory before */
        quit("chdir", 2);                   /* you starting reading its entries */

    while ((direntry = readdir(dir)) != NULL) { /* Read each entry in directory*/
        if (lstat(direntry->d_name, &statbuf) < 0) { /* dname must be in */
            perror("lstat");                /* current directory */
            continue;
        }
        if (S_ISDIR(statbuf.st_mode)) {             /* If file is a directory */
            file_type = statbuf.st_mode & S_IFMT;
            file_perm = statbuf.st_mode & ~S_IFMT;
            printf("%o %4o %s\n", file_type, file_perm, direntry->d_name);
        }
    }
    exit(0);
}
```

Fig. 23.12 `lsdir.c`

As we have done in a previous program (**lls.c**, Fig. 23.10), we first have to obtain a pointer to a DIR structure with **opendir**, and then use **readdir** to return a pointer (`direntry`) to a `dirent` structure. *However, this time we must change to the directory with* **chdir** *before we use* **readdir**.

Next, we extract the filename from `direntry` (`direntry->d_name`) and then use **lstat** to populate a `stat` structure (`statbuf`) with the attributes of the file. From this structure, we extract the `st_mode` member (`statbuf.st_mode`) and then use it with the `S_ISDIR` macro to filter out only directories. For each directory we find, we mask its `st_mode` value with `S_IFMT` and `~S_IFMT` to obtain the file type and permissions. We print both along with the filename.

Note that the **chdir** call is essential because the `d_name` member of the `dirent` structure evaluates to a filename without slashes. Without **chdir**, **lstat** would look for the file in the current directory (when it shouldn't be). Let's run this program with the root directory as argument; a censored list is shown below:

```
$ a.out /
40000   755 .
40000   755 ..
40000   700 lost+found
40000   755 usr
40000   755 var
40000   755 export
40000   755 etc
40000   755 sbin
40000  1777 tmp                    The 1 shows the sticky bit is set
40000   755 .dt
```

The first character of the first field shows 4 (representing a directory) as the file type; the other four octal digits (here, 0000) have been masked out (with S_IFMT). The second field shows the file's permissions. Note the entry for tmp; it shows the sticky bit set for the directory. You now have a command that lists only directory names including those beginning with a dot.

23.12 CHECKING A FILE'S ACCESS RIGHTS

There are a couple of mechanisms for checking a file's access rights. You can check each permission bit that's embedded in stat.st_mode, but that doesn't always have much meaning. A user running a program would often like to know whether she has the necessary access permissions without knowing the category (user, group or others) to which she belongs. We'll be discussing two ways of checking whether a file has the necessary permissions:

- By testing the individual members of the st_mode member of the stat structure. All the 12 permission bits can be tested in this way.
- Using the **access** system call, which looks at the *real* UID and *real* GID of the user running the program, and determines whether the file is accessible by the "real" user.

Both techniques have their advantages and limitations, but they can sometimes appear to contradict each other, so you must know the relationship between ownership and permissions well. We'll also make use of the SUID bit to highlight the distinction between real UID and effective UID, a point that was first raised in Section 9.4.

23.12.1 check_all_perm.c: Checking All 12 Permission Bits

In this section, we'll devise means to check every permission bit that's available in stat.st_mode. Recall from Section 23.11.2 that the S_IFMT mask has to be used in this way to extract the permissions from st_mode:

```
file_perm = statbuf.st_mode & ~S_IFMT;
```

To test for a specific permission, we need to AND file_perm with the symbolic constant that represents the permission. The expression returns true if the permission bit is on. For instance, to test a file for read permission for the others category, we should use this statement:

```
if (file_perm & S_IROTH)
```

Note that this is something we couldn't do with shell programming where all permission tests were applicable only to the *user* running the script. Let's use this feature to develop a program that tests a file for all 12 permissions. This program needs two functions to be developed. The first function, **print_permissions**, prints a file's permissions:

```
#include <stdio.h>
#include <sys/stat.h>
#include <unistd.h>
void print_permissions(char *fname, struct stat *addbuf) {
    if (lstat(fname, addbuf) < 0) {
        perror("stat");
        exit(1);
    } else
        printf("File: %s  Permissions: %o\n", fname, addbuf->st_mode & ~S_IFMT);
}
```

print_permissions takes the filename and address of a stat structure as its two arguments. It uses the **lstat** system call to populate the stat structure, addbuf. It prints the permissions obtained by masking st_mode with ~S_IFMT. Store this code in the file **print_permissions.c**, and compile it with **cc -c print_permissions.c** to generate **print_permissions.o**.

The next function, **check_permissions**, ANDs the expression representing all permissions with the symbolic constant representing a specific permission. If the result is true, a message is printed on the terminal:

```
void check_permissions(int perm, int flag, char *message) {
    if (perm & flag)
        printf("%s\n", message);
}
```

check_permissions uses three arguments—the permissions portion of stat.st_mode (like 0644), the permission to be tested (like S_IRUSR) and a message. Store this function too in a separate file, **check_permissions.c**, and then use **cc -c check_permissions.c** to generate the object code for it.

Our main program, **check_all_perm.c** (Fig. 23.13), makes use of both functions. It initially uses **print_permissions** to display a file's permissions and then calls **check_permissions** 12 times in a loop. For compactness, the program uses two arrays. perm_flag[] holds the numeric values of the 12 permissions (like perm_flag[0] = S_IRUSR, i.e., 0400). *mesg[] is an array of pointers to character strings, each representing a permission-specific message that is printed. By delegating some tasks to the two functions, the program has become fairly easy to comprehend.

Assuming that we have previously created the object files of the functions, let's compile this program first:

```
cc check_all_perm.c check_permissions.o print_permissions.o
```

Before running the program with each of the files, /usr/bin/passwd (the **passwd** command) and /etc/shadow, let's observe their listing:

```
$ ls -l /usr/bin/passwd /etc/shadow
-r--------    1 root     root             1055 Nov 21 15:59 /etc/shadow
-r-s--x--x    1 root     root            15368 May 28  2002 /usr/bin/passwd
```

The s in the permissions field of the listing of **passwd** shows the SUID bit set. This is the bit that makes **passwd** run with the powers of root, the program's owner, even when it is invoked by a nonprivileged user. Let's see whether the output of the program matches the information in the permissions field:

```
$ a.out /usr/bin/passwd
File: /usr/bin/passwd  Permissions: 4511            SUID is 4
User-readable
User-executable
Group-executable
Others-executable
SUID bit set
```

The first octal digit (4) in the four-octet permissions string signifies the presence of the SUID bit. The second octal digit (5) shows that the file has read and execute permission for the user. Now run this program on the other file:

```
$ a.out /etc/shadow
File: /etc/shadow  Permissions: 400
User-readable
```

```
/* Program: check_all_perm.c -- Checks all 12 permission bits of a file */

#include <stdio.h>
#include <sys/stat.h>
#include <fcntl.h>

void print_permissions(char *, struct stat *) ;
void check_permission(int, int, char *);

int main(int argc, char *argv[]) {
    int i, fd, perm;
    char *filename = argv[1];
    struct stat statbuf;
    mode_t perm_flag[] = {S_IRUSR, S_IWUSR, S_IXUSR, S_IRGRP, S_IWGRP, S_IXGRP,
                     S_IROTH, S_IWOTH, S_IXOTH, S_ISUID, S_ISGID, S_ISVTX };

    char *mesg[] = {"User-readable", "User-writable", "User-executable",
                  "Group-readable", "Group-writable", "Group-executable",
                  "Others-readable", "Others-writable", "Others-executable",
                  "SUID bit set", "SGID bit set", "Sticky bit set" };

    print_permissions(filename, &statbuf);

    perm = statbuf.st_mode & ~S_IFMT;
    for (i = 0; i < 12; i ++)
       check_permissions(perm, perm_flag[i], mesg[i]);
}
```

Fig. 23.13 **check_all_perm.c**

True, the file is user-readable, but as a non-root user we can't read this file. More often than not, we need to know whether a file is accessible to *us* irrespective of the user category to which we belong. This is what **access** does and it is taken up in the next topic.

23.12.2 access: Checking the Owner's Permissions

The **access** system call looks at the real UID and real GID of the process, and lets you know whether the "real" user has the necessary access rights. It uses this syntax:

```
int access(const char *path, int amode);
```

The first argument is the pathname and *amode* specifies the access permission to be tested, which can be one or more of these four values:

R_OK—Read permission OK
W_OK—Write permission OK
X_OK—Execute permission OK
F_OK—File exists

Checking for specific permissions makes sense only when the file exists, and **access** is frequently used with F_OK to make the test for existence before continuing with the program. The program, **faccess.c** (Fig. 23.14), makes this check for multiple files.

The program uses a **for** loop to iterate through a list of command line arguments representing filenames. For each argument, it performs all four tests with **access**. We'll now find out the access rights a nonprivileged user has to /etc/passwd and /etc/shadow, and compare the output with the listing:

```
$ ls -l /etc/passwd /etc/shadow
-r--r--r--   1 root     sys           9953 Nov 28 15:30 /etc/passwd
-r--------   1 root     sys           5425 Nov 28 15:30 /etc/shadow
$ a.out /etc/passwd /etc/shadow
/etc/passwd: Not writable  Not executable
/etc/shadow: Not readable  Not writable  Not executable
```

The listing shows that passwd is readable by all, but shadow is unreadable by group and others. It's obvious that the user running the program belongs to one of these two categories (probably, others), so **access** fails in the read test on shadow. This also implies that an attempt to open the file using the program represented by the source, **reverse_read2.c** (Fig. 23.6), should also fail:

```
$ reverse_read2 /etc/shadow
/etc/shadow: Permission denied
```

Yes, it does. **reverse_read2** here is the executable of **reverse_read2.c**. The story's not over yet; there's a way of making the file readable *with the same program* even though **access** will still fail in the read test. This is where the SUID bit comes in and is taken up next.

Note: You can OR the symbolic constants used by **access** to test for multiple permissions. For instance, **access("foo", R_OK | W_OK)** tests for both read and write permission.

```
/* Program: faccess.c --
            Determines a file's access rights using the read UID and GID */
#include <unistd.h>
#include <stdio.h>

void quit(char *, int);
int main(int argc, char *argv[]) {
    short count;
    for (count = 1; count < argc; count++) {
        printf("%s: ", argv[count]);

        if (access(argv[count], F_OK) == -1)
            quit("File not found", 1);
        if (access(argv[count], R_OK) == -1 )
            printf("Not readable ");
        if (access(argv[count], W_OK) == -1)
            printf("Not writable ");
        if (access(argv[count], X_OK) == -1)
            printf("Not executable ");

        printf("\n");
    }
    exit(0);
}
```

Fig. 23.14 faccess.c

23.12.3 How SUID Affects File Access

To continue with the exercise of making **shadow** readable by a nonprivileged user, let's assume for the two programs, **reverse_read2** and **faccess** (the executables for **reverse_read2.c** and **faccess.c**), considered in this section, that user sumit executes them and also owns them initially. To make **reverse_read2** work, we'll have to do two things—both from the root account:

1. Set the SUID bit of **reverse_read2**:

   # **chmod u+s reverse_read2 ; ls -l reverse_read2**
   -rwsr-xr-x   1 sumit   staff   7588 Feb 13 16:04 reverse_read2

2. Surrender the ownership of the file to root:

   # **chown root reverse_read2 ; ls -l reverse_read2**
   -rwsr-xr-x   1 root   staff   7588 Feb 13 16:04 reverse_read2

Now return from the superuser mode to the usual nonprivileged mode. With two important attributes changed, when you run this program now, *its effective UID this time becomes the owner of the file, i.e. root*. And since root has permissions to open /etc/shadow, the program can now read the file:

```
$ read_reverse2 /etc/shadow
```
                                                    Blank line
```
::::::56021:2CLXPgOdqjMPz:mahtrap
::::::03021:UGqdYyX2fYEs/:atnasus
::::::60021:*:ptf
......
```
                                                    The ftp user

The SUID bit has made all the difference here; it enabled us to read shadow. But what happens if we try out a similar exercise with **faccess**? Let's go through the usual steps of using **chmod** and **chown** before running the program:

```
# chmod u+s faccess ; ls -l faccess
-rwsr-xr-x   1 sumit      staff        7464 Dec  7 19:00 faccess
# chown root faccess ; ls -l faccess
-rwsr-xr-x   1 root       staff        7464 Dec  7 19:00 faccess
# [Ctrl-d]                              Quit superuser mode
$ echo $LOGNAME                         What is our real UID?
sumit                                   Real UID is still sumit, and
$ faccess /etc/shadow                   sumit has no access to the file
/etc/shadow: Not readable  Not writable  Not executable
```

Even though **reverse_read2** could read the file, **access** in **faccess** fails even though both programs have identical ownership and permission settings. The real UID is still sumit (since sumit has run **faccess**), and sumit doesn't have access rights to /etc/shadow. It makes no difference to **access** that **faccess** is running with root as its effective UID.

Note: From the above, we can conclude that there's no point in using **access** to check a file's access rights if the program using it has its SUID bit set. In such circumstances, it makes sense to use **open** and check whether it fails.

23.13 MODIFYING FILE ATTRIBUTES

Finally, let's terminate this chapter with a discussion on file attribute manipulation. The stat structure is useful for accessing a file's attributes but it can't be used to set them except in an indirect manner. To change these attributes, the system call library offers a number of functions, some of whom have identical command names:

- **link** and **unlink**—For creating a hard link and removing both a hard and symbolic link. This has already been discussed.
- **chmod** and **fchmod**—For changing file permissions.
- **chown**—This handles both ownership and group ownership.
- **utime**—This changes the file's modification and access times.

Each call in the list sets one or two file attributes to absolute values. Some of them (like **chmod** and **utime**) can be used in a relative manner also. For doing that, the general principle is to obtain the current value of the attribute from the stat structure and then add to or subtract from it.

23.13.1 chmod and fchmod: Changing File Permissions

There's nothing special to mention about these two calls except note that **chmod** identifies a file by its pathname while **fchmod** uses a file descriptor:

```
int chmod(const char *path, mode_t mode);
int fchmod(int fildes, mode_t mode);
```

The second argument (*mode*) represents the permissions, and can be used by OR'ing any number of the symbolic constants listed in Section 23.2.1. For instance, to set permissions in an absolute manner, this is how you should use the **chmod** call:

```
chmod ("foo", S_IRUSR | SIWUSR | S_IRGRP)              Same as chmod 640 foo
```

Unlike the **chmod** command, the **chmod** system call can't be used *directly* to set relative permissions. You'll have to first extract the current permissions from st_mode and then use **chmod** with the bit-wise

- OR combination of the existing permissions and the specific permission to be assigned.
- AND combination of the existing permissions and the complement of the specific permission to be removed.

To consider an example, you can assign execute permission to foo in two steps:

```
lstat("foo", &statbuf);
chmod("foo", statbuf.st_mode | S_IXUSR);              Adding a permission
```

To remove a permission, you have to use the AND operator with the complement of the permission. The first example below removes the user's execute permission, while the second one removes all permissions for the user:

```
chmod("foo", statbuf.st_mode & ~S_IXUSR);
chmod("foo", statbuf.st_mode & ~(S_IRUSR | S_IWUSR | S_IXUSR));
```

In a previous example *(23.12.3)*, we used the command **chmod u+s reverse_read2** to add SUID permission to the **reverse_read2** program. This can also be done from your C program:

```
chmod("reverse_read2", statbuf.st_mode | S_ISUID);
```

You may be wondering why we didn't use S_IFMT to extract the permissions from st_mode before applying **chmod**. Fortunately, **chmod** also accepts the entire st_mode (which includes the file type) as its second argument.

23.13.2 chown: Changing Ownership

Like its command counterpart, the **chown** system call is used to change both the owner and group owner. As with **stat**, there are three versions. One uses a pathname, the other a file descriptor and the third doesn't follow symbolic links:

```
int chown(const char *path, uid_t owner, gid_t group);
int fchown(int fildes, uid_t owner, gid_t group);
int lchown(const char *path, uid_t owner, gid_t group);
```

owner and *group* are represented by the numeric UID and GID, respectively. To change either the owner or group owner, set the unchanged argument to -1 (the first time we encounter -1 as an argument to a system call). Here are two examples:

```
chown("foo", 512, 100);                    UID changed to 512, GID to 100
fchown(4, -1, 100);                        UID unchanged, GID changed to 100
```

If the **chown** command can be used only by the superuser on your system, then the same restriction applies to the **chown** system call siblings also. Similarly, your system may permit changing your GID to only another group to which you also belong (supplementary group).

23.13.3 utime: Changing the Time Stamps

The last system call that we take up is **utime**. This call is used to change a file's modification and access times. It takes two arguments:

```
int utime(const char *path, const struct utimbuf *times);
```

The first argument is obviously the pathname. The second argument represents a pointer to a structure of type utimbuf. (Note the missing 'e'.) This structure contains two members of type time_t:

```
struct utimbuf {
    time_t actime                          Last access time
    time_t modtime                         Last modification time
};
```

These two members store the last access and modification time in seconds since the Epoch. To obtain the existing values for a file, you need to "stat" it and then examine the st_atime and st_mtime members in the stat structure. But to set them to different values, you'll have to populate the utimbuf structure before using **utime**.

23.13.4 atimemtime.c: Creating a File with Identical Time Stamps

Can you create a file having the same time stamps as another file, using UNIX commands? It's not as easy as you might think, but our next C program, **atimemtime.c** (Fig. 23.15), makes the task look simple. It requires two filenames as arguments; the time stamps of the first file are used to set the stamps for the second.

We first use **lstat** to fill up statbuf with the attributes of an existing file (argv[1]). Next, we populate the utimbuf structure with the two time stamps obtained from the previous lstat call. We open a second file (argv[2]), creating it if necessary, and then use **utime** to change its time stamps to the values in timebuf. This operation can be performed even if the file is not open; the file was opened simply to make sure that it's created if it doesn't exist.

Let's use this program to create a file with the same time stamps as one of the profiles—like .profile. Let's first see its time stamps:

```
$ cd ; ls -l ~/.profile ; ls -lu ~/.profile
-rw-r--r--  1 sumit    staff          61 Dec 12 20:14 .profile
-rw-r--r--  1 sumit    staff          61 Feb  2 12:33 .profile
```

```
/* Program: atimemtime.c --
                        Sets a file's time stamps to those of another file */
#include <sys/stat.h>
#include <fcntl.h>
#include <utime.h>

void quit(char *, int);
int main(int argc, char **argv) {
    struct stat statbuf;         /* To obtain time stamps for an existing file */
    struct utimbuf timebuf;      /* To set time stamps for another file */

    if (lstat(argv[1], &statbuf) == -1)
        quit("stat", 1);

    timebuf.actime  = statbuf.st_atime;  /* Setting members of timebuf with */
    timebuf.modtime = statbuf.st_mtime;  /* values obtained from statbuf */

    if (open(argv[2], O_RDWR | O_CREAT, 0644) == -1)
        quit("open", 2);
    close(argv[2]);                      /* Previously used open only to create it */

    if (utime(argv[2], &timebuf) == -1)  /* Sets both time stamps for file */
        qui("utime", 3);                 /* that was just created */
    exit(0);
}
```

Fig. 23.15 `atimemtime.c`

The last access time for this file (obtained with `ls -lu`) is generally the time we logged in, and it's a good idea to save this time by creating another file with identical time stamps. We'll move the `a.out` executable to the home directory before running it:

```
$ mv a.out $HOME; cd ; a.out .profile .logintime
$ ls -l .logintime ; ls -lu .logintime
-rw-r--r--   1 sumit   _staff              0 Dec 12 20:14 .logintime
-rw-r--r--   1 sumit    staff              0 Feb  2 12:33 .logintime
```

Note that the time stamps for the two files are identical. Using a C program, we have done something which we couldn't do using the UNIX commands and the shell.

23.14 CONCLUSION

We can now understand how commands like **cat** and **chmod** actually work. Moreover, using system calls we could do things that just can't be done using UNIX commands alone. Though we discussed file descriptors in this chapter, we didn't manipulate them. We must be able to open files in one process, pass on the descriptors to the child and then manipulate these descriptors to implement redirection and piping. The programmer's view of the process is presented in the next chapter.

WRAP UP

A *system call* is a routine built in the kernel to perform a specific function that requires communication with the system's hardware. It switches the CPU to *kernel mode* from *user mode*. It generally returns -1 on error. *Library functions* are built on top of the system calls, but can't do everything system calls can do. System calls and library functions are documented in sections 2 and 3, respectively, of the UNIX manual.

open returns a *file descriptor* that is used by the other I/O calls. It sets the opening *mode* (O_RDONLY, O_WRONLY or O_RDWR) and *status flags* that can create (O_CREAT) or truncate (O_TRUNC) a file. File permissions specified with O_CREAT are modified by the shell's umask setting.

read and **write** use a user-defined buffer whose size should be set equal to the size of the kernel buffer for best performance. **lseek** simply moves the file offset pointer, and can take it beyond EOF to create a *sparse* file. Unlike **read**, **write** returns immediately even though the actual writing can take place later.

All system calls set a global variable, errno, to a numeric value whose associated text can be printed with **perror** and **strerror**.

The kernel maintains three tables in memory when a file is opened. The *file descriptor table* stores all open descriptors. The descriptor table points to a *file table* that stores the opening mode, status flags and file offset. This table points to the *vnode table* that contains the inode information. The last two tables also maintain a reference count field.

Directories are usually handled with library functions because of the nonstandard format of the directory structure. **opendir** opens a directory to return a pointer to a DIR structure, which is subsequently used as argument by **readdir**. This function reads a directory entry to return a pointer to a dirent structure that contains the filename and inode number as its members. **chdir** changes the current directory and **getcwd** returns the pathname of the current directory.

Files can be hard linked (**link**) and symbolically linked (**symlink**), but **unlink** removes both. When **unlink** is invoked on an open file, the kernel removes the directory entry but its data blocks are deallocated only when the file is closed.

The inode information is maintained in the stat structure which is populated by **stat**, **lstat** and **fstat**. The file type and permissions are maintained in a single field, st_mode, which can be split into separate components using the S_IFMT mask. The S_ISxxx macros can be used to test for specific file types.

access tests a file's access rights using the *real* UID and *real* GID of the process. The SUID bit affects accessibility. Setting this bit on a program and changing its ownership to root gives the program the power of the superuser.

The **chmod** and **chown** calls do the same jobs as their command counterparts. **utime** is used to set a file's access and modification time stamps using a structure of type utimbuf.

Test Your Understanding

Incorporate error checking wherever possible and relevant. File I/O operations are to be performed using only the **read** and **write** system calls, and not library functions.

23.1 Explain the difference between *system calls* and *library functions*. What happens in the CPU when a system call is invoked?

23.2 What is a *file descriptor*, and what is it used for? Name the system calls that use a file descriptor as argument.

23.3 Why must we *immediately* check the value of errno after a system call fails, rather than later?

23.4 Specify how the **open** call is used to emulate the function performed by the shell's (i) > (ii) >> symbols.

23.5 Group the following symbolic constants into two categories and explain the significance of the categories: (i) O_RDONLY (ii) O_CREAT (iii) O_SYNC (iv) O_RDWR (v) O_TRUNC (vi) O_APPEND (vii) O_WRONLY. What is the role of the O_SYNC flag when using **write**?

23.6 Check the man pages of **open**, **dup**, **dup2**, **pipe** and **fcntl** and see if you find anything they have in common.

23.7 What is the difference between the *file descriptor table* and *file table*? Will each entry in the descriptor table have a separate file table associated with it?

23.8 Write a program that ascertains the size of the file descriptor table by opening a file repeatedly. Display the cause of the error that led to the aborting of the program.

23.9 Using only system calls, write a program that displays the contents of a file in uppercase. The filename is supplied as argument. How will you find out the ASCII values of the alphabetic characters using another program?

23.10 How will you create a (i) file with permissions 666, (ii) directory with permissions 777? Use only symbolic constants to represent the permissions.

23.11 Write a program that accepts a directory name as argument and then checks whether it exists as a directory. If it doesn't exist or exists as an ordinary file, then remove the file and create the directory. Also change to that directory and display the current directory.

23.12 Write a program that lists from the current directory all ordinary filenames whose size exceeds 100,000 bytes. Also remove all files whose size is 0 bytes.

23.13 Explain fully whether the following statement is true or not: It is possible to read and write a file even after it is deleted.

23.14 Write a program that removes the read, write and execute permissions for others in all files owned by the user running the program. The directory name is provided as argument. (HINT: Use **getuid** to obtain your own UID.)

23.15 Write a program that sets the user mask to zero before creating a file foo. Now, change the permissions of foo to (i) 764 (ii) 440. The previous value of the mask should be restored before program termination.

Flex Your Brain

Incorporate error checking wherever possible and relevant. File I/O operations are to be performed using only the **read** and **write** system calls, and not library functions.

23.1 Explain what an *atomic operation* is. How do you open a file and (i) truncate it if it exists, (ii) create it if it doesn't? What is the advantage of using **open** to create a file instead of **creat** which is designed for only that purpose?

23.2 Write a program that copies a file and accepts the source and destination as its two arguments. The destination can also be a directory.

23.3 Modify the program in 23.9 (Test Your Understanding) so that it displays the output in lowercase when invoked by the name **lower** and uppercase when invoked by **upper**. What else do you need to do to run it?

23.4 Explain why the selection of the buffer size used by **read** and **write** is crucial in writing efficient programs.

23.5 Write two programs that read /etc/passwd using (i) a single-character buffer, (ii) a buffer of 2048 bytes with **read**. Use the **time** command with each and compare their performance.

23.6 Devise an advisory locking mechanism which allows two programs **lock1.c** and **lock2.c** to read a file foo only if the file .lockfile doesn't exist. Both programs will first create the file if it doesn't exist, and remove it before termination.

23.7 Write a program to split the contents of a file into multiple files so that each file contains at most 10,000 bytes. Name the files foo.1, foo.2 and so forth.

23.8 Write a program that uses complete error checking to perform the following on an existing file foo: (i) opens foo and then deletes it without closing it, (ii) reads foo and displays its output, (iii) opens foo again. After the program has completed execution, check whether foo has actually been deleted. Explain your observations and the behavior of the **unlink** system call.

23.9 Write a program that moves a group of files to a directory. The file names are provided as arguments and the last argument is a directory. Provide adequate checks to ensure that the files exist and have the expected file type. If the last argument doesn't exist, then create a directory by that name.

23.10 Write code to create a file foo1 with the same permissions, modification time and access time as another file, foo2.

Systems Programming II —Process Control

The process abstraction enables us to understand the activities that take place in the computer. In this chapter—the second devoted to systems programming—we examine processes from the C programmer's point of view. We find here answers to some old questions. How can one program run another? How do we manipulate the shell's standard streams? How can we handle signals in our programs? We'll learn to do all that in this chapter, but only after we have enlarged our existing knowledge of processes acquired in Chapter 9.

To master the techniques of process control, we'll discuss the process control mechanism and associated data structures maintained by the kernel. We'll examine in some detail the fork-exec-wait cycle that will enable us to create processes using the system call library. We handled file descriptors in the previous chapter, but here we'll make use of the kernel's descriptor replicating properties to implement two important shell features—redirection and piping. Finally, we'll examine the elaborate signal handling mechanism and develop code that generates and handles signals.

WHAT YOU WILL LEARN

- Examination of the different segments of the *virtual address space* of a process.
- The other process abstractions—*user mode* and *kernel mode*, *context* and *context switching*.
- Analyze the control information held in the *process table*.
- Use **fork** to create a process, and study the environmental changes in the child.
- Terminate a process with **_exit** and **exit**, and examine the significance of the *exit status*.
- Use **wait** and **waitpid** to wait for a change of status in the child, and gather its exit status from the process table.
- How the system handles *orphan* and *zombie* processes.
- Replace the existing process address space with a new program using the *exec* family of functions.
- Understand the attributes of a pipe and create a pipeline using the **pipe** system call.
- The basics of signal handling and the concept of signal *disposition*.
- Install *signal handlers* with **signal** and generate signals with **kill**.

24.1 PROCESS ABSTRACTIONS

The basic concepts related to processes have been discussed in Chapter 9, but we need to expand that knowledge before we use system calls to create and control processes. UNIX supports **preemptive multitasking**, which means that the kernel preempts a process when its time period expires. However, the norms are sometimes relaxed, especially when a process invokes a system call.

Generally, a system call is allowed to complete even after the process has consumed its time slice, but the behavior of certain system calls necessitates the use of a different control mechanism. For instance, if a system call keeps the CPU idle (when waiting for an I/O operation to complete, for instance), the process blocks by *voluntarily* giving up control of the CPU. The process *sleeps* on an event, and when the event occurs the kernel wakes up the process so that it could start running again when its turn arrives.

The kernel allocates memory not only for the process image but also for control information that enables it to switch processes. We examine here two concepts—the process address space and the process table.

24.1.1 The Virtual Address Space

In general, processes have their origin in executable program files on disk. When you execute a C program, the program loader transfers the binary code from the on-disk program to memory. The kernel has to create additional space in memory as and when needed by the process (for invoking functions, for instance). This collection of memory locations that the process can access is referred to as its **virtual address space**. This space is organized into a number of segments (Fig. 24.1):

- The **text segment**   This segment contains the instructions to be executed. Multiple instances of one program will share this segment; three users running **vi** will use a single text segment.
- The **data segment**   This segment represents the constants, global and static variables used in the program.
- The **stack**   The stack stores the arguments and local variables of functions as well as the address to return to. It grows and shrinks in size as functions are invoked and complete execution.
- The **heap**   This segment is used to dynamically allocate memory during program runtime (using functions like **malloc**). The heap and stack are separated by unallocated space, and they grow at the expense of each other.
- Command line arguments and environment variables. These are generally found at the bottom of the stack (top in figure).

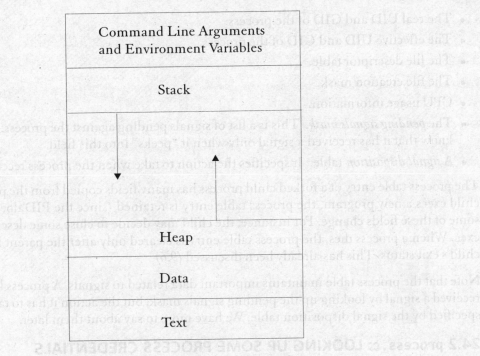

Fig. 24.1 The Process Virtual Address Space

The addresses of the process segments (text, data, stack, etc.) created by the linker are *virtual* because they don't point to physical memory locations. It is possible for all programs to have their virtual address space begin from address 0 and yet run without conflict. At runtime, the *Memory Management Unit* (MMU) converts these virtual addresses to nonconflicting physical memory locations using a set of *address translation maps*. The MMU contains a set of hardware registers that point to the translation maps of the currently running process.

Every process has a **context** that represents the entire environment available to the process when it is running. This environment includes the status of the hardware registers, the address space and the information maintained in the process table. The kernel saves the process context before it uses a **context switch** to force one process to vacate the CPU and make room for another. The kernel then sets the registers to point to the translation maps of the new process. Because every process has its own set of translation maps, one process can't access another's address space.

24.1.2 The Process Table

The attributes of every active process are stored in a fairly large structure that represents an entry in the **process table**. Modern UNIX systems no longer swap out portions of the process table to disk, but maintain the entire table in memory. The important attributes of the process table are:

- The PID and PPID of the process.
- The state of the process—whether running, sleeping, zombie, and so forth.

- The real UID and GID of the process.
- The effective UID and GID of the process.
- The file descriptor table.
- The file creation mask.
- CPU usage information.
- The *pending signals mask*. This is a list of signals pending against the process. The process can know that it has received a signal only when it "peeks" into this field.
- A *signal disposition* table. It specifies the action to take when the process receives a signal.

The process table entry of a forked child process has many fields copied from the parent. When the child execs a new program, the process table entry is retained (since the PID doesn't change) but some of these fields change. For instance, the child may decide to close some descriptors before an exec. When a process dies, the process table entry is cleared only after the parent has gathered the child's exit status. This has already been discussed *(9.6)*.

Note that the process table maintains important data related to signals. A process knows that it has received a signal by looking up the pending signals mask, but the action it has to take for a signal is specified by the signal disposition table. We have more to say about them later.

24.2 process.c: LOOKING UP SOME PROCESS CREDENTIALS

Our first program, **process.c** (Fig. 24.2), displays the PID and PPID of the current process along with the ownership credentials. Six system calls are used here, and their names reflect their function.

The process obtains its own PID and its parent's PID using the **getpid** and **getppid** calls. The program also prints the effective UID and GID, which normally are equal to the real UID and GID:

```
$ a.out
PID : 1035, PPID: 1028
UID : 102,  GID:   10
EUID: 102, EGID:   10
```
Real UID and GID are the same as their effective cousins

To understand how the SUID bit affects the effective UID, let's set the SUID bit of this executable from the superuser account and transfer the ownership to root. Confirm your actions by observing the listing:

```
/* Program: process.c -- Lists process and user credentials
                    The PID, PPID, real and effective UIDs and GIDs */
#include <stdio.h>
int main(void) {
    printf("PID : %4d, PPID: %4d\n", getpid(), getppid());
    printf("UID : %4d,  GID: %4d\n", getuid(), getgid());
    printf("EUID: %4d, EGID: %4d\n", geteuid(), getegid());
    exit(0);
}
```

Fig. 24.2 process.c

```
# chmod u+s a.out ; chown root a.out ; ls -l a.out
-rwsr-xr-x     1 root      sumit        12211 Dec 17 09:49 a.out
```

Now quit the superuser mode and run the program again. The effective UID now becomes the owner of the file (root, whose UID is 0):

```
$ a.out
PID : 1041, PPID: 1028
UID :  102, GID:  10
EUID:    0, EGID:  10
```

Recall that we had carried out a similar exercise with the program represented by **reverse_read2.c** in the previous chapter *(23.12.3)*. The SUID setting there allowed a nonprivileged user to read a file that is otherwise readable only by root.

24.3 CREATING A PROCESS

The basic mechanism of process creation was discussed in Section 9.4; we need to examine the concepts in some detail now. The entire process life cycle is built around four system calls—**fork**, *exec* (not a system call really), **wait** and **_exit**. It's important for the systems programmer to know how to create processes because many important functions can't be performed in a single process. For instance, to build a pipeline you need to create at least two processes.

24.3.1 fork: Replicating the Current Process

The forking mechanism uses the **fork** system call to create a process. Except for PIDs 0, 1, 2, and possibly 3, which the kernel creates "by hand", every process in the system owes its creation to **fork**. It has a simple syntax but returns in an unusual manner:

```
pid_t fork(void);                         Copies current process to child
```

After **fork** returns, the parent and child have different PIDs and PPIDs, and that's probably the only major difference between them. At this point, there are two processes with practically identical constituents, and they both continue execution at the statement *following* **fork** (code before **fork** ignored by child). To be able to distinguish between the original and its replica, **fork** returns twice with two different values:

- Zero in the child, which is safe because no process can be created with that PID.
- The PID of the child in the parent, so the parent can later access the child with this PID.

When **fork** is invoked, the kernel replicates the address space of the current process (its text, data, stack, etc.). It also creates a separate entry in the process table containing several fields copied from the entry of the parent. This includes the file descriptors, current directory and umask value. Because the child runs in its own address space, changes made to these parameters don't affect the parent.

Even though the child has separate copies of all descriptors allocated in the parent, *the original descriptor and its copy share the same file table.* This means that the file offset pointer set by an I/O operation in the parent is seen by the child using a copy of the descriptor.

The size of the process table places a restriction on the total number of processes that the machine can support. If an attempt to fork a process violates this restriction, **fork** returns -1.

24.3.2 fork.c: A Simple Child Creation Program

You may find the behavior of **fork** a little confusing initially, so let's demonstrate its effect with a simple program, **fork.c** (Fig. 24.3). We simply fork a process and then use **getpid** and **getppid** to obtain the PID and PPID of both parent and child.

Since **fork** returns two different values, we need to examine this return value to distinguish between parent and child. Observe from the output below that the first and second **printf** statements are executed in the parent, and the third one in the child. The final **printf** is executed by both processes. We'll discuss the significance of the **sleep** call after observing the output:

```
$ a.out
Before forking
CHILD -- PID: 1556 PPID: 1555
Both processes continue from here                        This statement runs in child ...
PARENT -- PID: 1555 PPID: 1450, CHILD PID: 1556
Both processes continue from here                        ... as well as in parent
```

```c
/* Program: fork.c -- A simple fork
                    Shows PID, PPID in both parent and child */
#include <stdio.h>
#include <sys/types.h>

int main(void) {
   pid_t pid;

   printf("Before fork\n");
   pid = fork();                            /* Replicates current process */

   if (pid > 0) {                           /* In the parent process; make sure */
      sleep(1);                             /* that parent doesn't die before child */
      printf("PARENT -- PID: %d PPID: %d, CHILD PID: %d\n",
                    getpid(), getppid(), pid);
   }
   else if (pid == 0)                       /*In the child process */
      printf("CHILD -- PID: %d PPID: %d\n", getpid(), getppid());
   else {                                   /* pid must be -1 here */
      printf("Fork error\n");
      exit(1);
   }
   printf("Both processes continue from here\n");      /*In both processes */
   exit(0);
}
```

Fig. 24.3 fork.c

In this program run on Solaris, the child runs first. But on Linux, the parent runs before the child. POSIX doesn't specify any sequence, so you can't write programs based on the assumption that one runs before the other. We deliberately introduced the **sleep** call to ensure that the parent doesn't die before the child. The consequences of letting the parent die first are examined in Section 24.7.

Note: The standard I/O library that includes functions like **printf** maintains an additional set of buffers. These buffers are different from the buffer cache available in the kernel. Forking copies these buffers as well, which means that the same buffers are available to the child. This creates problems when using functions like **printf** with **fork**.

Unlike **write**, **printf** is *line-buffered* when writing to the terminal. This means that the buffer contents are written to the terminal only when a newline is encountered. **printf** is, however, *fully-buffered* when writing to disk; the buffer is written when it is full. Redirect the output of the program, **fork.c** to a file, and you'll find the program behaving differently.

24.3.3 getenv and setenv: Handling Environment Variables

Forking also transmits the parent's environment to the child since environment variables are constituents of the process address space. These variables are available in the environ[] variable, which you may need to define in your C program like this:

```
extern char **environ;
```

Like argv[] (used as the second argument to **main**), this represents an array of pointers to char, except that this array stores pointers to environment variable strings of the form *name=value*. POSIX specifies two functions, **getenv** and **setenv**, to obtain and set these values:

```
char *getenv(const char *name);
int setenv(const char *envname, const char *envval, int overwrite);
```

getenv returns a pointer to the value of a variable, whose string representation is passed to it as the *name* argument. For instance, you can obtain the current value of PATH in this manner:

```
char *path = getenv("PATH");                    Obtains value from environ[] variable
```

setenv uses three arguments; the first two are used to pass the variable name and value. The third argument, *overwrite*, determines whether an existing value of a variable will be overwritten. If the variable is already defined and *overwrite* is nonzero, its existing value is updated. However, the value is left alone if *overwrite* is zero. This is how you can reset the PATH variable to include only the current directory:

```
setenv("PATH", ".", 1);
```

BSD created **setenv**, and even though POSIX recommends its use, it is not available on many SVR4 systems including Solaris. If you don't find **setenv** on your machine, then use SVR4's **putenv** (not preferred by POSIX) which accepts a pointer to char as its only argument. The strings pointed to have the form *name=value*. The previous **setenv** call can be replaced with **putenv("PATH=.")**.

24.3.4 `childenv.c`: Studying the Environment

The following program, **childenv.c** (Fig. 24.4), demonstrates how the parent is affected by three changes made to a child's environment. Henceforth, we'll be using a **switch** construct to separate parent code from child code.

We first obtain and print the current directory using **getcwd**. The **switch** statement tests for three possible types of return values from **fork**. The first checks for a **fork** error. Next, **switch** checks for a child, where we make three changes to the child's environment. We set x to 200, the PATH variable to a dot (with **setenv**), and change the current directory (with **chdir**). We also print some of the old and changed values as seen in the child.

Once again, we let the parent sleep for two seconds to ensure that the child dies before the parent continues beyond **fork**. Let's now check whether the changes made in the child's environment are visible in the parent:

```
$ a.out
BEFORE FORK -- Current directory: /users1/home/staff/sumit
CHILD -- Inherited value of x: 100
CHILD -- Changed value of x: 200
CHILD -- Inherited value of PATH: /usr/bin::/usr/local/bin:/usr/ccs/bin
CHILD -- New value of PATH: .
CHILD -- Current directory changed to: /etc
PARENT -- Value of x after change by child: 100
PARENT -- Current directory is still: /users1/home/staff/sumit
PARENT -- Value of PATH is unchanged: /usr/bin::/usr/local/bin:/usr/ccs/bin
```

It shouldn't surprise us that the changes made in the child are not visible in the parent; x still has the value 100, PATH retains its old value and the current directory remains /users1/home/staff/sumit. A child process maintains its own copies of these parameters.

Putting a parent to sleep for an arbitrary time interval isn't a satisfactory method of ensuring that the child dies before the parent. Ideally, in most situations, the parent should *wait* for the death of the child. This it does by invoking **wait**, which is taken up soon after discussing **exit** and **_exit**.

24.4 _exit AND exit: PROCESS TERMINATION

Except for some daemon processes that live as long as the machine is up, most processes will eventually die. When a process dies, the kernel closes all open files and frees the memory associated with the process (like the address space). Whether or not it also frees the process table entry depends on whether the parent has waited for the child's death. Before we get into what exactly the parent waits for, let's first understand that a process can terminate in any of the following ways:

- By falling through to the end of the program. This happens when you don't include an explicit **exit** or **return** call in **main**. The process then invokes an implicit **return**.
- By an explicit **return** statement in the **main** function.
- By the **exit** function or **_exit** system call anywhere in the program.
- On receipt of a signal which may terminate the process.

```
/* Program: childenv.c -- Changes child's environment and then checks
                          the effect in parent */
#include <stdio.h>
#include <sys/types.h>
#define PATH_LENGTH 30

int main(void) {
    pid_t pid;
    int x = 100;
    char newdir[PATH_LENGTH + 1];      /* Additional space required for \0 */

    getcwd(newdir, PATH_LENGTH);        /*Get current directory before fork */
    printf("BEFORE FORK -- Current directory: %s\n", newdir);

    pid = fork ();
    switch (pid) {
      case -1:
        perror("fork");                              /* fork error */
        exit(1);                                     /* Parent exits */
      case 0:      /* Child */
        printf("CHILD -- Inherited value of x: %d\n", x);
        x = 200 ;                                    /* Change x in child */
        printf("CHILD -- Changed value of x: %d\n", x);
        printf("CHILD -- Inherited value of PATH: %s\n", getenv("PATH"));
        setenv("PATH", ".", 1);  /* Change PATH here; use putenv("PATH=.") */
                                 /* if setenv() not supported */
        printf("CHILD -- New value of PATH: %s\n", getenv("PATH"));
        if (chdir("/etc") != -1) {                   /* "cd" to /etc */
            getcwd(newdir, PATH_LENGTH);             /* Do a "pwd" */
            printf("CHILD -- Current directory changed to: %s\n", newdir);
        }
        break;
        exit(0);
      default:    /* Parent */
        sleep(2);                                    /* Allow child to complete */
        getcwd(newdir, PATH_LENGTH);                 /*Getting new directory */
        printf("PARENT -- Value of x after change by child: %d\n", x);
        printf("PARENT -- Current directory is still: %s\n", newdir);
        printf("PARENT -- Value of PATH is unchanged: %s\n", getenv("PATH"));
        exit(0);
    }
}
```

Fig. 24.4 childenv.c

We'll discuss signal handling later; in this section, we examine the **exit** library function and **_exit** system call. We have used **exit** in every C program used in this text. **_exit** is one of the four basic system calls used in the process life cycle. Both **_exit** and **exit** share an identical syntax:

```
void _exit(int status);
void exit(int status);
```

Both functions work in a manner similar to the shell's built-in **exit** command that is used in shell scripts. The **_exit** call closes all open files and terminates a process but doesn't bother about performing other cleanup operations. We generally avoid its use because **exit** internally calls **_exit** but makes a program terminate gracefully.

When a process terminates by any of the methods described at the beginning of the section, the kernel sends a signal (SIGCHLD) to the parent informing it of the child's death. If termination is on account of invoking **exit** (or **_exit**), the argument used with **exit** eventually finds its way to the process table. This value, called the **exit status**, is picked up by the parent by invoking the **wait** or **waitpid** system call. We'll soon discuss how this value is actually extracted from an argument used with **wait** or **waitpid**.

Note: The shell's **exit** command and the **exit** and **_exit** calls in a C program often return control to the shell. In the shell, the exit status is stored in the shell variable $? (status in the C shell).

24.5 WAITING TO PICK UP CHILD'S EXIT STATUS

After a process has forked a child, more often than not, it is followed by a call to exec. You know what exec does; it replaces the child's address space with that of a new program *(9.4)*. We'll be taking up exec shortly, but note that whether a call to exec is finally made or not, the two processes run independently. So what does the parent do while the child executes? It can do two things:

- Wait to gather the child's exit status.
- Continue execution without waiting for the child (and pick up the exit status later, if at all).

The first is the normal shell behavior when we enter a command. The shell exhibits its nonwaiting role when it runs a job in the background. The two system calls involved in waiting are **wait** and **waitpid**. We take up **wait** first.

24.5.1 wait: Waiting for Death of Child

When a child terminates, its exit status is placed along with other information in the process table. The parent picks up this exit status using the **wait** system call. The call uses a pointer to an int variable as its only argument:

```
pid_t wait(int *stat_loc);
```

When there's at least one child process running, **wait** blocks until a child dies. It then returns the PID of the first dying child and places its exit status in *stat_loc*. The kernel then clears the slot in the process table that was allocated to the child. The parent resumes operation with the statement following **wait**.

The variable *stat_loc*, representing the *termination status*, doesn't contain only the exit status but some other things as well—like the process state and the signal that caused the process to be in that state. Separate macros are available to obtain the complete information. The exit status itself is stored in the least eight significant bits of *stat_loc*. The WEXITSTATUS macro used with *stat_loc* as argument fetches this value.

Note: Even though we explained the use of **wait** with reference to a dying child, **wait** is not merely concerned with death of a process but a change in its state. This can be caused by, say, a signal suspending a process. The termination status stores both the state and the signal responsible for the change.

24.5.2 wait.c: Using wait and WEXITSTATUS

In this program, **wait.c** (Fig. 24.5), the parent opens a file and writes one line of data to it. After forking, the child writes one more line to the same file. This should be possible since the child inherits the parent's file descriptors. Meanwhile, the parent waits for the child to die, and when it does, it invokes the WEXITSTATUS macro to gather the exit status from the process table. Finally, the parent writes a third line to the file.

```
/* Program: wait.c -- Uses wait to obtain child's termination status.
                      The WEXITSTATUS macro fetches the exit status. */
#include <stdio.h>
#include <fcntl.h>
#include <sys/wait.h>

int main(int argc, char **argv) {
    int fd, exitstatus;
    int exitval = 10;                  /* Value to be returned by child */

    fd = open(argv[1], O_WRONLY | O_CREAT | O_TRUNC, 0644);
    write(fd, "Original process writes\n", 24);    /* First write */

    switch(fork()) {
        case 0:
            write(fd, "Child writes\n", 13);         /* Second write */
            close(fd);              /* Closing here doesn't affect parent's copy */
            printf("CHILD: Terminating with exit value %d\n", exitval);
            exit(exitval);          /* Can also use _exit(exitval) */

        default:
            wait(&exitstatus);      /* Waits for child to die */
            printf("PARENT: Child terminated with exit value %d\n",
                    WEXITSTATUS(exitstatus));        /* Extracting exit status */
            write(fd, "Parent writes\n", 14);        /* Third write */
            exit(20);               /* Value returned to shell; try echo $? */
    }
}
```

Fig. 24.5 wait.c

We used the **write** call three times in this program. In each case, we had to specify as **write**'s third argument, the length of the string written to the file. The filename itself is obtained as a command line argument. We have raised concerns about the sequence of operations before—whether the parent runs first or the child runs first after the fork. Once we use **wait**, such concerns disappear as the parent can't continue execution until the child dies.

Let's now run this program with a filename as argument and then observe the sequence in which the three lines appear:

```
$ a.out foo
CHILD: Terminating with exit value 10
PARENT: Child terminated with exit value 10
$ cat foo
Original process writes
Child writes
Parent writes
```

We have been able to run the parent in synchronism with the child. We have also achieved a rudimentary form of *inter-process communication* (IPC); the parent knows the child's exit status.

24.5.3 `waitpid`: A More Powerful Waiting Mechanism

wait suffers from a number of limitations. It blocks until a child dies, and there's nothing the process invoking it can do until that happens. Further, if a parent spawns several children, **wait** returns the moment one of them dies; it can't wait for a process with a specific PID to die. Finally, **wait** can't handle *process groups* (discussed in the next section).

Overcoming these limitations is important in process management, and for these reasons the use of **waitpid** is recommended over **wait**. **waitpid** takes three arguments:

```
pid_t waitpid(pid_t pid, int *stat_loc, int options);
```

The second argument, *stat_loc*, has the same significance as in **wait**; the termination status of the process is stored there. The *options* setting enables **waitpid** to run in nonblocking mode, but there are other functions. The *pid* can take four types of values:

* If *pid* is -1, **waitpid** blocks until a child dies or changes state.
* If *pid* > 0, **waitpid** waits for a specific process with *pid* as its PID.
* If *pid* = 0, **waitpid** waits for any process belonging to the same process group as the process invoking the call.
* If *pid* < -1, **waitpid** waits for any process whose PGID is the same as the absolute value of *pid* (PGID is process group-id, and is explained in the next section).

The behavior of **waitpid** is also controlled by the *options* setting. This can be zero or a bit-wise OR of the constants WNOHANG, WUNTRACED and WCONTINUED. We consider only the two following settings of *options*:

* If *options* is 0, **waitpid** blocks until the child changes state, but the behavior of the process is also influenced by the way *pid* is specified.

- If *options* is set to WNOHANG, **waitpid** behaves in a nonblocking manner; it returns immediately regardless a child has changed state or not.

For emulating **wait(&status)**, we need to use **waitpid(-1, &status, 0)**. We'll use **waitpid** in an example later in the chapter.

24.6 PROCESS GROUPS

Every process belongs to a **process group** (a Berkeley feature that lets you control a group of processes working for a common cause). Each process in the group has the same *process group-id* (PGID). The group has a leader whose PGID is the same as its PID. The **waitpid** system call can be made to wait for any member of a process group to die. The **kill** system call can also send a signal to all processes in a process group.

The shell's handling of the process groups of its children depends on whether it supports job control. In the Bourne shell, a command run from the shell has the same PGID as the shell itself. That is not so in the other three shells (C shell, Korn and Bash) supporting job control where every command is placed in its own process group. A pipeline that represents a job in these three shells also forms a process group.

You can have several process groups in a *session*, but only one of them would be a *foreground process group*; the rest would be *background process groups*. A foreground process group is directly connected to the session's controlling terminal. This means that you can use your keyboard to input data to the processes in the group as well as send them signals. When you press *[Ctrl-c]*, all processes in the foreground process group receive the SIGINT signal and respond accordingly (usually, terminate).

A background process group can't be sent signals from the terminal though they can receive signals by other means (with **kill**, for instance). A background process group may or may not be allowed to write to the terminal depending on how the system is set up, but if it tries to read from the terminal, then the terminal driver notices this and immediately issues a signal to suspend the process group. This explains why you can't use **vi foo &**.

24.7 ZOMBIES AND ORPHANS

Though the normal shell behavior is to wait for a child to die, that is not always practicable. With most shells today supporting job control, it is usual for a process or process group to be in the background or remain in a suspended state. However, there are two things that can happen if the parent doesn't wait for the child to die:

- The child dies while the parent is still alive.
- The parent dies while the child is still alive.

If the child dies first, the kernel empties the process address space but retains the process table entry. The child is said to be in a **zombie** state *(9.6)*. A zombie is actually not a process at all, so you can't kill it. The only reason for a child to remain in the zombie state is the "hope" that the parent may eventually call **wait** or **waitpid** to pick up the exit status and clear the process table slot. The **ps** output shows zombie processes as the string <defunct> in the last column.

When the parent dies first, the child becomes an **orphan** since the parent isn't just there to pick up its exit status. The kernel clears the process table slot of the parent, but before doing so, it checks whether there are any processes spawned by the parent that are still alive. When it finds one, it makes **init** its parent by changing the PPID field of the child. This is what happens when we run a job with **nohup** and then kill the shell by logging out *(9.7.2)*.

The following program, **orphan.c** (Fig. 24.6), also creates an orphan but doesn't require that we log out. Here, the parent exits immediately after creating the child. The child sleeps for two seconds to let the parent die and then prints a message.

After running the program, let's check the exit status as returned by the program to the shell:

```
$ a.out                                          ...no response for 2 seconds...
CHILD: Adopted by init now, PPID: 1
$ echo $?
10
```

It's the parent, not the child, that returned the exit status to the shell. Because **init** acquired the parentage of the child, **init** also collected the exit status. **init** is so designed that it can run numerous child processes without blocking, but is smart enough to collect the exit status of its children as and when they die. Using **waitpid**, you can do that too in your programs.

24.8 exec: THE FINAL STEP IN PROCESS CREATION

More often than not, we don't stop at fork. We want to run a separate program in a forked process. This is done by doing an exec. This operation replaces the entire address space (text, data and stack) with that of the new program. Since the stack is also replaced, the call to exec doesn't return unless it results in an error. The forking mechanism is responsible for creating processes, but it's exec that actually executes programs on a UNIX system.

Many attributes inherited during a fork don't change with an exec. For instance, the previous program's file descriptors, the current and root directory, umask settings and the environment remain the same. Since no new process is created, the PID doesn't change across an exec.

```
/* Program: orphan.c -- Creates an orphan by letting child sleep for 2 minutes
                        Parent doesn't call wait and dies immediately */
#include <stdio.h>
int main(void) {
    int pid;
    if ((pid = fork()) > 0)              /* Parent */
        exit(10);                        /* Parent exits without calling wait */
    else if (pid == 0) {                 /* Child */
        sleep(2);                        /* Lets parent die in this time frame */
        printf("CHILD: Adopted by init now, PPID: %d\n", getppid());
        exit(0);
    }
}
```

Fig. 24.6   orphan.c

The exec operation can be performed by six members of a family of one system call and five library functions, which we'll refer to simply as "exec" or the "exec family". There's no system call named exec; rather, there's only one—**execve**, on top of which five library functions are built.

The entire set can be grouped into two parts, which we'll call the "execl" set and the "execv" set, because the function names begin with the string **exec** followed by either an l or a v. Two of the members also have the names **execl** and **execv**; the other four are simple derivatives of them and have more similarities than differences.

Tip: First, commit to memory this simple statement: The l in **execl** (and its variants) represents a fixed *list* of arguments, while the v in **execv** (and its variants) signifies a *variable* number of arguments.

24.8.1 execl: The Key Member of the "l" Series

As noted in the Tip above, **execl** is used with a list comprising the command name and its arguments:

```
int execl(const char *path, const char *arg0, ... /*, (char *) 0 */);
```

The syntax may appear daunting, but it is not; in fact, it is quite simple. We use **execl** when we know the number of arguments in advance. The first argument is the pathname (*path*) which could be an absolute or a relative pathname. The arguments to the command to run are represented as separate arguments beginning with the name of the command (*arg0*). The ellipsis representation in the syntax (... /*) points to the varying number of arguments.

To consider an example, here's how we use **execl** to run the **wc -l** command with the filename **foo** as argument:

```
execl("/bin/wc", "wc", "-l", "foo", (char *) 0);
```

execl doesn't use PATH to locate **wc**, so we must specify the pathname as its first argument. *The remaining arguments are specified exactly in the way they will appear as **main**'s arguments in **wc**.* So, argv[0] in **wc**'s **main** is **wc**, the name of the command itself.

HOW IT WORKS: Why a Null Pointer is Required

To understand why we follow the argument list with a null pointer ((char *) 0), let's first understand how arguments are passed to a C program. By convention, we use this syntax for **main** when a program is run with arguments:

```
int main(int argc, char *argv[]) {
```

The startup routine that eventually runs **main** populates *argv[] (an array of pointers to char) with the string arguments specified in the command line. A null pointer is also placed at the end of the array. The number of arguments (excluding the null pointer) is then evaluated and assigned to argc. When **main** runs, it knows the number of arguments passed to it.

When we use exec to run a program, there's no provision to specify the number of arguments (no argc); exec has to fill up argc "by hand." The only way for **execl** to know the size of the argument list is to keep counting until it encounters the null pointer. That's why this pointer must be specified in every member of the **execl** series.

Let's use **execl** in our next program, **execl.c** (Fig. 24.7), to run the **wc -l -c** command with /etc/passwd as argument. Because a successful **execl** never returns, the **printf** statement is not executed:

```
$ a.out
    166    9953 /etc/passwd
```

We can also use NULL in place of (char *) 0. Note that to be able to use **execl**, we must know the number of arguments in advance because each argument is specified as a separate argument to **execl**. Often, the size of the argument list is known only at runtime. The solution is **execv**, which we'll take up next.

24.8.2 execv: The Key Member of the "v" Series

To run a command with any number of arguments, you must use one of the functions of the "execv" set. In this section, we discuss the **execv** function before we discover the advantages that are found in its variants. **execv** needs an array to work with:

```
int execv(const char *path, char *const argv[]);
```

Like in **execl**, *path* represents the pathname of the command to run. The second argument represents an array of pointers to char (of the same type as **main**'s argv[]). The array is populated by addresses that point to strings representing the command name and its arguments, in the form they are passed to the **main** function of the program to be exec'd. In this case also, the last element of *argv*[] must be a null pointer.

We'll use **execv** in the next program, **execv.c** (Fig. 24.8), to run the **grep** command with two options to look up the author's name in /etc/passwd. In this program, we populate the array *cmdargs*[] with the strings comprising the command line to be executed by **execv**. Note that the first argument to **execv** still remains the pathname of the command. Here's the run:

```
$ a.out
15:sumit:x:102:10::/users1/home/staff/sumit:/usr/bin/bash
```

You might say that this sequence could have been run by **execl** also, but observe the way we used **execv** in the program. Since we pass the address of an array element as its second argument (cmdargs being the same as &cmdargs[0]), it implies that we can input *any* command line during runtime. Our next program will be used in that way.

```
/* Program: execl.c -- Uses execl to run wc */
#include <stdio.h>
int main(void) {
    execl("/bin/wc", "wc", "-l", "-c", "/etc/passwd", (char *) 0);
    printf("execl error\n");
}
```

Fig. 24.7 execl.c

```
/* Program: execv.c -- Stuffs all command line arguments to an array
                        to be used with execv */
#include <stdio.h>
int main(int argc, char **argv) {
    char *cmdargs[] = { "grep", "-i", "-n", "SUMIT", "/etc/passwd", NULL };
    execv("/bin/grep", cmdargs);                 /* Execute another program */
    printf("execv error\n");
}
```

Fig. 24.8 execv.c

24.8.3 exec_and_fork.c: Running exec in a Child Process

The previous two programs used **execl** and **execv** in the current process. We normally don't use exec like this; often we do an exec in a child process so that the parent is free to do what it likes. In the following program, **exec_and_fork.c** (Fig. 24.9), the command line to execute is specified as the program's arguments. We also fork a process, run **execv** in the child and then make the parent wait for the child's death.

Here we take advantage of the facilities available in a program's startup routine to fill up **main**'s argv[]. We didn't bother about including the null pointer here because that is automatically done when you pass command line arguments to a program. Instead, we pass the absolute pathname of the command to run as the first argument, and the *entire* command line as the remaining arguments.

```
/* Program: exec_and_fork.c.c --
            Uses fork, exec and wait to run a UNIX command */
#include <stdio.h>
#include <wait.h>

int main(int argc, char **argv) {
    int returnval ;                      /* Used by wait */

    switch(fork()) {
      case 0:                            /* Run command in child */
          if ((execv(argv[1], &argv[2]) < 0)) {
              fprintf(stderr, "execl error\n");
              exit(200);
          }
      default:                           /* In the parent */
          wait(&returnval);              /* After the command has completed ... */
          fprintf(stderr, "Exit status: %d\n", WEXITSTATUS(returnval));
          exit (0);
    }
}
```

Fig. 24.9 exec_and_fork.c

This command line is accessed by **execv** as the address of argv[2]. The program doesn't terminate immediately after exec in the way the previous two programs did:

```
$ a.out /bin/grep grep -i -n SUMIT /etc/passwd
15:sumit:x:102:10::/users1/home/staff/sumit:/usr/bin/bash
Exit status: 0
```

The shell does a similar thing with our input except that we don't provide input to the shell in the way we did above. Even if we ignore this program's inability to handle redirection and wild-card interpretation, it still has the following drawbacks:

- We need to know the location of the command file because neither **execl** nor **execv** will use PATH to locate it.
- The command name is specified twice—as the first two arguments.
- These calls can't be used to run a shell script but only binary executables.
- The program has to be invoked every time we need to run a command.

To be able to run programs in a simpler and easier way, we need to discuss the derivatives of **execl** and **execv**. There are four of them, and after we examine them in the next section, we 'll use one of them to design a rudimentary shell program that has none of the limitations presented above.

24.8.4 The Other Members of the "l" and "v" Series

execlp *and* **execvp**   The requirement to provide the pathname of the command makes the previous exec calls somewhat inconvenient to use. Fortunately, help is at hand in the form of the **execlp** and **execvp** functions that use PATH to locate the command. They behave exactly like their other counterparts but overcome two of the four limitations discussed in the previous section. First, the first argument need not be a pathname; it can be a command name. Second, these functions can also run a shell (or **awk** or **perl**) script. Here's their syntax:

```
int execlp(const char *file, const char *arg0, ... /*, (char *)0 */);
int execvp(const char *file, char *const argv[]);
```

Note that *pathname* has now become *file*; the other arguments remain the same. To show how **execlp** works, just replace the line containing the **execl** call in the program **execl.c** (Fig. 24.7), with this one:

```
execlp("wc", "wc", "-l", "foo", (char *) 0);
```

Now the first and second arguments are the same. To run the program, **execv.c** (Fig. 24.8), that uses **execv**, just change **execv** to **execvp** without disturbing the arguments. When running it, the first two command line arguments can again be the same. You'll find these calls easier to work with.

Note: To run shell, **awk** or **perl** scripts with exec, use **execlp** or **execvp**. By default, exec spawns a Bourne shell to read the commands in the script, but you can override that by providing an interpreter line at the top of the script. For instance, if you have #!/bin/ksh as the interpreter line, exec will call up the Korn shell.

---

execle *and* **execve**   All of the previous four exec calls silently pass the environment of the current process to the exec'd process by making available the environ[] variable to the overlaid process. Sometimes, you may need to provide a different environment to the new program—a restricted shell, for instance. In that case, we need to use the remaining members of the exec family, **execle** and **execve**:

```
int execle(const char *path, const char *arg0, ... /*,
           (char *) 0, char *const envp[]*/);
int execve(const char *path, char *const argv[], char *const envp[]);
```

Unlike the other four members, both **execle** and **execve** use an additional argument to pass a pointer to an array of environment strings (of the form *variable=value*) to the program. It's *only* this environment that is available in the exec'd process, not the one stored in environ[].

We are back to *path* once again; these functions behave more like **execl** and **execv** in that they use the command pathname as the first argument. However, they retain one advantage of **execlp** and **execvp**: They can also run a shell script provided the script contains an interpreter line. The last one, **execve**, is the only system call in the exec family; the others internally invoke **execve**.

24.9 shell.c: A PROGRAM WITH A SHELL-LIKE CAPABILITY

We'll now round up discussions on process creation by devising a program, **shell.c** (Fig. 24.10), that mimics the shell's behavior in executing a command that is input by the user. The parent repeatedly displays a prompt, and **execvp** is run with user input in a child process. To keep things simple, we define arrays of fixed sizes so that the following restrictions apply: Command lines can't be longer than 200 characters and the number of arguments can't exceed 40. The program doesn't permit use of the special characters, so no redirection and piping are allowed.

The program prints the Shell> prompt and reads user input into the buffer buf. The program terminates if the user enters **exit**. The **strtok** (string tokenizer) function then parses the command line (buf, its first argument) on whitespace (DELIM, its second argument). The function is a little unusual; in the first call, it returns the first word which is assigned to clargs[0]. However, subsequent calls to **strtok** will return the other words only if the first argument is null. That's why the strings were extracted in two stages. Once *clargs[] is populated with the words extracted from user input, a null pointer is added so that the program knows the number of elements of the array to read.

Next, the process forks and runs **execvp** in the child, using the arguments that were obtained with **strtok**. The parent waits for the child's death and prints the exit status every time a command is run. Finally, it initializes the arrays, buf and clargs, before beginning the next cycle. Here's a sample run:

```
$ a.out
Shell> grep joker /etc/passwd
Exit status of command: 1                    grep returns 1 if pattern not found
Shell> date
Mon Mar 10 16:18:28 IST 2003
Exit status of command: 0
Shell> pwd                                   Is this the shell builtin?
/users1/home/staff/sumit
```

```c
/* Program: shell.c -- Accepts user input as a command to be executed. Uses
                       the strtok library function for parsing command line */
#include <stdio.h>
#include <unistd.h>
#include <string.h>                         /* For strtok */
#include <wait.h>

#define BUFSIZE 200                         /* Maximum size of command line */
#define ARGVSIZE 40                         /* Maximum number of arguments */
#define DELIM "\n\t\r "                     /* White-space delimiters for strtok */

int main(int argc, char **argv) {
    int i, n ;
    char buf[BUFSIZE+1];                    /* Stores the entered command line */
    char *clargs[ARGVSIZE];                 /* Stores the argument strings */
    int returnval ;                         /* Used by wait */
    for (;;) {                              /* Loop forever */
        n = 1;
        write(STDOUT_FILENO, "Shell> ", 7);  /* Display a prompt */
        read(STDIN_FILENO, buf, BUFSIZE);    /* Read user input into buf */
        if (!strcmp(buf, "exit\n"))
            exit(0);                         /* Terminate if user enters exit */
                                             /* Now parse buf to extract the */
        clargs[0] = strtok(buf, DELIM);      /* first word */
                                             /* Continue parsing until ... */
        while ((clargs[n] = strtok(NULL, DELIM)) != NULL)
            n++;                             /* ... all words are extracted */

        clargs[n] = NULL;                    /* Set last argument pointer to NULL */
        switch(fork()) {
            case 0:                          /* Run command in child */
                if ((execvp(clargs[0], &clargs[0])) < 0)
                    exit(200);               /* We'll check this value later */
            default:                         /* In the parent */
                wait(&returnval);            /* After the command has completed ... */
                printf("Exit status of command: %d\n", WEXITSTATUS(returnval));
                for (i = 0; i <=n; i++)      /* ... initialize both ... */
                    clargs[i] = "\0";        /* the argument array  ... */
                for (i = 0; i <BUFSIZE+1; i++)
                    buf[i] = '\0';           /* .... and buffer that stores command */
                                             /* line, so next command can work with */
        }
                                             /* an initialized buffer and argument */
    }
                                             /* array. */
}
```

Fig. 24.10 shell.c

```
Exit status of command: 0
Shell> ls -lu /usr/bin/pwd                    Now check the access time of on-disk pwd
-r-xr-xr-x   1 root      bin      4360 Mar 10 16:18 /usr/bin/pwd
Exit status of command: 0                     Disk file has just been accessed!
Shell> exit
$ _
```

This "shell" runs all external commands using **execvp**. Note how the program correctly prints the exit status after executing each command. The exec calls can't execute shell builtins (because there's no shell here), so every command that we input must exist as an on-disk executable. This must be true for the **pwd** command also, and we confirmed this by checking the last accessed time for the file and comparing it with the **date** output.

Tip: As can be seen from the code of the previous program, it's tedious to parse a line into word-strings and then populate an array with pointers to these strings. You can make the shell do this work for you by passing the shell itself as the first two arguments to **execlp**. All shells support a -c option that takes a command line as argument to be executed. For instance, you can run the **ls** command *with wildcards and redirection to save the output* by using **sh -c "ls *.c > list"**. To use this with **execlp**, we need to use **execlp("sh", "sh", "-c", "ls *.c > list")**. The first three arguments will always be the same; the entire command line can be supplied as a single fourth argument!

Note: Often, you'll find it more convenient to use the **system** library function which is built on top of the **fork**, exec and **wait** calls. **system** takes the entire command line (which can also be a shell builtin or a shell script) as a single argument:

```
system("ls -lu /etc/passwd > foo")
```

The function uses a shell (by default, Bourne) to execute the command, and also makes use of PATH. **system** works with redirection and can also run a pipeline.

24.10 FILE DESCRIPTOR MANIPULATION

The previous program can't handle redirection or connect two commands in a pipe. To be able to do that, we must first understand a special feature available in the UNIX kernel to manipulate file descriptors. You'll recall that the kernel always allocates the lowest available integer as the new file descriptor when you open a file. This implies that if you close standard output and then open a disk file foo, the descriptor for the file would be 1:

```
close(STDOUT_FILENO);                         Next open returns 1 as file descriptor
open("foo", O_WRONLY | O_CREAT |O_TRUNC, S_IRUSR | S_IWUSR);
printf("This statement goes to foo; standard output redirected\n");
```

Place these three statements in a program with the necessary #include statements (fcntl.h, sys/stat.h and unistd.h), and you'll find that the output of the **printf** statement has been "redirected" to foo. This isn't the way the shell actually performs redirection, but it has an important message to convey:

If you want to perform a read or write operation on a file foo *using a specific file descriptor that is already allocated to* bar, *then close* bar *before you open* foo. foo *should then get the descriptor that was previously allocated to* bar.

We'll now see how this concept is used to implement redirection and piping.

24.10.1 dup: Duplicating a File Descriptor

At the outset, let's clearly understand the difference between opening a file twice and duplicating the descriptor of an open file. When a file is opened twice—either in the same or in a different process—the two file descriptors point to *separate* file table entries. This means that they have their own separate file offsets. However, when you duplicate a file descriptor, both descriptors point to the *same* file table, which means that they share the same offset. This behavior—also shared by **fork** *(24.3.1)*—is required to achieve redirection and piping.

We'll consider here two system calls that duplicate file descriptors—**dup** and **dup2**. The first one has a very simple syntax:

```
int dup(int fildes);
```

Here, **dup** duplicates the file descriptor *fildes* and returns the lowest numbered descriptor available for allocation. Assuming that the standard descriptors 0, 1 and 2 are allocated, and there's no other file open in that process, **dup(1)** will return the value 3. This is one way of creating another handle to access standard output.

Let's use this feature in our next program, **dup.c** (Fig. 24.11), to run any filter that obtains input from redirected standard input and writes to redirected standard output. The program accepts the first argument as the input filename, the second argument as the output filename, and the remaining arguments as the command line to be executed.

We use **dup** to replicate the file descriptors returned by opening the two files (argv[1] and argv[2]). Because we previously closed the respective standard streams, we *should* get them back by using **dup**. Let's now use the program to run **wc** (the third argument) to save the word count of /etc/passwd (the first argument) in passwd.cnt (the second argument):

```
$ a.out /etc/passwd passwd.cnt wc -l
$ cat passwd.cnt
    37 /etc/passwd
```

We have said this before as a UNIX user *(8.5.1)*, and we say this again—this time as a systems programmer: **wc** didn't open /etc/passwd but obtained its input from standard input. We have achieved the effect of redirection except that we didn't use the < and > symbols and relied on the program to identify the first two arguments as the filenames to be used for redirection.

24.10.2 dup2: A Better Way of Replicating a Descriptor

The reason why we used the word "should" (twice in the program annotations and once in the paragraph prior to the previous one) is that we assume that nothing untoward will occur after **close** and before **dup**. However, this behavior is not guaranteed; a signal handler (covered later) could

```
/* Program: dup.c -- Uses dup to achieve both input and output redirection
                     Closes standard streams first before using dup */
#include <unistd.h>
#include <stdio.h>
#include <sys/stat.h>
#include <fcntl.h>
#define MODE600 (S_IRUSR | S_IWUSR)

int main(int argc, char **argv) {
    int fd1, fd2;
    fd1 = open(argv[1], O_RDONLY);
    fd2 = open(argv[2], O_WRONLY | O_CREAT | O_TRUNC, MODE600);

    close(STDIN_FILENO);
    dup(fd1);                         /* This should return descriptor 0 */
    close(STDOUT_FILENO);
    dup(fd2);                         /* This should return descriptor 1 */

    execvp(argv[3], &argv[3]);     /* Execute any filter */
    printf("Failed to exec filter");
}
```

Fig. 24.11 **dup.c**

create a file in this time interval. In that case, that file will be allocated the descriptor that we wanted from **dup**. The program will then fail.

To overcome this problem, we use the **dup2** system call that uses two arguments:

   int dup2(int *fildes*, int *fildes2*);

dup2 replicates *filedes* to *filedes2* and returns it. If *filedes2* is already open, **dup2** closes it first. **dup2** thus combines the actions of **close** and **dup** that were used in succession in the previous program, except that **dup2** performs both functions as a single atomic operation *(23.1.3)*; a signal can't interrupt an atomic operation.

There are two problems with the previous program. First, doing an exec in a single process leaves us with nothing more to do since exec doesn't return. Further, by closing standard output, we ensured that we can't write to the terminal again. Ideally, files to be used for redirection should be opened in a separate child process. The child should manipulate the descriptors before exec'ing the program which uses these descriptors.

To fall in line with the shell's approach to redirection, let's repeat the previous exercise, using **dup2** this time. In this program, **dup2.c** (Fig. 24.12), file opening, descriptor manipulation and also the exec are done in a child process. The parent simply forks and waits for the child to die. The program uses the **quit** function developed in the previous chapter to handle error messages.

To demonstrate how the parent correctly obtains the exit status of the command run by the child let's use the program to run **grep** twice:

```
/* Program: dup2.c -- Opens files in the parent and uses
                      dup2 in the child to reassign the descriptors */
#include <unistd.h>
#include <stdio.h>
#include <sys/stat.h>
#include <fcntl.h>
#include <wait.h>

#define OPENFLAGS (O_WRONLY | O_CREAT | O_TRUNC)
#define MODE600 (S_IRUSR | S_IWUSR)

void quit(char *message, int exit_status) ;

int main(int argc, char **argv) {
    int fd1, fd2, rv, exit_status;

    if (fork() == 0) {                    /* Child */
        if ((fd1 = open(argv[1], O_RDONLY)) == -1)
            quit("Error in opening file for reading\n", 1);
        if ((fd2 = open(argv[2], OPENFLAGS, MODE600)) == -1)
            quit("Error in opening file for writing\n", 1);
        dup2(fd1,0);                      /* Closes standard input simultaneously */
        dup2(fd2,1);                      /* Closes standard output simultaneously */
        execvp(argv[3], &argv[3]);        /* Execute command */
        quit("exec error", 2);
    } else {                              /* Parent */
        wait(&rv);                        /* Or use waitpid(-1, &rv, 0) */
        printf("Exit status: %d\n", WEXITSTATUS(rv));
    }
}
```

Fig. 24.12 dup2.c

```
$ a.out /etc/passwd passwd.cnt grep joker
Exit status: 1                                    joker not found in /etc/passwd
$ a.out /etc/passwd passwd.cnt grep sumit
Exit status: 0                                    sumit found in /etc/passwd
$ cat passwd.cnt
sumit:x:500:500:sumitabha das:/home/sumit:/bin/bash
```

grep here is used only with the pattern as argument; it obtained its input from standard input, which was redirected using **dup2** to originate from /etc/passwd. Further, the standard output of **grep** was also redirected with **dup2** to passwd.cnt.

24.10.3 fcntl: Recommended over dup and dup2

POSIX calls **dup** and **dup2** "redundant" functions, and advocates the use of the **fcntl** system call. Space constraints don't permit a thorough examination of this versatile system call, but **you should** at least know that descriptor replication is one of **fcntl**'s numerous functions. Here are the **fcntl** equivalents to **dup** and **dup2**:

dup *and* dup2	fcntl *Equivalents*
fd = dup(*filedes*);	fd = fcntl(*fildes*, F_DUPFD, 0);
fd = dup2(*fildes*, *fildes2*);	close(*fildes2*);
	fd = fcntl(*fildes*, F_DUPFD, *fildes2*);

Note that **fcntl** loses its atomicity when emulating **dup2** because it is preceded by the **close** call. POSIX recommends the use of signal blocking to avoid this problem.

Note: There are basically two ways of duplicating a file descriptor—using **fork**, and using **dup** and **dup2** (or their **fcntl** equivalents). **fork** makes a copy of the parent's descriptor available in the child, while **dup** and **dup2** do the same in the current process. In either case, the end result is that both original and copy share the same file table, i.e. the same file offset, opening modes and status flags.

24.11 pipe: INTER-PROCESS COMMUNICATION

UNIX has very elaborate schemes for two processes to communicate with each other. At a very rudimentary level, we have seen how the child communicates its exit status to the parent. Later in this chapter, we'll see how the kernel sends a signal to another process. In this section, we discuss the piping mechanism available in the shell.

To understand how a pipe enables one process to send its standard output to another's standard input, imagine doing a similar thing using a disk file instead. One process could write to the file and the other could read from it. This just won't work because if the reader is faster than the writer, it will often catch up with the writer and read EOF. There's no flow control mechanism that would make one process block until the other has completed its job. Besides, the size of the file grows as the data continues to flow from the writer to the reader. Operating system theorists have a name for this—the *producer-consumer* problem.

The pipe solves both these problems. It is a half-duplex communication channel, which means that data flows in only one direction. It is a type of file which can be used with **read** and **write**, but is created with the **pipe** system call:

```
int pipe(int fildes[2]);
```

pipe takes an array of 2 integers as its only argument, which it populates with two file descriptors. Whatever is written to *fildes*[1] can be read from *fildes*[0]; the significance of 0 and 1 have been retained in the pipe as well. A call to **write** on *fildes*[1] populates a fixed-sized buffer (about 4-8 KB), while a call to read on *filedes*[0] drains the buffer so the next **write** can fill it up again.

If the buffer is found to be empty during a read, the operation will block until the buffer is written. Similarly, a write to a buffer that has not yet been read will block too. The data is read on first in-first out basis (FIFO), and expectedly, the pipe's file type is FIFO which can be checked with the S_ISFIFO macro.

Although a pipe is most commonly shared by two processes, a trivial example shows its use in a single process:

```
int n, fd[2];
char buf[100];
pipe(fd);                               Fills up fd[2] with 2 descriptors
write(fd[1], "abcdefgh", 8 );           Writing to one file descriptor
n = read(fd[0], buf, 100);              and reading it back from another
write(STDOUT_FILENO, buf, n);           Printing what was read from pipe
```

The **pipe** call here generates two file descriptors, fd[0] and fd[1]. We simply write the string abcdefgh to fd[1], read it back from fd[0], and then write the same string to standard output. There's not much to learn from here except that numerous possibilities open up when a pipe is used by two processes. This is taken up next.

24.11.1 Using pipe with fork

To make **pipe** work in tandem with **fork**, the usual procedure is to create the pipe before forking a process. Because **fork** duplicates all open descriptors, a call to **pipe** before a **fork** connects two descriptors to each end of the pipe. To use the pipe, we don't need all four of them, but only one at each end. Data here can flow in either direction, but assuming that the parent writes to the pipe and the child reads it, we must close the pipe's read end in the parent and write end in the child. This is what the program, **pipe.c** (Fig. 24.13), does.

The **pipe** call returns two descriptors, fd[0] and fd[1], which should have the values 3 and 4 in this program. This example assumes data flowing from parent to child, so the parent doesn't need the read end (fd[0]), while the child doesn't need the write end (fd[1]), the reason why these descriptors have been closed. The program outputs the string that's written to the pipe:

```
$ a.out
Writing to pipe
```

This is the string **write** wrote to fd[1] and **read** gathered from fd[0]. In real-life though, you use separate programs on either side of the shell's pipe symbol, |. So you'll naturally expect to be able to do a similar thing with **pipe**. This means that you have to connect the standard output of one program to fd[1] and standard input of the other to fd[0]. How does one do that?

24.11.2 pipe2.c: Running UNIX Commands in a Pipe

The next program, **pipe2.c** (Fig. 24.14), addresses this issue. Apart from closing the unneeded file descriptors associated with the pipe, the program also uses **dup2** to replicate the other descriptors—both in the parent and the child. We reverse the data flow here—from the child to the parent—just to prove that the direction of flow is irrelevant.

To understand how the program works, let's first examine the sequence of statements that are executed in the child process. We first close (fd[0]), the descriptor for the read end of the pipe. We don't need it since the child writes (not reads) to the pipe. Next, we replicate fd[1] with **dup2** to give us the descriptor used by standard output. At this stage, the file descriptor for standard output points to the write end of the pipe. This means we don't need the original descriptor (fd[1]) that was connected to the same end of the pipe; so we close it.

```
/* Program: pipe.c -- Shares a pipe between two processes.
                      We want the data to flow from the parent to the child */
#include <stdio.h>
#include <unistd.h>

void quit(char *, int);
int main(void) {
    int n, fd[2];                       /* fd[2] to be filled up by pipe() */
    char buf[100];                      /* Buffer to be used by read() */

    if (pipe(fd) < 0)                   /* fd[0] is read end */
        quit("pipe", 1);                /* fd[1] is write end */

    switch (fork()) {                   /* Pipe has four descriptors now */
        case -1: quit("Fork error", 2);
        case 0: close(fd[1]);           /* CHILD-Close write end of pipe */
                n = read(fd[0], buf, 100); /* and read from its read end */
                write(STDOUT_FILENO, buf, n);
                break;
        default: close(fd[0]);          /* PARENT-Close read end of pipe */
                write(fd[1], "Writing to pipe\n", 16); /* write to write end */
    }
    exit(0);
}
```

Fig. 24.13 pipe.c

Having now closed both the original read and write ends of the pipe, we are left with only the descriptor for standard output that is now connected to the pipe's write end. Invoking **execvp** to run the **cat** command ensures that **cat**'s output is connected to the pipe's write end.

If we apply a similar line of reasoning to the statements in the parent, we'll end up in a situation where the standard input of **tr** is connected to the read end of the pipe. We have been able to establish a pipeline between **cat** and **tr**. On running the program, you should see the entries in planets, but after conversion to uppercase:

```
$ a.out
SATURN
EARTH
MERCURY
JUPITER
```

Compare this output with that obtained from the program, **reverse_read2.c** (Fig. 23.2), which displayed the contents of planets, but in reverse order.

A pipe is meant for one-way communication, and that's how we used it in these examples. The two programs that we considered lead us to an obvious conclusion: Two processes can use a pipe for communication only when they share a common ancestor. In these cases, the ancestor is the process

```
/* Program: pipe2.c -- Runs two programs in a pipeline
                       Child runs cat, parent runs tr */
#include <unistd.h>
#include <stdio.h>

void quit(char *message, int exit_status) ;
int main(void) {
  int fd[2];                               /* To be filled up by pipe() */

  if (pipe(fd) < 0)                        /* Now have four descriptors for pipe */
     quit("pipe", 1);
  switch (fork()) {
     case -1: quit("fork", 2);

     case 0: close(fd[0]);                 /* CHILD - Close read end first */
             dup2(fd[1], STDOUT_FILENO);   /* Connect stdout to  write end */
             close(fd[1]);                 /* and close original descriptor */
             execlp("cat", "cat", "/etc/hosts.equiv", (char *) 0);
             quit("cat", 3);

     default: close(fd[1]);                /* PARENT - Close write end first */
              dup2(fd[0], STDIN_FILENO);   /* Connect stdin to read end */
              close(fd[0]);                /* and close original descriptor */
              execlp("tr",     ", "'[a-z]'","'[A-Z]'", (char *) 0);
              quit("tr", 4);
  }
}
```

Fig. 24.11 **pipe2.c**

represented by a.out, but in the UNIX command line, the shell is the common ancestor of all processes in a pipeline (not strictly true).

24.12 SIGNAL HANDLING

We were introduced to signals in Chapter 9 where we used them to kill processes. But generally **speaking**, a signal is a mechanism used by the kernel to communicate the occurrence of an event to **a** process. The process often responds by terminating itself, but there are other actions the process can take—ignore it or invoke a user-defined function for instance. The action that a signal will take on receipt of a signal is known as its **disposition**.

A signal is represented by an integer and its symbolic name. For instance, SIGINT represents the signal number 2, and you'll recall having used signal names (without the SIG prefix) as arguments to the **kill** *(9.9.1)* and **trap** *(14.15)* commands. We must use signal names rather than their numbers in our programs because the same signal is sometimes represented by two different names on SVR4 and BSD systems. The name-number translation map is defined in <signal.h> (<bits/signum.h> in Linux).

The event that generates a signal can take place in the hardware, in the operating system or elsewhere. To be more specific, signals can be generated from the following sources:

- The keyboard   There are three signals that have their origin in the keyboard, and they all affect the current foreground job (or process group). *[Ctrl-c]* generates the SIGINT signal which terminates the process. *[Ctrl-\]* generates SIGQUIT which directs a process to produce a core dump (a file named core in the current directory). *[Ctrl-z]* , the suspend key, sends SIGTSTP to all processes of the foreground process group in a shell that supports job control.

- From the hardware   Signals can be generated on account of an arithmetic exception (SIGFPE), illegal instruction (SIGILL) or memory access violation (SIGSEGV). They all result in termination of the process.

- From a C program   The system call library offers some functions that generate signals. The alarm system call generates SIGALRM after the expiry of a specified time. The **abort** call generates SIGABRT which terminates a process. The **raise** and **kill** functions can generate any signal.

- From other sources   When a child dies, the kernel sends the SIGCHLD signal to the parent. When a background job tries to read from the terminal, the terminal driver generates the SIGTTIN signal and stops the process. You can also send many of these signals using the **kill** command, a technique with which you are familiar by now.

24.12.1 Signal Disposition

How a process responds to a signal depends on how things are set up in the program representing the process. This could be a little confusing to understand at first, so let's first simplify matters by noting that none of the programs considered in the previous chapter as well as the ones of this chapter (up to this point) has any code that handles signals. If any of them receives a signal, there are mainly three things that it can do with it:

- *Ignore the signal.*   The process continues running as if nothing has happened. This is true of the SIGCHLD signal that is sent to the parent when a child dies. The parent actually ignores the signal, but user-defined code in the parent often invokes **wait** or **waitpid** to pick up the exit status of the child.

- *Terminate the process.*   This is the default disposition of most signals. For instance, SIGINT and SIGHUP terminate the process. Both *[Ctrl-c]* and **kill -s INT** generate SIGINT. Signals generated by hardware errors also usually terminate a process.

- *Suspend (stop) the process.*   This happens when you press *[Ctrl-z]* from the keyboard (which generates SIGTSTP) or send the SIGSTOP signal from your program.

One of these would be the default disposition for a particular signal. However, you can override the default action and *catch* the signal using the **signal** system call. Contrary to what you would like to believe, this call doesn't generate a signal but only specifies its disposition. Using **signal**, you can do these things:

- *Ignore the signal.*   Even if the default disposition may not ignore a signal, you can still ignore it in your program.

- *Restore the default (in case the default was changed earlier).*

- *Invoke a signal handling function.* This function is automatically invoked when the process receives a signal for which the invocation of the signal handler is the current disposition.

In the remaining sections of this chapter, we'll discuss how the **signal** call is used to specify all three possible dispositions presented above. The last one—invoking a signal handling function—will be the focus of attention.

Note: Irrespective of the action you take, there are two signals that you can neither ignore nor catch by invoking a signal handler. They are SIGKILL and SIGSTOP. It's necessary for the superuser to have the powers to kill any process (with SIGKILL) or stop it (with SIGSTOP). If the superuser didn't have these powers, runaway processes could bring life to a standstill.

24.12.2 How the Kernel Handles Signals

Like a process, a signal has to go through a number of phases in its own life cycle. A signal is first *generated* and then *delivered* to a process. A signal is considered to be delivered when the signal disposition has occurred—even if the disposition is to ignore the signal. Until the signal is delivered, it is considered to be *pending*.

When a signal is sent to a process, the kernel sets a bit in the **pending signals mask** field of the process table *(24.1.2)* to indicate that a signal of a specific type has been received by the process. This field has a bit reserved for each type of signal. The process checks this field and the **signal disposition table** *(24.1.2)*. Accordingly the process decides to ignore, terminate or invoke a signal handler.

The kernel gets cautious when the process is in the midst of execution of a system call. If the process is sleeping on the completion of a disk I/O, the kernel allows the system call to complete before performing signal delivery. However, if the process is waiting to take input from the terminal, the kernel will abort the call and wake up the process. That is reasonable because waiting for terminal input could be a wait forever.

24.12.3 The System Calls

This chapter discusses the signal handling mechanism that has been in use ever since BSD modified the SVR4 implementation. These signals are considered *unreliable* for reasons that are discussed later. The adverse qualification need not deter you from using them; these calls work very well on most occasions. These are the calls that we are going to discuss:

- **signal** This call doesn't send a signal but specifies the disposition, i.e., how a process should behave when it receives a signal.
- **kill** This call behaves in identical manner to the **kill** command. Like "signal", the name "kill" is a misnomer too; it's **kill** that sends a signal, but it doesn't necessarily kill a process. A library function, **raise**, uses **kill** to send any signal to the current process.
- **alarm** The **alarm** call is used in the next example to set a timer that generates the SIGALRM signal after the timeout period. The library function **sleep** uses **alarm**.
- **pause** This is like the shell's **read** statement. It holds up program execution until a signal is received.

The important signals are listed along with their default disposition in Table 24.1. We'll now take up some of these calls in developing programs that handle signals. We begin with a detailed examination of the **signal** call.

Table 24.1 Signals and Default Disposition

Signal Name	*Significance*	*Default Action*
SIGINT	Terminal interrupt (*[Ctrl-c]*)	Terminate
SIGQUIT	Terminal quit (*[Ctrl\]*)	Terminate with core dump
SIGTSTP	Terminal stop (*[Ctrl-z]*)	Stop
SIGABRT	Abnormal termination (**abort** call)	Terminate
SIGCHLD	Change of child's status	Ignore
SIGCONT	Continue stopped child	Continue
SIGALRM	Timer (set by **alarm** call); sends signal after expiry of timeout period	Terminate
SIGHUP	Hangup signal	Terminate
SIGTERM	Software termination	Terminate
SIGPIPE	Write to pipe with read ends closed	Terminate
SIGILL	Illegal instruction	Terminate with core dump
SIGFPE	Arithmetic exception	Terminate with core dump
SIGSEGV	Segmentation violation; process attempts to access memory outside its own address space	Terminate with core dump
SIGKILL	Sure kill	Terminate; can't be caught
SIGSTOP	Process stop	Stop; can't be caught

24.13 signal: INSTALLING A SIGNAL HANDLER

A signal's disposition is set with the **signal** system call. The call *installs* a handler by specifying it as one of its two arguments. Installation makes the program aware of the action to take. **signal** returns the previous handler as shown by the syntax:

```
void (*signal(int sig, void (*func)(int)))(int);
```

This is how the POSIX prototype indicates that **signal** takes two arguments—the signal number (*sig*) and a pointer to a signal handling function (**func*). The handler takes one argument, the signal number (the second int), and returns nothing (the second void). **signal** itself returns a pointer to the previous handler, which takes one argument (the final int) and also returns nothing (the first void).

If you find this too much to accept, then consider this comforting syntax taken from the Linux man page:

```
sighandler_t signal(int signum, sighandler_t handler);
```

Strictly speaking, the second argument to **signal** need not always be a pointer to a signal handling function; it can also be one of these two values:

SIG_IGN   Ignore the signal.

SIG_DFL   Revert to the default disposition.

So a signal handler can specify either a handler or one of the two constants shown above as the disposition for the signal. Here are two typical signal installations:

```
signal(SIGALRM, alrm_handler);        Installs a handler
signal(SIGINT, SIG_IGN);              Changes default disposition to ignore
```

The first example installs the **alrm_handler** function which is invoked by the process when it receives SIGALRM. The second example sets the disposition to ignore on receipt of SIGINT. This means that the interrupt key can't terminate this program. You can make use of this protective feature to place this statement at the beginning of a critical section of code that you won't like to be interrupted. You can then revert to the default disposition by placing this statement after the critical code section:

```
signal(SIGINT, SIG_DFL);                   Restores the default disposition
```

Signal handlers are executed in the user mode. Let's now write our first signal handling program to catch the SIGALRM signal.

24.13.1 Catching the SIGALRM Signal

This program, **signal.c** (Fig. 24.15), uses the **alarm** call to set up a timer which times out in 5 seconds. The program prompts the user for a filename which is displayed if the user inputs it in 5 seconds. If the user is late in responding, SIGALRM is generated, which invokes a signal handler to set the default filename to foo.

We declare the prototype of the **alrm_handler** function before the **main** section. In the program body, we install this function with **signal**, checking for SIG_ERR, the only error that **signal** can return. The user is prompted for a filename, and the **alarm** timer sets off immediately thereafter. The filename is displayed if it is entered in the timeout period. But if the timeout occurs, SIGALRM is generated which leads to the execution of **alrm_handler**. This function prints the signal number and the default filename. It also explicitly terminates the program with **exit**.

Before we discuss what the second **signal** call is doing in this function, lets' execute this program twice—with and without a filename. We'll then verify the correctness of the signal number with the **kill -l** output:

```
$ a.out
Enter filename: signal.log
Filename: signal.log
$ a.out
Enter filename:                                   Nothing entered in 5 seconds
Signal 14 received, default filename: foo
$ kill -l | grep 14                               What is signal 14?
13) SIGPIPE     14) SIGALRM     15) SIGTERM     16) SIGUSR1
```

```
/* Program: signal.c -- Waits for 5 seconds for user input and then
                        generates SIGALRM that has a handler specified */
#include <stdio.h>
#include <unistd.h>
#include <signal.h>
#define BUFSIZE 100

void alrm_handler(int signo);                  /* Prototype declarations for */
void quit(char *message, int exit_status);  /* signal handler and quit */

char buf[BUFSIZE] = "foo\0";                   /* Global variable */
int main(void) {
    int n;
    if (signal(SIGALRM, alrm_handler) == SIG_ERR)   /* signal returns SIG_ERR */
        quit("sigalrm", 1);                          /* on error */

    fprintf(stderr, "Enter filename: ");
    alarm(5);                                  /* Sets alarm clock; will deliver */
    n = read(STDIN_FILENO, buf, BUFSIZE);   /* SIGALRM in 5 seconds */
    if (n > 1)                                 /* Will come here if user inputs */
        printf("Filename: %s\n", buf);         /* string within 5 seconds */
    exit(0);
}

void alrm_handler(int signo) {        /* Invoked with process receives SIGALRM */
    signal(SIGALRM, alrm_handler);    /* Resetting signal handler */
    fprintf(stderr, "\nSignal %d received, default filename: %s\n", signo, buf);
    exit(1);
}
```

Fig. 24.15 `signal.c`

24.13.2 Why signal is Unreliable

Why did we reinstall the signal handler in the same handling function? We need to move back in time a bit to discover that the original signals in System V were unreliable in that a signal's disposition was reset to the default *before* the handler was invoked. A second signal of the same type would then be subject to the default disposition. However, if we need the disposition to be persistent, we must reinstall the handler at the beginning of the handling function.

This approach works most of the time, but there's a finite probability of it leading to a **race condition.** In this situation, two or more events act on the same resource, and the sequence in which they are serviced determines the eventual outcome of the race. Here, if a second signal of the same type arrives *after* the disposition is reset to the default and *before* the handler is reinstalled, the default action will be taken. If the default action is to terminate the process, the handler won't be given a chance to reinstall itself.

Linux used BSD signals, and they are different; the signal disposition is not reset to the default. If you are running this program on Linux, you need not reinstall the handler. However, reinstallation is a safe thing to do because you are assured that the disposition is persistent regardless of the system the program is running on. However, all signals that are handled by **signal** are unreliable for other reasons also; a signal can get lost and can't be blocked.

Note: POSIX recommends the use of *reliable* system calls for which it provides the interface for a large number of them. In the POSIX system, it's **sigaction** and not **signal** that sets a signal's disposition. A POSIX signal can be *blocked,* and can be delivered only when it is *unblocked* (both with **sigprocmask**). We are constrained to drop discussions on the POSIX signal handling functions in this edition.

24.13.3 Catching Terminal-Generated Signals

Having seen how **signal** is used to handle SIGALRM that is generated in the program, and how the signal handler is reinstalled every time it is called, let's use these ideas in the program, **signal2.c** (Fig. 24.16), to develop two signal handlers for the SIGINT and SIGTSTP signals that are sent from the keyboard. We'll also ignore the SIGQUIT signal.

Using three **signal** calls, we set the disposition of three different signals. Since we are using unreliable signals, we reset the signal handlers every time we invoke them. Note the use of SIG_IGN in one **signal** call which sets the disposition to ignore for SIGQUIT. *[Ctrl-z]* generates SIGTSTP, but we catch it to display a message but without stopping the process. We also catch *[Ctrl-c]* (SIGINT), but to terminate it only when the key is pressed twice.

The **for** loop makes the **pause** system call run in a loop. **pause** simply suspends execution until it receives any signal, in which case it returns with the EINTR error. Let's now run this program by pressing all three key sequences in turn:

```
$ a.out
Press [Ctrl-z] first, then [Ctrl-c]
[Ctrl-\]                                  Signal ignored
[Ctrl-z]
Can't stop this program                   From tstp_handler
[Ctrl-c]
Press again                               From int_handler
[Ctrl-c]
Quitting: Interrupted system call         From int_handler
```

All three signal handlers can be seen at work here. So far, we have been handling signals; in the next section, we'll use **kill** to generate them.

24.14 killprocess.c: THE FINAL PROGRAM USING kill

Before we take up the final program featured in this chapter, we have a new system call to discuss— **kill**. Like its command counterpart, the **kill** system call sends a signal to one or more processes:

```
int kill(pid_t pid, int sig);
```

```
/* Program: signal2.c -- Handles SIGINT and SIGTSTP generated from terminal
                     Requires two [Ctrl-c]s to terminate */
#include <stdio.h>
#include <unistd.h>
#include <signal.h>

void quit(char *message, int exit_status) ;
void tstp_handler(int signo);                    /* Handler for [Ctrl-z] */
void int_handler(int signo);                     /* Handler for [Ctrl-c] */
int n, count = 0;

int main(void) {
    signal(SIGTSTP, tstp_handler);      /* Disposition for these two signals */
    signal(SIGINT, int_handler);        /* set to enter respective handlers */
    signal(SIGQUIT, SIG_IGN);           /* Disposition set to ignore */

    fprintf(stderr, "Press [Ctrl-z] first, then [Ctrl-c]\n");
    for (;;)
      pause();                          /* Will return on receipt of signal */
}

void tstp_handler(int signo) {
    signal(SIGTSTP, tstp_handler);              /* Not entirely reliable */
    fprintf(stderr, "Can't stop this program\n");  /* same signal can reset */
}                                               /* disposition to default */

void int_handler(int signo) {                   /* Will terminate program */
    signal(SIGINT, int_handler);                /* on second invocation */
    (++count == 1) ? printf("Press again\n") : quit("Quitting", 1);
}
```

Fig. 24.16 signal2.c

Generally, we obtain the PID of the child using **pid = fork()**, and then use, say, **kill(pid, SIGTERM)** to kill the child with SIGTERM. The *pid* in the syntax doesn't always represent a single PID; like in **waitpid** *(24.5.3)*, *pid* can take on four types of values with identical meaning. This means that you can send a signal to a process group also.

It's time for consolidation; so let's demonstrate the combined use of the fork-exec-wait and signal handling mechanisms. The program, **killprocess.c** (Fig. 24.17), runs a command that is input by the user and prints the exit status if the command completes in 5 seconds. If it doesn't, then the parent uses **kill** to send a SIGTERM signal to kill the child process.

This time we use a single signal handling function to handle both SIGCHLD and SIGALRM. The parent forks a child which then uses **execvp** to run a user-specified program supplied as one or more command line arguments. Note that this time the parent doesn't wait for the child's death after the fork. It starts a timer with **alarm(5)**, which on expiry issues the SIGALRM signal. The parent issues **pause**, which returns on receipt of any signal.

```
/* Program: killprocess.c -- Uses fork and exec to run a user-defined program
                            and kills it if it doesn't complete in 5 seconds.*/
#include <stdio.h>
#include <sys/types.h>
#include <sys/wait.h>
#include <signal.h>

pid_t pid;
int main(int argc, char **argv) {
    int i, status;
    void death_handler(int signo);          /* A common signal handler this time */

    signal(SIGCHLD, death_handler);    /* death_handler is invoked when a */
    signal(SIGALRM, death_handler);    /* child dies or an alarm is received */

    switch (pid = fork()) {
        case -1: printf("Fork error\n");
        case  0: execvp(argv[1], &argv[1]);    /* Execute command */
                 perror("exec");
                 break;
        default: alarm(5);      /* Will send SIGALRM after 5 seconds */
                 pause();       /* Will return when SIGCHLD signal is received */
                 printf("Parent dies\n");
    }
    exit(0);
}

void death_handler(int signo) {            This common handler picks up the */
    int status;                         /*  exit status for normal termination */
    signal(signo, death_handler);       /* and sends the SIGTERM signal if */
    switch (signo) {                    /* command doesn't complete in 5 seconds */
        case SIGCHLD: waitpid(-1, &status, );      /* Same as wait(&status); */
                      printf("Child dies; exit status: %d\n",
                                        WEXITSTATUS(status));
                      break;
        case SIGALRM: if (kill(pid, SIGTERM) == 0)
                         fprintf(stderr, "5 seconds over, child killed\n");
    }
}
```

Fig. 24.17   killprocess.c

One of two signals can wake up the parent here—either SIGCHLD or SIGALRM. In the signal handling function, we take into account two other possibilities; the child may or may not complete execution in 5 seconds. If it does, SIGCHLD is issued and **death_handler** invokes **waitpid** to pick up the exit status of the child. Otherwise, **death_handler** waits for SIGALRM and then kills the process with **SIGTERM**.

We'll run the program twice—once with a program that completes in 5 seconds and then with one that doesn't:

```
$ a.out date
Thu Apr  3 14:49:57 IST 2003
Child dies; exit status: 0
Parent dies
$ a.out find /home -name a.out -print
/home/sumit/personal/project8/a.out
/home/sumit/personal/books_code/glass_ables/12/a.out
/home/sumit/personal/books_code/stevens_c/ch08/a.out
    ...after 5 second time interval ......
5 seconds over, child killed
Parent dies
```

kill can be used to send a signal to the current process also. You need to use **getpid** to specify the PID here, but the **raise** library function does this work for us. **raise(SIGTERM)** is equivalent to **kill(getpid(), SIGTERM)**.

24.15 CONCLUSION

We covered some of the basic process internals in this chapter and the system calls that are used for process control. Space constraints don't permit inclusion of topics covering the advanced forms of IPC—like semaphores, message queues and shared memory. But the message is clear; there are a lot of places you can go from here. Pursuing IPC eventually leads us to the world of socket programming. You should also learn the fully reliable signal handling mechanism that is mandated by POSIX and offered by Solaris and Linux.

WRAP UP

A process runs in its own *virtual address space* comprising the text, data, stack and heap segments. The virtual addresses are translated into physical addresses at runtime by the *Memory Management Unit* (MMU).

A program has a *context*. Within a context, a process can run either in *user mode* or *kernel mode*, the latter being used when the kernel runs on the user's behalf while servicing a system call. The kernel performs a *context switch* to preempt one process to let another use the CPU.

The *process table* contains all control information related to a process. The table contains both the *pending signal mask* and the *signal disposition* for every signal that the process may receive.

The **fork** system call creates a process by replicating the existing address space. **fork** returns twice—zero in the child and its own PID in the parent. The child has a separate copy of the parent's environment, and hence changes made in it don't affect the parent.

The environment variables are available in the variable, *environ[]. A variable can be set with **setenv** or **putenv** and retrieved with **getenv**.

A process exits by invoking **exit** with an argument that represents the *exit status*. This number is retrieved by the parent with **wait** or **waitpid**. Unlike **wait**, **waitpid** can wait for a specific child to die and also need not block until the child dies.

If the parent dies before the child, the child turns into an *orphan*, which is immediately adopted by **init**. If the parent is alive but doesn't invoke **wait**, the child is transformed to a *zombie*. A zombie is a dead process whose address space has been freed but not the entry in the process table.

The exec family of functions replaces the complete address space of the current process with that of a new program. **execl** and **execlp** work with a fixed list of arguments; the latter uses PATH to locate the program. **execv** and **execvp** work in a similar manner, but with a variable list. Shell and **perl** scripts can be run by **execlp** and **execvp**. A successful exec doesn't return.

dup replicates a file descriptor and returns the lowest unallocated value. **dup2** allows us to choose the descriptor we want by closing it if it is already open. In either case, original and copy both share the same file table. POSIX recommends the use of **fcntl**.

pipe creates a buffered object that returns two file descriptors. Data written to one descriptor can be read back from the other. To create a pipeline of two commands, first create a pipe before a **fork**, then use **dup2** to replicate the pipe's descriptors in both parent and child so as to connect standard input and standard output to the two ends of the pipe. Finally, close all unneeded descriptors.

A *signal* is a mechanism by which a process is made aware of the occurrence of an event. When a process receives a signal, it may allow the default *disposition* to occur, ignore the signal or invoke a *signal handler*. Every signal handler is *installed* with the **signal** call. The signals SIGKILL and SIGSTOP can't be caught. The **kill** system call can send any signal to a process.

Test Your Understanding

24.1 If two users execute the same program, are the memory requirements doubled?

24.2 Why do we say that the address space of a process is *virtual*?

24.3 What is the significance of the stack and heap segments in the address space of a process? Why does the kernel need a separate stack for each process?

24.4 What is *kernel mode*? Does a separate process run in this mode?

24.5 When does a process voluntarily relinquish control of the CPU?

24.6 Name the system calls discussed in this chapter that return one or more file descriptors.

24.7 Write a program that forks twice. Display the PIDs and PPIDs of all three processes.

24.8 Redirect the output of **fork.c** (Fig. 24.3) to a file and explain the change in behavior.

24.9 A file may have more than one vnode table in memory. True or False?

24.10 The completion of process execution doesn't mean that the process is dead. True or false?

24.11 Write a program that accepts two small numbers (< 50) as arguments and then sums the two in a child process. The sum should be returned by the child to the parent as its exit status and the parent should print the sum.

24.12 Write a shell script containing only one statement: **exit 123456**. Now run the script and issue **echo $?** from the shell. Explain why the value provided in the script differs with $?.

24.13 Write a program that uses **write** to output the message hello dolly to the standard error. Manipulate file descriptors in such a way that makes it possible to save the error message using **a.out > foo** and not with **a.out 2>foo**.

24.14 Why are the attributes of an open file held in two tables rather than one?

24.15 In what ways can a process behave when it receives a signal? What is special about the SIGSTOP and SIGKILL signals?

24.16 Use the **kill** command to find the number of signals available on your system and then write a program that ignores all of them. Is it possible to do so?

Flex Your Brain

24.1 What is *context switching*?

24.2 What is the role of the Memory Management Unit in process switching. Why can't one process corrupt the address space of another?

24.3 Write a program that displays all environment variables.

24.4 Modify the program in 24.11 (Test Your Understanding) so that process A creates B and B creates C. The summation should be performed in C and the result returned to B as the exit status. B should double the summed value and return the product to A as the exit status. Will the program work with large numbers?

24.5 Name three advantages **waitpid** has over **wait**. Why can't a background process be terminated with the interrupt key?

24.6 Explain the difference in treatment meted out by the kernel to zombies and orphans.

24.7 Write a program that prompts for a command line to be executed and then uses an exec function to run it. The command line can contain shell metacharacters including redirection and piping symbols. (HINT: Take advantage of the shell's -c option.)

24.8 Write a program that runs the **ls -lids** command, but specifies a separate environment for the exec'd process. The new environment should have only the HOME and PATH variables. Prove that the MAIL and TERM variables are not available in the new process.

24.9 What are the structural changes that take place in memory when (i) a file is opened twice, (ii) its descriptor is replicated.

24.10 Does each entry in the file descriptor table have a separate file table associated with it?

24.11 Look up the man page for any shell and understand the significance of the -c option. Next, write a program that prompts for a command, which is executed with **exec**, and **sh -c**. Try using the program with both external and internal (shell) commands. Does this program behave properly even when using wild-cards and pipes?

24.12 Invoke the command **vi foo &**, and explain why you can't input text to the editor.

Advanced System Administration

In this revisit to the system administrator's domain, we take a closer look at the ways and means a UNIX system should be administered. The routine duties of an administrator, like monitoring the disk space and taking backups, have already been discussed in Chapter 15. But administration also involves handling problems, and system problems can be quite grave and unexpected. The file system might crash or a user may delete a supposedly secure file. The system administrator must have thorough knowledge of practically every system component.

The administrator has to often devise scripts for automating some operations that need to be carried out regularly. He must be able to configure the system's initialization scripts. All of these functions are system-dependent, and it's no wonder that POSIX doesn't address administrative issues. Since you could have easier access to a Linux machine for testing these functions, many examples in this chapter assume a Linux system.

WHAT YOU WILL LEARN

- Enforce *password aging* with **passwd** so that passwords are changed regularly.
- Restrict a user's activities with the *restricted shell*.
- The concept of a *partition* and *file system*, and the functions of its four components.
- Create a partition and file system on a Linux machine with **fdisk** and **mkfs**.
- *Mount* and *unmount* file systems with **mount** and **umount**, and examine their configuration file, /etc/fstab.
- Check and repair file systems with **fsck**.
- The significance of **init** *run levels*, and how they control startup and shutdown.
- How **init** uses /etc/inittab and *rc* scripts to start and stop the system's daemons.
- Consider the other options of **find** that aid in the backup process.

TOPICS OF SPECIAL INTEREST

- The different types of file systems that you'll find on UNIX machines.
- A detailed examination of the behavior of **init** and the organization of the *rc* files and scripts responsible for starting and stopping services.
- How the **xargs-find** combination can often speed up execution time.

25.1 MAINTAINING SECURITY

The administrator must exercise diligence in enabling access to some of the system's services. At times, he has to prevent some users from using a specific service. Modern times have seen several instances of hackers who manage to get into a system mainly because of the negligence of the administrator.

25.1.1 Password Aging

Systems having /etc/shadow use an elaborate scheme for administering the change of password. It is called **password aging** which should be used by the administrator to force users to change their passwords after a predetermined time. A line in this file contains several fields containing the attributes of the user's password. Most of these fields can be updated by using the **passwd** command with suitable options.

The -n option sets its argument equal to the minimum number of days for which a password has to be retained. The -x option sets the maximum limit. Here are some examples of their usage for the user oracle:

```
passwd -n 12 oracle          Minimum 12 weeks before password can be changed
passwd -x 24 oracle          Maximum 24 weeks before password must be changed
```

In the interests of security, it may be sometimes necessary for you to lock a user account. You can do that with **passwd**'s -l (lock) option. The -u option restores the account. You can also force a user to change her password at the next login with the -f option.

25.1.2 Restricted Shell

To restrict the activities of a user, you should set up the user account with a special restricted shell. This shell once had the name **rsh**, but today **rsh** represents the command with which you remotely run a program. The better shells today have restricted versions—**rbash** and **rksh**. Either of them has to be specified in the last field of /etc/passwd. A user with a restricted shell can't do any of the following things:

- Use the **cd** command, which means that she can't change directories.
- Redefine the PATH, which makes it impossible to access commands placed in other directories.
- Redefine the SHELL so the user can't change to a nonrestricted shell.
- Use a pathname containing a /, which means a command can't be executed with either a relative or an absolute pathname.
- Use the > and >> operators to create or append to files.

In this environment, a user can only execute programs in the directories specified in a new unchangeable PATH. This generally is set to only the current directory. If the user needs to run some of the system commands in /bin and /usr/bin, place links of those commands in the user's restricted directory.

Note: If you don't have a separate restricted shell on your system, use the standard shells with the -r option to enforce that behavior (**sh -r**, **bash -r** or **ksh -r**). Since you can't place these entries in /etc/passwd, run a normal shell there and use **exec** to execute them from the startup file. Make sure to set the PATH to just one directory.

25.1.3 Allowing a User to Shut Down Only

Shutting down the system requires root privilege, and the administrator is not expected to divulge the root password to anyone. There's still a way of allowing a user to shut down the system without allowing her direct access to the shell. The trick is to first create an ordinary user account (say, shut) with **useradd**:

```
useradd -u 210 -g group -s /bin/sh -d /home/shut -m shut
```

Next, you have to confer root status on this user by changing the UID in /etc/passwd from 210 to 0, the one used by root. This can't be done directly by **useradd** because it won't permit reuse of the root UID, and must be done manually by editing /etc/passwd. The **shutdown** command must be placed in the user's .profile (preferably preceded by **exec**) so she can't do anything else.

25.2 PARTITIONS AND FILE SYSTEMS

The system administrator must understand the file system internals well because it is his job to maintain it in a healthy and correct state. He must display his efficiency in fixing inconsistencies that tend to crop up from time to time and ensure that loss of data is minimum. When the system refuses to boot, he must not panic and reinstall the entire system. In this section and the following ones, we discuss the tools UNIX provides for maintaining file systems.

Like other operating systems, UNIX requires a formatted hard disk. Today, disks (both IDE and SCSI) come preformatted, so this is one thing you don't have to bother about. After the disk has been formatted, the next step is to divide it into **partitions**. Each partition can be considered to be a logically independent disk that is accessed by its own device file. Dividing a disk into a number of partitions has a number of distinct advantages:

- Separate partitions prevent potential encroachment conflicts that may arise between the various data areas.
- If there's corruption in one area, other areas are effectively shielded from this evil influence.
- If the system has an adequate number of partitions, each partition can be backed up separately onto a single volume of tape.

After the disk has been partitioned, it's still not ready for use. A **file system** *(11.1)* has to be created on each partition. Unlike a partition, a file system is organized in the form of a directory structure with its own root. But it also has space set aside (outside the directory structure) for maintaining information (like inodes) on the files it stores. Every file system has these four components:

- The *boot block*—This block contains a small boot program and the partition table.
- The *superblock*—It contains global information about the file system. Additionally, it also

maintains a free list of inodes and data blocks that can be immediately allocated by the kernel when creating a file.

- The *inode blocks*—This region contains the inode for every file of the file system.
- The *data blocks*—All data and programs created by users reside in this area.

The operating system usually resides on multiple file systems, and every file system has these four components. At the time of booting, these file systems combine (using a technique known as *mounting*) and appear to the user as a single file system. In the forthcoming sections, we'll use the `fdisk` command to create partitions, `mkfs` to create file systems and the `mount` and `umount` commands to mount and unmount file systems. Before we do that, let's briefly discuss the significance of the four file system components.

Note: The words *partition* and *file system* are often used synonymously, especially when a partition contains a single file system. However, this is not always the case. Some systems like Solaris break up a partition into *slices*, with a file system in each slice. Linux allows the creation of an *extended* partition, with multiple *logical* partitions in each extended partition. Each logical partition then contains a file system. In this way, it's possible to have multiple file systems in a single partition.

25.2.1 The Boot Block

The first block of a file system is known as the **boot block**, containing a small bootstrap program—often referred to as the **Master Boot Record (MBR)**. The program is loaded into memory when the system is booted (hence the name). It may, in turn, load another program from the disk, but eventually it loads the kernel into memory. However, the bootstrapping program is read in from the boot block of only one file system (the main one, called the *root* file system). For other file systems, this block is simply kept blank.

25.2.2 The Superblock

The boot block is followed by the **superblock**, the "balance sheet" of every UNIX file system. It contains global file information about disk usage and availability of data blocks and inodes. Its information should, therefore, be correct for healthy operation of the system. This is mainly what it contains:

- The size of the file system.
- The block size used by the file system.
- The number of free data blocks available and a partial list of immediately allocable free data blocks.
- Number of free inodes available and a partial list of immediately usable inodes.
- Last time of updating.
- The state of the file system (whether "clean" or "dirty").

The kernel maintains a copy of the superblock in memory. It also periodically updates the disk copy with the contents of the memory copy. Because the two copies are not in *sync* (one more recent than the other), the integrity of the file system is compromised when the power to the machine is improperly cut off. The **sync** command (discussed later) writes the memory copy to disk and ensures that the disk copy is never newer than the memory copy. When booting, the system checks for a possible mismatch between the two, and accordingly brands the file system "dirty" or "clean".

UNIX refuses to boot if the superblock is corrupt. To overcome this problem, many systems (like Solaris and Linux) have multiple superblocks written on different areas of the disk. If one superblock is corrupt, the system can be directed to use another.

Note: The kernel always maintains a copy of the superblock in memory. The in-memory copy actually contains the latest and correct file system status rather than its disk copy.

25.2.3 Inode Blocks

The **inode blocks** contain all inodes. When a file is created, an inode is allocated here. Even though the inode contains all file attributes (except its name), it doesn't store the inode number. Since the inodes are laid out sequentially, the kernel uses simple arithmetic to identify the inode by using the inode number as the index in this "array" of inodes, i.e. by its position in this list. The **ls** command looks up a directory to know the inode number of a file, and then reads the inode to obtain the file's attributes.

Apart from file attributes, the inode contains an array of 13 to 15 pointers to disk block addresses. Most of them are actual addresses of disk blocks containing the file's data. The other pointers hold addresses of disk blocks that contain the *addresses* of other data-bearing disk blocks. We'll not elaborate on this point in this edition, but be assured that this array of 13 to 15 pointers ultimately keep track of *every* disk block used by a file. The details of this scheme can be found in the Web site.

When a file is opened, the kernel copies its inode from disk to memory. Like for the superblock, the kernel works with the memory copy which is maintained in a structure known as *vnode*. A perpetually running process (named **update** or **bdflush**) uses **sync** periodically to write this memory copy to disk.

25.2.4 Data Blocks

All file data are stored in the data blocks, which occupy most of the file system. Most UNIX tools like **find**, **df** and **du** assume a block size of 512 bytes (1024 in Linux). **find** interprets the argument used with -size as the number of 512-byte blocks. **df** and **du** report on disk usage in 512-byte blocks. We often call this the **physical block size**, being the size of a disk sector—the smallest addressable disk area.

The physical block is useful for reporting purposes only. However, disk allocation takes place using a different block size—often 1024 bytes. We call this the **logical block size**, and it is set at the time of installation of the system. This block size also determines the largest file size that the system can accommodate. However using an entire block for read/write operations means that even if you have to write three bytes of data into a 1024-byte disk block, 1021 bytes will simply be wasted. A pity, but that is the price one has to pay for having a well-organized and consistent file system.

There's yet another block size, the one *actually* used for doing I/O. As we have discussed before *(15.7.1)*, all disk I/O takes place through a pool of buffers maintained by the kernel, and a command like **cat** never accesses the disk directly. Even though your logical block size could be 1024 bytes, the size of each kernel buffer could be 8192 bytes on your system. The kernel will then read in 8192 bytes from disk. It will also write that many bytes in a single I/O operation. This is the size we use in our C programs for the buffer used by **read** and **write** *(23.4)*. The st_blksize member of the stat structure *(23.11)* also points to this figure.

Even though disk blocks are numbered consecutively, you'll often find a file's data are arranged in noncontiguous blocks. When a file expands, the kernel may not find its adjacent blocks free. The remaining data then have to be written to the next free block, wherever it may be. This, no doubt, leads to disk **fragmentation**, and consequently increases the overheads of read/write operations. However, this fragmentation also allows files to be enlarged or reduced at will, and helps keep wastage to a minimum.

25.3 THE STANDARD FILE SYSTEMS AND THEIR TYPES

The preceding discussions related to a single file system. In real life, modern UNIX systems are invariably set up with multiple file systems, each meant for a specific purpose. If you have multiple disks, every such disk must have at least one file system on it. However, a single file system, until recently, could not span multiple disks. In general, most UNIX systems will always have these file systems:

- The **root file system**   This file system contains the bare-bones UNIX—the root directory, the /bin, /etc, /dev and /lib directories, i.e., all tools and utilities that are just sufficient to keep the system going. When the system is booted in single-user mode, this is the only file system available to the system administrator.

- The **boot file system**   This contains the UNIX kernel and other boot programs.

- The **swap file system**   When the system memory is heavily loaded, the kernel moves processes out of memory and to this file system. When these swapped processes are ready to run, they are loaded back to memory. Users can't access this file system directly.

Apart from these essential file systems, your computer would in all probability have additional ones. System files should be kept separate from data files created by users, and hence a separate file system is usually made for them. You might have a /home or /export/home file system to house all users. You could also have /usr, /var and /tmp as separate file systems.

Initially, there were only two types of file systems—the ones from AT&T and Berkeley. Over time, many more file system types have made their entry into the UNIX system. You need to know the following file systems which you'll encounter often:

- **s5**   Before SVR4, this was the only file system used by System V, but today it is offered by SVR4 by this name for backward compatibility only. This file system has a single superblock. It also can't handle filenames longer than 14 characters.

- **ufs**   This is how the Berkeley Fast File System is known to SVR4 and adopted by most UNIX systems. Performance of this file system is considerably better than s5. It uses multiple superblocks with each cylinder group storing a superblock. Unlike s5, ufs supports 255-character filenames, symbolic links and disk quotas.

- **ext2** or **ext3**   This is the standard file system on Linux. Like ufs, it uses multiple superblocks and symbolic links.

- **iso9660** or **hsfs**   This is the standard file system used by CD-ROMs. It features DOS-style 8+3 filenames, but since UNIX uses longer filenames, hsfs also provides Rock Ridge extensions to accommodate them.

- **msdos** or **pcfs**   Most UNIX systems also support DOS file systems. You can create this file system on a floppy diskette and transfer files to it for use on a Windows system. Some systems like Linux can also directly access a DOS file system on the hard disk.

- **proc** or **procfs**   This can be considered a pseudo-file system maintained in memory. It stores data of each running process and appears to contain files but actually contains none. Users can obtain most process information including their PIDs directly from here.

Commands handling file systems (like **mkfs** and **mount**) use an option to describe the file system, the reason why you should know the file system you are using.

25.4 `fdisk`: CREATING PARTITIONS

UNIX fragmentation becomes quite evident when it comes to creating partitions. Different versions of UNIX use different tools for partitioning a disk. Though the principles are broadly similar, there are significant differences in details. The system administrator probably won't allow you to create or delete partitions on his system, so we'll create them on a Linux system using the **fdisk** command.

Let's use **fdisk** to create a partition on the first IDE hard disk to hold the Oracle RDBMS software. Modern versions of Linux require the device name of the hard disk as argument:

```
fdisk /dev/hda
```

To print the partition table, use the **p** command:

```
Disk /dev/hda: 255 heads, 63 sectors, 784 cylinders
Units = cylinders of 16065 * 512 bytes
   Device Boot    Start      End    Blocks   Id  System
/dev/hda1   *         1      217   1743021    5  Extended
/dev/hda2           218      478   2096482+   7  HPFS/NTFS
/dev/hda4           620      784   1325362+  83  Linux native
/dev/hda5             1        5     40099+  82  Linux swap
/dev/hda6             6      217   1702858   83  Linux native
```

This 6.5 GB disk contains 784 cylinders of 160652 X 512 bytes each, and containing a number of partitions. Partitions in Linux behave more like their DOS counterparts. As stated before, you can create a *primary* partition with one file system in it, or an *extended* partition containing multiple *logical* partitions.

Linux has a simple scheme for naming partition devices. The first IDE hard disk as a whole is represented by /dev/hda, while individual partitions in this disk take on names hda1, hda2, and so forth. hda2 here is a primary partition housing an NTFS file system used by Windows; this disk contains another operating system also. The second hard disk will have the name /dev/hdb with similar numeric extensions.

Observe that partition 1 (hda1) uses the same cylinders as partitions 5 (hda5) and 6 (hda5). hda1 is an extended partition containing a logical partition hda6 and the swap partition hda5. There's another Linux system on partition 4 (hda4). The active partition is indicated by an * in the second column. We also have cylinders between 479 and 619 unused, so we can use that space to create a partition. This will be partition 3.

The **m** command of **fdisk** shows you all its internal commands of which the following subset should serve our purpose:

```
Command (m for help): m
Command action    Condensed list
   a   toggle a bootable flag
   d   delete a partition
   l   list known partition types
   m   print this menu
   n   add a new partition
   p   print the partition table
   q   quit without saving changes
   w   write table to disk and exit
```

To create a partition, we have to use the **n** command, supply the partition number and the starting and ending cylinder numbers:

```
Command (m for help): n                          Adding a partition
Command action
   l   logical (5 or over)                        Note this
   p   primary partition (1-4)
p                                                 Opting for primary partition
Partition number (1-4): 3
First cylinder (479-784, default 479): 479        Choosing default
Last cylinder or +size or +sizeM or +sizeK (479-619, default 619): 619
```

Linux is smart enough to suggest default cylinder values, but we preferred to enter the values explicitly. Now use **p** again to view the new partition:

```
Device     Boot   Start      End    Blocks   Id  System
/dev/hda1    *        1      217   1743021    5  Extended
/dev/hda2           218      478   2096482+   7  HPFS/NTFS
/dev/hda3           479      619   1132582+  83  Linux native      New partition
/dev/hda4           620      784   1325362+  83  Linux native
/dev/hda5             1        5     40099+  82  Linux swap
/dev/hda6             6      217   1702858   83  Linux native
```

We now have a new partition, hda3, occupying over 1 GB of space. Now that the partition table has been modified, we have to write it to the boot block with the **w** command. You may be prompted to reboot the system which will make the new file system available for use.

Note: To have multiple file systems on one Linux partition, you must first have an extended partition and then create multiple logical partitions on this extended partition.

25.5 `mkfs`: CREATING A FILE SYSTEM

Now that we have created a partition, we need to create a file system on this partition to make it usable. Though frontend tools are available today, they generally operate through **mkfs**—the universal file system creation tool. Sticking to Linux and the partition that we created recently, we'll use **mkfs** with the -t option to specify the type of file system:

```
# mkfs -t ext2 /dev/hda3
mke2fs 1.14, 9-Jan-1999 for EXT2 FS 0.5b, 95/08/09
Linux ext2 filesystem format
Filesystem label=
283560 inodes, 1132582 blocks
56629 blocks (5.00%) reserved for the super user
First data block=1
Block size=1024 (log=0)
Fragment size=1024 (log=0)
139 block groups
8192 blocks per group, 8192 fragments per group
2040 inodes per group
Superblock backups stored on blocks:
        8193, 16385, 24577, 32769, 40961, 49153, 57345, 65537, 73729, 81921,
        90113, 98305, 106497, 114689, 122881, 131073, 139265, 147457, 155649,
    ..... Condensed list .....
Writing inode tables: done
Writing superblocks and filesystem accounting information: done
```

This creates an ext2 file system—the standard Linux file system that uses a block size of 1024 bytes. Note the multiple superblocks that are uniformly (8192 blocks) spaced apart. Since we didn't specify the number of blocks, **mkfs** used default values for the number of inodes and data blocks. The increase of one can only be achieved at the expense of the other. Generally, you won't need to disturb the default values unless you are handling a huge number of very small files.

Tip: From the output of the **mkfs** command you should keep a record of the block addresses that contain copies of the superblock. If the main superblock gets corrupt, then you would need to use **fsck** with an alternate superblock number.

25.6 MOUNTING AND UNMOUNTING FILE SYSTEMS

A file system is a self-contained entity with its own tree structure and root directory. It just sits there in a standalone mode; the main file system doesn't even know of its existence. These file systems unite to become a *single* file system at the time of booting. The root file system then becomes the *main* file system, and its root directory is also the directory of the unified file system. This happens by a process known as **mounting**, when all secondary file systems mount (attach) themselves to the main file system at different points.

The UNIX **mount** and **umount** commands are used for mounting and unmounting file systems. The point at which mounting takes place is called the **mount point**. This is usually an empty directory. After mounting you see a single file system instead of two separate ones. You can then copy and move files between the two file systems.

25.6.1 mount: Mounting File Systems

The **mount** command is used to mount file systems. When mounting a new file system, it takes two arguments—the device name of the file system and the mount point. Before mounting a file system, an empty directory (say, /oracle) must first be made available in the main file system. The root directory of the new file system has to be mounted on this directory.

mount uses an option to specify the type of file system. This option varies across UNIX flavors. This is how we use **mount** to mount a file system on the /oracle directory on Solaris and Linux systems:

```
mount -F ufs /dev/dsk/c0t3d0s5 /oracle          Solaris
mount -t ext2 /dev/hda3 /oracle                 Linux
```

After the device is mounted, the root directory of the file system created by **mkfs** loses its separate identity. It now becomes the directory /oracle and is made to appear as if it's part of the main file system. The user now sees a single file system in front of her, quite oblivious of the possibility that a file moved from /oracle to /home may have actually traversed two hard disks!

Even though **mount** here used the device name and mount point as its arguments, we'll soon learn to set things up in a way that allows **mount** to be used with one argument. The mount point (/oracle) is normally an empty directory, but if it is not, then its files can't be seen if a file system is mounted on this mount point. The files are seen again when the file system is unmounted.

25.6.2 umount: Unmounting File Systems

Unmounting is achieved with the **umount** command (note the spelling!), which requires either the file system name or mount point as argument. The file system that we just created and mounted can be unmounted by using any of these commands:

```
umount /oracle                      Specify either mount point or
umount /dev/hda3                     device name—here a Linux device
umount /dev/dsk/c0t3d0s5            ... and a Solaris device here
```

Unmounting a file system is sometimes not possible. Just as you can't remove a directory unless you are placed in a directory above it, you can't unmount a file system unless you are placed above it. If you try to do that, this is what you'll see:

```
# pwd
/oracle
# umount /dev/hda3
umount: /oracle: device is busy
```

Now move out of the mount point (/oracle) and repeat the **umount** command; it should work now.

25.6.3 /etc/fstab: Configuring mount

Observe the **df** command output shown in Section 15.6.1, and you'll find that it shows the free space for every file system separately. These file systems have to be mounted for **df** to be able to report on them, and this mounting takes place during system startup. They are also unmounted when the system is shut down. The system's initialization scripts run the **mount** and **umount** commands with the -a (all) option to mount all file systems that are listed in **mount**'s configuration file.

This file is generally /etc/fstab (file system table), but Solaris uses the SVR4-styled /etc/vfstab having a different format. There are some minor differences in options too. We'll consider a few lines of /etc/fstab on an old Linux system:

```
# Mount device   Mount Point    File System Type    mount Options
/dev/hda5        swap           swap                defaults         0   0
/dev/hda6        /              ext2                defaults         1   1
/dev/hda2        /dosc          vfat                defaults         0   0
/dev/hda3        /oracle        ext2                defaults         1   2
/dev/hdc         /mnt/cdrom     iso9660             ro,noauto,user   0   0
/dev/fd0         /floppy        auto                noauto,user      0   0
none             /proc          proc                defaults         0   0
```

When you use **mount -a**, all file systems listed in this file are mounted sequentially (unless specified otherwise). At system startup, the same command is executed, so you always find mounted file systems available on your machine. The shutdown sequence runs **umount -a**.

Each line in /etc/fstab provides the mounting specifications for a single file system. The list includes the floppy drive and CD-ROM too. The first two columns show both the arguments used by **mount**—the device name and mount point. Once you have placed an entry for a file system in this file, you can then use **mount** with simply one argument:

```
mount /dev/hda3                 Both these commands
mount /oracle                   will now work
```

Let's briefly describe the other entries in fstab. The noauto option implies that the file system is mounted manually and not with **mount -a**. The user option implies that you can issue the command as an ordinary user. A 1 in the fifth field indicates that the file system has to be backed up (dumped) with the **dump** command.

mount, when used by itself, lists all mounted file systems. This output is seen on a Solaris system:

```
# mount
/ on /dev/dsk/c0t0d0s0 read/write/setuid/largefiles on Thu Apr 20 10:00:10 2000
/proc on /proc read/write/setuid on Thu Apr 20 10:00:10 2000
/dev/fd on fd read/write/setuid on Thu Apr 20 10:00:10 2000
/oracle on /dev/dsk/c0t0d0s3 setuid/read/write/largefiles on Thu Apr 20 10:00:15
   2000
/u01 on /dev/dsk/c1t3d0s1 setuid/read/write/largefiles on Thu Apr 20 10:00:15 20
00
/u02 on /dev/dsk/c1t3d0s3 setuid/read/write/largefiles on Thu Apr 20 10:00:15 20
00
/u03 on /dev/dsk/c1t3d0s4 setuid/read/write/largefiles on Thu Apr 20 10:00:15 20
00
```

25.6.4 mount Options

The third column in /etc/fstab shows the type of file system that **mount** needs to know. When mounting file systems not listed in this file, **mount** works with a default file system type (ufs in Solaris and ext2 in Linux), but if the file system you are mounting is of a different type, you need to use an option (-F in Solaris and -t in Linux):

```
mount -F hsfs -r /dev/dsk/c0t6d0s0 /cdrom       CD-ROM — Solaris
mount -F pcfs /dev/diskette /floppy             DOS diskette — Solaris
mount -t iso9660 /dev/cdrom /mnt/cdrom          CD-ROM — Linux
mount -t vfat /dev/hda1 /windows                Windows partition — Linux
mount -t msdos /dev/fd0 /floppy                 DOS diskette — Linux
```

mount can be run with a number of special options which themselves are preceded by the -o option. Many of these options are file system-specific. These options are grouped together with the comma as delimiter. Although they are used here with Linux device names, most of the options are universally applicable:

```
mount -o ro /dev/sdb3 /usr/local               Read only
mount -o exec /dev/cdrom /mnt/cdrom            Allows binary execution
mount -o rw,remount /dev/hda3 /home            Remounts in read-write mode
```

The first one mounts a file system in read-only mode; **mount** has a synonym for it though—the -r option. The second one lets you run executable files directly from the CD-ROM itself (exec). If you have mounted a file system as read-only, then to remount it as read-write, you don't need to unmount it first. Just use the rw and remount options together.

25.7 fsck: FILE SYSTEM CHECKING

The built-in UNIX feature of delaying the updating of the disk superblock and the inode blocks by their memory copies *(25.2.2)* leaves scope for file system inconsistency. If the power goes off before the superblock is written to disk, the file system loses its integrity. There are many discrepancies that could lead to file system corruption, and the most common ones are listed below:

- Two or more inodes claiming the same disk block.
- A block marked as free but not listed in the superblock.
- A used block marked as free.
- An inode neither marked free nor in use, or having a bad block number that is out of range.
- Mismatch between the file size specified in the inode and the number of data blocks specified in the address array.
- A corrupt superblock containing erroneous summary data.
- A file not having at least one directory entry or having an invalid file type specified in the inode.

The **fsck** (file system consistency check) command is used to check and repair a damaged file system. It's generally run when a file system fails to mount. On many systems including Solaris, file systems are marked as "dirty" or "clean." **fsck** then checks only the dirty file systems during the next startup. The command can also be used with the name of the file system as argument:

```
# fsck /dev/rdsk/c0t3d0s5
** /dev/rdsk/c0t3d0s5
** Phase 1 - Check Blocks and Sizes
** Phase 2 - Check Pathnames
** Phase 3 - Check Connectivity
** Phase 4 - Check Reference Counts
```

fsck conducts a check in five phases, and the output above is obtained when the file system is consistent. However, when it is corrupt, messages and questions are seen on the system console, which you have to answer correctly. This is what **fsck** does in each phase:

- *Phase 1* Validates the inodes for correctness of format and the block numbers for bad and duplicate blocks. **fsck** declares a block BAD if the block number is out of range and DUP if it is claimed by another inode.

- *Phase 2* Checks all directory entries, starting from root, for OUT OF RANGE inode numbers detected in Phase 1. **fsck** corrects the errors either by removing the entire directory or the file.

- *Phase 3* Looks for unreferenced directories and stores their files in /lost+found for later examination. The files here are named after their inode numbers. You must make sure this directory is always available on every file system because **fsck** won't create it on its own.

- *Phase 4* Checks the link count as stored in the inode with the directory entries, and prompts for the file's removal or reconnection (to the /lost+found directory), depending on the extent of damage caused. **fsck** then compares the free inode count it computes with the figure stored in the superblock.

- *Phase 5* Finally, **fsck**'s free-block count is compared with the figure maintained in the superblock. A salvage operation may be carried out with the user's approval, which will replace the erroneous free block list with a newly computed one.

When used without options, **fsck** prompts you before repairing any damage that it has detected. It's generally safe to answer every question with a y. **fsck -y** (-a in Linux) assumes that all answers are in the affirmative, and proceeds without waiting for a response.

If the superblock is corrupt beyond repair, then **fsck** must be used with the -b option (-o b=*n* in Solaris, where *n* is the block number) to specify an alternate superblock number. This list is displayed by **mkfs** when initializing the file system.

The administrator should always perform the **fsck** check with the file systems in unmounted condition. Since the root file system can't be unmounted, the check on this file system should be made in single-user mode. Occasionally, the file system is so corrupt that rectification simply becomes impossible, and reinstallation of the system remains the only alternative.

Tip: fsck often outputs the inode numbers of files which it considers suspect in integrity. You should note down these numbers for further investigation. You should also have a look in the /lost+found directory if you find a file missing after a system crash.

25.8 SYSTEM STARTUP AND init

Normally, there are no problems with either the startup or shutdown procedure. Both are run by automated shell scripts which are changed infrequently. Yet, the administrator needs to know the exact sequence of steps that the system follows during the two events. Things do go wrong, especially during startup, and he must be able to fix them. For that, he needs to have detailed knowledge of the system process cycle, and the role played by the initialization scripts in /etc.

There are several processes which are initiated at system startup. The kernel is loaded into memory, and it then starts spawning further processes. The most important of these is **/sbin/init** having PID 1, which is responsible for the birth of all subsequent processes. You must know the behavioral pattern of **init** for two vital reasons:

- It controls the system **run levels** (states), and decides which processes to run for each run level. Most of these processes are daemons *(9.3)*, and they keep running all the time.
- It spawns a **getty** process at every terminal so users can log in.

Recall the output of the **ps -e** command *(9.3)* which showed many of these processes. **lpsched** (**lpd** in Linux) monitors the line printer spooler for jobs that have been queued for printing. **inetd** is the master Internet daemon which spawns further daemons as and when required. Most daemons have **init** as their parent.

25.8.1 init Run Levels

As just mentioned, **init** controls the run level of a UNIX system. Each run level is normally a single digit (0 to 6), or an **s** or **S**. A distinct set of processes (mostly, daemons) is scheduled to run in each of these states. The significance of a few of these run levels shown below is system-dependent. Normally, the system would be in any one of these run levels:

0—System shutdown.

1—System administration mode (local file systems mounted).

2—Multiuser mode (NFS not available).

3—Full multiuser mode.

5—The graphical environment mode in Linux.

6—Shutdown and reboot mode.

s or S—Single-user mode (file systems mounted).

When the system is booted, **init** first enters run level 1 or S, which places the system in single-user mode. This mode is used by the administrator to perform his administrative tasks, like checking the file system or taking an offline backup. You can't use either the printer or the terminals because their corresponding system daemons (**lpsched** and **getty**) are not running. The role of run level 1 is system-variant; on many systems, 1 and S have identical roles.

Depending on your system, the normal multiuser mode is implemented in either of the two run levels—2 or 3. You can change your run level by using the **init** command (or its link, **telinit**) with the run level as argument:

```
init 2                          Switches to multiuser mode
init 3                          Can also use telinit 3
```

Both **init 0** and **init 6** are used to shut down the system. When the run level 6 is specified, the system will be shut down and immediately rebooted. Run level 1 keeps the machine in shutdown state so that power can be switched off.

Tip: To know the run level you are in, use the **who -r** command. Linux users can also use the **runlevel** command from the root account.

25.8.2 Using /etc/inittab

To understand how **init** works, you must familiarize yourself with the contents of /etc/inittab. **init** takes all its instructions from this file. Its fields determine the processes that should be spawned for each of the **init** states, and the programs to run at the communication ports. Each line of the file contains four fields as revealed by a few sample lines taken from a Solaris system:

```
fs::sysinit:/sbin/rcS sysinit          >/dev/msglog 2<>/dev/msglog </dev/console
is:3:initdefault:
s0:0:wait:/sbin/rc0           >/dev/msglog 2<>/dev/msglog </dev/console
s1:1:respawn:/sbin/rc1         >/dev/msglog 2<>/dev/msglog </dev/console
s2:23:wait:/sbin/rc2           >/dev/msglog 2<>/dev/msglog </dev/console
s3:3:wait:/sbin/rc3          >/dev/msglog 2<>/dev/msglog </dev/console
s6:6:wait:/sbin/rc6          >/dev/msglog 2<>/dev/msglog </dev/console
```

All of the things you see happening on startup owe their ultimate origin to entries like these. A typical inittab entry takes this form:

label:*run_levels*:*action*:*command*

label is simply used to identify the entry and has no real significance. The second field, *run_levels*, shows the run levels for which this line is applicable. The *action* and *command* (with all its arguments) to execute comprise the last two fields.

Let's now examine one of the lines of inittab. The line with the label s2 provides this directive: "For run levels 2 or 3, run the **/sbin/rc2** program and wait for it to complete before moving on to the other lines of this file." msglog is a special file that is used for logging all messages.

When **init** is executed with a specific run level as argument, it reads all lines that match that run level, and executes the commands specified there in sequence. A blank run level (here, in the first line) means the command has to be run for all run levels. **init** also obtains the default run level by reading the line that shows initdefault as the action. Here, the system boots to run level 3.

respawn and wait are two of the actions that **init** understands. There are others, and here are some of the important ones:

- sysinit—Used for initializing the system. The system may check the "dirtiness" of file systems, activate swap partitions and set the hostname. It may also ask for input from the administrator.

- respawn—Makes sure a process restarts on termination. This is always required for the **getty** process.
- boot—Executes only when inittab is read the first time. **init** ignores any run-level fields placed here.
- off—Kills the process if it is running.
- ctrlaltdel—Executes the **shutdown** command (Linux only).

Using telinit q   As administrator, you can also insert or modify statements in /etc/inittab. You can change the default run level, or add and modify entries when adding a new terminal or modem to the system. But then you have to use the **telinit** command to let **init** reread its configuration file:

```
telinit q                                          A directive to init
```

init and **telinit** are symbolically linked, and in most cases, they can be used interchangeably. However, **telinit** uses the -t option to indicate to **init** the number of seconds that **init** has to wait before it starts killing processes—something that happens during system shutdown.

25.8.3 init and getty

/etc/inittab will always have at least one line that specifies running a program to produce a login prompt on the console and other terminals (if supported). We deliberately didn't include this line in the sample lines shown previously because Solaris uses a nonstandard program for handling this function. Rather, these lines from a Linux machine illustrate the relationship between **init** and the **mingetty** (the "getty" of Linux) program:

```
1:2345:respawn:/sbin/mingetty tty1
2:2345:respawn:/sbin/mingetty tty2
```

Either line provides this directive: "For run levels 2, 3, 4 or 5, run the **mingetty** program (with tty1 or tty2 as argument) and recreate (respawn) the process when it dies, i.e., when the user logs out." It's because of lines like these that you see the login: prompt on your terminal. Recall from Section 9.4.1 that the **getty** process execs **login**, which in turn execs a shell.

LINUX: Because of /etc/inittab, you can have multiple *virtual* consoles on your Linux machine. Use *[Ctrl][Alt]* and a function key to bring up a new screen. In this way, you can have multiple login sessions on a single machine.

25.8.4 The *rc* Scripts

init and /etc/inittab completely control the way the system is booted and powered down. Moreover, when the system changes a run level, **init** looks up inittab to identify the processes that should and shouldn't be running for the new run level. It first kills the processes that shouldn't be running and then spawns those that should be.

Every inittab specifies the execution of some **rc (run command) scripts** placed in /etc or /sbin. These scripts have the names **rc0, rc1, rc2**—one for each run level. This is evident from the following lines in /etc/inittab that were also shown at the beginning of Section 25.8.2:

```
s0:0:wait:/sbin/rc0      >/dev/msglog 2<>/dev/msglog </dev/console
s2:23:wait:/sbin/rc2      >/dev/msglog 2<>/dev/msglog </dev/console
s3:3:wait:/sbin/rc3      >/dev/msglog 2<>/dev/msglog </dev/console
```

init executes the script specific to that run level. However, **rc2** runs in both states 2 and 3. Each rc script further specifies the execution of a series of scripts in the directory /etc/rc*n*.d. This means that for run level 2, **init** executes **/etc/rc2**, which in turn executes the scripts in /etc/rc2.d.

Now, let's turn our attention to the scripts in the /etc/rc*n*.d directories. These directories hold two types of files as shown by this listing of /etc/rc2.d:

```
K07dmi          S69inet          S74xntpd          S90wbem
K07snmpdx       S70uucp          S75cron           S92volmgt
K16apache       S71ldap.client   S75savecore       S93cacheos.finish
K28nfs.server   S71rpc           S76nscd           S94ncalogd
S01MOUNTFSYS    S72autoinstall   S80lp             S95ncad
S20sysetup      S72slpd          S85power          S99dtlogin
S21perf         S73cachefs.daemon S88sendmail
```

The scripts here fully initialize the system by mounting file systems, setting up the network and activating the other daemons. They are executed in two batches. When the system enters run level 2, **rc2** executes (in ASCII sequence) all scripts beginning with K (the "kill" scripts) with the **stop** argument. This kills all processes that shouldn't be running at this level. It then executes the scripts beginning with S (the "start" scripts) with the **start** argument. If you look up the **rc2** script, you'll find two **for** loops doing that.

As system administrator, you must understand how these scripts work. You should also be able to identify the script that starts a specific service. The filenames generally provides the clue, but sometimes you may need to use **grep** to look for names of specific daemons (like **httpd**, **sendmail**, **lpsched**, **inetd**, etc.) in these files.

Note: A script in rc*n*.d beginning with S is meant to start a service, while one beginning with K is meant to kill one. The kill scripts are executed before the start ones. They are all run from the corresponding **/etc/rc*n*** (or **/etc/rc.d/rc** with the argument *n* in Linux) script where *n* signifies the run level.

LINUX: The rc Files

The initialization files in Linux were originally based on BSD, but now have a strong System V flavor. However, the rc files and directories here are all under one roof—/etc/rc.d. Moreover, instead of using rc*n*, Linux uses a single file, **rc**, with different arguments as shown below in these lines from /etc/inittab:

```
l0:0:wait:/etc/rc.d/rc 0
l1:1:wait:/etc/rc.d/rc 1
l2:2:wait:/etc/rc.d/rc 2
```

All scripts in the rc*n*.d directories are executed from **/etc/rc.d/rc**. The sequence for Linux goes like this: For switching to run level *n*, **init** executes **/etc/rc.d/rc** *n*, which executes the scripts in **/etc/rc.d/rc*n*.d**.

25.9 SHUTDOWN AND THE sync OPERATION

The administrator uses the **shutdown** command to bring the system down. The command uses its -i option to direct **init** to change its run level. The possible **init** levels for this are 0, 1 and 6. The corresponding rc script is then invoked, and so are the kill scripts. File systems are unmounted and processes are killed, and the system is placed in single-user mode, rebooted or simply powered down. At run level 1, the machine is not technically shut down since all processes normally active in the single-user mode continue to live.

shutdown also performs a very important task; it invokes **sync** to write all memory resident data to disk. This includes the superblock, inodes and data blocks that are cached in memory. The **update** daemon calls **sync** every thirty seconds during normal system operation. When the command is entered manually, the prompt is returned, signifying that writing has been scheduled; the actual writing could take place later.

There's one occasion when **sync** must not be used. When **fsck** rebuilds the file system, the in-memory copies of the superblock and other tables may sometimes contain old and inaccurate information. In this unusual case, the information on disk is more *recent* than the memory copy. **fsck** may then flash the following message:

```
***** BOOT UNIX (NO SYNC!) *****
```

The file system has developed a serious problem here and the system warns you that if you use **sync** to write the incorrect memory information to disk, all the good work done by **fsck** would be lost. Instead, you should *immediately press the reset button without using* **sync**, and reboot the system. This must be done before the next **sync** operation automatically writes this incorrect information to disk.

25.10 BACKUPS

Some files are modified more often than others, while some are not accessed at all for months, if not years. How often the data changes in the system influences the backup strategy and determines the frequency of backup. The classical theory is that there should be a complete backup of all files once a week, and a daily incremental backup of only those files that have been modified. This routine can vary depending on the size and nature of installation, but can be used as a rough thumb rule.

25.10.1 Using find for Incremental Backups (-newer)

The **find** command *(11.7)* can match a file with practically every attribute. You can use it for performing incremental backups. First, you have to stamp a zero-byte file with the present system date and time whenever you go in for a backup. Subsequent backups will only select those files newer than this file. The following script lines show a simple implementation:

```
find /home -newer .last_time -print | cpio -o > /dev/rct0
touch .last_time
```

These two lines can be used together any time, and **touch** ensures that the last backup time is stored in the file's modification time stamp. You can use **tar** too, using command substitution:

```
tar -cvf /dev/rct0 `find /home -type f -newer .last_time -print`
touch .last_time
```

The type has to be specified as f because if it is not, **find** shows the directory as part of its output, which is interpreted by **tar** to include all files of the directory. This means files would be backed up twice.

25.10.2 Using find for Backing Up File Systems

In addition to the routine backups, you must back up individual file systems. Backing up the root file system generally requires other file systems to be unmounted so that **find** doesn't find any files in their mount points. Using **find**'s -mount option, you can perform a backup of just the root file system without traversing the other file systems, *while keeping them mounted*:

```
find / -depth -mount -mtime -1 -print | cpio -ocvB -0 /dev/rct0
```

This backs up the files of the root file system that have been modified in less than a day; **find** doesn't traverse the other file systems. The -depth keyword makes sure the files in the directories are acted upon before the directory itself. If the -mtime keyword is omitted, then the pipeline sequence makes a complete backup of the root file system.

Whenever peripherals are added or removed from the system, the configuration files in the root file system are changed. You must have a complete backup of both the boot and root file systems after the system has been fully configured. You can then go in for incremental backups as and when the system configuration changes.

If the system crashes and UNIX has to be reinstalled, you wouldn't obviously like to go through the tedious process of installing all peripherals separately. You can avoid that if you first install the *minimal* components of the operating system from the installation media, and then restore just the boot and root file systems from the backup.

Tip: You must back up the root file system on tape immediately after installation of the system. Subsequently, you must take further backups (normally, incremental) whenever the root system files are modified.

25.10.3 xargs: Building a Dynamic Command Line

There's one problem with using **find**'s -exec operator *(11.7.3)* with a UNIX command. If **find** produces a list of 200 files for removal, **rm** has to be executed 200 times. **xargs** comes to our rescue here as it lets **rm** (or, for that matter, any UNIX command) be used just once with 200 filenames as arguments.

xargs is one of UNIX's dark horses—a command not well appreciated or understood. It breaks up data supplied as standard input into a list and provides this list to the command used as its argument. The following command lines do the same thing except that the second one does it much faster:

```
find /usr/preserve -mtime +30 -exec rm -f {} \;
find /usr/preserve -mtime +30 -print | xargs rm -f
```

xargs here obtains the file list from **find** and supplies a *single* set of arguments to **rm**. So even if **find** selects 30 files, **rm** is executed only once.

Commands usually have limits on the number of arguments they can handle. **xargs** uses the -n option to provide the specified number of arguments for a single invocation of the command:

```
find / -name core -size +1024 -print | xargs -n20 rm -f
```

If **find** locates 100 files, **rm** will be invoked five times—each time with 20 filenames as arguments. Isn't this a useful tool?

25.10.4 Maintaining a Table of Contents

It's always preferable to maintain a file list for every backup. When a user asks for a particular file to be restored, you can first look up these lists so you know exactly which tape has to be used. Both **tar** and **cpio** use the -v option to display each filename as it is being accessed; the output has to be redirected to a separate file. You can always use a filename based on the current date, but the system also can do that for you:

```
tar cvf /dev/rct0 /home > homelist_`date "+%d%b%y"`
find /home -depth -print | cpio -ov > /dev/rct0 2>homelist_`date "+%d%b%y"`
```

Either of these commands can produce a file typically named homelist_17Nov03. A **grep** command can now be used, suitably framed with a regular expression, to look for any file. If the files are quite big, then they should be kept in compressed form. Apart from these selective lists, you must periodically maintain a complete list of *all* files of the system:

```
ls -lRF / > file_system.lst
```

Restoration with a wrong **tar** or **cpio** option often disturbs the file's attributes. A file's original attributes can be looked up from this list.

25.11 CONCLUSION

You can well imagine that system administration is demanding but not daunting. A system administrator must be productive and prompt in his actions. Fortunately, UNIX provides a wealth of tools that are at his disposal. Today, most systems have elaborate GUI-based applications that take some load off the administrator. If you aspire to be an administrator yourself, then you must be able to see what's happening behind the big picture.

> **WRAP UP**
>
> For enforcing security, the administrator should enforce *password aging* to force users to change their passwords regularly. For certain users, he may assign a restricted shell so the user can execute only a fixed set of commands.

A UNIX *file system* is held in a *partition* and consists of the *boot block, superblock,* inode and data blocks. The boot block contains a small program that eventually loads the kernel. The superblock contains details of free inodes and data blocks. Every inode contains 13 to 15 disk block addresses that keep track of all blocks used by a file.

Every UNIX system has the swap and root file systems. Most systems use the ufs file system which permit multiple superblocks, symbolic links and disk quotas. Linux uses the ext2 and ext3 file systems. There are different file system types for CD-ROMs (hsfs or iso9660), DOS disks (pcfs, vfat or msdos) and a pseudo-file system for processes (proc or procfs).

On Linux systems, **fdisk** is used to create, delete and activate partitions. Linux allows the creation of one *extended* partition to hold multiple *logical* partitions.

mkfs creates file systems. Each file system is unknown to the root file system until it is *mounted* (**mount**). **mount** takes mounting instructions from /etc/fstab (/etc/vfstab in Solaris). **umount** unmounts file systems.

fsck checks the integrity of file systems. It corrects inconsistencies by either deleting files or moving the unconnected ones to /lost+found. The root file system must be checked in single-user mode.

The **init** daemon maintains the system at a *run level*. The single-user mode (S or 1) is used for checking file systems. The multiuser mode (2 or 3) starts the system daemons and activates the network. **init** reads /etc/inittab which contains instructions to run **getty** at all terminals and the system's *rc* scripts. Processes are killed with the "K" scripts and started with the "S" ones.

shutdown uses **sync** to write the memory contents of the superblock to the file system. Sometimes, when the disk status is newer, "syncing" should not be done.

The administrator exploits **find**'s -newer option for incremental backups, and -mount for backing up the root file system without traversing other file systems. He should have a table of contents for each backup.

Test Your Understanding

25.1 How will you ensure that the password is changed after every four weeks?

25.2 A user after logging in is unable to change directories or create files in her home directory. How can that happen?

25.3 Discuss the significance of the boot, root and swap file systems.

25.4 Which file system can't be unmounted and why?

25.5 _____ creates, modifies and deletes partitions. _____ creates a file system. _____ makes a consistency check of one or more file systems.

25.6 When can **mount** work with only one argument? When is unmounting of a file system not possible?

25.7 Where is the file system mounting information kept in (i) SVR4, (ii) Linux?

25.8 What is *run level*? How do you determine and set the default run level of your system?

25.9 What should you do immediately after you have made changes to /etc/inittab?

25.10 Where are the startup scripts for multiuser operation located in (i) SVR4, (ii) Linux?

25.11 Devise a sequence using **find** and **xargs** that removes all files named a.out. The **rm** command should work with 20 filenames in each invocation.

Flex Your Brain

25.1 Name five features of the restricted shell.

25.2 Why do we install the UNIX system on multiple partitions?

25.3 What facilities do UNIX systems offer to counter superblock corruption?

25.4 Discuss the role of the **sync** command in maintaining the system in a consistent state. When must not you use **sync**?

25.5 Name the important features of the ufs file system. What is the significance of the proc file system?

25.6 What are the precautions you need to take when using **fsck**? What does **fsck** normally do with an unconnected file?

25.7 Describe the two main functions of **init**. What is the significance of run levels 0, 1 and 6?

25.8 You plan to use **tar** to back up all files you have worked with today. How do you plan the backup activity?

25.9 What is the significance of the *start* and *kill* scripts? How are they organized on (i) an SVR4 system, (ii) Linux?

25.10 Devise a sequence which shows whether the printer daemon is running, irrespective of whether the system is SVR4 or Linux.

The C Shell—Programming Constructs

The C shell was developed at UCB by Bill Joy, the architect of **vi**. This shell is used today mainly for its interpretive features. These features have also influenced the design of the Korn and Bash shells. The latter shells have completely superseded the C shell in power and versatility because they have more powerful programming constructs. If you are looking for an improved C shell, then use the Tcsh shell that is available in Linux.

Specifying the Interpreter

There are two ways of running a C shell script. Either use the **csh** command with the script name:

    csh *script_name*

or invoke it by name but only after after providing the interpreter line at the top of the script:

    #!/bin/csh

If the latter technique is used but the script doesn't have the interpreter line, the Bourne shell is used. (Linux uses Bash in this situation.) Every C shell script also executes the rc file, ~/.cshrc.

Interactive and Noninteractive Scripts

To make a script pause to read the standard input, you need to assign the special parameter, $<, to a variable. Input, which can comprise multiple words, is treated as a quoted string:

```
#!/bin/csh
echo "Enter filename: \c"
set flname = $<
echo "File: $flname"
```

A script can also be run noninteractively by passing command line arguments that are saved in a list or array named $argv. The arguments are individually accessed with $argv[1], $argv[2] etc. Further, $#argv is set to the number of arguments. To maintain compatibility with the other shells, the C shell also allows the use of $1 and $2, and so forth. Tcsh also allows the use of $#.

Computation

Unlike the Bourne shell, integer computing is built into the C shell. The arithmetic operators are standard (+, -, *, / and %). While variable assignment can be made with **set** or **setenv**, this shell offers a special operator, @, for performing computation:

```
% set x=5
% @ y = 10                                    A space after @
% @ sum=$x + $y
% @ product = $x * $y
% @ quotient = $y/$x                          Space around / required
@: Badly formed number
% @ quotient = $y / $x
```

Incrementing numbers is done in these ways:

```
@ x = $x + 1
@ x++
```

The @ must be followed by whitespace even if the = need not have any around it. The arithmetic operators must also be surrounded by whitespace.

Arrays and Lists

As discussed in Chapter 10, the C shell uses the **set** statement to define a local variable and **setenv** to define an environment variable. By default, **set** displays all local variables, but note that one variable (path) is set and evaluated differently:

```
% set path = (/bin /usr/bin /usr/local/bin /usr/dt/bin .)
% echo $path
/bin /usr/bin /usr/local/bin /usr/dt/bin .
```

Like argv, path is an array or list of five elements. The first element is accessed by $path[1], the second by $path[2], and so on. The number of elements in the list is indicated by $#path:

```
% echo $path
/bin /usr/bin /usr/local/bin /usr/dt/bin .
% echo $path[3]
/usr/local/bin
% echo $#path
5
```

Values can be put into an array with the **set** statement and **shift** also works with arrays:

```
% set numb = ( 9876 2345 6213 )              Like set 9876 2345 6213
% echo $numb[1]
9876
% echo $#numb                                Entire list stored in $numb[*]
3
% shift numb                                 Uses array name too
% echo $numb[1]
2345
```

The Comparison and Logical Operators

Before we take up the **if** statement, let's take a look at the operators that are used in expressions in a control command used with **if**. Numeric comparison is identical to **awk** which uses the operators <, >, ==, !=, >=, etc. The complete list is shown in Table 18.1. String comparison also uses the == and != operators, but the C shell is clearly superior to the Bourne shell because it supports two more operators for matching wild-cards:

- =~ Matches a wild-card expression
- !~ Doesn't match a wild-card expression

The same operators are used by **perl** with identical meaning except that **perl** uses them to match regular expressions.

You can also use the && and || operators in the same way you used them with **awk**, the Bourne shell and **perl**.

The **if** Statement

Like the Bourne shell, the **if** conditional takes three forms as shown in Section 14.6. However, there are three differences:

- The keyword **then** must be in the same line as **if**.
- The statement is terminated with **endif** and not **fi**.
- The control command is enclosed within parentheses (unless it is a UNIX command.

Let's examine these three forms using only examples. The first form also shows the use of numeric comparison, but note the second form which matches $response with any string that begins with y or Y:

```
if ( $#argv != 2 ) then
    echo Two parameters required
endif
```

```
if ( $response =~ [yY]* ) then
    echo You answered yes
else
    echo You answered no
endif
```

Form 1   Form 2

The third form uses the **if-else** clause (multiple times, if required) but only a single **endif**. Here's the meat of the script, **emp3a.sh** (Chapter 14), modified here to run in the C shell:

```
if ( $# == 0 ) then
    echo "Usage: $0 pattern file" >/dev/tty
else if ( $# == 2 ) then
    grep "$1" $2 || echo "$1 not found in $2" >/dev/tty
else
    echo "You didn't enter two arguments" >/dev/tty
endif
```

Form 3

As a variant of Form 1, you can have single-line conditionals when there is no **else** clause. The **then** and **endif** keywords are not used:

```
if ( $#argv == 2 ) @ size = $1 * 512 ; echo Size of $2 is $size bytes
```

When executing a UNIX command as the control command, the command itself should be surrounded by a matched pair of curly braces and not parentheses:

```
if { grep "director" emp.lst } then
```

Note that either the () or {} enclosures have to be provided with the control command used with **if**.

Testing File Attributes

Even though the C shell doesn't have a **test** statement, you can still test file attributes. This shell supports a limited set of operators, and many of them are used in the Bourne shell as well:

-f *file*	True if *file* is an ordinary file.
-d *file*	True if *file* is a directory.
-r *file*	True if *file* is readable.
-w *file*	True if *file* is writable.
-x *file*	True if *file* is executable.
-e *file*	True if *file* exists.
-o *file*	True if *file* exists and has a size of zero.

The following code shows the use of some of these operators:

```
if ( -f $1 ) then
    if ( ! -r $1 ) then
        echo "File exists but is not readable"
    else
        echo "File is readable"
    endif
else
    echo "File doesn't exist"
endif
```

The switch Statement

The **switch** statement is based on its namesake in the C language. Like **case**, the construct matches an expression for more than one alternative. The keywords used are **endsw**, **case**, **default** and **breaksw**. Here's a snippet of code that is similar to the script, **menu.sh**, developed in Chapter 14:

```
cat << END
        MENU
   1. List of files
   2. Processes of user
   3. Exit
Enter your option:
```

```
END
set choice = $<
switch ($choice)
    case 1:                          # Note the :
        ls -l ; breaksw
    case 2:
        ps -f ; breaksw
    case 3:
        exit
    default:                         # Use when previous matches fail
        echo "Invalid option"
endsw
```

The **breaksw** keyword moves control out of the construct after a successful match is found. If this word is not provided, then control "falls through" the end of the construct and performs all actions associated with *all* **case** options. The **default** keyword is used as the last option.

The while and foreach Loops

There are two loops—**while** and **foreach** (instead of **for**). Both loops have three major differences with their counterparts in the other shells:

- The loop condition (or the list) is to be enclosed within parentheses.
- The **do** keyword is not used.
- The loop is terminated with **end** instead of **done**.

Let's consider the **while** loop first. This simple sequence entered at the prompt runs the **ps** command four times:

```
% set x = 1
% while ( $x < 5 )                   Can also use while { true }
?   ps -f                            PS2 for C shell is ?
?   sleep 5
?   @ x++
? end
```

The **foreach** loop also has differences with its Bourne rival, but has been emulated by **perl**. The keyword **foreach** replaces **for**, and the **in** keyword is not required. The example in Section 14.12 can be reframed like this:

```
% foreach file (chap20 chap21 chap22 chap23)
?   cp $file ${file}.bak
?   echo $file copied to $file.bak
? end
```

Here, each component of the four-item list is assigned to the variable **file** until the list is exhausted. There are other ways of using a list:

```
foreach item ( `cat clist` )
foreach fname ( *.c )                All C programs in current directory
foreach fname ( $* )                 Script arguments
```

The goto Statement

Though this construct is hardly used by programmers today, the **goto** statement often provides a convenient mechanism to exit a section of code if used with caution. The statement specifies a *label* to branch to. The following code snippet uses **goto** to terminate a script after branching to the label named endblock:

```
if ( $#argv == 0 ) then                     # No arguments entered
    goto endblock
else
    grep $1 emp.lst
    exit                    # Required to stop intrusion into endblock
endif

endblock:
echo "You have not keyed in an argument"
```

The **exit** statement here has the same significance as the **break** statement used with **switch**. It ensures that control doesn't fall through after completion of **grep**. If the statement is not provided, the error message will appear irrespective of whether an argument was supplied or not.

The repeat Statement

If a single command has to be repeated a finite number of times, you can use the **repeat** statement:

```
% repeat 3 date
Sat Apr 26 10:46:25 IST 2003
Sat Apr 26 10:46:25 IST 2003
Sat Apr 26 10:46:25 IST 2003
```

The onintr Statement

The **onintr** statement (**trap** in Bourne) specifies the commands to be executed when a interrupt signal is sent to the script. It is normally placed at the beginning of a shell script:

```
% cat onintr.csh
#!/bin/csh
onintr cleanup
cut -c1-10 index > $$
cut -c21- index > $$.1
paste $$ $$.1 > pastelist
rm $$ $$.1
exit                        # Required to stop intrusion into cleanup

cleanup:
rm $$ $$.1
echo "Program interrupted"
```

Like the **goto** statement, the **onintr** statement is followed by a label. Execution branches to that label when the interrupt key is pressed. You may also like to ignore the signal and continue processing. In that case, you should make the program immune to such signals by using **onintr** with a -:

```
onintr -
```

vi/vim Command Reference

This appendix presents the features of the **vi/vim** editor. For convenience, commands and their customization parameters are grouped together. Most of these commands have been discussed in Chapters 7 and 20. The following points must be noted before you use this reference:

- Many commands can be used with a *repeat factor* (**vi**).
- **vim** (but not **vi**) supports a *region* as a contiguous text block which can be manipulated with commands. A region is defined with **v**, followed by a navigation command.
- The screen is cleared and redrawn with *[Ctrl-l]*.
- The **:set** command is used to customize the editor environment.

Navigation

Command	Function
h	Move cursor left
l (or *[Spacebar]*)	Move cursor right
k (or *[Ctrl-p]*)	Move cursor up
j (or *[Ctrl-n]*)	Move cursor down
[Ctrl-f]	Scroll full page forward
[Ctrl-b]	Scroll full page backward
[Ctrl-d]	Scroll half page forward
[Ctrl-u]	Scroll half page backward
1G	Move to beginning of file
40G	Move to line 40
G	Move to end of file
[Ctrl-g]	Display current line number and percentage of file
:set number	Show all lines numbered

Navigation along a Line

The **B**, **E** and **W** commands perform the same functions as their lowercase counterparts except that they ignore punctuation.

Command	Function
b	Move back to beginning of word
e	Move forward to end of word
w	Move forward to beginning of word
0 or |	Move to beginning of line
30|	Move to column 30
^	Move to first character of first word in line
$	Move to end of line

Inserting Text

Command	Function
i	Insert text to left of cursor
20i-*[Esc]*	Insert 20 hyphens
I	Insert text at beginning of line
[Ctrl-v][Ctrl-b]	Insert *[Ctrl-b]* character
[Ctrl-v][Esc]	Insert *[Esc]*
a	Append text to right of cursor
A	Append text at end of line
o	Open line below
O	Open line above
:set showmode	Display message when **vi** is in input mode
:set sm	Show momentarily match to a) and }
:set ts=*n*	Set tab stops to *n* (default: 8)
:set ai	Next line starts at previous indented level

Deleting and Moving Text

Command	Function
x	Delete character under cursor
6x	Delete character under cursor and five characters on right
X	Delete previous character
dd	Delete current line
4dd	Delete four lines
64dd	Delete 64 lines
dw	Delete word
d0 (d and zero)	Delete to beginning of line
d$	Delete to end of line
d	Delete region (**vim** only)
p	Put deleted text below (for complete lines) or right (partial lines)
P	Put deleted text above (for complete lines) or left (partial lines)

Command	Function
"add	Delete current line to buffer a
"ap	Restore contents from buffer a
J	Join current line with next line
xp	Transpose two characters

Changing Text

Command	Function
r*ch*	Replace single character under cursor with *ch*
R	Replace text from cursor to right
s	Replace single character under cursor with any number of characters
S	Replace entire line
cw	Change word
c	Change text of region (**vim** only)
~	Reverse case of scanned text or region
!tr '[a-z]' '[A-Z]'	Convert region to uppercase (**vim** only)
!tr '[A-Z]' '[a-z]'	Convert region to lowercase (**vim** only)

Copying Text

Command	Function
yy	Copy current line
6yy	Copy six lines
yw	Copy word
y	Copy region (**vim** only)
p	Put copied text on right or below
P	Put copied text on left or above
"ayy	Copy current line to buffer a
"ap	Restore contents from buffer a

Starting the Editor

Command	Function
vi +100 foo	Open file at line 200
vi +/*pat* foo	Open file at first occurrence of pattern *pat*
vi + foo	Open file at end
vi foo1 foo2	First open file foo1; use :n to switch to foo2, etc.
vi -r foo	Recover buffer from swap file
vi -R foo	Open file in read-only mode

Saving and Quitting

Command	Function
:w	Save file and remain in editing mode
:w bar	Like *Save As* ..... in Microsoft Windows
:w! bar	As above, but overwrite existing file bar
:n1,n2w foo	Write lines *n1* to *n2* to file foo
:n1,n2w >> foo	Append lines *n1* to *n2* to file foo
:.w foo	Write current line to file foo
:$w foo	Write last line to file foo
:x	Save file and quit editing mode
:wq	As above
:q	Quit editing mode when no changes are made to file
:q!	Quit editing mode but after abandoning changes

Editing Multiple Files

You can't use :e, :n and :rew unless the current file is saved (and autowrite is not set). The ! placed after the command overrides the safety feature.

Command	Function
:e foo	Stop editing current file and edit file foo
:e! foo	As above, but after abandoning changes made to current file
:e!	Load last saved version of current file
[Ctrl- ^]	Return to most recently edited file
:n	Edit next file (when **vi** is invoked with multiple filenames)
:set autowrite (aw)	Write current file automatically before switching files with :n
:rew	Rewind file list to start editing first file (when **vi** is invoked with multiple filenames)
:r foo	Insert contents of file foo below current line

Multiple Windows (vim)

Command	Function
:sp	Split current window in two
:new	Open a new blank window
[Ctrl-w][Ctrl-w]	Toggle between windows
:on	Make current window the only window
:q	Quit current window
:qa	Quit all windows
:xa	Save and quit all windows
[Ctrl-w] +	Increase window size
[Ctrl-w] -	Decrease window size

Search and Repeat

The search pattern *pat* can be a string as well as a regular expression. **vi** uses a separate set of key sequences for searching for a character in a line.

Command	Function
/*pat*	Search forward for *pat*
?*pat*	Search backward for *pat*
/printf	Search forward for printf
?[0-9]$	Search backward for a numeral at end of line
/^#	Search forward for # at beginning of line
n	Repeat search in same direction of previous search
N	Repeat search in opposite direction of previous search
:set wrapscan (ws)	Continue search by moving to other end of file
:set ignorecase (ic)	Ignore case when searching
:set magic	Retain meaning of regular expression characters
f*c*	Search forward for character *c* in current line
F*c*	Search backward for character *c* in current line
;	Repeat last forward search for character in current line
,	Repeat last reverse search for character in current line

Substitution

The source pattern *s1* can also be a regular expression. In the address, the dot indicates the current line while the $ signifies the last line. 1,$ addresses the entire file.

Command	Function
:.s/*s1*/*s2*/	Replace first occurrence of *s1* with string *s2* in current line
:1,$s/*s1*/*s2*/	Replace first occurrence of *s1* with string *s2* in entire file
:1,$s/echo/printf/g	Globally replace echo with printf
:1,$s/*s1*/*s2*/gc	Globally and interactively replace *s1* with *s2*
:1,$s/#//g	Globally remove #
:3,10s/^/#/	Insert a # at beginning of lines 3 to 10
:$s/$/;/	Insert a ; at end of last line
:1,$s/*s1*/*s2*/g	Globally replace *s1* with string *s2*
:1,$s/HEAD/<&>/g	Globally replace HEAD with <HEAD>

Marks and Bookmarks

Command	Function
ma	Set mark a
'a	Move to mark a
''	Toggle between current and previous positions

Redoing and Undoing

Command	Function
.	Repeat last command
u	Undo last editing command (All previous commands in **vim**)
[Ctrl-r]	Redo last undo (**vim** only)
U	Undo all changes made to current line
"4p	Restore 4th recent line deletion from buffer

Abbreviating Text

Command	Function
:ab *stg name*	Abbreviate *name* to *stg*
:unab *stg*	Kill abbreviation *stg*
:ab	List all abbreviations

Key Mapping

Command	Function
:map *key commands*	Map *key* to *commands*
:map! *key commands*	Map *key* to *commands* in Input Mode
:unmap *key*	Kill Command Mode map *key*
:unmap! *key*	Kill Input Mode map *key*
:map	Display all Command Mode maps
:map!	Display all Input Mode maps

Interface To UNIX

The editor can be suspended with *[Ctrl-z]* only for those shells that enable job control.

Command	Function
:!*cmd*	Run UNIX command *cmd*
:!%	Execute current file as a shell or **perl** script
:r !*cmd*	Insert output of command *cmd* below current line
:r !head -n 3 foo	Insert first three lines of foo below current line
:sh	Escape to UNIX shell
[Ctrl-z]	Suspend editor (Use **fg** to return to **vi**)
:!cc %	Compile currently edited C program
:!javac %	Compile currently edited Java program

The Howto

How to do or display	Command
abbreviate a command sequence	alias
add a user account (superuser only)	useradd
add a user group (superuser only)	groupadd
address all users (superuser only)	wall
arithmetic (integer) computation noninteractively	expr
arithmetic computation using the shell	(( )) or let
assign values to positional parameters	set
back up files specified in command line	tar
beginning of file	head
calendar of month or year	cal
cancel print job	cancel, lprm
change case of text	tr
change current directory	cd *dirname*
change current directory to home directory	cd or cd $HOME
change filename extension	basename, expr
change file's group ownership	chgrp
change file's last modification or access time	touch
change file's ownership	chown
change file's permissions	chmod
change login shell without involving administrator	chsh
change own password	passwd
change password of any user (superuser only)	passwd *username*
check current directory	pwd
check in SCCS/RCS file	delta, ci
check out SCCS/RCS file	get, co
check file system integrity (superuser only)	fsck
clear screen	tput clear

How to do or display	*Command*
command documentation	`man`
command history	`history`
command introduction in single line	`whatis`
command type (external, internal or alias)	`type`
commands containing keyword	`apropos`
compile C program	`cc, gcc`
compress file (to .bz2)	`bzip2`
compress file (to .gz)	`gzip`
compress multiple files to a single file (to .zip)	`zip`
concatenate files	`cat`
control access to X server	`xhost`
convert file from DOS to UNIX	`dos2unix`
convert file from UNIX to DOS	`unix2dos`
copy directory tree	`cp -r`
copy file	`cp`
copy file between machines	`ftp, scp, sftp`
copy file to and from DOS diskette	`doscp, mcopy`
copy floppy diskette or tape media	`dd`
count number of lines containing a pattern	`grep -c`
count number of lines, words and characters	`wc`
create archive of C object files	`ar`
create file	`cat >, echo >, vi`
create links to a file	`ln`
create SCCS/RCS file	`admin, ci`
create specification file for **cron**	`crontab`
create symbolic links to a file	`ln -s`
cut columns or fields from file	`cut`
default file permissions	`umask`
delay command execution in a script	`sleep`
device name of current terminal	`tty`
difference between two files (as **sed**-like instructions)	`diff`
difference between two files (character-wise list)	`cmp`
directory list	`ls -l | grep "^d"`
disk space utilization	`du`
duplicate standard input stream	`tee`
echo a message	`echo, printf`
edit file	`vi`
end of file	`tail`

How to do or display	*Command*
execute command in background and log out	nohup
execute command on remote machine without logging in	ssh
execute command with arguments from standard input	xargs
execute commands from a shell in X window	xterm
execute shell script without spawning sub-shell	. (dot), source
file attributes	ls -l
file content	cat
file content (compressed) (.Z or .gz)	zcat
file content in DOS diskette	doscat, mtype
file content in k columns	pr -k
file content one page at a time	more, less
file content with headings and page numbers	pr
file list	ls
file list containing a pattern	grep -l
file list in DOS diskette	dosdir, mdir
find files by name or any other attribute	find
format DOS floppy diskette	dosformat, mformat
format UNIX floppy diskette	fdformat
free disk space	df
free space in memory and swap	top
generate public/private key pair	ssh-keygen
handle signal from shell script	trap
input data to shell script interactively	read
join two files laterally	paste
kill job	See "terminate"
lines common to two files or unique to one	comm
lines containing one or more of multiple patterns	grep -E, egrep, fgrep
lines containing pattern	grep
lines in ASCII collating sequence	sort
lines in double space	pr -d -t
lines in numeric sequence	sort -n
lines in reverse order	tail -r
lines not containing pattern	grep -v
lines sorted ignoring case	sort -f
lines that are repeated	uniq -d
lines that occur only once	uniq -u
log in to remote machine	telnet, slogin
log session	script

How to do or display	*Command*
mail message	`mailx`
maintain group of C programs	`make`
manipulate individual fields in a line	`awk, perl`
maximum file size	`ulimit`
modify user account (*superuser only*)	`usermod`
monitor growth of file	`tail -f`
mount file system	`mount`
move files to another directory	`mv`
move job to background	`bg`
move job to foreground	`fg`
multiple segments from a file	`sed`
name of local host	`hostname`
number lines including empty lines	`pr -n -t`
octal value of character	`od`
operating system name	`uname`
operating system release	`uname -r`
pass variable value to sub-shell	`export, setenv`
print file	`lp, lpr`
print queue	`lpstat, lpq`
process ancestry	`ps -f, ps f`
process attributes	`ps`
process HTML form data	`perl`
remove duplicate lines	`sort -u`
remove duplicate lines from sorted file	`uniq`
remove empty directory	`rmdir`
remove empty or blank lines	`grep -v, sed`
remove file	`rm`
remove newline character from text	`tr -d`
remove nonempty directory	`rm -r`
remove user account (*superuser only*)	`userdel`
rename file or directory	`mv`
replace current shell with another program	`exec`
replace pattern	See "substitute"
restore files from backup media	`tar`
SCCS/RCS activity	`prs, rlog`
SCCS/RCS history	`sact, rlog`
schedule job for one-time execution	`at`
schedule job for repeated execution	`cron`

How to do or display	*Command*
schedule one-time job when system load permits	`batch`
search a file for one or more patterns	See "lines containing"
send signal to process	`kill`
set default file permissions *(superuser only)*	`umask`
set maximum file size *(superuser only)*	`ulimit`
set run level of system *(superuser only)*	`init`
set system date *(superuser only)*	`date`
set terminal characteristics	`stty`
shift positional parameters to next lower-numbered one	`shift`
shut down system *(superuser only)*	`shutdown, init`
sound beep	`echo "\007"`
squeeze multiple spaces to single space	`tr -s`
start SSH authentication agent	`ssh-agent`
string length	`expr`
substitute one character for another	`tr`
substitute one pattern for another	`sed`
substring extracted from larger string	`expr`
substring position within larger string	`expr`
superuser from nonprivileged account	`su`
system date	`date`
system memory usage	`top`
system run level	`who -r, runlevel`
terminate last background job	`kill $!`
terminate login session	`exit, logout`
terminate process	`kill`
terminate shell script	`exit`
test connectivity of host	`ping`
uncompress `.bz2` file	`bunzip2`
uncompress `.gz` file	`gunzip`
uncompress `.zip` file	`unzip`
unmount file system	`umount`
users and their activities	`who`
World Wide Web pages with graphics	`netscape, mozilla`
write buffer contents to disk *(superuser only)*	`sync`
write different segments of file to different files	`sed`

Solutions to Test Your Understanding

CHAPTER 1

1.1 The ASCII value.

1.2 So other people can't see it, otherwise they can use it to gain unauthorized access to the system.

1.3 Kernel, shell. **1.4** (i) ls (ii) ps (iii) who

1.5 No, it doesn't. UNIX is insensitive to the presence of spaces around the >, < and | symbols.

1.6 The number of files in the current directory.

1.7 Since the * matches all files in the current directory, both **echo** and **ls** output the same strings, except that **echo**'s output is cluttered.

1.8 The command in double quotes displays the value of SHELL, but the command in single quotes simply displays the quoted string.

1.9 False, a program is an executable file that resides on disk. A process is created in memory by executing the program.

1.10 Ken Thompson and Dennis Ritchie.

1.11 Because it is written in C, a high level language.

1.12 X/OPEN was a standards body now merged with The Open Group, which owns the UNIX trademark.

1.13 The **vi** editor, C shell, symbolic links and TCP/IP.

1.14 X Window System.

1.15 The Free Software Foundation is responsible for the development of most of the application tools and the shell. The kernel was created by Linus Torvalds.

CHAPTER 2

2.1 Files, processes.

2.2 False, there can be only one kernel, but there can be multiple shells.

2.3 The shell scans the command for some special characters and recreates the command structure. It then passes on the command to the kernel for execution. Because the shell does all this work on behalf of the user, it's known as an *interpreter*.

2.4 False, they must use the same system calls.

2.5 The **man** command on the machine, newsgroups and FAQs on the Internet.

2.6 The : must be a command that does nothing. The command **type :** indicates that the command is built into the shell.

2.7 False, you can use uppercase and provide extensions to command filenames.

2.8 That is because the commands there are most often used by users and would be located faster.

2.9 The command that occurs first in the PATH list would require no special treatment. The other command needs to be used with a pathname.

2.10 By a dot.

2.11 **cd** and **pwd** are internal commands of the shell.

2.12 An option is also an argument but generally begins with a hyphen.

2.13 Linux; its commands often have double-hyphenated options.

2.14 The secondary prompt is generally a > or ?, and appears when the *[Enter]* key is pressed before the command specification is complete.

2.15 Press **n** repeatedly.

2.16 A program that displays text on the screen a page at a time. **more** and **less** are two standard pagers used by **man**.

2.17 *[Ctrl-c]* or *[Delete]*

2.18 No, the buffer associated with the keyboard stores all input.

CHAPTER 3

3.1 12 days were skipped in September for adjustment purposes.

3.2 `cal 1752 | more`   **3.3** `date +"%d/%m/%Y"`

3.4 Not as an ordinary user.

3.5 `echo "\007"` or `echo -e "\007"` (Bash)

3.6 Make the setting `scale=3`.

3.7 Use the **script session.1st** command at the beginning of your login session.

3.8 /var/mail (SVR4) and /var/spool/mail (Linux)

3.9 **mailx** is used without arguments when checking for incoming mail, and with one or more arguments when sending mail.

3.10 That the message has been viewed.

3.11 Yes, you can; two or more users can log in with the same username.

3.12 The command is run by romeo who is logged in from a host named *pc123* at the date and time shown. romeo's terminal file is pts/10.

3.13 The password is stored in encrypted form in the file /etc/shadow.

3.14 First enter the command **stty echo**. If that doesn't work, try **stty sane**.

CHAPTER 4

4.1 255 characters. The / and null can't be used as filename characters.

4.2 (i) Difficult to remove such a file. (ii) Many commands interpret such filenames as options.

4.3 Yes, UNIX filenames are case-sensitive.

4.4 (i) cd ; pwd (ii) echo $HOME (iii) Locate the sixth field in the line pertaining to your username in /etc/passwd.

4.5 The directory doesn't change.

4.6 The command **cd ../../mail** will take you there with the minimum number of keystrokes.

4.7 **ls ..** displays all filenames in the parent directory, but **ls -d ..** shows .. as the parent directory without displaying its contents.

4.8 Use **mkdir -p share/man/cat1**, which creates all intermediate directories.

4.9 The directory c_progs is not empty or the command is executed in the directory itself.

4.10 No, **echo** is also a shell builtin which is executed by default.

4.11 (i) ls -F (ii) ls -a   **4.12** ls -laR /

CHAPTER 5

5.1 The same file three times in succession.

5.2 Use **cp -r bar1 bar2**. If bar2 exists, then bar1 becomes a subdirectory of bar2.

5.3 The contents of the file are displayed on the terminal.

5.4 rm -rf foo

5.5 (i) bar1 becomes a subdirectory of bar2. (ii) bar1 is renamed to bar2.

5.6 There are two file types: block special and character special.

5.7 lp -d arjun -n3 /etc/passwd

5.8 All lines are terminated by *[Ctrl-m]*.

5.9 Create a file with these characters and then use **od -bc foo**.

5.10 comm -12 foo1 foo2   **5.11** The two files are identical.

CHAPTER 6

6.1 2048.

6.2 In /etc/passwd.

6.3 (i) 756 (ii) 640 (iii) 124

6.4 (i) r-xrw-rwx (ii) rw--w--wx (iii) r--w--x

6.5 He can read but not write unless he changes the permissions.

6.6 The owner of the file.

6.7 You can copy once but not subsequently because the copy is now write-protected.

6.8 You can create a directory in /tmp (permissions—rwxrwxrwt) but not in /bin (rwxr-xr-x). group and others can't write in /bin, but they can write in /tmp.

6.9 No, she can't, because the owner's permissions override her group's.

6.10 On a BSD-based system, only the superuser can use **chown** to change the owner of a file. However, a user can change her own group with **chgrp** but only to one to which she also belongs.

6.11 Recursively changes (i) the owner of all files in the current directory, including the hidden files. (ii) the group of all files but doesn't include the hidden files.

CHAPTER 7

7.1 You didn't press *[Esc]* before using **50k**. Press *[Ctrl-w]* to erase the text followed by *[Esc]*.

7.2 Take the cursor to the end of has and press sve*[Esc]*.

7.3 (i) 0 (ii) o   **7.4** :q!   **7.5** :x, :wq and ZZ

7.6 Use **0, 5w, 4s**, enter counter and press *[Esc]*.

7.7 (i) 7 (ii) 2   **7.8** (i) 40| (ii) 0 (iii) $

7.9 Only (iii) and (iv) because they change the contents of the editing buffer. (i) and (ii) merely perform navigation without changing the buffer in any way.

7.10 Take the cursor to t and use **xp**.

7.11 **d** and **y** are operators but **j** and **$** are commands that can be used singly. An operator can either be doubled by itself (like **dd**) or combined with a Command Mode command.

7.12 Use **5J** with the cursor on the top-most line.

7.13 Use **/printf** and then use **N**.

7.14 Because you pressed o*[Esc]* before pressing the dot.

CHAPTER 8

8.1 Because they mean nothing to the command. A * is expanded to match all filenames in the current directory.

8.2 The command lists all filenames where a dot occurs anywhere in the filename except at the beginning.

8.3 The command **rm .[!.]*** removes all files beginning with a dot except . and ... **rm *** doesn't remove these files.

8.4 chap[a-cx-z]

8.5 Yes, because 3 has a higher value than e in the ASCII collating sequence.

8.6 (i) *[!0-9] (ii) ????*

8.7 When there is only one file in the current directory and that file is also a directory.

8.8 The terminal, redirection and pipe.

8.9 `ls -lRa $HOME > home.ls`

8.10 `( echo "<html>" ; cat foo.html ; echo "</html>" ) > htmlfile`

8.11 They expect input from standard input, the terminal by default. Press *[Ctrl-d]* to send EOF and return to the shell.

8.12 This is quite troublesome; **rm \-*** or **mv \-*** won't work. First create a directory bar2 at the same hierarchical level as bar. Next, move all files except this file to bar2 with **mv [!-]* ../bar2**. Now, move up with **cd ..**, remove bar with **rm -r bar**, and rename bar2 to bar.

8.13 Precede the space with a backslash: echo >\ *[Enter]*
When you use **ls | od -bc**, you'll find the octal value 040 at that position.

8.14 Legitimate, the **bc** command reads standard input from bar and writes standard output to foo.

8.15 Press a \ before pressing *[Enter]*. **8.16** (ii)

8.17 `mailx `cat foo` < message.txt`

8.18 $SHELL is evaluated in double quotes only.

8.19 No, it doesn't. The shell interprets x as a command and = and 10 as its arguments.

8.20 (i) $x evaluates to null and =5 is executed as a command, which usually results in an error. (ii) The string pwd, =, and the output of the **pwd** command are concatenated and saved in the directory variable.

8.21 (iv)

CHAPTER 9

9.1 The PID is a unique number assigned to a process by the kernel. The PPID is the PID of the parent.

9.2 The **init** process with the PID 1, and the parent of all shells.

9.3 ps -e (SVR4) and ps aux (Linux)

9.4 Shell scripts. The sub-shell reads and executes each statement in the script.

9.5 cd, pwd, echo **9.6** ps -f -u timothy (ps --user timothy in Linux)

9.7 (i) kill -s KILL (ii) kill -1

9.8 Use **kill $!**, which should work on most shells.

9.9 ps -e | mailx charlie

9.10 No, use an & as well to run it in the background.

9.11 First press *[Ctrl-z]* to suspend the process and escape to the shell prompt. Enter **fg** to continue the suspended process and bring up **vi** once again.

9.12 The **find** command runs at 21:30 hours every day.

9.13 Use the **time** command with both and note the real time.

CHAPTER 10

10.1 It is set by /etc/passwd. If you *directly* reassign the value of HOME, **cd** used without an argument will take you to the new value of $HOME. However, the home directory continues to be what has been specified in /etc/passwd.

10.2 The file vt220 will be available in /usr/share/lib/terminfo/v on Solaris systems.

10.3 PATH=$PATH:..   **10.4** alias lh="ls .[!.]*"   **10.5** (i) r (ii) !!

10.6 (i) r tar sh=pl (ii) !tar:s/sh/pl   **10.7** set -o vi

10.8 The next command should be **more $_**.

10.9 $_ represents a file in the current directory but has no execute permission.

10.10 cd ~henry

10.11 First use **cd /usr/include**, then **cd ../lib**. Now, every time you use **cd -**, the current directory toggles between the two.

10.12 /etc/profile is executed when a user logs in, and before her own .profile is executed.

10.13 No, Bash will read only .bash_profile.

10.14 False; a script runs only the rc file.

CHAPTER 11

11.1 The filename which is stored in the directory.

11.2 The file has a single inode with a link count of three. The file can be accessed by three pathnames.

11.3 ln *.c bar

11.4 (i) False, **rm** removes both. (ii) False, a symbolic link has a separate inode.

11.5 (i) ln foo1 foo2 (ii) ln -s foo1 foo2. If you delete the hard link foo2, the link count drops to 1 and the file exists. Deleting the symbolic link foo2 removes only the link, but the main file still exists.

11.6 Use **ls -i** and see whether they have the same inode number. It's quite possible for two files in two separate file systems to have the same inode number, so a comparison with **cmp** must also return success.

11.7 Remove the read permission from the directory for others.

11.8 The directory was writable by group and others.

11.9 Use **umask 006** in your .profile.

11.10 False, the access time of a file is not changed by a lookup of the inode.

11.11 Find out its last access time with **ls -lu foo**.

11.12 **touch** sets the modification and access time to the current time. The administrator uses **touch** to change these times whenever he finds files to be wrongly stamped. Wrong time stamps can result in inclusion or exclusion of a file from a backup.

11.13 The UID, GID, the time of last modification and access.

11.14 `touch -m 09301030 foo`

11.15 (i) `find /bin /usr/bin -name "z*" -print`
(ii) `find /bin /usr/bin \( -name "*.html -o -name "*.java" \) -print`

11.16 `find /home/henry -type f -print | wc -l`

11.17 The access time of foo doesn't change when using the >> symbols, even though the file has been modified.

CHAPTER 12

12.1 (i) `pr -t -d foo` (ii) `ls | pr -t -3`

12.2 **head** picks up 10 lines from each file, but precedes each group with a header that shows the filename.

12.3 `ps | tail +2`

12.4 Run a.out in the background with & and then use **tail -f foo**.

12.5 No, you can use only one of the options, -c and -f.

12.6 `sort -t"|" -k 5.4 emp.lst`

12.7 First cut out the date field and then extract the year:
`cut -d"|" -f5 emp.lst | cut -c7- | sort | uniq -c`

12.8 `cut -d"|" -f4 emp.lst | sort -u | pr -t -n`

12.9 `PATH=`echo $PATH | cut -d: -f2-``

12.10 (i) `uniq foo` (ii) `sort -u foo`   **12.11** `tr '[a-z]' '[A-Z]' < emp.lst`

CHAPTER 13

13.1 (i) **grep** searches for a in files b and c. (ii) The command doesn't work because <HTML> is not quoted, and the shell interprets the < and > symbols as redirection characters.

13.2 It searches for an asterisk at the beginning of the line. Because the * loses its special meaning when not preceded by a character, the \ isn't really required.

13.3 (i) The longest pattern starting with a and ending with b, as close to the left of the line as possible. (ii) At least one character in the line. (iii) The } as the only character in the line.

13.4 Use **grep -E** with these patterns: (i) `SIG(STOP|TSTP)` (ii) `SIGTT(IN|OU)` (iii) `harris(|on)`

13.5 g* could match nothing but gg* matches at least one g.

13.6 `grep pattern foo | tail -n 1`

13.7 `find . -name "*.c" -print | grep -v "/.*/"`

13.8 Displays the usernames of those using the shell evaluated from $SHELL. The second $ anchors the pattern at the end of the line.

13.9 `numb=`grep -l printf *.c | wc -l``

13.10 `grep -E "^[0-9]+\.[0-9]+ |^[0-9]+\.[0-9]+\.[0-9]+ " chap??`

13.11 `ls -lut `grep -l wait *.c``

13.12 `alias lsdir="ls -l | grep "^d"`

13.13 `cat * | grep -E "f?printf"`

13.14 (i) `sed -n '3,10p' foo` (ii) `sed -n '$!p' foo`

13.15 (i) `sed 'p' foo` (ii) `sed -n 'a\`

                          `'p foo`

13.16 `sed 's/Linux/Red Hat &/g' foo`

13.17 `sed 's/^/    /' foo`

13.18 Look for the locations where the | occurs and then use the TRE:

        `sed 's/\([^|]*\|\)\([^ ]*\) \([^|]*\)/\1\3 \2/' emp.lst`

CHAPTER 14

14.1 (i) x10$ (ii) 1010

14.2 Use !/usr/bin/ksh as the interpreter line or use **ksh** *script_name*.

14.3 $0 was used in the program.

14.4 The exit status is the value returned by a command to its parent. It is available in $?.

14.5 ```
case $LOGNAME in
     henry|romeo) case `tty` in
                  *tty0[56]) ;;
                          *) echo "You cannot use this terminal" ; exit
                  esac ;;
               *) echo "You are not authorized to use script" ; exit ;;
esac
```

14.6 **test** is a shell builtin and thus the script doesn't execute. The script can still be run with **sh test** or **./test**.

14.7 Only **grep** returns a false exit status if the pattern is not found; **sed** and **find** don't.

14.8 (i) Without using **expr**:
```
echo "Enter a long string: \c"
read name
case $name in
??????????*) ;;
          *) echo "String shorter than 10 characters"
esac
```

(ii)    The **case** construct in (i) can be replaced with this:
```
if [`expr "$name" : '.*'` -lt 10] ; then
    echo "String shorter than 10 characters"
fi
```

14.9 `expr "$x" : '\(.*\)/[^/]*'`

14.10 ```
file=$1                        # Save filename before set overwrites it
if [ -f $file ] ; then         # If file exists
    set -- `ls -l $file`
```

```
        echo "The last modification time of $file is $6 $7 $8"
    else
        echo "File not found" ; exit 2
    fi
```

14.11
```
cd $1
for file in * ; do
    if [ -f ../$2/$file ] ; then
        cmp $file ../$2/$file >/dev/null 2>/dev/null && rm ../$2/$file
    fi
done
```

14.12
```
[ $# -eq 0 ] && { echo "Usage: $0 filename" ; exit ;}
case $1 in
    *.gz) program=gunzip ; ufilename=`basename $1 .gz` ;;
    *.bz2) program=bunzip2 ; ufilename=`basename $1 .bz2` ;;
    *.zip) program=unzip ; ufilename=`basename $1 .zip` ;;
esac
if [ -f "$ufilename" ] ; then
    echo "Uncompressed file $ufilename exists; Quitting"
else
    $program $1
fi
```

14.13 Use this script, and then use **:n** to call up the next file and the **n** command to locate each occurrence of the pattern. (**n** repeats the last pattern search in **vi**.)
```
pattern="$1"
set -- `grep -l "$pattern" *`
[ $# -gt 0 ] && vi +/"$pattern" "$@"  || echo "$1 not found"
```

14.14 Both execute an infinite loop (i) unconditionally. (ii) only if script is run with at least one argument.

14.15
```
for file in "$@" ; do
    if [ -f $file ] ; then
        ufile=`echo $file | tr '[a-z]' '[A-Z]'`
        if [ -f $ufile ] ; then
            echo "$ufile also exists"
        else
            mv $file $ufile
        fi
    else
        echo "$file doesn't exist"
    fi
done
```

14.16
```
OLDIFS="$IFS"              # Save old value of IFS
IFS=:                      # before changing it
set -- $PATH
for directory in "$@" ; do
    if [ ! -d $directory ] ; then
        echo "$directory doesn't exist"
```

```
        elif [ ! -x $directory ] ; then
            echo "$directory doesn't have search permission"
        fi
done
IFS=$OLDIFS              # Restore old value of IFS
```

CHAPTER 15

15.1 In /sbin and /usr/sbin. The PATH for a superuser doesn't include the current directory.

15.2 It doesn't ask for the old password.

15.3 s indicates that the SUID bit is set, and t signifies the sticky bit.

15.4 The password encryption was world-readable in /etc/passwd of older systems. This made it vulnerable to attack by hackers. However, /etc/shadow is not world-readable.

15.5 SHELL and HOME.   **15.6** usermod -s /bin/bash romeo

15.7 For each file, ls obtains the numeric UID and GID from the inode and then looks up /etc/passwd for the name representation of UID, and /etc/group for the name representation of GID.

15.8 Printing, network services and user logins are not available in single-user mode.

15.9 -perm 1000 matches a file having exactly those permissions, but -perm -1000 matches only 1 (the sticky bit) and ignores the other three octal digits.

15.10 Use **shutdown -y -g0**. Linux allows us to use *[Ctrl][Alt][Del]*.

15.11 He should place the following statement in the crontab file: 00 09-22 * * 1,2,3,4,5 df -t

15.12 du -s .

15.13 (i) doscp *.htm *.html /dev/fd0 (ii) mcopy *.htm *.html a:

CHAPTER 16

16.1 The screen, keyboard and mouse.

16.2 The window manager client takes care of window management.

16.3 Yes, by using the -display option of the client or setting the DISPLAY variable before invoking the client.

16.4 Merely by selecting it with the mouse.

16.5 **xhost** determines whether other hosts can write to the local machine's display. **xhost +** enables the display to be written by all remote hosts.

16.6 The nonuniformity of the desktop made a user feel uncomfortable when changing to a different machine.

16.7 To provide four separate virtual desktops.

16.8 The commands will all be executed and then X will be terminated.

16.9 By using the -xrm option with the resource string.

CHAPTER 17

17.1 TCP monitors transmission of segments with an elaborate system of timeouts and retransmission facilities. These ensure that a missing or corrupted segment will make reassembly impossible.

17.2 It simulates a network without actually connecting to one. If a machine is not connected to a network, the TCP/IP tools can still be tested using the loopback address.

17.3 The port number specifies the application responsible for generating the packet, and also specifies the one receiving it.

17.4 Use the **hostname** command.

17.5 You did not use **ftp**'s **binary** command before starting the transfer, and the machine's default mode is not binary.

17.6 You can't upload files to an anonymous FTP site.

17.7 Because the authentication parameters and data are transmitted in clear text, which can be easily intercepted. The Secure Shell (SSH) encrypts transmission, so it is increasingly used today.

17.8 Trying out every possible key combination. The longer the key, the more the possible number of combinations.

17.9 Symmetric key.

17.10 Unlike a password, a passphrase allows the use of spaces. A passphrase also protects the private key.

17.11 **scp** must be used to copy a directory structure between a local and a remote UNIX machine; **ftp** can't copy directories.

17.12 *aero*, *biz*, *pro* are three new entrants.

17.13 The file has to be maintained in every host of a network.

17.14 The MUA hands over outgoing mail to the MTA, which connects directly to its peer at the destination to transmit the message. The MTA finally invokes the MDA to deliver the mail to the user's mailbox.

17.15 The original SMTP protocol used 7-bit ASCII for mail messages. Binary attachments had to be encoded using base64 to make this possible. The MIME standard requires such encoded data to be preceded by the headers Content-Type: and Content-Transfer-Encoding:.

17.16 Hypertext is a system of organizing information by which references can be made to other documents in the same or different server. The concept is not restricted to text but applies to images as well.

17.17 A CGI program is a separate program that accepts a request passed by the HTTP server. The server invokes the program which does all the processing work, creates fresh HTML code and passes it back to the server.

CHAPTER 18

18.1   Both print the entire line. **print** is not necessary if the selection criteria is specified.

18.2   (i) awk 'NR <= 5' foo (ii) awk 'NR == 5, NR == 10' foo (iii) awk 'NR >= 20' foo
         (iv) awk '/negroponte/' foo

18.3   awk '{ x= NR % 2 ; if (x == 1) print }' foo

18.4   awk '$0 !~ /^ *$/' foo

18.5   awk 'length > 100 && length < 150' foo

18.6   This one needs a small tweak: awk '{print $NF}' foo

18.7   awk -F: '{
              if ($6 > 6000)
                  print > "foo1"
              else
                  print > "foo2"
         }' emp.lst

18.8   ls -lR $HOME | awk ' $6 ~ /^Jan/ && $7 ~ /^6/ && $8 ~ /^11/'

18.9   find . -type f -ls | awk '{tot += $7} END { print tot}'

18.10   echo "DOCUMENT LIST" | \
         awk '{ for (k = 1 ; k < (55 - length($0)) / 2 ; k++)
                  printf "%s"," "
                  print $0 }'

18.11   echo "DOCUMENT LIST" | \
         awk '{ k = 0
                  while (k < (55 - length($0))/2) {
                      printf "%s", " " ; k++
                  }
                  print $0
              }'

18.12   #!/bin/sh
         user=$1
         grep "$user" /etc/passwd >/dev/null || { echo "Not valid user" ; exit ; }
         find / -type f -user $user -ls 2>/dev/null | awk '{tot += $7 }
         END {print tot }'

18.13   awk '{ y = 127 - length($0)
                  printf "%s", $0
                  if (y > 0)
                      for (i = 0; i < y; i++)
                          printf "%s", " "
                  printf "\n"
              }' foo

18.14   awk '{ for (i=1; i<=NF; i++) {
                  row[NR]+= $i
                  col[i]+= $i

```
        }
        printf "%s", $0
        printf " %d\n", row[NR]
} END { for (i=1; i<=NF; i++)
            printf "%d ", col[i]
        printf "\n"
    }' foo
```

CHAPTER 19

19.1 All commands to be executed with -e. (i) Treats \t literally and prints it, but only if **print** statement is enclosed within double quotes. (ii) Prints a tab. (iii) Prints romeo.com as @heaven is interpreted as an array.

19.2 `perl -ne 'print "$.\t" . $_' foo`

19.3 `perl -e 'print "UNIX" x 20 . "\n" ;'`

19.4
```
#!/usr/bin/perl
print("Enter three numbers: ") ;
$reply = <STDIN> ;
($n1, $n2, $n3) = split(/\s+/, $reply) ;
$max = $n1 ;
$max = $n2 if $n2 > $n1 ;
$max = $n3 if $n3 > $max ;
print("The maximum number is $max\n") ;
```

Try generalizing this program to handle any number of inputs using **split** and a **foreach** loop.

19.5
```
#!/usr/bin/perl
open(INFILE, "/etc/passwd");
while (<INFILE>) {
    split(/:/);
    print if ($_[2] == 1);
}
```

19.6 **perl** does this quite easily:
```
#!/usr/bin/perl
$x="A" ;
while (<>) {
    print $x++ . ". " . $_ ;
}
```
After Z., the program prefixes an A and prints AA., AB., AC., etc.

19.7
```
#!/usr/bin/perl
open (INFILE, "$ARGV[1]") ;
while (<INFILE>) {
    if (/$ARGV[0]/) {
        print ; exit ;
    }
}
```

19.8 `perl -ne 'print if /director/ ? ($x=2) : (--$x> 0)' emp.lst`

19.9
```
#!/usr/bin/perl
$number = 1 ;
while ( $number != 0 ) {
    print ("Enter a number: ") ;
    $number = <STDIN> ;
    chop ($number) ;
    if ( $number != 0 ) {
        $total+= $number ;
    }
}
print "The total is $total\n" ;
```

19.10 `perl -p -i -e "tr/[a-z]/[A-Z]/" foo`

19.11
```
#!/usr/bin/perl
print "String : ";
$a = <STDIN>;
print "Number of times : ";
chop ($b = <STDIN>);
$c = $a x $b;
print "The result is : \n$c";
```

19.12 `perl -e '$x=A ; print $x++ while $y++ < 26'`

19.13 (ii)

19.14
```
#!/usr/bin/perl
print("Enter a number: ") ;
$number = <STDIN> ;
if ( $number > 255 || $number < 0 ) {
    print("Not a valid number\n") ;
} elsif ($number > 223) {
    print("C\n") ;
} elsif ($number > 126) {
    print("B\n") ;
} else {
    print("A\n") ;
}
```

19.15
```
#!/usr/bin/perl
# Note that you can assign a null string with qw
@month = qw/'' Jan Feb Mar Apr May Jun Jul Aug Sep Oct Nov Dec/ ;
$i = 1 ;
while ($i <= 12) {
    print $i . ". " . $month[$i] . "\n" ;
    $i++ ;
}
```

19.16 `perl -ne 's/(\w+)/\u$1/g ; print' foo`

19.17 `perl -p -i -e "tr/[a-z]/[A-Z]/" foo`

19.18 All existing files will be **overwritten:**

```
#!/usr/bin/perl
$file = $ARGV[0];
open (INFILE, "$file");
$i = 1;
while (<INFILE>) {
    $lines = $. % 10 ;
    if ($lines == 1) {
        $sfile = "$file.$i";
        $i++;
        open(FILEOUT, ">$sfile");
    }
    print FILEOUT $_;
    if ($lines == 0 ) {           # Written 10 lines already
        close(FILEOUT);           # So close the file
    }
}
```

19.19
```
#!/usr/bin/perl
$file = $ARGV[0] ;
if (-e $file) {
    if (-B $file) {
        print("$file is a binary file\n") ;
    } else {
        print("$file is not a binary file\n") ;
    }
} else {
    print("$file does not exist\n") ;
}
```

CHAPTER 20

20.1 /* searches the entire file for an asterisk, while f* looks for it in the current line only.

20.2 First use **0** to move to the beginning of the line and then use **2df.**. For subsequent lines, you can repeat the operation with the dot.

20.3 Use **:e foo** to open foo, and then use *[Ctrl- ^]* to toggle between the two files.

20.4 Make the setting **:set autowrite** in .exrc.

20.5 An operator like **d** and **y** can work only when it is used with a Command Mode command or by itself.

20.6 Use the command **"a5yy** on the first of the lines to be copied. Bring up the second file with **:e** *filename*, move to the right location and press **"ap**.

20.7 You should have used **"a20yy** for copying and **"ap** for pasting.

20.8 (i) :e! (ii) :0r foo   **20.9** :!cc %

20.10 Unabbreviate it: :unab re*[Enter]*

20.11 :map #1 /loop^M^M"ay/end loop^M

CHAPTER 21

21.1 Export the variable with **export**.

21.2 **script** runs a separate sub-shell, and a variable defined in a sub-shell is not visible in the parent shell.

21.3 The current directory is one of the environmental parameters inherited by a child process. Since the child cannot alter the environment of its parent, the original directory is restored after the death of the script, which is executed in a sub-shell. To make the change permanent, execute the script with the . command.

21.4 `size() { ls -l $* | awk '{ tot += $5 } END {print tot}' }`

21.5 A shell function always executes in the current shell. An **exit** statement will terminate the shell itself, and may log the user out.

21.6 If the script is invoked without any argument, $1 would be null and flname would be set to emp.1st.

21.7
```
rmi() {
    [ $# -gt 1 ] && option="-i"
    rm $option $*
}
```

21.8
```
rd() {
    dir=`pwd`
    cd ..
    rm -r $dir
}
```

21.9 Run the program from the .profile with **exec**.

CHAPTER 22

22.1 Compiling, assembling and linking.

22.2 as and ld.   **22.3** Yes.

22.4 **cc** assumes a library name to have the lib prefix and .a suffix. The library files are in /lib and /usr/lib, and the include files in /usr/include.

22.5 **make** will report an error if **cc** is not preceded by a tab.

22.6 The compiler automatically includes object files in this library without an explicit instruction.

22.7 (i) Has smaller executables since the library code is not included in the executable. (ii) Easier maintenance since a modification made to a library doesn't require modification of the programs using the library.

22.8 (i) admin -i foo s.foo (ii) get -e s.foo (iii) delta s.foo

22.9 Because they are displayed by the **prs** command.

22.10 When you make a change to a delta that is not the latest one. A branch delta uses a set of four numbers, so 1.2.1 is not a valid SID.

CHAPTER 23

23.1 System calls are built into the kernel, but library functions are built on top of them. When a system call is invoked, the processor switches to the kernel mode and returns to the user mode when the call completes.

23.2 A file descriptor is an integer that is allocated when a file is opened. It is used by all system calls that perform some operation on the file—like **read**, **write**, **close** and **lseek**.

23.3 Because the value of errno can change later with subsequent system calls even if they return success.

23.4 (i) fd = open("foo", O_WRONLY | O_TRUNC) ;
(ii) fd = open("foo.txt", O_WRONLY | O_APPEND) ;

23.5 (i), (iv) and (vii) are opening mode flags; the rest are status flags. A file can be opened in one of the modes, but each mode can be associated with one or more status flags. O_SYNC ensures that **write** doesn't return until the physical write to disk has been completed.

23.6 They all return a file descriptor.

23.7 The file descriptor table contains all allocated file descriptor entries. Each entry points to its associated file table which contains the file's mode flags, status flags, file offset pointer and reference count. Each file descriptor is associated with a separate file table entry except when **dup**, **dup2** and **fork** are used.

23.8 This program terminates when the file descriptor table overflows:
```
#include <fcntl.h>
#include <sys/stat.h>
#define BUFSIZE 1024
int main(void) {
    int fd;                 /* File descriptors for read and write */
    while (1) {
        if ((fd = open("/etc/passwd", O_RDONLY)) == -1) {
          perror("open");
          exit (1);
        }
        printf("File des: %d\n", fd);
    }
    exit(0);
}
```

23.9
```
#include <fcntl.h>
#include <unistd.h>
int main(int argc, char **argv) {
    int fd, n;
    char u ;
    fd = open(argv[1], O_RDONLY) ;
    while ((n = read(fd, &u, 1)) > 0) {
        if (u >=97 && u <= 122)         /* Testing for lowercase alphabet */
            u -= 32;                    /* and changing it to uppercase */
        write(STDOUT_FILENO, &u, 1);
```

```
        }
        close(fd);
}
```

The following program displays the ASCII values of the alphabets:

```
#include <stdio.h>
int main(void) {
    char c ;
    for (c ='A'; c <= 'Z'; c++)
        printf("%d\n", c);
    for (c ='a'; c <= 'z'; c++)
        printf("%d\n", c);
}
```

23.10 (i) umask(0);
```
    fd = open("foo", O_WRONLY | O_CREAT, S_IRUSR | S_IWUSR | S_IRGRP |
                     S_IWGRP | S_IROTH | S_IWOTH);
```

(ii) umask(0);
```
    mkdir("foofoo", S_IRWXU | S_IRWXG | S_IRWXO);
```

23.11
```
#include <sys/stat.h>
#include <stdio.h>
#include <unistd.h>
int main(int argc, char **argv) {
    struct stat statbuf;
    int exists = 1;

    if ((access(argv[1], F_OK) == 0)) {
        lstat(argv[1], &statbuf);
        if (S_ISREG(statbuf.st_mode)) {
            unlink(argv[1]);
            exists = 0;
        }
    } else
        exists = 0;

    if (exists == 0)
        mkdir(argv[1], S_IRWXU | S_IRGRP | S_IXGRP | S_IROTH | S_IXOTH);
}
```

23.12
```
#include <sys/types.h>
#include <sys/stat.h>
#include <stdio.h>
#include <dirent.h>
int main(void) {
    DIR *dir; off_t size;
    struct dirent *direntry;   struct stat statbuf;

    if ((dir = opendir(".")) != NULL)
        while ((direntry = readdir(dir)) != NULL)
            if (lstat(direntry->d_name, &statbuf) == 0)
```

```
            if (S_ISREG(statbuf.st_mode))
                if ((size = statbuf.st_size) > 100000)
                    printf("%s: %d\n", direntry->d_name, size);
                else if (size == 0)
                    unlink(direntry->d_name);
    }
```

23.13 The `unlink` system call removes the directory entry for a file, but the inode of the file is freed only when there are no pointers to it. As long as the file is open, the file table points to the inode table. I/O can be performed on the open file, but the file can't be opened by another process because its name is not present in the directory.

23.14 Assuming that the files are available in the current directory, this program should work:

```c
#include <sys/types.h>
#include <sys/stat.h>
#include <stdio.h>
#include <dirent.h>

int main(void) {
    DIR *dir; off_t size;
    struct dirent *direntry;  struct stat statbuf;

    if ((dir = opendir(".")) != NULL)
        while ((direntry = readdir(dir)) != NULL)
            if (lstat(direntry->d_name, &statbuf) == 0)
                if (getuid() == statbuf.st_uid)
                    chmod(direntry->d_name, statbuf.st_mode & ~S_IRWXO);
}
```

23.15
```c
#include <fcntl.h>
#include <sys/stat.h>
int main(void) {
    int fd;
    mode_t old_mode;
    old_mode = umask(0);                        /* No mask */
    fd = open("foo", O_WRONLY | O_CREAT, S_IRUSR | S_IWUSR |
                                         S_IRGRP | S_IROTH);
    chmod("foo", S_IRWXU | S_IRGRP | S_IWGRP | S_IROTH);
    system("ls -l foo");
    fchmod(fd, S_IRUSR | S_IRGRP);      /* Can use fchmod also */
    system("ls -l foo");
    umask(old_mode);                            /* Revert to previous mask */
    exit(0);
}
```

CHAPTER 24

24.1 No, the text segment is shared.

24.2 Because the addresses specified in the executable don't point to actual memory locations.

24.3 The stack stores the local variables and arguments of a function while the heap memory is used when a process needs to dynamically create memory. Since the kernel may be concurrently executing on behalf of several processes, it needs a separate stack for each process.

24.4 A mode of the processor where any machine instruction can be executed. No separate process runs in this mode.

24.5 When a process makes a system call that keeps the CPU idle.

24.6 dup, dup2, fcntl and pipe.

24.7
```
#include <sys/types.h>
#include <stdio.h>
int main(void) {
    pid_t pid, pid2;
    if (fork() > 0)
        fork();
    printf("PID: %d PPID: %d\n", getpid(), getppid());
}
```

24.8 The statement Before fork occurs twice in the file. I/O buffers are copied during a fork and the standard library functions like **printf** are fully buffered when writing to a file. That's why the **printf** statement in the parent was not written to the terminal when the output was redirected.

24.9 False.

24.10 True, the process is removed from the process table only after the parent has picked up the exit status. Until that happens, the process remains in the zombie state.

24.11
```
#include <stdio.h>
#include <fcntl.h>
#include <sys/wait.h>
int main (int argc, char **argv) {
    int a, b, c, status;
    switch(fork()) {
        case 0:
            a = atoi(argv[1]);
            b = atoi(argv[2]);
            c = a + b ;
            exit(c);

        default:
            wait(&status);
            printf("The sum of the two numbers is %d\n", WEXITSTATUS(status));
            exit(20);
    }
}
```

24.12 The exit status is actually 8 bits long, and the value set inside the shell script is a large value. $? only stores the last 8 bits.

24.13
```
#include <unistd.h>
int main (void) {
    dup2(STDOUT_FILENO, STDERR_FILENO);
    write(2, "Hello Dolly\n", 12);
    exit(0);
}
```

24.14 Because there are some attributes of an open file that need to be replicated during a fork, and some that must not be. For a parent and child to be able to write the same file without conflict, the descriptor needs to be replicated but not the offset pointer. This is possible only if these parameters are held in two separate tables.

24.15 A process can either ignore a signal, perform the default action or catch it to execute a signal handling function. The SIGSTOP and SIGKILL signals can't be either ignored or caught, and will always perform the default action.

24.16 The output of this program will always show two lines for the SIGKILL and SIGSTOP signals:

```
#include <stdio.h>
#include <signal.h>
int main (void) {
    int i;
    for (i = 1; i <= 32; i++)
        if (signal(i, SIG_IGN) == SIG_ERR)
            printf("Signal %d can't be ignored\n", i);
}
```

CHAPTER 25

25.1 `passwd -x 28` *username*

25.2 The user is running a restricted shell.

25.3 The boot file system contains the UNIX kernel. The root file system contains the essential utilities that keep the system running. The swap file system stores the process images when they can't be held in memory.

25.4 The root file system because it contains the essential utilities that keep the system running.

25.5 (i) fdisk (ii) mkfs (iii) fsck

25.6 **mount** can work with only one argument when the mount point and device name are specified in /etc/fstab. Unmounting is not possible when the user executing **umount** is placed in a directory inside the file system.

25.7 (i) /etc/vfstab (ii) /etc/fstab

25.8 Run level represents the state the system is in; some services run only at specified run levels. The default run level is set in the line containing initdefault in /etc/inittab.

25.9 `telinit q`

25.10 (i) /etc/rc*n*.d (ii) /etc/rc.d/rc*n*.d where *n* is the run level.

25.11 `find / -name a.out -print | xargs -n20 rm -f`

Appendix E

Glossary

absolute pathname A pathname which begins with a /, indicating that the file has to be referenced in an absolute manner—from root. See also **relative pathname**.

access time A file's time stamp representing the date and time a file was last accessed. A file is considered to be accessed if it is read, written or executed. The access time is stored in the inode and displayed by **ls -lu**.

action A component of an **sed**, **awk** or **perl** instruction which acts on text specified by an **address**. It normally uses a single character to represent an action for **sed**, but could be a complete program in case of **awk** and **perl**. Also known as **internal command**.

address A component of an **sed**, **awk** or **perl** instruction which specifies the lines to be affected by the **action**. The specification could be made with a single line number or a range of them, or with a regular expression or a pair of them, or any combination of the two.

alias Term used to refer to a command sequence by another name. Aliasing is available in **csh**, **bash** and **ksh** to abbreviate long command sequences.

Anonymous FTP A public FTP site where users use the login name "anonymous" and the email address as the password to gain access. Most downloadable software are hosted in these sites. Doesn't permit uploading of files.

archive Term used to a store a group of files as a single unit—either on magnetic media or as a single disk file. Refers to such units created by **tar**, **cpio** and **zip**. Also refers to a library of object files.

argument The words following a command. It can be an option, an expression, an instruction, a program or one or more filenames. Options can also have their own arguments.

ASCII collating sequence The sequence used by ASCII (American Standard Code for Information Interchange) to number characters. Control characters occupy the top slots, followed by numerals, uppercase letters, and then lowercase. Sequence followed by any UNIX command which sorts its output.

atomic operation Multiple actions that must be performed in entirety or not at all. A system call represents an atomic operation.

attachment A file that is sent along with an email message. Attachments can be binary files that can be viewed by a mail client either inline or using a **plugin** or **helper application**.

background job   One or more related processes that run without being waited for by their parent. A command, when terminated by the & symbol, runs in the background. See also **foreground job**.

block device   A hard disk, tape unit or floppy drive where output is written to and read from in units of blocks rather than bytes. Is indicated by the character **b** in the first character of the permissions field of the listing. See also **character device**.

boot block   A special area in every file system. For the **root file system**, this block contains the boot procedure and the partition table, while for others it is left blank.

browser   A program used to view HTML pages of the World Wide Web. Common Web browsers include Netscape and Internet Explorer (for Microsoft Windows and selected UNIX flavors). Linux is shipped with Netscape, Mozilla and Konqueror.

brute force attack   A technique of trying out every possible key combination to decrypt data without knowledge of the key used to encrypt it.

BSD UNIX   A flavor of UNIX from the University of California, Berkeley. Berkeley introduced a number of enhancements like the **vi** editor, C shell, r-utilities, PPP and symbolic links. TCP/IP was first available on BSD UNIX.

buffer   A temporary storage that is often used to hold frequently requested information in memory, rather than on disk, thus speeding up data transfer. Used by **vi** to make a copy of a file before editing. See also **buffer cache**.

buffer cache   A pool of buffers maintained by the kernel to store data when doing I/O. All programs read from and write to these buffers unless explicitly directed to skip them.

cache   Same as **buffer**.

character   The smallest unit of information. The press of a key generates a single character, while ASCII has a set of 256 of them.

character device   A terminal or printer where output is written to and read from in streams of characters. Is indicated by the character **c** in the first character of the permissions field of the listing. See also **block device**.

child process   The process created by the parent process. The created process inherits some of the environmental parameters of its parent, but environmental changes made in the child are not available in the parent.

client-server   A two-tier scheme that allows two processes to run in a cooperative manner. The client process requests a service from a server process, generally running on a different host. X Window treats the concept in a reverse manner. See also **X server** and **X client**.

command   Normally the first word entered at the prompt. It is usually an executable file, but can also include the built-in statements (also known as **internal commands**) of the shell and other commands (like **mailx**, **vi**, etc.)

command failure   The **exit status** returned by a command on unsuccessful completion. A value greater than 0 indicates failure and 0 signifies success. See also **command success**.

command line A complete sequence of a command, its options, filenames and other arguments that are specified at the shell prompt. The shell executes a command only when it encounters a complete command line.

Command Mode One of the three modes available in the **vi** editor to let keystrokes be interpreted as commands to act on text. See also **Input Mode** and **ex Mode**.

command substitution A feature of the shell which executes a command enclosed within a pair of backquotes (``` `` ```) and uses its standard output to form the arguments of another command. Double quotes enable command substitution but not single quotes.

command success The **exit status** returned by a command on successful completion. A value of 0 indicates success, any other value signifies failure. See also **command failure**.

Common Desktop Environment (CDE) A standardized look and feel of the entire desktop under the X Window system now adopted by most UNIX vendors. Features a Front Panel from where applications can be launched, a File Manager and a Workspace Switch to allow the use of multiple desktops.

Common Gateway Interface (CGI) The interface offered by a Web server to pass on form data to an external application. The application processes the data and sends back the results to the server.

concatenation The combination of two or more entities. Term used in connection with the **cat** command and shell variables.

context address A form of addressing used by **sed**, **awk** and **perl** which uses a regular expression enclosed by a pair of /s. The lines containing the expression are affected by the action.

context switch Term used to refer to the change of the **process context** when the time quantum allocated to a process expires. It can also occur when the process invokes an I/O bound system call.

control command A command used in the command line of a shell, **awk** and **perl** conditional or loop to determine the control flow of the construct.

control file A text file used by some programs to take their instructions from. $HOME/.exrc, /etc/sendmail.cf, /etc/inittab and /etc/inetd are some of the control files to be found on a UNIX system.

cron The chronograph of the UNIX system. It executes the commands listed in a **crontab** file at a frequency specified by the various fields in the file. Is widely used for scheduling noninteractive jobs.

crontab A control file named after the user-id containing all instructions that need to be executed periodically. The **cron** command looks at this table every minute to execute any command scheduled for execution.

cryptography The science of protecting information using one or more keys. Symmetric cryptography uses a single key while asymmetric cryptography uses a **private key** and a **public key**.

current directory The directory in which the user is placed after using the **cd** command with an argument. Usually is set to the home directory during login time. See also **home directory**.

daemon   A process that runs continuously without a user specifically requesting it. It is usually not associated with a specific terminal. **cron**, **init**, **inetd**, **lpsched** and **sendmail** are important daemons that keep the system running.

DARPA set   The original set of TCP/IP utilities developed at the behest of DARPA and includes **telnet** and **ftp**.

delta   Term used to describe a version in the **Source Code Control System**.

device driver   A set of routines built into the kernel to handle a device. The kernel identifies the device driver from the device name used as argument to a command. The parameters passed by the kernel to the device driver are indicated by the **minor number** of the device.

device file   A file that represents a device. Provides a communication channel so that any interaction with the file actually results in activation of the physical device.

directory file   A file that contains the name and inode number of other files and subdirectories. Writing to a directory file is possible only by the kernel.

DNS   Same as **domain name system**.

domain   A common string used by several hosts as part of their fully qualified hostnames. Examples of top-level domains on the Internet are *com*, *edu*, *org* etc.

Domain Name System (DNS)   A service available on the Internet to convert hostnames to IP addresses, and vice versa. The database containing the mappings is distributed in a large network with consequent delegation of authority.

empty regular expression   A null string signified by two /s, which indicates that the string to be acted upon is the same as the last string searched. Used by **sed** in performing substitution.

encryption   A method of encoding a string of characters into a seemingly random character sequence. Used for storing the password of every user of the system. See also **secure shell**.

environment variable   A shell variable that is visible in all processes run by a user. The **export** and **setenv** commands create environment variables. HOME, TERM and SHELL are common environment variables. See also **local variable**.

escape sequence   A character that is preceded by a \ and has a special meaning. Escape sequences are used by **echo**, **printf**, **awk** and **perl**. For instance, \t represents a tab.

escaping   The use of the \ immediately before a character to indicate that the following character should be treated literally. Mostly used to remove the special meaning of a character, but sometimes is also used to emphasize it. See also **quoting**.

ex Mode   A mode available in the **vi** editor to let **ex** commands act on text. An indispensable mode for substitution, handling multiple files and customizing the editor. Also known as **Last Line Mode**. See also **Command Mode** and **Input Mode**.

exec   The mechanism used by a process to overwrite itself with the code of a new program. Usually follows the **fork** operation. Also represents a family of six C functions that actually do the job.

exit status   A value returned by a program after execution. A value 0 indicates successful (true) execution. In a C program, the **wait** system call directs the parent to pick up the child's exit status.

export   A built-in shell command which makes the environment of the parent process available in the child process. The statement is used with variables.

Extended Regular Expression (ERE)   An enhanced regular expression used by **grep -E**, **egrep**, **awk** and **perl** which allows the specification of multiple patterns. Uses the metacharacters ?, +, (,) and |.

file   A container for storing information. An ordinary file contains data. A directory file contains filenames. A device file provides the interface to access a physical device. A symbolic link points to the file that actually contains the information.

file attributes   A set of parameters stored in the inode which describe the characteristics of a file. They consist of the type, ownership, permissions, time stamps, size, number of links and an array of disk block addresses.

file descriptor   A small integer that is returned by the **open** system call when a file is opened. Each descriptor, maintained in the file descriptor table, points to the **file table**. The first three entires are usually allocated to the shell's standard streams.

file offset pointer   The location within the file where the next read or write operation will take place. This location is maintained in the **file table** and is updated every time a read or write operation on the file takes place.

file ownership   One of the attributes of a file. The user creating or copying a file is generally the owner as well. The owner of a file has certain privileges which are denied others. Ownership can be surrendered only by the superuser on a BSD-based system.

file permissions   Term used to describe a file's read, write and execute permissions available to three categories of users—**user**, **group** and **others**. Can be altered only by the owner of the file with **chmod**.

file system   A hierarchical structure of files and directories having its separate root directory. Every hard disk has at least one file system on it, which is attached to the **root file system** with the **mount** command.

file table   A structure maintained in memory that contains the file's opening modes, status flags, position of the offset pointer and a reference count field. Two file descriptors point to the same file table when a process forks or when a descriptor is replicated using **dup**, **dup2** or **fcntl**.

file time stamps   A set of three dates and times representing the date of last modification, access and change of inode of a file. This information is stored in the inode and displayed with various options to **ls**.

File Transfer Protocol (FTP)   A TCP/IP application protocol that transfers files between two remote machines. The **ftp** command uses this protocol.

filehandle   The logical name of a file used by I/O statements in **perl**.

filter   A program that uses a character stream as standard input, manipulates its contents and writes it to the standard output. The shell's redirection and piping features can be used with these programs.

foreground job   Refers to a job where the parent waits for execution to complete. You can run only one job in the foreground. See also **background job**.

fork   The mechanism of process creation by replicating the address space of the existing process. The copied process inherits the open files of its parent, current directory and exported variables. A fork is usually followed by an **exec**. Features a system call by that name.

FQDN   See **fully qualified domain name**.

Free Software Foundation   Same as **GNU**.

Fully Qualified Domain Name (FQDN)   A set of dot-delimited strings representing the domains and sub-domains to which the host belongs. The FQDN of a host is unique on the Internet.

getty   A process that runs at every free terminal to monitor the next login. Is spawned by **init** and execs the **login** program whenever a user tries to log in.

GNU   An organization founded by Richard Stallman which expands to GNU's Not UNIX, but now known as the Free Software Foundation. Many of the tools available on Linux have been developed by GNU or distributed under its license. The GNU license requires all developers to make the source code public.

Graphical User Interface (GUI)   The component of the X Window system that controls its look and feel.

group   A category of user understood by the **chmod** command. More than one user may belong to a group, and a set of file permissions is associated with this category. See also **owner** and **others**.

Group-Id (GID)   The group name or number of the user, which is allotted by the system when creating a user account. The name and its numeric representation are maintained in /etc/group, while the numeric value is also available in /etc/passwd. See also **user-id**.

hard link   See **link**.

helper application   An external program invoked by a browser to handle a special file format. Unlike a **plugin**, a helper application views files in a separate window. The file's extension, content type and the external program needed to handle it are specified in mime.types and mailcap.

here document   A form of standard input (<<) that forms part of the command line itself signifying that the input is *here*. Especially useful when used with commands that don't accept a filename as argument.

history   The facility to store, recall and execute previous commands in **csh**, **bash** and **ksh**. Also features a command by that name in these shells.

home directory   A field in /etc/passwd that indicates the directory where a user is placed on login. The **cd** command switches to the home directory when used without arguments. Same as **login directory**.

home page   Term used to refer to the first page presented to the user on connecting to a Web site.

host   A computer or device in a network having a separate IP address.

hostname   The name of a host that is unique in the network. Often used on the Internet with a series of dot-delimited strings to represent a **fully qualified domain name**. Features a command by that name which both displays and sets the hostname.

hosts file   Refers to the file /etc/hosts that contains the hostname-IP address mappings.

Hyper Text Markup Language (HTML)   The language used to code Web documents. Uses tags to transfer control to another document on another machine. HTML documents can be used to view animation or video or play audio.

Hyper Text Transfer Protocol (HTTP)   The application protocol that retrieves HTML documents from a Web server. It is *stateless* in that a connection has no knowledge of the state of the previous connection. HTTP 1.1 supports **keep-alive** (persistent) connections.

hypertext   A link placed in one document with the <A HREF> tag which points to a location in another document in the same machine or another. The World Wide Web is a collection of these documents. See also **Web page**.

in-line editing   Feature available in the Korn shell and Bash to recall and edit previous commands with **vi**-like commands. Is enabled with **set -o vi**.

in-place editing   Term used in **perl** to edit a file and write the output back to the same file without using redirection.

infinite loop   A **while**, **until** or **for** loop which never terminates. The **break** (**last** in **perl**) statement is used to switch control out of the loop.

init   A process having the PID number 1, which is responsible for the creation of all major processes. **init** runs all the system's daemons and the **getty** process at terminal ports. Can also be used as a command to set the system to a specific **run level**.

inode   A structure that stores all file attributes except the filename. Maintained in a special area of the disk and a copy is loaded into memory when a file is opened. See also **vnode table**.

inode number   A number identifying an inode for a file which is unique in a single file system. Displayed with **ls -i**.

Input Mode   One of the three modes of the **vi** editor. Any key depression is interpreted as input and the mode is terminated by pressing *[Esc]*. See also **Command Mode** and **ex Mode**.

instruction   A combination of an **address** and **action** used by **sed** and **awk**. The address specifies the lines to be affected by the action.

internal command   Name given to a sub-command of many UNIX tools like **vi**, **more**, **mailx** and **sed** commands, and the shell.

Internet   The super network of networks connected by the TCP/IP protocol with facilities of email, file transfer, remote login and the World Wide Web. See also **World Wide Web**.

Internet address   Same as **IP address**.

Internet daemon   A **daemon** that listens on multiple ports and invokes other daemons for FTP, TELNET and POP services. Available as the file **inetd** or **xinetd**.

interrupt   The sending of a signal (SIGINT) to a process with the intention of terminating it. A specific key is assigned this job, usually *[Ctrl-c]* or *[Delete]*, though it can be reassigned with the **stty** command.

Interval Regular Expression (IRE)   A regular expression that uses a single or a comma-delimited pair of numbers, enclosed by a matched pair of escaped curly braces (\{ and \}). The two numbers indicate the minimum and maximum number of times that the single character preceding it can occur. Used by **grep**, **sed** and **perl** commands. **perl** drops the \ in its implementation.

IP address   A string of four dot-delimited octets used to describe the logical address of a machine in a TCP/IP network. Same as **Internet address**.

iteration   The repeating of a loop's instruction set as long as the **control command** returns true. Term used in connection with the **while**, **until** and **for** loops.

job   A group of processes working toward a common goal. A pipeline is a simple example of a job. All processes in a job have the same process group-id (PGID).

job control   A feature provided in most shells (except Bourne) of moving jobs between foreground and background and suspending them. A job can be moved to foreground and background with **fg** and **bg**, respectively.

keep-alive connection   A feature available in HTTP 1.1 that allows multiple resources to be fetched in a single (persistent) connection. The server holds the connection for a certain time to allow further requests. Persistent connections speed up Web access.

kernel   The part of the UNIX operating system which is responsible for the creation and management of files and processes. Is loaded into memory when the machine is booted and interacts directly with the machine hardware. All system calls are built into the kernel.

kernel mode   A mode of the CPU used by the kernel when it runs on behalf of the user process. In this mode, the kernel can access any memory location. A switch from **user mode** to kernel mode takes place when the user program invokes a system call.

kill   A misnomer, actually signifies the sending of a signal to a process—often with the intention of terminating it. Features a command and system call by the name.

kill script   An **rc script** beginning with K that is used to kill a service. See also **start script**.

Last Line Mode   Same as **ex Mode**.

library function   A C function available in the standard library that performs most of the common programming tasks. Library functions encapsulate the **system calls** they internally use and often provide more convenient interfaces than the ones offered by system calls.

line   A sequence of characters terminated by the newline character.

line address   A form of addressing used by **sed**, **awk** and **perl** to specify a single line or a group of contiguous lines. Represented as a single line number or a pair of them to limit the boundaries of the text.

link   A file attribute stored in the inode that allows a file to be referred to by more than one name. Same as **hard link**. See also **symbolic link**.

listing   The output obtained with the **ls -l** command showing seven attributes of a file.

local variable   A variable that is visible only in the process or a **perl** subroutine where it is defined. See also **environment variable**.

login   A process that overlays the **getty** program when the user enters a login name. It execs the shell process on successful login.

login directory   Same as **home directory**.

login name   Same as **user-id**.

magic   Term used in **vi** to refer to the special meaning of a character used in a regular expression. The magic is turned off by using the **ex Mode** command **set nomagic**.

Mail Delivery Agent (MDA)   The agency responsible for delivering mail to the user. Receives a mail message from the **Mail Transport Agent** and appends it to a text file in /var/mail (/var/spool/mail in Linux).

Mail Transport Agent (MTA)   The agency responsible for transporting mail across a network. Sender's MTA hands over mail to recipient's MTA. SMTP is the standard protocol used by MTAs.

Mail User Agent (MUA)   The client program that is used to send and receive mail. The MUA looks at the spool directory in /var/mail (/var/spool/mail in Linux) for incoming mail. It also hands over outgoing mail to the **Mail Transport Agent**. **mailx**, **pine** and Netscape Messenger are common MUAs.

mailbox   A text file named after the username, usually in /var/mail (/var/spool/mail in Linux), and contains incoming mail that has not been viewed. Binary attachments are held in this file in encoded form. See also **mbox**.

major number   One of the parameters of the listing of a device file which indicates the device driver required to access the device. Similar devices have the same major number. See also **minor number**.

makefile   A control file used by the **make** command to determine the programs that need to be recompiled. Has the name makefile or Makefile in the user's working directory.

man page   The UNIX documentation as viewed by the **man** command. Every command, system configuration file, system call and library function is associated with a man page.

mbox   A file where a mail message is saved after it has been viewed. Many character-based mail clients use $HOME/mbox as the default mbox. See also **mailbox**.

metacharacter   Term used to describe any character that means something special to the shell. The meaning is reversed by preceding the character with a \. Concept also extends to special characters used by certain commands as part of their syntax.

minor number   One of the parameters of the listing of a device file which indicates the special characteristics of the device. Can be interpreted to mean the parameters passed on to the device driver. See also **major number**.

modification time   One of the time stamps of a file stored in the inode which represents the date and time the contents of a file were last modified. One of the attributes displayed by the listing.

mounting   The process of attaching a standalone **file system** to another file system. Also features a command by the name **mount**. See also **unmounting**.

MULTICS   An operating system whose development work was aborted to give way to the UNIX operating system. Many of the features of UNIX owe their origin to MULTICS.

Multipurpose Internet Mail Extensions (MIME)   A standard used on the Internet to encode and decode binary files. Also useful in encoding multiple data formats in a *single* mail message. Features two headers—Content-Type and Content-Transfer-Encoding.

name server   A dedicated service used on the Internet to convert the **fully qualified domain name** of a host to its IP address and vice versa. A name server is queried by a **resolver** and may either provide the answer or the address of another name server.

newline   The character generated by hitting *[Enter]*. Used as the delimiter between two lines and forms one of the characters of **whitespace**.

newsgroup   An offline discussion group on the Internet which originated from the UNIX-based USENET. Netscape Messenger also handles newsgroups.

nonprivileged user   An ordinary user having no superuser privileges.

option   A string normally beginning with a -, which changes the default behavior of a command. Multiple options can generally be combined with a single - symbol.

ordinary file   The most common file of the UNIX system represented by programs, data and text. It contains data but not the end-of-file mark. Also known as **regular file**.

orphan   A process whose parent has died. Orphans are adopted by **init**.

others   A category of user understood by the **chmod** command. A user who is neither the owner nor a group owner of a file belongs to this class. One set of file permissions is associated with this category. See also **owner** and **group**.

overlay   Same as **exec**.

owner   The creator of a file having complete authority of determining its contents and permissions. Understood as **user** by the **chmod** command. The string and numeric representations are stored in /etc/passwd. See also **group** and **others**.

packet   Term applied to describe a fragmented unit of data in a TCP/IP network.

pager   A tool that displays output one screen at a time. **more** and **less** are the standard pagers on UNIX and Linux systems.

Parent Process-ID (PPID)   The **process-id** of the parent process which is stored in the **process table** for every process.

passphrase   A secret string used to protect a user's **private key**. Unlike a **password**, a passphrase can contain spaces.

password   A secret string used by a user for authentication during login. The code is not flashed on the terminal, but is stored in an encrypted manner in /etc/shadow. Also features a command with a similar name (**passwd**) to change the password.

PATH   A shell variable that contains a colon-delimited list of directories that the shell will look through to locate a command invoked by a user. The PATH generally includes /bin and /usr/bin for nonprivileged users and /sbin and /usr/sbin for the superuser.

pathname   A sequence of one or more filenames using a / as a delimiter. All except the last filename have to be directories. See also **relative pathname** and **absolute pathname**.

pending signals mask   A field maintained in the **process table** that shows the signals that have been received for a process. The kernel looks up this field and the **signal disposition** table to determine the action to be taken.

ping   The sending of packets to a remote host to check the connectivity of the network. Also features a command by that name.

pipe   A buffered object that allows one-way data transmission through its two ends using flow control. Whatever is written to one end is read from the other. Features a system call by that name. Used to create a **pipeline**.

pipeline   A sequence of two or more commands used with the | symbol so that the input of one command comes from the output of the other. See also **pipe**.

plugin   A small program that is installed in a browser to handle special file formats which can't be handled by the browser. Unlike a **helper application**, a plugin can't be invoked separately.

port number   A number used to identify a TCP/IP application and defined in /etc/services. Servers use fixed port numbers but clients use random port numbers. A packet has two port numbers, one for each end of the channel.

positional parameters   The external arguments to a shell script which are read into a series of special variables designated as $1, $2, $3, etc. These parameters can be renumbered with the **shift** command.

POSIX   A set of standard interfaces that are based on the UNIX operating system. POSIX compliance ensures that a set of programs developed on one machine can be moved to another without recoding. POSIX.1 represents the standard for the application programming interface for the C language. POSIX.2 provides the interface for the shell and utilities.

Post Office Protocol (POP)   The TCP/IP protocol used for fetching mail from a mail server. POP is often used over a dialup line to fetch Internet mail.

private key   A key used for encrypting or decrypting data, but which doesn't leave the user's machine. Often protected by a **passphrase**. Data encrypted with this key can only be decrypted with the **public key**, and vice versa.

process   An instance of a running program and created by the **fork** system call. Usually is followed by an **exec**. Most of the shell's internal commands are executed without creating a process.

process address space   The memory locations that a process can access and includes the text, data, heap and stack segments.

process birth   Term used to refer to the creation of a process. The process is created when the command representing it is invoked, and dies when command execution is complete. The **fork** system call gives birth to a process.

process context   The complete environment that is seen by the process when it runs. Includes a hardware context (the state of the CPU registers) and a software context (the address space, process credentials). The kernel saves the context of the current process before running a new one.

process death   Term used to refer to the termination of a process. The process dies when the command representing it has completed execution.

process group   A collection of processes having some common attributes. In shells supporting job control, each job or process is placed in its own process group. A process group can be suspended and killed by sending a signal to the leader of the group.

Process Group-ID (PGID)   A common number allotted to a group of processes. The group leader has its PGID equal to the PID. See also **process group**.

process table   A structure maintained in memory containing the attributes of every active process running in the system. Also maintains the exit status of a terminated process until fetched by its parent.

Process-ID (PID)   A unique number allotted to a process by the kernel when it is born.

profile   A startup file used and maintained by every user in the home directory. Instructions in this file are executed during login time without spawning a sub-shell. However, /etc/profile is executed before the user's own profile.

prompt   A string that shows the position of the cursor. The appearance of a prompt generally indicates that the previous command has completed its run. Can be customized by setting the value of the shell variable PS1.

public key   A key used for encrypting or decrypting data, but which is distributed to all. Data encrypted with this key can only be decrypted with the **private key**, and vice versa.

quoting   Enclosing a group of characters in single or double quotes to remove their special meaning. Though the shell ignores all special characters enclosed in single quotes, double quotes permit evaluation of $ as a variable and ` for **command substitution**.

r-utilities A set of TCP/IP tools developed by Berkeley as alternatives to the **DARPA set**. The tools include **rlogin**, **rcp** and **rsh** and are inherently insecure. Has been superseded by tools of the **secure shell** (SSH) suite.

race condition A situation where two or more events contend for the same resource and the eventual outcome is determined by the sequence in which the events are serviced.

rc script A shell script maintained in the home directory that is automatically executed when creating a sub-shell. Also refers to a set of scripts in /etc that start the daemons that should run for a specific **run level** and kill the ones that shouldn't. See also **start script** and **stop script**.

recursion A characteristic feature of some UNIX commands to descend a specified directory to access all subdirectories under this directory, and beyond. **ls**, **rm**, **chmod**, **chown** and **chgrp** use a special option to do that, while **find** and **tar** do it compulsorily.

redirection Term used in the shell to reassign the standard input and standard output of a command. The default source and destination of a data stream can be redirected to point to a disk file or to a pipe.

regular expression An ambiguous expression containing some special characters which is expanded by a *command* to match more than one string. Should be quoted to prevent interference from the shell. See also **wild-card**.

regular file Same as **ordinary file**.

relative pathname A pathname which specifies the location of a file using the symbols . and .. to refer to the current and parent directories, respectively. See also **absolute pathname**.

remote login Connecting to a remote machine using a username and password. All commands entered after logging in are actually executed on the remote machine. See also **telnet** and **secure shell**.

repeat factor A feature available in the **vi** editor and the **more** and **less** commands of using a number to prefix any command. It usually repeats the command that number of times.

resolver A set of library routines used by a TCP/IP application to query a **name server** for resolving a domain name to the IP address. The resolver also looks up /etc/resolv.conf.

revision Term used to describe a version in the **Revision Control System**.

Revision Control System (RCS) An implementation of the document maintenance system as described in the **Source Code Control System (SCCS)**.

root The top-most directory in every file system which has no parent. Is indicated by the / symbol. Also signifies a user who uses the login name root to log on to the superuser account.

root file system The main file system containing the essential utilities needed to keep the system running. All other file systems are mounted at different mount points of this file system.

root name server A server running **DNS** that specifies the name servers of the top-level domains like *.com*, *.edu*, *.org* etc. Thirteen of them handle all top-level name server queries on the Internet.

router   A special device that routes packets from one network to another.

run level   Term used to refer to the various states that a UNIX system can be in. The run level is determined by the argument of the **init** command, and the action to be taken is specified in /etc/inittab. Different **rc scripts** are executed depending on the value of this run level.

secure shell (SSH)   A suite of networking tools that enable remote login, file transfer and command execution. Unlike with the older tools like **telnet** and **ftp**, communication with the secure shell is totally encrypted.

server   See **client-server architecture**.

Set-User-ID (SUID)   A special mode of a file indicated by the letter **s** in the permissions field. The effective user-id of a process having this bit set is the owner of the file and not the user running the program. This property lets users modify important system files by using a specific command, rather than directly.

shared library   A group of object files that are loaded into memory only during runtime. Several programs can share the same library code. See also **static library**.

shell   The command interpreter of the UNIX system which runs perpetually at every occupied terminal. The shell processes a user request and interacts with the kernel to execute the command. It also possesses a programming capability.

shell function   A group of statements executed as a bunch in the current shell. A shell function accepts parameters and can return only a numeric value.

shell script   An ordinary file containing a set of commands, which is executed in an interpretive manner in a sub-shell. All the shell's internal commands and external UNIX commands can be specified in a script.

signal   The notification made by the kernel that an event has occurred. A signal has a default disposition (action to take) but it can be overridden by a user-defined **signal handler**. Signals SIGKILL and SIGSTOP can't be ignored or handled otherwise. See also **signal disposition** and **signal handler**.

signal disposition   The action to be taken when a signal occurs. Every signal has a default disposition, maintained in the signal disposition table, which could be to terminate, stop the process or to ignore the signal. The disposition can be changed by using a **signal handler** except for the SIGKILL and SIGSTOP signals.

signal handler   A user-defined function in a C program that catches a signal and makes it behave in a manner that is different from the default. Signals SIGKILL and SIGSTOP can't be caught.

signature file   A file named .signature in a user's home directory. It is used to enter a person's details that must accompany every mail message. Most mail user agents are configured to automatically attach the file with every outgoing message.

Simple Mail Transfer Protocol (SMTP) The TCP/IP protocol used to transport email data across the Internet. The SMTP client communicates with the SMTP server at the other end and *directly* delivers the message. **sendmail** is the most common implementation of SMTP.

sleep Term used to refer to the temporary suspension of a process. Also features a command and library function by that name.

Source Code Control System (SCCS) An optimized document maintenance system that stores one version in full and only the changes needed to generate the other versions. Also features checks to prevent multiple users from editing the same version. See also **Revision Control System (RCS)**.

spawn The creating of a child process. However, most of the internal statements of the shell are executed without creating a process. See also **process birth**.

standard error The destination used by the diagnostic output stream to write its output. Includes all error messages generated by UNIX commands. The default destination of this stream is the terminal but can be redirected to any file.

standard input The source opened by the shell to accept information as a stream of characters. By default, the keyboard is assigned this source, but it can also come from a file, a pipeline or a **here document**.

standard output The destination used by commands to send output to. Used by all UNIX commands that send output to the terminal. The default destination can also be reassigned to divert output to another file or a pipeline.

start script An **rc script** beginning with S that is used to start a service. See also **kill script**.

static library A group of object files bundled into an archive. A program using a static library contains the object code of the library. See also **shared library**.

sticky bit A special mode assigned to a file or a directory and indicated by the letter t in the permissions field. The executable code of an ordinary file gets stuck in the swap area once it has been executed. A directory with the sticky bit set can be shared by a group of users, where one user can't tamper with another user's files.

stop script An **rc script** beginning with K that is used to stop a service. See also **start script**.

sub-shell A second shell created by the parent shell. It is normally required for executing a shell script or a group of commands with the () operators. Changes made in a sub-shell are not available in the parent.

subroutine A group of statements executed as a bunch in **perl**—like a shell function. Subroutines use arguments which are stored in the array @_. **perl** uses the & symbol to call a subroutine.

superblock A special area in every file system which contains important information on the file system. Includes a list of free data blocks and inodes. The disk copy is regularly updated with the memory copy by the **sync** command.

superuser Same as **system administrator**.

suspend The stopping of a job. The job may later be resumed either in the background or foreground. This feature is available in **csh**, **ksh** and **bash**.

swapping Refers to the movement of currently inactive processes from memory to the swap area of the disk (swapping out). Also refers to the transfer of these processes from the swap area to memory when ready for execution (swapping in).

symbolic link A file which points to the location of another file or directory. Unlike hard links, a symbolic link can link files across file systems. Can be used to link directories also. See also **link**.

symlink Same as **symbolic link**.

sync Term used to describe the synchronization of the superblock and inodes with their respective memory versions. Also features a command by that name which the kernel uses to write the memory data to disk.

system administrator The person responsible for the management of system resources. The administrator can change any file attribute and kill any user process. Uses a special user account (generally, root) to perform administrative duties. Also known as **superuser**.

system call A routine defined in the kernel which performs the basic operations of the computer, like opening a file and creating a process. All UNIX commands and library functions are written in terms of system calls. Processor switches from **user mode** to **kernel mode** when executing a system call.

system process A process which runs in the system during booting without being specifically requested for by a user. **init**, **getty**, **cron** and **lpsched** are some of the system processes. See also **daemon**.

tab A single character which simulates a contiguous set of spaces. Is generated by hitting a specific key or *[Ctrl-i]*. Forms one of the characters of **whitespace**. Useful for aligning columns.

tagged regular expression (TRE) Term used to indicate the grouping of a regular expression with an escaped pair of parentheses, \(and \). This group is repeated elsewhere in the line by using the tag *n* or $*n* (**perl**), where *n* is a number between 1 and 9. Used by **grep**, **sed** and **perl** commands.

TCP/IP Expands to Transmission Control Protocol/Internet Protocol—a collection of protocols used for networking computers that use different operating systems and different hardware. Ensures reliable transmission with full error-correction facilities.

The Open Group Owner of the UNIX standard and the originator of The Single UNIX Specification. Includes X/OPEN in its fold. Also maintains the X Window system.

toggle switch A command that reverses the effect of its immediate previous invocation. **ftp** has a few commands that act as toggle switches.

Top-Level Domain (TLD) A domain immediately below the root (.) domain. Not allotted to a specific country. TLDs comprise the generic domains *com, edu, org, net, museum, biz.* etc.

umask   A number maintained in the shell that determines a file's default permissions. This number is subtracted from the system's default to obtain a file's actual permissions. The value can be displayed and set by using a command of the same name.

Uniform Resource Locator (URL)   A string of characters that specifies a resource on the Web. Comprises the protocol, the FQDN of the site and the path name of the file.

unmounting   The process of disengaging a file system from the main file system. The **umount** command performs this unmounting. See also **mounting**.

user   The owner of a file as understood by the **chmod** command. See also **group** and **others**.

user mode   A mode of the CPU when running a program. In this mode, the program has no access to the memory locations used by the kernel. See also **kernel mode**.

User-ID (UID)   The name used by a user to gain access to the system. A list of authorized names is maintained in /etc/passwd along with their numeric representations. Also known as **login name** and **username**. See also **group-id**.

username   Same as **user-id**.

virtual console   A system of using multiple screens and logins from a single UNIX machine. A new screen is opened by using *[Alt]* and a function key.

vnode table   The image of the inode in memory. Contains apart from the inode information, a reference count that shows the number of processes that point to the table. A file can't be properly deleted as long as this table is open.

wait   Term used to refer to the inaction of a parent process while a child is running. Normally, the parent waits for the death of the child to pick up its **exit status**. Also features a shell built-in command and a system call by that name.

wake   Term used to indicate the termination of a dormant activity when an event occurs. The kernel wakes up a sleeping process when a specific event has occurred (like the completion of I/O).

Web page   An HTML document containing text and graphics that is presented in the form of a page at every Web site. A Web page has links with other pages—often on different machines.

Web server   A TCP/IP application that runs the HTTP protocol. The World Wide Web serves all resources through Web servers.

whitespace   A contiguous sequence of spaces, tabs or newlines. The default value of the IFS variable. Used as delimiter by the shell to parse command line arguments and by the **set** statement to assign its arguments to positional parameters.

wild-card   A special character used by the *shell* to match a group of filenames with a single expression. The * and ? are commonly used wild-card characters. See also **regular expression**.

word   A contiguous string of characters not containing whitespace. **wc** can count words, and **vi** enables cursor movement using a word as a navigational unit.

World Wide Web   A service on the Internet featuring a collection of linked documents and images. The browser (client) fetches these resources from a Web server using the HTTP protocol.

wraparound   A feature provided by the **vi** editor for resuming the search for a pattern from the other end of a file. The entire file is thus searched irrespective of the cursor position at the time of commencement of search.

X client   An X program which performs a specific function and uses the X server for display. **xterm** is a common X client found in every X Window system.

X server   The program in X Window which controls the display including the monitor, mouse and keyboard. X clients write their output to this program. If the display changes, only the server needs to change and not the clients.

X Window System   The graphical component of the UNIX system. X clients write their output to the server which is responsible for their display on separate windows.

zipped file   Any file that is compressed with the **gzip**, **zip** or **bzip2** commands. They are decompressed with **gunzip**, **unzip** and **bunzip2**.

zombie   A dead process whose exit status has not been picked up by its parent using **wait**. Zombies clog the process table and can't be killed.

Bibliography

There's an abundance of material on UNIX available both in print as well as on the Internet. Apart from the UNIX documentation, the following textbooks and journals served as handy references:

General Reading

UNIX System V: A Practical Guide, Third Edition by Mark G. Sobell (Addison-Wesley), 1995, Menlo Park, California

Harley Hahn's Student Guide to Unix by Harley Hahn (The McGraw-Hill Companies), 1996, Berkeley, California

Your UNIX: The Ultimate Guide by Sumitabha Das (Tata McGraw-Hill), 2001, New Delhi

The UNIX Operating System by Kaare Christian, Susan Richter (John Wiley), 1993, New York

UNIX: The Textbook by Syed Mansoor Sarwar, Robert Koretsky and Syed Aqeel Sarwar (Addison-Wesley Longman), 2001

UNIX Made Easy—UNIX and Linux Basics and Beyond by John Muster (Tata McGraw-Hill), 2002, New Delhi

Running Linux, Third Edition by Matt Welsh, Matthias Kalle Dalheimer and Lar Kaufman (O'Reilly & Associates), 1999, Sebastopol, California

References

UNIX in a Nutshell by Arnold Robbins (Shroff Publishers and Distributors), 1998, Mumbai

The UNIX Programming Environment by Brian Kernighan & Rob Pike (Prentice-Hall of India), 1984, New Delhi

The Design of the UNIX Operating System by Maurice Bach (Prentice-Hall of India), 1986, New Delhi

UNIX Internals—The New Frontiers by Uresh Vahalia (Pearson Education Asia), 1996, New Delhi

Solaris Internals—Core Kernel Architecture by Jim Mauro and Rochard McDougall (Sun Microsystems Press), 2001, Palo Alto, California

UNIX Power Tools by Shelley Powers, Jerry Peek, Tim O'Reilly and Mike Loukides (Shroff Publishers and Distributors), 2002, Mumbai

Systems Programming

Advanced Programming in the UNIX Environment by W. Richard Stevens (Pearson Education Asia), 1993, New Delhi

UNIX for Programmers and Users by Graham Glass and King Ables (Prentice-Hall), 1993, Upper Saddle River, New Jersey

Beginning Linux Programming by Richard Stones and Neil Matthew (Shroff Publishers and Distributors), 1999, Mumbai

Topical Reading

Advanced UNIX — A Programmer's Guide by Stephen Prata (SAMS), 1986, New Delhi

Learning the Korn Shell by Bill Rosenblatt and Arnold Robbins (Shroff Publishers and Distributors), 2002, Mumbai

Learning the bash Shell by Cameron Newham and Bill Rosenblatt (O'Reilly & Associates), 1998, Sebastopol, California

Programming Perl by Larry Wall, Brett McLaughlin, Jon Orwant (O'Reilly & Associates), 2000, Sebastopol, California

Learning Perl by Randal Schwartz (Shroff Publishers and Distributors), 2001, Mumbai

System Administration

UNIX System Administration Handbook by Evi Nemeth, Garth Snyder, Scott Seebass and Trent Hein (Pearson Education), 2001, Addison-Wesley Longman (Singapore) Pte Ltd., New Delhi

Essential System Administration by A Eleen Frisch (Shroff Publishers and Distributors), 2002, Mumbai

Journals and Papers

The UNIX Time-Sharing System by Dennis Ritchie & Ken Thompson (Bell System Technical Journal, Vol 57, No 6), 1978, Murray Hill, New Jersey

UNIX Implementation by Ken Thompson (Bell System Technical Journal, Vol 57, No 6), 1978, Murray Hill, New Jersey

The UNIX Shell by Steve Bourne (Bell System Technical Journal, Vol 57, No 6), 1978, Murray Hill, New Jersey

Awk - A Pattern Scanning and Processing Language Programmer's Manual by Alfred Aho, Peter Weinberger & Brian Kernighan (Computing Science Technical Report No 118 of AT&T Bell Labs), Murray Hill, New Jersey

Index

. 75, 77, 84
. command 206, 207
.. 75, 77
.bash_history 200
.bash_login 205
.bash_profile 205
.bashrc 205, 207
.exrc 122, 124, 443
.forward 372
.kshrc 205, 207
.netrc 360
.profile 205-206, 449
.rhosts 363
.sh_history 200
.shosts 363
.signature 371-372
.vimrc 122, 443
.Xdefaults 348
.xinitrc 335, 338, 347-348
/bin 29, 74, 79, 308
/dev 79, 317
/dev/dsk 317, 318
/dev/null 160-161, 182
/dev/rdsk 317, 318
/dev/tty 154, 161, 164, 279, 289-290, 455
/etc 79
/etc/cron.d/at.allow 308
/etc/cron.d/at.deny 308
/etc/cron.d/cron.allow 308
/etc/cron.d/cron.deny 308
/etc/default/man 37
/etc/fstab 582
/etc/group 109, 232, 311-312

/etc/hosts 342, 354-355, 370
/etc/hosts.equiv 363
/etc/inittab 338, 586-587
/etc/mailcap 373
/etc/mime.types 373, 377
/etc/passwd 69, 109, 117, 147, 196, 197, 232, 311
   structure 312-313
/etc/profile 308
/etc/resolv.conf 369-370
/etc/shadow 309, 312, 313, 573
/home 80
/lib 79, 478
/lost+found 584
/sbin 79, 308
/tmp 79, 310
/usr/bin 29, 74, 79, 308
/usr/include 79
/usr/include/sys/signal.h 185
/usr/lib 79, 478
/usr/sbin 79
/usr/share/lib/terminfo 197
/usr/share/man 79
/usr/xpg4/bin 247, 254
/var 79
/var/mail 196, 311, 346
/var/spool/cron/crontabs 188
/var/spool/mail 196, 346
/var/tmp 310

A

Acrobat Reader 373, 378
admin (SCCS) 480
AIX 16

alias 199-200, 230
anonymous FTP 353, 360
Apple 333
apropos 37-38
ar 475-477
archive 98
ARPANET 17
as 467
ASCII 5
   collating sequence 13, 76, 219, 250
   octal value 47, 94, 241
   value 65, 404
at 187-188
 controlling access to 308
AT&T 15-16, 27, 335
atomic operation 494
awk 381-398
   -f option 388-389
   arrays 391-393
   BEGIN section 389-390
   comparison operators 385-386
   computation 388
   delimiter used 383
   END section 389-390
   ENVIRON 393
   fields 383
   for loop 396-398
   functions 393
   hash arrays 392, 397-398
   if statement 394-396
   logical operators (|| and &&) 386, 395
   numeric comparison 387
   operators table 387
   print statement 382
   printf statement 384
   redirection 384
   regular expression operators (~ and !~)
   386-387
   regular expressions 382, 386-387
   while loop 398

awk functions
   index 393
   int 393
   length 393
   split 394
   sqrt 393
   substr 394
   system 394
   table 395
awk variables 384-385, 388, 390-391
   FILENAME 391
   FS 390
   NF 390
   NR 383
   OFS 390
   table 391

B

Bach, Maurice 511
basename 293-294
bash See Bash shell
Bash shell 9, 12, 23, 147, 166, 182, 183, 194,
   197-207, 271, 286, 306, 357, 450-453, 545
   event number (!) 198, 200-201
   PS1 variable 197-198
   using $0 274
   using **echo** 47, 271
batch 188
   controlling access to 308
bc 49-50, 160
Berkeley Software Distribution (BSD) See
   BSD UNIX
Berners-Lee, Tim 373
bg 186
block size
   logical 576
   physical 576
blocking (waiting) 502, 534, 557
boot file system 577

Bourne shell 9, 12, 23, 147, 271, 286, 306, 545
Bourne, Steve 194
browser 373, 376-377
brute force attack 361
BSD UNIX 16, 89, 91, 116, 117, 120, 176
　　and TCP/IP 16, 17
buffer 33
buffer cache 318, 502
bunzip2 98, 100
bzip2 98, 100

C

C 22, 288, 384, 391, 493
　　program compilation 288, 467, 470-471
C shell 9, 12, 16, 23, 147, 158, 159, 182, 183,
　　194, 545
　　programming 594-599
cal 11, 45
Caldera Linux 18, 23
cancel 91-92
carriage return (CR) 97, 98, 359
cat 13-14, 83-84, 473
　　compared with **pr** 83
　　numbering lines 83
　　creating a file 83
cc 467
cd 69-70, 74, 75
　　compared with DOS 70
　　toggling with ~ 205
　　without a process 175, 448
　　without arguments 70
Cerf, Vinton 17
character, definition 6, 93
chgrp 117
chmod 110-115, 218, 360, 403, 525, 526
　　abbreviations table 112
　　recursive behavior 115
　　setting sticky bit 310
　　setting SUID bit 309

　　with octal numbers 113-114
　　within **vi** 443
chown 116-117, 310, 525, 526
Christian, Kaare 24
chsh 147
ci (RCS) 486-489
client-server 334, 356, 375
cmp 95
co (RCS) 487-488
col 162-163
comm 95-96
command 9, 10, 28
　　argument 11, 30
　　exit status 275, 542
　　external 29, 181
　　failure 246, 275-276
　　grouping with () 32
　　history 198, 200-201
　　in background 182
　　in-line editing 203-204
　　internal 29, 181
　　locating 28
　　option 30-31, 32
　　parsing 31, 169
　　substitution in previous 201-202
　　success 95, 275-276
command line 31
command substitution 165-166, 168, 169,
　　284, 292, 294, 296, 297
Common Desktop Environment (CDE) 177,
　　336-337, 338, 339, 344, 347
Common Gateway Interface (CGI) 375, 418
controlling terminal 176, 178
country-code top-level domain (ccTLD) 368
cp 84-85
　　copying directories 85
cpio 321-325
　　incremental backups 589-590
　　multivolume backups 323
　　options table 324

cron   178, 188-189, 310
   controlling access to 308
crontab   189-190
cryptography   360-362
   symmetric key algorithms   361, 362, 363
   asymmetric key algorithms   361-362
csh   See C shell
current directory   69, 74, 75, 179-180
cut   231-233, 237, 240, 284, 294

D

DARPA   17, 355, 356, 357
date   9-10, 12, 45-46, 74, 294
   used by system administrator   307
dd   320-321
Debian Linux   18
decryption   361
delta (SCCS)   482, 485
device file   66, 317-319
   block special   318
   character special   318
   listing   317
   major number   318
   minor number   318
   table   319
device driver   318
df   315-316
   in Linux   316
diff   96-97, 255
Digital UNIX   16
directory   13, 24, 28, 66, 211, 214, 513
   permissions   115-116, 216-217
dirent structure   513
disk fragmentation   577
domain   368
Domain Name System (DNS)   342, 354, 355, 363, 363, 368-370, 371
DOS   5, 6, 9, 28, 31, 67, 70, 77, 86, 97, 149, 319, 320-321

AUTOEXEC.BAT   9, 77, 205
   handling diskettes   320-321
dos2unix   97-98
doscat   321
doscp   320-321
dtfile (CDE)   344, 345
dtterm (CDE)   339
dtwm (CDE)   335-336
du   316-317
dump   582

E

echo   22-23, 29, 33, 46-47, 279
   escaping in   154
   in Linux   47, 271
   quoting in   153-154
effective GID   179-180, 536
effective UID   179-180, 525, 536
egrep   254, 255, 382
email   51-52, 370-373
   addressing scheme   51-52
   attachments   372
   automatic forwarding   372
   mailbox   51, 53
   mbox   51, 54
   message structure   372
   role of DNS   371
   signature file   371-372
encryption   361, 362
env   195, 449
environment variables   180, 194, 195-199
   BASH_ENV   207
   ENV   207
   HISTFILE   202
   HISTFILESIZE   202
   HISTSIZE   202
   HOME   69, 196, 313
   IFS   197, 294, 299
   LOGNAME   197

MAIL 196, 312, 346
MAILCHECK 196
PATH 28-29, 74, 169, 195, 306
PS1 196, 197
PS2 196
SHELL 147, 196, 313
TERM 124, 197
table 198
Epoch 46, 187
errno table 507
errno variable 504-506
escape sequence 47, 94
table 48
exec 179, 180
exit 15, 50, 117, 204, 339
exit status 179
export See shell variables
expr 285-287
compared with **basename** 294
compared with **let** 450
computation 286
string handling 286-287

F

fdformat 319
in Linux 319
fdisk (Linux) 578-579
fg 186
file 12, 24, 28, 65-66
access time 218-219
binary 65
compression 98
group ownership 107, 109, 116
inode modification time 218
links 107
modification time 108, 218-219
name 67, 108
offset pointer 495
ordinary 65

ownership 72, 107, 109, 116
parent-child relationship 67-68
permissions 107, 109-110, 114-115
size 108
text 24, 65
type 107
file command 92-93
file descriptor 158, 159, 180, 462-463, 495
manipulation 553-555
file descriptor table 509-510, 536
file system 67-68, 79-80, 211, 315, 574-578
clean/dirty 583
components 574-577
mounting 580-581
organization in SVR4 79-80
types 577-578
file table 509, 510-511, 537
filter 26, 61, 101, 159, 228
find 220-224
displaying listing 223
executing UNIX command 223-224
file size 317
file type 221
in backups 589-590
in Linux 220
inode number 221
operators 222
options table 223
permissions 221-222
SUID programs 310
unused files 222
used with **cpio** 322, 323
fork 179, 180
format 319
Free Software Foundation See GNU
Frequently Asked Questions (FAQ) 27
fsck 583-584, 589
ftp 97, 98, 179, 354, 355, 357-360, 367
ASCII mode 359
binary mode 359

in Linux 360
transferring files 358-359
with .netrc 360
fully qualified domain name (FQDN) 354,
    360, 368-369, 374, 375

G

gawk 381, 393
gcc 467, 475
GCOS 312
generic domains See top-level domains
    (TLDs)
get (SCCS) 481-482, 484-485
getty 180, 586
GID 109, 312
GNOME 337, 338, 339, 344
GNU 17-18, 194
Graphical User Interface See GUI
grep 246-249, 264
    -E option 249, 254, 255, 382
    counting lines 248
    deleting lines 247
    ignoring case 247
    line numbers 247
    options table 249
    quoting with 247
    patterns from file 248, 255
    with multiple patterns 248
group-id See GID
groupadd 311-312
GUI (Graphical User Interface) 17, 335
gunzip 98, 214
gzcat 100
gzip 98, 99-100, 214
    with tar 101
gzmore 100

H

head 230
    with ls 230

with vi 230
helper application 373, 374, 378
here document 296-297
history 200
home directory 68-69
hostname 352, 354, 357
hostname command 58, 352
hosts file See /etc/hosts
HP-UX 16, 317
httpd 353
Hyper Text Markup Language (HTML)
    373-374, 376
Hyper Text Transfer Protocol (HTTP) 373, 375
    Keep-Alive 375
hypertext 373

I

IBM 336
id 109
ident (RCS) 489-490
IEEE 27
inetd 178, 179
init 180-181, 182, 183, 184, 585-589
    and getty 180-181, 585, 586
    rc script 587-588
    run level 313-314, 585
inode 107, 211, 212, 214, 315, 576
    number 73, 87, 211
Internet 17, 352, 355, 368
    and ARPANET 17, 368
    domains table 370
internet 352
Internet Message Access Protocol (IMAP) 371
intranet 352
IP address 353
    resolving 354-355, 369

J

job 185
  control 185-187

jobs 186
Joy, Bill 120, 194

K

Kahn, Robert 17
KDE 337, 338, 339, 344
kernel 22, 25, 212
kernel mode 493
Kernighan, Brian 5
keys
    [Backspace] 6
    [Ctrl-\] 561
    [Ctrl-c] 7, 39, 60, 545, 561
    [Ctrl-d] 15, 40, 41, 83, 204, 347
    [Ctrl-g] 95
    [Ctrl-h] 39, 60
    [Ctrl-i] 30, 95, 260
    [Ctrl-j] 40, 95
    [Ctrl-l] 95
    [Ctrl-m] 40, 97
    [Ctrl-q] 40
    [Ctrl-s] 40
    [Ctrl-u] 39, 60
    [Ctrl-z] 130, 186, 561
    [Ctrl] 7
    [Ctrl][Alt][Del] 315
    [Delete] 7, 39, 60
    [Enter] 6, 10, 31
    [Tab] 30, 94, 95, 260
    function keys 7
kill 184-185, 187
  Korn shell 9, 12, 23, 147, 166, 194, 197-207,
    271, 286, 306, 450-453, 545
  event number (!) 198, 200-201
  PS1 variable 197-198
Korn, David 194
ksh See Korn shell

L

ld 467
less 34, 88, 90
  commands table 90
library functions 24, 493
  closedir 513
  exec 546-553
  exit 540-542
  getcwd 512
  getenv 539
  opendir 513
  perror 504, 505
  printf buffering 539
  raise 569
  readdir 513
  rewinddir 513
  setenv 539
  strerror 504-505
  system 553
line, definition 93
linefeed (LF) 65, 95, 97, 98, 153, 359
link (hard) 212-214, 215
link (soft) See symbolic link
Linux 16, 17-18, 24, 30, 34, 176, 189, 231,
    247, 317, 337, 338, 342, 348, 359, 401, 433
  --help option 38-39
ln 213-214
localhost 371
logging in 7-8
logging out 15
login 180, 586
logout 15
lp 91, 92, 162
lpq 92
lpr 91, 92
lprm 92
lpsched 178
ls 13, 75-78
  displaying hidden files 77

displaying inode number 211-212
displaying time stamps 218-219
in Linux 75
listing (-1) 13, 106-108
listing directory (-d) 108
options table 78
recursive behavior 78
with directories 77-78
lynx 377

M

magic number 93
Mail 52
Mail Delivery Agent (MDA) 370, 371
Mail Transport Agent (MTA) 370, 371
Mail User Agent (MUA) 370, 371
mailx 12, 52-55, 58, 179
   internal commands table 55
   with here document 296
make 471-475
   cleaning up 474
   dependency tree 472
   macros in 474-475
   redundancies 473-474
   with **ar** 477
makefile 471
man 33-38, 162-163
   -f option 38
   -k option 37-38
   documentation table 37
   navigation 34
   PAGER variable 37
   sample page for **wc** 36
Mandrake Linux 18
Massachusetts Institute of Technology (MIT)
   17, 334, 344
Master Boot Record (MBR) 575
McNealy, Scott 16
Memory Management Unit (MMU) 535
metacharacter 13, 26, 32, 146

Microsoft 17, 333
mingetty (Linux) 586
mkdir 71, 72, 73
mkfs 580
Moolenaar, Bram 120
more 34, 88-90, 94
   and **vi** 90
   commands table 90
   in a pipeline 89-90, 163
   pattern search in 89
Motif window manager 335, 336
mount 581-583
mount point 581
Mozilla 179, 339, 346, 371, 377
mtools (Linux) 321
MULTICS 16
multipart message 377
Multipurpose Internet Mail Extensions
   (MIME) 372-373, 375, 377-378
   Content-Transfer-Encoding header 372-373
   Content-Type header 372-373
mv 87
   compared with **rename** system call 516
   with **find** 224
mwm 336

N

name server 369-370
Netscape 346, 371, 377, 378
newline character See linefeed (LF)
newsgroups 27
nice 183-184
nohup 182-183, 184
Novell 16, 336
nroff 376

O

octal numbers 113
od 94-95

Open Look window manager 335
operating system 4-5, 22
orphan process 182, 546

P

pager 34
parent PID (PPID) 174, 176
partition 211, 574
passphrase 363
passwd 9, 55-56, 180, 310, 522-523
   used by system administrator 308-309, 573
password 8
   aging 573
   encryption 56, 312
   framing rules 56-57
paste 233-234, 237
   joining lines 234
PATH See shell variables
pathname
   absolute 69, 73-74
   relative 74-75
perl 265, 282, 375, 401-428
   -e option 402
   -n option 407
   array 408-409, 411-412
   array, built-in (@_) 415
   array (@ARGV) 410-411
   associative array 417-418
   associative array (%ENV) 419
   chop function 403-404
   command substitution in 413
   concatenation (. and x) 405
   current line number ($.) 408
   default variable ($_) 407-408, 412, 413, 420
   diamond operator (<>) 406
   die function 410
   file handling 423-424
   file tests 425
   filehandle 424

for loop 413
foreach loop 412-413
functions 402
grep function 416-417
if conditional 403
in-place editing 423
interpreter line 402
interval regular expression (IRE) 422
join function 415-416
list 408-409
operators 404-405
quoting 404
qw function 410
range operator (..) 408
regular expression 420-423
regular expression table 422
require statement 427
s function 420-421
select function 424
split function 413-415
string functions 405-406
subroutine 426-427
tagged regular expression (TRE) 422-423
tr function 420-421
variables 402, 404-405
while loop 406
Pike, Rob 5
ping 356
pipe 14, 161-164, 183
PKUNZIP 102
PKZIP 102
plugin 373, 378
port number 353-354
Portable Document Format (PDF) 349, 372, 373
POSIX 11, 24, 26, 27-28, 38, 50, 52, 89, 166, 231, 247, 249, 393, 476, 512, 539, 557
Post Office Protocol (POP3) 371
Postscript 92, 349
pr 229-230

prs (SCCS) 482, 484
printf 48-49
    compared with C 49
process 12, 24, 174-175
    and kernel 174
    and program 174
    attributes inherited 179-180
    background 182, 185, 338, 339
    child 175
    compared with file 24, 175
    context 535
    context switch 535
    creation 179
    daemon 178, 353-354
    data segment 534, 535
    heap 534, 535
    killing 184
    parent 175
    stack 534, 535
    states 181-182
    text segment 534, 535
    virtual address space 534-535
    process groups 544, 545
    waiting for death of 175
process table 174, 535-536
process-id (PID) 174
procmail (Linux) 371
prompt string 8, 10, 33, 116, 196, 357
    for root 306
ps 12, 176-178, 183, 188
    options table 177
pwd 69
    without a process 175

R

race condition 565
r-utilities 355, 363
rcs (RCS) 486
real GID 179-180, 536
real UID 179-180, 526, 536

RealAudio 377
RealVideo 377
reboot 314
Red Hat Linux 18, 337
redirection See shell
regular expression 26, 89, 249-255
    [] 250-251
    . (dot) 252, 253
    * 251-252, 253
    ^ 252-253, 258, 261, 387
    $ 252-253, 258, 261, 387
    ? 254
    + 254
    | 254-255
    () 255, 264-265
    & 263
    {} 263-264
    basic (BRE) 249-254
    compared with wild-cards 249, 251, 252
    escaping 253
    extended (ERE) 254-255, 386
    interval (IRE) 263-264
    listing only directories 253
    multiple patterns 254-255
    repeated pattern 263
    table 250, 255
    tagged (TRE) 263, 264-265, 287
    triple role of ^ 253
Request for Comments (RFC) 353, 372
resolver 354, 369
Revision Control System (RCS) 486-490
    compared with SCCS 487
Ritchie, Dennis 15-16, 18, 22, 309, 493
rlog (RCS) 489
rm 85-87, 215
    danger in using with * 149
    recursive behavior 86
    used with **find** 224
rmdir 71-72, 73

root directory 28, 67-68
root file system 211, 577, 580
router 352

S

sact (SCCS) 483-484, 485
sample database (emp.1st) 228
SCO UNIX 326
scp 367-368
script 50-51, 98
secure shell (SSH) 357, 362-368
    configuring 362-366
    host key generation 362-363
    session key generation 363
    trusted hosts 363
sed 249, 255-262, 264, 265
    compressing multiple spaces 262
    context addressing 258
    deleting blank lines 260
    doublespacing text 259-260
    inserting text 259
    instructions from file 257
    internal commands table 266
    line addressing 256-257
    multiple instructions 256, 257
    quoting with 257
    regular expressions 258, 261
    remembered pattern 262
    repeated pattern 263
    substitution 260-262
    writing selected lines 258-259
sendmail 178, 179, 353, 372
set 195
    +o 204
    -o 204
    ignoreeof 204
    noclobber 204
set-group-id (SGID) 309-310
set-user-id (SUID) 180, 309-310, 522-523,
    525-526, 536-537

sftp 367
sh See Bourne shell
shared library 478
shell 5, 9, 22-23, 29, 146-147, 194
    -c option 553
    aliases 199
    creation mechanism 179-180
    escaping 152-153, 167
    escaping \ 153, 259
    escaping newline 153
    escaping space 153
    positional parameters 167
    process 174-175
    quoting 152, 153-154, 165, 167
    redirection 13, 32, 53, 154-160, 169, 279,
        290
    restricted 573
    shell escape 196
shell metacharacters
    ; 32
    < 155-156, 160
    << 296-297
    > 13-14, 83, 103, 146, 157, 160, 204
    >> 157
    >| 204
    1>&2 455
    2> 158-159
    2>&1 455
    () 32, 157, 447-448
    {} 447-448
    \ 153
    ` 165
    | 14, 26, 103, 162
    ~ 69, 205
    $ 15, 166
    = 166
    & 182, 183, 185
shell parameters
    $$ 174-175, 176, 259
    $? 275-276

$! 185
$# 273, 274, 281, 285, 294
$* 273, 274, 281, 294
"$@" 281
$0 274, 288
table 275
shell programming 27, 270-302, 447-464
  # 271
  #! 271
  (()) 450
  [] synonym for **test** 280
  . (dot) command 449-450
  arrays 450-451
  break 300
  case statement 283-285
  continue 300
  eval 365, 459-460
  exec 461-464
  exit 275
  export See shell variables
  file test 278, 282-283
  file test table 283
  for loop 291-294
  here document 296-297
  if conditional 277-278
  interpreter line 271, 447
  let for computation 450
  logical operators (&& and ||) 276
  numerical comparison 278-279
  parameter substitution 453-454
  positional parameters 273-275, 292, 294, 295
  read statement 272-273
  set -- 296
  set -x 298-299
  set statement 294
  shell function 456-459
  shell functions and aliases 199
  shell script 27, 181, 271
  shift statement 295

string comparison 278, 280-282
string handling 286-287, 452-453
test operators table 279, 282, 283
test statement 278-283
trap statement 297-298, 301
until loop 291
while loop 289-291
with /dev/tty 279, 289-290, 455
shell script See shell programming
shell variables 15, 166-169, 292, 297
  concatenation 168
  export 37, 195, 448-449
shell wild-cards 147-151, 169, 292, 323
  * 26, 85, 86, 93, 146, 148-149, 285
  ? 149, 285
  ! 150
  [] character class 150, 285
  {} 150-151
  dot matching 149
  table 148
Shockwave 377
shutdown 314, 589
  in Linux 315
SID (SCCS ID) 479
signals 184, 297-298, 560-562
  blocking 566
  disposition 560
  disposition table 536, 562
  pending signals mask 536, 562
  reliable 566
  table 563
  unreliable 565-566
  SIGABRT 561
  SIGALRM 561
  SIGCHLD 561
  SIGFPE 561
  SIGHUP 298, 561
  SIGILL 561
  SIGINT 184, 298, 545, 560, 561

SIGKILL 184, 562
SIGQUIT 561
SIGSEGV 561
SIGSTOP 184, 561, 562
SIGTERM 184, 298
SIGTSTP 561
SIGTTIN 561
Simple Mail Transfer Protocol (SMTP)
   371, 372
Single UNIX Specification 27-28
sleep 290-291
slogin 366
Solaris 16, 92, 97, 116, 117, 176, 231, 248, 314,
   315, 317, 327, 338, 343, 348, 359, 401
sort 234-237, 242
   in **vi** 433-434
   numeric 236
   options table 237
   primary key 234
   removing repeated lines 236
   secondary key 234-235
Source Code Control System (SCCS) 97,
   478-486
   branch delta 479, 484-485
   checking in 478
   checking out 478
   compared with **diff** 478
   compared with RCS 487
   delta 478-479
   identification keywords 485-486
   lock file 481
   SCCS file 479
source 206, 207
ssh 341, 342, 364, 365, 366-367
ssh-add 365
ssh-agent 365
ssh-keygen 363-364
sshd 362
Stallman, Richard 17

standard error 155, 158, 159
standard input 155-156, 228
   significance of - 156, 164
standard output 155, 156-157, 165, 228
startx 338, 347
stat structure 516-517
static library 477-478
sticky bit 310
stty 40, 59-61, 187
   setting options 60-61
su 116, 306-307
Sun Microsystems 16, 335
SunOS 8, 16, 58
superblock 574-575, 580, 583, 584
superuser See system administrator
supplementary groups 117, 311
SuSE Linux 18, 337
SVR3 See System V Release 3
SVR4 See System V Release 4
swap file system 577
symbolic link 16, 215, 272
   dangling 215
   fast 215
   in Linux 215
sync 589
system administrator 7, 10, 116, 188, 189,
   231, 306
   privileges 307-308
system calls 22, 24, 282, 425, 493-494, 534
   error handling 504-506
   _exit 540-542
   abort 561
   access 524
   alarm 562, 567
   chdir 512
   chmod 526, 527
   chown 526, 527-528
   close 497
   creat 496

dup 510, 554, 556
dup2 510, 554-555, 556
fchdir 512
fchmod 526, 527
fchown 527-528
fcntl 511, 556-557
fork 510, 537-538, 557
fstat 517
ftruncate 502
getpid 536
getppid 536
kill 545, 562, 566-567
lchown 527-528
link 515, 526
lseek 500, 502, 505
lstat 517
mkdir 515
open 495-496, 510
pause 562, 566
pipe 557-558
putenv 539
read 497-498, 502
rename 516
rmdir 515
signal 561, 562-564
sleep 538-539
stat 516-517
symlink 515
truncate 502
umask 496, 503-504
unlink 515-516, 526
utime 526, 528
wait 542-543, 545
waitpid 542, 544-545
write 498, 502-503
System V 176, 317, 318, 326
System V Interface Definition 27
System V Release 3 16
System V Release 4 16

T

tail 231
tar 98, 100-101, 325-328, 591
  compared with **cpio** 325
  in Linux 102, 327
  multivolume backup 326
  options table 328
TCP/IP 17, 178, 342, 352-354
tee 164, 232
telinit 586
telnet 341, 355, 356-357
The Open Group 16, 27
Thompson, Ken 15-16, 18, 22
tilde substitution 205
time 190
top-level domains (TLDs) 368
Torvalds, Linus 17
touch 219-220
tput clear 10-11
tr 239-241, 242
  changing case of text 240
  complementing 241
  compressing characters 240
  deleting characters 240
  escape sequences 241
  with ASCII octal values 241
trap 297-298
troff 376
Tru64 UNIX 16
tty 59
type 28, 154

U

UID 109, 116, 312
ulimit 308
umask 218
umount 581, 582
uname 58
  in Linux 59

unget (SCCS)   483
Uniform Resource Locator (URL) 373, 374, 375, 376
uniq 238-239, 241-242
University of California, Berkeley 16
UNIX 5
   history 15-17
   multiprogramming 5, 25
   multitasking 25, 534
   multiuser 25
   run level See **init**
   shutdown 314
   startup 313-314
unix2dos 97-98
unzip 98, 102-103
user mode 493
user-id See UID
useradd 312, 574
userdel 313
usermod 147, 313
username 8
utimbuf structure 528

V

version control 478
vi 120-144, 197, 203, 262, 403, 431-44
   abbreviate command 443
   aborting session 129
   appending text 125
   buffers in 128
   changing text 433
   clearing screen 123
   Command Mode 121, 122
   command reference 600-605
   current cursor position 121
   current line 121, 134
   deleting 135
   deleting with operators 135, 432
   escape to shell 130

ex Mode 122, 128-131, 435-437
ex Mode table 131, 437
executing C program 443
executing shell script 443
filtering text 433-434
Input Mode 121, 122, 124-128, 340
Input Mode table 128
inserting command output 436
inserting control character 439
inserting file 436
inserting text 124-125
joining lines 137
keys with no function 124
Last Line Mode See **vi**, ex Mode
map command 442-443
marking text 440
moving text 135-136
moving text between files 438
multiple files 435
named buffers 437
navigation 131-134
numbered buffers 438-439
opening new line 124, 126
operator-command table 434
operators 134, 431-435
quitting 129
recovering from crash 130
reloading last saved file 435
repeat factor 122, 126, 132, 203
repeating last command 138, 139
repeating search 139, 440
replacing text 124, 126-127
role of **!** 129, 435
role of *[Esc]* 121, 124, 125, 127
saving 128
search for character 439-440
search for pattern 138-139
search-repeat table 140, 440
set autoindent 441

set autowrite 436
set ignorecase 441
set nomagic 441
set number 441
set showmatch 441-442
set showmode 124
set tabstop 442
set options table 442
substituting text 140-141
suspending 130
toggling between two files 436, 437
undoing 123, 137
multiple line deletions 438-439
word in 132
writing lines 129-130
yanking text 136-137, 432-433
vim 120, 124, 340
redoing 137
splitting the window 436-437
substituting text 141
text completion 127
undoing 137
vnode table 511

W

wait 179
wall 307-308, 314
Wall, Larry 401
wc 14, 93-94, 155, 162, 164
whatis 38
whitespace 30
who 11-12, 57-58, 161-162, 164
displaying run level 314
used with **cut** 233
window manager See X Window
Windows 5, 6, 17, 24, 25, 29, 67, 98, 149, 215, 320, 336, 359, 378, 436
WINZIP 98
word, definition 30, 93
World Wide Web 373-378

X

X See X Window
X Window 177, 334-336, 437
-display option 341, 342
client 334, 335
command line options 343-344
command options table 344
copying text 339-341
DISPLAY variable 341, 342
resources 348
server 334
window manager 335-336
X/OPEN 16
Portability Guide 27
xargs 590-591
xbiff 346
xcalc 341, 345
xclipboard 340-341, 437
xclock 345, 349
xdm 338
XENIX 16
xfm 344
xhost 341
xinit 338, 347
xkill 347
xload 346-347
xrdb 348-349
xterm 338-339, 343, 344, 347, 348

Z

zcat 100
zip 98, 102-103
zmore 100
zombie process 181, 545

The ls Command (Include -1 option for listing)

Command	Displays
ls -a	All filenames including those beginning with a dot
ls -d .*	Only filenames beginning with a dot
ls -R	Recursive file list
ls -l	Long listing in ASCII collating sequence
ls /etc	Filenames in /etc
ls -d /etc	Only /etc
ls -ld /etc	Listing of /etc
ls -l /etc	Listing of all filenames in /etc
ls -lRa /	Recursive listing of all filenames in file system
ls -t	Filenames sorted by last modification time
ls -u	Filenames sorted by last access time
ls -i	Inode number

Switching Directories (Setting CDPATH makes navigation easier)

Command	Action
cd ~sharma	Switches to home directory of sharma
cd ~/sharma	Switches to directory $HOME/sharma
cd -	Toggles between current and previous directory
cd	Switches to $HOME

Wild-cards vs Regular Expressions (EREs available in grep -E, egrep and awk)

Wild-card	Regular Expression	Matches
*	.*	Any number of characters including none
?	.	A single character
-	*	Zero or more occurrences of the previous character
-	g*	Nothing or g, gg, ggg, etc.
-	g?	Nothing or g (ERE)
-	g+	g, gg, ggg, etc. (ERE)
[ijk]	[ijk]	i, j or k
[b-m]	[b-m]	Any character between b and m
[!b-m]	[^b-m]	Any character not between b and m
[!a-zA-Z0-9]	[^a-zA-Z0-9]	Any non-alphanumeric character
-	^#include	#include at beginning of line
-	*/$	*/ at end of line
-	^MARK$	MARK as only word in line
-	^$	Lines containing nothing
-	GIF|JPEG	GIF or JPEG (ERE)
-	(lock|ver)wood	lockwood or verwood (ERE)

Filters

Command	*Displays from* **foo**
head -n 5 foo	First 5 lines
tail -n 3 foo	Last 3 lines
tail +5 foo	Lines 5 through end
cut -d":" -f1,3 foo	Fields 1 and 3 delimited by :
cut -f5- foo	Fields 5 through end delimited by tab
sort -t: -k 2 foo	Lines delimited by : and sorted on field 2
sort -n foo	Lines sorted numerically
sort -u foo	Only unique lines
uniq foo	Only unique lines
uniq -u foo	Only nonrepeated lines
uniq -c foo	Frequency of occurrence of each line and the line
tr ':' '/' < foo	Lines after replacing : with /
tr '[a-z]' '[A-Z]' < foo	Lines after conversion to uppercase
tr -s ' ' < foo	Lines after squeezing multiple contiguous spaces to single space
tr -d '\012' < foo	All characters except newline
grep "printf" foo	Lines containing printf
grep -v "printf" foo	Lines not containing printf
grep -l 'printf' foo*	Filenames containing printf
sed -n '5,9p' foo	Lines 5 through 9
sed 's/echo/printf/' foo	After replacing first occurrence of echo with printf in each line
sed 's/echo/printf/g' foo	After globally replacing echo with printf
sed 's/;$//' foo	After deleting every ; at end of line

The find Command (Search assumed to start from /)

Command	*Matches Filename(s)*
find / -name a.out -print	a.out
find / -name "*.c" -print	with .c extension
find / ! -name "*.[ch]" -print	Other than .c and .h
find / -type d -print	Only directories (f for regular, l for symlink)
find / -user henry -print	Owned by henry
find / -size +4 -print	Having size greater than 4 blocks
find / -size 2048c -print	With exactly 2048 characters
find / -mtime +180 -print	Modified 180 days back or more
find / -type f -atime +365 -exec rm {} \;	Not accessed in a year or more, and removes them
find / -type f -atime +365 -ok rm {} \;	As above, but after user confirmation
find / -type d -perm -0070 -print	Directories having all permssions for group
find / -perm -4000 -ls	With SUID bit set and displays listing
find / -type f -newer /etc/passwd -print	Newer than /etc/passwd (only regular files)

Shell Parameters

Expression	Significance
$#	Number of command line arguments
$0	Name of executed command
$*	All parameters as a single string
"$@"	As above, but quoted strings treated as separate arguments
$?	Exit status of last command
$$	PID of the current shell
$!	PID of the last background job

test Expressions

String Comparison (e.g. if [$stg = "yes"] ; then ....)

Expression	True if
$s1 = $s2	String s1 and s2 are identical
$s1 != $s2	String s1 and s2 are not identical
-n $stg	String stg is not a null string
-z $stg	String stg is a null string

Integer Comparison (e.g. if [$count -gt 4] ; then ....)

Expression	True if
$n1 -gt $n2	Integer n1 is greater than integer n2
$n1 -ge $n2	Integer n1 is greater than or equal to integer n2
$n1 -eq $n2	Integer n1 is equal to integer n2
$n1 -ne $n2	Integer n1 is not equal to integer n2
$n1 -le $n2	Integer n1 is less than or equal to integer n2
$n1 -lt $n2	Integer n1 is less than integer n2

File Attribute Testing (e.g. if [-f foo] ; then ....)

Expression	True if
-e foo	foo exists
-s foo	foo has a size greater than zero
-r foo	foo is readable
-w foo	foo is writable
-x foo	foo is executable
-f foo	foo is a regular file
-d foo	foo is a directory
-L foo	foo is a symbolic link
-u foo	foo has SUID bit set
-g foo	foo has SGID bit set
-k foo	foo has sticky bit set